# PARKIN ◆ POWELL ◆ MATTHEWS

# ECONOMICS

## STUDY GUIDE

### THIRD EDITION

# PARKIN ◆ POWELL ◆ MATTHEWS
# ECONOMICS

# STUDY GUIDE

## THIRD EDITION

**Brian Atkinson** *formerly of University of Central Lancashire*

and

Avi J. Cohen *York University*

Harvey B. King *University of Regina*

Mark Rush *University of Florida*

**ADDISON-WESLEY**

HARLOW, ENGLAND ◆ READING, MASSACHUSETTS ◆ MENLO PARK, CALIFORNIA ◆ NEW YORK
DON MILLS, ONTARIO ◆ AMSTERDAM ◆ BONN ◆ SYDNEY ◆ SINGAPORE ◆ TOKYO
MADRID ◆ SAN JUAN ◆ MILAN ◆ MEXICO CITY ◆ SEOUL ◆ TAIPEI

Addison Wesley Longman Limited
Edinburgh Gate
Harlow
Essex CM20 2JE
England
*and Associated Companies throughout the world.*

| | |
|---|---|
| Commissioning Editor: | Paula Harris |
| Senior Production Editor: | Susan Harrison |
| Editor: | Lee Hodder |
| Editorial Assistant: | Anna Herbert |
| Production Control Manager: | Jim Allman |
| Production Assistant: | Alison Martin |
| Cover Designer: | Kevin Ancient |
| Cover Design Artist: | Mark Surridge |
| Typesetter: | Meridian Colour Repro Limited, Pangbourne |
| Technical Illustrator: | Margaret Macknelly Design, Tadley |
| Printer: | Short Run Press, Exeter |

First printed 1997.

ISBN 0-201-40398-6

**British Library Cataloguing-in-Publication Data**
A catalogue record for this book is available from
the British Library.

**Acknowledgements**
The publishers would like to thank the following for permission to reproduce material: Oxford University Press;
Macmillan Ltd; OECD; International Labour Organisation; Gower Publishers; Office for Official Publications of the
European Communities; Causeway Press; The Economics & Business Education Association; The Society of
Motor Manufacture Traders; *Economic/Social Trends*, 1996 Crown Copyright 1996, Reproduced by permission of
the Controller of HMSO and of the Office for National Statistics; The Economist, London.

# CONTENTS

# INTRODUCTION

## Before You Begin . . .

Our experience has taught us that what first-year economics students want most from a study guide is help in mastering course material in order to do well in examinations. We have developed this *Study Guide* to respond specifically to that demand. Using this *Study Guide* alone, however, is not enough to guarantee that you will do well in your course. In order to help you overcome the problems and difficulties that most first-year students encounter, we have some general advice on how to study, as well as some specific advice on how best to use this *Study Guide*.

## Some Friendly Advice

The study of economics requires a different style of thinking from what you may encounter in other courses. Economists make extensive use of assumptions to break down complex problems into simple, analytically manageable, parts. This analytical style, while not ultimately more demanding than the styles of thinking in other disciplines, feels unfamiliar to most students and requires practice. In order to do well we suggest:

*Don't rely solely on your previous knowledge of economics*. If you have taken economics before you will have seen the material on supply and demand on which your tutor will lecture in the first few weeks. Don't be lulled into feeling that the course will be easy. Your previous knowledge of economic concepts will be very useful, but it will not be enough to guarantee high marks in exams. Your tutors will demand much more detailed knowledge of concepts and ask you to apply them in new circumstances.

*Keep up with the course material on a weekly basis*. Read the appropriate chapter in the textbook *before*

your tutor lectures on it. In this initial reading, don't worry about details or arguments you can't quite follow – just try and get a general understanding of the basic concepts and issues. You may be amazed at how your tutor's ability to teach improves when you come to class prepared. As soon as your tutor has finished covering a chapter, complete the corresponding *Study Guide* chapter. Avoid cramming the day before or even just the week before an exam. Because economics requires practice, cramming is an almost certain recipe for failure.

*Keep a good set of lecture notes*. Good lecture notes are vital for focusing your studying. Your tutor will only lecture on a subset of topics from the textbook. The topics your tutor covers in a lecture should usually be given priority when studying. You should also give priority to studying the figures and graphs covered in lectures.

*Use your tutor for help*. When you have questions or problems with course material, ask for help. Remember, tutors are there to help you learn. We are often amazed at how few students come to see us to ask for help. Don't be shy. The personal contact that comes from one-to-one tutoring is professionally gratifying for us as well as (hopefully) beneficial for you.

*Form a study group*. A very useful way to motivate your studying and to learn economics is to discuss the course material and problems with other students. Explaining the answer to a question *out loud* is a very effective way of discovering how well you understand the question. When you answer a question in your head only, you often skip steps in the chain of reasoning without realizing it. When you are forced to explain your reasoning aloud, gaps and mistakes quickly appear, and you (and your fellow group members) can quickly correct your reasoning. The Short Answer questions and the Discussion questions in the *Study Guide* and the Review questions at the end of each textbook chapter are good study group material. You also might get together *after* having worked the problems in the *Study Guide* chapter, but *before* looking at the answers, and help each other solve unsolved problems.

*Work old exams*. One of the most effective ways of studying is to work through exams your tutor has given in previous years. Old exams give you a feel for the style of question your lecturer may ask, and give you the opportunity to get used to time pressure if you force yourself to do the exam in the allotted time. Some institutions keep old exams in the library, others in the department. Students who have previously taken the course are usually a good source as well. Remember, though, that old exams are a useful study aid only if you use them to *understand* the reasoning behind each question. If you simply memorize answers in the hopes that your instructor will repeat the identical question, you are likely to fail. From year to year, examiners routinely change the questions or change the numerical values for similar questions.

*Use the other study aids*. In addition to the *Study Guide* you will benefit from using *Economics in Action* software. This is truly interactive tutorial software available for IBM-compatible computers. It is an integrated tutorial, graphing, demonstration and testing program that covers all the main themes in the textbook using three modes. The tutorial mode places you in an economics-related job situation and leads you through assignments that reveal and explore economic concepts and principles. The free mode allows you to interact with economic models by changing parameters and observing the effects on graphs. The quiz mode gives you graphical or data-related multiple-choice questions. When you select an answer, you are given a detailed explanation (and graphical illustration) of why your answer is right or wrong. All software modes are closely integrated with the textbook.

## Using the Study Guide

You should only attempt to complete a chapter in the *Study Guide* after you have read the corresponding textbook chapter once and listened to your lecturer lecture on the material. Each *Study Guide* chapter contains the following sections.

**Chapter in Perspective**. The purpose of this first section is to briefly situate the material of a particular textbook chapter in the context of what has come before and what will follow. Since you will see so much detailed information throughout the course, we try to paint the bigger picture for you in broad strokes so that you don't feel lost. This is the 'look at the forest instead of the trees' section.

**Helpful Hints**. Where you encounter difficulty in mastering concepts or techniques, you will not be alone. Many students find certain concepts difficult and often make the same kinds of mistakes. We have seen these common mistakes often enough to have learned how to help students avoid them. These hints point out these mistakes and offer tips for avoiding them. The hints focus on the most important concepts, equations and techniques for problem solving.

**Key Figures and Tables**. In the textbook, key figures and tables are identified with the textbook icon. Here, we group together summaries of the key figures and tables to help you focus your study on the most important diagrams. The list of Key Figures and Tables in the *Study Guide* is shorter than in the main text. This should help your revision by making it easier for you to focus on a few particularly important aspects. The summaries in this section are similar to those in the textbook captions, but use slightly different language. If you are having trouble understanding particular figures, these additional summaries should prove helpful. If you have understood the figure or table in the textbook, you may skip or skim the summary here.

**Self-Test**. Besides the Helpful Hints, this will be the most useful section of the *Study Guide*. The questions are designed to give you practice and to test the skills and techniques you must master to do well in exams. There are plenty of the types of questions you are most likely to encounter in your course exams – True/False and Multiple-Choice questions.

There are other types of questions, described below, each with a specific pedagogical purpose. Before we describe the seven parts of the Self-Test section, here are some general tips that apply to all of the parts.

Use a pencil to write your answers in the *Study Guide*. This will allow you to erase your mistakes and have neat, completed pages from which to study.

Draw graphs wherever they are applicable. Some questions will ask explicitly for graphs; many others will not but require a chain of reasoning that involves shifts of curves on a graph. *Always draw the graph.* Don't try and work through the reasoning in your head – you are much more likely to make mistakes that way. Whenever you draw a graph, even in the margins of the *Study Guide*, label the axes. You may think that you can keep the labels in your head, but you will be confronting many different graphs with many different variables on the axes. Avoid confusion and label. As an added incentive, remember that on exams where graphs are required, examiners will deduct marks for unlabelled axes.

Do the Self-Test questions as if they were real exam questions, which means do them *without looking at the answers.* This is the single most important tip we can give you about effectively using the *Study Guide* to improve your exam performance. Struggling for the answers to questions that you find difficult is one of the most effective ways to learn. The athletic adage – no pain, no gain – applies equally well to studying. You will learn the most from right answers you had to struggle for and from your wrong answers and mistakes. Only after you have attempted all of the questions should you look at the answers. When you finally do check the answers, be sure to understand where you went wrong and why the right answer is correct.

If you want to impose time pressure on yourself to simulate the conditions of a real exam, allow two minutes for each Multiple-Choice question and one minute for each True/False question. The other types of question vary considerably in their time requirements, so it is difficult to give generally applicable time estimates for them. However, we believe that such time pressure is probably not a good idea for *Study Guide* questions. A state of mind of relaxed concentration is best for work in the *Study Guide*. Use old exams if you want practice with time pressure.

The seven parts of the Self-Test section are:

## Concept Review.
This part contains simple 'recall' questions, designed to check your memory of basic terms and concepts. These questions should build your confidence. If you have understood the terms and concepts in the chapter, you should get very few of these questions wrong. This part is not a test of deep understanding or of mastery of analytical skills.

## True or False.
These questions test your basic knowledge of chapter concepts as well as your ability to apply the concepts. These are the first questions to challenge your understanding to see if you can identify mistakes in statements using basic concepts.

## Multiple Choice.
These more difficult questions test your analytical abilities by asking you to apply concepts to new situations, to manipulate information and to solve numerical and graphical problems.

Read each question and all five choices carefully before you answer. Many of the choices will be plausible and will differ only slightly. You must choose the one *best* answer. A useful strategy in working these questions is first to eliminate any obviously wrong choices and then to focus on the remaining alternatives. Be aware that sometimes the correct answer will be 'none of the above choices is correct'. Don't get frustrated or think that you are dim if you can't immediately see the correct answer. These questions are designed to make you work to find the correct choice.

## Short Answer.
Each chapter contains several Short Answer questions. These are straightforward, confidence-building questions about basic concepts. They can generally be answered in a few sentences or, at most, in one paragraph. These questions are useful to answer out loud in a study group.

## Problems.
The best way to learn to do economics is to do problems. Each Self-Test includes numerical or graphical problems. In many chapters, this will be the most challenging part of the Self-Test. It is also likely to be particularly helpful for deepening your understanding of the chapter material. We have, however, designed the questions to teach as much as to test. We have purposefully arranged the parts of each question to lead you through the problem-solving analysis in a gradual and sequential fashion, from easier to more difficult parts.

## Discussion Questions.
These are questions that are suitable for you to talk about in seminars or with your friends in order to clarify your thinking.

## Data Questions.
Each chapter includes a data question. These have been chosen to test your ability to apply economic concepts to 'real life situations'. Since real life does not come in well-defined chapters, the questions often require you to use ideas from earlier chapters. For reasons of space, the answers are not always set out in full but instead refer you to parts of the main text.

**Answers**. The Self-Test is followed by answers to all of the questions. Be sure not to look at the answers until you have attempted to answer all of the questions. When you do finally look at the answers, use them to understand where you went wrong and why the right answer is correct. The detailed answers to the Problems should be especially useful in clarifying and illustrating typical chains of reasoning involved in economics analysis. If the answers alone do not clear up your confusion, go back to the appropriate sections of the textbook. If that still does not suffice, ask your tutor for help or go to your study group members, and get help and clarification.

If you effectively combine the use of the textbook and the *Study Guide*, you will be well prepared for exams. Equally importantly, you will also have developed analytical skills and powers of reasoning that will benefit you throughout your life and in whatever career you choose.

## Do You Have Any Friendly Advice For Us?

We have attempted to make this *Study Guide* as clear as possible, and to avoid errors. No doubt, we have not succeeded entirely, and you are the only judges who count in evaluating our attempt. If you discover errors, or if you have other suggestions for improving the *Study Guide*, please write to us. In future editions, we will try and acknowledge the names of all students whose suggestions help us improve the *Study Guide*. Send your correspondence to:

The Business Editor
Addison Wesley Longman Publishers
Edinburgh Gate
Harlow
Essex
CM20 2JE

E-mail: b&e.feedback@awl.co.uk

## Acknowledgements

This *Study Guide* has benefited from help and advice from many sources. In particular it has drawn on the American and Canadian Study Guides, and I would like to thank all those who helped in preparing these editions.

Brian Atkinson

# Chapter 1    What is Economics?

---

## Chapter in Perspective, Text Pages 5–24

The fundamental economic problem is scarcity. Because wants exceed the resources available to satisfy them, we cannot have everything we want and must make choices. This problem leads to economizing behaviour – choosing the best or optimal use of the resources available. Economics, as a subject, is the study of how we use limited resources to try to satisfy unlimited wants. What economists do is also discussed.

    This chapter also introduces the *method* of economics: how economists use economic theory and models to answer economic questions and to analyse and understand how people and economic systems cope with the fundamental problem of scarcity. It also shows that, contrary to popular opinion, economists do agree on many issues.

---

## Helpful Hints

**1** The definition of economics (the study of how people use limited resources to try to satisfy unlimited wants) leads us directly to three important economic concepts – choice, opportunity cost and competition. If wants exceed resources, we cannot have everything we want and therefore must make *choices* among alternatives. In making a choice, we forgo other alternatives, and the *opportunity cost* of any choice is the value of the best forgone alternative. Also, if wants exceed resources, then wants and individuals must *compete* against each other for the scarce resources.

**2** Scientists use theory to abstract from the complex descriptive facts of the real world and focus only on those elements essential for understanding. Those essential elements are fashioned into models – highly simplified representations of the real world.

Economic models attempt to focus on the essential forces (competition, self-interest) operating in the economy while abstracting from less important forces (whims, advertising, altruism). Unlike physicists, economists cannot perform controlled experiments to test their models. As a result, it is difficult conclusively to prove or disprove a theory and its models.

**3** Remember that economic models are not claims that the real world is as simple as the model. Models claim to capture the simplified effect of some real force operating in the economy. Before drawing conclusions about the real economy from a model, we must be careful to consider whether, when we reinsert all the real-world complexities we have omitted from the model, the conclusions will be the same as in the model.

**4** The most important purpose of studying economics is not to learn lots of economic facts, but rather *how* to think about economics. The value of an economics education is the ability to think critically about economic problems and *to understand how* an economy works. This understanding of the essential forces governing how an economy works comes through the mastery of economic theory and model-building.

**5** This chapter is designed to give you a broad introduction to economics. It therefore covers a lot of ground. Don't worry if you find it a bit overwhelming; all the ideas in this chapter will be explored in greater detail later in the book.

## Key Figure

**Figure 1.2 A Picture of an Economy with Households, Firms and Governments, text page 18** This illustrates the flow of goods and services as well as flows of money in the economy. There are three groups of decision makers (households, firms and governments) and two groups of markets (goods markets and factor markets). Households supply factors of production to firms through factor markets for which they receive payment of wages, interest, rent and profits. Firms supply goods and services to households through goods markets for which they receive money payments. Governments collect taxes (money flows) from both households and firms and supply goods and services to both in addition to other benefits (transfer payments) to households and subsidies to firms.

This figure is important because it highlights the *interdependence* between households, firms and governments. What any one group can do depends on what the other groups do. This interdependence is coordinated through competition and the market mechanism.

# SELF-TEST

## CONCEPT REVIEW

**1** The fundamental and pervasive fact that gives rise to economic problems is _____ . This simply means that human wants _____ the resources available to satisfy them. The inescapable consequence is that people must make _____ .

**2** When we choose an action, the value of the best forgone alternative is the _____ cost of that action.

**3** The process of evaluating the costs and benefits of our choices in order to do the best we can with limited resources is called _____ or _____ .

**4** An economy is a mechanism that determines _____ is produced, _____ it is produced, and _____ _____ it is produced.

**5** The three groups of decision makers in the economy are _____ , _____ and _____ .

**6** Factors of production are classified under three general headings. The physical and mental resources of human beings are called _____ . Natural resources are called _____ . Manufactured goods used in production (for example, machines and factories) are called _____ .

**7** While all economies must have some way of coordinating choices, there are two fundamental mechanisms. The _____ mechanism relies on the authority of some kind of central planning, while the _____ mechanism relies on the adjustment of _____ in economic markets. A(n) _____ economy has elements of both of these fundamental mechanisms.

**8** An economy that is economically linked with other economies in the world is called _____ .

**9** Statements about what *is* are called _____ statements, while those about what *ought* to be are called _____ statements.

**10** The branch of economics that studies the choices of individual households and firms is called _____ , while the branch that studies behaviour of the economy as a whole is called _____ .

**11** The cost of a small increase in an activity is called a(n) _____ cost. The benefit that arises from a small increase in benefit is called a(n) _____ benefit.

## TRUE OR FALSE

___ **1** Scarcity is a problem only for capitalist (market) economies.

___ **2** Economics is the study of how to use unlimited resources to satisfy limited wants.

___ **3** The notion of opportunity cost is illustrated by the fact that because Fred studied for his economics examination last night he was unable to see a film with his friends.

___ **4** Competition is a contest for command over scarce resources.

___ **5** The opportunity cost of any action is the cost of all forgone alternatives.

___ **6** A mixed economy is one in which there is both internal and international trade.

___ **7** The United Kingdom is a pure market economy.

___ **8** Careful and systematic observation and measurement are basic components of any science.

___ **9** Economics is not a science since it deals with the study of wilful human beings and not inanimate objects in nature.

___ **10** An increase in the income tax rate will cause total tax revenue to fall. This is an example of a positive statement.

___ **11** A positive statement is about what *is*, while a normative statement is about what *will* be.

___ **12** Economic models are of limited value in helping us understand the real world because they abstract from the complexity of the real world.

___ **13** Macroeconomics includes the study of the causes of inflation.

___ **14** Testing an economic model requires comparing its predictions against real-world events.

___ **15** When the predictions of a model conflict with the relevant facts, a theory must be discarded or modified.

## MULTIPLE CHOICE

**1** The fact that human wants cannot be fully satisfied with available resources is called the problem of
**a** opportunity cost.
**b** scarcity.
**c** normative economics.
**d** what to produce.
**e** for whom to produce.

**2** The problem of scarcity exists
**a** only in economies that rely on the market mechanism.
**b** only in economies that rely on the command mechanism.
**c** in all economies.
**d** only when people have not optimized.
**e** now but will be eliminated with economic growth.

**3** When the government chooses to use resources to build a dam, those resources are no longer available to build a road. This illustrates the concept of
**a** a market mechanism.
**b** macroeconomics.
**c** opportunity cost.
**d** a closed economy.
**e** cooperation.

**4** Renata has the chance either to attend an economics lecture or to play tennis. If she chooses to attend the lecture, the value of playing tennis is
**a** greater than the value of the lecture.
**b** not comparable to the value of the lecture.
**c** equal to the value of the lecture.
**d** the opportunity cost of attending the lecture.
**e** zero.

**5** Which of the following is an example of capital as a factor of production?
**a** money held by Shell
**b** a Shell bond
**c** a building owned by Shell
**d** all of the above
**e** none of the above

**6** All of the following are factors of production *except*

   **a** natural resources.

   **b** tools.

   **c** labour.

   **d** government.

   **e** land.

**7** A closed economy is one that has

   **a** more exports than imports.

   **b** more imports than exports.

   **c** strict government control of production.

   **d** no economic links between households and government.

   **e** no economic links with other economies.

**8** A normative statement is a statement regarding

   **a** what is usually the case.

   **b** the assumptions of an economic model.

   **c** what ought to be.

   **d** the predictions of an economic model.

   **e** what is.

**9** 'The rich face higher income tax rates than the poor' is an example of

   **a** a normative statement.

   **b** a positive statement.

   **c** a descriptive statement.

   **d** a theoretical statement.

   **e** **b** and **c**.

**10** An economic model is tested by

   **a** examining the realism of its assumptions.

   **b** comparing its predictions with the facts.

   **c** comparing its descriptions with the facts.

   **d** the Testing Committee of the Royal Economic Society.

   **e** all of the above.

**11** When economists say that people are rational, it means they

   **a** do not make errors of judgement.

   **b** make the best decision from their perspective.

   **c** act on complete information.

   **d** will not later regret any decision made now.

   **e** do not let emotion influence decisions.

**12** The branch of economics that studies the decisions of individual households and firms is called

   **a** macroeconomics.

   **b** microeconomics.

   **c** positive economics.

   **d** normative economics.

   **e** home economics.

**13** All of the following are microeconomic questions *except*

   **a** technological change.

   **b** wages and earnings.

   **c** distribution of wealth.

   **d** production.

   **e** consumption.

## SHORT ANSWER

**1** What is meant by scarcity and why does the existence of scarcity mean that we must make choices?

**2** If all people would only economize, that would solve the problem of scarcity. Agree or disagree and explain why.

**3** Explain the interdependence that exists between households and firms in textbook Figure 1.2 on page 18 (ignore governments for this question).

**4** Why are European economies considered to be mixed?

## PROBLEMS

**1** Assume that it takes 1 hour to travel from London to Glasgow by aeroplane and 5 hours by train. Further, suppose that the air fare is £100 and the train fare is £60. Which mode of transport has the lower opportunity cost for the following people?

   **a** a person who can earn £5 an hour.

   **b** a person who can earn £10 an hour.

   **c** a person who can earn £12 an hour.

**2** Suppose the government builds and staffs a hospital in order to provide 'free' medical care.

   **a** What is the opportunity cost of the free medical care?

   **b** Is it free from the perspective of society as a whole?

**3** Indicate whether each of the following statements is positive or normative. If it is normative (positive), rewrite it so that it becomes positive (normative).

   **a** The government ought to reduce the size of the deficit in order to lower interest rates.

   **b** Government imposition of a tax on tobacco products will reduce their consumption.

**4** Suppose we examine a model of plant growth which predicts that, given the amount of water and sunlight, the application of fertilizer stimulates plant growth.
  **a** How might you test the model?
  **b** How is the test different from what an economist could do to test an economic model?

## DISCUSSION QUESTIONS

**1** 'Economic theories are useless because the models on which they are based are unrealistic.' Is this a good argument?

**2** Does everything have an opportunity cost?

## DATA QUESTIONS

**1** Two-thirds of the Netherlands lies below sea level. In 1953 a huge storm flooded large parts of the country, killing more than 2,000 people. This caused the Dutch to devote huge resources to the 'Delta Project' – a massive sea barrage which prevents the sea encroaching on to the land.

But the problem remains. If global warming becomes a reality, then the sea will rise and the Netherlands will again become vulnerable to storms. Hence it is not surprising that the Dutch are world leaders in the search for sources of energy that do not pollute the atmosphere and for measures to reduce the effects of pollution. Thus the Dutch propose to plant large numbers of trees across the world to absorb carbon dioxide.
  **a** What is meant by 'opportunity cost'? How can this concept be related to the above passage?
  **b** Distinguish between command and market economies. Which decision-making mechanism do you think was used by the Dutch in making the decisions outlined above? Why did they choose this mechanism?

**2** Saving lives costs money. More important, it needs resources. There are lots of examples of this. Every year children are killed when they run on to the road. It would be possible to reduce this number by improving road safety education and by building safety barriers along the road side. This is often done outside schools, but it could be done on a much wider scale. Similarly 'sleeping policemen' would reduce the speed of cars on housing estates.

Another example of how more resources could save lives is in medicine. If everyone had regular medical check-ups then diseases would be caught early and treatment would be more successful.
  **a** Why don't governments take such measures and so save lives?
  **b** How do you think market mechanisms would approach the problem of allocating resources to medicine?

# ANSWERS

## CONCEPT REVIEW

**1** scarcity; exceed; choices

**2** opportunity

**3** optimizing; economizing

**4** what; how; for whom

**5** households; firms; government

**6** labour; land; capital

**7** command; market; prices; mixed

**8** open

**9** positive; normative

**10** microeconomics; macroeconomics

**11** marginal; marginal

## TRUE OR FALSE

**1 F** Scarcity is a universal fact.

**2 F** It is the study of limited resources and unlimited wants.

**3 T** The opportunity cost is the alternative forgone.

**4 T** True by definition.

**5 F** It is the best alternative forgone.

**6 F** A mixed economy uses markets and command mechanisms.

**7 F** It is a mixed economy.

**8 T** All sciences have these characteristics.

**9 F** Science is not defined by subject but by method.

**10 T** Positive because it can be tested.

**11 F** Normative statements are about what *ought* to be.

**12 F** The abstraction is what makes them useful.

**13 T** Inflation affects the whole society.

**14 T** Test predictions, not assumptions.

**15 T** A model's predictions must be consistent with the facts to become part of accepted theory.

## MULTIPLE CHOICE

**1 b** Definition.

**2 c** With infinite wants and limited resources, scarcity will never be eliminated.

**3 c** The road is a forgone alternative.

**4 d** Choosing the lecture means its value is greater than tennis. Tennis is the best alternative forgone.

**5 c** Capital defined as manufactured goods used in production.

**6 d** Government is a decision maker, not a factor.

**7 e** Definition.

**8 c** Key word for normative statements is *ought*.

**9 e** Positive statements describe facts about what is.

**10 b** If its predictions do not match the facts, it is discarded.

**11 b** Rational choice is an individual's best choice based on available information.

**12 b** Definition.

**13 c** c is a macroeconomic topic.

## SHORT ANSWER

**1** Scarcity is the universal condition that human wants always exceed the resources available to satisfy them. The fact that goods and services are scarce means that individuals cannot have all of everything they want. It is therefore necessary to choose among alternatives.

**2** Disagree. If everyone economized, then we would be making the best possible use of our resources and would be achieving the greatest benefits or satisfaction possible, given the limited quantity of resources. But this does not mean that we would be satisfying all of our limitless needs. The problem of scarcity can never be 'solved' as long as people have infinite needs and finite resources for satisfying those needs.

**3** Firms depend on households for the supply of factors of production. In exchange, households depend on firms for income. Households use that income to buy goods and services from firms, while firms depend on the money they get from household purchases to be able to purchase more factors of production in the next period and start the circular flow all over again.

**4** European economies are mixed because they rely on both market and command mechanisms. Most coordination is carried out through the market mechanism, but there are many economic decisions which are made or regulated either by governments or by the European Union.

## PROBLEMS

**1** The point here is to recognize that the opportunity cost of travel includes the best alternative value of travel time as well as the train or air fare.

  **a** Thus if the opportunity cost of the time spent travelling is the £5 an hour that could have been earned (but wasn't), the opportunity cost of train travel (in pounds) is the £60 train fare plus the £25 (£5 an hour times 5 hours) in forgone income for a total of £85.

  **b** In this case, the opportunity cost of air travel is the £100 air fare plus £10 in forgone income, for a total of £110. Therefore, for a person whose best alternative use of time is to earn £10 an hour, the opportunity cost of travelling by train is the same as the opportunity cost of travelling by air.

  **c** For a person who could have earned £12 an hour the opportunity cost of train travel (£120) exceeds the opportunity cost of air travel (£112).

**2 a** Even though medical care may be offered without charge ('free'), there are still opportunity costs. The opportunity cost of providing such health care is the best alternative use of the resources used in the construction of the hospital and the best alternative use of the resources (including human resources) used in the operation of the hospital.

**b** These resources are no longer available for other activities and therefore represent a cost to society.

**3 a** The given statement is normative. The following is positive: if the government reduces the size of the deficit, interest rates will fall.

**b** The given statement is positive. The following is normative: the government ought to impose a tax on tobacco products.

**4 a** The prediction of the model can be tested by conducting the following controlled experiment and carefully observing the outcome. Select a number of similar plots of ground that will be subject to the same amount of water and sunlight. Plant equal quantities of seeds in all the plots. In some of the plots apply no fertilizer and in some of the plots apply (perhaps varying amounts of) fertilizer. When the plants have grown, measure their size and compare growth in the fertilized plots and the unfertilized plots. If plant growth is greater in fertilized plots, we provisionally accept the model and the theory on which it is based. If plant growth is *not* greater in fertilized plots, we discard the theory (model), or modify its assumptions. Perhaps the effective use of fertilizer requires more water. Then construct a new model which predicts that given more water (and the same amount of sunlight), fertilized plants will grow larger than equivalently watered unfertilized plants. Test that model and continue modifying assumptions until predictions are consistent with the facts.

**b** Economists cannot perform such controlled experiments and must instead change one assumption at a time in alternative models and compare the resulting outcomes. Such differences in outcomes can then only be tested against variations in data that occur naturally in the economy. This is a more difficult and less precise model building and testing procedure than exists for the controlled fertilizer experiment.

## DISCUSSION QUESTIONS

**1** Economic theories are like maps, which are useful precisely because they abstract from the real world. They yield predictions that can be tested in the real world. Any attempt to include all the complexities of the real world would make a theory unmanageable.

**2** Virtually everything has an opportunity cost. For example, looking at a beautiful view has an opportunity cost in that time is spent watching it. So, from a wide perspective, every human activity has an opportunity cost.

## DATA QUESTIONS

**1 a** The opportunity cost of any action is the best alternative forgone. In this case the resources used to build the Delta Project and to plant trees could have been used for other purposes.

**b** When command mechanisms are used, decisions are made by the government while market mechanisms allocate resources through markets. In this example, it was the Dutch government which made the decisions. Hence it is an example of the command mechanism. The government did this because it decided that the market mechanism would not work in this case.

**2 a** Governments don't take such measures because resources are scarce. The land, labour and capital used to implement life-saving measures would have to be paid for by giving up something else.

**b** Markets would allocate resources to medicine just as they would to any other good or service – if people wanted some medical service, it would be provided if they could pay. Command economies would involve the government deciding which services should be provided, perhaps as a result of political pressure. Neither system would be able to provide all the medical services which everyone would like because the opportunity cost would be too high.

# Chapter 2  Making and Using Graphs

## Chapter in Perspective, Text Pages 25–43

As a science, economics is characterized by systematic observation and measurement as well as by the development of economic theory. In both of these components of economic science, the use of graphs plays an important role.

Economic theory describes relationships among economic variables and graphs offer a convenient way to represent such relationships. Moreover, representing data graphically can be extremely useful for quickly conveying information about general characteristics of economic behaviour. As we will see in the next few chapters, graphical analysis of economic relationships is especially helpful when we are interested in discovering the theoretical consequences of a change in economic circumstances.

This chapter reviews all the concepts and techniques you will need to construct and use graphs in this course.

## Helpful Hints

1 The chapters of the text discuss numerous relationships among economic variables. Many of these relationships will be represented and analysed graphically. Thus an understanding of graphs will greatly facilitate mastery of the economic analysis of later chapters.

2 If your experience with graphical analysis is limited, this chapter is crucial to your ability to understand readily later economic analysis. If you are experienced in the construction and use of graphs this chapter may be 'old hat'. Even in this case, the chapter should be skimmed and the Self-Test in this *Study Guide* completed. The main point is that you should be thoroughly familiar with the basic concepts and techniques of this chapter.

3 Slope is a *linear* concept since it is a property of a straight line. For this reason, the slope is constant along a straight line but is different at different points on a curved (non-linear) line. When we are interested in the slope of a curved line, we actually calculate the slope of a straight line. The text presents two ways of choosing such a straight line and thus two alternative ways of calculating the slope of a curved line: (1) slope across an arc, and (2) slope at a point. The first of these calculates the slope of the *straight line* formed by the arc between two points on the curved line. The second calculates the slope of the *straight line* that just touches (is tangent to) the curve at a point.

4 A straight line on a graph can also be described by a simple equation. The general form for the equation of a straight line is:

$$y = a + bx$$

If you are given such an equation, you can graph the line by finding the $y$-intercept (where the line intersects the vertical $y$-axis), finding the $x$-intercept (where the line intersects the horizontal $x$-axis), and then connecting these two points with a straight line:

To find the $y$-intercept, set $x = 0$.

$$y = a + b(0)$$
$$y = a$$

To find the $x$-intercept, set $y = 0$.

$$0 = a + bx$$
$$x = -a/b$$

Connecting these two points $((x = 0, y = a)$ and $(x = -a/b, y = 0)$ or $(0, a)$ and $(-a/b,0))$ yields the line in Fig. 2.1.

**Figure 2.1**

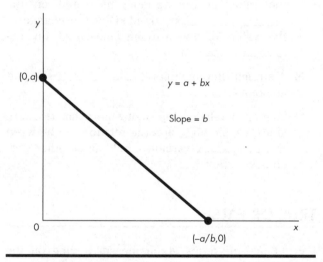

For any straight line with the equation of the form $y = a + bx$, the slope of the line is $b$.

To see how to apply this general equation, consider this example:

$$y = 4 - 2x$$

To find the $y$-intercept, set $x = 0$.

$$y = 4 - 2(0)$$
$$y = 4$$

To find the $x$-intercept, set $y = 0$.

$$0 = 4 - 2x$$
$$x = 2$$

Connecting these two points, (0,4) and (2,0), yields the line in Fig. 2.2.

**Figure 2.2**

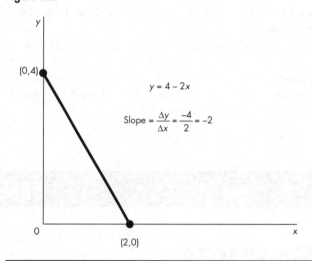

The slope of this line is –2. Since the slope is negative, there is a negative relationship between the variables $x$ and $y$.

## Key Figures

### Figure 2.9    Positive (Direct) Relationships, text page 33

Variables that move up and down together are positively related. Three different positive relationships are illustrated in this figure. In each case, as the variable measured on the horizontal axis increases, the variable measured on the vertical axis also increases. Part (a) illustrates a positive linear relationship while parts (b) and (c) illustrate positive relationships that are not linear.

### Figure 2.10    Negative (Inverse) Relationships, text page 34

This is a companion to Figure 2.9 and illustrates negative relationships. Variables that move in opposite directions are negatively related. Three different negative relationships are illustrated in this figure. In each case, as the variable measured on the horizontal axis increases, the variable measured on the vertical axis decreases.

### Figure 2.12    Maximum and Minimum Points, text page 35

The relationship in part (a) reaches a maximum. As the variable measured on the horizontal axis increases, the value of the variable measured on the vertical axis increases, reaches a maximum at point $a$ and then decreases. Similarly, the relationship in part (b) reaches a minimum at point $b$.

## Figure 2.13   The Slope of a Straight Line, text page 36

The slope of a straight line tells us how much and in what direction the variable on the vertical axis changes when the variable on the horizontal axis changes. The slope is computed by dividing the change in $y$ (the 'rise') by the change in $x$ (the 'run').

## Figure 2.14   The Slope of a Curve, text page 37

Slope is a linear concept, so even when we measure the slope of a curve, we do so by calculating the slope of a straight line. This figure illustrates the two ways of choosing a straight line to do this. Part (a) calculates the slope of the straight line that just touches (is tangent to) the curve at a point. Part (b) calculates the slope of the straight line formed by the arc between two points on the curved line.

# SELF-TEST

## CONCEPT REVIEW

**1** A graph that measures an economic variable on the vertical axis and time on the horizontal axis is called a(n) _____ - _____ graph.

**2** The tendency for a variable to rise or fall over time is called the _____ of the variable.

**3** Suppose the value of one economic variable is measured on the $x$-axis and the value of a second is measured on the $y$-axis. A diagram that plots the value of one variable corresponding to the value of the other is called a(n) _____ diagram.

**4** If two variables tend to move up or down together they exhibit a(n) _____ relationship. Such a relationship is represented graphically by a line that slopes _____ (to the right).

**5** Two variables that move in opposite directions exhibit a(n) _____ relationship. Such a relationship is represented graphically by a line that slopes _____ (to the right).

**6** Suppose variables $A$ and $B$ are unrelated. If we measure $A$ on the $y$-axis and $B$ on the $x$-axis, the graph of $A$ as we increase $B$ will be a(n) _____ line.

**7** The slope of a line is calculated as the change in the value of the variable measured on the _____ axis divided by the change in the value of the variable measured on the _____ axis.

**8** A straight line exhibits _____ slope at all points.

**9** To graph a relationship among more than two variables, we simply graph the relationship between _____ variables, holding all other variables constant.

## TRUE OR FALSE

___ **1** A time-series graph measures time on the horizontal axis.

___ **2** A time-series graph gives information about the level of the relevant economic variable, as well as information about changes and the speed of those changes.

___ **3** A two-variable time-series graph can help us see if the two variables tend to move together over time.

___ **4** A one-dimensional graph that represents measured rainfall along a horizontal line is an example of a scatter diagram.

___ **5** If the graph of the relationship between two variables slopes upward (to the right), the variables move up and down together.

___ **6** If variable *a* rises when variable *b* falls and falls when *b* rises, then the relationship between *a* and *b* is negative.

___ **7** The graph of the 'relationship' between two variables that are in fact unrelated will be either horizontal or vertical.

___ **8** The slope of a straight line is calculated by dividing the change in the value of the variable measured on the horizontal axis by the change in the value of the variable measured on the vertical axis.

___ **9** The slope of a curved line is not constant.

___ **10** If we want to graph the relationship among three variables, we must hold two of them constant as we represent the third.

___ **11** In Fig. 2.3, the relationship between *y* and *x* is first negative, reaches a minimum, and then becomes positive as *x* increases.

**Figure 2.3**

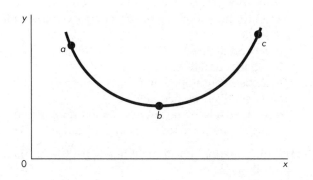

## MULTIPLE CHOICE

**Table 2.1**

| Year | x | y |
|------|-----|-----|
| 1994 | 6.2 | 143 |
| 1995 | 5.7 | 156 |
| 1996 | 5.3 | 162 |

**1** From the information in Table 2.1, it appears that
**a** *x* and *y* tend to exhibit a negative relationship.
**b** *x* and *y* tend to exhibit a positive relationship.
**c** there is no relationship between *x* and *y*.
**d** there is first a negative and then a positive relationship between *x* and *y*.
**e** there is first a positive and then a negative relationship between *x* and *y*.

**2** If variables *x* and *y* move up and down together, they are said to be
**a** positively related.
**b** negatively related.
**c** conversely related.
**d** unrelated.
**e** trendy.

**3** The relationship between two variables that move in opposite directions is shown graphically by a line that is
**a** positively sloped.
**b** relatively steep.
**c** relatively flat.
**d** negatively sloped.
**e** curved.

**4** What is the slope of the line in Fig. 2.4?
**a** 2
**b** 1/2
**c** 3
**d** 1/3
**e** −3

**Figure 2.4**

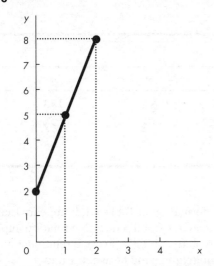

**5** If the line in Fig. 2.4 were to continue down to the $x$-axis, what would the value of $x$ be when $y$ is zero?

   **a** 0
   **b** 2
   **c** 2/3
   **d** −2/3
   **e** −3/2

**6** If the price of an umbrella is low and the number of rainy days per month is large, more umbrellas will be sold each month. On the other hand, if the price of an umbrella is high and there are few rainy days per month, fewer umbrellas will be sold each month. On the basis of this information, which of the following statements is true?

   **a** The number of umbrellas sold and the price of an umbrella are positively related, holding the number of rainy days constant.
   **b** The number of umbrellas sold and the price of an umbrella are negatively related, holding the number of rainy days constant.
   **c** The number of rainy days and the number of umbrellas sold are negatively related, holding the price of an umbrella constant.
   **d** The number of rainy days and the price of an umbrella are negatively related, holding the number of umbrellas sold constant.
   **e** None of the above statements is true.

**7** Given the data in Table 2.2, holding income constant, the graph relating the price of strawberries (vertical axis) to the purchases of strawberries (horizontal axis)

   **a** is a vertical line.
   **b** is a horizontal line.
   **c** is a positively sloped line.
   **d** is a negatively sloped line.
   **e** reaches a minimum.

**Table 2.2**

| Weekly family income (pounds) | Price per box of strawberries (pounds) | Number of boxes purchased per week |
|---|---|---|
| 300 | 1.00 | 5 |
| 300 | 1.25 | 3 |
| 300 | 1.50 | 2 |
| 400 | 1.00 | 7 |
| 400 | 1.25 | 5 |
| 400 | 1.50 | 4 |

**8** Consider the data in Table 2.2. Suppose family income decreases from £400 to £300 per week. Then the graph relating the price of strawberries (vertical axis) to the purchases of strawberries (horizontal axis) will

   **a** become negatively sloped.
   **b** become positively sloped.
   **c** shift to the right.
   **d** shift to the left.
   **e** no longer exist.

**9** Given the data in Table 2.2, holding price constant, the graph relating family income (vertical axis) to the purchases of strawberries (horizontal axis) is

   **a** a vertical line.
   **b** a horizontal line.
   **c** a positively sloped line.
   **d** a negatively sloped line.
   **e** a positively or negatively sloped line, depending on the price that is held constant.

**10** If the equation of a straight line is $y = 6 + 3x$, then the slope is

   **a** −3 and the $y$-intercept is 6.
   **b** −3 and the $y$-intercept is −2.
   **c** 3 and the $y$-intercept is 6.
   **d** 3 and the $y$-intercept is −2.
   **e** 3 and the $y$-intercept is −6.

# SHORT ANSWERS

**1** Draw a two-variable time-series graph that illustrates two variables that have a tendency to move up and down together. What would the scatter diagram for these two variables look like?

**2** Draw a graph of variables $x$ and $y$ that illustrates each of the following relationships:
**a** $x$ and $y$ move up and down together.
**b** $x$ and $y$ move in opposite directions.
**c** as $x$ increases $y$ reaches a maximum.
**d** as $x$ increases $y$ reaches a minimum.
**e** $x$ and $y$ move in opposite directions, but as $x$ increases $y$ decreases by larger and larger increments for each unit increase in $x$.
**f** $y$ is independent of the value of $x$.
**g** $x$ is independent of the value of $y$.

**3** What does it mean to say that the slope of a line is −2/3?

**4** Explain how we measure the slope of a curved line
**a** at a point.
**b** across an arc.

**5** How do we graph a relationship among more than two variables using a two-dimensional graph?

# PROBLEMS

**1** Consider the data in Table 2.3.
**a** Draw a time-series graph for the interest rate.
**b** Draw a two-variable time-series graph for both the inflation rate and the interest rate.
**c** Draw a scatter diagram for the inflation rate (horizontal axis) and the interest rate (vertical axis).
**d** Would you describe the general relationship between the inflation rate and the interest rate as positive, negative or unrelated?

**2** Compute the slope of the lines in Fig. 2.5(a) and (b).

**Table 2.3**

| Year | Inflation rate (per cent) | Interest rate (per cent) |
|------|---------------------------|--------------------------|
| 1987 | 5.4 | 6.4 |
| 1988 | 3.2 | 4.3 |
| 1989 | 3.4 | 4.1 |
| 1990 | 8.3 | 7.0 |
| 1991 | 11.8 | 7.9 |
| 1992 | 6.7 | 5.8 |
| 1993 | 4.9 | 5.0 |
| 1994 | 6.5 | 5.3 |
| 1995 | 8.6 | 7.2 |
| 1996 | 12.3 | 10.0 |

**Figure 2.5**

**(a)**

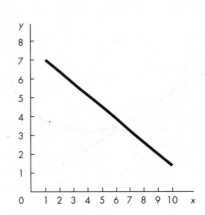

**(b)**

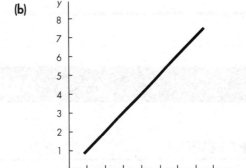

**3** Draw each of the following:
   **a** a straight line with slope –10 and passing through the point (2,80).
   **b** a straight line with slope 2 and passing through the point (6,10).

**4** The equation for a straight line is $y = 6 - 2x$.
   **a** Calculate:
     **i** the $y$-intercept
     **ii** the $x$-intercept
     **iii** the slope
   **b** Draw the graph of the line.

**5** Use the graph in Fig. 2.6 to compute the slope
   **a** across the arc between points *a* and *b*.
   **b** at point *b*.
   **c** at point *c*, and explain your answer.

**Figure 2.6**

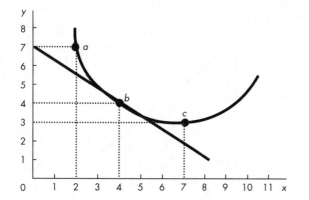

## DISCUSSION QUESTION

**1** Why do economists often use graphs instead of numbers?

## DATA QUESTIONS

Table 2.4 shows the percentage unemployment rate in the United Kingdom and in the European Union as a whole.

**Table 2.4**

|      | 1987 | 1988 | 1989 | 1990 | 1991 | 1992 | 1993 | 1994 | 1995 | 1996[1] |
|------|------|------|------|------|------|------|------|------|------|---------|
| **UK** | 10.6 | 8.7 | 7.3 | 7.0 | 9.8 | 10.1 | 10.4 | 9.6 | 8.8 | 8.6 |
| **EU** | – | – | – | – | 8 | 9.3 | 10.7 | 11.1 | 10.7 | 11.0 |

[1]Figures for 1996 are for the first part of the year.
Source: *Eurostatistics*, Tab 0601, Statistical Office of the European Community, July 1996.

Graph these data and answer the following questions:

**1** In what year was unemployment lowest in the United Kingdom? In the European Union as a whole?

**2** In what year was unemployment highest in the United Kingdom? In the European Union?

**3** Would these data support the hypothesis that unemployment was caused by international factors or by influences in one country?

**4** Was the unemployment record better in the United Kingdom or in the European Union as a whole?

# ANSWERS

## CONCEPT REVIEW

**1** time-series

**2** trend

**3** scatter

**4** positive; upward

**5** negative; downward

**6** horizontal

**7** vertical ($y$); horizontal ($x$)

**8** constant

**9** two

## TRUE OR FALSE

**1 T** Other variables are plotted on the vertical axis.

**2 T** The graph enables us to see the changes.

**3 T** A visual representation allows comparison.

**4 F** A scatter diagram shows the relationship between variables.

**5 T** This illustrates a positive relationship.

**6 T** A rise in one variable and a fall in another represents a negative relationship.

**7 T** Such a relationship can take any pattern.

**8 F** Slope is the change in the variable on the vertical axis divided by the change in the variable on the horizontal axis.

**9 T** Slope of a straight line is constant.

**10 F** Changes in more than one variable can be shown.

**11 T** Arc $ab$ would have a negative slope, arc $bc$ a positive slope.

## MULTIPLE CHOICE

**1 a** Higher values of $x$ are associated with lower values of $y$.

**2 a** Definition.

**3 d** Graph may be steep, flat or curved, but must have a negative slope.

**4 c** Change in vertical axis is 3 for each change in horizontal.

**5 d** Minus, because to the left of the $y$-axis.

**6 b c** would be true if we change 'negatively' to 'positively'. Can't judge **d** without additional information.

**7 d** Higher price is associated with lower purchases.

**8 d** At each price fewer boxes will be purchased.

**9 c** Sales increase as income increases.

**10 c** Use formula $y = a + bx$. Slope = $b$, $y$-intercept = $a$.

## SHORT ANSWER

**1** Figure 2.7(a) illustrates a two-variable time-series graph of two variables with a tendency to move up and down together. Figure 2.7(b) illustrates a scatter diagram for such variables.

**Figure 2.7**

**(a)**

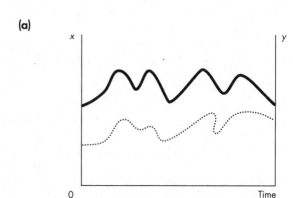

**(b)**

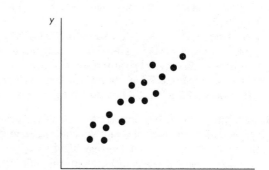

**2** Figures 2.8(a) to (g) illustrate the desired graphs.

**3** The negative sign in the slope of –2/3 means that there is a negative relationship between the two variables. The value of 2/3 means that when the variable measured on the vertical axis decreases by 2 units (the 'rise' or $\Delta y$), the variable measured on the horizontal axis increases by 3 units (the 'run' or $\Delta x$).

**Figure 2.8**

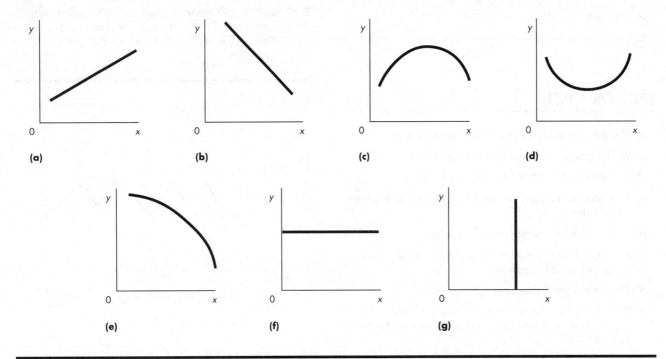

(a)   (b)   (c)   (d)

(e)   (f)   (g)

**4** In both cases we actually measure the slope of a straight line.
  **a** The slope at a point is measured by calculating the slope of the straight line that is tangent to (just touches) the curved line at the point.
  **b** The slope across an arc is measured by calculating the slope of the straight line that forms the arc.

**5** To graph a relationship among more than two variables, we hold all of the variables but two constant, and graph the relationship between the remaining two. Thus we can graph the relationship between any pair of variables, given the constant values of the other variables.

## PROBLEMS

**1 a** A time-series graph for the interest rate is given in Fig. 2.9(a).
  **b** Figure 2.9(b) is a two-variable time-series graph for both the inflation rate and the interest rate.
  **c** The scatter diagram for the inflation rate and the interest rate is given in Fig. 2.9(c).

**d** From the graphs in Fig 2.9(b) and (c), we see that the relationship between the inflation rate and the interest rate is generally positive.

**Figure 2.9**

**(a)**

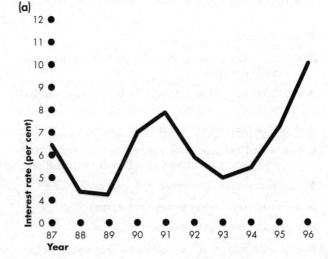

**(b)**

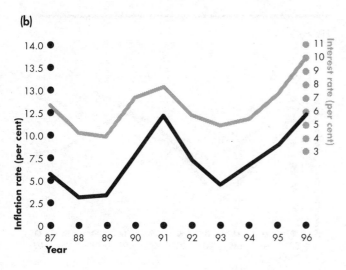

**Figure 2.10**

**(a)**

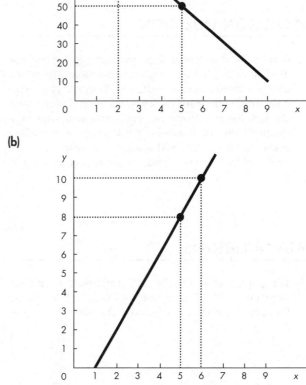

**(c)**

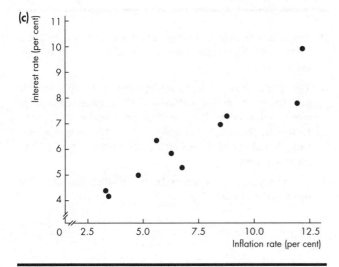

**(b)**

**2** The slope of the line in Fig. 2.5(a) is –2/3 and the slope of the line in Fig. 2.5(b) is 2.

**3 a** The requested straight line is graphed in Fig. 2.10(a).
   **b** The requested straight line is graphed in Fig. 2.10(b).

**4 a   i** To find the $y$-intercept, set $x = 0$.
$$y = 6 - 2(0)$$
$$y = 6$$

   **ii** To find the $x$-intercept, set $y = 0$.
$$0 = 6 - 2x$$
$$x = 3$$

   **iii** The slope of the line is –2, the value of the $b$ coefficient on $x$.

   **b** The graph of the line is shown in Fig. 2.11.

**Figure 2.11**

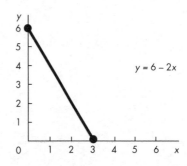

**5 a** The slope across the arc between points *a* and *b* is −3/2.

  **b** The slope at point *b* is −3/4.

  **c** The slope at point *c* is zero because it is a minimum point. Near a minimum point the slope changes from negative to positive and must pass through zero, or no slope, to do so.

## DISCUSSION QUESTION

**1** Graphs make understanding economics easier because they make it possible to picture relationships which may be hidden in a mass of figures. They can also make it easier to understand theory by showing how two variables are related. However, economists also make considerable use of numbers, particularly in economic research where statistical analysis can help make the relationship between variables more precise than is possible with graphs.

## DATA QUESTIONS

**1** The graph is shown in Fig. 2.12. The lowest unemployment rate in the United Kingdom was in 1990; in the European Union as a whole it was also 1990.

**Figure 2.12**

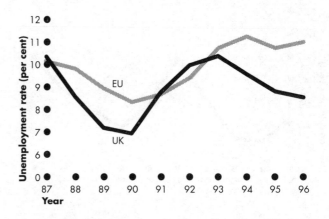

**2** The rate was highest in the United Kingdom in 1987 and 1993; in the European Union as a whole it was also highest in 1994.

**3** The graph shows that unemployment rates were similar and followed similar patterns. This suggests that they were determined by common international factors. However, there are differences, and this suggests that factors within countries (such as government policy) can have an effect.

**4** Unemployment was lower in the United Kingdom for most of the period.

# Chapter 3

# Production, Growth and Trade

---

## Chapter in Perspective, Text Pages 44–67

In the first chapter we learned that the existence of scarcity is the fundamental and pervasive social problem giving rise to economic activity. Because all individuals and all economies are faced with scarce resources choices must be made, each of which has an opportunity cost. Specialization in production is the key to obtaining maximum output from scarce resources, and leads to lowest opportunity costs. Since workers specialize as producers but consume a variety of goods and services, exchange is a necessary complement to specialization.

This chapter explains why specialization and exchange are the natural consequences of attempts to get the most from scarce resources (that is, to optimize). It also discusses the critical role of opportunity cost in explaining both why individuals and countries specialize in the production of goods and services and why tremendous gains occur from specialization and exchange.

---

## Helpful Hints

**1** This chapter reviews the absolutely critical concept of *opportunity cost* – the best alternative forgone – which was introduced in Chapter 1. A formula for opportunity cost, which works well in solving problems that involve moving up or down a production possibility frontier is:

$$\text{Opportunity cost} = \frac{\text{Give up}}{\text{Get}}$$

Opportunity cost equals the quantity of goods you must give up divided by the quantity of goods you will get.

Opportunity cost can also be related to the slope of the production possibility frontier (*PPF*). As we move down between any two points on the *PPF*, the opportunity cost of an additional unit of the good on the *horizontal* axis is:

$$| \text{ slope of } PPF |$$

The slope of the *PPF* is negative, but economists like to describe opportunity cost in terms of a positive quantity of forgone goods. Therefore, we must use the *absolute value* of the slope to calculate the desired positive number.

As we move up between any two points on the *PPF*, the opportunity cost of an additional unit of the good on the *vertical* axis is:

$$\left| \frac{1}{\text{slope of } PPF} \right|$$

**2** A production possibility frontier represents the boundary between attainable and unattainable levels of production for a fixed quantity of resources and a given state of technology. It indicates the best that can be done with existing resources and technology. Thus the production possibility frontier will shift out if the quantity of resources increases (for example, an increase in the stock of capital goods) or if there is an increase in the ability to produce (that is, a technological improvement).

**3** The text defines absolute advantage as a situation where one person has greater productivity than another in the production of all goods. We can also define *absolute advantage in the production of one good*. In comparing the productivity of two persons, this narrower concept of absolute advantage can be defined in terms of either greater output of the good per unit of inputs, or fewer inputs per unit of output. The text shows that the gains from trade depend on differing comparative advantages. People have a comparative advantage in producing a good if they can produce it at lower opportunity cost than others.

**4** This chapter gives us our first chance to develop and use an economic model. The model developed in the chapter is a representation of the production possibilities in the two-good world of Best Jeans Company. The model abstracts greatly from the complexity of the real world in which there are billions of people and numerous different kinds of goods and services. The model allows us to explain a number of phenomena that we observe in the world such as specialization and exchange. The model also has some implications or predictions. For example, countries that devote a larger proportion of their resources to capital accumulation will have more rapidly expanding production possibilities. The model can be subjected to 'test' by comparing these predictions with the facts we observe in the real world.

## Key Figures

**Figure 3.1 The Production Possibility Frontier for Jeans, text page 47**
A production possibility frontier is the boundary between attainable and unattainable levels of production for a fixed quantity of resources and a given state of technology. This figure illustrates the production possibility frontier for manufacturing two types of jeans. Each point on the frontier shows the *maximum* combinations of either straight leg or comfort fit jeans that can be produced with the resources and technology that are available. Points beyond the frontier are unattainable. Points inside the production possibility frontier are attainable but inferior.

**Figure 3.3 Increasing Opportunity Cost, text page 51**
The opportunity cost of a good is not constant. In this two-part figure, part (a) shows that as more video games are produced, more and more resources will have to be given up to produce them. This means that more and more books will have to be given up to produce the extra games. Part (b) shows the same thing applies when more and more books are produced – the opportunity cost rises in terms of games.

# SELF-TEST

## CONCEPT REVIEW

**1** The process of converting resources into goods and services is called _____ .

**2** Resources such as iron ore and running rivers are examples of _____ resources; the skill of a computer programmer and the physical strength of a bricklayer are examples of _____ resources; and a shoe factory and an olive-pitting machine are examples of _____ resources.

**3** The graphical representation of the boundary between attainable and unattainable production levels is called the _____ _____ _____ .

**4** The _____ _____ of a choice is the value of the best forgone alternative choice.

**5** Two key activities that can shift the production possibility frontier out are _____ progress and _____ accumulation.

**6** The opportunity cost of producing capital goods now in order to expand future production is forgone current _____ goods.

**7** If Marta can produce salad forks at a lower opportunity cost than Jill, we say that Marta has a(n) _____ advantage in the production of salad forks.

**8** The economic system that permits private individuals to own the capital resources used in production is called _____ .

**9** A system in which goods are traded directly for goods is known as _____ .

**10** In order for exchange to take place in such a system there must be a double _____ of wants.

## TRUE OR FALSE

___ **1** Increasing opportunity cost results from the equal usefulness of scarce resources in all activities.

**Figure 3.1**

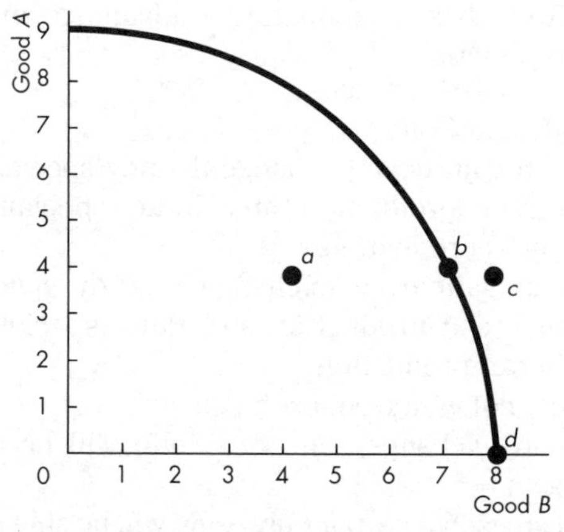

Refer to the production possibility frontier in Fig. 3.1 for Questions 2–7.

___ **2** At point *d*, 9 units of good *A* and 8 units of good *B* are produced.

___ **3** Point *a* is not attainable.

___ **4** The opportunity cost of increasing the production of good *B* from 7 to 8 units is 4 units of good *A*.

___ **5** Point *c* is not attainable.

___ **6** In moving from point *b* to point *d*, the opportunity cost of increasing the production of good *B* equals the absolute value of the slope of the production possibility frontier between *b* and *d*.

___ **7** The bowed out (concave) shape of a *PPF* reflects decreasing opportunity cost as we increase production of either good.

___ **8** Reducing the current production of consumption goods in order to produce more capital goods will shift the production possibility frontier inward in the future.

___ **9** Consider an economy with two goods, *X* and *Y*, and two producers, Bill and Joe. If Bill has a comparative advantage in the production of *X* then Joe must have a comparative advantage in the production of *Y*.

___ **10** Any time two individuals have different opportunity costs they can both gain from specialization and trade.

___ **11** The incentives for specialization and exchange do not depend on property rights but only on differing opportunity costs.

## MULTIPLE CHOICE

**1** If Harold can increase production of good *X* without decreasing the production of any other good, then Harold
  **a** is producing on his production possibility frontier.
  **b** is producing outside his production possibility frontier.
  **c** is producing inside his production possibility frontier.

**d** must have a linear production possibility frontier.

**e** must prefer good $X$ to any other good.

**2** The bowed out (concave) shape of a production possibility frontier

**a** is due to the equal usefulness of resources in all activities.

**b** is due to capital accumulation.

**c** is due to technological improvement.

**d** reflects the existence of increasing opportunity cost.

**e** reflects the existence of decreasing opportunity cost.

**3** The economy is at point $b$ on the production possibility frontier in Fig. 3.2. The opportunity cost of producing one more unit of $X$ is

**a** 1 unit of $Y$.

**b** 20 units of $Y$.

**c** 1 unit of $X$.

**d** 8 units of $X$.

**e** 20 units of $X$.

**4** The economy is at point $b$ on the production possibility frontier in Fig. 3.2. The opportunity cost of increasing the production of $Y$ to 50 units is

**a** 2 units of $X$.

**b** 6 units of $X$.

**c** 8 units of $X$.

**d** 20 units of $Y$.

**e** 30 units of $Y$.

**Figure 3.2**

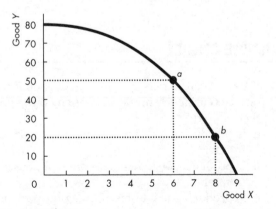

**5** Because productive resources are scarce, we must give up some of one good in order to acquire more of another. This is the essence of the concept of

**a** specialization.

**b** monetary exchange.

**c** comparative advantage.

**d** absolute advantage.

**e** opportunity cost.

**6** In general, the higher the proportion of resources devoted to technological research in an economy the

**a** greater will be current consumption.

**b** faster the production possibility frontier will shift outward.

**c** faster the production possibility frontier will shift inward.

**d** closer it will come to having a comparative advantage in the production of all goods.

**e** more bowed out will be the shape of the frontier.

In an 8-hour day, Andy can produce either 24 loaves of bread or 8 pounds of butter. In an 8-hour day, Rolfe can produce either 8 loaves of bread or 8 pounds of butter. Use this information to answer Questions 7 and 8.

**7** Which of the following statements is true?

**a** Andy has an absolute advantage in butter production.

**b** Rolfe has an absolute advantage in butter production.

**c** Andy has an absolute advantage in bread production.

**d** Andy has a comparative advantage in butter production.

**e** Rolfe has a comparative advantage in bread production.

**8** Andy and Rolfe

**a** can gain from exchange if Andy specializes in butter production and Rolfe specializes in bread production.

**b** can gain from exchange if Andy specializes in bread production and Rolfe specializes in butter production.

**c** cannot gain from exchange.

**d** can exchange, but only Rolfe will be able to gain.

**e** can exchange, but only Andy will be able to gain.

**9** Anything that is generally acceptable in exchange for goods and services is
  **a** a commodity.
  **b** a medium of exchange.
  **c** private property.
  **d** a barter good.
  **e** called an exchange resource.

**10** Which of the following is an advantage of a monetary exchange system over barter?
  **a** A monetary exchange system eliminates the basis for comparative advantage.
  **b** A monetary exchange system does not require a medium of exchange.
  **c** Only in a monetary exchange system can gains from trade be realized.
  **d** A monetary exchange system does not require a double coincidence of wants.
  **e** All of the above are advantages of a monetary exchange system over barter.

**11** Norway and the United Kingdom each produce both oil and apples using labour only. A barrel of oil can be produced with 4 hours of labour in Norway and 8 hours of labour in the United Kingdom; and 18 kilograms of apples can be produced with 8 hours of labour in Norway and 12 hours of labour in the United Kingdom. The United Kingdom has
  **a** an absolute advantage in oil production.
  **b** an absolute advantage in apple production.
  **c** a comparative advantage in oil production.
  **d** a comparative advantage in apple production.
  **e** none of the above.

Suppose a society produces only two goods – guns and butter. Three alternative combinations on its production possibility frontier are given in Table 3.1.

**Table 3.1   Production Possibilities**

| Possibility | Units of butter | Units of guns |
|-------------|-----------------|---------------|
| a | 8 | 0 |
| b | 6 | 1 |
| c | 0 | 3 |

Use the information in Table 3.1 to answer Questions 12 and 13.

**12** In moving from combination *b* to combination *c*, the opportunity cost of producing *one* additional unit of guns is
  **a** 2 units of butter.
  **b** 1/2 unit of butter.
  **c** 6 units of butter.
  **d** 1/6 unit of butter.
  **e** 3 units of butter.
  **f** 1/3 unit of butter.

**13** According to this production possibility frontier
  **a** a combination of 6 units of butter and 1 unit of guns would not employ all resources.
  **b** a combination of 0 units of butter and 4 units of guns is attainable.
  **c** resources are homogeneous.
  **d** the opportunity cost of producing guns increases as more guns are produced.
  **e** the opportunity cost of producing guns decreases as more guns are produced.

**14** In Germany, the opportunity cost of a bale of wool is 3 bottles of wine. In the United Kingdom, the opportunity cost of 1 bottle of wine is 3 bales of wool. Given this information,
  **a** the United Kingdom has an absolute advantage in wine production.
  **b** the United Kingdom has an absolute advantage in wool production.
  **c** Germany has a comparative advantage in wine production.
  **d** Germany has a comparative advantage in wool production.
  **e** no trade will occur.

## SHORT ANSWER

**1 a** Why is a production possibility frontier negatively sloped?
  **b** Why is it bowed out?

**2 a** In an economy with no tool-making possibilities (constant capital goods), what is the opportunity cost of moving from a point inside the production possibility frontier to a point on the frontier? Explain.
  **b** In a tool-making economy, what is the opportunity cost of current consumption?

**3** Lawyers earn £100 per hour while secretaries earn £8 per hour. Use the concepts of absolute and comparative advantage to explain why a lawyer, who is a better typist than her secretary, will still 'specialize' in doing only legal work and will 'trade' with the secretary for typing services.

**4** Explain, using a specific example of exchange, why a monetary exchange system is more efficient than barter.

**5** In *Reading Between the Lines,*

   **a** what do you think are the difficulties in estimating the size of the 'black economy'?

   **b** Explain what is meant by 'opportunity cost' and give an example from your own life as a student.

## PROBLEMS

**1** Suppose that an economy with unchanged capital goods (no tool-making) has the production possibility frontier shown in Table 3.2.

**Table 3.2   Production Possibilities**

| Possibility | Maximum units of butter per week | Maximum units of guns per week |
|---|---|---|
| a | 200 | 0 |
| b | 180 | 60 |
| c | 160 | 100 |
| d | 100 | 160 |
| e | 40 | 200 |
| f | 0 | 220 |

   **a** On graph paper, plot these possibilities, label the points and draw the production possibility frontier. (Put guns on the *x*-axis.)

   **b** If the economy moves from possibility *c* to possibility *d*, the opportunity cost *per unit of guns* will be how many units of butter?

   **c** If the economy moves from possibility *d* to possibility *e*, the opportunity cost *per unit of guns* will be how many units of butter?

   **d** In general terms, what happens to the opportunity cost of guns as the output of guns increases?

   **e** In general terms, what happens to the opportunity cost of butter as the output of butter increases? What do the results for possibilities *e* and *f* imply about resources?

   **f** If (instead of the possibilities given) the production possibility frontier were a straight line joining points *a* and *f*, what would that imply about opportunity costs and resources?

   **g** Given the original production possibility frontier you have plotted, is a combination of 140 units of butter and 130 units of guns per week attainable? Would you regard this combination as an efficient one? Explain.

   **h** If the following events occurred (each is a separate event, unaccompanied by any other event), what would happen to the production possibility frontier?

     **i** A new, easily exploited energy source is discovered.

     **ii** A large number of skilled workers immigrate into the country.

     **iii** The output of butter is increased.

     **iv** A new invention increases output per person in the butter industry but not in the guns industry.

     **v** A new law is passed compelling workers, who could previously work as long as they wanted, to retire at age 60.

**2** France and Germany each produce both wine and beer, using a single homogeneous input – labour. Their production possibilities are:

France has 100 units of labour and can produce a maximum of 200 bottles of wine *or* 400 bottles of beer.

Germany has 50 units of labour and can produce a maximum of 250 bottles of wine *or* 200 bottles of beer.

**Table 3.3**

|  | Bottles produced by 1 unit of labour | | Opportunity cost of 1 additional bottle | |
|---|---|---|---|---|
|  | Wine | Beer | Wine | Beer |
| France |  |  |  |  |
| Germany |  |  |  |  |

   **a** Complete Table 3.3.

Use the information in part (a) to answer the following questions.

   **b** Which country has an absolute advantage in wine production?

**c** Which country has an absolute advantage in beer production?

**d** Which country has a comparative advantage in wine production?

**e** Which country has a comparative advantage in beer production?

**f** If trade is allowed, describe what specialization, if any, will occur.

## DISCUSSION QUESTIONS

**1** Why bother to learn about production possibility curves with only two goods when every country produces millions?

**2** Why does economic growth inevitably involve some costs?

## DATA QUESTIONS

**The tailor and the shoemaker**

It is the maxim of every prudent master of a family never to attempt to make at home what it will cost him more to make than to buy. The tailor does not attempt to make his own shoes, but buys them off the shoemaker. The shoemaker does not attempt to make his own clothes, but employs a tailor…. What is prudence in the conduct of a private family can scarce be folly in that of a great kingdom…. If a foreign country can supply us with a commodity cheaper than we ourselves can make it, better buy it off them with some part of the produce of our own industry…

Source: Adam Smith, *The Wealth of Nations*, 1776.

**1** Explain what is meant by 'absolute advantage' and 'comparative advantage'. Do either of these concepts relate to the passage above? If so, how?

**2** Draw production possibility curves for the shoemaker and the tailor.

**3** How would they each benefit from specialization?

# ANSWERS

## CONCEPT REVIEW

**1** production

**2** natural; human; capital

**3** production possibility frontier

**4** opportunity cost

**5** technological; capital

**6** consumption

**7** comparative

**8** capitalism

**9** barter

**10** coincidence

**4 T** Moving from *b* to *d*, production of good *A* falls by 4 units.

**5 T** Outside *PPF.*

**6 T** See Helpful Hint 1.

**7 F** Reflects the increasing opportunity cost as increased production of either good.

**8 F** It will shift the *PPF out*ward.

**9 T** Because comparative advantage measures *relative* advantages.

**10 T** Different opportunity cost means different comparative advantage.

**11 F** Property rights are a prerequisite for specialization and exchange.

## TRUE OR FALSE

**1 F** Unequal usefulness.

**2 F** At *d*, 0 units of good *A* and 8 units of good *B* produced.

**3 F** Attainable but not a maximum.

## MULTIPLE CHOICE

**1 c** For zero opportunity cost, there must be unemployed resources.

**2 d** **a** would be true if *un*equal resources, **b** and **c** shift *PPF.*

**3 b** To increase quantity *X* to 9, must cut quantity *Y* from 20 to 0.

**4 a** To move from *b* to *a* quantity *X* falls from 8 to 6.

**5 e** Definition.

**6 b** Technological progress shifts *PPF* outward at cost of current consumption.

**7 c** Andy is three times as efficient in producing bread.

**8 b** Andy is more efficient in producing bread.

**9 b** Definition.

**10 d** Double coincidence of wants is a principal limitation of barter.

**11 d** The United Kingdom uses relatively few hours to produce apples.

**12 e** Give up 6 units of butter to get 2 units of guns: 6/2 = 3 units of butter per gun.

**13 d** Opportunity cost of a gun between *a* and *b* = 2 units of butter. Between *b* and *c* = 3 units of butter. **a** is on *PPF*, **b** outside *PPF*.

**14 c** Opportunity cost of wine in terms of bales of wool is Germany 1/3, United Kingdom 3. Opportunity cost of wool in terms of wine is Germany 3, United Kingdom 1/3.

# SHORT ANSWER

**1 a** The negative slope of the production possibility frontier reflects opportunity cost: in order to have more of one good, some of the other must be forgone.

  **b** It is bowed out because the existence of non-homogeneous resources creates increasing opportunity cost as we increase the production of either good.

**2 a** In an economy with no tool-making possibilities, a point inside the production possibility frontier represents unemployed or underutilized resources. By moving to a point on the frontier, more output can be produced from the same resources, simply by utilizing the resources more efficiently. Since resources do not have to be withdrawn from the production of any other good, the opportunity cost of moving to a point on the frontier is zero. This is the closest we get to a 'free lunch' in the discipline of economics.

  **b** In a tool-making economy, we can forgo current consumption to produce capital goods which subsequently increase future production and consumption. By consuming all that is currently produced, we forgo tool-making and, ultimately, increase future consumption.

**3** The lawyer has an absolute advantage in producing both legal and typing services relative to the secretary. Nevertheless, she has a comparative advantage in legal services, and the secretary has a comparative advantage in typing. To demonstrate these comparative advantages, we can construct a table of opportunity costs.

**Table 3.4  Opportunity Cost of 1 Additional Hour (pounds)**

|  | Legal services | Typing |
|---|---|---|
| Lawyer | 100 | 100 |
| Secretary | >100 | 8 |

Consider first the lawyer's opportunity costs. The lawyer's best forgone alternative to providing 1 hour of legal services is the £100 she could earn by providing another hour of legal services. If she provides 1 hour of typing, she is also forgoing £100 (1 hour) of legal services. What would the secretary have to forgo to provide 1 hour of legal services? She would have to spend several years as a student, forgoing years of income in addition to the tuition she must pay. Her opportunity cost is a large number, certainly greater than £100. If she provides 1 hour of typing, her best forgone alternative is the £8 she could have earned at another secretarial job. Thus Table 3.4 shows that the lawyer has a lower opportunity cost (comparative advantage) of providing legal services, and the secretary has a lower opportunity cost (comparative advantage) of providing typing services. It is on the basis of comparative advantage (not absolute advantage) that trade will take place from which both parties gain.

**4** The principal reason for the efficiency of a monetary exchange system relative to barter is that the monetary system does not require a double coincidence of wants to complete a successful exchange. For example, suppose you specialize in the production of apples but like to eat bananas. In a barter economy, you would probably not be able to complete an exchange with the first person you found who had bananas to trade. It would be necessary for that person also to want to trade the bananas for apples and not for carrots or some other good. In a monetary economy, you would always be able to make a successful exchange with the first person you found with bananas to trade since that person would be willing to accept money in exchange. Similarly, in a money exchange system, you would be able to sell your apples for money to the first person you found who wanted apples (even if that person did not have bananas to sell).

**5 a** The basic difficulty is that people will not say if they are breaking the law and not declaring income. This makes all such estimates unreliable, although this does not mean that they are useless – sometimes rough approximations are better than nothing.

  **b** The opportunity cost of any action is the next best alternative; so, for example, the opportunity cost of reading this is what you would have been doing if you were not reading this.

# PROBLEMS

**1 a** The graph of the production possibility frontier follows:

**Figure 3.3**

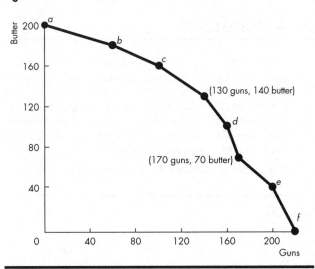

**b** In moving from *c* to *d*, in order to gain 60 units of guns, we must give up 160 – 100 = 60 units of butter. The opportunity cost per unit of guns is:

$$\frac{60 \text{ units butter}}{60 \text{ units guns}} = \frac{1 \text{ unit of butter per}}{\text{unit of guns}}$$

**c** In moving from *d* to *e*, in order to gain 40 units of guns, we must give up 100 – 40 = 60 units of butter. The opportunity cost per unit of guns is:

$$\frac{60 \text{ units butter}}{40 \text{ units guns}} = \frac{1.5 \text{ units of butter per}}{\text{unit of guns}}$$

**d** The opportunity cost of producing more guns increases as the output of guns increases.

**e** Likewise, the opportunity cost of producing more butter increases as the output of butter increases.

Increasing opportunity costs imply that resources are non-homogeneous, that is, they are not equally useful in gun and butter production.

**f** Opportunity costs would always be constant, regardless of the output of guns or butter. The opportunity cost per unit of guns would be:

200/220 = 10/11 units of butter

The opportunity cost per unit of butter would be:

220/200 = 1.1 units of guns

Constant opportunity costs imply that resources are homogeneous, that is, they are equally useful in gun and butter production.

**g** This combination is outside the frontier and, therefore, is not attainable. Since the economy cannot produce this combination, the question of efficiency is irrelevant.

**h i** Assuming that both goods require energy for their production, the entire frontier shifts out to the north-east.

**Figure 3.4**

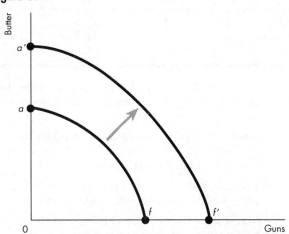

**ii** Assuming that both goods use skilled labour in their production, the entire frontier shifts out to the north-east.

**iii** The frontier does not shift. An increase in the output of butter implies a movement *along* the frontier to the left, not a shift of the frontier itself.

**iv** The new invention implies that for every level of output of guns, the economy can now produce more butter. The frontier swings to the right, but remains anchored at point *f*.

**v** The entire frontier shifts in towards the origin.

**Figure 3.5**

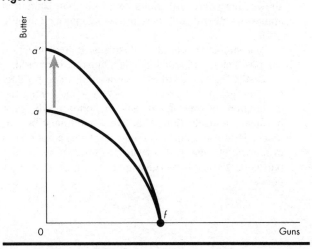

**2 a** The completed table is shown as Table 3.5.

**Table 3.5**

| | Bottles produced by 1 unit of labour | | Opportunity cost of 1 additional bottle | |
|---|---|---|---|---|
| | Wine | Beer | Wine | Beer |
| France | 2 | 4 | 2.0 beer | 0.5 wine |
| Germany | 5 | 4 | 0.8 beer | 1.25 wine |

**b** Germany, which can produce more wine (5 bottles) per unit of input, has an absolute advantage in wine production.

**c** Neither country has an absolute advantage in beer production, since beer output (4 bottles) per unit of input is the same for both countries.

**d** Germany, with the lower opportunity cost (0.8 beer), has a comparative advantage in wine production.

**e** France, with the lower opportunity cost (0.5 wine), has a comparative advantage in beer production.

**f** The incentive for trade depends only on differences in comparative advantage. Germany will specialize in wine production and France will specialize in beer production.

## DISCUSSION QUESTIONS

**1** All economic models involve simplification. The lessons that can be learned from the simple two-good *PPF* carry over into the real world; for example, the two-good *PPF* shows that there are limits to production, and this applies whether or not there are two goods or 2 million goods.

The simple model also illustrates that production can be efficient or inefficient – just like the real world.

Lastly, the two-good *PPF* shows that once production is efficient – a point on the *PPF* – increasing the production of one good has an opportunity cost because the production of the other good must be curtailed. This also applies to countries. Once a country is producing efficiently, if it wishes to produce more of a particular good, it has to give up the production of other goods.

**2** There is an opportunity cost to economic growth. As more and more of particular goods are produced, resources are being used that could have been used to produce other goods. In addition, some people would argue that economic growth imposes costs in terms of pollution.

## DATA QUESTIONS

**1** Absolute advantage occurs when one person or country has greater productivity than another in the production of all goods. A person has comparative advantage if that person can produce a good at a lower opportunity cost than another person. In the case in question, the shoemaker has a comparative advantage in producing shoes and the tailor in producing clothes.

**2** The production possibility curves are shown in Fig. 3.6.

**Figure 3.6**

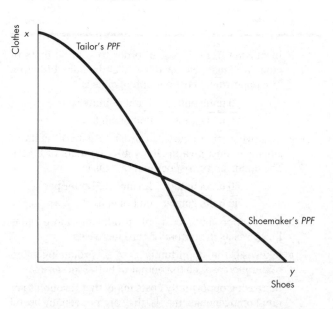

**3** Both tailor and shoemaker would benefit if they specialize and exchange their products. In Fig. 3.6, total output would be $x$ units of clothes and $y$ shoes. This exceeds the output if both tailor and shoemaker produced both clothes and shoes. Self-sufficiency means lower levels of output.

# Chapter 4

# Demand and Supply

## Chapter in Perspective, Text Pages 68–96

This is perhaps the most important chapter in the book. The concepts of demand and supply are so powerful they can be applied to a wide variety of situations. It is therefore important that you master the ideas in this chapter.

Most formal exchange takes place in 'markets' at prices determined by the interaction of buyers (demanders) and sellers (suppliers) in those markets. There are markets for goods (such as wheat or textbooks), for services (such as haircuts or tattoos), for financial assets (such as IBM shares, pounds sterling or government bonds). Demand and supply are powerful tools that economists use to explain how much will be traded and at what price. Careful use of these tools will allow us to explain a wide array of economic phenomena and even predict changes in prices and quantities traded.

## Helpful Hints

1 Specific examples will help you understand economic ideas. For example, when analysing complementary goods, think about hamburgers and chips; when discussing substitute goods, think about hamburgers and hot dogs. This will help reduce the 'abstractness' of the economic theory.

2 The statement 'price is determined by demand and supply' is a shorthand way of saying that price is determined by all of the factors affecting demand (such as prices of other goods, income, population, preferences) and all of the factors affecting supply (such as prices of other goods, prices of factors of production, technology). The benefit of using demand and supply *curves* is that they allow us systematically to sort out the influences on price of each of these separate factors.

Changes in the factors affecting demand shift the demand curve and move us up or down the given supply curve. Changes in the factors affecting supply shift the supply curve and move us up or down the given demand curve.

Any demand and supply problem requires you to sort out these influences carefully. In so doing, *always draw a graph*, even if it is just a small graph in the margin of a true–false or multiple-choice problem. As you become comfortable with graphs, you will find that they are effective and powerful tools for systematically organizing your thinking.

Note that when you draw a graph, you should be sure to *label* the *axes*. As the course progresses, you will encounter many graphs with different variables on the axes. It is easy to become confused if you do not develop the habit of labelling the axes.

**3** Another common mistake among students is a failure correctly to *distinguish between a shift in a curve and a movement along a curve*. This distinction applies to both demand and supply curves.

Consider demand curves. The quantity of a good demanded depends on its own price, the prices of related goods, income, population and preferences. The term 'demand' refers to the relationship between the price of a good and the quantity demanded, holding constant all the other factors on which the quantity demanded depends. This demand relationship is represented graphically by the demand curve. Thus the effect of a change in price on quantity demanded is already reflected in the slope of the demand curve; that is, the effect of a change in the price of the good itself is given by a movement along the demand curve. This is referred to as a change in quantity demanded.

On the other hand, if one of the other factors affecting the quantity demanded changes, the demand curve itself will shift; that is, the quantity demanded at each price will change. This shift of the demand curve is referred to as a change in demand. The critical thing to remember is that a change in the price of a good will not shift the demand curve, it will only cause a movement along the demand curve. Similarly, it is just as important to distinguish between shifts in the supply curve and movements along the supply curve.

*Remember*: it is shifts in demand and supply curves that cause the market price to change, not changes in the price that cause demand and supply curves to shift.

**4** When analysing the shifts of demand and supply curves in related markets (for example, for substitute goods like beer and wine), it often seems as though the feedback effects from one market to the other can go on endlessly. To avoid confusion, stick to the rule that each curve (demand and supply) for a given market can shift a maximum of *once*.

# Key Figures and Tables

## Figure 4.2 The Demand Curve, text page 72

A demand schedule is a table that lists the quantities consumers demand at each price, if everything else remains constant. For example, if the price of a tape is £1.50, consumers would be willing to buy 2 million tapes per week, assuming that other things (like income and the price of a Walkman) remain unchanged. The law of demand is illustrated by the fact that as the price of a tape increases, *ceteris paribus*, the quantity of tapes that consumers would be willing to buy decreases.

A demand curve is the graphical representation of the relationship between the quantity demanded of a good and its price, holding constant all other influences on consumers' planned purchases. Price appears on the vertical axis and quantity demanded on the horizontal axis. The demand curve tells us how many tapes consumers will be willing to buy in a week at each price, other things held constant. The law of demand is reflected in the negative slope of the demand curve.

## Figure 4.4 A Change in Demand Versus a Change in the Quantity Demanded, text page 75

This figure distinguishes between a change in demand (represented by a shift in the demand curve) and a change in the quantity demanded (represented by a movement along a given demand curve). Remember that a change in the price of a good or service implies that the quantity demanded changes. Since this is exactly the relationship represented by the demand curve, the change in quantity demanded is represented by a movement along the demand curve. If there is a change in any of the other factors affecting the willingness of consumers to buy at a given price, then we say there is a change in demand, which is represented by a shift in the demand curve itself.

## Figure 4.5 The Supply Curve, text page 77

A supply schedule is a table that lists the quantities that producers will plan to sell at each price, if everything else remains constant. For example, if the price of a tape is £1.50, producers will plan to sell 6 million tapes per week, assuming that other things (such as the technology used to produce tapes) remain unchanged. The law of supply is illustrated by the fact that as the price of a tape increases, *ceteris paribus*, the quantity of tapes that producers plan to supply increases.

A supply curve is the graphical representation of the relationship between the quantity of a good supplied and its price, holding constant all other influences on producers' planned sales. The supply curve tells us how many tapes producers will be willing to sell per week at each price, other things remaining the same. The law of supply is reflected in the slope of the supply curve.

**Figure 4.7  A Change in Supply Versus a Change in the Quantity Supplied, text page 79**
This figure distinguishes between a change in supply (represented by a shift in the supply curve) and a change in the quantity supplied (represented by a movement along a given supply curve). Remember that a change in the price of a good or service implies that the quantity supplied changes. Since this is the relationship represented by the supply curve, the change in quantity supplied is represented by a movement along the supply curve. If there is a change in any of the other factors affecting the willingness of producers to sell at a given price, then we say there is a change in supply, which is represented by a shift in the supply curve itself.

**Figure 4.8  Equilibrium, text page 80**
In this figure, the demand and supply curves are combined in the same graph in order to examine the price and quantity traded that leave both buyers and sellers satisfied. Equilibrium price is defined as the price at which the quantity demanded is equal to the quantity supplied. The equilibrium price (90 pence in the example) can be identified using either the table or the diagram. The idea of equilibrium as a point of rest is also illustrated. Note that when the price is below the equilibrium price there is a shortage, which will cause the price to rise towards equilibrium. When the price is above the equilibrium price, there is a surplus, which will cause the price to fall towards equilibrium. Only at the equilibrium price will there be no tendency for the price to change.

**Table 4.1  The Demand for Tapes, text page 74**
This table specifies the law of demand: the quantity demanded increases as the price of the good or service falls and decreases as the price rises. These changes are represented by movements along the demand curve. The factors that cause changes in demand are also listed. Changes in these factors will cause the demand curve to shift. Note that the table assumes that tapes are a normal good, since a rise in income will cause the demand for tapes to increase. If the good in question is inferior, a rise in income will cause demand to decrease whereas a fall in income will cause demand to increase. As implied by the name, most goods and services are normal.

**Table 4.2  The Supply of Tapes, text page 78**
In parallel with Table 4.1, this table specifies the law of supply: the quantity supplied increases as the price rises and decreases as the price falls. These changes are represented by movements along the supply curve. The factors that cause changes in supply are also listed. Changes in these factors will cause the supply curve to shift.

# SELF-TEST

## CONCEPT REVIEW

**1** The _____ _____ of a good or service is the amount that consumers are willing and able to purchase at a particular price.

**2** The law of demand states that, other things remaining the same, the higher the _____ of a good, the _____ is the quantity demanded.

**3** A demand _____ is a list of the quantities of a good demanded at different _____.

**4** A demand curve illustrates the _____ price that consumers are willing to pay for the last unit of a good purchased.

**5** The demand curve for most goods will shift to the right if income _____, or if the price of a substitute _____, or if the price of a complement _____, or if the size of the population _____.

**6** A good is said to be _____ if the demand for it increases as income increases and _____ if demand decreases as income increases.

**7** The amount of a good or service that producers plan to sell at a particular price is called the _____ _____.

**8** The law of supply states that the _____ the price of a good, the _____ the quantity supplied.

**9** A supply curve shows the quantity supplied at each given _____ .

**10** A decrease in supply is represented by a shift to the _____ in the supply curve.

**11** The supply curve will shift to the right if the price of a complement in production _____ , or if the price of a substitute in production _____ , or if there is a technological _____ , or if the price of a productive resource _____ .

**12** An increase in the price of a good will cause an increase in the _____ ; this is represented by a(n) _____ movement along the supply curve.

**13** The price at which the quantity demanded equals the quantity supplied is called the _____ price.

**14** If the price is above equilibrium, a(n) _____ will exist, causing the price to _____ .

**15** When demand increases, the equilibrium price will _____ and the quantity traded will _____ .

**16** When supply increases, the equilibrium price will _____ and the quantity traded will _____ .

**17** If demand increases and supply increases, then we know that the quantity traded must _____ ; but the equilibrium price may increase, decrease or remain unchanged.

## TRUE OR FALSE

___ **1** The law of demand tells us that as the price of a good rises the quantity demanded decreases.

___ **2** The negative slope of a demand curve is a result of the law of demand.

___ **3** An increase in the price of apples will shift the demand curve for apples to the left.

___ **4** Hamburgers and chips are complements. If Burger Bar reduces the price of chips, the demand for hamburgers will increase.

___ **5** A supply curve shows the maximum price at which the last unit will be supplied.

___ **6** A demand curve is a graphical representation of the relationship between the price of a good and quantity demanded given the level of income, prices of other goods, population and preferences.

___ **7** A cost-reducing technological improvement will shift a supply curve to the right.

___ **8** If we observe a doubling of the price of mozzarella cheese (an ingredient in pizza), we will expect the supply curve for pizzas to shift to the left.

___ **9** When a cow is slaughtered for beef, its hide becomes available to make leather. Thus beef and leather are substitutes in production.

___ **10** If the price of beef rises, we would expect to see an increase in the supply of leather and in the quantity of beef supplied.

___ **11** If the current price is such that the quantity demanded exceeds the quantity supplied, the price will tend to rise.

___ **12** If demand increases, we would predict an increase in equilibrium price and a decrease in quantity traded.

___ **13** If potatoes are inferior goods, we would expect an increase in income to result in a fall in the price of potatoes.

___ **14** A decrease in the supply of a good will result in a decrease in both the equilibrium price and the quantity traded.

## MULTIPLE CHOICE

**1** Which of the following could *not* cause an increase in demand for a commodity?
**a** an increase in income
**b** a decrease in income
**c** a decrease in the price of a substitute
**d** a decrease in the price of a complement
**e** an increase in preferences for the commodity

**2** If Hamburger Helper is an inferior good, then, *ceteris paribus*, a decrease in income will cause
   **a** a leftward shift of the demand curve for Hamburger Helper.
   **b** a rightward shift of the demand curve for Hamburger Helper.
   **c** a movement up along the demand curve for Hamburger Helper.
   **d** a movement down along the demand curve for Hamburger Helper.
   **e** none of the above.

**3** Good $A$ is a normal good if
   **a** an increase in the price of a complement causes the demand for $A$ to decrease.
   **b** an increase in income causes the demand for $A$ to increase.
   **c** an increase in the price of a substitute causes the demand for $A$ to increase.
   **d** it satisfies the law of demand.
   **e** income and the demand for $A$ are negatively correlated.

**4** A decrease in quantity demanded is represented by a
   **a** rightward shift of the supply curve.
   **b** rightward shift of the demand curve.
   **c** leftward shift of the demand curve.
   **d** movement upward and to the left along the demand curve.
   **e** movement downward and to the right along the demand curve.

**5** The price of a good will tend to fall if
   **a** there is a surplus at the current price.
   **b** the current price is above equilibrium.
   **c** the quantity supplied exceeds the quantity demanded at the current price.
   **d** all of the above are true.
   **e** none of the above is true.

**6** The fact that a decline in the price of a good causes producers to reduce the quantity of the good supplied illustrates
   **a** the law of supply.
   **b** the law of demand.
   **c** a change in supply.
   **d** the nature of an inferior good.
   **e** technological improvement.

**7** A shift of the supply curve for salami will be caused by

   **a** a change in preferences for salami.
   **b** a change in the price of a related good that is a substitute in consumption for salami.
   **c** a change in income.
   **d** a change in the price of salami.
   **e** none of the above.

**8** Which of the following will shift the supply curve for good $X$ to the left?
   **a** a decrease in the wages of workers employed to produce $X$
   **b** an increase in the cost of machinery used to produce $X$
   **c** a technological improvement in the production of $X$
   **d** a situation where quantity demanded exceeds quantity supplied
   **e** all of the above

**9** If a resource can be used to produce either good $A$ or good $B$, then $A$ and $B$ are
   **a** substitutes in production.
   **b** complements in production.
   **c** substitutes in consumption.
   **d** complements in consumption.
   **e** normal goods.

**10** If the market for pencils is in equilibrium, then
   **a** pencils must be a normal good.
   **b** producers would like to sell more at the current price.
   **c** consumers would like to buy more at the current price.
   **d** there will be a surplus.
   **e** quantity traded equals quantity demanded.

**11** A shortage is the amount by which quantity
   **a** demanded exceeds quantity supplied.
   **b** traded exceeds quantity supplied.
   **c** traded exceeds quantity demanded.
   **d** demanded exceeds the equilibrium quantity.
   **e** supplied exceeds the equilibrium quantity.

**12** A surplus can be eliminated by
   **a** increasing supply.
   **b** government raising the price.
   **c** decreasing the quantity demanded.
   **d** allowing the price to fall.
   **e** allowing the quantity traded to fall.

The market for coffee is initially in equilibrium with supply and demand curves of the usual shape. Pepsi is a substitute for coffee; cream is a complement for coffee. Questions 18–20 concern the market for *coffee*.

Assume that all *ceteris paribus* assumptions continue to hold *except* for the event(s) listed. Answer each question without considering the others.

**13** Coffee is a normal good. A decrease in income will
   **a** increase the price of coffee and increase the quantity demanded of coffee.
   **b** increase the price of coffee and increase the quantity supplied of coffee.
   **c** decrease the price of coffee and decrease the quantity demanded of coffee.
   **d** decrease the price of coffee and decrease the quantity supplied of coffee.
   **e** cause none of the above.

**14** An increase in the price of Pepsi will
   **a** increase the price of coffee and increase the quantity demanded of coffee.
   **b** increase the price of coffee and increase the quantity supplied of coffee.
   **c** decrease the price of coffee and decrease the quantity demanded of coffee.
   **d** decrease the price of coffee and decrease the quantity supplied of coffee.
   **e** cause none of the above.

**15** A technological improvement lowers the cost of producing coffee. At the same time, preferences for coffee decrease. The *quantity traded* of coffee will
   **a** rise.
   **b** fall.
   **c** remain the same.
   **d** rise or fall depending on whether the price of coffee falls or rises.
   **e** rise or fall depending on the relative shifts of demand and supply curves.

**16** If both demand and supply increase, then
   **a** price will rise and quantity traded will increase.
   **b** price will fall and quantity traded will increase.
   **c** price could either rise or fall and quantity traded will increase.
   **d** price will rise and quantity traded could either increase or decrease.

   **e** price will fall and quantity traded could either increase or decrease.

**17** Which of the following will definitely cause an increase in the equilibrium price?
   **a** an increase in both demand and supply
   **b** a decrease in both demand and supply
   **c** an increase in demand combined with a decrease in supply
   **d** a decrease in demand combined with an increase in supply
   **e** none of the above

## SHORT ANSWER

**1** Explain the difference between wants and demands.

**2** Suppose we observe that the consumption of peanut butter increases at the same time as its price rises. What must have happened in the market for peanut butter? Is the observation consistent with the law of demand?

**3** The price of personal computers has continued to fall even in the face of increasing demand. Explain.

**4** Brussels sprouts and carrots are substitutes in consumption and, since they can both be grown on the same type of land, substitutes in production too. Suppose there is an increase in the demand for Brussels sprouts. Trace through the effects on price and quantity traded in both the Brussels sprout and carrot markets. (Keep in mind Helpful Hint 4.)

**5** In *Economics in History*, explain how, when demand and supply are in stable equilibrium, 'if any accidents should move the scale of production from its equilibrium position, there will be instantly brought into play forces tending to push it back to that position'.

## PROBLEMS

**1** The information given in Table 4.1 is about the behaviour of buyers and sellers of fish at the market on a particular Saturday.

### Table 4.1 Demand and Supply Schedules for Fish

| Price per fish | Quantity demanded | Quantity supplied |
|---|---|---|
| £0.75 | 270 | 45 |
| £1.00 | 260 | 135 |
| £1.25 | 245 | 185 |
| £1.50 | 225 | 225 |
| £1.75 | 200 | 250 |
| £2.00 | 170 | 265 |
| £2.25 | 135 | 280 |
| £2.50 | 105 | 290 |
| £2.75 | 80 | 300 |
| £3.00 | 60 | 310 |
| £3.25 | 45 | 315 |
| £3.50 | 35 | 320 |

a On graph paper, draw the demand curve and the supply curve. Be sure to label the axes. What is the equilibrium price?

b We will make the usual *ceteris paribus* assumptions about the demand curve so that it does not shift. List four factors that we are assuming do not change.

c We will also hold the supply curve constant by assuming that three factors do not change. List them.

d Explain briefly what would happen if the price were initially set at £2.75.

e Explain briefly what would happen if the price were initially set at £1.

f Explain briefly what would happen if the price were initially set at £1.50.

2 The market for wine in the United Kingdom is initially in equilibrium with supply and demand curves of the usual shape. Beer is a close substitute for wine; cheese and wine are complements. Use demand and supply diagrams to analyse the effect of each of the following (separate) events on the equilibrium price and quantity traded in the UK wine market. Assume that all of the *ceteris paribus* assumptions continue to hold except for the event listed. For both price and quantity traded, you should indicate in each case whether the variable rises, falls, remains the same, or moves ambiguously (may rise or fall).

a The income of consumers falls (wine is a normal good).

b Early frost destroys a large part of the world grape crop.

c A new churning invention reduces the cost of producing cheese.

d A new fermentation technique is invented that reduces the cost of producing wine.

e A government study is published which suggests that wine drinking is linked to higher rates of heart disease.

f Costs of producing both beer and wine increase dramatically.

3 Table 4.2 lists the demand and supply schedules for cases of peanuts.

### Table 4.2 Demand and Supply Schedules for Cases of Peanuts per Week

| Price per case | Quantity demanded (cases) | Quantity supplied (cases) |
|---|---|---|
| £70 | 20 | 140 |
| £60 | 60 | 120 |
| £50 | 100 | 100 |
| £40 | 140 | 80 |
| £30 | 180 | 60 |

a Draw the demand and supply curves for peanuts. Be sure to label the axes properly. Label the demand and supply curves $D_0$ and $S_0$ respectively.

b What are the equilibrium price and quantity traded in the peanut market? On your diagram, label the equilibrium point a.

c Is there a surplus or a shortage at a price of £40? How much?

d Suppose the population grows sufficiently that the demand for peanuts increases by 60 cases per week at every price.

   i Construct a table (price, quantity demanded) of the new demand schedule.

   ii Draw the new demand curve on your original graph and label it $D_1$.

   iii Label the new equilibrium point b. What are the new equilibrium price and quantity traded?

## DISCUSSION QUESTIONS

**1** What is the difference between a move along a curve and a movement of a curve?

**2** The law of demand and supply says that a fall in demand will lead to a fall in price. But observation would suggest that in the real world prices hardly ever fall. So how do we explain this difference?

## DATA QUESTIONS

**Setting sail for happier returns**
Holidaymakers: this could be your last cross-Channel summer bonanza. Enjoy it while it lasts. The government last week allowed P&O to seek cooperation with its seafaring rivals in the Straits of Dover. P&O is expected to suggest to its arch rival Stena Line that they collaborate on Channel crossings, which could mean anything from joint pricing and sailing to a merger of assets. By next summer the current 11 P&O and Stena ships could be replaced by only six. They will have 50 per cent of the cross-channel drive-on market, compared with Eurotunnel's 40 per cent, with the remainder shared between Hoverspeed and Sea France.

Since Eurotunnel commenced operation the total market has grown, but there is overcapacity both on and under the water and fares have dropped by 20 per cent on average.

Source: Adapted from *The Observer (Business Supplement)*, 21 July 1996. Published by permission of The Observer©.

**1** Draw diagrams to show the effect that Eurotunnel had on the price of a cross-Channel journey.

**2** What will be the effect on price if the ferry firms cut the number of ferries? What will be the effect on Eurotunnel?

# ANSWERS

## CONCEPT REVIEW

**1** quantity demanded
**2** price; lower
**3** schedule; prices
**4** highest
**5** increases; increases; decreases; increases
**6** normal; inferior
**7** quantity supplied
**8** higher; higher
**9** price
**10** left
**11** increases; decreases; improvement; increases
**12** quantity supplied; upward
**13** equilibrium
**14** surplus; fall
**15** increase; increase
**16** decrease; increase
**17** increase

## TRUE OR FALSE

**1 F** As price rises, quantity demanded decreases.
**2 T** The law of demand states that as price falls, quantity increases.
**3 F** It will cause a movement *along* the curve.
**4 T** A meal of hamburger and chips is now cheaper.
**5 F** Supply curve shows minimum price at which last unit supplied.
**6 T** The demand curve holds constant all factors except quantity and price.
**7 T** More will be supplied at each price.
**8 T** An increase in the price of a factor of production leads to a fall in supply.
**9 F** Beef and leather are complements in production because they are produced together.
**10 T** For complements in production, an increase in the price of one good leads to an increase in quantity supplied and an increase in the supply of the other good.
**11 T** Price rises when demand exceeds supply.
**12 F** An increase in demand will lead to an increase in quantity.

**13 T** For inferior goods, an increase in income leads to a fall in demand and a fall in price.

**14 F** A decrease in supply will lead to a rise in price.

## MULTIPLE CHOICE

**1 c** A fall in the price of a substitute causes an increased demand for the substitute and therefore a fall in demand for the other good.

**2 b** Changes in income shift the demand curve rather than causing moves along it.

**3 b** Definition.

**4 d** Decrease in quantity is caused by a change in price and a movement along a curve.

**5 d** Demand shifts left.

**6 a** Definition.

**7 e** **a**, **b** and **c** affect demand. **d** would cause a move along the supply curve.

**8 b** A rise in the price of a factor shifts the supply curve left.

**9 a** As alternatives, they are substitutes.

**10 e** Definition.

**11 a** Shortage occurs when demand exceeds supply.

**12 d** Other answers make surplus larger.

**13 d** Demand shifts left.

**14 b** Demand shifts right.

**15 e** Supply shifts right and demand shifts left.

**16 c** Both shifts will increase quantity but have opposite effects on price.

**17 c** Both shifts will increase price.

## SHORT ANSWER

**1** Wants reflect our unlimited desires for goods and services without regard to our ability or willingness to make the sacrifices necessary to obtain them. The existence of scarcity means that many of those wants will not be satisfied. On the other hand, demands refer to plans to buy and, therefore, reflect decisions about which wants to satisfy.

**2** The observation that the consumption of peanut butter increases at the same time as the price of peanut butter rises is entirely consistent with the law of demand (that is, a negatively-sloped demand curve). It simply reflects the fact that the demand for peanut butter has increased (that is, the demand curve has shifted out to the right).

**3** Owing to the tremendous pace of technological advance, not only has the demand for personal computers been increasing, but the supply has been increasing as well. Indeed, supply has been increasing much more rapidly than demand, which has resulted in falling prices. Thus *much* (but not all) of the increase in sales of personal computers reflects a movement down along a demand curve rather than a shift in demand.

**4** The answer to this question requires us to trace through the effects on the two graphs in Fig. 4.1(a) and (b) – one for the Brussels sprout market and one for the carrot market. The sequence of effects occurs in order of the numbers on the graphs.

### Figure 4.1

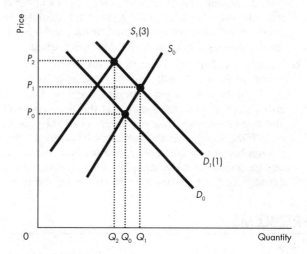

**(a) Brussels sprouts**

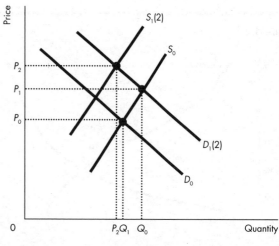

**(b) Carrots**

Look first at the market for Brussels sprouts. The increase in demand shifts the demand curve to the right from $D_0$ to $D_1$ (1), and the price of Brussels sprouts rises. This price rise has two effects (2) on the carrot market. Since Brussels sprouts and carrots are substitutes in consumption, the demand curve for carrots shifts to the right from $D_0$ to $D_1$. And, since Brussels sprouts and carrots are substitutes in production, the supply curve of carrots shifts to the left from $S_0$ to $S_1$. Both of these shifts in the carrot market raise the price of carrots, causing feedback effects on the Brussels sprout market. But remember the rule (Helpful Hint 4) that each curve (demand and supply) for a given market can shift a maximum of *once*. Since the demand curve for Brussels sprouts has already shifted, we can only shift the supply curve from $S_0$ to $S_1$ (3) because of the substitutes in production relationship. Each curve in each market has now shifted once and the analysis must stop. We can predict that the net effects are increases in the equilibrium prices of both Brussels sprouts and carrots, and indeterminate changes in quantities traded in both markets.

**5** If some 'accident' occurs, such as bad weather cutting output of food, this will lead to a fall in supply. The result will be a rise in price. In turn, this will stimulate growth in supply in the future and the price rise will also reduce demand. The eventual result will be equilibrium. If the accident should lead to a fall in demand then the result will be a fall in price, causing more people to buy the good and at the same time causing firms to cut production. Again, the result will be a new equilibrium.

# PROBLEMS

**1 a** The demand and supply curves are shown in Fig. 4.2. The equilibrium price is £1.50 per fish.

**b** Prices of other (related) goods; income; population; preferences.

**c** Prices of other (related) goods; prices of factors of production; technology.

**d** At a price of £2.75, quantity supplied (300) exceeds quantity demanded (80). Fish sellers find themselves with surplus fish. Rather than be stuck with unsold fish (which yield no revenue), some sellers cut their price in an attempt to increase the quantity of fish demanded. Competition forces other sellers to follow suit, and the price falls until it reaches the equilibrium price of £1.50, while quantity demanded increases until it reaches the equilibrium quantity of 225 units.

**e** At a price of £1, the quantity demanded (260) exceeds the quantity supplied (135) – there is a shortage. Unrequited fish buyers bid up the price in an attempt to get the 'scarce' fish. As prices continue to be bid up as long as there is excess demand, quantity supplied increases in response to higher prices. Price and quantity supplied both rise until they reach the equilibrium price (£1.50) and quantity (225 units).

**f** At a price of £1.50, the quantity supplied exactly equals the quantity demanded (225). There is no excess demand (shortage) or excess supply (surplus), and, therefore, no tendency for the price or quantity to change.

**2** The demand and supply diagrams for parts (a) to (e) are shown in Fig. 4.3.

Questions like part (f) require the examination of two separate but related markets – the beer and wine markets. Since this kind of question often causes confusion for students, here is a more detailed explanation of the answer.

## Figure 4.2

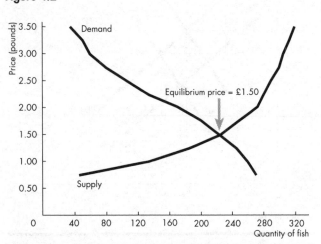

## Figure 4.3

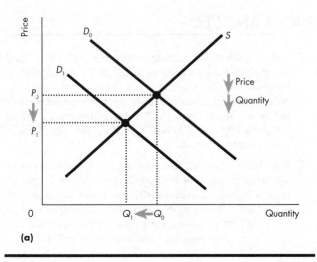

(a)

# Figure 4.3

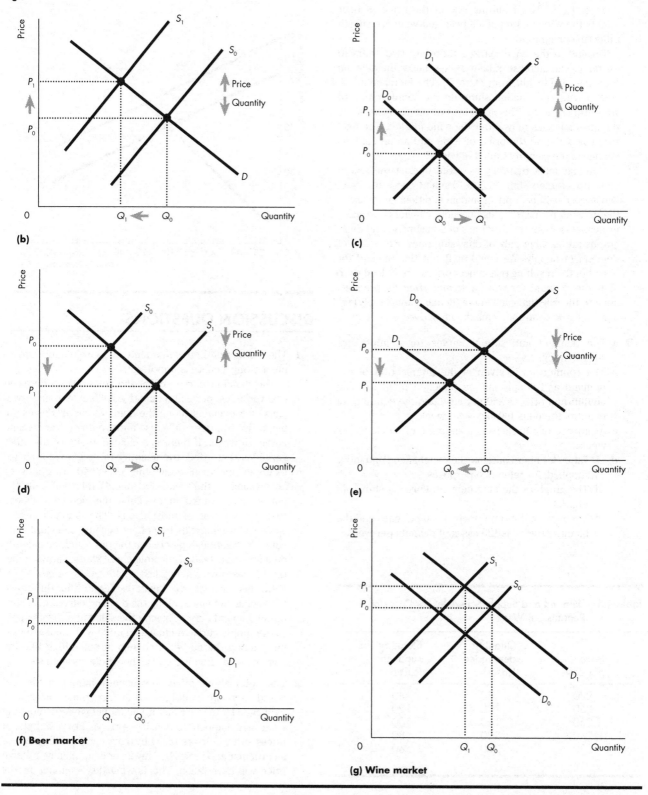

(b)

(c)

(d)

(e)

(f) Beer market

(g) Wine market

Look first at the beer market. The increase in the cost of beer production shifts up the supply curve of beer from $S_0$ to $S_1$. The resulting rise in the price of beer affects the wine market since beer and wine are substitutes (in consumption).

Turning to the wine market, there are two shifts to examine. The increase in beer prices causes the demand for wine to shift out from $D_0$ to $D_1$. The increase in the cost of wine production shifts up the supply curve of wine from $S_0$ to $S_1$. This is the end of the analysis, since the question asks only about the wine market. The final result is a rise in the price of wine and an ambiguous change in the quantity traded of wine.

Many students rightfully ask: 'But doesn't the rise in wine prices then shift out the demand curve for beer, causing a rise in beer prices and an additional increase in the demand for wine?' This question, which is correct in principle, is about the dynamics of adjustment, and these graphs are capable only of analysing once-over shifts of demand or supply. We could shift out the demand for beer, but the resulting rise in beer prices would lead us to shift the demand for wine a *second time*. In practice, stick to the rule that each curve (demand and supply) for a given market can shift a maximum of *once*.

**3 a** The demand and supply curves for peanuts are shown in Fig. 4.4.
   **b** The equilibrium is given at the intersection of the demand and supply curves (labelled point *a*). The equilibrium price is £50 per case and the equilibrium quantity traded is 100 cases per week.
   **c** At a price of £40 there is a shortage of 60 cases per week.
   **d** **i** Table 4.3 also contains the (unchanged) quantity supplied, for reference purposes.
      **ii** The graph of the new demand curve is shown in Fig. 4.4.
      **iii** The new equilibrium price is £60 per case and the quantity traded is 120 cases of peanuts per week.

**Table 4.3  Demand and Supply Schedules for Cases of Peanuts per Week**

| Price per case | Quantity demanded (cases) | Quantity supplied (cases) |
|---|---|---|
| £70 | 80 | 140 |
| £60 | 120 | 120 |
| £50 | 160 | 100 |
| £40 | 200 | 80 |
| £30 | 240 | 60 |

**Figure 4.4**

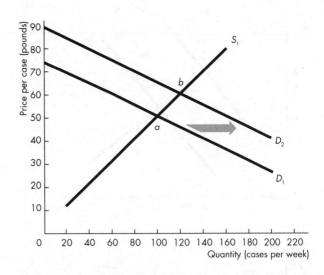

## DISCUSSION QUESTIONS

**1** The distinction between a shift in a curve and a movement along a curve is important.

The demand curve shows the relationship between two variables: price and quantity. A change in price will cause a movement along the demand curve. For example, a rise in price will cause a move down the demand curve. However, if there is a change in any of the other variables that affect the quantity of goods we buy (for example, incomes, competing or substitute goods or advertising in the case of demand) this will shift the entire curve. For example, a fall in our income will mean that we buy less of most goods. The demand curve's slope cannot show us this effect because the slope indicates the relationship between the price and the quantity demanded. Instead, the whole curve shifts, showing that (in this case) we will buy less whatever the price.

In this answer we have discussed the difference between a movement along the demand curve and a shift in the demand curve. Exactly the same arguments apply to the supply curve. A change in price will cause a movement along the curve. A change in something like the cost of production will cause the whole curve to shift.

**2** The point about prices not usually falling in the real world but often doing so in economic models is explained by the fact that in the model we are predicting what will happen to *relative* prices. For example, if prices as a whole are rising by 5 per cent and the price of a particular good rises by only 2 per cent, then its relative price will have fallen. This is what the economic model predicts and, as relative price changes are frequent in the real economy, the model is extremely useful.

What causes prices as a whole to change is discussed later in the book when we talk about inflation.

## DATA QUESTIONS

**1** The effect of Eurotunnel's entry into the cross-Channel market is shown in Fig. 4.5. This new large firm meant that there was a substantial increase in supply. This is shown by the move from $S_0$ to $S_1$ in part (a). The result is a fall in price from $P_0$ to $P_1$.

**2** If P&O and Stena cut the supply, the result will be as shown in part (b). The supply curve will move upward to the left and the result will be a rise in price. Eurotunnel will benefit from this higher price since it means less competition so it will also be able to charge higher prices.

**Figure 4.5**

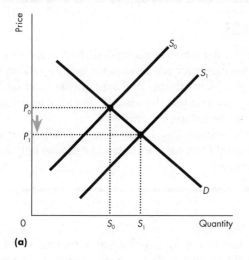

**(a)**

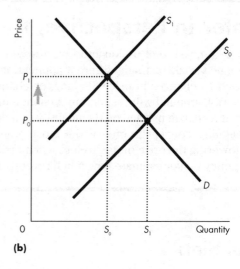

**(b)**

# Chapter 5    **Elasticity**

---

## Chapter in Perspective, Text Pages 97–121

Elasticity is a measure of the quantitative *responsiveness* of quantity demanded or supplied to changes in other key economic variables. Using different applications of elasticity, we can calculate how much quantity demanded will respond to changes in price, income, or changes in the prices of substitutes or complements, and by how much quantity supplied will respond to a change in price. Similarly, we can use the idea of elasticity to calculate the effect of a change in price on the quantity of a good that firms will be willing to supply.

The elasticity concept is one of the most practical concepts in economics. It can help a company decide whether lowering the price of its product will increase or decrease total revenue from sales. It can also help a government policy maker estimate how much revenue a sales tax will raise.

---

## Helpful Hints

**1** There are many elasticity formulae in this chapter, but they are all based on *responsiveness*. All of the demand and supply elasticity formulae measure the *responsiveness (sensitivity) of quantity* (demanded or supplied) to changes in something else. Thus percentage change in quantity is always in the numerator of the relevant formula.

**2** The complete formula for calculating the price elasticity of demand between two points on the demand curve is:

$$\eta = \left| \frac{\% \, \Delta \text{ quantity demanded}}{\% \, \Delta \text{ price}} \right|$$

$$= \left| \left( \frac{\Delta Q}{Q_{ave}} \right) \bigg/ \left( \frac{\Delta P}{P_{ave}} \right) \right|$$

The law of demand assures us that price and quantity demanded always move in opposite directions along any demand curve. Thus without the absolute value sign, the formula for the price elasticity of demand would yield a negative number. Whenever you see the often-used shorthand term, *elasticity of demand*, remember that it means the absolute value of the *price* elasticity of demand.

**3** Elasticity is *not* the same as slope (although they are related). Along a straight-line demand curve the slope is constant, but the elasticity varies from infinity to zero as we move down the demand curve.

**4** One of the most practical and important uses of the concept of price elasticity of demand is that it allows us to predict the *effect on total revenue* of a change in price. A fall in price will increase total revenue if demand is elastic, leave total revenue unchanged if demand is unit elastic, and decrease total revenue if demand is inelastic. Because price and quantity demanded always move in opposite directions along a demand curve, a fall in price will cause an increase in quantity demanded. Since total revenue equals price × quantity, the fall in price will tend to decrease total revenue, while the increase in quantity demanded will increase total revenue. The net effect depends on which of these individual effects is larger.

The concept of price elasticity of demand conveniently summarizes the net effect. For example, if demand is elastic, the percentage change in quantity demanded is greater than the percentage change in price. Hence with a fall in price, the quantity effect dominates and total revenue will increase. If, however, demand is inelastic, the percentage change in quantity demanded is less than the percentage change in price. Hence with a fall in price, the price effect dominates and total revenue will decrease.

**5** Two other important elasticity concepts are the income elasticity of demand and the cross elasticity of demand.

Income elasticity of demand:

$$\eta_Y = \frac{\% \, \Delta \text{ quantity demanded}}{\% \, \Delta \text{ income}}$$

$$= \left(\frac{\Delta Q}{Q_{ave}}\right) \Big/ \left(\frac{\Delta Y}{Y_{ave}}\right)$$

Cross elasticity of demand:

$$\eta_X = \frac{\% \, \Delta \text{ quantity demanded of good } A}{\% \, \Delta \text{ price of good } B}$$

$$= \left(\frac{\Delta Q^A}{Q^A_{ave}}\right) \Big/ \left(\frac{\Delta P^B}{P^B_{ave}}\right)$$

Notice that these two elasticity formulae do *not* have absolute value signs and can take on either positive or negative values. In the case of income elasticity of demand, the response of quantity demanded to an increase in income will be positive for a normal good and negative for an inferior good. In the case of cross elasticity of demand, the response of the quantity demanded of good $A$

to an increase in the price of good $B$ will be positive if the goods are substitutes and negative if the goods are complements.

# Key Figures and Table

## Figure 5.4 Elasticity Along a Straight-line Demand Curve, text page 103

When the slope of a straight-line demand curve is constant, the elasticity varies systematically as we move down it. The elasticity decreases as the price of the good falls and the quantity demanded rises. In the price range above the midpoint of a straight-line demand curve, demand is elastic, at the midpoint elasticity is 1 (demand is unit elastic), and in the price range below the midpoint, demand is inelastic.

## Figure 5.8 Income Elasticity of Demand, text page 108

The three graphs in this figure illustrate relationships between income (measured on the horizontal axis) and quantity demanded (measured on the vertical axis). Part (a) shows a relationship in which the quantity demanded increases as income increases, but the quantity demanded increases by a greater percentage than income. Thus the income elasticity is greater than 1. In part (b) quantity demanded and income again increase together but the percentage change in quantity demanded is less than the percentage change in income. The income elasticity is between 0 and 1. The first part of the relationship in part (c) is similar to that of part (b). However, as income continues to increase, eventually the quantity demanded reaches a maximum and thereafter decreases. At the point of maximum quantity demand, the income elasticity is 0 and it is negative for higher levels of income.

## Table 5.3 A Compact Glossary of Elasticities of Demand, text page 110

Three kinds of elasticities of demand are presented in this chapter: price elasticities, income elasticities and cross elasticities of demand. The purpose of this table is to summarize the economic meaning of these measures as they assume values in alternative ranges. Table 5.3 should serve as an excellent study device. You should understand and memorize all the information contained in the table.

# SELF-TEST

## CONCEPT REVIEW

**1** A units-free measure of the responsiveness of quantity demanded to price changes is given by the _____ _____ of demand.

**2** The (price) elasticity of demand is calculated as the percentage change in the _____ _____ divided by the percentage change in the _____ .

**3** If the (price) elasticity of demand is between 0 and 1, demand is said to be _____ ; if it is greater than 1, demand is said to be _____ ; if it is equal to 1, demand is said to be _____ _____ .

**4** A good that has many good substitutes is likely to have demand that is _____ . If only a small proportion of income is spent on a good, its demand is likely to be _____ .

**5** As time passes after a change in the price of a good, demand will tend to become more _____ .

**6** If demand is elastic, an increase in the price implies that revenue (expenditures) will _____ .

**7** A measure of the responsiveness of the quantity demanded of a good to changes in income is given by the _____ _____ of demand.

**8** The income elasticity of demand is calculated as the percentage change in the _____ _____ divided by the percentage change in _____ .

**9** The income elasticity is _____ for inferior goods.

**10** The responsiveness of the quantity demanded of one good to a change in the price of a complement or substitute is given by the _____ _____ of demand.

**11** The cross elasticity of demand with respect to the price of a substitute is _____ . The cross elasticity of demand with respect to the price of a complement is _____ .

**12** The elasticity of supply is a measure of the responsiveness of the _____ _____ to changes in _____ .

**13** To illustrate the initial change in quantity supplied induced by a sudden change in price we use the _____ supply curve. To illustrate the response of quantity supplied after all technologically possible long-run adjustments in the production process have been made we use the _____ supply curve.

**14** The long-run supply curve will generally be more _____ than a short-run supply curve, which will be more _____ than the momentary supply curve.

## TRUE OR FALSE

___ **1** The price elasticity of demand measures how responsive prices are to changes in demand.

___ **2** A horizontal demand curve is perfectly inelastic.

___ **3** The demand for petrol is likely to become more inelastic with the passage of time after a price increase.

___ **4** If substitutes for a good are more readily available, demand for it will be more inelastic.

___ **5** If total revenue falls following an increase in price, demand must be inelastic.

___ **6** If your expenditures on toothpaste are a small proportion of your total income, your demand for toothpaste is likely to be inelastic.

___ **7** The more narrowly we define a good, the more elastic is its demand.

___ **8** Long-run demand is more inelastic than short-run demand because there is more opportunity for substitution.

___ **9** If the income elasticity of the demand for turnips is positive, then turnips are an inferior good.

**10** The effect of the change in the price of one good on the quantity demanded of another good is measured by the cross elasticity of demand.

**11** We would expect the cross elasticity of demand between hamburgers and hot dogs to be negative.

**12** If goods *A* and *B* are substitutes, then a decrease in the demand for *A* will lead to a decrease in the equilibrium price of *B*.

**13** Supply will generally be more inelastic in the long run than in the short run.

**14** For a linear demand curve, demand is more elastic at higher price ranges than at lower price ranges.

**15** If a 10 per cent increase in the price of good *A* causes a 6 per cent decrease in the quantity of good *B* demanded, the cross elasticity of demand between *A* and *B* is 0.6.

**16** If a 9 per cent increase in price leads to a 5 per cent decrease in quantity demanded, total revenue has decreased.

## MULTIPLE CHOICE

**1** Two points on the demand curve for volleyballs are shown in Table 5.1.

Table 5.1

| Price per volleyball (pounds) | Quantity demanded |
|---|---|
| 19 | 55 |
| 21 | 45 |

What is the elasticity of demand between these two points?
a 2.5
b 2.0
c 0.5
d 0.4
e none of the above

**2** The fact that butter has margarine as a close substitute in consumption
a makes the supply of butter more elastic.
b makes the supply of butter less elastic.
c makes the demand for butter more elastic.
d makes the demand for butter less elastic.
e does not affect butter's elasticity of supply or demand.

**3** If the price elasticity of demand is 2, then a 1 per cent decrease in price will
a double the quantity demanded.
b reduce the quantity demanded by half.
c increase the quantity demanded by 2 per cent.
d reduce the quantity demanded by 2 per cent.
e increase the quantity demanded by 0.5 per cent.

**4** A good will have a more price inelastic demand
a the higher its price.
b the larger the percentage of income spent on it.
c the longer the time elapsed.
d if it is a luxury good.
e if it has no close substitutes.

**5** If the demand for frozen orange juice is price elastic, then a severe frost that destroys large quantities of oranges is likely to
a reduce the equilibrium price of juice but increase total consumer spending on it.
b reduce the equilibrium quantity of juice as well as total consumer spending on it.
c reduce both the equilibrium quantity and the price of juice.
d increase the equilibrium price of juice as well as total consumer spending on it.
e increase the equilibrium price of juice but leave total consumer spending on it constant.

**6** If a 4 per cent rise in the price of peanut butter causes the total revenue from peanut butter sales to fall by 8 per cent, then demand for peanut butter
a is elastic.
b is inelastic.
c is unit elastic.
d has an elasticity of 0.5.
e has an elasticity of 2.

**7** Tina and Brian work for the same recording company. Tina claims that they would be better off by increasing the price of their tapes while Brian claims that they would be better off by decreasing the price. It can be concluded that

a Tina thinks the demand for tapes has price elasticity of zero and Brian thinks price elasticity equals one.

b Tina thinks the demand for tapes has price elasticity equal to one and Brian thinks price elasticity equals zero.

c Tina thinks the demand for tapes is price elastic and Brian thinks it is price inelastic.

d Tina thinks the demand for tapes is price inelastic and Brian thinks it is price elastic.

e Tina and Brian should stick to singing and forget about economics.

**8** Given the relationship shown in Fig. 5.1 between total revenue from the sale of a good and the quantity of the good sold, then

a this is an inferior good.

b this is a normal good.

c the elasticity of demand is zero.

d the elasticity of demand is infinity.

e the elasticity of demand is one.

**Figure 5.1**

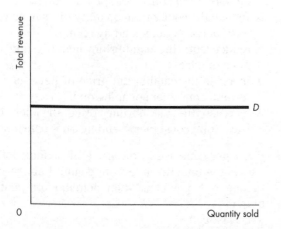

**9** If an increase in price causes a decrease in total revenue then price elasticity of demand is

a negative.

b zero.

c greater than zero but less than one.

d equal to one.

e greater than one.

**10** If a 4 per cent decrease in income (at a constant price) causes a 2 per cent decrease in the consumption of books then

a the income elasticity of demand for books is negative.

b books are a necessity and a normal good.

c books are a luxury and a normal good.

d books are an inferior good.

e **a** and **d** are true.

**11** Luxury goods tend to have income elasticities of demand which are

a greater than one.

b greater than zero but less than one.

c positive.

d negative.

e first positive and then negative as income increases.

**12** If a 10 per cent increase in income causes a 5 per cent increase in quantity demanded (at a constant price), what is the income elasticity of demand?

a 0.5

b −0.5

c 2.0

d −2.0

e none of the above

**13** The cross elasticity of the demand for white tennis balls with respect to the price of yellow tennis balls is probably

a negative and high.

b negative and low.

c positive and high.

d positive and low.

e zero.

**14** A decrease in the price of $X$ from $6 to $4 causes an increase in the quantity of $Y$ demanded (at the current price of $Y$) from 900 to 1,100 units. What is the cross elasticity of demand between $X$ and $Y$?

a 0.5

b −0.5

c 2

d −2

e **a** or **b**, depending on whether $X$ and $Y$ are substitutes or complements

**15** When price goes from £1.50 to £2.50, quantity supplied increases from 9,000 to 11,000 units. What is the price elasticity of supply?
a 0.4
b 0.8
c 2.5
d 4.0
e none of the above

**16** The magnitude of *both* the elasticity of demand and the elasticity of supply depend on
a the ease of substitution between goods.
b the proportion of income spent on a good.
c the time elapsed since the price change.
d the technological conditions of production.
e none of the above factors.

**17** The long-run supply curve is likely to be
a more elastic than momentary supply but less elastic than the short-run supply curve.
b less elastic than momentary supply but more elastic than the short-run supply curve.
c less elastic than both momentary and short-run supply curves.
d more elastic than both momentary and short-run supply curves.
e vertical.

## SHORT ANSWER

**1** In each of the following, compare the price elasticity of demand for each pair of goods and explain why demand for one of the goods is more elastic than demand for the other.
a IBM personal computers before the development of other 'clone' personal computers versus IBM personal computers after the production of such clones
b Television sets versus matches
c Electricity just after an increase in its price versus electricity two years after the price increase

**2** Why does demand tend to be more elastic in the long run?

**3** Why does supply tend to be more elastic in the long run?

**4** Which demand curve in Fig. 5.2 ($D_A$ or $D_B$) is more elastic in the price range $P_1$ to $P_2$? Explain why. [*Hint:* use the formula for price elasticity of demand.]

Figure 5.2

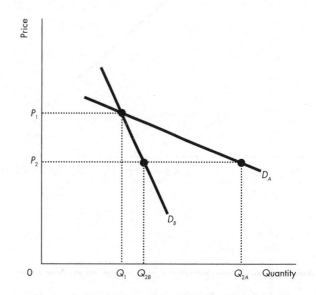

**5** In *Reading Between the Lines*, explain
a why some markets can be described as 'cut throat'.
b how knowledge of price elasticity can lead to the 'rewards of a better pricing strategy'.

## PROBLEMS

**1** a Given the demand curve in Fig. 5.3, complete the second and third columns of the table in this figure: $\eta$ (the price elasticity of demand) and $\Delta TR$ (the change in total revenue) as the price falls from the higher price to the lower price. Describe the relationship between elasticity and change in total revenue as price falls (moving down the demand curve).

**Figure 5.3**

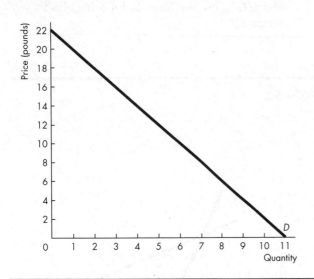

| ΔP (pounds) | η | ΔTR (pounds) | η | ΔTR' (pounds) |
|---|---|---|---|---|
| 16–14 | | | | |
| 14–12 | | | | |
| 12–10 | | | | |
| 10–8 | | | | |
| 8–6 | | | | |

**b** Suppose income, which initially was £10,000, increases to £14,000, causing an increase in demand: at every price, quantity demanded increases by 2 units. Draw the new demand curve and label it $D'$. Use this new demand curve to complete the last two columns of the table in Fig. 5.3 for η (the new price elasticity of demand) and $\Delta TR'$ (the new change in total revenue).

**c** Using the price range between £16 and £14, explain why $D'$ is more inelastic than $D$.

**d** Calculate the income elasticity of demand, assuming the price remains constant at £12. Is this a normal or an inferior good? Explain why you could have answered the question even without calculating the income elasticity of demand.

**2** Table 5.2 gives the demand schedules for good $A$ when the price of good $B$ ($P_B$) is £8 and when the price of good $B$ is £12. Complete the last column of the table by computing the cross elasticity of demand between goods $A$ and $B$ for each of the three prices of $A$. Are $A$ and $B$ complements or substitutes?

**Table 5.2 Demand Schedules for Good A**

| | $P_B = £8$ | $P_B = £12$ | |
|---|---|---|---|
| $P_A$ | $Q_A$ | $Q'_A$ | $\eta_X$ |
| 8 | 2,000 | 4,000 | |
| 7 | 4,000 | 6,000 | |
| 6 | 6,000 | 8,000 | |

## DISCUSSION QUESTION

**1** 'The mathematics for calculating the elasticity of demand are not necessary; the slope of a diagram will do just as well.' Discuss.

## DATA QUESTIONS

Table 5.3 gives figures of income elasticity of various foods.

**Table 5.3**

| | Income elasticity |
|---|---|
| All foods | −0.01 |
| Frozen convenience meats | −0.36 |
| Fresh fruit | 0.48 |
| Fruit juices | 0.94 |
| Bread | −0.25 |
| Tea | −0.56 |
| Coffee | 0.23 |

Source: Adapted from *Household Food Consumption and Expenditure Report*, Ministry of Agriculture, Fisheries and Food, 1990.

**1** Explain what is meant by 'income elasticity of demand'.

**2** What is meant by saying that the income elasticity of all foods is −0.01?

**3** Assume that incomes continue to rise in the next few years and that income elasticities of demand remain constant. What will be the effect on firms producing the goods mentioned in the table?

# ANSWERS

## CONCEPT REVIEW

**1** price elasticity
**2** quantity demanded; price
**3** inelastic; elastic; unit elastic
**4** elastic; inelastic
**5** elastic
**6** decrease
**7** income elasticity
**8** quantity demanded; income
**9** negative
**10** cross elasticity
**11** positive; negative
**12** quantity supplied; price
**13** momentary; long-run
**14** elastic; elastic

## TRUE OR FALSE

**1 F** It measures the responsiveness of quantity to changes in price.
**2 F** Definition.
**3 F** Elasticity increases as time passes.
**4 F** More substitutes lead to greater elasticity.
**5 F** Revenue increases when price rises and demand is elastic.
**6 T** The smaller the proportion of income spent on a good, the lower the elasticity.
**7 T** Narrow definitions are associated with more substitutes.
**8 F** In the long run more substitutes will be produced.
**9 F** For inferior goods, as income increases less is demanded.
**10 T** Definition.
**11 F** Cross elasticity is positive for substitutes.
**12 T** Follows from definition.
**13 F** Supply becomes more elastic in the long run.
**14 T** Elasticity changes along a straight line.
**15 F** Cross elasticity is *minus* 0.6.
**16 F** Percentage increase in price is greater than the percentage fall in quantity, so total revenue increases.

## MULTIPLE CHOICE

**1 b** $(-10/50)/(2/20) = -2$
**2 c** Closer substitutes lead to more elastic demand.
**3 c** $Q$ and $P$ are always inversely related on demand curve.
**4 e** **a** and **d** irrelevant, elasticity falls with smaller proportion of income spent on a good and shorter elapsed time.
**5 b** Supply curve will shift to the left; the rise in price will lead to a bigger fall in demand.
**6 a** If increase in price leads to a fall in total revenue, elasticity must be greater than one.
**7 d** Better off means increased total revenue. If demand is elastic a price cut will increase revenue.
**8 e** Note total revenue on $y$-axis. Since total revenue is constant as quantity increases (and presumably price falls), elasticity = 1.
**9 e** Definition.
**10 b** Income elasticity >0, so normal good. Necessities tend to have income elasticity <1.
**11 a** See previous answer. **c** is correct, but **a** is best answer.
**12 a** Positive, because income and price move in the same direction.
**13 c** Close substitutes, so cross elasticity is positive and high.
**14 b** Substituting into formula gives $(200/1,000)/(-2/5) = -0.5$
**15 a** Substituting into formula gives $(2,000/10,000)/(1/2) = 0.4$.
**16 c** **a** and **b** affect price elasticity only; **d** affects supply elasticity only.
**17 d** Definition. Momentary supply curve most vertical.

## SHORT ANSWER

**1 a** The demand for IBM personal computers will be more elastic after the production of clone personal computers since there would then be more readily available substitutes.
 **b** The demand for television sets will be more elastic since they will generally take a larger proportion of consumer income.

**c** The demand for electricity after the passage of two years will be more elastic since consumers will have more time to find substitutes for electricity (for example, a gas stove).

**2** Demand is more responsive to price changes (more elastic) in the long run because more substitutes become available to consumers. Not only are new goods invented but consumers also learn about and begin to use new substitutes.

**3** Supply is more elastic in the long run because the passage of time allows producers to find better (more efficient) ways of producing that are not available in the short run. The responsiveness of production to an increase in price will increase as firms have time to discover and implement new technologies or to increase the scale of operation.

**4** $D_A$ is more elastic than $D_B$. To see why, look at the formula for price elasticity of demand:

$$\eta = \left| \frac{\% \, \Delta \text{ quantity demanded}}{\% \, \Delta \text{ price}} \right|$$

The percentage change in price is the same for the two demand curves. But the percentage change in quantity is greater for $D_A$. At $P_1$, the initial quantity demanded is the same for both demand curves ($Q_1$). With the fall in price to $P_2$, the increase in quantity demanded is greater for $D_A$ (to $Q_{2A}$) than for $D_B$ (to $Q_{2B}$). Therefore $D_A$ is more elastic than $D_B$. (See Fig. 5.4.)

**5 a** 'Cut throat' implies that sellers are forced to cut prices. This would be the case where competition is strong, and also where price elasticity of demand is high. This would mean that any seller with higher prices would sell very little.

**b** Where demand for a good is inelastic, firms can increase their prices without losing much custom. Hence revenue will rise when they increase prices. Where demand is elastic, total revenue will be increased if prices are cut, but whether or not this is profitable will depend on other factors such as what happens to costs when output rises.

# PROBLEMS

**1 a** The completed columns of the table attached to Fig. 5.3 are shown here in Table 5.4. The second and third columns of the table show that as price falls, total revenue increases when demand is elastic; total revenue remains constant when demand is unit elastic; total revenue falls when demand is inelastic.

**Figure 5.4**

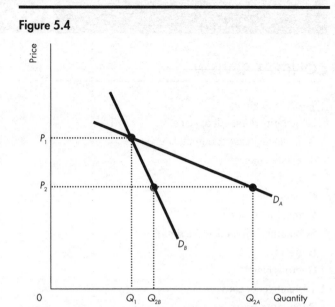

**Table 5.4**

| $\Delta P$ (pounds) | $\eta$ | $\Delta TR$ (pounds) | $\eta$ | $\Delta TR'$ (pounds) |
|---|---|---|---|---|
| 16–14 | 2.14 | +8 | 1.36 | +4 |
| 14–12 | 1.44 | +4 | 1.00 | 0 |
| 12–10 | 1.00 | 0 | 0.73 | −4 |
| 10–8 | 0.69 | −4 | 0.53 | −8 |
| 8–6 | 4.67 | −8 | 0.37 | −12 |

**Figure 5.5**

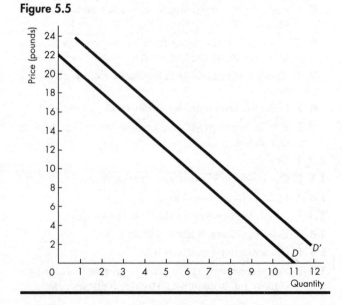

**b** The new demand curve is labelled $D'$ (Fig. 5.5). The last two columns of the table have been completed on the basis of the new demand curve.

**c** Since they are parallel, $D'$ and $D$ have exactly the same slope. Thus we know that for a given change in price, the change in quantity demanded will be the same for the two curves. However, elasticity is determined by *percentage* changes, and the percentage change in quantity demanded is different for the two curves (although the percentage change in price will be the same). For a given percentage change in price, the percentage change in quantity demanded will always be less for $D'$. For example, as the price falls from £16 to £14 (a 13 per cent change), the quantity demanded increases from 5 to 6 units along $D'$ but from 3 to 4 units along $D$. The percentage change in quantity demanded is only 18 per cent along $D'$ and 29 per cent along $D$. Since the percentage change in price is the same for both curves, $D'$ is more inelastic than $D$.

**d** Income increases from £10,000 to £14,000. At a constant price of £12, the increase in income, which shifts out the demand curve to $D'$, increases the quantity consumers will demand from 5 units to 7 units. Substituting these numbers into the formula for the income elasticity of demand yields:

$$\eta_Y = \left(\frac{\Delta Q}{Q_{ave}}\right) \bigg/ \left(\frac{\Delta Y}{Y_{ave}}\right)$$

$$= \left(\frac{2}{6}\right) \bigg/ \left(\frac{4{,}000}{12{,}000}\right) = +1$$

The income elasticity of demand is a positive number, since both $Q$ and $Y$ are positive. Therefore this is a normal good. We already knew that from the information in part (b), which stated that the demand curve shifted out to the right with an increase in income. If this were an inferior good, the increase in income would have shifted the demand curve in to the left, and the income elasticity of demand would have been negative.

**2** The cross elasticities of demand between $A$ and $B$ are listed in the table. Since the cross elasticities are positive, we know that $A$ and $B$ are substitutes.

## DISCUSSION QUESTION

**1** It is true that the slope of a diagram is a useful quick way to discuss elasticity, but it is imprecise. Changing the scale on the axes will change the slope of the curve and so might give a misleading impression. Numerical answers avoid this difficulty.

**Table 5.5 Demand Schedules for Good A**

| $P_A$ | $P_B = £8$ $Q_A$ | $P_B = £12$ $Q'_A$ | $\eta_X$ |
|---|---|---|---|
| 8 | 2,000 | 4,000 | 1.67 |
| 7 | 4,000 | 6,000 | 1.00 |
| 6 | 6,000 | 8,000 | 0.71 |

## DATA QUESTIONS

**1** Income elasticity of demand is a measure of the responsiveness of demand for a good to a change in income.

**2** When we say that the income elasticity of demand for all food is –0.01 we mean that as incomes rise there is little effect on the demand for foods as a whole, although this conceals some significant changes in the demand for particular foods. This is not surprising; if our incomes doubled, most of us would not double our food consumption, although we might eat more of some luxury foods.

**3** If incomes rise while income elasticities remain unchanged, then sales of goods such as fresh fruit and fruit juice will rise faster than incomes. Hence producers of such goods will prosper, other things remaining the same. However, producers of goods with negative income elasticities will find that their sales fall.

# Chapter 6    **Markets in Action**

---

## Chapter in Perspective, Text Pages 122–146

This chapter extends the theory of demand and supply by focusing on markets in action. In particular, it examines various types of government intervention in the economy. This can take several forms. Governments intervene in markets such as housing and labour because they believe that markets fail. Hence they introduce schemes such as minimum wage legislation to help low-paid workers. They intervene on a huge scale by imposing taxes on goods and services. Governments also affect markets by prohibiting some products, particularly drugs, and the chapter examines the effect that this has on the quantity and price of such products.

The chapter also examines another type of intervention: that of the European Union in the market for agricultural products.

---

## Helpful Hints

**1** In the real world we frequently observe market regulation by governments in the form of price constraints of one type or another. It is thus important to study the effects of such regulation in its own right. Another significant benefit of exploring the effects of government regulation, however, is a clearer and deeper understanding of how markets work when, by contrast, the government does *not* affect the normal operation of markets.

Whenever something happens to disturb an equilibrium in an unregulated (free) market, the desires of buyers and sellers are brought back into balance by price movements. If prices are controlled by government regulation, however, the price mechanism can no longer serve this purpose. Thus 'balance' must be restored in some other way. In the case of price ceilings, black markets are likely to arise. If black markets cannot develop because of strict enforcement of the price ceiling, then demanders will be forced to bear the costs of increased search activity, waiting in queues, or something else.

**2** In any market with a legal price ceiling set below the market-clearing price, we will observe excess quantity demanded, because the price cannot increase to eliminate it. As a consequence, the value of the last unit of the good available will exceed the controlled price, and therefore demanders are willing to engage in costly activities up to the value of that last unit (for example, search activity, queuing and black market activity) in order to obtain the good.

Furthermore, if the price is allowed to increase in response to a decrease in supply or an increase in demand, there are incentive effects for suppliers to produce more and demanders to purchase less (that is, movements along the supply and demand curves). Indeed, it is the response to these incentives that restores equilibrium in markets with freely adjusting prices. If, however, the price cannot adjust, these price-induced incentive effects do not have a chance to operate.

# Key Figures

### Figure 6.1 The Gelderland Housing Market in 1995, text page 125

In January 1995, the Gelderland province of the Netherlands suffered a devastating flood which wrecked homes and businesses. Figure 6.1 illustrates the response of the unregulated housing market. Part (a) shows the position before the flood, with demand equalling supply at the going rent. Part (b) shows how the stock of housing fell as a result of the flood, and how the housing market responded to bring about equilibrium again.

### Figure 6.3 A Market for Unskilled Labour, text page 128

This figure illustrates the consequences of a decrease in the demand for labour in an unregulated market for unskilled labour. Part (a) illustrates the market in an initial equilibrium. Then a labour-saving machine is invented which shifts the demand for labour curve to the left; from $D$ to $D_A$ in part (b). If the wage rate is allowed to adjust freely, wages and employment will fall in the short run. At the lower wage, some workers have the incentive to leave the unskilled labour market to seek training that qualifies them for higher paying jobs. This causes the short-run supply curve of labour to shift to the left; from $SS$ to $SS_A$. As a result, the wage rate begins to rise while employment falls.

### Figure 6.5 The Sales Tax, text page 131

To producers, the imposition of a sales tax is similar to the effect of a rise in the price of raw materials; it causes less to be supplied at each price. This causes the supply curve to shift to the left leading to a fall in quantity and a rise in price.

### Figure 6.8 The Market for a Prohibited Drug, text page 135

This figure shows that *selling* an illegal drug adds costs so that supply falls to $S + CBL$, resulting in a lower quantity consumed and a higher price. If *buying* drugs becomes illegal, demand will fall, resulting in a lower quantity and price.

### Figure 6.12 The European Union's Agricultural Price Support System, text page 142

The demand curve in this figure is the familiar downward-sloping line marked $D$. Without any EU intervention, food would be supplied to Europe from all over the world, and the supply curve would be horizontal. The CAP imposes a tariff which shifts the supply curve to $S +$ tariff. This leads to a higher price, causing European farmers to increase their supply. The result is a surplus since consumers are not willing to buy all the food supplies at this higher price.

# SELF-TEST

## CONCEPT REVIEW

1  In an unregulated housing market, a sudden decrease in the supply of housing would cause rent to _____ in the short run and thus create an incentive for the construction of new housing to _____ in the long run.

2  A(n) _____ _____ is a regulation making it illegal to charge a rent higher than a specified level.

3  If a price ceiling is below the market clearing price, an excess quantity _____ of the relevant good will exist. In such a situation two mechanisms will tend to arise in order to achieve equilibrium. We will observe an increase in _____ activity as demanders spend more time trying to find a seller. In addition, illegal markets, called _____ markets, may arise in order to satisfy demand.

**4** The invention of a new labour-saving technology will cause the demand curve for unskilled labour to shift to the _____ . If the labour market is unregulated, the wage rate will _____ .

**5** Unemployment will be created if a legal minimum wage is established, which is _____ the market clearing wage rate.

**6** A tax on expenditure will lead to a(n) _____ in price and a(n)_____ in quantity.

**__ 10** A specific tax is set as a fixed amount per unit of the commodity.

**__ 11** The imposition of a sales tax shifts the supply curve upward by the amount of the tax.

**__ 12** The CAP shifts income from consumers to farmers.

**__ 13** If penalties are imposed on both sellers and buyers in a market for prohibited goods, the price remains constant and the quantity bought decreases.

## TRUE OR FALSE

**__ 1** In an unregulated housing market, higher rents will result in an increase in the quantity of housing supplied.

**__ 2** When rents in an unregulated housing market rise owing to a decrease in supply, people who are unable to pay the higher rents will not get housing.

**__ 3** In a housing market with rent ceilings, there will be a strong incentive to construct new housing.

**__ 4** If a rent ceiling exceeds people's willingness to pay, search activity and black markets will arise.

**__ 5** Search activity will tend to be greater in unregulated markets than in markets with price ceilings.

**__ 6** The black market price of a good is usually below the regulated price.

**__ 7** An increase in the minimum wage will reduce the number of workers employed.

**__ 8** In an unregulated labour market a decline in the demand for labour causes the wage rate to increase.

**__ 9** The impact of minimum wage laws on un-employment among young workers tends to be about the same as it is for older workers.

## MULTIPLE CHOICE

**1** The short-run supply curve for rental housing is positively sloped because
 **a** the supply of housing is fixed in the short run.
 **b** the current stock of buildings will be used more intensively as rents rise.
 **c** the cost of constructing a new building increases as the number of buildings increases.
 **d** the cost of constructing a new building is about the same regardless of the number of buildings in existence.
 **e** new buildings will be constructed as rents rise.

**2** Rent ceilings imposed by governments
 **a** keep rental prices below the unregulated market price.
 **b** keep rental prices above the unregulated market price.
 **c** keep rental prices equal to the unregulated market price.
 **d** increase the stock of rental housing.
 **e** increase the intensity of use of the current stock of rental housing.

**3** Which of the following is *not* a likely outcome of rent ceilings?
 **a** a black market for rent-controlled housing
 **b** long waiting lists of potential renters of rent-controlled housing
 **c** a short-run shortage of housing
 **d** black market prices below the rent ceiling prices
 **e** increased search activity for rent-controlled housing

**4** In an unregulated market which of the following is *not* a likely result of the sudden destruction of a large proportion of the stock of housing?
   **a** higher rental prices
   **b** a shortage of rental housing
   **c** more basement apartments offered for rent
   **d** more families sharing living quarters
   **e** the construction of new rental housing

**5** A price ceiling set below the equilibrium price will result in
   **a** excess supply.
   **b** excess demand.
   **c** the equilibrium price.
   **d** an increase in supply.
   **e** a decrease in demand.

**6** A price floor set below the equilibrium price results in
   **a** excess supply.
   **b** excess demand.
   **c** the equilibrium price.
   **d** an increase in supply.
   **e** a decrease in demand.

**7** If the minimum wage is set at £2 per hour in Fig. 6.1, what is the level of unemployment in millions of hours?
   **a** 50
   **b** 40
   **c** 20
   **d** 10
   **e** 0

**8** In Fig. 6.1, if the minimum wage is set at £6 per hour, what is the level of unemployment in millions of hours?
   **a** 50
   **b** 40
   **c** 20
   **d** 10
   **e** 0

**9** Which of the following types of labour would be most significantly affected by an increase in the legal minimum wage?
   **a** professional athletes
   **b** young, unskilled labour
   **c** skilled union workers
   **d** university professors
   **e** self-employed labour

**Figure 6.1**

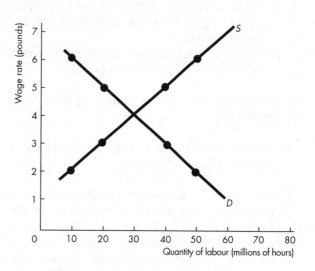

**10** A minimum wage law creates
   **a** gainers
   **b** losers
   **c** gainers and losers
   **d** a decrease in supply
   **e** an increase in hours worked

**11** The burden of a sales tax falls on
   **a** consumers
   **b** governments
   **c** consumers and governments
   **d** producers
   **e** consumers and producers

**12** The Common Agricultural Policy of the European Union
   **a** forces the Union to buy surplus food
   **b** increases farm incomes
   **c** increases the price paid by consumers
   **d** sets a common external tariff
   **e** all of the above

**13** Which of the following combinations would generally yield the greatest price fluctuations?
   **a** large supply shifts and inelastic demand
   **b** large supply shifts and elastic demand
   **c** large supply shifts and perfectly elastic demand
   **d** small supply shifts and inelastic demand
   **e** small supply shifts and elastic demand

# SHORT ANSWER

**1** **a** Suppose there is a significant reduction in the supply of petrol. Explain how an unregulated market adjusts.

**b** What is it that induces consumers willingly to reduce their consumption of petrol?

**2** Explain the effects of the imposition of a minimum wage.

**3** Explain what happens when the government imposes an expenditure tax.

**4** Suppose the Nudist party wins the next election and passes a law making clothes illegal. Unfortunately for the Nudists, the police don't take the law seriously and put little effort into enforcement. Use a diagram to explain why the black market price of now illegal clothes will be close to the unregulated equilibrium price.

**5** In the *Reading Between the Lines* article

**a** why do you think that the European Union wants to reduce the curbs on imports of alcohol into Finland?

**b** Why do you think that so many governments tax alcohol?

# PROBLEMS

**1** Suppose that the market for rental housing is initially in long-run equilibrium. Use graphs to answer the following:

**a** Explain how an unregulated market for rental housing would adjust if there is a sudden significant increase in demand. Consider what will happen to rent and the quantity of units rented in the short run and in the long run. Be sure to discuss the effect on incentives (in both the short run and the long run) as the market-determined price (rent) changes.

**b** Now explain how the market would adjust to the increase in demand if rent ceilings are established at the level of the initial equilibrium rent. What has happened to supplier incentives in this case?

**2** Answer the following, given the information about the demand for and supply of mineral water in Table 6.1.

**a** What is the equilibrium price of mineral water and the equilibrium quantity of mineral water traded?

**Table 6.1**

| Price (pounds per litre) | Quantity demanded (millions of litres per day) | Quantity supplied |
|---|---|---|
| 1.40 | 8 | 24 |
| 1.30 | 10 | 22 |
| 1.20 | 12 | 20 |
| 1.10 | 14 | 18 |
| 1.00 | 16 | 16 |
| 0.90 | 18 | 14 |

**b** Suppose that the quantity of mineral water supplied suddenly declines by 8 million litres per day at every price. Construct a new table of price, quantity demanded and quantity supplied, and draw a graph of the demand curve and the initial and new supply curves. Assuming that the market for mineral water is unregulated, use either your table or your graph to find the new equilibrium price of mineral water and the new equilibrium quantity of mineral water traded.

**c** How has the change in price affected the behaviour of demanders? the behaviour of suppliers?

**d** Suppose that the government imposes a price ceiling of £1 per litre of mineral water at the same time as the decrease in supply reported in part **b**.

  **i** What is the quantity of mineral water demanded?

  **ii** What is the quantity of mineral water supplied?

  **iii** What is the quantity of mineral water actually sold?

  **iv** What is the excess quantity of mineral water demanded?

  **v** What is the highest price demanders are willing to pay for the last litre of mineral water available?

**vi** Consider someone who values mineral water as in **d v**. How long would that consumer be willing to queue to buy 10 litres of mineral water if the best alternative was to work at a wage rate of £8 per hour?

## DISCUSSION QUESTION

**1** 'It seems to me that when taxes rise, the poor consumer pays all the tax. Am I right?' Discuss.

## DATA QUESTIONS

**The cost of the Common Agricultural Policy (CAP)**

The costs of the CAP are considerable and include:

◆ The cost of buying and storing surplus produce
◆ Payments to farmers for structural improvements
◆ Transfers from consumers in the form of higher prices

It is not possible to make precise calculations of these costs because these depend in part on the effect of European surpluses on the world price of food. These surpluses are sold on the world market and force down the world price of many commodities. Thus one result is that there is a fall in the incomes of developing country farmers.

Within Europe, the costs and benefits are not distributed evenly since large farmers benefit much more than those with only small farms.

**1** What are the aims of the CAP?

**2** Draw a diagram to show the effect of European food exports on the world price of food.

**3** Who benefits and who loses from the CAP system?

**4** How can the surpluses be eliminated?

# ANSWERS

## CONCEPT REVIEW

**1** increase; increase

**2** rent ceiling

**3** demanded; search; black

**4** left; fall

**5** above

**6** rise; fall

## TRUE OR FALSE

**1 T** Movement up supply curve is unobstructed by the ceiling.

**2 T** At equilibrium, all who can afford housing get it, but not necessarily all who need it.

**3 F** Returns on investment in housing will be low.

**4 F** The rent ceiling will have little effect.

**5 F** Because people will search for bargains.

**6 F** Black market prices are higher.

**7 T** Increase in minimum wage leads to a fall in quantity demanded.

**8 F** Wage will fall.

**9 F** Greater impact on young workers because they have lower wages.

**10 T** Definition.

**11 T** Taxes reduce supply since they are similar to an increase in raw material prices.

**12 T** Consumers face higher prices, farmers receive more than the equilibrium price.

**13 F** Supply shifts to the right.

## MULTIPLE CHOICE

**1 b** **c, d**, and **e** refer to the long run.

**2 a** Definition **d** and **e** result of increase in rent in unregulated market.

**3 d** Black markets cause shortages and lead to prices above the official price.

**4 b** Price would rise and stimulate supply as after Gelderland province flood.

**5 b** Draw a graph. No change in *ceteris paribus* assumptions so no shift in supply or demand.

**6 c** A price floor below the equilibrium will have no effect.

**7 e** Floor below equilibrium price does not prevent market from reaching equilibrium.

**8 b** Quantity supplied (50) > quantity demanded (10).

**9 b** Lowest wage labour.

**10 c** Some will gain from higher wages, some will not find employment at higher wage.

**11 e** Both consumers and producers bear tax burden depending on elasticity.

**12 e** These are the effects of intervention.

**13 a** Draw graph to see.

## SHORT ANSWER

**1 a** If the market for mineral water is initially in equilibrium and there is a significant reduction in the supply of mineral water, there will be excess quantity demanded at the existing price. As a result, the price of mineral water will rise, which will cause movements along the new supply curve and the demand curve. As the price rises there will be a price-induced increase in quantity supplied and a price-induced decrease in quantity demanded. The price will continue to rise until the excess quantity demanded is eliminated.

**b** It is the price increase that causes consumers to reduce their desired consumption of mineral water.

**2** Minimum wage legislation stops employers paying their workers wages lower than a minimum set by government. The result is that some people benefit and others lose. Employers lose because they have to pay higher wages. Other losers include those who cannot find work since the higher wages cause firms to reduce their demand for labour. The main benefit accrues to those low-paid workers who receive higher wages as a result of the pay increase. The exact results will depend on the level at which the minimum wage is set and on the elasticity of demand and supply of labour. If these are both inelastic, the result will be only a small fall in employment. If they are elastic, there will be a considerable fall in employment.

**3** An expenditure tax results in a rise in prices and a fall in the quantity of goods bought and sold. This is illustrated in Fig. 6.2.

**Figure 6.2**

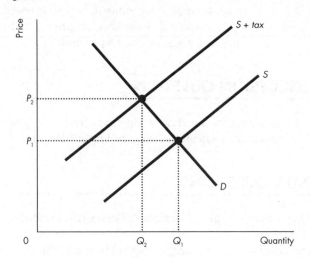

The tax will shift the supply curve to the left (the vertical distance between the supply curves measures the extent of the tax). The result is a rise in price from $P_1$ to $P_2$ and a fall in quantity from $Q_1$ to $Q_2$. The extent of these changes depends on the shape of the demand curve, that is, on its elasticity.

**4** The clothing market is illustrated in Fig. 6.3. The demand curve is $D$ and the supply curve is $S$. Since police enforcement is lax, the cost of breaking the law *(CBL)* is small for both buyers and sellers, so the demand and supply curves move only a short distance and the effect is small.

**5 a** A major aim of the European Union is to have a single market for goods. Restrictions by governments on imports prevent competition and are a barrier to the creation of the single market.

**b** Demand for alcohol is inelastic (because it has few competitors and is addictive). This means that governments can tax it without significantly reducing the demand. Hence they can raise fairly large sums of money, and firms will not suffer much from falling sales.

## PROBLEMS

**1 a** Figure 6.4 corresponds to an unregulated market for rental housing. The initial demand, short-run supply and long-run supply curves are $D_0$, $SS_0$ and $LS$ respectively. The market is initially in long-run equilibrium

**Figure 6.3**

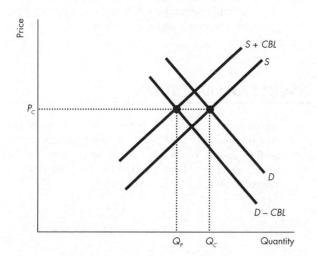

**Figure 6.4**

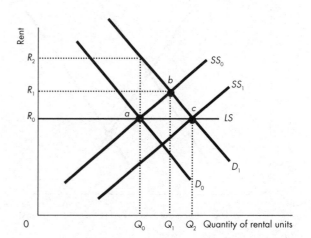

at point $a$ corresponding to rent $R_0$ and quantity of rental units $Q_0$. Demand then increases to $D_1$, creating excess quantity demanded of $Q_2 - Q_0$ at the initial rent. In the short run, in an unregulated market, rent will rise to $R_1$ to clear the market and the equilibrium quantity of housing rented is $Q_1$ (point $b$). Note that as the rent rises, the quantity of rental housing supplied increases (a movement from point $a$ to point $b$ along supply curve $SS_0$) as the existing stock of housing is used more intensively. Also the quantity of housing demanded decreases (a movement from point $c$ to point $b$ along demand curve $D_1$). Together, these movements eliminate the excess quantity demanded. The higher rent also provides an incentive to construct new housing in the long run. This is illustrated by the shift in the supply curve from $SS_0$ to $SS_1$. Lastly, a new long-run equilibrium is achieved at point $c$, with rent restored to its original level and the number of units rented equal to $Q_2$.

**b** We now use the graph in Fig. 6.4 to discuss the behaviour of a market with a rent ceiling set at $R_0$. Again we start in the same long-run equilibrium at point $a$. Once again we observe an increase in demand from $D_0$ to $D_1$. In this case, however, the rent cannot rise to restore equilibrium. There will be no incentive to use the existing stock of housing more intensively in the short run or to construct new housing in the long run. The quantity of rental housing supplied will remain at $Q_0$. Since the last unit of rental housing is valued

at $R_2$, but rent is fixed at $R_0$, demanders of rental housing will be willing to bear additional costs up to $R_2 - R_0$ (in the form of additional search activity or illegal payments) in order to obtain rental housing.

**2 a** The equilibrium price of mineral water is £1 per litre since, at that price, the quantity of mineral water demanded is equal to the quantity supplied (16 million litres per day). The equilibrium quantity of mineral water traded is 16 million litres of mineral water per day.

**b** The new table and graph are shown in Table 6.2 and Fig. 6.5.

**Table 6.2**

| Price (pounds per litre) | Quantity demanded (millions of litres per day) | Quantity supplied |
|---|---|---|
| 1.40 | 8 | 16 |
| 1.30 | 10 | 14 |
| 1.20 | 12 | 12 |
| 1.10 | 14 | 10 |
| 1.00 | 16 | 8 |
| 0.90 | 18 | 6 |

**Figure 6.5**

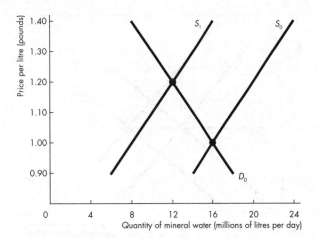

The new equilibrium price is £1.20 per litre since, at that price, the quantity of mineral water demanded equals the new quantity supplied (12 million litres per day). The new equilibrium quantity traded is 12 million litres of mineral water per day.

**c** The increase in price has caused the quantity of mineral water demanded to decrease by 4 million litres per day (from 16 to 12 million). Given the new supply curve $S_1$, the increase in price from £1 to £1.20 per litre increases the quantity of mineral water supplied by 4 million litres per day (from 8 to 12 million).

**d** **i** At the ceiling price of £1, the quantity demanded is 16 million litres per day.
   **ii** The quantity supplied is 8 million litres per day.
   **iii** The quantity of mineral water actually sold is 8 million litres per day. When, at a given price, quantity demanded and quantity supplied differ, whichever quantity is the *lesser* will determine the quantity actually sold.
   **iv** The excess quantity of mineral water demanded is 8 million litres per day.
   **v** The highest price consumers are willing to pay for the last unit of mineral water supplied (the 8 millionth litre per day) is £1.40. You can obtain this answer from your graph by imagining a vertical line from the quantity 8 million litres up to where it intersects the demand curve at £1.40. The demand curve shows the highest price consumers would be willing to pay for that last litre supplied.
   **vi** The regulated price of mineral water is £1 per litre but the value to the consumer of the last litre is £1.40, so the consumer would be willing to bear

costs of £4 above the regulated price of mineral water to obtain 10 litres (£0.40 × 10 litres). If the best alternative is to earn £8 per hour, the consumer would be willing to spend up to half an hour queuing to buy the 10 litres.

## DISCUSSION QUESTION

**1** Appearances can be deceptive. Prices certainly rise after the imposition of a tax, although usually not by the full amount of the tax. When firms show the full amount of value added tax (VAT) to be paid, this may conceal a fall in the price before tax.

## DATA QUESTIONS

**1** The objectives of the CAP are to increase agricultural productivity, to increase farm incomes, to stabilize prices and to ensure reasonable prices for agricultural products.

**2** The effect of the European Union's food surpluses on the world market are shown in Fig. 6.6. The result is a fall in world prices and an increase in quantity.

**Figure 6.6**

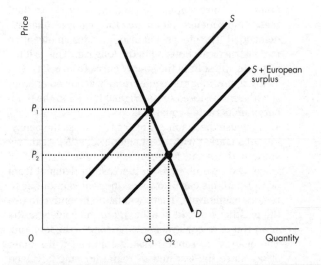

**3** Large farmers in particular benefit. The biggest losers are consumers and developing country farmers who cannot compete with subsidized European exports.

**4** Several measures can be used to reduce surpluses. These include cutting the price at which the European Union buys agricultural products, selling surpluses abroad at low prices, imposing quotas which limit the quantity of food farmers are allowed to produce, and paying farmers to set aside land, that is, to let land lie fallow.

In recent years the European Union has taken some of these measures, and as a result surplus stocks have fallen.

# Chapter 7  **Utility and Demand**

---

## Chapter in Perspective, Text Pages 151–170

The fundamental economic concept of demand was introduced in Chapter 4. There we assumed that as the price of a good rises, the quantity demanded will decline. Assuming this law of demand allowed us to draw a number of useful conclusions, and make predictions about the behaviour of prices and quantity traded. Our confidence in these results would be enhanced if it were not necessary to assume the law of demand – if this could be derived as a prediction of a more fundamental theory. This is the major task of this chapter. Not only is the law of demand derived as a prediction of the marginal utility theory, but other results that had previously been assumed (for example, a change in income causes a shift in demand) also turn out to be predictions.

This chapter and the next greatly deepen our understanding of the forces underlying the law of demand and associated concepts.

---

## Helpful Hints

**1** The concept of utility is an extremely useful abstract device that allows us to think more clearly about consumer choice. Marginal utility theory assumes that an individual is able to judge whether the additional satisfaction per pound spent on good $X$ is greater or less than the additional satisfaction per pound spent on $Y$. If it is greater, then the decision is to consume an additional unit of $X$. How much greater is irrelevant for the decision.

**2** The marginal utility per pound spent on good $X$ can be written as $MU_X/P_X$ where $MU_X$ is the marginal utility of the last unit of $X$ consumed and $P_X$ is the price of a unit of good $X$. The consumer equilibrium (utility-maximizing) condition for goods $X$ and $Y$ can thus be written:

$$\frac{MU_X}{P_X} = \frac{MU_Y}{P_Y}$$

This implies that, in consumer equilibrium, the ratio of marginal utilities will equal the ratio of prices of the two goods:

$$\frac{MU_X}{MU_Y} = \frac{P_X}{P_Y}$$

**3** If an individual is not in consumer equilibrium, then the equation above is not satisfied. For example, consider spending all of your income on a consumption plan where:

$$\frac{MU_X}{P_X} > \frac{MU_Y}{P_Y}$$

or, equivalently

$$\frac{MU_X}{MU_Y} > \frac{P_X}{P_Y}$$

Since $P_X$ and $P_Y$ are given, this means that $MU_X$ is 'too large' and $MU_Y$ is 'too small'. Utility can be increased by increasing consumption of $X$ (and thereby decreasing $MU_X$ owing to the principle of diminishing marginal utility) and decreasing consumption of $Y$ (and thereby increasing $MU_Y$ owing to diminishing marginal utility).

**4** Table 7.7 in the text on page 162 is a good review device.

## Key Figures and Table

### Figure 7.1 Individual and Market Demand Curves, text page 153

The market demand curve is obtained by adding the quantities demanded at each price by each individual. Figure 7.1 illustrates this in a market with two individuals. At each price, the quantity demanded in the market is equal to the quantity demanded by these two people. This is illustrated graphically and in a table.

### Figure 7.3 Total Utility and Marginal Utility, text page 156

This figure shows the relationship between total and marginal utility. As more of a good is consumed total utility rises, but at a diminishing rate because marginal utility falls as more is consumed.

### Figure 7.4 Equalizing Marginal Utility per Pound Spent, text page 159

This shows that as more of a good is consumed its utility will fall and rational consumers will therefore consume more of other goods.

### Figure 7.5 A Fall in the Price of Cinema Tickets, text page 160

When the price of a cinema ticket falls, Lisa buys more cinema tickets and this is shown in part (a) by a movement along the demand curve. Since, for Lisa, films and cola are substitutes, the fall in the price of films causes a shift in her demand for cola, and this is shown in part (b).

### Figure 7.6 A Rise in the Price of Cola, text page 161

The increase in the price of cola will cause a movement along the demand curve for cola, and also a shift in the demand curve for films so that more films are demanded.

### Figure 7.7 Consumer Surplus, text page 164

Consumer surplus is the difference between the most a person is willing to pay for a good (its value to that person) and its price (the amount actually paid). This figure illustrates the calculation of consumer surplus by examining Lisa's demand for films.

### Table 7.7 Marginal Utility Theory, text page 162

This table summarizes the assumptions, implications and predictions of marginal utility theory. Note particularly that the first prediction is the law of demand.

# SELF-TEST

## CONCEPT REVIEW

**1** The _____ demand curve is the sum of the quantities demanded by each individual at each _____ .

**2** The benefit or satisfaction a person receives from the consumption of a good or a service is called _____ .

**3** The additional utility a person receives from consuming one more unit of a good is called _____ _____ .

**4** As consumption increases, marginal utility _____ . This is called the principle of _____ marginal utility.

**5** We assume that a household will choose quantities to consume so as to _____ utility subject to its income and the prices it faces.

**6** The marginal utility per pound spent is the marginal utility of the last unit of a good consumed divided by its _____ .

**7** Utility will be maximized if the marginal utility per pound spent is _____ for all goods.

**8** Marginal utility theory predicts that if the price of one good rises, _____ of it will be consumed and _____ of other goods will be consumed.

**9** Marginal utility theory predicts that the higher household income is, the _____ is the quantity consumed of all normal goods.

**10** The difference between the value of a good and its price is called _____ _____ .

## TRUE OR FALSE

___ **1** Market demand is the sum of all individual demands.

___ **2** Total utility equals the sum of the marginal utilities for all units consumed.

___ **3** The principle of diminishing marginal utility means that as consumption of a good increases, total utility declines.

___ **4** The principle of diminishing marginal utility means that as consumption of a good increases, total utility increases but at a decreasing rate.

___ **5** A consumer equilibrium exists when a consumer has allocated his or her income in a way that maximizes total utility.

___ **6** A household will be maximizing utility if the marginal utility per pound spent is equal for all goods and all its income is spent.

___ **7** When the price of good X rises, the marginal utility from the consumption of X decreases.

___ **8** If the marginal utilities from consuming two goods are not equal, then the consumer cannot be in equilibrium.

___ **9** If the marginal utility per pound spent on good X exceeds the marginal utility per pound spent on good Y, total utility will increase by increasing consumption of X and decreasing consumption of Y.

___ **10** Marginal utility theory predicts that if the price of a good falls, consumption of substitute goods will rise.

___ **11** Utility cannot be observed or measured.

___ **12** The value of a good is always the price of the good.

___ **13** The principle of diminishing marginal utility guarantees that consumers will always make some consumer surplus.

___ **14** Consumer surplus is the difference between the value of a good and its price.

___ **15** If a shift in supply decreases the price of a good, consumer surplus increases.

___ **16** The diamond–water paradox illustrates that relative prices actually reflect total utility rather than marginal utility.

## MULTIPLE CHOICE

**1** Marginal utility equals
   **a** total utility divided by price.
   **b** total utility divided by the total number of units consumed.
   **c** the slope of the total utility curve.
   **d** the inverse of total utility.
   **e** the area below the demand curve but above market price.

**2** If Ms Petersen is maximizing her utility in the consumption of goods A and B, which of the following statements must be true?
   **a** $MU_A = MU_B$

   **b** $\dfrac{MU_A}{P_A} = \dfrac{MU_B}{P_B}$

   **c** $\dfrac{MU_A}{P_B} = \dfrac{MU_B}{P_A}$

**d** $TU_A = TU_B$

**e** $\dfrac{TU_A}{P_A} = \dfrac{TU_B}{P_B}$

**3** If a consumer is in equilibrium, then
  **a** total utility is maximized given the consumer's income and the prices of goods.
  **b** marginal utility is maximized given the consumer's income and the prices of goods.
  **c** marginal utility per pound spent is maximized given the consumer's income and the prices of goods.
  **d** the marginal utility of the last unit of each good will be the same.
  **e** none of the above is true.

**4** If Renata is maximizing her utility and two goods have the same marginal utility then
  **a** she will buy only one of them.
  **b** she will buy equal quantities of them.
  **c** she will be willing to pay the same price for each of them.
  **d** she will get the same total utility from each of them.
  **e** none of the above is true.

**5** Shelley is maximizing her utility in her consumption of mink coats and Porsches. If the marginal utility of her last purchased mink coat is twice the marginal utility of her last purchased Porsche, then we do not know with certainty that
  **a** Shelley buys twice as many mink coats as Porsches.
  **b** Shelley buys twice as many Porsches as mink coats.
  **c** Shelley buys more Porsches than mink coats, but we do not know how many more.
  **d** the price of a mink coat is twice the price of a Porsche.
  **e** the price of a Porsche is twice the price of a mink coat.

**6** Total utility equals
  **a** the sum of the marginal utilities of each unit consumed.
  **b** the area below the demand curve but above the market price.
  **c** the slope of the marginal utility curve.
  **d** the marginal utility of the last unit divided by price.

**e** the marginal utility of the last unit consumed multiplied by the total number of units consumed.

**7** Samir consumes apples and bananas and is in consumer equilibrium. The marginal utility of the last apple is 10 and the marginal utility of the last banana is 5. If the price of an apple is £0.50, then what is the price of a banana?
  **a** £0.05
  **b** £0.10
  **c** £0.25
  **d** £0.50
  **e** £1

**8** The value of a good is defined as the
  **a** market price.
  **b** average price paid by individuals in a market.
  **c** cost of producing the good.
  **d** highest price an individual is willing to pay.
  **e** total utility to an individual of all units of the good.

**9** The difference between the value of a good and its price is known as
  **a** excess demand.
  **b** excess supply.
  **c** consumer surplus.
  **d** consumer excess.
  **e** marginal utility.

**10** The demand schedule for marbles is shown in Table 7.1.

**Table 7.1 Demand Schedule for Marbles**

| Price per marble (pounds) | Quantity demanded |
|---|---|
| 10 | 1 |
| 9 | 2 |
| 8 | 3 |
| 7 | 4 |
| 6 | 5 |

If the actual price is £7, what is total consumer surplus?
  **a** £3
  **b** £4
  **c** £6

**d** £12

**e** £27

**11** The high price of diamonds relative to the price of water reflects the fact that at typical levels of consumption

**a** the total utility of water is relatively low.

**b** the total utility of diamonds is relatively high.

**c** the marginal utility of water is relatively high.

**d** the marginal utility of diamonds is relatively low.

**e** none of the above is true.

## SHORT ANSWER

**1** A consumer is initially maximizing his or her utility in the consumption of goods $A$ and $B$ so that:

$$\frac{MU_A}{P_A} = \frac{MU_B}{P_B}$$

The price of $A$ then rises as a result of the shift in supply shown in Fig. 7.1. Use the above condition for utility maximization to explain how the consumer will move to a new utility-maximizing equilibrium. Show the connection between your explanation and the change on the diagram.

**Figure 7.1**

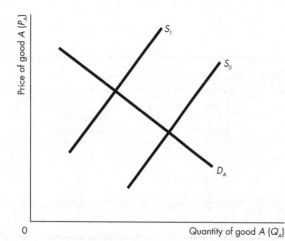

**2** Explain why the consumer equilibrium condition and the principle of diminishing marginal utility imply the law of demand.

**3** How does marginal utility theory resolve the diamond–water paradox of value?

**4** In the *Reading Between the Lines* article, explain why 'They maximize their utility per pound spent on meats equal to the utility per pound spent on meat substitutes'.

## PROBLEMS

**1** Table 7.2 gives the demand schedules for broccoli for three individuals: Tom, Jana and Ted.

**Table 7.2  Individual Demand for Broccoli**

| Price per kilogram (pounds) | Quantity demanded (kilograms per week) | | |
|---|---|---|---|
| | Tom | Jana | Ted |
| 0.50 | 10 | 4 | 10 |
| 0.75 | 9 | 2 | 7 |
| 1.00 | 8 | 0 | 4 |
| 1.25 | 7 | 0 | 1 |

**a** Calculate the market demand schedule.

**b** On a single diagram, draw the individual demand curves for Tom, Jana and Ted, as well as the market demand curve.

**2** Suppose that John spends his entire income of £8 on tennis rackets and books. The price of a tennis racket is £2 and the price of a book is £4. The marginal utility of each good is independent of the amount consumed of the other good.

**Table 7.3**

| Quantity | Marginal utility | |
|---|---|---|
| | Books | Rackets |
| 1 | 20 | 36 |
| 2 | 18 | 32 |
| 3 | 16 | 20 |
| 4 | 8 | 16 |

**a** If John is maximizing his utility, how many units of each good should he purchase?

**b** If John's income rises to £24, how many units of each good should he purchase?

**c** Using the information above, calculate John's income elasticity of demand for books.

**3** Andy's weekly demand schedule for pizzas is shown in Table 7.4.

**Table 7.4 Demand Schedule for Pizzas**

| Price per pizza (pounds) | Quantity demanded |
|---|---|
| 15 | 1 |
| 12 | 2 |
| 10 | 3 |
| 9 | 4 |
| 8 | 5 |

If the price of a pizza is £9, what is Andy's consumer surplus for the following number of pizzas that he buys at that price?

**a** first pizza

**b** second pizza

**c** total number of pizzas

## DISCUSSION QUESTIONS

**1** What is the point of learning something so remote from reality as marginal utility theory?

**2** 'Marginal utility theory suggests that as the price of a good rises, less will be consumed. But I rent only one flat. How does marginal utility theory explain this?'

## DATA QUESTIONS

**Music, love and utility**

Duke Orsino. 'If music be the food of love, play on:
   Give me excess of it, that, surfeiting,
   The appetite may sicken, and so die.
   … Enough! no more:
   'Tis not so sweet now as it was before.'

Source: Shakespeare, *Twelfth Night*, Scene 1.

**1** Explain the effect of music on love in terms of utility theory.

**2** In the play Orsino wants his love to die because his love for Olivia is not returned. What would be the effect on the utility of music for him if she also loved him?

# ANSWERS

## CONCEPT REVIEW

**1** market; price

**2** utility

**3** marginal utility

**4** decreases; diminishing

**5** maximize

**6** price

**7** equal

**8** less; more

**9** greater

**10** consumer surplus

## TRUE OR FALSE

**1 T** Definition.

**2 T** Definition.

**3 F** *Marginal* utility falls as more is consumed.

**4 T** Because marginal utility is positive but diminishing.

**5 T** Because any change would reduce utility.

**6 T** Definition.

**7 F** Rise in price leads to a fall in quantity and hence a rise in marginal utility.

**8 F** If prices are unequal, then marginal utilities must be unequal for consumers to be in equilibrium.

**9 T** Because it moves the ratio of marginal utility/price towards equality.

**10 F** More of the good will be consumed and less of substitute goods.

**11 T** Utility is an abstract concept.

**12 F** Price can be greater or less than value.

**13 T** Willingness to pay is greater than price for all units consumed except the last.

**14 T** Definition.

**15 T** The shift in supply leads to an increase in quantity consumed, so there are more units where consumers are willing to pay more than the price.

**16 F** Relative prices reflect marginal utility.

## MULTIPLE CHOICE

**1 c** Definition.

**2 b** Definition.

**3 a** Consumers maximize total utility. **c** and **d** are wrong because *MU/P* are equal for total utility maximization.

**4 c** From maximum condition of equal *MU/P*. There is no necessary relation between *MU* and quantity or total utility.

**5 d** From maximum condition of equal *MU/P*. No necessary relation between *MU* and quantity.

**6 a** **b** is consumer surplus. For **c**, *MU* = slope of the total utility curve. **d** and **e** are nonsense.

**7 c** Solve $10/0.5 = 5/P_b$ for $P_b$.

**8 d** Definition.

**9 c** Definition.

**10 c** For four marbles consumed, consumer surplus = $(10 - 7) + (9 - 7) + (8 - 7) + (7 - 7)$.

**11 e** For diamonds: *TU* is relatively low, *MU* relatively high. For water: *TU* is relatively high, *MU* relatively low.

## SHORT ANSWER

**1** When the price of A rises, *ceteris paribus*:

$$\frac{MU_A}{P_A} = \frac{MU_B}{P_B}$$

The consumer is no longer in equilibrium. In order to restore the equality in the equilibrium condition, the consumer must change his consumption to make $MU_A$

rise and $MU_B$ fall. (The consumer cannot change the prices of A and B.) Since marginal utility diminishes with increases in quantity consumed, the consumer must decrease consumption of A and increase consumption of B. Decreased consumption of A moves the consumer up to the left on the demand curve, from the initial intersection of D and $S_0$ to the new intersection of D and $S_1$. In the new consumer equilibrium, equality will be restored in the equilibrium condition.

**2** Suppose we observe an individual in consumer equilibrium consuming $X_0$ units of good X and $Y_0$ units of good Y with the prices of X and Y given by $P_X$ and $P_Y$ respectively. This means that at consumption levels $X_0$ and $Y_0$, the marginal utility per pound spent on X equals the marginal utility per pound spent on Y. Now let the price of X increase to $P_X^1$. This increase implies that the marginal utility per pound spent on X declines and thus is now less than the marginal utility per pound spent on Y. To restore equilibrium, our consumer must increase the marginal utility of X and decrease the marginal utility of Y. From the principle of diminishing marginal utility we know that the only way to do this is to decrease the consumption of X and increase the consumption of Y. This demonstrates the law of demand since an increase in the price of X has been shown to require a decrease in the consumption of X to restore consumer equilibrium.

**3** The paradox of value is resolved by recognizing that while the total utility from consumption of water is large, the marginal utility from the last unit of water is small. Likewise, the total utility from the consumption of diamonds is small, but the marginal utility of the last unit of diamonds is large. If consumers are in equilibrium, then the requirement that the marginal utility per pound spent be the same for water and diamonds means that the price of water must be low and the price of diamonds must be high.

**4** If consumers gained more utility per pound of money by buying meat than they did by buying other goods such as meat substitutes, they would increase their utility by buying more meat. As they consumed more meat, its utility would gradually decline until the utility per pound spent equalled that spent on other goods. They would then be maximizing their utility.

## PROBLEMS

**1 a** The market demand schedule is obtained by adding the quantities demanded by Tom, Jana and Ted at each price.

### Table 7.5  Market Demand Schedule for Broccoli

| Price per kilogram (pounds) | Quantity demanded (kilograms per week) |
|---|---|
| 0.50 | 24 |
| 0.75 | 18 |
| 1.00 | 12 |
| 1.25 | 8 |

**b** Figure 7.2 illustrates the individual demand curves for Tom, Jana and Ted as well as the market demand curve.

### Figure 7.2

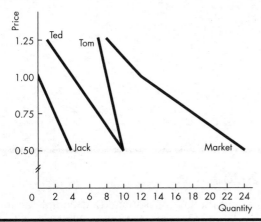

**2 a** The utility-maximizing combination of goods is shown in Table 7.6.

### Table 7.6

| | MU/P | |
|---|---|---|
| Quantity | Books | Rackets |
| 1 | 10 | 9 |
| 2 | 9 | 8 |
| 3 | 8 | 5 |
| 4 | 4 | 4 |

John should purchase 2 books and 1 racket. John spends all of his income (£8) and the marginal utility per pound spent is the same for books and rackets (9).

**b** John should purchase 4 books and 4 rackets. He spends all of his income (£24) and the marginal utility per pound spent is the same for books and rackets (4).

**c** The income elasticity of demand for books is:

$$\eta_y = \frac{\Delta Q/Q_{ave}}{\Delta Y/Y_{ave}}$$

**3 a** The most Andy would be willing to pay for the first pizza is £15, but the price is only £9. Therefore his consumer surplus is £6 (£15–£9).

**b** Andy's consumer surplus on the second pizza is the difference between the most he would be willing to pay (£12) and the price (£9). His consumer surplus is £3.

**c** At a price of £9, Andy will buy 4 pizzas. He will receive consumer surplus on the first three pizzas in the amount of £6, £3 and £1, respectively. Thus his total consumer surplus is £10.

## DISCUSSION QUESTIONS

**1** It is certainly true that no one goes into a shop and calculates marginal utility before buying. But that is not the point. Marginal utility theory is *not* trying to explain how people make decisions about what to buy. Instead it assumes that people attempt to maximize their utility and tries to explain how they respond to changes in prices and incomes. It is a theory of peoples' actions, not of their thoughts.

**2** The answer is that not all flats are identical. A rise in price would mean that some people would move to smaller flats or would be forced to share, so 'consuming' fewer flats.

## DATA QUESTIONS

**1** If we eat too many cakes the marginal utility of cakes will fall, and eventually we will be surfeited – turned off cakes altogether. Orsino hopes this will also be the case with the effect of music on love. More music means an increase in love, but eventually the marginal utility of love will diminish and become zero. Hence he will no longer want love.

**2** If Olivia falls in love with Orsino, the position will change (just as a drink may change the utility of another cake). Now he will want love – and music, but not too much. He will choose additional amounts of music until the satisfaction he gets from love is maximized. Note that this assumes that the music is free. If he was paying for the music, he would buy more music until the cost of the music equalled the benefit he obtained from it.

# Chapter 8    Possibilities, Preferences and Choices

---

## Chapter in Perspective, Text Pages 172–200

This chapter provides an alternative analysis of consumer choice and the law of demand that complements the marginal utility analysis of Chapter 7. Here, the analysis uses a model of consumer behaviour based on a budget equation that represents *possible choices* given a consumer's income and an indifference curve representation of *preferences*.

  The model allows more systematic analysis of what happens to quantity demanded when the price of a good changes and when income changes, as well as more insight into the distinction between normal and inferior goods. Compared with the marginal utility analysis, the budget equation/indifference curve model has the advantage that it does not depend on the abstract notion of utility. None the less, the two analyses of consumer choice have close parallels, which are outlined in Box 8.1 on text pages 199–200.

---

## Helpful Hints

**1** The consumer's problem is to do the best given the constraints faced. These constraints, which limit the range of possible choices, depend on income and the prices of goods and are represented graphically by the budget line. 'Doing the best' means finding the most preferred outcome consistent with those constraints. In this chapter, preferences are represented graphically by indifference curves. Thus, graphically, the consumer problem is to find the highest indifference curve attainable given the budget line. To make graphical analysis feasible, we restrict ourselves to choices between only two goods, but the same principles apply in the real world where the array of choices is much broader.

**2** Each of the two endpoints (the intercepts) of a budget line is just income divided by the price of the good on that axis. Connecting those endpoints with a straight line yields the budget line. The slope of the budget line provides additional information relevant for the consumer's choice between goods. The magnitude (absolute value) of the slope equals the relative price (or opportunity cost) of films in terms of cola. To put it in different words, the magnitude of the slope equals the number of units of cola it takes to buy one cinema ticket. More generally, the magnitude of the slope of the budget line $P_X/P_Y$) equals the relative price (or opportunity cost) of the good on the horizontal $x$-axis in terms of the good on the vertical $y$-axis; or the number of units of vertical-axis goods it takes to buy one unit of the horizontal-axis good.

**3** The marginal rate of substitution ($MRS$) is the rate at which a consumer gives up good $Y$ for an additional unit of good $X$ and still remains indifferent. The $MRS$ equals the magnitude of the slope of the indifference curve, $Q_Y/Q_X$.

Because indifference curves are bowed towards the origin (convex), the magnitude of the slope and, hence, the $MRS$ diminish as we move down an indifference curve. The diminishing $MRS$ means that the consumer is willing to give up less of good $Y$ for each additional unit of good $X$. As the consumer moves down an indifference curve, the consumer is coming to value good $Y$ more and value good $X$ less. This is easily explained by the principle of diminishing marginal utility, which underlies the equations in Box 8.1 on text pages 199–200.

At the top of the indifference curve, the consumer is consuming little $X$ and much $Y$, so the marginal utility of $X$ ($MU_X$) is high and the marginal utility of $Y$ ($MU_Y$) is low. Moving down the curve, as the quantity of $X$ consumed increases, $MU_X$ decreases; and as the quantity of $Y$ consumed decreases, $MU_Y$ increases. Thus the principle of diminishing marginal utility provides an intuitive understanding of why the $MRS$ diminishes as we move down an indifference curve.

**4** At the consumer's best affordable point, the budget line is just tangent to the highest affordable indifference curve, so the magnitude of the slope of the budget line equals the magnitude of the slope of the indifference curve.

**5** Understanding the distinction between the income and substitution effects of a change in the price of a good is sometimes a challenge for students. Consider a decrease in the price of good $A$. This has two effects that will influence the consumption of $A$. First, the decrease in the price of $A$ will reduce the relative price of $A$ and, second, it will increase real income. The substitution effect is the answer to the question: how much would the consumption of $A$ change as a result of the relative price decline if we also (hypothetically) reduce income by enough to leave the consumer indifferent between the new and original situations? The income effect is the answer to the following question: how much more would the consumption of $A$ change if we (hypothetically) restore the consumer's real income but leave relative prices at the new level?

## Key Figures

### Figure 8.1 The Budget Line, text page 173
Household consumption is limited by the level of household income and the prices of goods and services. A budget line graphically represents these limits to consumption choices. This figure illustrates a budget line faced by Lisa, who has a monthly income of £30 to be allocated between two goods: films and colas. The price of a cinema ticket is £6 and the price of a six-pack of cola is £3. The table indicates six possible allocations of Lisa's income, given these prices. The budget line simply represents these points graphically. To locate the budget line, find the end points by asking how many six-packs of cola could be purchased if all income is spent on cola (the $y$-intercept) and how many films could be seen if all income is spent on cinema tickets (the $x$-intercept). Then draw a straight line between the end points.

### Figure 8.4 A Preference Map, text page 177
A preference map is a series of indifference curves for the same individual. This figure illustrates three indifference curves in Lisa's preference map. Along each indifference curve, Lisa is indifferent among the alternative consumption combinations; each would make her equally happy. However, points on a higher indifference curve are preferred to points on a lower indifference curve.

### Figure 8.7 The Best Affordable Point, text page 180
Points along the budget line represent maximum affordable combinations of consumption goods.

Higher indifference curves represent more preferred consumption points. The objective of the consumer is to obtain the best (most preferred) affordable consumption point possible. Graphically, this means that a consumer will choose the consumption point that is on the budget line and also on the highest indifference curve possible. The best affordable point will always be a point where the budget line is just tangent to (that is, touches at one point only) the highest indifference curve possible. In this figure, this occurs at consumption point *c*. This is the best affordable consumption point because all other affordable points (on the budget line) intersect lower indifference curves. On the other hand, all points on higher indifference curves are not affordable.

# SELF-TEST

## CONCEPT REVIEW

**1** A _____ line describes the maximum amounts of consumption a household can undertake given its income and the prices of the goods it buys.

**2** Real income is income expressed in units of _____ .

**3** The price of one good divided by the price of another is called a(n) _____ price.

**4** If the quantity of good *A* consumed is measured on the horizontal axis and the quantity of good *B* consumed is measured on the vertical axis, an increase in the price of good *a* will make the budget line _____ . An increase in income will shift the budget line _____ .

**5** A(n) _____ curve shows all combinations of goods that would leave a consumer indifferent.

**6** Suppose we measure good *A* on the horizontal axis and good *B* on the vertical axis. The rate at which a person would give up good *B* to obtain more of good *A* is called the _____ rate of _____ . As the consumer increases consumption of good *A* (and decreases consumption of good *B* so as to remain indifferent), this rate _____ .

**7** The best affordable consumption point will be on both the _____ line and the highest attainable _____ curve.

**8** If the price of good *A* rises, the _____ effect will always imply that less of *A* will be consumed, while the _____ effect reinforces this only if *A* is a normal good.

**9** If a decrease in income causes an increase in the consumption of good *B*, then *B* is a(n) _____ good.

**10** As the wage rate rises, the substitution effect encourages _____ leisure and the income effect encourages _____ leisure.

## TRUE OR FALSE

____ **1** At any point on the budget line, all income is spent.

____ **2** An increase in the price of the good measured on the horizontal axis will make the budget line flatter.

____ **3** *Ceteris paribus*, an increase in the price of goods means that real income falls.

____ **4** An increase in income will cause an inward parallel shift of the budget line.

____ **5** Preferences depend on income and the prices of goods.

____ **6** We assume that more of any good is preferred to less of the good.

____ **7** An indifference curve shows all combinations of two goods which the consumer can afford.

____ **8** It is logically possible for indifference curves to intersect each other.

___ **9** The principle of the diminishing marginal rate of substitution explains why indifference curves are bowed towards the origin.

___ **10** The magnitude of the slope of an indifference curve is equal to the marginal rate of substitution.

___ **11** The marginal rate of substitution falls as consumption of the good measured on the $y$-axis falls and consumption of the good measured on the $x$-axis rises.

## MULTIPLE CHOICE

**1** Which of the following statements best describes a consumer's budget line?
  **a** the amount of each good a consumer can purchase
  **b** the limits to a consumer's set of affordable consumption choices
  **c** the desired level of consumption for the consumer
  **d** the consumption choices made by a consumer
  **e** the set of all affordable consumption choices

**2** If the price of the good measured on the vertical axis increases, the budget line will
  **a** become steeper.
  **b** become flatter.
  **c** shift inward but parallel to the original budget line.
  **d** shift outward but parallel to the original budget line.
  **e** shift inward and become steeper.

**3** If income increases, the budget line will
  **a** become steeper.
  **b** become flatter.
  **c** shift inward but parallel to the original budget line.
  **d** shift outward but parallel to the original budget line.
  **e** shift parallel but outward or inward depending on whether a good is normal or inferior.

**4** A change in income changes which aspect(s) of the budget equation?
  **a** slope and $y$-intercept
  **b** slope and $x$-intercept

  **c** $x$- and $y$-intercepts but not slope
  **d** slope only
  **e** none of the above

**5** Bill consumes apples and bananas. Suppose Bill's income doubles and the prices of apples and bananas also double. Bill's budget line will
  **a** shift inward but not change slope.
  **b** remain unchanged.
  **c** shift outward but not change slope.
  **d** shift outward and become steeper.
  **e** shift outward and become flatter.

**6** Suppose good $X$ is measured on the horizontal axis and good $Y$ on the vertical axis. The marginal rate of substitution is best defined as the
  **a** relative price of good $X$ in terms of good $Y$.
  **b** relative price of good $Y$ in terms of good $X$.
  **c** rate at which a consumer will give up good $Y$ in order to obtain more of good $X$ and remain indifferent.
  **d** rate at which a consumer will give up good $X$ in order to obtain more of good $Y$ and remain indifferent.
  **e** slope of the budget line.

**7** In general, as a consumer moves down an indifference curve, increasing consumption of good $X$ (measured on the horizontal axis),
  **a** more of $Y$ must be given up for each additional unit of $X$.
  **b** a constant amount of $Y$ must be given up for each additional unit of $X$.
  **c** less of $Y$ must be given up for each additional unit of $X$.
  **d** the relative price of $Y$ increases.
  **e** the relative price of $Y$ decreases.

**8** Consider the budget line and indifference curve in Fig. 8.1. If the price of good $X$ is $2, what is the price of good $Y$?
  **a** $0.37
  **b** $0.67
  **c** $1.50
  **d** $2.67
  **e** impossible to calculate without additional information

**9** When the price of a good changes, the change in consumption that leaves the consumer indifferent is called the
  **a** utility effect.

**Figure 8.1**

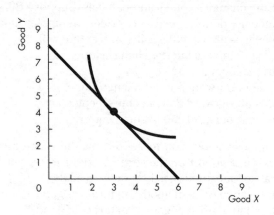

**Figure 8.2**

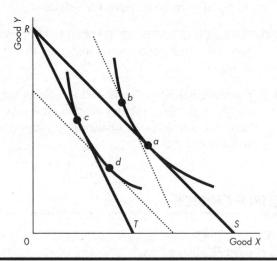

**b** substitution effect.
**c** income effect.
**d** price effect.
**e** Giffen effect.

**10** When the price of a normal good rises, the income effect
  **a** increases consumption of the good and the substitution effect decreases consumption.
  **b** decreases consumption of the good and the substitution effect increases consumption.
  **c** and the substitution effect both increase consumption of the good.
  **d** and the substitution effect both decrease consumption of the good.
  **e** is always larger than the substitution effect.

**11** The initial budget line labelled *RS* in Figure 8.2 would shift to *RT* as a result of
  **a** an increase in the price of good *X*.
  **b** a decrease in the price of good *X*.
  **c** a decrease in preferences for good *X*.
  **d** an increase in the price of good *Y*.
  **e** an increase in real income.

**12** When the initial budget line labelled *RS* in Fig. 8.2 shifts to *RT*, the substitution effect is illustrated by the move from point
  **a** *a* to *b*.
  **b** *a* to *c*.
  **c** *a* to *d*.
  **d** *b* to *d*.
  **e** *d* to *c*.

**13** When the initial budget line labelled *RS* in Fig. 8.2 shifts to *RT*, the income effect is illustrated by the move from point
  **a** *a* to *b*.
  **b** *a* to *c*.
  **c** *a* to *d*.
  **d** *b* to *c*.
  **e** *b* to *d*.

**14** Over the last 100 years, the quantity of labour supplied has fallen as wages have increased. This indicates that the income effect
  **a** and the substitution effect have both discouraged leisure.
  **b** and the substitution effect have both encouraged leisure.
  **c** discouraging leisure has been dominated by the substitution effect encouraging leisure.
  **d** encouraging leisure has dominated the substitution effect discouraging leisure.
  **e** has not affected the labour–leisure choice.

## SHORT ANSWER

**1** Why is an indifference curve negatively sloped?

**2** Use the principle of diminishing marginal utility to explain why the marginal rate of substitution diminishes as we move down an indifference curve.

**3** Suppose the price of a normal good falls. Without the use of graphs, distinguish between the income and substitution effects of this price decline.

**4** The *Economics in History* article shows that many more women now go out to work than formerly. Use the ideas in this chapter to explain why.

# PROBLEMS

**1** Jan and Dan both like bread and peanut butter and have the same income. Since they each face the same prices, they have identical budget lines. Currently, Jan and Dan consume exactly the same quantities of bread and peanut butter; they have the same best affordable consumption point. Jan, however, views bread and peanut butter as close (although not perfect) substitutes, while Dan considers bread and peanut butter to be quite (but not perfectly) complementary.
  **a** On the same diagram, draw a budget line and representative indifference curves for Jan and Dan. (Measure the quantity of bread on the horizontal axis.)
  **b** Now suppose the price of bread declines. Graphically represent the substitution effects for Jan and Dan. For whom is the substitution effect greater?

**2** Kurt consumes both coffee and whisky. The initial price of coffee is £1 per unit and the price of whisky is £1.50 per unit. Kurt's initial income is £12.
  **a** What is the relative price of coffee?
  **b** Derive Kurt's budget equation and draw his budget line on a graph. (Measure coffee on the horizontal axis.)
  **c** On your graph, draw an indifference curve so that the best affordable point corresponds to 6 units of coffee and 4 units of whisky.
  **d** What is the marginal rate of substitution of coffee for whisky at this point?
  **e** Show that any other point on the budget line is inferior.

**3** Given the initial situation described in Problem 2, suppose Kurt's income now increases.
  **a** Illustrate graphically how the consumption of coffee and whisky are affected if both goods are normal. (Numerical answers are not necessary. Just show whether consumption increases or decreases.)
  **b** Draw a graph showing the effect of an increase in Kurt's income if whisky is an inferior good.

**4** Return to the initial circumstances described in Problem 2. Now suppose the price of coffee doubles to £2 per unit while the price of whisky remains at £1.50 per unit and income remains at £12.
  **a** Draw the new budget line.
  **b** Why is the initial best affordable point (label it point *r*) no longer the best affordable point?
  **c** Using your graph, show the new best affordable point and label it *t*. What has happened to the consumption of coffee?
  **d** Decompose the effect on the consumption of *X* into the substitution effect and the income effect. On your graph, indicate the substitution effect as movement from point *r* to point *s* (which you must locate) and indicate the income effect as movement from point *s* to point *t*.

# DISCUSSION QUESTIONS

**1** Why should we bother to use indifference curves to derive demand curves? Why not just use demand curves?

**2** What is the difference between demand curves and indifference curves?

# DATA QUESTION

### Age and mobility
Look at almost any bus. The passengers will not be a cross-section of the public as a whole because those with high incomes will tend to travel by car. Hence those on the bus will usually be from the poorer sections of society, particularly old people.

People that want to increase the mobility of old people make two suggestions. The first is a subsidy that allows old people to travel at a reduced price. The second is to increase the pensions paid to old people so that they have more money to spend on goods, including buses.

**1** Draw budget lines and indifference curves to illustrate:
  **a** the effect of a subsidy on the choice between bus travel and all other goods.
  **b** the effect of an increase in income for old people.

# ANSWERS

## CONCEPT REVIEW

  **1** budget
  **2** goods
  **3** relative
  **4** steeper; outward
  **5** indifference
  **6** marginal; substitution; diminishes
  **7** budget; indifference
  **8** substitution; income
  **9** inferior
  **10** less; more

## TRUE OR FALSE

  **1 T** Definition.
  **2 F** The budget line will move to the left.
  **3 T** Real income = income/price of goods.
  **4 F** Rightward parallel shift.
  **5 F** Definition.
  **6 T** One of three fundamental assumptions about preferences.
  **7 F** Definition of budget line.
  **8 F** Logically impossible.
  **9 T** Definition.
  **10 T** Definition.
  **11 T** Describes downward movement along indifference curve.

## MULTIPLE CHOICE

  **1 b a** should be combinations of goods, **c** about indifference curves, **d** about best affordable point, **e** includes area inside budget line.
  **2 b** $y$-intercept shifts down, $x$-intercept is unchanged.
  **3 d** Increase in income does not change slope, but increase in $x$- and $y$-intercepts.
  **4 c** Change in income does not change slope but does change intercepts.
  **5 b** Numerators and denominators of both intercepts double, so intercepts do not change.
  **6 c** Definition. **a** and **b** relate to the slope of the budget line. *MRS* = **e** only at best affordable point.
  **7 c** Owing to diminishing *MRS*. **d** and **e** are wrong since relative price relates to budget line, not indifference curve.
  **8 c** Income = £12 (£2 × 6 units $X$) so price of $Y$ = £12/8 units $Y$.
  **9 b** Definition.
  **10 d** Both work in same direction. Rise in price leads to fall in consumption.
  **11 b** With the same income there is a fall in quantity of $X$ that can be purchased.
  **12 a** Budget line with new prices tangent to original indifference curve.
  **13 d** Hypothetically restore original income (reverse increase in real income), but keep prices constant at new level.
  **14 d** Substitution effect always discourages leisure. But rise in wages leads to rise in income and an increase in leisure (since leisure is a normal good).

# SHORT ANSWER

**1** An indifference curve tells us how much the consumption of one good must change as the consumption of another good decreases in order to leave the consumer indifferent (no better or worse off). It is negatively sloped because the goods we measure on the axes are both desirable. This means that as we *decrease* the consumption of one good, in order to not be made worse off, consumption of the other good must *increase*. This implies a negative slope.

**2** As we move down an indifference curve we change the combination of goods consumed by increasing the quantity of one good consumed and decreasing the quantity of the other good consumed. As consumption of a good increases its marginal utility falls because of the principle of diminishing marginal utility. Thus the value of the numerator on the right-hand side of the equation below decreases:

$$\text{Marginal rate of substitution} = \frac{\text{Marginal utility of } X}{\text{Marginal utility of } Y}$$

As consumption of $Y$ decreases, each previous $X$ consumed yields higher marginal utility. Thus the value of the denominator on the right-hand side of the equation increases. The effect of both a decrease in the numerator and an increase in the denominator is that the ratio $MU_X/MU_Y$ falls as we move down an indifference curve, corresponding to a diminishing marginal rate of substitution on the left-hand side of the equation.

**3** A decrease in the price of a good will have two effects on the consumption of the good. First, if all other prices remain constant, when the price of one good falls, real income increases. The substitution effect is the increase in consumption of the good resulting from the fall in its relative price accompanied by a hypothetical reduction in real income, which leaves the consumer indifferent between the new and initial situations. The income effect for a normal good is the further increase in consumption of the good when we hypothetically restore the consumer's real income but leave relative prices unchanged at the new level.

**4** Most people have some choice about how they spend their time. In recent years the educational standards of women have risen, thus increasing the amount of money that they can earn. This has meant a move along the supply of labour curve so that they now spend less time at home and more at paid work, that is, there is a strong substitution effect, although for many women this is not a choice between 'leisure' and work, but between paid and unpaid work.

# PROBLEMS

**1  a** Initially, Jan and Dan are at point $c$ on the budget line labelled $AB$ in Fig. 8.3. Jan's indifference curve is illustrated by $I_J$. Note that her indifference curve is close to a straight line reflecting the fact that bread and peanut butter are close substitutes. On the other hand, since Dan considers bread and peanut butter to be complementary, his indifference curve, $I_D$, is more tightly curved.

**Figure 8.3**

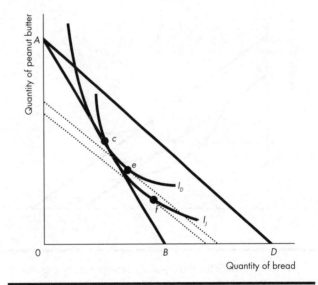

**b** If the price of bread declines, the budget line will become flatter, such as the line labelled $AD$ in Fig. 8.3. In order to measure the substitution effect we find the point on the original indifference curve that has the same slope as the new budget line. Since Dan's indifference curve is more sharply curved, it becomes flatter quite rapidly as we move away from point $c$. Thus the substitution effect is quite small: from $c$ to point $e$. Since Jan's indifference curve is almost a straight line, the substitution effect must be much larger: from point $c$ to point $f$.

**2  a** The relative price of coffee is the price of coffee divided by the price of whisky:

$$\frac{£1}{£1.50} = \frac{2}{3}$$

**b** Let $P_c$ be the price of coffee, $P_w$ be the price of whisky, $Q_c$ be the quantity of coffee, $Q_w$ be the quantity of whisky, and $y$ be income. The budget equation, in general form, is:

$$Q_w = \frac{y}{P_w} - \frac{P_c}{P_w} Q_c$$

Since $P_c$ = £1, $P_w$ = £1.50, and $y$ = £12, Kurt's budget equation is specifically given by:

$$Q_w = 8 - \tfrac{2}{3} Q_c$$

The graph of this budget equation, the budget line, is given by the line labelled $AB$ in Fig. 8.4.

## Figure 8.4

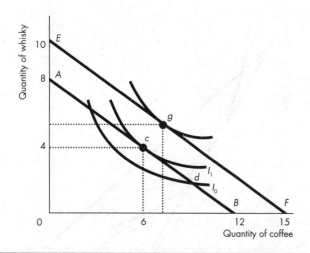

c If the best affordable point corresponds to 6 units of coffee and 4 units of whisky, then the relevant indifference curve must be tangent to (just touch) the budget line $AB$ at $c$, which is indifference curve $I_1$.

d The marginal rate of substitution is given by the magnitude of the slope of the indifference curve at point $c$. We do not know the slope of the indifference curve directly but we can easily compute the slope of the budget line. Because at point $c$ the indifference curve and the budget line have the same slope, we can obtain the marginal rate of substitution of coffee for whisky. Since the slope of the budget line is –2/3, the marginal rate of substitution is 2/3. For example, Kurt is willing to give up 2 units of whisky in order to receive 3 additional units of coffee and still remain indifferent.

e Since indifference curves cannot intersect each other and since indifference curve $I_1$ lies everywhere above the budget line (except at point $c$), we know that every other point on the budget line is on a lower indifference curve. For example, point $d$ lies on indifference curve $I_0$. Thus every other point on the budget line is inferior to point $c$.

**3 a** An increase in income will cause a parallel outward shift of the budget line, for example, to $EF$ in Fig. 8.4. If both coffee and whisky are normal goods, Kurt will move to a point like $g$ at which the consumption of both goods has increased.

**b** If whisky is an inferior good, then its consumption will fall as income rises. This is illustrated in Fig. 8.5. Once again the budget line shifts from $AB$ to $EF$, but Kurt's preferences are such that his new consumption point is given by a point like $g'$ where the consumption of whisky has actually declined.

## Figure 8.5

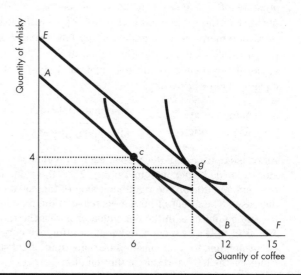

**4 a** Kurt's initial budget line is given by $AB$ and the initial best affordable point by $r$ in Fig. 8.6. The new budget line following an increase in the price of coffee to £2 (income remains at £12) is represented by $AH$.

**b** After the price increase, point $r$ is no longer the best affordable point since it is no longer even affordable.

**c** The new best affordable point (labelled $t$ in Fig. 8.6) indicates a decrease in the consumption of coffee.

**d** The substitution effect of the increase in the price of coffee is indicated by the movement from $r$ to $s$ in Fig. 8.6. This gives the effect of the change in relative prices while keeping Kurt on the same indifference curve. The income effect is indicated by movement from point $s$ to point $t$.

# DISCUSSION QUESTIONS

**1** There are two main reasons for using indifference curves. First, economists usually assume that rational

**Figure 8.6**

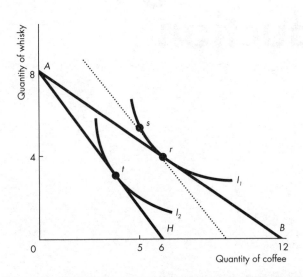

**Figure 8.7**

individuals attempt to maximize their satisfaction, and indifference curves make use of this assumption to derive demand curves by rational argument.

Second, the indifference curve approach allows us to analyse income and substitution effects, and these concepts are important in several areas of economics. So indifference curves are a useful tool of analysis.

**2** Demand curves show us how much of a good will be bought at different prices. Indifference curves show us different combinations of goods that give a consumer equal satisfaction.

# DATA QUESTION

**1 a** Old people's original budget line is *AB* in Fig. 8.7, and they will maximize satisfaction at point *x* on indifference curve $I_1$. A subsidy for bus travel will shift the budget line to *CB* and satisfaction will be maximized at point y on $I_2$. They will consume considerably more bus travel and a little more of other goods.

**b** An increase in income will shift the entire budget line from *AB* to *CD* as shown in Fig. 8.8. However, since bus travel is an inferior good, they will move along budget line *CD* to position *y* on indifference curve $I_2$. The result will be a fall in the consumption of bus travel and an increase in the consumption of other goods such as taxis and private motoring.

**Figure 8.8**

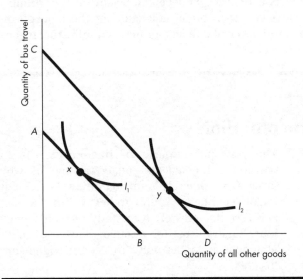

# Chapter 9    Organizing Production

This chapter begins the analysis of firms' choices and the principles underlying supply. The analysis here focuses on key differences that exist in how firms organize production.

  The first difference relates to types of firms. While there are common characteristics shared by all firms, there are different forms of business organization, each with pros and cons. The second difference relates to types of business finance. Concepts you read about every day in the business press – bonds, shares, present value, price–earnings ratios – are examined, as well as a difference between the accountant's and the economist's concepts of cost that depend crucially on opportunity cost. The third difference relates to the concepts of technological versus economic efficiency and the concepts of firm versus market coordination. The efficiency of firms (as institutions) make them a primary coordinating mechanism through which market economies tackle the problem of scarcity.

## Helpful Hints

1  The principal purpose of this chapter is to develop a fundamental understanding of why firms exist. Since it is obvious they do exist, it might seem better simply to begin with that fact and turn immediately to a study of their behaviour. Taking firms for granted, however, would eliminate an opportunity to acquire significant insights.

2  The chapter defines several important economic concepts.

a  The concept of present value is fundamental in thinking about the value today of an investment or of future amounts of money. The intuition behind present value is that a pound today is worth more than a pound in the future because today's pound can be invested to earn interest. To calculate the value *today* of a sum of money that will be paid in the future, we must discount that future sum to compensate for the forgone interest. The *present value* of a future sum of money is the amount that, if invested today, will grow as large as that future sum, taking into account the interest that it will earn.

**b** In this chapter, we again meet our old friend opportunity cost. Here we look at the costs firms face with a special emphasis on the differences between historical cost measures used by accountants and opportunity cost measures used by economists. Historical cost includes only explicit, out-of-pocket costs. Opportunity cost, which is the concept of cost relevant for economic decisions, includes *explicit costs and imputed costs*. Important examples of imputed costs include the owner's/investor's forgone interest, forgone rent and forgone income. These differences in cost measures between accountants and economists lead to differences in profit measures as well, as outlined here.

**Accountants**
Historical costs    = Explicit costs
Accounting profits = Revenues − Explicit costs

**Economists**
Opportunity costs  = Explicit costs +
                     Imputed costs

Economic profits   = Revenues − (Explicit costs
                     + Imputed costs)

Imputed costs, which economists include but accountants exclude, are the key difference between accountants' and economists' measures of cost and profit.

**c** It is important to distinguish between technological efficiency and economic efficiency. The difference is critical since economic decisions will be made only on the basis of economic efficiency. Technological efficiency is an engineering concept and occurs when it is not possible to increase output without increasing inputs. There is no consideration of input costs. Economic efficiency occurs when the *cost* of producing a given output is at a minimum. All technologically efficient production methods are not economically efficient. But all economically efficient methods are also technologically efficient.

## Key Tables

**Table 9.1 The Pros and Cons of Different Types of Firm, text page 209**
There are three main types of business organizations: sole proprietorship, partnership and company. This table presents some of the characteristics of these types of firms in the form of lists of advantages and disadvantages of each.

**Table 9.2 Mike's Mountain Bikes, Revenue, Cost and Profit Statement, text page 215**
Accounting costs and opportunity costs are usually *not* equal. As a result, accounting profit and economic profit will not be equal. This table illustrates the differences using the example of Mike's Mountain Bikes.

**Table 9.3 Four Ways of Making 10 TV Sets a Day, text page 216**
There are generally many technological methods available to produce a given quantity of a particular good, each of them using a different combination of inputs. The firm must choose which of these input combinations it will use. For a given set of input prices, a profit-maximizing firm will choose the method (input combination) that has least cost. It will choose the economically efficient method. This table gives the costs associated with four different methods of producing 10 TV sets a day. Remember that the economically efficient method depends critically on input prices. Note that when input prices change, the economically efficient method can change.

# SELF-TEST

## CONCEPT REVIEW

**1** An institution that organizes resources it has purchased or hired to produce and sell goods and services is called a(n) _____ .

**2** There are three main forms of business organizations. The two simpler forms are a(n) _____ (which has a single owner) and a(n) _____. In these two forms owners face _____ liability. The third more complicated form is a(n) _____ in which owners face _____ liability.

**3** Firms can raise money by selling _____, which are legal obligations to pay specified amounts at specified future dates. Companies can also raise money by issuing _____ .

**4** An agent is a person or firm hired by a _____ to do a specified job.

**5** In assessing costs, accountants measure _____ cost, which values resources at the prices originally paid for them. Economists measure _____ cost.

**6** The change in the market price of a durable input over a given period is called economic _____ .

**7** _____ efficiency is achieved when the cost of producing a given output is as low as possible. _____ efficiency is achieved when no more output can be produced without increasing inputs.

**8** Firms coordinate economic activity when they can do so more efficiently than _____ .

**9** The costs associated with finding a buyer, reaching agreement about exchange and ensuring the fulfilment of the agreement are _____ costs.

**10** _____ of _____ exist when the cost of producing a unit of output falls as we produce more.

**11** Economies that are derived from the size of the firm rather than from the amount of machinery are called economies of _____ .

## TRUE OR FALSE

___ **1** A firm purchases or hires factors of production and organizes production of goods and services.

___ **2** A partnership has joint unlimited liability.

___ **3** The residual claimants of a company are its bond holders.

___ **4** The perpetual 'life' of a company is an advantage over other forms of business

organizations when it comes to raising large sums of money.

___ **5** A cooperative is a firm that has equal total costs and total revenue.

___ **6** Historical cost is more likely to be the same as opportunity cost when firms use their own funds rather than borrow.

___ **7** In general, opportunity cost will be greater than historical cost.

___ **8** When a firm produces using a machine it owns, its opportunity cost is lower than if it had rented the machine.

___ **9** The opportunity cost of using stocks is the current replacement cost.

___ **10** A production process that is economically efficient may become economically inefficient if the relative prices of inputs change.

## MULTIPLE CHOICE

**1** Which of the following statements is *not* true of firms?
a Firms are like markets in that they are an institution for coordinating economic activity.
b Firms organize factors of production in order to produce goods and services.
c Firms sell goods and services.
d Technologically efficient firms can eliminate scarcity.
e Firms include Crown corporations.

**2** What is a firm called that has two or more owners with joint unlimited liability?
a a proprietorship
b a partnership
c a conglomerate
d a company
e none of the above

**3** What is a *disadvantage* of a company relative to a proprietorship or partnership?
a owners have unlimited liability
b profits are taxed as corporate profits and as dividend income to shareholders
c there is difficulty in raising money
d perpetual life
e none of the above

**4** The owner's stake in a business is called
  **a** present value.
  **b** redemption value.
  **c** historical cost.
  **d** equity capital.
  **e** preferred stock.

**5** Historical cost calculates the value of resources at the
  **a** original purchase price.
  **b** original purchase price minus depreciation.
  **c** original purchase price minus economic depreciation.
  **d** current market price.
  **e** value of the best forgone alternative.

**6** The construction cost of a building is £100,000. The conventional depreciation allowance is 5 per cent per year. At the end of the first year the market value of the building is £80,000. For the first year, the depreciation cost is
  **a** £20,000 to an accountant or an economist.
  **b** £5,000 to an accountant or an economist.
  **c** £5,000 to an accountant but £20,000 to an economist.
  **d** £20,000 to an accountant but £5,000 to an economist.
  **e** none of the above.

**7** John operates his own business and pays himself a salary of £20,000 per year. He was offered a job that pays £30,000 per year. What is the opportunity cost of John's time in the business?
  **a** £10,000
  **b** £20,000
  **c** £30,000
  **d** £50,000
  **e** zero

**8** The rate of interest is 10 per cent per year. If you invest £50,000 of your own money in a business and earn *accounting* profits of £20,000 after one year, what are your *economic* profits?
  **a** £20,000
  **b** £15,000
  **c** £5,000
  **d** £2,000
  **e** −£15,000

**9** Which of the following statements is *true*?
  **a** All technologically efficient methods are also economically efficient.
  **b** All economically efficient methods are also technologically efficient.

  **c** Technological efficiency changes with changes in relative input prices.
  **d** Technologically efficient firms will be more likely to survive than economically efficient firms.
  **e** None of the above statements is true.

**10** Firms will be more efficient than the market as a coordinator of economic activity when firms have
  **a** lower transactions costs.
  **b** lower monitoring costs.
  **c** economies of scale.
  **d** economies of team production.
  **e** all of the above.

**11** Economies of scale exist when
  **a** transactions costs are high.
  **b** transactions costs are low.
  **c** hiring additional inputs does not increase the price of inputs.
  **d** the cost of producing a unit of output falls as the output rate increases.
  **e** the firm is too large and too diversified.

## SHORT ANSWER

**1** Compare the historical cost and opportunity cost approaches in each of the following cases:
  **a** depreciation cost
  **b** the firm borrows money to finance its operation
  **c** the firm uses its own funds rather than borrowing

**2** Distinguish between technological efficiency and economic efficiency.

**3** Markets and firms are alternative ways of coordinating economic activity that arises because of scarcity. Why is it that both firms and markets exist?

## PROBLEMS

**1** Suppose that there are two technologically efficient methods of producing 1 tonne of wheat.

Method 1 requires 20 machine hours plus 20 human hours.

Method 2 requires 100 human hours.

Country *A* has a highly developed industrial economy, while country *B* is less developed. In country *A* the price of an hour of human labour (the wage rate) is £8, while the wage rate in country *B* is £4. The price of a machine hour is £20 in both countries. Which method is economically efficient in country *A*? in country *B*? Explain.

**2** Consider countries *A* and *B* described in Problem 1.
   **a** What wage rate in country *B* would make the two methods equally efficient in country *B*?
   **b** What price of a machine hour would make the two methods equally efficient in country *A*?

## DISCUSSION QUESTIONS

**1** What is the difference between a 'normal profit' and an 'economic profit'? Why does the difference matter?

**2** How can a situation be technologically efficient and not economically efficient?

## DATA QUESTIONS

**Firms and markets**
No one knows who invented firms, or even markets, but both play crucial roles in the modern economy. In addition to conventional, privately owned 'firms', there are many kinds of formal organizations that play a part in the economic life of the country, for example, charities such as War on Want, educational institutions such as schools and other bodies such as athletics clubs. All have economic influences. Nevertheless, it is true that firms have a profound effect on the economy. Many of these are small. In 1993 in the United Kingdom there were 129,000 business establishments and of these 90,000 employed fewer than 10 people. At the other extreme, 516 huge businesses employed a total of 381,000 people.

In some circumstances, firms will be used to allocate resources. This will occur when they represent a more efficient method of organizing production. In other circumstances, markets will be used to allocate resources.

**1** List some economic agents that are not firms.

**2** Comment on the variation in the size of firms given in the text.

**3** When will firms 'represent a more efficient method of organizing production'?

**4** When will markets be used to allocate resources?

# ANSWERS

## CONCEPT REVIEW

**1** firm

**2** proprietorship; partnership; unlimited; company; limited

**3** bonds; shares

**4** principal

**5** historical; opportunity

**6** depreciation

**7** Economic; technological

**8** markets

**9** transactions

**10** Economies; scale

**11** scope

## TRUE OR FALSE

**1 T** Definition.
**2 T** This is the legal status.
**3 F** Bond holders have priority status.
**4 T** The legal status gives confidence to lenders.
**5 F** A cooperative is a form of organization where owners have equal shares.
**6 F** More likely to be different.
**7 T** Usually true, but it depends on the existence of imputed costs.

**8 F** Opportunity cost is equal whether or not the machine is owned or rented.

**9 T** Definition of opportunity cost.

**10 T** Economic efficiency depends on prices; if these change so does the efficiency of the process.

## MULTIPLE CHOICE

**1 d** Scarcity can never be eliminated.

**2 b** Definition.

**3 b d** is an advantage; **a, c** are disadvantages of proprietorship and partnership.

**4 d** Definition.

**5 a** Definition.

**6 c** Accountant's depreciation = (5 per cent) × £100,000. Economist's depreciation = change in market value.

**7 c** Forgone income.

**8 b** Economic profits = accounting profits − imputed costs = £20,000 − (0.10 × £50,000).

**9 b c** is true for economic efficiency; the reverse of **d** is true.

**10 e** Definition.

**11 d** Definition.

## SHORT ANSWER

**1 a** From the historical cost approach, depreciation cost is computed as a prespecified percentage of the original purchase price of the capital good, with no reference to current market value. The opportunity cost approach measures economic depreciation cost as the change in the market value of the capital good over the period in question.

**b** If a firm borrows money, the historical and opportunity cost approaches will be the same; both will include the explicit interest payments.

**c** If a firm uses its own funds rather than borrowing, the historical and opportunity cost approaches will again differ. The historical cost will be zero since there are no explicit interest payments. The opportunity cost approach recognizes that those funds could have been loaned out and thus the (imputed) interest income forgone is the opportunity cost.

**2** A method is technologically efficient if it is not possible to increase output without increasing inputs. A method is economically efficient if the cost of producing a given level of output is as low as possible. Technological efficiency is independent of prices while economic efficiency depends on the prices of inputs. An economically efficient method of production is always technologically efficient, but a technologically efficient method is not necessarily economically efficient.

**3** As we saw in the text example on page 218, car repair can be coordinated by the market or by a firm. The institution (market or firm) that actually coordinates in any given case will be the one that is more efficient. In cases where there are significant transactions costs, economies of scale, or economies of team production, firms are likely to be more efficient, and we will see firms dominate the coordination of economic activity. But the efficiency of firms is limited and there are many circumstances in which we observe market coordination of economic activity because it is more efficient.

## PROBLEMS

**1** Both production methods are technologically efficient. To find the economically efficient production method we want to know which of the methods has the lower cost of producing 1 tonne of wheat. In country $A$, the price of an hour of labour is £8 and the price of a machine hour is £20. Thus the cost of producing 1 tonne of wheat is £560 using method 1 and £800 using method 2. Therefore method 1 is economically efficient for country $A$.

The price of an hour of labour is £4 in country $B$ and thus it will face different costs of producing 1 tonne of wheat. Under method 1, the cost will be £480 but under method 2, which uses only labour, the cost will be £400. So method 2 is economically efficient for country $B$.

The reason for this difference is that economic efficiency means producing at lowest cost. If the relative prices of inputs are different in two countries, there will be differences in the relative costs of production using alternative methods.

**2 a** If the wage rate in country $B$ were to increase to £5 an hour, then production of 1 tonne of wheat would be £500 under either method. How did we obtain this answer? Express the cost under method 1 ($C_1$) and the cost under method 2 ($C_2$) as follows:

$$C_1 = 20\,P_m + 20\,P_h$$
$$C_2 = 100\,P_h$$

where $P_m$ is the price of a machine hour and $P_h$ is the price of a human hour (the wage rate). We are given that $P_m$ = £20 and asked to find the value of $P_h$ that makes the two methods equally efficient; the value of $P_h$ that makes $C_1 = C_2$. Thus we solve the following equation for $P_h$:

$$20P_m + 20P_h = 100P_h$$
$$20(\$20) + 20P_h = 100P_h$$
$$\$400 = 80P_h$$
$$\$5 = P_h$$

**b** If the price of a machine hour is $32, production of 1 tonne of wheat would be $800 under either method in country *A*. This question asks: given the wage rate of $8 ($P_h$) in country *A*, what value of $P_m$ makes $C_1 = C_2$? Thus we solve the following equation for $P_m$:

$$20P_m + 20P_h = 100P_h$$
$$20P_m + 20(\$8) = 100(\$8)$$
$$20P_m = \$640$$
$$P_m = \$32$$

## DISCUSSION QUESTIONS

**1** Every business owner supplies some input into the business. One of these inputs is entrepreneurial talent, and normal profit is the payment for these services. Because normal profit is a payment for services rendered (perhaps implicitly), it is part of the firm's opportunity costs.

An economic profit equals the firm's revenues minus its opportunity costs. Because opportunity costs already include normal profit, an economic profit is a profit over and above a normal profit.

**2** Technological efficiency merely reflects a firm's inputs and the resulting outputs. A situation is technologically efficient when producing more output without using more inputs is impossible.

Economic efficiency occurs when the cost of producing a given amount of output is as low as possible. A firm which is economically efficient will also be technologically efficient, but it is possible for a firm to be technologically efficient but not economically efficient. This will occur if it uses the wrong mix of inputs. For example, if the local McDonalds employed economics professors to cook its burgers it might be technologically efficient, but it would not be economically efficient because the cost of wages would be too high.

## DATA QUESTIONS

**1** Other economic agents include cooperatives, nationalized industries and government departments.

**2** In some industries there are economies of scale. These exist when the cost of producing a unit of output falls as the quantity produced increases. Hence in industries such as car production, firms tend to be large. When the product does not permit economies of scale – for example, in hairdressing or plumbing – the enterprise remains small.

**3** Firms achieve lower transactions costs, economies of scale and economies of team production.

**4** Markets are used to allocate resources when firms do not provide an optimal solution.

# Chapter 10  Output and Costs

---

## Chapter in Perspective, Text Pages 225–255

In a modern market economy, goods and services are produced primarily by firms. In Chapter 9 we saw that firms exist because they provide economically efficient ways of organizing factors of production for producing and selling goods and services. In this chapter we begin to analyse the production and cost constraints that firms face, and thus how efficiency is pursued.

What kinds of costs do firms face? How do these costs change as a firm's planning horizon changes? How will a firm, motivated by the desire to maximize profit, decide how much output to produce? When will a firm hire more labour? When will it increase its plant size? This chapter begins to answer these questions.

---

## Helpful Hints

**1** There is a simple and fundamental relationship between production functions and cost functions.

The chapter begins with the short-run production function and the concepts of total product, marginal product and average product. This is followed by the short-run cost function and the concepts of total cost, marginal cost, average variable cost and average total cost.

All of these seemingly disparate concepts are related to the law of diminishing returns. The law states that as a firm uses additional units of a variable input, while holding constant the quantity of fixed inputs, the marginal product of the variable input will eventually diminish. This law explains why the marginal product and average product curves eventually fall, and why the total product curve becomes flatter. When productivity falls,

costs increase, and the law explains the eventual upward slope of the marginal cost curve. The marginal cost curve, in turn, explains the U-shape of the average variable cost and average total cost curves. When the marginal cost curve is below the average variable (or total) cost curve, the average variable (or total) cost curve is falling. When marginal cost is above the average variable (or total) cost curve, the average variable (or total) cost curve is rising. The marginal cost curve intersects the average variable (or total) cost curve at the minimum point on the average variable (or total) cost curve.

Use the law of diminishing returns as the key to understanding the relationships between the many short-run concepts and graphs in the chapter. Pay most attention to the unit cost concepts and graphs – especially marginal cost, average variable cost and average total cost – because these will be used the most in later chapters to analyse the behaviour of firms. Be sure to thoroughly understand text Figure 10.5(b) on page 234. It is the most important figure in the chapter.

**2** You will probably draw the unit cost graph with the marginal cost, average variable cost and average total cost curves many times in this course. Here are some hints on drawing the graph quickly and easily.

   **a** Be sure to label the axes; quantity of output *(Q)* on the horizontal axis and average cost on the vertical axis.

   **b** Draw a shallow U-shaped curve (see Fig. 10.1) and mark its minimum point. Then pick a second point above and to the right of that first minimum point. Draw another shallow U-shaped curve whose minimum point passes through your second point. Draw an upward-sloping marginal cost curve which passes through the two minimum points. The marginal cost curve can have a small downward-sloping section at first, but this is not important for subsequent analysis. Finally, label the curves.

   **c** Any time a test question asks about these curves, *draw a graph* before you answer.

---

**Figure 10.1**

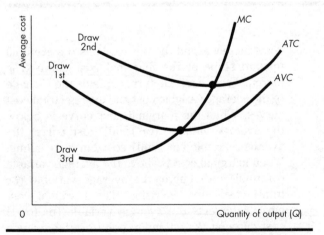

**3** Be sure to understand how economists use the terms *short run* and *long run*. These terms do not refer to any notion of calendar time. They are better thought of as planning horizons. The short run is a planning horizon short enough for, while some inputs are variable, at least one input

to be fixed not varied. The long run refers to a planning horizon that is long enough for all inputs to be varied.

**4** The later sections of the chapter explain the long-run production function and cost function when plant size is variable. While diminishing returns was the key for understanding short-run costs, the concept of returns to scale is the key for understanding long-run costs. Returns to scale are the increase in output relative to the increase in inputs when *all inputs* are increased by the same percentage. Returns to scale can be increasing, constant, or decreasing, and correspond to the downward-sloping, horizontal and upward-sloping sections of the long-run average cost curve.

# Key Figures and Table

### Figure 10.2  Marginal Product, text page 229

This figure illustrates how to calculate marginal product from total product. Marginal product of labour is the increase in total product resulting from the use of an additional unit of labour. Part (a) illustrates the total product curve and indicates the addition to total product associated with each additional unit of labour. Notice that the slope of the total product curve, $TP/L$, is equal to marginal product. Thus if you know the total product curve, you can always derive the marginal product curve.

When graphing the marginal product curve, as in part (b), notice that marginal product is plotted midway between the corresponding units of labour, emphasizing that marginal product is the result of *changing* inputs. For example, the marginal product of changing from 0 to 1 worker is 4 jumpers, and the value 4 is plotted midway between 0 and 1 workers.

### Figure 10.5  Short-run Costs, text page 234

In the short run, total cost *(TC)* is divided into total fixed cost *(TFC)* and total variable cost *(TVC)*. Part (a) illustrates the total cost, total fixed cost and total variable cost curves. Since $TC = TFC + TVC$, the vertical distance between the $TC$ and $TVC$ curves is equal to $TFC$, which by definition is constant (fixed).

The graph in part (b) is one of the most important graphs in all of microeconomics, and you must understand it thoroughly. The curves for average total cost

*(ATC)*, average fixed cost *(AFC)* and average variable cost *(AVC)* are derived by taking the values for *TC*, *TFC* and *TVC* and dividing by quantity of output. Since these are average values for a fixed quantity of output, they are plotted directly above the corresponding units of output. On the other hand, marginal cost *(MC)* is the *change* in total cost (or equivalently, in total variable cost) resulting from a one-unit increase in output. It is plotted in the graph in part (b) midway between the corresponding units of output. The *ATC*, *AVC* and *MC* curves are crucially important. The *ATC* and *AVC* curves are both U-shaped. The *MC* curve is also U-shaped and intersects the *ATC* and *AVC* curves at their minimum points. The *MC* curve is below the *ATC* and *AVC* curves when *ATC* and *AVC* are falling, and above the *ATC* and *AVC* curves when they are rising. The less important *AFC* curve falls continuously as output increases. See Helpful Hint 2 for tips on how to draw the crucially important curves.

**Table 10.3 A Compact Glossary of Costs, text page 235**
This handy table summarizes the relationships between various definitions of cost.

# SELF-TEST

## CONCEPT REVIEW

**1** The profits of a firm are limited by two types of constraints: _____ constraints, which are conditions under which the firm can buy its inputs and sell its output, and _____ constraints, which limit the feasible ways in which inputs can be converted into output.

**2** A production process that uses large amounts of capital relative to labour is called a(n) _____-_____technique while a(n)_____ - _____ technique uses a large amount of labour relative to capital.

**3** The term economists use for a period of time in which the quantities of some inputs are fixed while others can be varied is the _____ _____. The period of time in which all inputs are variable is the _____ _____ .

**4** The total product curve is a graph of the maximum output attainable at each level of a _____ input, given the amount of fixed inputs. The change in total product resulting from a one-unit increase in labour input, holding the quantity of capital constant, is called the _____ _____ of labour. The average product of labour is _____ _____ divided by the units of _____ .

**5** If marginal product is greater than average product, then average product must be _____ . Marginal product _____ average product when average product reaches a maximum.

**6** The shape of the marginal product curve can be described as follows: it first _____, reaches a _____ and then _____ as labour inputs increase.

**7** Increasing marginal returns occur when the marginal product of an additional worker is _____ than the marginal product of the previous workers. As more of a variable input is used, holding other inputs fixed, the marginal product of the variable input begins to decline. This is a statement of the law of _____ _____ .

**8** $TC = FC +$ _____ .

**9** Marginal cost is the increase in total cost resulting from a one-unit increase in _____ .

**10** If the average variable cost curve is decreasing, then the marginal cost curve must be _____ the average variable cost.

**11** If output increases by 20 per cent when all inputs are increased by 10 per cent, the production process is said to display _____ _____ to _____ .

**12** If a firm is experiencing constant returns to scale, a 10 per cent increase in inputs will result in a _____ per cent _____ in output. When the long-run average cost curve rises, there are _____ returns to scale.

**13** A technological advance will tend to _____ product curves and _____ cost curves.

## TRUE OR FALSE

___ **1** All economically efficient production methods are also technologically efficient.

___ **2** The short run is a time period in which there is at least one fixed input and at least one variable input.

___ **3** All inputs are fixed in the long run.

___ **4** Marginal product is given by the slope of the total product curve.

___ **5** Average product can be measured as the slope of a line drawn from the origin to a point on the total product curve.

___ **6** The average product curve cuts the marginal product curve from above at the maximum point on the marginal product curve.

___ **7** Average total cost, average variable cost and average fixed cost are all U-shaped.

___ **8** Average variable cost reaches its minimum at the level of output at which average product is a maximum.

___ **9** In the real world, marginal cost curves are rarely upward sloping.

___ **10** A firm producing on the downward-sloping part of its average total cost curve is said to have excess capacity.

___ **11** By capacity, economists mean the physical limits of production.

___ **12** If average total cost is greater than marginal cost, then average total cost must be increasing.

___ **13** Increasing returns to scale means that the long-run average cost curve is negatively sloped.

___ **14** In the long run, the total cost and total variable cost curves are the same.

## MULTIPLE CHOICE

**1** In economics, the short run is a time period
 **a** of one year or less.
 **b** in which all inputs are variable.
 **c** in which all inputs are fixed.
 **d** in which there is at least one fixed input and at least one variable input.
 **e** in which all inputs are variable but the technology is fixed.

**2** The average product of labour can be measured as the
 **a** slope of a straight line from the origin to a point on the total product curve.
 **b** slope of the total product curve.
 **c** slope of a straight line from the origin to a point on the marginal product curve.
 **d** slope of the marginal product curve.
 **e** change in output divided by the change in labour input.

**3** A field of ripe corn is waiting to be harvested. Labour is the only variable input, and the total product (in kilograms) of various numbers of workers is given in the table.

**Table 10.1**

| Number of workers | Total product |
|---|---|
| 0 | 0 |
| 1 | 300 |
| 2 | 700 |
| 3 | 1,000 |
| 4 | 1,200 |

Diminishing returns *begin* when you add which worker?
 **a** 1st worker
 **b** 2nd worker
 **c** 3rd worker
 **d** 4th worker
 **e** there are no diminishing returns since total product always rises

**4** When the marginal product of labour is less than the average product of labour
 **a** the average product of labour is increasing.
 **b** the marginal product of labour is increasing.

**c** the total product curve is negatively sloped.

**d** the firm is experiencing diminishing returns.

**e** none of the above is true.

**5** The vertical distance between the *TC* and *TVC* curves is

**a** decreasing as output increases.

**b** increasing as output increases.

**c** equal to *AFC*.

**d** equal to *TFC*.

**e** equal to *MC*.

**6** The marginal cost *(MC)* curve intersects the

**a** *ATC*, *AVC* and *AFC* curves at their minimum points.

**b** *ATC* and *AFC* curves at their minimum points.

**c** *AVC* and *AFC* curves at their minimum points.

**d** *ATC* and *AVC* curves at their minimum points.

**e** *TC* and *TVC* curves at their minimum points.

**7** Marginal cost is the amount by which

**a** total cost increases when one more worker is hired.

**b** fixed cost increases when one more worker is hired.

**c** variable cost increases when one more worker is hired.

**d** total cost increases when one more unit of output is produced.

**e** fixed cost increases when one more unit of output is produced.

**8** A firm's fixed costs are £100. If total costs are £200 for one unit of output and £310 for two units, what is the marginal cost of the second unit?

**a** £100

**b** £110

**c** £200

**d** £210

**e** £310

**9** If *ATC* is falling then *MC* must be

**a** rising.

**b** falling.

**c** equal to *ATC*.

**d** above *ATC*.

**e** below *ATC*.

**10** In the long run

**a** only the scale of plant is fixed.

**b** all inputs are variable.

**c** all inputs are fixed.

**d** a firm must experience decreasing returns to scale.

**e** none of the above is true.

**11** The marginal cost curve slopes upward because of

**a** diminishing marginal utility.

**b** diminishing returns.

**c** technological inefficiency.

**d** economic inefficiency.

**e** none of the above statements.

**12** Constant returns to scale means that as all inputs are increased

**a** total output remains constant.

**b** average total cost remains constant.

**c** average total cost increases at the same rate as inputs.

**d** long-run average cost remains constant.

**e** long-run average cost rises at the same rate as inputs.

**13** The long-run average cost curve

**a** shifts upward when fixed costs increase.

**b** shifts downward when fixed costs increase.

**c** is the short-run average total cost curve with the lowest cost.

**d** traces the minimum points on all the short-run average total cost curves for each scale of plant.

**e** traces the minimum short-run average total cost for each output.

**14** A firm will want to increase its scale of plant if

**a** it persistently produces on the upward-sloping part of its short-run average total cost curve.

**b** it persistently produces on the downward-sloping part of its short-run average total cost curve.

**c** it is producing below capacity.

**d** marginal cost is below average total cost.

**e** marginal cost is below average variable cost.

The following questions relate to the Appendix to this chapter (text pages 248–255).

**15** Figure 10.2 shows a series of isoquants. Which of the following combinations of labour and capital could *not* produce 30 units of output?

**a** 8 units of labour and 1 unit of capital

**b** 7 units of labour and 2 units of capital

**c** 5 units of labour and 3 units of capital

**d** 2 units of labour and 6 units of capital

**e** 1 unit of labour and 8 units of capital

**Figure 10.2**

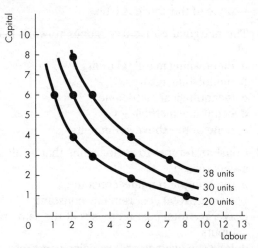

**16** In Fig. 10.2, what is the marginal rate of substitution of capital for labour as labour is increased from 2 to 3 units if output is kept constant at 38 units?
 **a** 1/2
 **b** 1
 **c** 2
 **d** 3
 **e** 6

**17** In Fig. 10.2, 6 units of capital and 2 units of labour are currently in use. What is the marginal product of an additional unit of labour?
 **a** 6
 **b** 8
 **c** 10
 **d** 18
 **e** cannot be determined without additional information

## SHORT ANSWER

**1** What market constraints does a firm face on its ability to make profits?

**2** Why does a steeper slope of the total product curve imply a higher level of the marginal product curve?

**3** Why is it the case that the marginal product curve must intersect the average product curve at its maximum point?

**4** What is the difference, if any, between diminishing returns and decreasing returns to scale?

**5** In the *Reading Between the Lines* article, explain why: 'Excess capacity means that individual refineries are not operating at minimum average total cost. This is a common problem in manufacturing.'

## PROBLEMS

**1** For a given scale of plant, Table 10.2 gives the total monthly output of golf carts attainable using varying quantities of labour.

**Table 10.2   Monthly Golf Cart Production**

| Workers (per month) | Output (units per month) | Marginal product | Average product |
|---|---|---|---|
| 0 | 0 | | |
| 1 | 1 | | |
| 2 | 3 | | |
| 3 | 6 | | |
| 4 | 12 | | |
| 5 | 17 | | |
| 6 | 20 | | |
| 7 | 22 | | |
| 8 | 23 | | |

 **a** Complete the table for the marginal product and average product of labour. (Note that marginal product should be entered midway between rows to emphasize that it is the result of *changing* inputs – moving from one row to the next. Average product corresponds to a *fixed* quantity of labour and should be entered on the appropriate row.)
 **b** Label the axes and draw a graph of the total product curve *(TP)*.
 **c** On a separate piece of paper, label the axes and draw a graph of both marginal product *(MP)* and average product *(AP)*. (Marginal product should be plotted midway between the corresponding units of labour, as in text Figure 10.2 on page 229, while average product should be plotted directly above the corresponding units of labour, as in text Figure 10.3 on page 230.)

**2** Now let's examine the short-run costs of golf cart production. The first two columns of Table 10.2 are reproduced in the first two columns of Table

10.3. The cost of 1 worker (the only variable input) is $2,000 per month. Total fixed cost is $2,000 per month.

**Table 10.3 Short-run Costs**

| Workers (per month) | Output (units per month) | TFC (£) | TVC (£) | TC (£) | MC (£) | AFC (£) | AVC (£) | ATC (£) |
|---|---|---|---|---|---|---|---|---|
| 0 | 0 | 2,000 | | | | | | |
| 1 | 1 | | | | | | | |
| 2 | 3 | | | | | | | |
| 3 | 6 | | | | | | | |
| 4 | 12 | | | | | | | |
| 5 | 17 | | | | | | | |
| 6 | 20 | | | | | | | |
| 7 | 22 | | | | | | | |
| 8 | 23 | | | | | | | |

**a** Given this information, complete Table 10.3 by computing total fixed cost *(TFC)*, total variable cost *(TVC)*, total cost *(TC)*, marginal cost *(MC)*, average fixed cost *(AFC)*, average variable cost *(AVC)* and average total cost *(ATC)*. Your completed table should look like text Table 10.2 on page 233, with marginal cost entered midway between the rows.

**b** Label the axes and draw the *TC*, *TVC* and *TFC* curves on a single graph.

**c** Label the axes and draw the *MC*, *ATC*, *AVC* and *AFC* curves on a single graph. Be sure to plot *MC* midway between the corresponding units of output.

**d** Now suppose that the price of a worker increases to $2,500 per month. Construct a table for the new *MC* and *ATC* curves (output, *MC*, *ATC*). Label the axes and draw a graph of the new *MC* and *ATC* curves. What is the effect of the increase in the price of the variable input on these curves?

**3** Figure 10.3 gives a sequence of short-run *ATC* curves numbered 1 to 7 corresponding to seven different factory sizes.
  **a** Draw the long-run average cost curve on Fig. 10.3.
  **b** If the desired level of output is 100 units per day, what is the best factory size? (Give the number of the associated short-run *ATC* curve.)
  **c** If the desired level of output is 200 units per day, what is the best factory size?

**Figure 10.3**

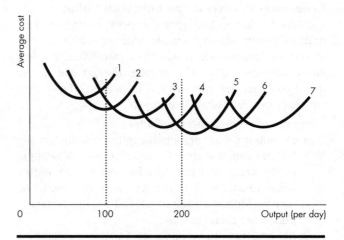

**4** This question relates to the Appendix to this chapter (text pages 248–255).

In country *A* the price of labour is $8 per unit and the price of capital is also $8 per unit. In country *B*, the price of labour is $4 per unit and the price of capital is $8 per unit. Country *B* is a low-wage economy. Consider the production problem faced by two firms, one in each country, which both produce the same good. Firm 1 is in country *A* and firm 2 is in country *B*. Both firms have access to the same production technology, and therefore the same production function.

**a** Draw a graph of an isoquant and isocost line for firm 1 which illustrates the least-cost production techniques for some level of output.

**b** Now consider firm 2. As the firms have the same production function, their isoquants are identical. On the same graph as part **a**, illustrate the least-cost production technique for firm 2, using the same level of output.

**c** Using the same graph, show that the combinations of labour and capital used by
  **i** firm 1 is more expensive than the combination used by firm 2 when the price of labour is as in country *B*.
  **ii** firm 2 is more expensive than the combination used by firm 1 when the price of labour is as in country *A*.

## DISCUSSION QUESTION

**1** Why is marginal cost an important concept?

## DATA QUESTIONS

### Economies of scale in the European Union

Increased trade and sharper competition triggered by market integration will enable firms to make savings linked to larger-scale production. Empirical studies show that the bigger the market, the greater is the move towards the size needed to achieve the necessary economies of scale to compete.

There are three complicating factors:

a Potential gains vary significantly by industry: the fall in costs resulting from economies of scale is of the order of 1 per cent for sectors like petroleum products, but reaches 3–6 per cent for heavy electrical equipment and means of transport other than cars.

b In addition to economies in the production process, firms may realize economies in research, marketing and finance.

c These economies of scale take time to achieve.

Taking just manufacturing industries, the total cost savings to be had from economies of scale for production would be about 60 billion ecu. In addition, there would be substantial economies in other sectors, particularly services. Moreover, learning 'on the job' means that as larger quantities are produced the unit cost falls. Thus given a doubling of overall production, unit costs will fall by an average of 10 per cent in refining and car manufacturing and 20 per cent in aircraft manufacture.

Source: Adapted from *1992: The benefits of a single market* (The Cecchini Report), Wildwood House, 1988, pp. 77 and 78.

1 Explain what is meant by 'economies of scale'.

2 Why do you think some industries benefit more from economies of scale than others?

3 Draw points on average cost curves for (a) cars, and (b) aircraft manufacture.

4 If large firms benefit from substantial economies of scale, why are not all industries made up of enormous firms?

# ANSWERS

## CONCEPT REVIEW

1 market; technological
2 capital-intensive; labour-intensive
3 short run; long run
4 variable; marginal product; total product (output); labour
5 rising; equals
6 increases; maximum; decreases
7 greater; diminishing returns
8 $VC$
9 output
10 below
11 increasing returns; scale
12 10; increase; decreasing
13 raise; lower

## TRUE OR FALSE

1 **T** Definition.
2 **T** Definition.
3 **F** All inputs are variable in the long run.
4 **T** Change in $TP$/Change in $L$.
5 **T** Geometrical relationship.
6 **F** This would be true if the terms 'average product' and 'marginal product' were switched.
7 **F** See cost curve diagrams.
8 **T** $AVC = TVC/Q = WL/Q = W/(Q/L) = W/AP$
9 **F** Marginal costs sometimes fall, sometimes rise.
10 **T** Could increase output up to capacity (quantity associated with minimum $ATC$).
11 **F** Capacity = capacity associated with minimum $ATC$.
12 **T** Draw curves to check.
13 **T** Definition.
14 **T** All costs are variable in the long run.

## MULTIPLE CHOICE

1 **d** Definition.
2 **a** Equals $TP/L$.
3 **c** $MP$ 1st = 3. $MP$ 2nd = 4. $MP$ 3rd = 3.
4 **d** When $MP < AP$, $MP$ is falling (diminishing returns), $AP$ is falling and $TP$ is positively sloped.

**5 d** $TC = TFC + TVC$. Distance is constant.

**6 d** $AFC$ always falls, $TC$ and $TVC$ always rise.

**7 d** Definition.

**8 b** Fixed costs are irrelevant. Change in $TC$/Change in quantity = ($310 – $200) / (2 – 1).

**9 e** $MC$ could be rising or falling below $ATC$ when $ATC$ is falling.

**10 b** Definition. All returns to scale possible in long run.

**11 b** Diminishing returns will cause marginal costs to rise.

**12 d** $LRAC$ is horizontal.

**13 e** Definition. **a** and **b** apply to the short run since fixed costs.

**14 a** **b** and **c** plant too big. **d** and **e** relate to short run.

**15 a** This isoquant would produce only 20 units.

**16 c** Read off from move along 38-unit isoquant.

**17 b** Read off from move along 30-unit isoquant.

**4** The law of diminishing returns states that as a firm uses additional units of a variable input, *while holding constant the quantity of fixed inputs*, the marginal product of the variable input will eventually diminish. Decreasing returns to scale occur when a firm increases *all of its inputs by an equal percentage,* and this results in a lower percentage increase in output. Diminishing (marginal) returns is a short-run concept since there must be a fixed input. Decreasing returns to scale is a long-run concept since all inputs must be variable.

**5** Uncertainty is the fundamental reason why firms do not operate at the bottom of the average cost curve and so have excess capacity. If they could predict sales and costs accurately, they would operate accordingly. Instead, they often build on a large scale to take advantage of economies of scale but find that sales are not large enough to increase output so that it is at the most efficient level.

Excess capacity is not limited to manufacturing; for example, supermarkets could serve more customers, and so could be said to have excess capacity.

# SHORT ANSWER

**1** Every firm is constrained by the supply of inputs it uses and by the demand for the output it produces. Because of the law of supply, firms, in general, can obtain more inputs only if they are willing to pay more for them. On the other hand, given the law of demand, firms, in general, can sell more of their output only if they are willing to drop the price.

**2** Marginal product is equal to the slope of the total product curve since it is defined as the change in total product resulting from an increase in the variable input. Since a steeper slope means a larger slope, it also means a higher marginal product.

**3** Since the average product curve first rises and then falls, when average product is rising, marginal product must be greater than average product, and when average product is falling, marginal product must be lower than average product. If this is the case, then the marginal product curve intersects the average product curve at its maximum point. In order for average product to increase, it must have been *pulled up* by a larger increase in product from the last unit of input. Therefore the marginal product is higher than average product. Similarly, when average product is falling, it must have been *pulled down* by a lower marginal product. When average product is at its maximum, it is neither rising nor falling, so marginal product cannot be higher or lower than average product. Therefore marginal product must be equal to average product.

# PROBLEMS

**1 a** The completed table is shown as Table 10.4.

Table 10.4  Monthly Golf Cart Production

| Workers (per month) | Output (units per month) | Marginal product | Average product |
|---|---|---|---|
| 0 | 0 | | 0 |
| | | ...1 | |
| 1 | 1 | | 1.00 |
| | | ...2 | |
| 2 | 3 | | 1.50 |
| | | ...3 | |
| 3 | 6 | | 2.00 |
| | | ...6 | |
| 4 | 12 | | 3.00 |
| | | ...5 | |
| 5 | 17 | | 3.40 |
| | | ...3 | |
| 6 | 20 | | 3.33 |
| | | ...2 | |
| 7 | 22 | | 3.14 |
| | | ...1 | |
| 8 | 23 | | 2.88 |

**b** Figure 10.4 gives the graph of the total product curve.

**c** Figure 10.5 gives the graphs of marginal product and average product.

**Figure 10.4**

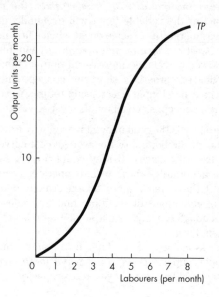

**Table 10.5  Short-run Costs**

| Workers (per month) | Output (units per month) | TFC (£) | TVC (£) | TC (£) | MC (£) | AFC (£) | AVC (£) | ATC (£) |
|---|---|---|---|---|---|---|---|---|
| 0 | 0 | 2,000 | 0 | 2,000 | | | | |
| | | | | | 2,000 | | | |
| 1 | 1 | 2,000 | 2,000 | 4,000 | | 2,000 | 2,000 | 4,000 |
| | | | | | 1,000 | | | |
| 2 | 3 | 2,000 | 4,000 | 6,000 | | 667 | 1,333 | 2,000 |
| | | | | | 667 | | | |
| 3 | 6 | 2,000 | 6,000 | 8,000 | | 333 | 1,000 | 1,333 |
| | | | | | 333 | | | |
| 4 | 12 | 2,000 | 8,000 | 10,000 | | 167 | 667 | 833 |
| | | | | | 400 | | | |
| 5 | 17 | 2,000 | 10,000 | 12,000 | | 118 | 588 | 706 |
| | | | | | 667 | | | |
| 6 | 20 | 2,000 | 12,000 | 14,000 | | 100 | 600 | 700 |
| | | | | | 1,000 | | | |
| 7 | 22 | 2,000 | 14,000 | 16,000 | | 91 | 636 | 727 |
| | | | | | 2,000 | | | |
| 8 | 3 | 2,000 | 8,000 | 18,000 | | 87 | 696 | 783 |

**b** The *TC*, *TVC* and *TFC* curves are graphed in Fig. 10.6.

**c** The *MC*, *ATC*, *AVC* and *AFC* curves are graphed in Fig. 10.7.

**d** The new *MC* and *ATC* curves (and the associated table) are given in Fig. 10.8. The original curves, $MC_1$ and $ATC_1$, are indicated for reference. The new curves are labelled $MC_2$ and $ATC_2$. Both curves have shifted upward as a result of an increase in the price of labour.

**Figure 10.5**

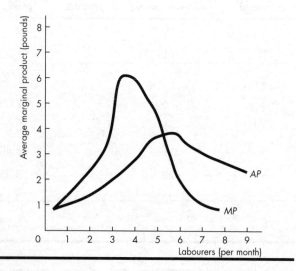

**2  a** The completed table is given as Table 10.5.

**Figure 10.6**

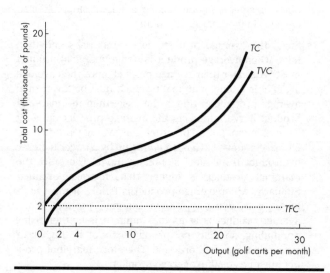

**Figure 10.7**

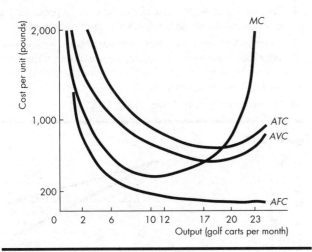

**Figure 10.8**

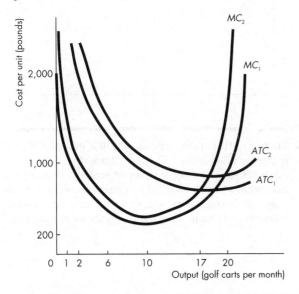

| Output | MC (£) | ATC (£) |
|---|---|---|
| 0 | | 0 |
| 1 | ...2,500 | 4,500 |
| 3 | ...1,250 | 2,333 |
| 6 | ......833 | 1,583 |
| 12 | ......417 | 1,000 |
| 17 | ......500 | 853 |
| 20 | ......833 | 850 |
| 22 | ...1,250 | 886 |
| 23 | ...2,500 | 957 |

**3 a** The long-run average cost curve is indicated in Fig. 10.9 by the heavy line tracing out the lowest short-run average total cost of producing each level of output.

**Figure 10.9**

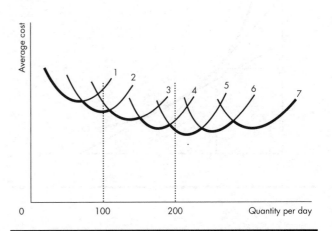

**b** If the desired level of output is 100 units, the best plant size is the one associated with short-run average total cost curve 2.

**c** If the desired level of output is 200 units, the best plant size is the one associated with short-run average total cost curve 5.

**4 a** See Fig. 10.10. The isoquant for the chosen level of output is the curve $Q$. Since firm 1 is in country $A$ where the prices of labour and capital are the same, the slope of the isoquant line is 1 in absolute value. The least-cost isoquant line for firm 1 is given by the line labelled $AA$, which is tangent to the isoquant at point $a$. Thus for firm 1, the least-cost combination is $L_1$ units of labour and $K_1$ units of capital.

**b** The isoquant for firm 2 is the same as for firm 1. In this case the slope of the isoquant lines is 1/2 in absolute value and the least-cost isoquant for firm 2 is the line labelled $BB$, which is tangent to the isocost at point $b$. Thus for firm 2 the least cost combination is $L_2$ units of labour and $K_2$ units of capital.

**c i** The input combination represented by point $a$ is more costly than the input combination represented by point $b$.

**ii** Point $b$ lies above the $AA$ isocost line and therefore must lie on a higher isocost line. This means that the input combination represented by point $b$ is more costly than the input combination represented by point $b$.

**Figure 10.10**

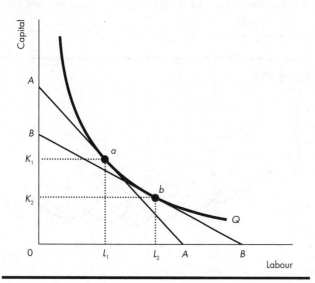

# DATA QUESTIONS

**1** Economies of scale exist when the cost of producing a unit of a good falls as the level of output increases.

**2** Some industries (such as car manufacture) enjoy considerable economies of scale, but in other industries (such as hairdressing and other personal services) there are few economies of scale.

**3** The cost curves are shown in Fig. 10.11.

**Figure 10.11**

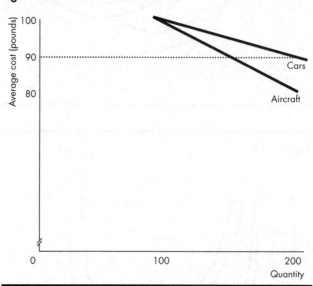

# DISCUSSION QUESTION

**1** The idea of the margin is fundamental in economics. Here we have been analysing marginal cost – the additional cost which a firm incurs when it expands production by one unit. When a firm is considering expansion, it will maximize profit if it continues to expand as long as the marginal revenue obtained by selling an additional unit exceeds the marginal cost of making that unit. This idea is fundamental to much economic analysis of firms.

**4** There are two main reasons why the economy is not completely dominated by large firms. First, there are often substantial diseconomies of scale so that growth may mean less efficiency. This is discussed in the text on page 238. Second, there is only a small market for some products so firms in these industries are inevitably small.

# Chapter 11 Competition

## Chapter in Perspective, Text Pages 258–283

This chapter combines the cost information of Chapters 9 and 10 with new revenue information in order to analyse the profit-maximization decisions of firms in a perfectly competitive market. The analysis includes derivations of both the individual firm supply curve and the industry supply curve. While we have previously simply assumed that supply curves are upward sloping, this chapter derives upward-sloping supply curves as a prediction of the theory of perfect competition. The theory also allows us to make precise predictions about the behaviour of firms and their responses to changes in market conditions. Although perfect competition does not occur frequently in the real world, the theory allows us to isolate the effects of competitive forces that are at work in *all* markets, even in those that do not match the assumptions of the theory of perfect competition.

## Helpful Hints

**1** Although perfectly competitive markets are quite rare in the real world, there are three important reasons to develop a thorough understanding of their behaviour.

First, many markets closely approximate perfectly competitive markets. Thus the analysis developed in this chapter gives direct and useful insights into the behaviour of these markets.

Second, the theory of perfect competition allows us to isolate the effects of competitive forces that are at work in *all* markets, even in those that do not match the assumptions of perfect competition.

Third, the perfectly competitive model serves as a useful benchmark against which to evaluate relative allocative efficiency.

**2** In the short run, a perfectly competitive firm cannot change the scale of its plant – it has fixed inputs. The firm is also a price taker; it always sells at the market price, which it cannot influence. Thus the only variable that the firm controls is its level of output. The short-run condition for profit maximization is to choose the level of output at which marginal revenue equals marginal cost. This is a general condition which, as we will see in subsequent chapters, applies to other market structures such as monopoly and monopolistic competition. Since for the perfectly competitive firm, marginal revenue is equal to price, this profit-maximizing condition takes a particular form: choose the level of output at which price is equal to marginal cost ($P = MC$).

**3** Many students have trouble understanding why a firm continues to operate at the break-even point, where economic profits are zero. The key to understanding lies in the definition of which costs are included in the average total cost curve. Recall from Chapter 9 that a firm's total costs are defined by the economist as *opportunity costs*, which include both explicit costs and *imputed costs*.

Imputed costs include the owners'/investors' forgone interest, forgone rent and forgone income. Therefore, at the break-even point where total revenue equals total cost (or, equivalently, average revenue equals average total cost), the owners/investors of the firm are earning a return on their investment which is equal to the best return that they could earn elsewhere. That is the definition of opportunity cost – the best alternative forgone. Economists sometimes refer to these imputed costs or best alternative return on investment as 'normal profits'. As the phrase implies, these are profits that could normally be earned in any other industry. At the break-even point, the firm is earning 'normal profits' even though its economic profits (sometimes called 'extra-normal profits') are zero. In earning 'normal profits', the firm is earning just as much profit as it could anywhere else, and is therefore totally content to continue producing in this industry.

**4** When the price of output falls below the break-even point, but is above the shutdown point, the firm will continue to produce even though it is making economic losses. In order to switch industries, the firm would have to shut down, which entails losing its total fixed costs.

As long as the price is above the shutdown point (minimum average variable cost), however, a firm will decide to produce since it will be covering total variable cost and part of total fixed cost. Thus its loss will be less if it continues to produce at the output where $P = MC$ than if it shuts down.

If the price falls below the shutdown point, a firm which produces output will not only lose its total fixed costs, it will lose additional money on every unit of output produced, since average revenue is less than average variable cost. Thus when the price is less than average variable cost, the firm will choose to minimize its loss by shutting down.

**5** In the long run, fixed costs disappear and the firm can switch between industries and change scale of plant without cost. Economic profits serve as the signal for the movement or reallocation of firm resources until long-run equilibrium is achieved. Firms will move out of industries with negative economic profits and into industries with positive economic profits. Only when economic profits are zero will there be no tendency for firms to exit or enter industries.

The fact that there are no restrictions on entry into the industry assures that economic profits will be zero and that firms will be producing at the minimum of their long-run average cost curves in long-run equilibrium.

**6** In long-run equilibrium, three conditions are satisfied for each firm in a competitive industry:
   **a** $MR = P = MC$. This implies that profits are maximized for each firm.
   **b** $P = ATC$. This implies that economic profits are zero and each firm is just earning 'normal profits'.
   **c** $P =$ minimum $LRAC$. This implies that production takes place at the point of minimum long-run average cost.

## Key Figures

### Figure 11.2 Total Revenue, Total Cost and Profit, text page 263

Profit is defined as total revenue minus total cost. In part (a) of this figure, the total revenue and total cost curves are both illustrated. Profit (or loss) is the vertical distance between them. In part (b), profit and loss are plotted against output as the profit curve in the graph. In the example, profit is a maximum when 9 jumpers are produced.

### Figure 11.3 Marginal Revenue, Marginal Cost and Profit-maximizing Output, text page 264

This figure illustrates the alternative profit-maximizing condition: marginal revenue *(MR)* equals marginal cost *(MC)*. Producing and selling one more unit of a good (jumpers in the example) adds both to revenue and to cost. If the addition to revenue *(MR)* is greater than the addition to cost *(MC)*, then profit will increase and the additional unit should be produced.

If, on the other hand, marginal revenue is less than marginal cost, profit will decrease and the additional unit should not be produced. Therefore, a profit-maximizing firm should produce each unit up to the point at which marginal revenue equals marginal cost.

This is illustrated with a table and corresponding graph for the example of Neat Knits. Producing each of the first up to the ninth sweater adds to profit ($MR > MC$), but the tenth sweater decreases profit ($MR < MC$). Nine sweaters is the profit-maximizing output at which the profit-maximizing condition, $MR = MC$, holds. Since, for a perfectly competitive firm, $MR = P$, the profit-maximizing condition can also be expressed as the output at which $P = MC$.

### Figure 11.6  Industry Supply Curve, text page 267
The industry supply curve is obtained by summing horizontally the individual supply curves of all of the firms in the industry. For a given price, this means moving horizontally to each individual firm's supply curve, reading off the quantity supplied, and summing these quantities.

### Figure 11.12  Allocative Efficiency, text page 277
Allocative efficiency is achieved when marginal social benefit *(MSB)* equals marginal social cost *(MSC)*. Additional output adds both to social benefit and to social cost.

If the addition to social benefit *(MSB)* is greater than the addition to social cost *(MSC)*, the additional unit should be produced.

If the marginal social benefit of an additional unit of output is less than the marginal social cost, it should not be produced. Allocative efficiency occurs where $MSB = MSC$.

If there are no external costs or benefits, the perfectly competitive industry supply curve is the marginal social cost curve and the industry demand curve is the marginal social benefit curve. Thus the competitive market equilibrium will achieve allocative efficiency.

# SELF-TEST

## CONCEPT REVIEW

**1** Perfect competition occurs in a market under the following conditions.
   **a** There are _____ firms, each selling a(n)_____ product.
   **b** There are _____ buyers.
   **c** There are no restrictions on _____ into the industry.

**2** A firm in a perfectly competitive market is said to be a price _____ since it cannot influence the price of the good it produces. Such a firm faces a demand curve that is perfectly_____ .

**3** We assume that the firm's single objective is to maximize its _____ .

**4** Total revenue divided by the total quantity sold is called _____ _____ . The change in revenue resulting from a one-unit increase in the quantity sold is called _____ _____ .

**5** In the case of perfect competition, average revenue and marginal revenue are both equal to _____ .

**6** An output at which total cost equals total revenue is called a _____ - _____ .

point. The point at which a firm's maximum profit (minimum loss) is the same regardless of whether the firm produces any output or not is called the _____ point.

**7** Profit is maximized when marginal revenue equals _____ _____ .

**8** Market price is determined by _____ demand and _____ supply.

**9** In the range of prices greater than the minimum average variable cost, a perfectly competitive firm's supply curve is the same as its _____ _____ curve. At prices below minimum average variable cost, the firm will produce _____ and make a loss equal to its _____ _____ _____ .

**10** New firms will enter a perfectly competitive industry if firms in the industry are making economic _____ . As new firms enter the industry, the price will _____ . If economic _____ are being made, firms will tend to exit the industry.

**11** Long-run equilibrium occurs in a perfectly competitive industry when economic profits are

_____ . Each firm will also be producing at the _____ point of its long-run average cost curve.

**12** Factors beyond the control of an individual firm that lower its costs as industry output increases are called _____ _____ . Factors beyond the control of an individual firm that raise its costs as industry output increases are called _____ _____ .

**13** _____ _____ occurs when no one can be made better off without making someone else worse off.

**14** Costs that are not borne by the producer but are borne by other members of society are called _____ _____ .
Benefits which accrue to people other than the buyer of a good are called _____ _____ .

___ **10** In long-run equilibrium, each firm in a perfectly competitive industry will be making zero economic profit.

___ **11** The entry of new firms into an industry will increase the price and increase the profit of each firm.

___ **12** Suppose a competitive industry is in long-run equilibrium when there is a substantial increase in total fixed costs. All firms will now be making economic losses and some firms will go out of business.

___ **13** If a firm is economically efficient, then it must be allocatively efficient.

___ **14** A firm is economically efficient if it is maximizing profit.

___ **15** Allocative efficiency occurs when marginal social benefit is greater than marginal social cost.

## TRUE OR FALSE

___ **1** In a perfectly competitive industry no single firm can exert a significant effect on the market price of a good.

___ **2** In a perfectly competitive industry there are no restrictions on entry into the industry.

___ **3** The industry demand curve in a perfectly competitive industry is horizontal.

___ **4** The objective of firms in a competitive industry is to maximize revenue.

___ **5** If marginal revenue is greater than marginal cost, a firm can increase profit by decreasing output.

___ **6** A firm is breaking even if its economic profit is zero.

___ **7** If the price is below the minimum average total cost, a firm will shut down.

___ **8** All firms in a competitive market will be maximizing profit in short-run equilibrium.

___ **9** The short-run industry supply curve is obtained as the horizontal sum of the supply curves of the individual firms.

## MULTIPLE CHOICE

**1** If a firm faces a perfectly elastic demand for its product, then
   **a** it is not a price taker.
   **b** it will want to lower its price to increase sales.
   **c** it will want to raise its price to increase total revenue.
   **d** its marginal revenue curve is equal to the price of the product.
   **e** it will always earn zero economic profits.

**2** A perfectly competitive firm is maximizing profit if
   **a** marginal cost equals price and price is above minimum average variable cost.
   **b** marginal cost equals price and price is above minimum average fixed cost.
   **c** total revenue is at a maximum.
   **d** average variable cost is at a minimum.
   **e** average total cost is at a minimum.

**3** In which of the following situations will a perfectly competitive firm earn economic profits?
   **a** $MR > AVC$
   **b** $MR > ATC$
   **c** $ATC > MC$
   **d** $ATC > AR$
   **e** $AR > AVC$

**4** The maximum loss a firm will experience in the short run is equal to
  **a** zero.
  **b** total costs.
  **c** total variable costs.
  **d** total fixed costs.
  **e** none of the above.

**5** The short-run industry supply curve is
  **a** the horizontal sum of the individual firm's supply curves.
  **b** the vertical sum of the individual firm's supply curves.
  **c** vertical at the total level of output being produced by all firms.
  **d** horizontal at the current market price.
  **e** none of the above.

**6** If a perfectly competitive firm in the short run is able to pay its variable costs and part, but not all, of its fixed costs, then it is operating in the range on its marginal cost curve that is
  **a** above the break-even point.
  **b** below the break-even point.
  **c** above the shutdown point.
  **d** below the shutdown point.
  **e** between the shutdown and break-even points.

**7** In a perfectly competitive industry, the market price is $10. An individual firm is producing the output at which $MC = ATC = \$15$. $AVC$ at that output is $10. What should the firm do to maximize its short-run profits?
  **a** shut down
  **b** expand output
  **c** contract output
  **d** leave output unchanged
  **e** insufficient information to answer

**8** In a perfectly competitive industry, the market price is $5. An individual firm is producing the level of output at which marginal cost is $5 and is increasing, and average total cost is $25. What should the firm do to maximize its short-run profits?
  **a** shut down
  **b** expand output
  **c** contract output
  **d** leave output unchanged
  **e** insufficient information to answer

**9** The maximum loss a firm will experience in long-run equilibrium is

  **a** zero.
  **b** its total cost.
  **c** its total variable cost.
  **d** its average total cost.
  **e** none of the above.

**10** The long-run competitive industry supply curve will be positively sloped if there are
  **a** external economies.
  **b** external diseconomies.
  **c** no external economies or diseconomies.
  **d** external costs.
  **e** external benefits.

**11** If an industry experiences external economies as the industry expands in the long run, the long-run industry supply curve will
  **a** be perfectly inelastic.
  **b** be perfectly elastic.
  **c** have a positive slope.
  **d** have a negative slope.
  **e** have allocative inefficiency.

## SHORT ANSWER

**1** Why will a firm in a perfectly competitive industry choose *not* to charge a price either above or below the market price?

**2** Why is the perfectly competitive firm's supply curve the same as the marginal cost curve above minimum average variable cost?

**3** Why will economic profits be zero in long-run equilibrium in a perfectly competitive industry?

**4** Suppose output is at a level such that marginal social benefit is greater than marginal social cost. Explain why this level of output is allocatively *inefficient*.

**5** Is the industry discussed in the *Reading Between the Lines* article in this chapter in perfect competition?

## PROBLEMS

**1 a** Table 11.1 gives the total cost structure for one of many identical firms in a perfectly competitive industry. Complete the table by computing total variable cost, average total cost, average variable cost and marginal cost at each level of output. (Remember, as in the problems in *Study Guide* Chapter 10, marginal cost should be entered midway between rows.)

**Table 11.1**

| Quantity (units per day) | Total cost (pounds) | Total variable cost (pounds) | Average total cost (pounds) | Average variable cost (pounds) | Marginal cost (pounds) |
|---|---|---|---|---|---|
| 0 | 12 | | | | |
| 1 | 24 | | | | |
| 2 | 32 | | | | |
| 3 | 42 | | | | |
| 4 | 54 | | | | |
| 5 | 68 | | | | |
| 6 | 84 | | | | |

b Complete Table 11.2 by computing the profit (per day) for the firm at each level of output if the price of output is £9, £11, or £15.

**Table 11.2**

| Quantity (units per day) | Profit $P = £9$ | Profit $P = £11$ | Profit $P = £15$ |
|---|---|---|---|
| 0 | | | |
| 1 | | | |
| 2 | | | |
| 3 | | | |
| 4 | | | |
| 5 | | | |
| 6 | | | |

c Consider the profit-maximizing output decision of the firm at alternative prices. How much will the firm produce if the price of output is £9? £11? £15? Explain each of your answers.

2 A firm will maximize profit if it produces every unit of output for which marginal revenue exceeds marginal cost. This is sometimes called the marginal approach to profit maximization. Using the marginal approach, determine the profit-maximizing level of output for the firm of Problem 1 when the price of output is £15. How does your answer here compare with your answer in **1c**?

3 a Consider a perfectly competitive industry in long-run equilibrium. All the firms in the industry are identical. Draw a two-part graph illustrating the long-run equilibrium for the industry (part (a) on the left) and for the typical firm (part (b) on the right). The graph of the firm should include the *MC, ATC, MR* and *LRAC* curves.

Assume that the *LRAC* curve is U-shaped as it is in Figure 11.9 on text page 271. Label the equilibrium price $P_0$, the equilibrium industry quantity traded $Q_0$ and the output of the firm $q_0$.

b Now suppose there is a decline in industry demand. Using your graphs from part (a),

i show what happens to market price, firm output, firm profits and industry quantity traded in the short run (assume that the shutdown point is not reached).

ii show what happens to market price, firm output, firm profits and industry quantity traded in the long run (assume that there are no external economies or diseconomies). What has happened to the number of firms?

## DISCUSSION QUESTIONS

1 Why do firms produce where $MR = MC$? Wouldn't it make more sense to produce where $MR$ exceeds $MC$ so that revenue exceeds costs?

2 Why should a business operate even though it incurs an economic loss?

## DATA QUESTIONS

**Perfect competition in the lead mining industry – a nineteenth century case study**

The structure of the lead mining industry has changed enormously over the last couple of centuries and today large firms account for great proportions of output. But the price at which they sell their product is still determined by market forces, and the producers have little control over the price of their product and are therefore price takers.

The Snailbeach Company worked a vein of ore in Shropshire. It took a lease in 1783 and continued to produce lead until 1912. Before analysing the firm it is worthwhile to outline the features of lead mining which made for a perfect market.

First, there were a large number of firms; in the early years of the eighteenth century most mines were worked as partnerships and needed only small amounts of capital to work what were in effect little more than shallow holes in the ground. The fixed costs of the company were therefore small.

The normal method of sale was for the company to put a sample of its ore into the market; buyers would inspect it and then make an offer for the whole lot. The price of lead was therefore determined by the market, thus satisfying the condition of perfect competition, which requires that the firm has no control over the price of the product it sells. In times of scarcity the price of lead was high, and in times of surplus or demand deficiency it fell. In consequence the price of lead exerted an enormous influence on the whole structure of the industry, determining profits, wages, and the opening up and closing down of enterprises.

During the 1860s demand increased to such an extent that a shortage of ore occurred. However, it was only a matter of time before the bubble burst. In the early 1870s lead ore was selling at between £13 and £14 a ton, but by 1890 the price had fallen to £7 a ton. The reason for the fall was an increased supply from overseas sources in Australia and America. With falling prices it was impossible for many firms to stay profitable, and many companies went out of business.

Source: Adapted from E. Brook, 'Perfect competition in the lead mining industry', *Economics*, Journal of the Economics and Business Education Association, Autumn 1970, **8**(5) No 35, 240–255.

**1** Outline the characteristic features of perfect competition. To what extent did the lead mining industry of the period satisfy the criteria needed for perfect competition?

**2** Draw diagrams to show the effect on the industry and the firm of an increase in demand for lead.

**3** Draw diagrams for the industry and the firm to show why prices fell between 1880 and 1890.

# ANSWERS

## CONCEPT REVIEW

**1** many; identical; many; entry

**2** taker; elastic

**3** profit

**4** average revenue; marginal revenue

**5** price

**6** break-even; shutdown

**7** marginal cost

**8** industry; industry

**9** marginal cost; nothing; total fixed cost

**10** profits; fall; losses

**11** zero; minimum

**12** external economies; external diseconomies

**13** Allocative efficiency

**14** external costs; external benefits

## TRUE OR FALSE

**1** **T** Each firm is a price taker.

**2** **T** Definition.

**3** **F** The individual firm's demand curve is horizontal. The industry demand curve is downward sloping.

**4** **F** Firm aims to maximize total profit.

**5** **F** Profits will increase if it increases output since each additional unit's revenue is greater than its cost.

**6** **T** Definition.

**7** **F** It would be true if $P <$ minimum $AVC$.

**8** **T** Otherwise they would be making losses.

**9** **T** Definition.

**10** **T** Otherwise new firms would enter and bring down profits till they reached zero.

**11** **F** New firms will lead to lower prices and profits.

**12** **T** $ATC$ will rise with no change in marginal cost. This will lead to losses and some firms will go bust.

**13** **F** It would be true if there are no external costs or benefits, otherwise it is false.

**14 T** Maximizing profit means minimizing costs.

**15 F** Allocative efficiency occurs when marginal social benefit equals marginal social cost.

## MULTIPLE CHOICE

**1 d** Firm can increase quantity without changing price, so *MR* from additional quantity = price.

**2 a** *AFC* is irrelevant. Maximizing profit does not equal maximizing revenue. **d, e** might be true, depending on *P*.

**3 b** Since *MR* = *AR*, *AR* > *ATC*. Multiply by *Q* gives *TR* > *TC*, so economic profits.

**4 d** Equals shutdown cost. Any potentially greater loss, firm will shut down.

**5 a** Definition. **c** is momentary supply curve. **d** is demand curve facing individual firm.

**6 e** If couldn't pay variable costs → below shutdown. If paying all variable and fixed costs → break even.

**7 c** Draw a graph. Firm should choose lower *Q* where *P* = *MC*. If *AVC* at current *Q* = £10, minimum *AVC* must be < £10, so new *Q* > minimum *AVC*.

**8 e** Firm is at *Q* where *P* = *MC*, but is losing money since *AR* < *ATC*. Need *AVC* information to determine if **a** or **d** is correct.

**9 a** Definition. Long-run equilibrium leads to zero economic profits.

**10 b** Rise in costs as industry quantity increases.

**11 d** Because fall in costs as industry *Q* rises.

## SHORT ANSWER

**1** If a firm in a perfectly competitive industry charged a price even slightly higher than the market price, it would lose all of its sales. Thus it will not charge a price above the market price. Since it can sell all it wants at the market price, it would not be able to increase sales by lowering its price. Thus it would not charge a price below the market price since this would decrease total revenue and hence profits.

**2** A perfectly competitive firm will want to supply the quantity that will maximize profit. This is done by equating marginal revenue and marginal cost. Since marginal revenue is equal to price for a perfectly competitive firm, the firm will produce the level of output at which price equals marginal cost. Since this is true for each

price above minimum *AVC*, the firm's supply curve is the same as its marginal cost curve above minimum *AVC*. For prices below minimum *AVC*, the firm will maximize profit (actually minimize loss) by shutting down. The loss from shutting down will be equal to total fixed cost. If the firm continued to produce at a price below minimum *AVC*, its loss would exceed total fixed cost.

**3** In a perfectly competitive industry, the existence of positive economic profits will attract the entry of new firms, which will shift the industry supply curve to the right, causing the market price to fall and firm profits to decline. This tendency will exist as long as there are positive economic profits. Similarly, the existence of economic losses will cause firms to exit from the industry, which will shift the industry supply curve to the left, causing the market price to rise and firm profits to rise (losses to decline). This tendency will exist as long as losses are being made. Thus the only point of rest in the long run (the only equilibrium) is one in which economic profits are zero.

**4** A level of output at which marginal social benefit is greater than marginal social cost is allocatively inefficient, because some people can be made better off without making anyone worse off if more is produced. Since the production of an additional unit of output will add more to social benefit than to social cost, those who bear the additional costs can be compensated out of the additional benefits (and thus be left no worse off) with some additional benefits left over (making those who receive the additional benefits better off).

**5** The container industry certainly has some of the characteristics of perfect competition. In particular, firms do not seem to be making monopoly profits. There are a number of firms in the industry, and the product is fairly similar (although one container ship cannot really be described as identical to all others). However, one characteristic of perfect competition is that there are no restrictions on entry. The container industry does have restrictions since it requires considerable capital to build even one ship.

## PROBLEMS

**1 a** The completed Table 11.1 is shown here as Table 11.3.

**b** The completed Table 11.2 is given here as Table 11.4. The values for profit are computed as total revenue minus total cost, where total revenue is price times quantity and total cost is given in Table 11.1.

## Table 11.3

| Quantity (units per day) | Total cost (pounds) | Total variable cost (pounds) | Average total cost (pounds) | Average variable cost (pounds) | Marginal cost (pounds) |
|---|---|---|---|---|---|
| 0 | 12 | 0 | – | – | |
| | | | | | ...12 |
| 1 | 24 | 12 | 24.00 | 12.00 | |
| | | | | | ...8 |
| 2 | 32 | 20 | 16.00 | 10.00 | |
| | | | | | ...10 |
| 3 | 42 | 30 | 14.00 | 10.00 | |
| | | | | | ...12 |
| 4 | 54 | 42 | 13.50 | 10.50 | |
| | | | | | ...14 |
| 5 | 68 | 56 | 13.60 | 11.20 | |
| | | | | | ...16 |
| 6 | 84 | 72 | 14.00 | 12.00 | |

## Table 11.4

| Quantity (units per day) | Profit $P = £9$ | Profit $P = £11$ | Profit $P = £15$ |
|---|---|---|---|
| 0 | -12 | -12 | -12 |
| 1 | -15 | -13 | -9 |
| 2 | -14 | -10 | -2 |
| 3 | -15 | -9 | 3 |
| 4 | -18 | -10 | 6 |
| 5 | -23 | -13 | 7 |
| 6 | -30 | -18 | 6 |

c If the price is £9, profit is maximized (actually loss is minimized) when the firm shuts down and produces zero units. If the firm chooses to produce, its loss will be at least £14, which is greater than the fixed cost loss of £12. Therefore the firm will minimize losses by shutting down. If the price is £11, the firm is still unable to make a positive economic profit. The loss is minimized (at £9) if the firm produces 3 units. At this price all of variable cost and part of fixed cost can be recovered. At a price of £15, the firm will maximize profit (at £7) at an output of 5 units per day.

2 The marginal approach to profit maximization states that the firm should produce all units of output for which marginal revenue exceeds marginal cost. For a perfectly competitive firm, marginal revenue equals price, so the approach states (equivalently) that the firm should produce every unit for which price exceeds marginal cost. If the price of output is £15, we can see from Table 11.3 that the firm should produce 5 units. Since the marginal cost of moving from the 4th to the 5th unit (£14) is less than price (£15), the 5th unit should be produced. The marginal cost of moving to the 6th unit (£16), however, is greater than price. It should not be produced. The answer obtained here is the same as the answer obtained in 1c.

3 a A long-run equilibrium in a perfectly competitive industry is illustrated in Fig. 11.1.

Part (a) illustrates industry equilibrium at the intersection of industry demand ($D_0$) and industry supply ($S_0$): point $a$ . The equilibrium industry quantity traded is labelled $Q_0$ and the equilibrium market price is labelled $P_0$.

Part (b) illustrates the situation for a single firm in long-run equilibrium. The firm is at point $a'$, the minimum point of both the short-run average total cost curve (ATC) and the long-run average cost curve (LRAC). The firm is producing the output labelled $q_0$ and earning zero economic profit.

b i The new short-run equilibrium is also illustrated in Fig. 11.1. The decrease in demand shifts the market demand curve to the left, from $D_0$ to $D_1$. The new market equilibrium is at point $b$. The price has fallen from $P_0$ to $P_1$ and the industry quantity traded has fallen from $Q_0$ to $Q_1$. The fall in price induces firms to reduce output as shown by the move from point $a'$ to point $b'$ on the MC curve in part (b). Since $P_1$ is less than minimum ATC, firms are making losses in the new short-run equilibrium.

ii The new long-run equilibrium is also illustrated in Fig. 11.1. Since losses are experienced in short-run equilibrium, firms will exit from the industry in the long run.

This will make the industry supply curve shift to the left causing the price to rise and thus reducing losses. Firms will continue to leave until the industry supply curve has shifted enough to eliminate losses, from $S_0$ to $S_1$. This gives a new long-run industry equilibrium at point $c$ and the price has returned to its initial level, $P_0$, but industry quantity traded has fallen to $Q_2$. As firms exit and the market price rises, remaining firms will increase their output (moving up the MC curve from point $b'$ to point $a'$) and their losses will be reduced. When sufficient firms have left the industry, the price will have risen (returned) to $P_0$ and firms will have returned to point $a'$ in part (b). At this point, each firm is again earning zero economic profit and firm output has returned to $Q_0$. But since there are now fewer firms, industry quantity traded is less.

**Figure 11.1**

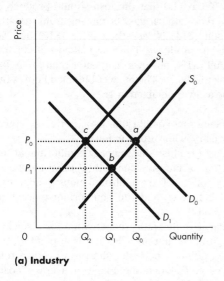

**(a) Industry**

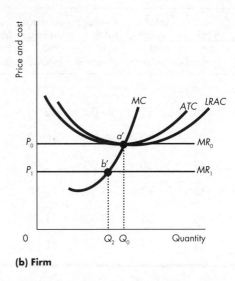

**(b) Firm**

## DISCUSSION QUESTIONS

**1** The basic assumption underlying most economic analysis is that firms attempt to maximize *total* profit; that is the difference between total costs and total revenue. This will occur if a firm expands output until $MR = MC$. If it ceased to expand while marginal revenue exceeded marginal cost, it would be losing some profit which it could obtain from producing one more unit of output, as long as the costs of producing that unit did not exceed the revenue obtained by selling it.

**2** Whenever the price of output falls below the break-even point (the minimum average total cost) but remains above the shutdown point (the minimum average variable cost), the firm continues to produce even though it is making an economic loss. The key idea here is that since a loss is inevitable, the owner wants to make it as low as possible. If the firm were to shut down it would still have to pay its fixed costs. The owner compares this loss to the loss incurred by continuing to operate. If the price exceeds the average variable cost, the owner loses less by continuing to operate. This is because some of the revenue obtained can be used to pay some of the fixed costs.

## DATA QUESTIONS

**1** The characteristic features of perfect competition are: many firms, identical product, many buyers, easy entry and perfect knowledge, and that existing firms have no advantage over new entrants. The lead industry in the nineteenth century satisfied many of these criteria, but we do not know that those involved had perfect knowledge about the product and the industry.

Moreover, the product was not identical – different samples of lead ore differed in quality. However, it is safe to conclude that the industry exhibited many of the characteristics of perfect competition.

**2** The position is shown in Fig. 11.2. In this figure the demand curve for the firm is horizontal because the Snailbeach Company has to take the price determined by the supply and demand for lead in the industry as a whole. It can then sell all the lead ore it wants at this price because it is only a small firm in a large industry. The original equilibrium is at price $P_0$ and quantity $Q_0$. The increase in demand will cause the demand curve to shift and a new equilibrium at price $P_1$ and quantity $Q_1$.

**3** Prices fell because there was a large increase in supply from overseas firms. This caused the supply curve to shift and the result was that price fell from $P_0$ to $P_1$ while quantity rose from $Q_0$ to $Q_1$ as shown in Fig. 11.3.

**Figure 11.2**

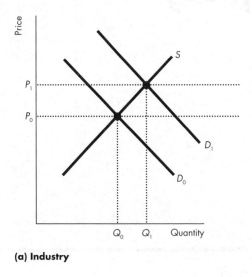

**(a) Industry**

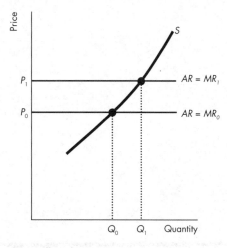

**(b) Snailbeach Company**

**Figure 11.3**

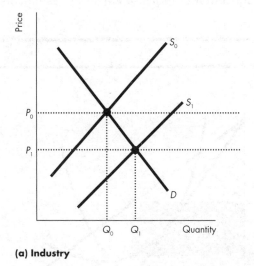

**(a) Industry**

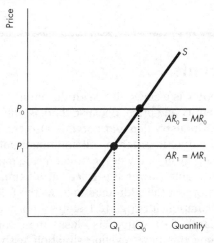

**(b) Snailbeach Company**

# Chapter 12 **Monopoly**

## Chapter in Perspective, Text Pages 284–309

The perfectly competitive firms of Chapter 11 are price takers. At the opposite extreme are industries in which there is a single firm, a monopoly. Unlike a perfectly competitive firm, a monopoly's output decision has a direct effect on price; it cannot sell more output unless it drops its price.

This chapter pursues the answers to numerous questions about monopoly. Why does monopoly exist? How does a monopoly choose how much to produce? What constraints on behaviour does a monopoly face? How much profit will a monopoly make? When will a monopoly charge different prices to different customers for the same good or service? How does a monopoly compare with perfect competition in terms of efficiency? Is monopoly always 'bad'?

## Helpful Hints

**1** A monopoly is a single firm with the ability to set both quantity and price. Because there is only one firm, the industry demand curve is also the firm demand curve. In order to sell additional output, the monopoly must lower the price. A single-price monopoly must lower the price on all units of output, not just the additional unit. As the following explanation for Fig. 12.1 states, this means that marginal revenue is less than price. Combining this new revenue situation with our familiar cost curves from Chapter 10 yields the important diagram shown in Fig. 12.1.

Notice the following:

**a** The rule for profit maximization is to find the quantity of output where $MR = MC$. This is the same rule that applies to a perfectly competitive firm.

**Figure 12.1**

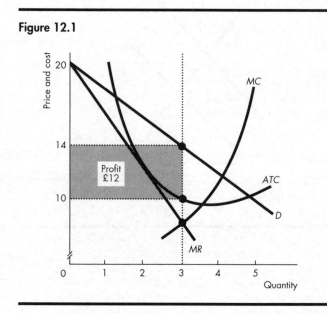

For a perfectly competitive firm *MR* is also equal to price, so the intersection of *MR* and *MC* yields the profit-maximizing output and price. That is not true for the monopolist. *MR* is not equal to price, and once the profit-maximizing output is identified, the monopolist still has to set the price.

**b** To find the profit-maximizing price, draw an imaginary vertical line up to the demand curve from the intersection of *MR* and *MC*. Then draw an imaginary horizontal line to the price axis to read the price.

**c** Understanding what the vertical and horizontal distances of the total profit area represent will make you less likely to make mistakes in drawing that area. The vertical distance is between the demand (or average revenue) curve and the average total cost curve. That distance measures average revenue minus average total cost, which equals average profit, or profit per unit. The horizontal distance is just the number of units produced. So the area of the rectangle (vertical distance × horizontal distance) = profit per unit × number of units = total profit. Do *not* make the mistake of drawing the vertical distance down to the intersection of *MC* and *MR*. That intersection has no economic meaning for the calculation of total profit.

**2** There is an easy trick for drawing the marginal revenue curve corresponding to any linear demand curve. The price intercept (where $Q = 0$) is the same as for the demand curve, and the quantity intercept (where $P = 0$) is exactly *half* of the output of the demand curve. The marginal revenue curve is, therefore, a downward-sloping straight line whose slope is twice as steep as the slope of the demand curve.

**3** Price discrimination can only be profitable for a monopoly if different groups have different elasticities of demand for the good. The monopoly can then treat each group as a separate market and produce where $MR = MC$ for each group.

# Key Figures

**Figure 12.2 Demand and Marginal Revenue for a Single-price Monopoly, text page 288**
This figure illustrates the relationship between the demand and marginal revenue curves for a single-price monopoly using the example of Cut and Dry's hairdressing salon. If the firm wants to sell one more unit of output, it must lower its price. This has two effects on revenue. First, the sale of an additional unit will increase revenue by the amount of the price. However, since the firm must also *drop the price on previous units*, revenue on these will decrease. The net change in revenue, the marginal revenue, will thus be less than price and the marginal revenue curve will lie below the demand curve.

**Figure 12.4 A Single-price Monopoly's Output and Price, text page 292**
Table 12.2 on text page 291 reports the revenues and costs for Cut and Dry's hairdressing salon. This information is used to illustrate how a single-price monopoly will choose the profit-maximizing output and price.

Part (a) of the figure shows the total revenue and total cost curves facing the firm. Profit is a maximum when the vertical amount by which total revenue exceeds total cost is a maximum. For Cut and Dry's hairdressing salon, this turns out to be 3 haircuts per hour.

Part (b) shows the total profit curve itself; it is derived from the figure in part (a) by taking the difference between total revenue and total cost at each level of output. Profit is maximized when this curve reaches its maximum. Part (c) shows that profit is a maximum at the quantity where marginal revenue is equal to marginal cost. The diagram of marginal cost and marginal revenue in part (c) is the most important and useful of the three diagrams.

**Figure 12.8 Monopoly and Competition Compared, text page 298**
This figure compares the price and quantity results in a monopoly industry with the price and quantity results if the same industry were competitive.

A competitive industry will produce at the intersection of the industry supply and demand curves (labelled *S* and *D* in the figure). Thus a competitive industry will produce the quantity *C* and charge the price $P_C$.

If the same industry became a single-price monopoly, its marginal cost curve would be the supply curve of the competitive industry. A profit-maximizing single-price monopoly will produce the output level at which marginal revenue equals marginal cost. Thus the monopoly will produce the quantity *M* and charge the price $P_M$. The single-price monopoly output is lower than for a competitive industry and the price is higher than the competitive price. A perfectly price-discriminating monopoly produces the competitive output *C* and charges a different price (all above $P_C$) for each unit sold.

# SELF-TEST

## CONCEPT REVIEW

**1** A firm that is the single supplier of a good in an industry is called a(n) _____ . The key feature of such an industry is the existence of _____ preventing the entry of new firms.

**2** A monopoly that charges the same price for every unit of output it sells is called a(n) _____ - _____ monopoly.

**3** The demand curve facing a monopoly firm is the _____ demand curve.

**4** For a monopoly charging a single price, the average revenue curve is the _____ curve and the marginal revenue curve is _____ the average revenue curve.

**5** The output range over which total revenue is rising is the same as that over which marginal revenue is _____ . This is the same range of input over which the (price) elasticity of demand is _____ than 1. If elasticity of demand is _____ than 1, marginal revenue is _____ . This implies that a profit-maximizing monopoly will never produce an output in the _____ range of its demand curve.

**6** Unlike a perfectly competitive firm, a monopoly's decision to produce more or less of a good will affect the _____ of the good.

**7** A profit-maximizing monopoly will want to produce less if, at the current level of output, marginal _____ is greater than marginal _____ .

**8** Unlike a perfectly competitive firm, a monopoly can be making positive economic _____ in the long run.

**9** The practice of charging some customers a higher price than others for exactly the same good is called _____ _____ . This kind of pricing policy can be seen as an attempt by the monopoly to capture all or part of the consumer _____ .

**10** Charging different prices to different groups of customers will increase the profits of a monopoly only if the groups of customers have different _____ of demand for the product. A monopoly that charges different prices to different groups of customers will produce _____ than would a monopoly that charges a single price.

**11** If a perfectly competitive industry is taken over by a single monopoly firm, output will _____ and the price will _____ . The reduction in consumer and producer surplus resulting from this new monopoly is called the _____ loss.

**12** The activity of creating monopoly is called _____ _____ . If there are no barriers to such activity, the value of the resources used up in the process will, in equilibrium, be _____ _____ the monopoly's profit.

**13** A firm that has a decrease in average total cost when it increases the number of different goods it produces is said to have economies of _____ .

## TRUE OR FALSE

___ **1** Natural monopoly can arise because of economies of scale.

___ **2** For a single-price monopoly, average revenue always equals price.

___ **3** Over the output range where total revenue is decreasing, marginal revenue is positive.

___ **4** The marginal revenue curve lies below the demand curve for a single-price monopoly because when the price is lowered to sell additional units of output, it must be lowered on all units of output.

___ **5** A profit-maximizing single-price monopoly will produce only in the elastic range of its demand curve.

___ **6** The supply curve of a monopoly firm is its marginal cost curve.

___ **7** A monopoly will always make economic profits.

___ **8** Price discrimination occurs when a firm charges one group of customers more than another or when a firm gives quantity discounts.

___ **9** A monopoly can acquire all of the consumer surplus for itself if it practises perfect price discrimination.

___ **10** Price discrimination is an attempt by a monopolist to capture the producer surplus.

___ **11** For a perfect price-discriminating monopolist, the demand curve is also the marginal revenue curve.

___ **12** A monopoly industry with large economies of scale and scope may produce more output and charge a lower price than does a perfectly competitive industry.

## MULTIPLE CHOICE

**1** Which of the following is a natural barrier to the entry of new firms in an industry?
   **a** licensing of professions
   **b** economies of scale
   **c** issuing a patent
   **d** a public franchise
   **e** all of the above

**2** In order to increase sales from 7 units to 8 units, a single-price monopoly must drop the price from £7 per unit to £6 per unit. What is marginal revenue in this range?
   **a** £48
   **b** £6
   **c** £1
   **d** −£1
   **e** none of the above

**3** A single-price monopoly will maximize profits if it produces the output where
   **a** price equals marginal cost.
   **b** price equals marginal revenue.
   **c** marginal revenue equals marginal cost.
   **d** average revenue equals marginal cost.
   **e** average revenue equals marginal revenue.

**4** If a profit-maximizing monopoly is producing at an output at which marginal cost exceeds marginal revenue, it
   **a** should raise price and lower output.
   **b** should lower price and raise output.
   **c** should lower price and lower output.
   **d** is making losses.
   **e** is maximizing profit.

**5** A single-price monopoly never operates
   **a** on an elastic portion of the demand curve.
   **b** on a portion of the demand curve that is unit elastic.
   **c** on an inelastic portion of the demand curve.
   **d** at a quantity where marginal revenue is positive since total revenue is not at a maximum.
   **e** under any of the above conditions.

**6** For the single-price monopoly depicted in Fig. 12.2, when profit is maximized quantity is
   **a** 3 and price is £3.
   **b** 3 and price is £6.
   **c** 4 and price is £4.
   **d** 4 and price is £5.
   **e** 5 and price is £4.

**Figure 12.2**

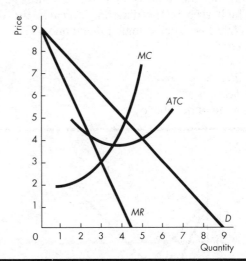

**7** If the monopoly depicted in Fig. 12.2 is maximizing profit, what is the total profit?
   **a** £3
   **b** £4
   **c** £6
   **d** £9
   **e** none of the above

**8** A perfect price-discriminating monopoly
  **a** has a demand curve which is also its average revenue curve.
  **b** will maximize revenue.
  **c** is assured of making a profit.
  **d** will produce the quantity at which the marginal cost curve intersects the demand curve.
  **e** will be allocatively inefficient.

**9** Table 12.1 lists marginal costs for the XYZ firm. If XYZ sells 3 units at a price of £6 each, what is its producer surplus?
  **a** £2
  **b** £6
  **c** £7
  **d** £9
  **e** £12

**Table 12.1**

| Quantity | Marginal cost |
|----------|---------------|
| 1 | 2 |
| 2 | 3 |
| 3 | 4 |
| 4 | 5 |

**10** Consider the industry demand curve in Fig. 12.3. Which area in the diagram indicates the deadweight loss from a single-price monopoly?
  **a** *eacf*
  **b** *acd*
  **c** *abd*
  **d** *bcd*
  **e** none of the above

**Figure 12.3**

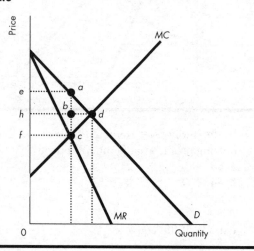

**11** Which area in Fig. 12.3 indicates the deadweight loss from a perfect price-discriminating monopoly?
  **a** *eacf*
  **b** *acd*
  **c** *abd*
  **d** *bcd*
  **e** none of the above

**12** Why is the quantity of output produced by a single-price monopoly allocatively inefficient?
  **a** average social cost exceeds average social benefit
  **b** marginal social cost exceeds marginal social benefit
  **c** average social benefit exceeds average social cost
  **d** marginal social benefit exceeds marginal social cost
  **e** none of the above

**13** Activity for the purpose of creating monopoly is
  **a** called rent seeking.
  **b** illegal in the United Kingdom.
  **c** called price discrimination.
  **d** called legal monopoly.
  **e** costless.

## SHORT ANSWER

**1** Does a single-price monopoly produce in the elastic or inelastic range of its demand curve? Why?

**2** Explain why the output of a competitive industry will always be greater than the output of the *same* industry under single-price monopoly.

**3** Under what circumstances would a monopoly be more efficient than a large number of competitive firms? Illustrate graphically such a situation where a monopoly produces more and charges a lower price than would be the case if the industry consisted of a large number of perfectly competitive firms.

**4** With reference to the *Reading Between the Lines* article, explain what is meant by a cartel and say why cartels are undesirable.

# PROBLEMS

**1** Keith's Lunch has two kinds of customers for lunch: stockbrokers and retired senior citizens. The demand schedules for lunches for the two groups are given in Table 12.2.

Keith has decided to price discriminate between the two groups by treating each demand separately and charging the price that maximizes profit in each of the two submarkets. Marginal cost and average total cost are equal and constant at £2 per lunch.

**a** Complete Table 12.2 by computing the total and marginal revenue associated with stockbroker demand ($TR_{SB}$ and $MR_{SB}$) as well as the total and marginal revenue associated with senior citizen demand ($TR_{SC}$ and $MR_{SC}$). (Remember that marginal revenue should be entered midway between rows.)

**b** What are the profit-maximizing output and price for stockbrokers?

**c** What are the profit-maximizing output and price for senior citizens?

**d** What is total profit?

**e** Show that the total profit in part (d) is the maximum by comparing it with total profit if instead Keith served

  **i** 1 additional lunch *each* to stockbrokers and senior citizens.

  **ii** 1 less lunch *each* to stockbrokers and senior citizens.

**2** Figure 12.4 gives the demand, marginal revenue and marginal cost curves for a certain industry. In this problem we consider how consumer and producer surplus are distributed under each of four ways of organizing the industry. In each case redraw any relevant part of Fig. 12.4 and then **(1)** indicate the region of the graph corresponding to consumer surplus by drawing horizontal lines through it; **(2)** indicate the region corresponding to producer surplus by drawing vertical lines through it; and **(3)** indicate the region (if any) corresponding to deadweight loss by putting dots in the area.

**a** The industry consists of many perfectly competitive firms.

**b** The industry is a single-price monopoly.

**c** The industry is a price-discriminating monopoly charging two prices: $P_1$ and $P_3$.

**d** The industry is a perfect price-discriminating monopoly.

## DISCUSSION QUESTIONS

**1** Can you think of a couple of rules that you can use to determine, first, how much is produced, and second, how much is charged?

**2** How does price discrimination reduce the amount of consumer surplus?

**Table 12.2**

| | Stockbrokers | | | Senior citizens | | |
|---|---|---|---|---|---|---|
| Price (P) (pounds) | Quantity demanded ($Q_D$) (lunches) | Total revenue ($TR_{SB}$) (pounds per lunch) | Marginal revenue ($MR_{SB}$) (pounds per lunch) | Quantity demanded ($Q_D$) (lunches) | Total revenue ($TR_{SC}$) (pounds per lunch) | Marginal revenue ($MR_{SC}$) (pounds per lunch) |
| 8 | 0 | | | 0 | | |
| 7 | 1 | | | 0 | | |
| 6 | 2 | | | 0 | | |
| 5 | 3 | | | 1 | | |
| 4 | 4 | | | 2 | | |
| 3 | 5 | | | 3 | | |
| 2 | 6 | | | 4 | | |
| 1 | 7 | | | 5 | | |
| 0 | 8 | | | 6 | | |

**Figure 12.4**

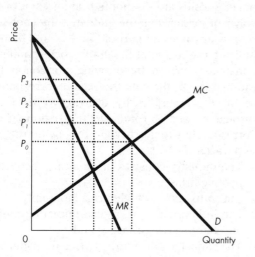

## DATA QUESTIONS

**Table 12.3   Return Rail Fares from Preston to London, 1995**

| Ticket type | Fare (£) |
|---|---|
| First | 142 |
| Standard | 96 |
| Leisure First | 65 |
| APEX First | 53 |
| Supersaver | 33 |
| APEX | 25 |
| SUPERAPEX | 19 |

Young Persons and Senior Citizens railcards give a discount of one-third on most fares.

1 Explain how the conditions required for successful price discrimination apply to this market.

2 Show how the rail company benefits from charging different prices for similar services (similar, but in this case not identical, because, for example, the seats in a first class carriage differ from those in standard class).

# ANSWERS

## CONCEPT REVIEW

1 monopoly; barriers

2 single-price

3 industry

4 demand; below

5 positive; greater; less; negative; inelastic

6 price

7 cost; revenue

8 profits

9 price discrimination; surplus

10 elasticities; more

11 decrease; increase; deadweight

12 rent seeking; equal to

13 scope

## TRUE OR FALSE

1 **T** Natural monopolies have high fixed costs.

2 **T** Average of all (equal) prices of a product = price.

3 **F** *MR* is negative.

4 **T** Draw curves to verify this.

5 **T** If it produced in the inelastic range it would increase profits by increasing price.

6 **F** Monopoly has no supply curve.

7 **F** Monopoly gives no guarantee of profits if consumers are unwilling to buy the product.

8 **T** Definition.

9 **T** Definition.

10 **F** It is an attempt to capture consumer surplus.

11 **T** Demand curve gives revenue for each successive unit.

12 **T** This is one of the advantages of monopoly.

## MULTIPLE CHOICE

**1 b** Others are legal barriers.

**2 d** $TR$ ($P$ = £7) = £7 × 7 = £49. $TR$ ($P$ = £6) = £6 × 8 = £48, $MR$ = change in $TR$ = £48 – £49.

**3 c** All firms will maximize profits if they produce where $MR = MC$.

**4 a** Draw graph. If $MC$ exceeds $MR$ firm should cut production, so increasing $MR$ and cutting $MC$.

**5 c** Since $TR$ falls needlessly, $MR$ must always be > 0 to intersect (positive) $MC$.

**6 b** Profit is maximized where $MR = MC$.

**7 c** ($AR - ATC$) × $Q$ = (£6 – £4) × 3

**8 d** Same outcome as perfectly competitive industry, so **e** wrong. $D = MR$ so **a** wrong. Profit maximizing, so **b** wrong.

**9 d** Sum of ($P - MC$) for each unit of output.

**10 b** Sum of lost producer *(bcd)* and consumer *(abd)* surplus compared to competitive outcome.

**11 e** Deadweight loss is zero.

**12 d** $MSB$ measured on demand curve, $MSC$ on $MC$ curve.

**13 a** Definition. Activity has costs.

## SHORT ANSWER

**1** A single-price monopoly will always produce in the elastic range of the demand curve. The reason is straight-forward. Marginal cost is always positive. Thus the profit-maximizing condition that marginal cost equals marginal revenue must be satisfied over the range of output for which marginal revenue is positive, the elastic range.

**2** A competitive industry will produce the level of output at which the industry marginal cost curve intersects the demand curve facing the industry. A single-price monopoly will produce at the level of output at which the industry marginal cost curve intersects the monopoly marginal revenue curve. Since the marginal revenue curve lies below the demand curve, this implies a lower level of output in the monopoly industry.

**3** A monopoly would be more efficient than perfect competition if the monopoly has sufficient economies of scale and/or scope. These economies must be large enough for the monopoly to produce more than the competitive industry and sell it at a lower price. Figure 12.5 illustrates such a situation. The important feature is that the marginal cost curve for the monopoly must not

only be lower than the supply curve of the competitive industry, but it must also be sufficiently lower so that it intersects the $MR$ curve at an output greater than $C$ (the competitive output). Such a situation could arise if there are extensive economies of scale and/or scope.

### Figure 12.5

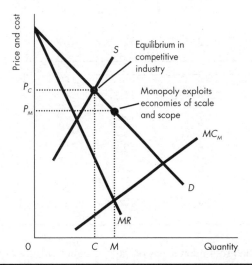

**4** A cartel is a group of firms that has entered into an agreement to restrict output so as to increase prices and profits. In this case six companies are suspected of forming a cartel in the heating-pipe manufacturing industry. This is undesirable because consumers in Denmark have been faced with prices up to 50 per cent higher than in Sweden. This is possible because the firms are alleged to have colluded to restrict output. Thus the supply curve moves to the left and results in higher prices. The other feature in this case is that it is suggested that members of the cartel have targeted a non-member's customers, to the disadvantage of a possible competitor.

## PROBLEMS

**1 a** The completed table is given in Table 12.4.
For stockbrokers, equilibrium output occurs where $MC = MR = 2$, $Q_{SB} = 3$, $P_{SB} = 5$.
For senior citizens, equilibrium output occurs where $MC = MR = 2$, $Q_{SC} = 2$, $P_{SC} = 4$.

**b** The profit-maximizing output for stockbrokers occurs when $MC = £2 = MR_{SB}$. This is at 3 lunches and the price is £5 per lunch to stockbrokers.

# Table 12.4

| Price (P) (pounds) | Stockbrokers | | | | Senior citizens | | |
|---|---|---|---|---|---|---|---|
| | Quantity demanded (Q_D) (lunches) | Total revenue (TR_SB) (pounds per lunch) | Marginal revenue (MR_SB) (pounds per lunch) | | Quantity demanded (Q_D) (lunches) | Total revenue (TR_SC) (pounds per lunch) | Marginal revenue (MR_SC) (pounds per lunch) |
| 8 | 0 | 0 | | | 0 | 0 | |
| | | | ...7 | | | | ...0 |
| 7 | 1 | 7 | | | 0 | 0 | |
| | | | ...5 | | | | ...0 |
| 6 | 2 | 12 | | | 0 | 0 | |
| | | | 3 | | | | ...0 |
| 5 | 3 | 15 | | | 1 | 5 | |
| | | | 1 | | | | 3 |
| 4 | 4 | 16 | | | 2 | 8 | |
| | | | -1 | | | | 1 |
| 3 | 5 | 15 | | | 3 | 9 | |
| | | | 3 | | | | -1 |
| 2 | 6 | 12 | | | 4 | 8 | |
| | | | -5 | | | | -3 |
| 1 | 7 | 7 | | | 5 | 5 | |
| | | | -7 | | | | -5 |
| 0 | 8 | 0 | | | 6 | 0 | |

c  The profit-maximizing output for senior citizens occurs when $MC = £2 = MR_{SC}$. This occurs at 2 lunches and the price to senior citizens is £4 per lunch.

d  Since average total cost is also £2 per lunch, the total cost is £2 × 5 lunches = £10. Total revenue is £15 from stockbrokers and £8 from senior citizens, or £23. Thus total profit is £13.

e  i  If Keith served 1 additional lunch each to stockbrokers and senior citizens, that would make 4 lunches for stockbrokers (at £4/lunch) and 3 lunches for senior citizens (at £3/lunch). Since average total cost is £2 per lunch, the total cost is £2 × 7 lunches = £14. Total revenue is £16 from stockbrokers and £9 from senior citizens, or £25. Thus total profit is £11, less than the £13 in part d.

ii  If Keith served 1 less lunch each to stockbrokers and senior citizens, that would make 2 lunches for stockbrokers (at £6/lunch) and 1 lunch for senior citizens (at £5/lunch). Since average total cost is £2 per lunch, the total cost is £2 × 3 lunches = £6. Total revenue is £12 from stockbrokers and £5 from senior citizens, or £17. Thus total profit is £11, less than the £13 in part d.

2  a  Under perfect competition, price equals marginal cost. The amount of consumer surplus is given by the area under the demand curve but above the price $(P_0)$ while the amount of producer surplus is given by the area above the MC curve but below the price. See Fig. 12.6(a).

b  If the industry is a single-price monopoly, price will be greater than MC and output will be less than under competition. Consumer surplus is still given by the area under the demand curve but above the price $(P_2)$, while producer surplus is given by the area above the MC curve but below the price up to the monopoly level of output. The remaining part of the large triangle is a deadweight loss since it is the amount of surplus under competition that is lost under a single-price monopoly. See Fig. 12.6(b).

c  Similar reasoning allows us to establish regions in Fig. 12.6(c) corresponding to consumer surplus, producer surplus and deadweight loss.

d  Under perfect price discrimination, all of the potential surplus is captured by the producer and there is no deadweight loss (or consumer surplus). See Fig. 12.6(d).

## DISCUSSION QUESTIONS

1  Two mechanical rules help you to remember how a profit-maximizing monopolist selects price and output. First, find the output by using the $MR = MC$ rule. Second, find the price. To do this draw a vertical line up from where the MR and MC curves intersect until you reach the demand curve. Then draw a horizontal line to the vertical axis to find the price.

2  Price discrimination measures the difference between how much consumers actually pay and how much they

**Figure 12.6**

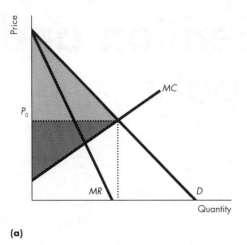

(a)

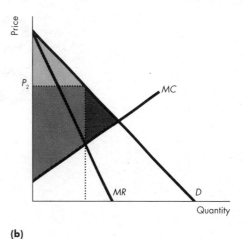

(b)

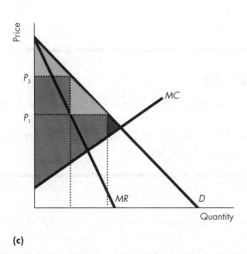

(c)

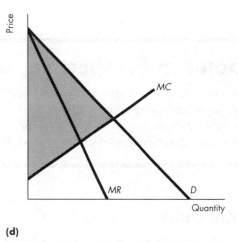

(d)

would be willing to pay. Through price discrimination, the monopoly can reduce this difference. Consumers who value the service a lot and are willing to pay high prices do pay high prices. Those who do not value it so much and are not willing to pay high prices obtain it for less. Thus a price-discriminating monopolist moves the price closer to what consumers are willing to pay, and so reduces consumer surplus.

## DATA QUESTIONS

**1** Price discrimination is the practice of charging a higher price to some customers than to others for an identical item, or charging an individual customer a higher price on a small purchase than on a large one. It can be used only when it is impossible for a buyer to sell the good and when customers have different elasticities. In the case of rail journeys, the company can easily differentiate among people sitting in first class or standard class seats; similarly it can distinguish among people travelling on early trains who have to pay the full standard fare and those travelling later.

**2** The manufacturer benefits by obtaining a higher revenue (price times quantity) by charging a higher price when demand is inelastic and a lower price when demand is elastic.

# Chapter 13

# Monopolistic Competition and Oligopoly

---

## Chapter in Perspective, Text Pages 310–339

Perfect competition and strict monopoly are quite rare. Most firms that we observe seem to lie somewhere between these two polar cases.

This chapter explores the behaviour of the in-between firms that populate the real world. We will discover that the tools of analysis developed in the previous two chapters will take us a long way.

---

## Helpful Hints

1 It is important not only to know the different key characteristics of the alternative forms of market structure (see Table 13.2 on text page 314 for a review) but also to understand how these characteristics explain differences in firm behaviour.

2 We continue to assume that all firms are profit-maximizers. In spite of this common objective, the equilibrium price and level of output will be different for each of the market structures. This is because of differences in the nature of constraints faced by firms in each of the four types of market structures. For example, except in the case of perfect competition, firms face downward-sloping demand curves and thus have some control over the price of the good they sell.

In these cases, profit-maximizing firms will (typically) produce less than would have been produced in the competitive case and will charge a price higher than the competitive price.

3 In graphing a monopolistically competitive firm in long-run equilibrium, be sure that the *ATC* curve is tangent to the demand curve at the same level of output at which the *MC* and *MR* curves intersect. Also be sure that the *MC* curve intersects the *ATC* curve at the minimum point on the *ATC* curve.

4 This chapter explains the use of elementary game theory to help understand oligopoly. Be sure to understand the prisoners' dilemma game because it illustrates, simply, the most important game theory concepts (rules, strategies, payoffs), which

are then used in more complex game theory models like those of repeated games.

Understand the incentives faced by the players and why a particular outcome is an equilibrium. The key to finding the equilibrium of a simple game is carefully to construct and examine the payoff matrix.

# Key Figures and Tables

## Figure 13.3 Monopolistic Competition, text page 317

This figure illustrates the output and pricing decisions of a monopolistically competitive firm in both the short run and the long run. In the short run, the firm can make either a positive profit, as illustrated in part (a) of the figure, or a loss. When firms are making profits, new firms will enter, causing the demand curves of existing firms to shift to the left. Prices and firms' profits will fall. Similarly, if firms are making losses in the short run, some will leave the industry, which will increase prices and profits (that is, reduce losses).

In long-run equilibrium, illustrated in part (b) of the figure, firms will be making zero profits and there will be no more tendency for firms to either exit or enter the industry.

## Figure 13.6 Costs and Demand, text page 325

If there are no barriers to entry, an industry will be characterized by duopoly if costs and industry demand are such that only two firms can survive in the long run. This figure illustrates such an industry using the example of two firms: Trick and Gear.

The firms have identical costs, which are shown in part (a). The minimum *ATC* of £6,000 occurs at the quantity of 3,000 switchgears per firm per week. Since, at a price of £6,000, the total quantity demanded in the industry is 6,000 switchgears per week, only two firms can survive in the long run.

## Figure 13.7 Colluding to Make Monopoly Profits, text page 326

The two firms of a duopoly industry obtain maximum total profit by colluding. This is illustrated in the figure once again using the example of Trick and Gear.

In order to maximize total profit, the firms will, together, behave as a single monopolist by producing the output at which *industry* marginal cost is equal to *industry* marginal revenue.

The firms will produce the quantity at which the *MC* and *MR* curves intersect (4,000 units) and charge the monopoly price obtained from the industry demand curve (£9,000). The firms then divide the production and the profits. As seen in part (a), each firm produces 2,000 switchgears per week and earns a profit of £2 million per week.

## Figure 13.9 Both Firms Cheat, text page 329

After the firms of a duopoly enter into a collusive agreement, each firm can either abide by the agreement or cheat by increasing output and reducing price.

Each firm has an incentive to cheat since it can increase its profit (at the expense of the non-cheating firm) by doing so. The case of both firms cheating is illustrated for Trick and Gear in this figure. The limit to the breakdown of the agreement is the competitive equilibrium. The limit for each firm is shown in part (a) and for the industry in part (b).

Once the collusive agreement has broken down by the cheating of the firms, successively lower prices will result until the price has fallen to the competitive level and both firms are making zero profit as seen in part (a). The industry output and price will be those associated with the competitive equilibrium, at the intersection of the industry marginal cost curve and the industry demand curve.

## Table 13.2 Market Structure, text page 314

This table summarizes the characteristics of the four market structures that have been discussed in this and previous chapters. These are, from most competitive to least competitive: perfect competition, monopolistic competition, oligopoly and monopoly. These are compared on the basis of the number of firms in the industry, the kind of product, the nature of any barriers to entry, the firm's control over price and the concentration ratio. The table also provides examples of each market structure. This table is an excellent study tool.

## Table 13.4 Duopoly Payoff Matrix, page 330

One way to analyse the interactive behaviour of firms in an oligopoly is to use game theory and construct a payoff matrix. A payoff matrix indicates the payoffs associated with the alternative strategy combinations of the players of the game. The payoff matrix for Trick and Gear is illustrated in this table. It indicates the profit for each firm that results from each of the four possible strategy pairs. Each firm then chooses its best strategy.

For example, Trick will consider its best strategy under each choice that Gear might make. If Gear cheats, Trick is better off by cheating (zero profit is better than a £1 million loss). If Gear complies, Trick is also better off by cheating (a £4.5 million profit is better than a £2 million profit). Thus Trick's dominant strategy is to cheat. The same analysis leads Gear to decide also to cheat. The result is a Nash equilibrium in which both firms cheat.

# SELF-TEST

## CONCEPT REVIEW

**1** The most commonly used measure of concentration is called the five-firm _____ _____. This is the percentage of _____ accounted for by the largest five firms in the industry.

**2** The market structure characterized by a large number of firms that compete with each other by making similar but slightly different products is called _____ _____. The market structure characterized by a small number of producers competing with each other is called _____.

**3** When profits are being made in a monopolistically competitive industry, firms will _____. If losses are being made, firms will _____. As a result, in a monopolistically competitive industry, in long-run equilibrium, each firm will make a(n) _____ economic profit and will have _____ capacity.

**4** The modern approach to understanding oligopoly uses _____ theory, a method of analysing strategic interaction invented by John von Neumann. In such a theory all the possible actions of each player are called _____ and the score of each player is called the _____.

**5** A market structure in which only two producers of a commodity compete with each other is called _____.

**6** The table that shows the payoffs for every possible action by each player for every possible action by the other player is called a(n) _____ _____.

**7** The equilibrium of a game like the prisoners' dilemma is called a(n) _____ equilibrium. A special case of such an equilibrium occurs when the best strategy for each player is the same regardless of the action taken by the other player. This is called a(n) _____ _____ equilibrium.

**8** A group of firms that has entered into a collusive agreement to restrict output and increase price and profits is called a(n) _____ . Each firm in the group can pursue one of two strategies: it can either comply or _____ .

**9** In a repeated game, the strategy in which a player begins by cooperating and then cheats only if the other player cheated the previous time the game was played is called a(n) _____-_____-_____ strategy.

**10** In a repeated game, the strategy in which a player cooperates if the other player cooperates, but plays the Nash equilibrium strategy forever thereafter if the other player cheats is called a _____ _____ .

**11** The equilibrium which results from each player responding rationally to a credible threat of a heavy penalty from the other player if the agreement is broken is called a(n) _____ equilibrium.

**12** _____ pricing is the practice of charging a price below the monopoly profit-maximizing price.

## TRUE OR FALSE

___ **1** A low concentration ratio indicates a low degree of competition.

__ **2** In a monopolistically competitive industry, each firm faces a downward-sloping demand curve.

__ **3** Product differentiation is what gives a monopolistically competitive firm some monopoly power.

__ **4** A critical difference between monopoly and monopolistic competition is that in the latter case there is free entry.

__ **5** If firms in a monopolistically competitive industry are making profits, we can expect to see their demand curves shift to the left as new firms enter.

__ **6** In long-run equilibrium, a monopolistically competitive firm will produce more output than that associated with the minimum point on its average total cost curve.

__ **7** An oligopolist will consider the reaction of other firms before it decides to cut its price.

__ **8** A Nash equilibrium occurs when *A* takes the best possible action given the action of *B* and *B* takes the best possible action given the action of *A*.

__ **9** If two players in a game face the same choices, there cannot be a dominant strategy equilibrium.

__ **10** If duopolists agree to collude, they can (jointly) make as much profit as a single monopoly.

__ **11** In the case of colluding duopolists in a non-repeated game, the dominant strategy equilibrium is for both firms to cheat.

## MULTIPLE CHOICE

**1** The four-firm concentration ratio measures the share of the largest four firms in total industry
a profits.
b sales.
c cost.
d capital.
e none of the above.

**2** Under monopolistic competition, long-run economic profits tend towards zero *because of*

a product differentiation.
b the lack of barriers to entry.
c excess capacity.
d inefficiency.
e the downward-sloping demand curve facing each firm.

**3** In the long run, the firm in monopolistic competition will
a face a perfectly elastic demand curve.
b produce more than the quantity that minimizes *ATC*.
c produce less than the quantity that minimizes *ATC*.
d produce the quantity that minimizes *ATC*.
e earn economic profits.

**4** Figure 13.1 represents a monopolistically competitive firm in short-run equilibrium. What is the firm's level of output?
a $Q_1$
b $Q_2$
c $Q_3$
d $Q_4$
e zero

**Figure 13.1**

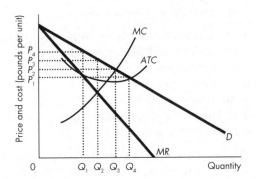

**5** What will be the price charged by the monopolistic competitor of Fig. 13.1?
a $P_1$
b $P_2$
c $P_3$
d $P_4$
e zero, since the firm has shut down.

**6** Refer again to the short-run situation illustrated in Fig. 13.1. We know that in the long run
   **a** there will be entry of new firms and each existing firm's demand will shift to the left.
   **b** there will be entry of new firms and each existing firm's demand will shift to the right.
   **c** existing firms will leave and each remaining firm's demand will shift to the left.
   **d** existing firms will leave and each remaining firm's demand will shift to the right.
   **e** there will be no change from the short run.

**7** Which of the following is true for perfect competition, monopolistic competition and single-price monopoly?
   **a** homogeneous product
   **b** zero long-run economic profits
   **c** short-run profit-maximizing quantity where $MC = MR$
   **d** easy entry and exit
   **e** none of the above

**8** The kinked demand curve theory
   **a** suggests that price will remain constant even with fluctuations in demand.
   **b** suggests how the current price is determined.
   **c** assumes that marginal revenue sometimes increases with output.
   **d** assumes that competitors will match price cuts and ignore price increases.
   **e** suggests none of the above.

**9** In the prisoners' dilemma with players Alf and Bob, the dominant strategy equilibrium is
   **a** both prisoners confess.
   **b** both prisoners deny.
   **c** Alf denies and Bob confesses.
   **d** Bob denies and Alf confesses.
   **e** indeterminate.

**10** The firms Trick and Gear form a cartel to collude to maximize profit. If this game is non-repeated, the dominant strategy equilibrium is
   **a** both firms cheat on the agreement.
   **b** both firms comply with the agreement.
   **c** Trick cheats while Gear complies with the agreement.
   **d** Gear cheats while Trick complies with the agreement.
   **e** indeterminate.

**11** Consider the same cartel consisting of Trick and Gear. Now, however, the game is repeated indefinitely and each firm employs a tit-for-tat strategy. The equilibrium is
   **a** both firms cheat on the agreement.
   **b** both firms comply with the agreement.
   **c** Trick cheats while Gear complies with the agreement.
   **d** Gear cheats while Trick complies with the agreement.
   **e** indeterminate.

**12** The equilibrium in Question 11 is called a
   **a** credible strategy equilibrium.
   **b** dominant player equilibrium.
   **c** duopoly equilibrium.
   **d** trigger strategy equilibrium.
   **e** cooperative equilibrium.

## SHORT ANSWER

**1** **a** Considering the geographical scope of markets, how might concentration ratios *understate* the degree of competitiveness in an industry?
   **b** How might they *overstate* the degree of competitiveness in an industry?

**2** Why will a firm in a monopolistically competitive industry always have excess capacity in long-run equilibrium?

**3** Compare the advantages and disadvantages of perfect competition and monopolistic competition in terms of allocative efficiency.

**4** Consider the case of two colluding duopolists in a non-repeated game. Why will both firms cheat on the agreement in equilibrium?

**5** In the *Reading Between the Lines* article in this chapter, why do you think that Sainsbury's emphasized increased market share?

## PROBLEMS

**1** Consider a single firm in a monopolistically competitive industry in the short run. On a grid similar to the grid shown in Fig. 13.2, draw a new graph for each of the following situations.

**Figure 13.2**

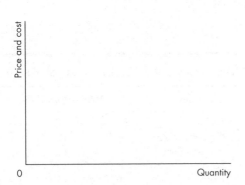

**Figure 13.3**

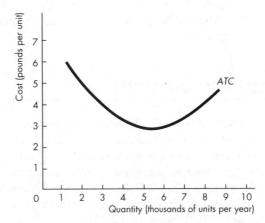

**(a)**

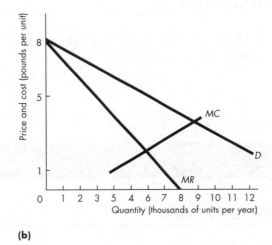

**(b)**

**a** The firm is making a profit.

**b** The firm is making a loss that will cause shutdown.

**c** The firm is making a loss but is still producing.

**d** Starting from the situation in **c**, explain what will happen in this industry and how your graph in **c** will be affected? (A new graph is not required.)

**e** The firm is in long-run equilibrium.

**2** A duopoly industry with no collusion consists of firms *A* and *B*, which are essentially identical. Currently, neither firm is advertising and each is making a profit of £5 million per year. If *A* advertises and *B* does not, *A* will make an annual profit of £12 million while *B* will make a loss of £5 million.

On the other hand, if *B* advertises and *A* does not, *B* will make a £12 million profit and *A* will make a loss of £5 million. If both advertise, each will make zero profit.

**a** Represent this duopoly as a game by identifying the players, strategies and possible outcomes.

**b** Construct the payoff matrix.

**c** What is the equilibrium outcome? Explain.

**3** Use the graphs given in Fig. 13.3 to answer this question. Figure 13.3(a) gives the average total cost *(ATC)* curve for each of two identical firms (call them *A* and *B*) in a duopoly. Figure 13.3(b) gives the market demand curve and the firms' joint marginal cost curve. Suppose these firms collude to maximize profit and agree to divide output equally *for a single year*.

**a** How much will each firm produce by the agreement and what price will they charge?

**b** What is each firm's average total cost and profit?

**c** Now suppose that firm *B* convinces *A* that demand has decreased and they must reduce their price by £1 per unit in order to sell the quantity agreed upon. Of course, demand has *not* decreased but *A* produces its agreed amount and charges £1 less per unit. Firm *B*, the cheater, also charges £1 less than the original agreement price but increases output sufficiently to satisfy the rest of the demand at this price.

**i** How much does *B* produce?

**ii** What is firm *A*'s average total cost and profit?

**iii** What is firm *B*'s average total cost and profit?

# DISCUSSION QUESTION

**1** Common rules make it easier to understand economics. One such rule is that firms will maximize profits if they produce where $MR = MC$. There is another rule that is common across all industries. Can you explain it? (Hint: it deals with when a firm earns an economic profit, that is, with the relationship between *P* and *ATC*).

# DATA QUESTIONS

**1** In Table 13.1, classify this industry as to market type.

**2** What is the five-firm concentration ratio in this industry?

**3** Why are there so few firms in this European industry?

**Table 13.1  Shares of the West European Car Market, 1996**

| Company | Market share (%) |
|---|---|
| Volkswagen | 17 |
| General Motors | 13 |
| Peugeot Group | 12 |
| Ford | 12 |
| Fiat | 11 |
| Renault | 10 |
| Rover (BMW) | 3 |
| Daimler Benz | 4 |
| Volvo | 2 |
| Others | 16 |

Source: Derived from data from Society of Motor Manufacture Traders.

# ANSWERS

## CONCEPT REVIEW

**1** concentration ratio; sales

**2** monopolistic competition; oligopoly

**3** enter; leave; zero; excess

**4** game; strategies; payoff

**5** duopoly

**6** payoff matrix

**7** Nash; dominant strategy

**8** cartel; cheat

**9** tit-for-tat

**10** trigger strategy

**11** cooperative

**12** Limit

## TRUE OR FALSE

**1 F** Low concentration ratio = high degree of competition.

**2 T** Firm will have to cut price to sell more.

**3 T** Creates a downward-sloping demand curve.

**4 T** Definition.

**5 T** Increase in supply moves curve to left.

**6 F** Profits would fall if it produced beyond the minimum point.

**7 T** Oligopoly involves strategic behaviour.

**8 T** Definition.

**9 F** Prisoners' dilemma players face same choices leading to dominant strategy equilibrium.

**10 T** With collusion they act like a monopoly.

**11 T** True for non-repeated game, but may be false for repeated game.

## MULTIPLE CHOICE

**1 b** Definition.

**2 b** **a** and **e** lead to possible profits, **c** and **d** are outcomes.

**3 c** Excess capacity at $Q$ where demand is tangent to downward slope $ATC$.

**4 b** Where $MR = MC$.

**5 c** Highest possible price to sell $Q_2$.

**6 a** Since firm is making profits, new firms will enter so each firm will sell less.

**7 c** **b** and **d** false for monopoly, **a** false for monopolistic competition.

**8 d** **a** is true if there are fluctuations in $MC$. **c** is false because $MR$ always falls as quantity rises.

**9 a** Outcome of game.

**10 a** Similar to prisoners' dilemma outcome.

**11 b** Cooperative equilibrium; each player responds rationally to credible threat of the other.

**12 e** Definition.

## SHORT ANSWER

**1 a** Since concentration ratios are calculated from a national perspective, if the actual geographical scope of the market is not national, the concentration ratio is likely to mis-state the degree of competitiveness in an industry. For example, if the actual market is global, the concentration ratio will understate the degree of competitiveness, and it will be too high. It is possible for a firm to have a concentration ratio of 100 because it is the only producer in the country, but to face a great deal of international competition.

**b** Similarly, when the scope of the market is regional, the degree of competitiveness is likely to be less than would be indicated by the simple concentration ratio.

**2** A firm is defined to have excess capacity if it is producing in the negatively-sloped portion of its average total cost curve. At the long-run equilibrium level of output (sales) in a monopolistically competitive industry, each firm will be earning zero profit and its average total cost curve will be tangent to its demand curve. Since the demand curve of a monopolistic competitor is downward sloping, so is the average total cost curve at that level of output. Therefore, the monopolistically competitive firm will have excess capacity in long-run equilibrium.

**3** The advantage of perfect competition is that it leads to production at minimum average total cost, while monopolistic competition leads to a higher average total cost with reduced output.

The advantage of monopolistic competition is that it leads to greater product variety, which consumers value, while in a perfectly competitive industry there is a single, identical product produced by all firms. Thus the loss in allocative efficiency (higher $ATC$) that occurs in monopolistic competition has to be weighed against the gain of greater product variety.

**4** Each firm's best strategy is to cheat regardless of the strategy of the other firm. Call the firms $A$ and $B$. Firm $A$ knows that if firm $B$ follows the collusive agreement, $A$ can increase its profit by cheating. If firm $B$ cheats, then firm $A$ knows that it must also cheat to minimize its loss of profit. Thus cheating is the dominant strategy for firm $A$. Accordingly, it is also the dominant strategy for firm $B$.

**5** Most conventional economic analysis rests on the assumption that firms attempt to maximize profits. Here Sainsbury's said 'it aimed to recapture lost market share'. There are two reasons for this. First, firms often want to be the biggest in their industry. Second, it may well be that increasing market share will bring higher profits, for example by allowing the firm to gain economies of scale. However, this is not certain; if market share rises because prices are cut, then this may lead to lower profits.

## PROBLEMS

**1 a** Figure 13.4(a) illustrates a monopolistically competitive firm making a profit in the short run. The important feature of the graph is that at the profit-maximizing output, price is greater than average total cost. Profit is given by the shaded area in the graph.

**b** Figure 13.4(b) illustrates a firm that will shut down in the short run since price is less than average variable cost at the profit-maximizing (loss-minimizing) level of output.

**c** Figure 13.4(c) illustrates a firm making a loss but continuing to produce. The loss is given by the shaded area in the graph. Note that, at the profit-maximizing output, price is less than $ATC$ but greater than $AVC$.

**d** Since firms are typically experiencing a loss, firms will leave the industry. This means that the demand curves facing each of the remaining firms will begin to shift out as they each attract some of the customers of the departing firms. As the firm demand curves shift out, losses are reduced. Firms will continue to have an

## Figure 13.4

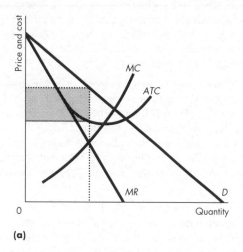

**(a)**

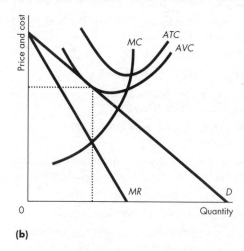

**(b)**

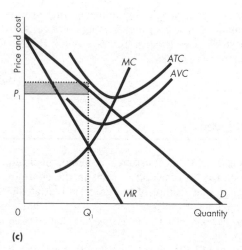

**(c)**

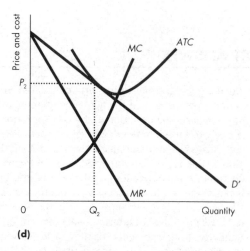

**(d)**

---

incentive to leave until losses have been eliminated. Thus firm demand curves will continue to shift out until they are tangent to the *ATC* curve.

**e** Figure 13.4(d) illustrates a typical monopolistically competitive firm in long-run equilibrium. The key feature is that the demand curve facing the firm is tangent to the *ATC* curve at the profit-maximizing output. Thus the firm is making zero profit.

**2 a** The players are firms *A* and *B*. Each firm has two strategies: to advertise or not to advertise. There are four possible outcomes: **(1)** both firms advertise, **(2)** firm *A* advertises but firm *B* does not, **(3)** firm *B* advertises but firm *A* does not, and **(4)** neither firm advertises.

**b** The payoff matrix is given in Table 13.2. The entries give the profit earned by firms *A* and *B* under each of the four possible outcomes.

**Table 13.2**

| Firm A | | Firm B | | Firm B | |
|---|---|---|---|---|---|
| | | **Advertise** | | **Not advertise** | |
| **Advertise** | A:<br>B: | 0<br>0 | | A:<br>B: | £12 million<br>−£15 million |
| **Not Advertise** | A:<br>B: | −£5 million<br>£12 million | | A:<br>B: | £5 million<br>£5 million |

c First consider how firm *A* decides which strategy to pursue. If *B* advertises, *A* can advertise and make zero profit or not advertise and make a £5 million loss. Thus firm *A* will want to advertise if firm *B* does.

   If *B* does not advertise, *A* can advertise and make a £12 million profit or not advertise and make a £5 million profit. Therefore, firm *A* will want to advertise whether firm *B* advertises or not. *B* will come to the same conclusion. Thus the dominant strategy equilibrium is that both firms advertise.

3 a The firms will agree to produce 3,000 units each and sell at a price of £5 per unit. We determine this by noticing (Fig. 13.3b) that the profit-maximizing (monopoly) output is 6,000 units for the industry (*MR = MC* at 6,000) at a price of £5. Since the firms have agreed to divide output equally, each will produce 3,000 units.

  b From Fig. 13.3(a) we determine that, at 3,000 units, each firm's average total cost is £4 per unit. Since price is £5, profit will be £3,000 for each firm.

  c  i At the new price of £4 the total quantity demanded is 8,000 units. Since *A* continues to produce 3,000 units this means that firm *B* will produce the remaining 5,000 units demanded.

ii Since firm *A* continues to produce 3,000 units, its average total cost continues to be £4 per unit. With the new price also at £4, firm *A* will make a zero profit.

iii Firm *B* has increased output to 5,000 units, which implies average total cost of £3 per unit. Thus given a price of £4, firm *B*'s profit will be £5,000.

## DISCUSSION QUESTION

1 One other rule works for a firm in any type of industry structure. In particular:

   ◆ if $P > ATC$ the firm earns an economic profit
   ◆ if $P = ATC$ the firm earns a normal profit
   ◆ if $P < ATC$ the firm suffers an economic loss.

## DATA QUESTION

1 An industry dominated by a few firms such as this is characterized by oligopoly.

2 The five-firm concentration ratio for this industry is $17 + 13 + 12 + 12 + 11 = 65\%$.

   Note that these figures are for the European market. They would be different if a particular country was considered to be the market.

3 The reason that there are so few firms in the industry is because there are huge barriers to entry. These are largely made up of research and development costs and heavy fixed costs of production, but firms add to these barriers by large-scale advertising expenditure, which creates an additional barrier.

# Chapter 14 · Pricing and Allocating Factors of Production

---

## Chapter in Perspective, Text Pages 344–369

This chapter explains how factor prices are determined. As with the prices of outputs of goods and services, the prices of productive inputs are determined in markets – markets for factors of production. These markets have many of the same characteristics as the markets for goods and services we examined in Chapters 11–13. Here we take a broad first look at markets for factors of production, leaving more detailed discussion of specific markets to later chapters.

---

## Helpful Hints

**1** The purpose of this chapter is to give a broad overview of the characteristics that are common to the markets for all factors of production. For example, the assumption that firms are profit-maximizers implies that they will hire each factor of production up to the point where marginal revenue product is equal to the marginal cost of the factor, regardless of whether the factor of production is labour, land or capital.

**2** Be sure to distinguish carefully between the marginal revenue product of a factor of production and the marginal revenue of a unit of output. As noted in the text, the marginal revenue product of a factor of production can be calculated by multiplying marginal revenue and marginal product ($MRP = MR \times MP$). We can think of this intuitively as follows: marginal product tells us how much more output we receive from using more of a factor, and marginal revenue tells us how much more revenue we receive from each unit of that additional output. Therefore, $MP$ times $MR$ tells us how much more revenue we receive from using more of the factor (the $MRP$).

## Key Figures and Tables

**Figure 14.1 Demand and Supply in a Factor Market, text page 347**
This figure depicts the market for a factor of production. The quantity of a factor demanded decreases as

the price of the factor increases, and the quantity of a factor supplied increases as the price of the factor increases.

Equilibrium occurs at the intersection of the demand and supply curves. The amount of total factor income is given by the area of the blue rectangle, which is the price of a unit of the factor *(PF)* times the quantity of factors hired *(QF)*.

### Figure 14.4 The Demand for Labour at Max's Wash 'n' Wax, text page 351

A firm's demand for labour curve is the same as its marginal revenue product curve of labour. This is illustrated in the figure using the example of Max's Wash 'n' Wax.

Part (a) shows the marginal revenue product curve *(MRP)*. This curve plots the values reported in Table 14.1 on text page 350. Notice that the values for *MRP* are plotted midway between the labour inputs used in their calculation. For example, the *MRP* of moving from 0 to 1 labourer is 20, so the value of 20 on the *MRP* curve is plotted midway between 0 and 1 labourers.

Part (b) constructs Max's demand for labour by asking how much labour Max would be willing to hire at alternative wage rates. Since Max is a profit-maximizer, he will want to hire labour up to the point where the marginal revenue product of labour is equal to the wage rate. For example, if the wage rate is $10 per hour, Max will hire 3 workers since marginal revenue product is $10 when 3 workers are hired. Other points on the labour demand curve can be obtained in a similar way. The result, as seen in part (b), is that the labour demand curve is the same as the *MRP* curve.

### Figure 14.8 Economic Rent and Transfer Earnings, text page 363

Total income received by the owners of a factor of production can be divided into two components: economic rent and transfer earnings. This figure illustrates the division. It shows the demand and supply curves for a factor of production. The total income received by the factor owners is given by the price of the factor *(PF)* times the quantity of the factor hired *(QF)*, which is the area of the green and yellow rectangle in the figure.

Transfer earnings are the part of income that is required to induce the supply of the factor. They are measured by the part of the income rectangle that lies below the supply curve, shown in yellow in the figure. Economic rent is the part of factor income that exceeds transfer earnings, shown in green in the figure.

### Table 14.2 Compact Glossary of Factor Market Terms, text page 352

While this chapter discusses a variety of specific factor markets, there are some important general terms that are used when discussing any factor markets. These terms are reviewed in this table, providing a handy resource for reference and review.

### Table 14.3 Two Conditions for Maximum Profit, text page 353

In previous chapters we learned that a profit-maximizing firm will choose the level of output at which marginal revenue equals marginal cost ($MR = MC$). In this chapter, we have seen that a profit-maximizing firm will hire a factor up to the level at which marginal revenue product equals the price of the factor ($MRP = PF$). This table demonstrates that these two profit-maximization conditions are equivalent.

### Table 14.4 A Firm's Demand for Labour, text page 354

This table summarizes the law of demand as it applies to labour. The quantity of labour demanded is negatively related to the price of labour (the wage rate) along a given demand for labour curve. The table also indicates the *ceteris paribus* assumptions that, if changed, cause the demand for labour curve to shift.

# SELF-TEST

## CONCEPT REVIEW

1  Owners of factors of production receive income from firms for the use of those factors of production. The payment for labour is called _____ , the payment for capital is called _____ and the payment for land is called _____ .

2  An increase in the demand for a factor of production will _____ that factor's income. If the supply curve for a factor of production is very elastic, the resulting change in quantity traded will be _____ and the change in price will be _____ .

**3** The demand for a factor as an input in the productive process rather than for its own sake is called a(n) _____ demand.

**4** The change in total revenue resulting from _____ an additional unit of _____ is called the marginal revenue product of labour. If a profit-maximizing firm finds that the marginal revenue product of labour exceeds the wage, the firm should _____ the quantity of labour it hires.

**5** The law of diminishing returns implies that the marginal revenue product curve will be _____ sloped. A firm's demand for labour curve will be based on its _____ _____ _____ curve.

**6** If the price of the good produced by firm *A* increases, the demand curve for labour hired by firm *A* will shift to the _____ . A technological change that increases the marginal product of labour will shift the demand curve for labour to the _____ .

**7** Other things remaining the same, the higher the elasticity of demand for a product, the _____ is the elasticity of demand for the labour that produces it. The more readily capital can be substituted for labour in production, the _____ elastic is the long-run elasticity of demand for labour.

**8** The lowest wage for which a household will supply labour to the market is called its _____ wage.

**9** An increase in the wage will have two effects on the quantity of labour supplied by a household. The income effect will lead to a(n) _____ in the quantity of labour supplied and the substitution effect will lead to a(n) _____ in the quantity of labour supplied.

**10** The income received by the owner of a factor of production that exceeds the amount just necessary to induce the owner to offer the factor for use is called _____ _____ . The income required to induce the supply of the factor is called _____ earnings.

## TRUE OR FALSE

**___ 1** When the elasticity of demand for labour is greater than 1, an increase in the supply of labour will lead to a decrease in labour income.

**___ 2** As long as the labour supply curve is positively sloped, an increase in the demand for labour will increase total labour income.

**___ 3** A profit-maximizing firm will hire the quantity of a factor of production for which the marginal revenue product equals the marginal cost of the factor.

**___ 4** The firm's demand for labour curve is the same as the average revenue product curve.

**___ 5** The market demand curve for labour is the horizontal sum of the individual firms' marginal revenue product of labour curves.

**___ 6** When discussing the short-run demand for labour, labour is considered to be the only variable input.

**___ 7** If the production of good *A* is labour intensive, the demand for labour used in the production of good *A* is likely to be rather inelastic.

**___ 8** The steeper the marginal product curve for labour, the less elastic is the firm's demand for labour.

**___ 9** The short-run elasticity of demand for labour depends on the substitutability of capital for labour in the production process.

**___ 10** If the wage rate increases, the substitution effect results in the household increasing the time spent in market activities and decreasing the time spent in non-market activities.

**___ 11** If the wage rate increases, the income effect results in the household increasing its demand for leisure.

**___ 12** The household supply curve for capital shows the relationship between the interest rate and the quantity of capital supplied.

# MULTIPLE CHOICE

**1** The income received by owners of factors of production are wages paid for labour,
  **a** profit paid for capital and interest paid for money.
  **b** dividends paid for capital and interest paid for money.
  **c** dividends paid for capital and rent paid for land.
  **d** interest paid for capital and rent paid for land.
  **e** profit paid for capital and rent paid for land.

**2** An increase in the supply of a factor of production will
  **a** increase the factor's income if the elasticity of factor demand is less than 1.
  **b** decrease the factor's income if the elasticity of factor demand is less than 1.
  **c** increase the factor's income if the elasticity of factor supply is less than 1.
  **d** decrease the factor's income if the elasticity of factor supply is less than 1.
  **e** always decrease the factor's income.

**3** The change in total revenue resulting from employing an additional unit of capital is the
  **a** marginal product of capital.
  **b** marginal revenue of capital.
  **c** marginal revenue cost of capital.
  **d** marginal revenue product of capital.
  **e** average revenue product of capital.

**4** When a firm is a price-taker in the labour market, its marginal revenue product of labour curve is also its
  **a** marginal cost curve for labour.
  **b** demand curve for labour.
  **c** supply curve of labour.
  **d** supply curve of output.
  **e** average revenue curve.

**5** A profit-maximizing firm will continue to hire units of a variable factor of production until the
  **a** marginal cost of the factor equals its marginal product.
  **b** marginal cost of the factor equals its average revenue product.
  **c** average cost of the factor equals its marginal revenue product.
  **d** marginal cost of the factor equals its marginal revenue product.
  **e** factor's marginal revenue product equals zero.

**6** Suppose a profit-maximizing firm hires labour in a competitive labour market. If the marginal revenue product of labour is greater than the wage, the firm should
  **a** increase the wage rate.
  **b** decrease the wage rate.
  **c** increase the quantity of labour it hires.
  **d** decrease the quantity of labour it hires.
  **e** shift to a more labour-intensive production process.

**7** The demand curve for a factor of production will shift to the right as a result of
  **a** a decrease in the price of the factor.
  **b** an increase in the price of the factor.
  **c** a decrease in the price of a substitute factor.
  **d** an increase in the price of a substitute factor.
  **e** a decrease in the price of output.

**8** A technological change that causes an increase in the marginal product of labour will shift
  **a** the labour demand curve to the left.
  **b** the labour demand curve to the right.
  **c** the labour supply curve to the left.
  **d** the labour supply curve to the right.
  **e** **b** and **d**.

**9** Other things remaining the same, the larger the proportion of total cost coming from labour, the
  **a** more elastic is the demand for labour.
  **b** less elastic is the demand for labour.
  **c** more elastic is the supply of labour.
  **d** less elastic is the supply of labour.
  **e** lower is the demand for labour.

**10** If the wage rate increases, the *substitution* effect will give a household an incentive to
  **a** raise its reservation wage.
  **b** increase its non-market activity and decrease its market activity.
  **c** increase its market activity and decrease its non-market activity.
  **d** increase both market and non-market activity.
  **e** decrease both market and non-market activity.

**11** If the wage rate increases, the *income* effect will give a household an incentive to
  **a** raise its reservation wage.
  **b** increase its non-market activity and decrease its market activity.
  **c** increase its market activity and decrease its non-market activity.

**d** increase both market and non-market activity.

**e** decrease both market and non-market activity.

**12** If the desire for leisure increased, the wage rate would
**a** rise and the quantity of labour hired would fall.
**b** rise and the quantity of labour hired would rise.
**c** fall and the quantity of labour hired would fall.
**d** fall and the quantity of labour hired would rise.
**e** fall and the quantity of labour demanded would rise.

**13** Economic rent is the
**a** price paid for the use of a hectare of land.
**b** price paid for the use of a unit of capital.
**c** income required to induce a given quantity of a factor of production to be supplied.
**d** income received that is above the amount required to induce a given quantity of a factor of production to be supplied.
**e** transfer earnings of a factor of production.

**14** Consider the supply schedule of a factor of production given in Table 14.1. If 4 units of the factor are supplied at a price of £8 per unit, what are the transfer earnings?
**a** £8
**b** £12
**c** £20
**d** £32
**e** none of the above

Table 14.1

| Price of a factor (pounds) | Quantity of factor supplied |
| --- | --- |
| 2 | 1 |
| 4 | 2 |
| 6 | 3 |
| 8 | 4 |
| 10 | 5 |

**15** Consider the supply schedule of a factor of production given in Table 14.1. If 4 units of the factor are supplied at a price of £8 per unit, what is the economic rent?
**a** £8
**b** £12

**c** £20
**d** £32
**e** none of the above

## SHORT ANSWER

**1** Why will an increase in the supply of a factor of production result in an increase in income if the demand for the factor has elasticity greater than 1, and result in a decrease in income if the elasticity of demand for the factor is less than 1?

**2** Why is the demand for a factor of production given by its marginal revenue product curve?

**3** Discuss the substitution and income effects on the quantity of labour supplied if the wage rate *decreases*.

**4** Are prices of retail goods in central London high because rents are high, or are rents high because prices are high? Explain.

**5** Read the *Economics in History* extract and summarize Malthus's views on population. Do you think that he was right?

## PROBLEMS

**1** Table 14.2 gives the total and marginal product schedules for a firm that sells its output in a competitive market and buys labour in a competitive market. Initially the price at which the firm can sell any level of output is £5 per unit and the wage rate at which it can purchase any quantity of labour is £15 per unit.
**a** Complete the first two blank columns in Table 14.2 by computing the $TR$ and $MRP_L$ corresponding to price of output = £5.
**b** The text informs us that the values obtained for the marginal revenue product of labour ($MRP_L$) are the same when they are computed by either of the following formulae:

$$MRP_L = \Delta TR/\Delta L$$
$$MRP_L = MR \times MP_L$$

where $\Delta TR$ = the change in total revenue, $\Delta L$ = the change in labour, $MR$ = marginal revenue and $MP_L$ = marginal product of labour. Show that these two formulae are equivalent for the case when the quantity of labour changes from 1 to 2 units.

**Table 14.2**

| Quantity of labour (L) (workers) | Output (Q) (units per hour) | Marginal product of labour $(MP_L = \Delta Q/\Delta L)$ (units per worker) | Total revenue $(TR = £5 \times Q)$ (pounds per hour) | Marginal revenue product $(MRP = \Delta TR/L)$ (pounds per worker) | Total revenue $(TR = £3 \times Q)$ (pounds per hour) | Marginal revenue product $(MRP_L = TR/L)$ (pounds per worker) |
|---|---|---|---|---|---|---|
| 0 | 0 | | | | | |
| | | ...12 | | | | |
| 1 | 12 | | | | | |
| | | ...10 | | | | |
| 2 | 22 | | | | | |
| | | ...8 | | | | |
| 3 | 30 | | | | | |
| | | ...6 | | | | |
| 4 | 36 | | | | | |
| | | ...4 | | | | |
| 5 | 40 | | | | | |
| | | ...2 | | | | |
| 6 | 42 | | | | | |

c If the firm maximizes profit, what quantity of labour will it hire? How much output will it produce?

d If total fixed cost is £125, what is the amount of profit?

e What is its profit if the firm hires one more unit of labour than the profit-maximizing quantity? One less unit of labour than the profit-maximizing quantity?

f Draw a graph of the demand for labour and the supply of labour and illustrate labour market equilibrium.

2 Now suppose that the market demand for the output of the firm in Problem 1 decreases, causing the price of output to decrease to £3 per unit. The total and marginal product schedules remain unchanged.

a Complete the last two blank columns in Table 14.2 by computing the *TR* and *MRP_L* corresponding to price of output = £3.

b If the wage remains at £15 per unit of labour, what is the profit-maximizing quantity of labour that the firm will hire? How much output will it produce?

c Total fixed cost continues to be £125. What is the amount of profit?

d Will the firm shut down in the short run? Explain.

e Draw a new graph of the new labour market equilibrium.

3 The price of output for the firm in Problem 2 remains at £3 but the wage now rises to £21 per unit of labour. The total and marginal product schedules remain unchanged.

a What happens to the demand curve for labour (the *MRP* of labour curve)?

b Under these circumstances, what is the profit-maximizing quantity of labour that the firm will hire? How much output will it produce?

c Total fixed cost continues to be £125. What is the amount of profit?

d Draw a graph of the labour market equilibrium.

## DISCUSSION QUESTION

1 What is the point of discussing the supply of labour when most people have no choice about the number of hours that they work?

## DATA QUESTIONS

### Increased Supply of Women in the Labour Force

**Increased real wages**   Real wages for women have been rising since World War II. Since 1970, part of this rise has been a consequence of the Equal Pay Act.

**Changes in demographic trends**   Labour force participation rates are higher for single women. In the United Kingdom, 40 per cent of all marriages end in divorce, and married women may choose to enter the labour market as a cushion against the financial loss of unearned income after divorce. In addition, the mean age of marriage has increased.

**Changes in the value of non-market time**   Labour-saving devices, supermarket dinners and shops full of commodities mean that women do not have to devote as much time to non-market work. Market goods have been substituted for non-market time at low prices.

**Changes in male earnings** A rise in male earnings might reduce the participation of women as their unearned income will rise. However, this effect is over-ridden by the rise in women's earnings.

**Keeping up with the Jones's** As individuals require an ever rising standard of living and equate that with increased consumption of market commodities, the value of non-market time falls.

*Source*: Adapted from Anna Palmer, 'Changes in Labour Force Participation', in G.B.J. Atkinson (ed),

*Developments in Economics*, **13**, 1997, Causeway Press.

**1** Why do you think women's real wages have been rising?

**2** How do non-market activities affect market activities?

**3** The extract deals with the supply of women's labour. What factors do you think might affect the demand for women's labour?

# ANSWERS

## CONCEPT REVIEW

**1** wages; interest; rent

**2** increase; large; small

**3** derived

**4** hiring; labour; increase

**5** negatively; marginal revenue product

**6** right; right

**7** higher; more

**8** reservation

**9** decrease; increase

**10** economic rent; transfer

## TRUE OR FALSE

**1 F** Fall in price leads to rise in income.

**2 T** Income is price times quantity.

**3 T** A specific example of the $MR = MC$ rule.

**4 F** Same as $MRP$ curve.

**5 T** The $MRP$ curve is the firm's demand for labour curve.

**6 T** Definition.

**7 F** Tends to be elastic.

**8 T** Steep $MRP$ curve means inelastic demand.

**9 F** Short-run elasticity of demand for labour depends on elasticity of demand for the product, labour intensity and slope of marginal product curve – capital cannot be substituted in short run.

**10 T** People will substitute work for leisure.

**11 T** Definition. Leisure is a normal good.

**12 T** Definition.

## MULTIPLE CHOICE

**1 d** Definition.

**2 b** Increase in factor of production with inelastic demand leads to increase in $PF \times QF$.

**3 d** Revenue from selling marginal product of capital.

**4 b** Shows quantity of labour hired at each wage rate.

**5 d** Where supply curve of factor to firm *(MC)* intersects with demand curve for factor *(MRP)*.

**6 c** Hiring more labour leads to more profit since $MRP > MC$. Firm cannot change wage.

**7 d** Firm demands more of the now relatively cheaper factor. **a** and **b** move along curve, **e** shifts curve leftward.

**8 b** Definition.

**9 a** Increase in wage leads to greater increase in total costs and increase in price of product. This leads to greater fall in sales and labour hired.

**10 c** Substitute work for leisure.

**11 b** Consume more normal goods including leisure, which entails working less.

**12 a** Labour supply would shift leftward.

**13 d** Definition. Price paid for land use is rent.

**14 c** £2 + £4 + £6 + £8.

**15 b** Total income (£32 = 4 × £8) minus transfer earnings (£20).

# SHORT ANSWER

**1** An increase in the supply of a factor of production will cause the price of the factor to decrease and the quantity of the factor hired to increase. Income received by the factor is equal to the price of the factor times the quantity hired. If the percentage increase in the quantity hired is greater than the percentage decrease in price (if the elasticity of demand for the factor is greater than 1), income will increase. Similarly, if the percentage increase in the quantity hired is less than the percentage decrease in price (if the elasticity of demand for the factor is less than 1), income will decrease.

**2** The marginal revenue product curve for a factor of production gives its demand curve because firms are profit maximizers. As a consequence, they will hire an additional unit of a factor of production until the marginal cost of the factor (its price) is equal to the additional revenue from its use (its *MRP*). Thus the quantity of the factor demanded at each price (the demand curve) is given by the *MRP* curve.

**3** If the wage rate decreases, households will have a tendency to shift from work to leisure (the substitution effect), thus reducing the quantity of labour supplied. The lower wage also decreases the household's income, causing the household to reduce its demand for leisure and other normal goods (the income effect) and thus increasing the quantity of labour supplied.

**4** Rents are high because prices are high. Land in central London has a perfectly inelastic supply, so the price of land (its rent) is determined entirely by demand for the land.

Demand is high because shop owners know that the prime retail location will allow them to charge higher prices and potentially earn higher profits than in other locations.

**5** Malthus argued that, if unchecked, population would grow at a geometric rate while food would grow only arithmetically. Hence the result would be wars, famines and plagues. Supporters of Malthus argue that these have only been prevented by such factors as the development of new land, for example, in the United States, and new techniques of food production. However, these cannot continue indefinitely. Critics argue that the determinants of population growth are more complex than Malthus supposed; for example, the growth of education and women's earnings has led to a fall in the number of births per woman.

# PROBLEMS

**1 a** The completed columns for *TR* and $MRP_L$ corresponding to price of output = £5 are shown in Table 14.3. The values for *TR* are obtained by multiplying the quantity of output by the price of output (£5). The values for $MRP_L$ between any two quantities of labour are obtained by dividing the change in *TR* by the change in quantity of labour.

**Table 14.3**

| Quantity of labour (L) (workers) | Output (Q) (units per hour) | Marginal product of labour $(MP_L = \Delta Q/\Delta L)$ (units per worker) | Total revenue $(TR = £5 \times Q)$ (pounds per hour) | Marginal revenue product $(MRP = \Delta TR/L)$ (pounds per worker) | Total revenue $(TR = £3 \times Q)$ (pounds per hour) | Marginal revenue product $(MRP_L = TR/L)$ (pounds per worker) |
|---|---|---|---|---|---|---|
| 0 | 0 |  | 0 |  | 0 |  |
|  |  | ...12 |  | ...60 |  | ...36 |
| 1 | 12 |  | 60 |  | 36 |  |
|  |  | ...10 |  | ...50 |  | ...30 |
| 2 | 22 |  | 110 |  | 66 |  |
|  |  | ...8 |  | ...40 |  | ...24 |
| 3 | 30 |  | 150 |  | 90 |  |
|  |  | ...6 |  | ...30 |  | ...18 |
| 4 | 36 |  | 180 |  | 108 |  |
|  |  | ...4 |  | ...20 |  | ...12 |
| 5 | 40 |  | 200 |  | 120 |  |
|  |  | ...2 |  | ...10 |  | ...6 |
| 6 | 42 |  | 210 |  | 126 |  |

**b** From **a**, the formula $MRP_L = TR/L$ yields a marginal revenue product of labour of 60 when the quantity of labour changes from 1 to 2 units. To confirm that the second formula ($MRP_L = MR \times MP_L$) gives the same answer when the quantity of labour changes from 1 to 2 units, substitute in the values for *MR* (£5, the price of an additional unit of output) and $MP_L$ (12 units of output). This yields the same marginal revenue product of labour as above; £5 × 12 units = £60.

**c** The firm maximizes profit by hiring labour up to the point where the *MRP* of labour is equal to the marginal cost of labour (the wage rate). That point occurs at 5 units of labour. The *MRP* of moving from 4 to 5 units of labour is 20, and the *MRP* of moving from 5 to 6 units of labour is 10. Thus by interpolation the *MRP* at exactly 5 units of labour is 15 (midway between 20 and 10). So when 5 units of labour are hired, the *MRP* of labour is equal to the wage rate (£15). Given that 5 units of labour are hired, the profit-maximizing output will be 40 units (from Table 14.3).

**d** To calculate profit, we must first calculate total revenue and then subtract total cost. Total revenue is £200 (40 units of output × £5 per unit) and total cost is also £200 – the sum of total variable (labour) cost of £75 (5 units of labour × £15 per unit) and total fixed cost of £125. Thus profit is zero.

e If the firm hires one more unit of labour (6 units), total revenue will be £210 (42 units of output × the £5 price). Total cost will be the £125 fixed cost plus £90 in total variable cost (6 units of labour × the £15 wage rate) or £215. Thus profit will be a negative £5 (a £5 loss).

If the firm hires one less unit of labour (4 units), total revenue will be £180 (36 units of output × the £5 price). Total cost will be the £125 fixed cost plus £60 in total variable cost (4 units of labour × the £15 wage rate) or £185. Thus profit will be a negative £5 (a £5 loss).

f The graph of labour market equilibrium appears in Figure 14.1. The demand for labour is given by the firm's $MRP_L$ curve which is labelled $D_0$ ($D_1$ will be discussed in Problem 2).

Notice that the values for $MRP$ are plotted midway between the corresponding quantities of labour. For example, $MRP$ of 60 is plotted midway between 1 and 2 units of labour.

Since the firm purchases labour in a perfectly competitive labour market, the supply of labour to the firm is perfectly elastic at the market wage rate. The labour supply curve is labelled $W$ = £15. The equilibrium is at the intersection of these curves, and corresponds to a wage rate of £15 and a quantity of labour hired of 5 units.

---

**Figure 14.1**

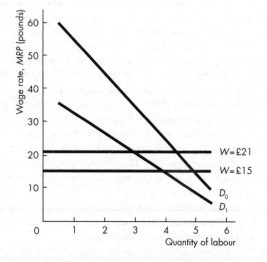

**2 a** The completed columns for $TR$ and $MRP_L$ corresponding to price of output = £3 are shown in Table 14.3. The values for $TR$ are obtained by multiplying

the quantity of output by the price of output (£3). The values for $MRP_L$ between any two quantities of labour are obtained by dividing the change in $TR$ by the change in quantity of labour.

**b** If the wage rate remains at £15, the profit-maximizing quantity of labour will fall to 4 units since $MRP_L$ equals the wage rate at 4 units of labour. The $MRP$ of moving from 3 to 4 units of labour is 18, and the $MRP$ of moving from 4 to 5 units of labour is 12. Thus by interpolation the $MRP$ at exactly 4 units of labour is 15 (midway between 18 and 12). Given that 4 units of labour are employed, the profit-maximizing output will be 36 units (from Table 14.3).

**c** Profit equals total revenue minus total cost. Total revenue is £108 (36 units of output × £3 per unit) and total cost is £185 – the sum of total variable (labour) cost of £60 (4 units of labour × £15 per unit) and total fixed cost of £125. Thus profit is –£77, or a loss of £77.

**d** The firm will not shut down since total revenue (£108) is enough to cover total variable cost (£60) and part of fixed cost. If the firm decided to shut down, it would lose the £125 of fixed cost rather than just £77.

**e** The graph of labour market equilibrium appears in Fig. 14.1. The new demand for labour is given by the firm's new $MRP_L$ curve, which is labelled $D_1$. The supply of labour has not changed; it continues to be horizontal at £15, the competitive market wage. The new equilibrium is at the intersection of these curves, and corresponds to a wage rate of £15 and a quantity of labour hired of 4 units.

**3 a** Since marginal revenue and the marginal product of labour are unaffected by a change in the wage rate, the demand curve for labour (the $MRP$ of labour) will remain at $D_1$.

**b** If the wage rate rises to £21, the profit-maximizing quantity of labour will fall to 3 units since $MRP_L$ equals the wage rate at 3 units of labour. Given that 3 units of labour are employed, the profit-maximizing output will be 30 units (from Table 14.3).

**c** Profit equals total revenue minus total cost. Total revenue is £90 (30 units of output × £3 per unit) and total cost is £188 – the sum of total variable (labour) cost of £63 (3 units of labour × £21 per unit) and total fixed cost of £125. Thus profit is –£98, or a loss of £98.

**d** See Figure 14.1. The relevant demand for labour curve continues to be $D_1$, but the labour supply curve reflects the rise in the competitive wage rate; it is now horizontal at a wage rate of £21 (labelled $W$ = £21). The equilibrium is at the intersection of these curves and corresponds to a wage rate of £21 and a quantity of labour hired of 3 units.

# DISCUSSION QUESTION

**1** While it is true that some people have little choice over the number of hours they work, others do have a choice. Many employers allow overtime and there are part-time jobs where the hours are flexible, and some people have more than one part-time job. Self-employed people can also extend the hours that they work.

# DATA QUESTIONS

**1** Women's real wages have been rising for a number of reasons. One is that real wages as a whole have been rising (for example, because of increased technology), and women have benefited from this as well as men. In addition, higher education is associated with higher incomes, and women's educational standards have been rising, leading to higher wages. Equal pay legislation has also had an effect. Lastly, there has been increased demand for the goods produced and services provided by women, and this increased demand has led to higher wages. Despite this, women's wages remain below those of men.

**2** Non-market activities, such as leisure, can have a strong effect on market activities, for example, a rise in incomes increases the demand for leisure. This will increase the demand for goods and services in the leisure industry, and it may also cause people to choose to do less work and to take more leisure.

**3** A number of factors have affected the demand for women's labour. One is that the demand for labour is a derived demand, so as the demand for goods rises, so does demand for labour. In particular, there has been a rise in the importance of services, and many jobs in these areas are considered to be women's jobs. This is reinforced by the rise in part-time jobs, predominantly done by women. Lastly, the increased education of women has narrowed the gap between educated women and men and enabled many women to take jobs which were previously held by educated men.

# Chapter 15  Labour Markets

---

## Chapter in Perspective, Text Pages 370–392

Labour markets play an important role in the economic well-being of almost every household since household income is determined largely by the operation of these markets. This chapter looks more carefully at labour markets to explain how wage rates and employment levels are determined. We investigate why some groups earn more than other groups: why skilled workers earn more than unskilled workers; why union workers earn more than non-union workers; why, on average, men earn more than women; and why there are differences in the average earnings of people from different ethnic groups.

---

## Helpful Hints

**1** This chapter introduces the concept of a monopsonist, a firm that is the only buyer in a market such as labour, for example. The monopsonist faces an upward-sloping supply of labour curve and, as a result, its marginal cost of labour curve (*MCL*) is different from the labour supply curve.

The monopoly, as the only seller in an output market, faces a downward-sloping demand curve. The marginal revenue from the sale of an additional unit of output is *less* than the selling price because the monopoly must *lower* the price on all previous units as well. Thus the *MR* curve lies *below* the demand curve for the monopoly. For the monopsonist in a labour market, the marginal cost of hiring an additional unit of labour is *higher* than the wage because the monopsonist must *raise* the wage on all previous units of labour as well. Thus the *MCL* curve lies *above* the supply of labour curve for the monopsonist.

**2** A particular labour market may *not* establish a wage rate and a level of employment in the simple sense of the intersection of demand and supply curves. The broader notion of labour market equilibrium includes determination of quantity and of the type of compensation scheme, of which time rates of pay (wage rates) are only one possibility. Equilibrium occurs when the market is at rest in the sense that no worker or firm has an incentive to change.

## Key Figures and Table

**Figure 15.1  Skill Differentials, text page 373**
Different workers receive different wages depending on their level of skill. This figure shows how differences in wages can be explained using the model of competitive labour markets. Part (a) shows that the demand for skilled labour is higher than the demand for unskilled labour because skilled labour has a

higher marginal revenue product. The vertical distance between the two demand curves gives the difference in marginal revenue product, which is the marginal revenue product of the skill.

Part (b) gives the supply curves for skilled and unskilled labour. It illustrates that the supply curve for skilled labour will lie above the supply curve for unskilled labour because skills are costly to obtain. As a result, skilled labour must receive a higher wage in order to induce workers to obtain the skill. The vertical distance between the two labour supply curves gives the required additional wage.

Part (c) puts together the demand and supply curves from parts (a) and (b) in order to look at the equilibrium wage rate for each type of labour. Not surprisingly, the equilibrium wage rate for skilled workers will be higher than that for unskilled workers.

### Figure 15.8 Discrimination, text page 383

This figure illustrates how discrimination will affect wage rates and employment. Part (a) shows that discrimination against a particular group of workers (in this case, black female investment advisers) will reduce wages and employment below what they would have been without discrimination. The prejudice of customers makes the marginal revenue product of the workers who are discriminated against $(MRP_{DA})$ lower than the marginal revenue product without discrimination $(MRP)$.

Part (b) shows that customer prejudice in favour of a particular group (in this case, white male investment advisers) makes the marginal revenue product of the workers who are discriminated in favour of $(MRP_{DF})$ higher than the marginal revenue product without discrimination. This will raise wages and employment above what they would have been without discrimination.

### Table 15.1 A Compact Glossary on Labour Relations, text page 375

This table conveniently brings together much of the terminology associated with trade unions. It provides definitions of terms used frequently in analysing the operation of unions in the economy.

# SELF-TEST

## CONCEPT REVIEW

1 The demand curve for skilled labour lies _____ the demand curve for unskilled labour, because the marginal revenue product of skilled workers is _____ than that of unskilled workers. The supply curve for skilled labour lies _____ the supply curve for unskilled labour, because skills are costly to acquire.

2 Education and training can be viewed as investments in _____ capital. The value of that capital is the _____ _____ of the extra future earnings that result from the increased education or training.

3 A market in which there is only one buyer is called _____ . If there is only one firm that buys labour, the wage rate will be _____ than the marginal cost of labour. A situation in which a single seller of labour, such as a union, faces a single buyer of labour is called _____ monopoly.

4 Four possible explanations of wage differentials between the sexes are discussed in Chapter 15. The first is concerned with job types. The second is discrimination. The third is that the two groups have differences in _____ capital. The fourth is that there are differences in the degree of _____ in market and non-market activities.

5 A formula for calculating a person's income is called a(n) _____ rule. If the formula is based solely on the number of hours the person works, it is called a(n) _____ rate. If the formula is based on the amount of output the worker produces it is called a(n) _____ rate. A rule that allocates a certain fraction of the firm's profit to employees is called _____ - _____ .

**6** Often, either worker effort or worker output are difficult, if not impossible, to observe. An individual who sets a rule for compensating workers, which motivates the worker to choose activities advantageous to the individual is called a(n) _____ . Each worker in such a situation is called a(n) _____ .

# TRUE OR FALSE

___ **1** The marginal revenue product of unskilled workers is lower than that of skilled workers.

___ **2** The vertical distance between the labour supply curves for skilled and unskilled workers is the marginal revenue product of the skill.

___ **3** The larger the marginal revenue product of the skill and the more costly it is to acquire, the smaller is the wage differential between skilled and unskilled workers.

___ **4** Unions support minimum wage laws in part because they increase the cost of unskilled labour, a substitute for skilled union labour.

___ **5** A firm that is a monopsonist in the labour market must compete with other firms for the labour it hires.

___ **6** The more elastic is labour supply, the less opportunity a monopsonist has to make an economic profit.

___ **7** In a monopsonistic labour market, the introduction of a minimum wage that is above the current wage will raise the wage but reduce employment.

___ **8** The evidence suggests that, after allowing for the effects of skill differentials, union workers earn no more than non-union workers.

___ **9** Economic theory tells us that discrimination in employment will result in wage differentials.

___ **10** If males on average earn more than females, we can conclude that there must be discrimination.

# MULTIPLE CHOICE

**1** Which of the following is *not* a reason why the wage of skilled workers exceeds the wage of unskilled workers?
   **a** The market for skilled workers is more competitive than the market for unskilled labour.
   **b** The marginal revenue product of skilled workers is greater than that of unskilled workers.
   **c** The cost of training skilled workers is greater than the cost of training unskilled workers.
   **d** Skilled workers have acquired more human capital than unskilled workers.
   **e** The demand curve for skilled workers lies to the right of the demand curve for unskilled workers.

**2** The economic value of the increase in human capital owing to additional education is
   **a** the money cost of the additional education.
   **b** the money cost of the additional education plus forgone earnings.
   **c** the present value of all expected future earnings.
   **d** the present value of all extra expected future earnings that are the result of the additional education.
   **e** none of the above.

**3** Which of the following would unions be *least* likely to support?
   **a** increasing the legal minimum wage
   **b** restricting immigration
   **c** encouraging imports
   **d** increasing demand for the goods their workers produce
   **e** increasing the marginal product of union labour

**4** The most important way in which unions increase wages is by
   **a** increasing the marginal (physical) product of labour.
   **b** increasing the marginal revenue product of labour.
   **c** increasing the demand for labour.
   **d** decreasing the supply of labour.
   **e** increasing the marginal cost of labour.

**5** Figure 15.1 illustrates a monopsonist in the labour market (*MCL* = marginal cost of labour). The profit-maximizing wage rate and quantity of labour hired will be
   **a** $4 per hour and 800 hours of labour.

**b** £4 per hour and 400 hours of labour.
**c** £7 per hour and 600 hours of labour.
**d** £9 per hour and 400 hours of labour.
**e** none of the above.

**Figure 15.1**

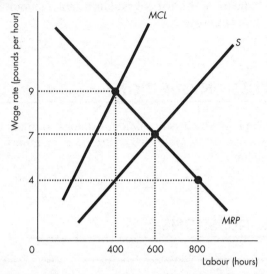

**6** If the labour market illustrated in Fig. 15.1 became competitive, the equilibrium wage rate and quantity of labour hired would be
**a** £4 per hour and 800 hours of labour.
**b** £4 per hour and 400 hours of labour.
**c** £7 per hour and 600 hours of labour.
**d** £9 per hour and 400 hours of labour.
**e** none of the above.

**7** Wage differentials between males and females can be explained by
**a** occupational differences.
**b** human capital differences.
**c** degree of specialization differences.
**d** discrimination.
**e** all of the above.

**8** Which of the following cases is most likely to be characterized by a time rate of pay?
**a** Individual effort is readily observed but individual contribution to output is not.
**b** Individual effort is not readily observed but individual contribution to output is.
**c** Neither individual effort nor individual contribution to output is readily observable.
**d** Monitoring costs are high.
**e** None of the above statements is most likely.

## SHORT ANSWER

**1** Members of trade unions earn wages well above the minimum wage. Even so, why is it in the interest of a union to support increases in the legal minimum wage?

**2** Bob and Sue form a household. They have decided that Sue will fully specialize in market activity and Bob will pursue activities both in the job market and in the household. If most households are like Bob and Sue, why would the result be a difference between the earnings of men and women, even if there is no discrimination?

**3** Many large firms are owned by a group of shareholders who hire managers to run the firm. Why is profit-sharing a good compensation scheme for top management in such a firm?

**4** In the *Reading Between the Lines* article, why do you think that the author used median wages as a measure of average?

## PROBLEMS

**1** Figure 15.2 shows the demand and supply of skilled and unskilled labour. $S_U$ and $S_S$ are the supply curves for unskilled and skilled workers, respectively, and $D_U$ and $D_S$ are the demand curves for unskilled and skilled workers, respectively.

**Figure 15.2**

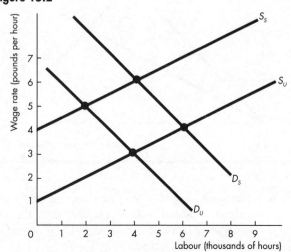

**a** What is the marginal revenue product of skill if 5,000 hours of each kind of labour are hired?

**b** What is the amount of extra compensation per hour required to induce the acquisition of skill at the same level of hiring?

**c** What are the equilibrium wage and quantity of labour in the market for skilled labour?

**d** What are the equilibrium wage and quantity of labour in the market for unskilled labour?

**2** Yuri has an opportunity to increase his human capital by taking a training course that will raise his income by £100 every year for the rest of his life. Assume that there are no other benefits of the course. The cost of the course is £1,200 and Yuri's best alternative investment pays an interest rate of 10 per cent per year for the rest of his life. Should Yuri pay the £1,200 and take the course? Explain.

**3** Figure 15.3 illustrates a profit-maximizing monopsonist in the labour market.

**Figure 15.3**

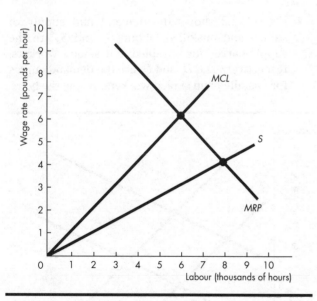

**a** What wage rate will the monopsonist pay and how much labour will be employed? What is the value of labour's marginal revenue product at this level of employment?

**b** If this were a competitive labour market with the same marginal revenue product curve, what would the equilibrium wage rate and the level of employment be?

**c** Now suppose the government imposes a minimum wage of £4 per hour. What wage rate will the monopsonist pay and how much labour will be employed?

## DISCUSSION QUESTION

**1** Explain why it is possible for unions to lower the wages of workers who are not members of unions.

## DATA QUESTIONS

**Table 15.1 Wages in Non-agricultural Activities: Earnings Per Hour (National Currencies)**

| | | 1987 | 1989 | 1991 | 1993 |
|---|---|---|---|---|---|
| Denmark | M | 102 | 112 | 121 | – |
| | F | 83 | 93 | 101 | – |
| France | M | 42 | 45 | 49 | 53 |
| | F | 34 | 36 | 40 | 42 |
| Germany | M | 19 | 20 | 22 | 25 |
| | F | 14 | 15 | 17 | 18 |
| Netherlands | M | 21 | 22 | 24 | 25 |
| | F | 16 | 17 | 18 | 20 |
| United Kingdom | M | 4.2 | 4.8 | 5.7 | 6.2 |
| | F | 2.9 | 3.4 | 4.0 | 4.4 |

*Source: Yearbook of Labour Statistics 1995*, © International Labour Organisation, Geneva.

**1** Analyse these statistics and comment on your results, noting in particular:

**a** In which countries is the difference between male and female pay

**i** the greatest?

**ii** the least?

**b** What reasons do you think explain these differences?

**2** Why, on average, do men earn more than women?

# ANSWERS

## CONCEPT REVIEW

**1** above; greater; above

**2** human; present value

**3** monopsonist; lower; bilateral

**4** human; specialization

**5** compensation; time; piece; profit-sharing

**6** principal; agent

## TRUE OR FALSE

**1 T** Demand for unskilled workers is to the left of the demand for skilled workers.

**2 F** Vertical distance is compensation for cost of acquiring skill.

**3 F** The larger is the wage differential.

**4 T** Increase in the price of a substitute leads to rise in demand for union labour.

**5 F** Definition. Monopsonist is sole buyer.

**6 T** Draw diagram to verify this.

**7 F** True for competitive market.

**8 F** Union members earn more than non-union members with similar skills.

**9 T** Discrimination means that those discriminated against earn less.

**10 F** Differences may be owing to discrimination, human capital differences and/or specialization.

## MULTIPLE CHOICE

**1 a** Wage differences are not owing to competitive differences. In any case, an increase in competitiveness would lead to a fall in skilled wages.

**2 d** Return on investment in additional education.

**3 c** Increase in imports would lead to a fall in sales of domestic products and hence in demand for domestic labour.

**4 d** **a**, **b** and **c** are indirect ways.

**5 b** Quantity of labour is where *MCL* intersects *MRP*. Then the lowest wage required for labour to supply that quantity (on supply curve).

**6 c** Where *S* intersects *MRP*.

**7 e** All can contribute to differentials.

**8 a** Lazy individuals can be sacked so no need to pay by results.

## SHORT ANSWER

**1** An increase in the minimum wage will increase the cost of hiring unskilled labour, which will tend to increase the demand for skilled labour; which is a substitute.

**2** If Sue specializes in market activity while Bob is diversified, it is likely that Sue's earning ability will exceed Bob's owing to the gains from her specialization. If most households followed this pattern of specialization, the income of women would exceed that of men even without discrimination.

**3** In this case the owners (shareholders) are the principals and the top managers are the agents. Neither the effort nor the output of the managers can be easily monitored. But since the decisions of managers have a direct and significant bearing on the profit of the firm, their incentive is to make decisions that maximize profit if they share in any increase in profit through a profit-sharing compensation scheme.

**4** The usual measure of average is the mean, which in this case would involve dividing the total earnings of women executives by their number. However, this method is often unsuitable for measuring average earnings since it can give too much influence to a few extremes; for example, in this case one or two women earning millions would distort the picture. On the other hand, calculating the median involves finding the middle number; for example, the median of 3, 3, 4, 4, 10 is 4. Hence the median is often used to measure average wages.

## PROBLEMS

**1 a** The marginal revenue product of skill is the difference between the marginal revenue products of skilled versus unskilled labour; the vertical distance between the demand curves for skilled and unskilled labour. In Fig. 15.2, the marginal revenue product of skill is £3 per hour when 5,000 hours of each kind of labour are employed.

**b** Since labour supply curves give the minimum compensation workers are willing to accept in return for supplying a given quantity of labour, the extra compensation for skill is the vertical distance between the supply curves of skilled and unskilled labour. At 5,000 hours of employment for both kinds of labour, this is £3 per hour.

**c** In equilibrium in the market for skilled labour, the wage rate will be £6 per hour and employment will be 4,000 hours of labour. This occurs at the intersection of the $D_S$ and $S_S$ curves.

**d** In equilibrium in the market for unskilled labour, the wage rate will be £3 per hour and employment will be 4,000 hours of labour. This occurs at the intersection of the $D_U$ and $S_U$ curves.

**2** Yuri should take the course only if the value of the course exceeds the cost of the course. The cost of the course is £1,200 while the value of the course is the present value of the extra £100 in income Yuri can expect to receive each year for the rest of his life. The present value of this income stream is the amount of money which, if invested today at 10 per cent (Yuri's best alternative return), would yield an equivalent stream of income. Thus the present value of the extra income is £1,000. Since this is less than the cost of the training course, Yuri should not take it.

**3 a** The profit-maximizing monopsonist will hire additional labour up to the point where the marginal cost of labour *(MCL)* equals the marginal revenue product of labour *(MRP)*. Referring to Fig. 15.3, this means that the monopsonist will hire 6,000 hours of labour. The wage rate is given by the labour supply curve *S* and, for 6,000 hours of labour, will be £3 per hour. This is less than the £6 per hour marginal revenue product of labour.

**b** In a competitive market, the wage rate would be £4 per hour and 8,000 hours of labour would be employed.

**c** If the government establishes a minimum wage at £4 per hour, the marginal cost of labour to the monopsonist becomes constant at £4 per hour (up to 8,000 hours of labour). Thus equating the marginal cost of labour and the marginal revenue product of labour leads to a wage rate of £4 and 8,000 hours of labour employed.

## DISCUSSION QUESTION

**1** If unions are successful in their demands for higher wages, employers may respond by cutting the quantity of labour that they employ. The unemployed workers may then migrate to other industries, and this increase in supply may then lead to a fall in wages for these workers, some of whom will not be union members.

## DATA QUESTIONS

**1 a** The overwhelming fact is that in all countries men earn significantly more than women, and that this difference is persistent, despite equal pay legislation.
   **i** The difference (at the end of the period) is greatest in the United Kingdom.
   **ii** Denmark is the country with the least difference.

**b** There are many possible reasons, but one is that Denmark (and to a lesser extent other continental European countries) have social legislation which not only reduces discrimination but also encourages women to obtain human capital and to specialize in occupations that are well paid. The United Kingdom has a high percentage of women workers, but many of these are in low-paying occupations.

**2** The explanations for the lower pay earned by women are: discrimination, differences in human capital and differences in degree of specialization. These are discussed in detail in the main text, pages 381–387, and there is no need to repeat the arguments here.

# Chapter 16 Capital and Natural Resource Markets

---

## Chapter in Perspective, Text Pages 393–415

This chapter continues a more detailed examination of markets for specific factors of production and we expand our understanding of capital and natural resource markets. What determines interest rates and share prices? How are the prices of natural resources determined? Can we rely on market forces to regulate the use of exhaustible resources? These and related issues are discussed in this chapter.

---

## Helpful Hints

**1** A profit-maximizing firm will hire an additional unit of a factor as long as the factor's use adds more to revenue than to cost; in other words, as long as its marginal revenue product ($MRP$) is greater than its marginal cost ($MC$). The profit-maximizing quantity will be the quantity at which the marginal revenue product of a factor is just equal to its marginal cost. Since in a competitive market the marginal cost is the price of the factor ($P_F$), this profit-maximizing condition becomes $MRP = P_F$ in a competitive factor market. This implies that the demand curve for a factor is given by its $MRP$ curve.

**2** The profit-maximizing condition given in Helpful Hint 1 is easy to apply in the case of capital

markets in which capital is rented. The profit-maximizing firm will rent capital up to the point at which the marginal revenue product per rental period is equal to the rental price.

If, however, a firm considers purchasing capital rather than renting it, we must be careful in applying the profit-maximizing condition. The reason is that capital is generally operated over more than one period and will generate marginal revenue products that are distributed over time. The purchase price, however, must be paid now. Therefore, in order to compare the purchase price ($P_F$) with the stream of marginal revenue products, we must compute the present value of that stream.

In the case of capital that will be used over more than one period, the profit-maximizing condition becomes: hire an additional unit of capital

147

until the present value of the stream of marginal revenue products is equal to the price of the unit of capital. Since the net present value is defined as the difference between the present value of the stream of marginal revenue products and the price of the unit of capital, an equivalent condition is: the net present value of the last unit of capital is zero.

**3** Note that financial analysts equate a *rise* in bond prices with a *fall* in interest rates.

## Key Figures

**Figure 16.1 Capital Market Flows, text page 396**
This shows the major participants in capital markets and indicates the directions of interactions among them.

**Figure 16.5 Capital Market Equilibrium, text page 403**
Equilibrium in the capital market is achieved at the interest rate at which the quantity of capital demanded is equal to the quantity of capital supplied. For the example illustrated in this figure, the equilibrium interest rate is 5 per cent and the equilibrium quantity of capital traded is £10 billion.

# SELF-TEST

## CONCEPT REVIEW

**1** There are two broad classes of assets. Those that are paper claims against a household, firm, or government are called _____ assets, and physical capital such as buildings, factories and machinery are called _____ assets.

**2** A _____ market is a market in which company shares are traded. A _____ market is a market in which the bonds or debentures of companies or governments are traded.

**3** A firm maximizes its net worth when the _____ _____ of the marginal revenue product of capital is equal to the price of capital. Thus an increase in the interest rate means that the quantity of capital demanded will _____ .

**4** The quantity of capital supplied depends on the _____ decisions of households. As the interest rate increases, the substitution effect causes a(n) _____ in the quantity of capital supplied by the household; the income effect causes a(n) _____ in the quantity of capital supplied if the household is a net borrower. If the proportion of young people in the population increases, we would expect to see the capital supply curve shift to the _____ .

**5** A takeover occurs when the stock market value of a firm is _____ than the present value of expected future profits from operating the firm. A merger occurs when the two firms involved think that by combining their assets, their combined stock market value will _____ .

**6** Natural resources that can be used only once and not replaced are called _____ natural resources. According to the Hotelling Principle, the market for the stock of such a resource will be in equilibrium when the price of the resource is expected to rise over time, at a rate equal to the _____ _____ .

**7** The price at which it no longer pays to use a natural resource is called its _____ price.

**8** The higher the interest rate, the _____ will be the current price of a natural resource. The higher the marginal revenue product of a natural resource, the _____ will be its current price. The larger the initial stock of a natural resource, the _____ will be its current price.

## TRUE OR FALSE

___ **1** If we add depreciation to net investment, we have gross investment.

**2** Portfolio decisions determine a person's wealth.

**3** The quantity of capital is an example of a flow.

**4** If the price of a unit of capital exceeds the present value of its marginal revenue product, a profit-maximizing firm should buy it.

**5** If the net present value of an investment is positive, a profit-maximizing firm will buy the item.

**6** A new machine that is expected to last one year and, at the end of the year, increase firm revenue by £1,050, sells at a price of £1,000. The firm should buy the machine if the interest rate is 6 per cent.

**7** If a cheap substitute for oil is developed, we would expect to see the choke price for oil decline.

**8** The higher the interest rate, the lower is the current price of a natural resource.

**9** The economic model of exhaustible natural resources implies that the market will provide an automatic incentive to conserve as the resource gets closer to being depleted.

## MULTIPLE CHOICE

**1** Which of the following is a real asset?
  **a** a shovel
  **b** IBM shares
  **c** money
  **d** a General Motors bond
  **e** all of the above

**2** Which of the following is an example of a stock?
  **a** investment
  **b** depreciation
  **c** capital
  **d** income
  **e** none of the above

**3** The decline in the value of capital resulting from its use over time is given by
  **a** the level of saving.
  **b** investment.
  **c** net investment.

  **d** gross investment minus net investment.
  **e** net present value.

**4** Firms that are primarily engaged in taking deposits, making loans and buying securities are called
  **a** brokers.
  **b** financial intermediaries.
  **c** insurance companies.
  **d** monopsonists.
  **e** pension funds.

**5** A profit-maximizing firm will choose to buy an extra unit of capital whenever
  **a** the present value of the flow of marginal revenue product is greater than zero.
  **b** the cost of capital exceeds the present value of the flow of marginal revenue product.
  **c** the cost of capital equals the present value of the flow of marginal revenue product.
  **d** net present value is greater than zero.
  **e** none of the above occurs.

**6** Which of the following would cause the supply of capital curve to shift to the right?
  **a** an increase in the proportion of young households in the population
  **b** an increase in the interest rate
  **c** a decrease in the interest rate
  **d** an increase in average household income
  **e** an increase in the marginal revenue product of capital

**7** A machine that costs £2,000 will generate marginal revenue product of £1,100 at the end of one year and the same amount at the end of two years. What is the net present value of the machine if the rate of interest is 10 per cent?
  **a** −£90.91
  **b** −£49.90
  **c** 0
  **d** £90.91
  **e** £1,909.09

**8** Bond $A$ is more risky than bond $B$. Then, in equilibrium,
  **a** the interest rate on $A$ must be higher than that on $B$.
  **b** the interest rate on $A$ must be lower than that on $B$.
  **c** the interest rate on $A$ must be equal to the interest rate on $B$.

**d** no one will want to buy bond *A*.

**e** only those who prefer risk will buy bond *A*.

**9** A *takeover* of a firm is likely to occur when

  **a** the stock market value of the firm is higher than expected future profit from operating the firm.

  **b** the stock market value of the firm is lower than expected future profit from operating the firm.

  **c** current firm profit is higher than expected future profit from operating the firm.

  **d** current firm profit is lower than expected future profit from operating the firm.

  **e** interest rates are low.

**10** Which of the following is an exhaustible natural resource?

  **a** coal

  **b** land

  **c** water

  **d** trees

  **e** none of the above

**11** The yield on a stock of a natural resource is the

  **a** rate of interest on the loan used to buy the resource.

  **b** marginal revenue product of the resource.

  **c** marginal revenue product of the resource divided by its price.

  **d** marginal revenue product of the resource multiplied by the market interest rate.

  **e** rate of change in the price of the resource.

**12** The current price of a natural resource is higher when

  **a** its marginal revenue product is lower.

  **b** the stock of the resource remaining is larger.

  **c** the interest rate is lower.

  **d** the choke price is lower.

  **e** none of the above is true.

## SHORT ANSWER

**1** Why does the quantity of capital demanded increase when the interest rate falls?

**2** Suppose firms *A* and *B* earned the same amount of profit per share in the most recent year but that the price of a share of stock in firm *A* is higher than for firm *B*.

  **a** What does this imply about the two firms' price–earnings ratios?

  **b** What does this reflect about expected future profits of the two firms?

**3** Why will the market for the stock of an exhaustible natural resource be in equilibrium only if the price of the resource is expected to rise at a rate equal to the rate of interest?

**4** Why does a higher interest rate imply a lower current price of an exhaustible resource?

**5** How would pro-market economists use the information in the *Reading Between the Lines* article to argue that markets can help solve environmental problems?

## PROBLEMS

**1** Larry's Lawn Care began the year with a stock of capital equal to £100,000. The value of that stock of capital depreciated by 12 per cent during the year. Larry also bought £10,000 worth of new lawn care equipment during the year. What was Larry's gross investment during the year? Net investment?

**2** Larry's Lawn Care is considering the purchase of additional lawn mowers. These lawn mowers have a life of 2 years and cost £120 each. Marginal revenue products for each year are given in Table 16.1.

Table 16.1

| Number of lawn mowers | MRP in first year (pounds) | MRP in second year (pounds) | NPV (r = 0.05) (pounds) | NPV (r = 0.10) (pounds) | NPV (r = 0.15) (pounds) |
|---|---|---|---|---|---|
| 1 | 100 | 80 | | | |
| 2 | 80 | 64 | | | |
| 3 | 72 | 62 | | | |

  **a** Complete Table 16.1 by computing net present values *(NPV)* if the interest rate is 5 per cent (*r* = 0.05), 10 per cent (*r* = 0.10), or 15 per cent (*r* = 0.15).

  **b** How many lawn mowers will Larry's purchase if the interest rate is 15 per cent? 10 per cent? 5 per cent?

  **c** Construct an approximate lawn mower demand curve for Larry's by graphically representing the three points identified in **b** and drawing a curve through them.

**3** Gunk is an exhaustible natural resource and we are running out of it. There are only 1,215 barrels of gunk remaining. Table 16.2 gives the marginal revenue product schedule for gunk.

Table 16.2

| Barrels of gunk per year | Marginal revenue product (pounds) |
|---|---|
| 0 | 14.64 |
| 133 | 13.31 |
| 254 | 12.10 |
| 364 | 11.00 |
| 464 | 10.00 |
| 555 | 9.09 |

**a** Draw a graph of the demand curve for gunk (as a flow).
**b** What is the choke price of gunk?
**c** Suppose that the interest rate is 10 per cent.
  **i** What is the current equilibrium price of a barrel of gunk? How did you determine this?
  **ii** If the current year is year 1, complete Table 16.3 for each year until the stock of gunk is exhausted.

Table 16.3

| Year | Price (pounds per barrel of gunk) | Initial stock of gunk (barrels) | Final stock of gunk (barrels) |
|---|---|---|---|
| 1 | | 1,215 | |
| 2 | | | |
| 3 | | | |
| 4 | | | |
| 5 | | | |

## DISCUSSION QUESTION

**1** Why does a higher interest rate lower the price of a bond?

## DATA QUESTIONS

**Controlling the Price of Raw Materials**

The prices of many raw materials such as copper, tin and rubber are highly sensitive to fluctuations in the business cycle because they are used extensively in industries which are subject to considerable fluctuations. In many cases producers – and in some cases consumers – have formed organizations which attempt to fix the price of their product. OPEC is the best known, and in the past it has proved successful in increasing the price of oil. In recent years, however, it has proved less successful. In the case of copper, in 1967 a group of producers formed an organization called Conseil Intergovernmental des Pays Exportateurs de Cuivre (CIPEC). Its aim was to secure an increase in the growth of real earnings of copper exports. As with OPEC, CIPEC faces considerable difficulties in achieving this goal.

**1** Why are the prices of raw materials usually 'highly sensitive to fluctuations in the business cycle'?

**2** What factors determine the price and the quantity of natural resources such as copper?

**3** Why do you think that OPEC has been unable to raise the price of oil in recent years?

# ANSWERS

## CONCEPT REVIEW

**1** financial; real
**2** stock; bond
**3** present value; decrease
**4** savings; increase; decrease; left
**5** lower; increase
**6** exhaustible; interest rate
**7** choke
**8** lower; higher; lower

# TRUE OR FALSE

**1 T** Net investment = gross investment – depreciation.

**2 F** Other factors also influence wealth.

**3 F** Quantity of capital is a stock.

**4 F** Reverse is true.

**5 T** Definition.

**6 F** Present value = £1,050/(1 + 0.06) = £990.56. *NPV* = £990.56 – £1,000 = –£9.44. Since *NPV* is negative, don't buy.

**7 T** Less demand for oil so people would stop using it, even at a lower price.

**8 T** Inverse relationship.

**9 T** Because price will rise.

# MULTIPLE CHOICE

**1 a** Others are financial assets.

**2 c** Others are flows.

**3 d** Equals depreciation.

**4 b** Definition.

**5 d** When the present value of the flow of the marginal product exceeds the cost of capital.

**6 d a** would cause a leftward shift, **b** and **c** movements along supply curve, **e** shifts demand curve.

**7 a** *NPV* = [£1,100/(1.1) + £1,100/(1.1)²] – £2,000.

**8 a** Higher return is necessary to compensate for higher risk if investors are to hold the bond.

**9 b** Definition.

**10 a** Others are non-exhaustible natural resources.

**11 e** Definition.

**12 c** Reverse of **a** and **b** is true. No direct relation between current and choke prices.

# SHORT ANSWER

**1** Profit-maximizing firms will demand capital as long as the present value of the stream of future marginal revenue product from the new capital exceeds the price of the new capital; in other words, as long as its net present value is positive. Since a lower interest rate implies that the present value of any given future stream of marginal revenue product will be larger, the net present value will be positive for a larger quantity of additional capital and thus more capital will be purchased. Therefore the quantity of capital demanded increases as the interest rate falls.

**2 a** The price–earnings ratio is the current price of a share of stock divided by the most recent profits per share. Thus the price–earnings ratio of firm *A*'s stock is greater than the price–earnings ratio of firm *B*'s stock. This implies that, although the recent profits (per share) of the two firms may be the same, future profits (per share) for firm *A* are expected to be higher than those for firm *B*.

**b** The price of a share of stock represents the present value of *expected* future profits, so a higher price implies higher expected future profits.

**3** The yield on the stock of an exhaustible resource is the percentage rate of change in the price of the resource. For the market for the stock of the resource to be in equilibrium, there must be no incentive for movement into or out of the market. This will be the case only if the yield on the stock of the exhaustible resource is the same as the yield on other assets, which is given by the rate of interest.

**4** A rise in interest rates reduces the current price and increases the use.

**5** When demand is higher than supply, the markets' response will be a rise in price. This will have two effects. It will choke off some demand, leading to an increase in demand for substitutes, in this case such materials as steel, plastics and straw. On the supply side, a high price will stimulate production, for example, new plantations and increased use of recycled paper.

# PROBLEMS

**1** Gross investment is £10,000, the amount of the purchase of new capital. Net investment is –£2,000, the amount of gross investment minus depreciation of £12,000.

**2 a** Completed Table 16.1 is shown as Table 16.4. *NPV* is calculated as the present value of the stream of marginal revenue products resulting from an investment minus the cost of the investment. For lawn mowers with a 2-year life, the *NPV* is calculated using the following equation:

$$NPV = \frac{MRP_1}{1 + r} + \frac{MRP_2}{(1 + r)^2} - P_L$$

where $MRP_1$ and $MRP_2$ are the marginal revenue products in the first and second years, respectively, and $P_L$ is the price of a lawn mower. The values of $MRP_1$ and $MRP_2$ are given in Table 16.1 for 1, 2 and 3 lawn mowers and $P_L$ is given as £120. The values for NPV given in Table 16.4 are obtained by substituting these values into the above equation and evaluating the expression for the alternative values of $r$, the interest rate.

## Table 16.4

| Number of lawn mowers | MRP in first year (pounds) | MRP in second year (pounds) | NPV (r = 0.05) (pounds) | NPV (r = 0.10) (pounds) | NPV (r = 0.15) (pounds) |
|---|---|---|---|---|---|
| 1 | 100 | 80 | 47.80 | 37.02 | 27.45 |
| 2 | 80 | 64 | 14.24 | 5.62 | -2.04 |
| 3 | 72 | 62 | 4.81 | -3.31 | -10.51 |

**b** If the interest rate is 15 per cent, only one additional lawn mower will be purchased since the second lawn mower has negative net present value. If the rate of interest is 10 per cent, 2 lawn mowers will be purchased, and if the rate of interest is 5 per cent, 3 lawn mowers will be purchased.

**c** The approximate lawn mower demand curve is illustrated in Fig. 16.1. The curve indicates that, at an interest rate of 15 per cent, 1 lawn mower will be demanded. At an interest rate of 10 per cent, 2 lawn mowers will be demanded, and at an interest rate of 5 per cent, 3 lawn mowers will be demanded.

## Figure 16.1

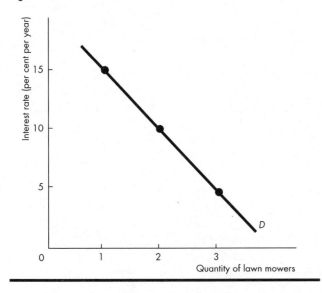

**3 a** The demand curve for gunk is given by the marginal revenue product curve. It is illustrated in Fig. 16.2.

## Figure 16.2

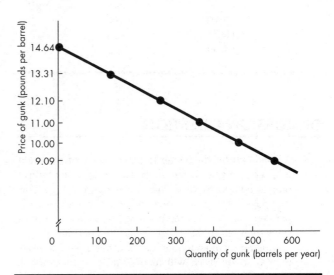

**b** The choke price for gunk is £14.64. This is the price that is high enough for the resource not to be used at all.

**c i** If the interest rate is 10 per cent, the current price of a barrel of gunk is £10. We know that the current (equilibrium) price must be such that if the price of gunk is increasing at a rate of 10 per cent per year (equal to the rate of interest), the stock will be depleted just as the choke price is achieved. We can find the current price by noting that (1) the choke price is £14.64 and (2) the remaining stock is 1,215 barrels and working backwards.

Since the price of gunk is growing at the rate of 10 per cent per year, the price in the year before the choke price is reached must be £14.64 (the choke price) divided by 1.10 (1 + the 10 per cent growth rate of price) or £13.31. From Table 16.2 (and recognizing that gunk is just depleted as the £14.64 price is reached) we can infer that 133 barrels of gunk would be purchased in that year. Proceeding in a similar manner, working backwards until all 1,215 barrels of gunk have been purchased, we discover that the current equilibrium price must be £10.

**ii** Using the procedure outlined in **c**, Table 16.3 can be completed as shown in Table 16.5.

**Table 16.5**

| Year | Price (pounds per barrel of gunk) | Initial stock of gunk (barrels) | Final stock of gunk barrels) |
|------|------|------|------|
| 1 | 10.00 | 1,215 | 751 |
| 2 | 11.00 | 751 | 387 |
| 3 | 12.10 | 387 | 133 |
| 4 | 13.31 | 133 | 0 |
| 5 | 14.64 | 0 | |

## DISCUSSION QUESTION

1  A bond entitles the owner to a fixed number of pounds in interest a year. If the interest rate rises, the interest on a bond doesn't vary. This means that if I buy a bond that pays £100 a year forever when interest rates are 10 per cent, the price of the bond will be £1,000. If interest rates then fall to (say) 5 per cent, the bond will be generating an income double that of other financial instruments, so its price will also double, in this case to £2,000. Hence lower interest rates mean that bond prices rise. Similarly, when interest rates rise, bond prices can be expected to fall.

## DATA QUESTIONS

1  Demand for raw materials fluctuates considerably over time. When the economy is booming demand rises very quickly; when the economy is in recession demand falls very quickly. One reason for this is that manufacturers increase their stocks when times are good but cut them when depression occurs.

2  The factors which determine the price and the flow of a natural resource such as copper are the rate of interest, the demand for the flow and the stock of the resource remaining. These are discussed in detail in the text on pages 405–412.

3  The earnings of OPEC members depend on the demand for and the supply of copper. The factors which affect demand are discussed above in Questions 1 and 2; they are difficult for any organization to control. OPEC attempts to control the price by restricting supply. However, individual members may break ranks to increase their own sales if they think it will benefit them

# Chapter 17  Uncertainty and Information

## Chapter in Perspective, Text Pages 416–437

This chapter explains how people make decisions when they are uncertain about the consequences, and why it pays to buy insurance and disseminate information. It also looks at a variety of markets in which uncertainty and information play important roles.

## Helpful Hints

**1** The existence of risk and uncertainty is an objective feature of reality. How decision makers cope with uncertainty, however, depends on their attitudes towards risk. Some people are more risk averse than others.

A utility of wealth schedule reflects a person's degree of risk aversion. Economists believe that most people's utility of wealth schedules exhibit diminishing marginal utility as wealth increases. However, for two people, for example Alexis and Madeleine, Alexis's marginal utility of wealth may decrease at a faster rate than Madeleine's. Alexis would be more risk averse than Madeleine and less likely to undertake risky ventures that offer the possibility of a high return at the cost of a greater probability of loss. *Ceteris paribus*, Alexis would be less likely to undertake risky ventures because she will attach a relatively greater utility weight to the probable decrease of wealth from a loss than to the probable increase in wealth from a success. Because of these relative weights, a risk-averse person is also more likely to take out insurance against loss.

**2** Two important concepts for analysing choice under uncertainty are expected wealth and expected utility. Expected wealth (sometimes called expected value) is the average wealth arising from all possible outcomes. It is computed as the weighted average of the wealth associated with each possible outcome, where the weights are the probabilities of each outcome. For example, if there are three possible outcomes yielding wealth of $W_1$, $W_2$, and $W_3$, and the probabilities associated with these outcomes are $p_1$, $p_2$, and $p_3$, respectively, then expected wealth equals

$$(W_1 \times p_1) + (W_2 \times p_2) + (W_3 \times p_3).$$

Expected utility is the average utility arising from all possible outcomes. It is calculated in the same way. If the utilities associated with each possible wealth outcome are $U_1$, $U_2$, and $U_3$, respectively, then expected utility equals

$$(U_1 \times p_1) + (U_2 \times p_2) + (U_3 \times p_3).$$

In analysing choice under uncertainty, we must first calculate expected wealth. But a decision is ultimately based on the expected utility associated with that expected wealth.

155

## Key Figures

**Figure 17.1 The Utility of Wealth, text page 419**
This figure assumes that utility can be measured. Increasing wealth means taking more risks, so the utility of wealth curve flattens out.

**Figure 17.2 Choice under Uncertainty, text page 419**
In part (a) Tania gets a summer job that enables her to save ℒ5,000 and gives a utility of 80. However, there is an alternative. Tania can take a selling job. If she is successful she will be able to save ℒ9,000 (utility 95); if she is unsuccessful she will be able to save only ℒ3,000 (utility 65 units). Her *expected* utility averages these two possibilities and is 80 units, but the expected wealth is ℒ6,000 – ℒ1,000 more than in the first job.

So the expected utility between these two jobs is the same. Which will she choose? In Tania's case, the extra ℒ1,000 just compensates for the extra risk.

**Figure 17.6 Optimal-search Rule, text page 424**
Finding things out costs time. It would be foolish to spend a week to find the cheapest packet of drawing pins in London – the cost would exceed the benefit.

In this figure, the marginal cost of search is constant – shown by a horizontal line. As the lowest price found declines, the marginal utility (expected benefits) of searching further also falls.

The optimum-search rule is to search until the reservation price (the highest price the buyer is willing to pay) is found and then to buy at the lowest found price.

# SELF-TEST

## CONCEPT REVIEW

1 Facing uncertainty, it is rational to maximize _____ _____ , that is, the average utility for all possible events.

2 The utility of wealth schedule describes attitudes towards _____. Increased wealth leads to increased utility, but the _____ _____ of wealth declines.

3 People buy insurance to reduce _____. Insurance works by _____ risks. It is profitable because people are risk _____ .

4 Buyers searching for the lowest price use the _____ search rule, that is, they search until the expected _____ of search equal the marginal _____ of search, then buy.

5 Moral _____ arises when there is a post-agreement incentive to increase personal benefits at the expense of others who are uninformed.

6 Risk in financial markets can be lowered by _____ asset holdings (don't put all your eggs in one basket), buying in _____ markets and _____ markets (taking positions in forward markets without necessarily taking delivery of goods).

## TRUE OR FALSE

___ 1 Risk is a state in which more than one event may occur, but we don't know which one.

___ 2 The more rapidly your marginal utility of wealth diminishes, the less risk averse you are.

___ 3 A risk-neutral person has a constant marginal utility of wealth.

___ 4 If Petro-Anglia drills in an uncharted region of the Atlantic Ocean without any idea of the likelihood of striking oil, Petro-Anglia faces uncertainty rather than risk.

___ 5 Risk neutrality makes insurance possible and profitable.

___ 6 Advertising increases the price of the goods advertised.

___ 7 Advertising for search goods is designed mainly to inform rather than persuade.

___ 8 If you are careless with matches because you know you have fire insurance, an adverse selection problem exists.

___ 9 The rational expectation of price is the price at which expected demand equals expected supply.

___ **10** In an efficient market, the actual price is rarely equal to the expected future price.

___ **11** If prices in an efficient market are volatile, expectations about future prices must be volatile.

## MULTIPLE CHOICE

**1** The more rapidly a person's marginal utility of wealth diminishes, the
a more risk inclined the person is.
b more risk neutral the person is.
c more risk averse the person is.
d more likely it is that the person has a moral hazard problem.
e less likely the person is to take out insurance.

**2** The expected value of a game that gives a 50 per cent chance of winning £60 and a 50 per cent chance of winning nothing is
a £10.
b £20.
c £30.
d £60.
e none of the above.

**3** On a normal utility of wealth curve diagram with wealth on the horizontal axis and utility on the vertical axis, the marginal utility of wealth is
a a point on the horizontal axis.
b a point on the vertical axis.
c an area under the utility of wealth curve.
d the slope of a ray from the origin to a point on the utility of wealth curve.
e the slope of the utility of wealth curve.

**4** Goods whose quality can be assessed only after they are bought are called
a private information goods.
b search goods.
c experience goods.
d inferior goods.
e lemons.

**5** The buyer's reservation price is
a the lowest price that the buyer is willing to pay.
b the highest price that the buyer is willing to pay.
c the price equating the expected marginal benefit and marginal cost of searching.
d a and c.
e b and c.

**6** According to the utility of wealth schedules in Table 17.1,
a Chloe is more risk averse than Esther.
b Esther is more risk averse than Chloe.
c Chloe is risk neutral, while Esther is risk averse.
d Esther is risk neutral, while Chloe is risk averse.
e it is impossible to calculate risk aversion and risk neutrality.

**Table 17.1**

| Wealth (pounds) | Utility (units) | |
| --- | --- | --- |
| | Chloe | Esther |
| 0 | 0 | 0 |
| 20 | 45 | 60 |
| 40 | 80 | 90 |
| 60 | 110 | 100 |
| 80 | 130 | 105 |

**7** Chloe's expected wealth from an investment opportunity that will pay either £40 or £80 with equal probability is
a £60.
b £105.
c £120.
d £210.
e none of the above.

**8** Which compensation scheme is most likely to be efficient in the case of a chief executive officer of a corporation?
a commission on sales
b share of total firm profits
c salary based on years of employment
d tournament-like prize
e b and d

**9** Which compensation scheme is most likely to be efficient in the case of a salesperson?
a hourly wage rate
b commission on sales
c share of total firm profits
d salary based on years of employment
e none of the above

**10** A rational expectation of a price is not
a based on forecasts of expected demand *(ED)*.
b based on forecasts of expected supply *(ES)*.
c the price at which *ED = ES*.

**d** necessarily equal to actual price.

**e** a forecast that uses all relevant available information.

**11** Ann must choose Option *A* or Option *B*. Option *A* guarantees her £10,000. Option *B* gives her £5,000 with probability 0.5 and £15,000 with probability 0.5. Having a normal utility of wealth curve, Ann will

**a** prefer and choose *A*.

**b** prefer and choose *B*.

**c** prefer *A* but choose *B*.

**d** prefer *B* but choose *A*.

**e** be indifferent between *A* and *B*.

**12** If there are three possible events and each has a probability of occurrence of one-third, then

**a** neither uncertainty nor risk exists.

**b** uncertainty exists, but not risk.

**c** risk exists, but not uncertainty.

**d** both uncertainty and risk exist.

**e** there is not enough information to distinguish between uncertainty and risk.

**13** In an efficient market, which of the following statements is false?

**a** The current price is equal to the expected future price.

**b** The current price embodies all available information.

**c** No forecastable profit opportunities exist.

**d** Prices are stable.

**e** Expectations are subject to fluctuations.

**14** An efficient compensation scheme

**a** cannot incorporate the effects of luck.

**b** will not be accepted by the agent.

**c** splits revenues equally between the agent and principal.

**d** maximizes the agent's expected income.

**e** maximizes the principal's expected profit.

**15** Optimizing buyers will devote additional resources searching for information when

**a** expected marginal benefit is positive.

**b** expected marginal benefit is less than the marginal cost of searching.

**c** expected marginal benefit equals the marginal cost of searching.

**d** marginal cost of searching is positive.

**e** none of the above.

**16** If buyers cannot assess the quality of used cars and there are no warranties,

**a** only bad used cars will be sold.

**b** only good used cars will be sold.

**c** good cars will be sold at a higher price than bad cars.

**d** there is a moral hazard problem.

**e** there is no adverse selection problem.

**17** In a forward market, a contract is made today for an exchange at a future date. The typical forward contract specifies

**a** price but not quantity.

**b** quantity but not price.

**c** both price and quantity.

**d** neither price nor quantity.

**e** none of the above.

**18** Stock market prices are volatile because

**a** expectations are irrational.

**b** expectations change frequently owing to new information.

**c** stock markets are inefficient markets.

**d** shareholders do not behave like inventory holders.

**e** all of the above statements are true.

## SHORT ANSWER

**1** If you agree to pay the first £200 worth of damage (£200 excess), your car insurance premium might be £1,000 per year. But if you agree to a £500 deductible, your insurance premium might be £800 per year. Why do insurance companies charge premiums that are related inversely to the total loss that the customer agrees to bear?

**2** Many large firms are owned by a group of shareholders who hire managers to run the firm. Why is profit sharing a good compensation scheme for top management in such a firm?

**3** Define a rational expectation and explain how to go about calculating the rational expectation of a future price.

**4** What is meant by an efficient market? Explain why the current market price will always be equal to the expected future price in an efficient market.

**5** Reread the *Reading Between the Lines* article in this chapter. Why do you think that results of exams such as A levels matter to employers?

# PROBLEMS

**1** Table 17.2 presents the utility of wealth schedules for Peter and Mary. Who is more risk averse, Peter or Mary? Explain.

**Table 17.2**

| Wealth (pounds) | Utility (units) | |
|---|---|---|
| | Peter | Mary |
| 0 | 0 | 0 |
| 20 | 100 | 60 |
| 40 | 150 | 110 |
| 60 | 175 | 150 |
| 80 | 187 | 180 |
| 100 | 193 | 200 |

**2** Table 17.3 presents Leonard's utility of wealth schedule. Leonard is considering an investment project that will pay either zero or £20,000 with equal probability.

**Table 17.3  Leonard's Utility of Wealth**

| Wealth (thousands of pounds) | Utility (units) |
|---|---|
| 0 | 0 |
| 4 | 52 |
| 5 | 60 |
| 8 | 79 |
| 10 | 87 |
| 15 | 98 |
| 20 | 104 |

**a** What is Leonard's expected wealth from the project?
**b** What is Leonard's expected utility?
**c** What is Leonard's cost of risk?
**d** Is Leonard willing to undertake the project if it costs him £5,000?

**3** Dylan owns some land on which he usually grows vegetables. This year he has accepted a job as a barman and will not be able to tend the vegetable patch. Dylan is thinking of hiring Thomas, who has some gardening experience, to grow vegetables for him.

Thomas has been milking cows for a dairy farmer, and working hard for £30 per day. From conversations with Thomas, Dylan gathers that Thomas places a value of £10 on relaxation – Thomas prefers to relax rather than to work, but a day of working for £10 or a day of relaxing are equally acceptable.

Dylan knows that total income from growing vegetables depends on how hard the cultivator works and on weather conditions. Table 17.4 gives the alternative total incomes from the possible combinations of work effort and weather conditions. There is a 50–50 chance of good or bad weather.

**Table 17.4  Total Income from Vegetable Growing (pounds per day)**

| Weather | Worker's effort | |
|---|---|---|
| | Works hard | Relaxes |
| Good | £160 | £80 |
| Bad | £80 | £80 |

Dylan is considering two alternative compensation schemes:

Scheme 1  Dylan pays Thomas £31 per day.
Scheme 2  Dylan pays Thomas £10 per day plus 26 per cent of the total income from vegetable growing.

Using this information, work out which compensation scheme Dylan should adopt. Remember that an efficient compensation scheme has two features. It must maximize profit for the principal and be acceptable to the agent (make the agent at least as well off as in the best alternative job).

**4** The expected demand for and supply of wheat are given in Table 17.5.

**Table 17.5**

| Price (pounds/tonne) | Expected quantity demanded | Expected quantity supplied |
|---|---|---|
| | (millions of tonnes per year) | |
| 400 | 140 | 350 |
| 350 | 180 | 320 |
| 300 | 220 | 290 |
| 250 | 260 | 260 |
| 200 | 300 | 230 |
| 150 | 340 | 200 |

**a** If nothing happens to change expectations, what is the rational expectation of the price of a tonne of wheat? Of the quantity of wheat traded?

**b** Suppose that actual demand is exactly as expected but that the weather turns out to be better than usual for growing wheat. Actual wheat production (momentary supply) is 40 million tonnes greater than the quantity expected. What is the quantity of wheat actually traded? What is the actual price of a tonne of wheat?

**c** How much wheat would farmers have supplied if they had accurately forecast the price in **b**?

## DISCUSSION QUESTION

**1** Explain what an efficient market is and then say why prices fluctuate and why profit opportunities can't be predicted.

## DATA QUESTIONS

### South African Insurance

The spread of HIV, the virus that causes AIDS, is a worry to life insurers all over the world. Its proliferation is worst in Africa, which is home to roughly half of all people infected with HIV. But sub-Saharan Africa, whose average GDP per head is just $460, is largely outside the net of the life insurance industry. The exception is South Africa, where the industry is coming up with some imaginative ideas to deal with the problem.

Some 4.3 per cent of South Africa's population is now infected with HIV, and among the country's economically active population the infection rate is 10.4 per cent, and rising fast.

The virus is now predominantly found among heterosexuals, especially black city dwellers. Southern Life found that if it did nothing, the future cost of AIDS-related death would push premiums so high it would hurt the overall market. So it launched a policy to exclude anyone with HIV. To qualify, people must test negative for the virus every five years.

*Source*: Adapted from *The Economist*, 17 August 1996, p. 67. Copyright © *The Economist*, London, 17 August 1996.

**1** Using the concept of income elasticity of demand, explain why sub-Saharan Africa 'is largely outside the net of the life insurance industry'.

**2** Use the concepts of moral hazard and adverse selection to explain Southern Life's action.

# ANSWERS

## CONCEPT REVIEW

**1** expected utility

**2** risk; marginal utility

**3** risk; pooling; averse

**4** optimal; costs; benefits

**5** hazard

**6** diversifying; forward; futures

## TRUE OR FALSE

**1 F** Definition. Uncertainty.

**2 F** More risk averse.

**3 T** Definition. Linear marginal utility of wealth curve.

**4 T** Risk means probabilities could be estimated.

**5 F** Risk aversion.

**6 F** Advertising is costly, but it may cut price through increased competition and greater economies of scale.

**7 T** Quality can be assessed before buying.

**8 F** Moral hazard problem.

**9 T** Definition.

**10 F** Actual price = expected future price.

**11 T** Definition.

## MULTIPLE CHOICE

**1 c** Moral hazard irrelevant. More likely to insure.

**2 c** $(\$60 \times 0.5) + (\$0 \times 0.5)$.

**3 e** Change in utility/change in wealth.

**4 c** Definition.

**5 e** Definition.

**6 b** Marginal utility of wealth diminishes more rapidly.

**7 a** $(\$40 \times 0.5) + (\$80 \times 0.5)$.

**8 e** Strong connection effort/competition and profit.

**9 b** Directly links unmonitored effort to outcome.

**10 d** Equals actual price on average.

**11 a** Expected value *A* and *B* equal, but *A* less risky, so preferable.

**12 d** Definitions. Risk is subset of uncertainty.

**13 d** Prices fluctuate with changes in expectations.

**14 e** Designed by principal and must be acceptable to agent.

**15 e** When expected marginal benefit > marginal cost.

**16 a** Opposite **d, e** true.

**17 c** Definition.

**20 b** Only source of change in efficient market.

## SHORT ANSWER

**1** By allowing customers to pay lower premiums if they agree to bear a higher share of total damages, insurance companies alleviate the adverse selection problem. High-risk drivers know that they are accident prone and are willing to pay higher premiums for nearly full coverage, while low-risk drivers know that they seldom have accidents and will choose lower premiums with lower coverage. With deductibles, the adverse selection problem of high-risk people driving low-risk people out of the market is less likely to occur. The insurance company can charge differential premiums that reflect the different risks that it is insuring.

**2** The owners (shareholders) are the principals and the top managers are the agents. Neither the effort nor the output of the managers can be monitored easily. But since the decisions of managers have a direct and significant bearing on the profit of the firm, their incentive is to make decisions that maximize profit if they share in any increase in profit through a profit-sharing compensation scheme.

**3** A rational expectation is the forecast that uses all of the relevant information available about past and present events and that has the least possible error. The rational expectation of a future price is the price at which expected quantity demanded equals expected quantity supplied. Thus to calculate the rational expectation of a price, we must forecast, using all available and relevant information, the variables that determine the expected demand and expected supply curves.

The forecast of expected demand depends on the expected values of the prices of substitutes and complements in consumption, income, population and preferences. The forecast of expected supply depends on the expected values of the prices of substitutes and complements in production, the prices of resource inputs and technology.

**4** An efficient market is one in which the actual price embodies all available relevant information. The price will thus be equal to the rational expectation of the future price and there will be no forecastable profit opportunities. The current market price will always be equal to the expected future price in an efficient market because any deviation would be eliminated immediately since it provides an expected profit opportunity.

**5** In part, exams act as a 'screening device' making it easier for employers to select the best candidates. But there is a lot of evidence to suggest that highly educated people are more productive than those with less education. Hence exams enable them to select workers who will be more productive.

## PROBLEMS

**1** To find out who is more risk averse, we must determine whose marginal utility of wealth decreases faster as wealth increases. Table 17.6 presents the total and marginal utility of wealth for Peter and Mary. Since Peter's marginal utility of wealth decreases faster than Mary's, Peter is the more risk averse.

**2 a** Leonard's expected wealth is $(\$0 \times 0.5) + (\$20,000 \times 0.5) = \$10,000$.

**b** Leonard's expected utility is $(0 \times 0.5) + (104 \times 0.5) = 52$ units.

**c** Uncertain wealth of zero or $20,000 yields expected wealth of $10,000 and expected utility of 52 units. From Table 17.3, we can see that certain (no-risk) wealth of $4,000 also yields utility of 52 units. The cost of risk is $6,000, the amount by which expected wealth must be increased beyond no-risk wealth to give the same utility as the no-risk situation (£10,000–£4,000).

## Table 17.6

| Wealth (pounds) | Peter | | Mary | |
|---|---|---|---|---|
| | Total utility (units) | Marginal utility (units) | Total utility (units) | Marginal utility (units) |
| 0 | 0 | | 0 | |
| | | ...100 | | ...60 |
| 20 | 100 | | 60 | |
| | | ...50 | | ...50 |
| 40 | 150 | | 110 | |
| | | ...25 | | ...40 |
| 60 | 175 | | 150 | |
| | | ...12 | | ...30 |
| 80 | 187 | | 180 | |
| | | ...6 | | ...20 |
| 100 | 193 | | 200 | |

d For Leonard, the forgone utility of the £5,000 cost of investing in the project (60 units) is greater than the expected utility of the risky project (52 units). Leonard is not willing to undertake the project.

**3** Total income depends on whether Thomas works hard or relaxes and whether there is good or bad weather. The probability of good or bad weather is 0.5.

If Thomas works hard, expected total income is (£160 × 0.5) + (£80 × 0.5) = £120.

If Thomas relaxes, expected total income is (£80 × 0.5) + (£80 × 0.5) = £80.

To see which compensation scheme is efficient, calculate the outcome of each scheme for the principal and the agent.

**Scheme 1:** Dylan (principal) pays Thomas (agent) £31 per day. Will Thomas work hard or relax? If Thomas relaxes, he receives £31. Since he does not have to exert himself, the value of relaxing is also £31. If Thomas works hard, he also receives £31, but since he has to exert himself, the value of working hard is £31 – £10 = £21. Thomas will choose to relax. Expected total income will be £80 per day, with £31 going to Thomas and £49 going to Dylan.

**Scheme 2:** Dylan (principal) pays Thomas (agent) £10 plus 26 per cent of the total income from vegetable growing. If Thomas relaxes, he receives £10 + (0.26 ×

£80) = £30.80. Since he does not have to exert himself, the value of relaxing is also £30.80. If Thomas works hard, he receives £10 + (0.26 × £120) = £41.20. Since he has to exert himself, the value of working hard is £41.20 – £10 = £31.20. Thomas will choose to work hard. Expected total income will be £120 per day, with £41.20 going to Thomas and £78.80 going to Dylan.

Both Dylan and Thomas are better off under compensation scheme 2. But is Thomas better off growing vegetables under compensation scheme 2 than he would be milking cows? If Thomas milks cows, he earns £30, but since he has to work hard, the value to him is £30 – £10 = £20. This is lower than the value he receives working hard growing vegetables under scheme 2. Therefore, compensation scheme 2 is more efficient.

**4 a** The rational expectation of the price of a tonne of wheat is £250 since, at that price, expected quantity demanded equals expected quantity supplied. The rational expectation of the quantity of wheat traded is 260 million tonnes.

**b** The momentary supply turns out to be 300 million tonnes, 40 million tonnes more than the 260 million expected. Thus the quantity of wheat traded is 300 million tonnes. To clear the market of the 300 million tonnes (where momentary supply intersects demand), the actual price of a tonne of wheat must be £200.

**c** If farmers had accurately forecast the price of £200 per tonne, they would have produced 230 million bushels of wheat. Thus farmers would regret having produced too much wheat (300 million tonnes instead of 230 million tonnes).

## DISCUSSION QUESTION

**1** An efficient market has three characteristics, namely that the actual price equals the expected future price, that it embodies all the available information and that there are no forecastable profit opportunities. Most economists believe that the stock market is an efficient market.

So why do share prices fluctuate? They fluctuate when new information becomes available; for example, if new information about future dividends becomes available it will affect the price of a firm's shares. Forecastable profit opportunities are ruled out because the price changes to reflect the new information.

# DATA QUESTIONS

**1** The concept of income elasticity of demand suggests that as incomes rise, people spend relatively more on some goods and services. Insurance is one of these. However, most of Africa is poor, so money goes on goods such as food. Only those with higher incomes will take out life insurance.

**2** The moral hazard problem is that a person with insurance coverage for a loss has less incentive to take precautions to avoid such a loss. In this case, however, it might be thought that the possession of life insurance would not normally cause people to take life-threatening risks.

Adverse selection is more central in this case. People exposed to HIV might well take out insurance to protect their families. The insurance company in this case is seeking to reduce adverse selection by excluding those most at risk.

# Chapter 18  **Market Failure and Public Choice**

---

## Chapter in Perspective, Text Pages 441–464

In this chapter we discover that there are circumstances in which markets fail to allocate goods and services efficiently. For example, if competitive markets are efficient, why is there so much pollution? As a result of such *market failure* to achieve efficiency, there are additional opportunities for government to improve allocation. This chapter begins a discussion of how an 'ideal' government might proceed to do so. In the next chapter we examine the behaviour of actual governments.

---

## Helpful Hints

**1** The criterion economists use to judge the success of the market is allocative efficiency. Allocative efficiency means that the economy is producing all goods and services up to the point at which the marginal cost is equal to the marginal benefit. In such a state, no one can be made better off without making someone else worse off.

When the market fails to achieve this 'ideal' state of efficiency, we call it *market failure*. The market can fail by producing too little if the marginal benefit of the last unit exceeds the marginal cost. On the other hand, the market can fail by producing too much if the marginal cost of the last unit exceeds the marginal benefit.

**2** All goods provided by the government are not necessarily public goods. A public good is defined by the characteristics of non-rivalry and non-excludability, not by whether or not it is publicly provided. For example, local authorities provide swimming pools and residential refuse collection but neither of these is a pure public good in spite of the fact that they may be provided by the government.

**3** A private good is a rival in consumption. Therefore, to obtain the demand curve for the whole economy, we sum the individual marginal benefit (demand) curves *horizontally*. However, the economy's marginal benefit curve for a public good is obtained by summing the individual marginal benefit curves *vertically*. This is the relevant marginal benefit curve for evaluating the efficient provision level of the public good. (See the discussion of Key Figure 18.5).

**4** A competitive market will result in the quantity being traded at which the marginal private cost is equal to the marginal private benefit. The efficient quantity is the quantity at which marginal social cost is equal to marginal social benefit.

The difference between *marginal social cost* and *marginal private cost* is external cost, and the difference between *marginal social benefit* and *marginal private benefit* is external benefit. When third parties are affected, there are external costs or benefits and competitive markets will not be efficient.

**5** Competitive markets with externalities are not efficient because some of the costs or benefits are *external*. If these costs or benefits could be *internalized* somehow, then the market would be efficient. Two approaches to internalizing externalities are discussed in this chapter.

The first is to define clearly and strictly enforce property rights. Then costs imposed on non-participants in a transaction can be recovered through the legal process and will thus be borne by those making the transaction decision: the costs will become internal (private).

The second approach to internalizing externalities is to tax activities that generate external costs and subsidize activities that generate external benefits. By charging a tax equal to the external cost, the entire cost becomes internal. Similarly, by paying a subsidy in the amount of external benefits, the entire benefit becomes internal.

**6** Public choice theory provides a theory of the political marketplace that parallels the economic theory of the market for goods and services. In political markets the demanders are voters while in ordinary markets the demanders are consumers. In both cases, demanders are concerned about their own costs and benefits. The suppliers in political markets are politicians and bureaucrats, and again they are concerned about their own costs and benefits.

One way to analyse this market is to use the median voter theorem. This predicts that successful politicians will appeal to the median voter.

# Key Figures

## Figure 18.5 Benefits of a Public Good, text page 449

If one person consumes a unit of a private good, that unit cannot be consumed by anyone else. However, the consumption of a public good by one person does not reduce the amount available for others. This implies that the economy's marginal benefit curve (demand curve) for a private good is obtained by summing the individual marginal benefit (demand) curves *horizontally* (see Chapter 7).

For a public good, however, the economy's marginal benefit curve is obtained by summing the individual marginal benefit curves *vertically*; by adding up the individual marginal benefits at each quantity. This is illustrated in the figure by considering an economy in which there are two individuals, Lisa and Max, who receive benefits from defence satellites, a public good. Their marginal benefit curves are given in parts (a) and (b) of the figure. The economy's marginal benefit curve is given in part (c) as the *vertical* sum of the marginal benefit curves of Lisa and Max.

## Figure 18.6 The Efficient Quantity of a Public Good, text page 450

The efficient scale of provision of a public good is the amount that maximizes net benefit, which is total benefit minus total cost. Part (a) of this figure graphs the total cost (*TC*) and total benefit (*TB*) curves. Net benefit is given by the vertical distance between the two curves. We find that this distance (net benefit) is a maximum at a quantity of 2 satellites. Thus 2 satellites is the efficient scale of provision.

Part (b) illustrates an alternative way to find the same result. The efficient scale of provision is achieved if satellites are produced up to the level at which marginal benefit equals marginal cost. The marginal benefit (*MB*) and marginal cost (*MC*) curves are shown in part (b). Marginal benefit equals marginal cost at a quantity of 2 satellites.

## Figure 18.7 Provision of a Public Good in a Political System, text page 451

This builds on Fig. 18.6 to show that given informed voters, competition between political parties will maximize the perceived net benefit accruing to voters. This is because provision will be at the level where the distance between total benefit (*TB*) and total cost (*TC*) is greatest.

**Figure 18.10  An Excise Tax, text page 456**
This shows the effects of the imposition of an excise tax on petrol. The result is a rise in price, a fall in quantity and a deadweight loss of producer and consumer surplus. The advantage is the tax revenue gained by government, which is shown by the quantity multiplied by the amount of the tax.

# SELF-TEST

## CONCEPT REVIEW

**1** If an unregulated market economy is unable to achieve allocative efficiency in all circumstances, we have _____ _____ .

**2** There are two classes of economic theories of government behaviour. Public _____ theories predict that government will pursue actions that will achieve allocative efficiency. Public _____ theories study the behaviour of government as the outcome of individual choices made by voters, politicians and bureaucrats.

**3** A good which, if consumed by one person, cannot be consumed by another is called a(n) _____ good. There are two important features of such a good. The fact that Bob's consumption of a good means that Sue cannot consume the same good illustrates the feature of _____ . If Sue has purchased a good, she owns it and can keep others from using it. This illustrates the feature of _____ .

**4** A good which, if consumed by one person, is necessarily also consumed by everyone else is called a(n) _____ _____ good.

**5** Someone who consumes a good without paying for it is called a(n)_____ _____ . When such individuals are prevalent in the consumption of a particular good, the amount of that good provided by the private market will be _____ than the allocatively efficient amount.

**6** The maximum amount a person would be willing to pay for one more unit of a public good is the _____ _____ of that good to the individual.

**7** A cost or a benefit arising from a transaction which affects someone other than the direct parties in the transaction is called a(n)_____ . When a chemicals firm dumps its waste into the river, it kills a large number of fish downstream. This is an example of an external _____ . When a neighbour plants flowers on the border of your property, you benefit. This is an example of an external _____ .

**8** A legally established title to the sole ownership of a resource is a(n) _____ _____ _____ .

**9** The marginal cost borne directly by the producer of a good is called the marginal _____ cost. This marginal cost together with the marginal external cost is the marginal _____ cost.

**10** If there are external costs in the production of steel (for example pollution), the output of steel produced by the market will be _____ than the allocatively efficient level.

**11** The _____ voter theorem predicts that successful political parties will pursue policies that maximize the net _____ of the _____ voter.

**12** A(n) _____ tax is a tax on the sale of a particular commodity.

## TRUE OR FALSE

— **1** Restriction of output by monopolies is an example of market failure.

**2** According to the public choice theory of government behaviour, not only is there the possibility of market failure, but there is also the possibility of 'government failure'.

**3** The existence of public goods gives rise to the free-rider problem.

**4** Any good made available by the government is a public good.

**5** The economy's marginal benefit curve for a public good is obtained by adding the marginal benefits of each individual at each quantity of provision.

**6** The private market will produce much less than the efficient quantity of pure public goods.

**7** If the production of a good involves no external cost, then marginal social cost is equal to marginal private cost.

**8** If, at the current level of production of good A, marginal social benefit is less than marginal social cost, then output of good A should increase to achieve allocative efficiency.

**9** The government can enhance allocative efficiency by subsidizing the production of goods that generate external benefits and taxing the production of goods that generate external costs.

**10** The public choice theory of government behaviour assumes that politicians and bureaucrats are motivated primarily by concern for the public interest.

**11** In order to be elected, a politician will tend to choose policies that appeal to the median voter.

**12** It is irrational for voters to be uninformed about an issue as important as defence.

## MULTIPLE CHOICE

**1** Which of the following is *not* a source of market failure?
a the existence of public goods
b external costs
c external benefits
d an unequal distribution of income
e the existence of monopolies

**2** A good that exhibits both rivalry and excludability is a(n)
a private good.
b public good.
c government good.
d mixed good.
e external good.

**3** Governments provide pure public goods like national defence because
a governments are more efficient than private firms at producing such goods.
b of the free-rider problems, which result in underproduction by private markets.
c people do not value highly national defence.
d of the potential that private firms will make excess profits.
e of external costs.

**4** Which of the following goods has the non-excludability feature?
a a city bus
b a toll-bridge
c a lighthouse
d a museum
e all of the above

**5** The economy's total demand curve for a public good is obtained by
a summing the individual marginal cost curves horizontally.
b summing the individual marginal cost curves vertically.
c summing the individual marginal benefit curves horizontally.
d summing the individual marginal benefit curves vertically.
e none of the above methods.

**6** The total benefit of a given level of provision of a public good can be obtained by
a adding the marginal benefit of each level of provision up to the given level.
b adding the marginal benefit of each level of provision and then subtracting the marginal cost of each level of provision.
c adding the net benefit of each level of provision up to the given level.
d multiplying net benefit by the quantity of the public good provided.
e none of the above methods.

**7** Figure 18.1 depicts the demand for good *A* as well as the marginal private cost (*MPC*) and marginal social cost (*MSC*) associated with the production of good *A*. Production of the sixth unit of output generates an external
  **a** cost of £1.50.
  **b** cost of £3.
  **c** cost of £6.
  **d** benefit of £3.
  **e** benefit of £6.

**Figure 18.1**

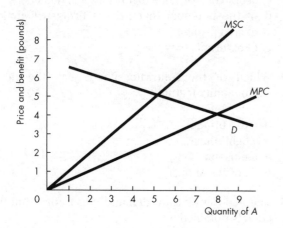

**8** In Fig. 18.1, how many units of good *A* will be produced in an unregulated market?
  **a** 0 units
  **b** 5 units
  **c** 6 units
  **d** 8 units
  **e** impossible to calculate without additional information

**9** In Fig. 18.1, what is the allocatively efficient quantity of good *A*?
  **a** 0 units
  **b** 5 units
  **c** 6 units
  **d** 8 units
  **e** impossible to calculate without additional information

**10** Figure 18.2 depicts the demand curve for good *B* as well as the marginal social benefit *(MSB)* and marginal cost *(MC)* curves. How many units of good *B* will be produced and consumed in an unregulated market?
  **a** 0 units
  **b** 3 units
  **c** 5 units
  **d** 6 units
  **e** 9 units

**Figure 18.2**

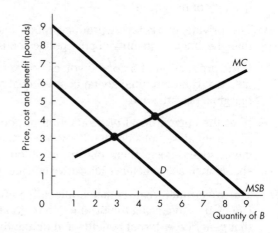

**11** In Fig. 18.2, what is the allocatively efficient quantity of good *B*?
  **a** 0 units
  **b** 3 units
  **c** 5 units
  **d** 6 units
  **e** 9 units

**12** In Fig. 18.2, which of the following government policies would induce the market to achieve allocative efficiency?
  **a** Tax the production of *B* in the amount of £3 per unit.
  **b** Tax the production of *B* in the amount of £4 per unit.
  **c** Subsidize the consumption of *B* in the amount of £1 per unit.
  **d** Subsidize the consumption of *B* in the amount of £3 per unit.
  **e** Subsidize the consumption of *B* in the amount of £4 per unit.

**13** Public choice theory
  **a** argues that government has a tendency to conduct policies that help the economy towards allocative efficiency.
  **b** argues that politicians and bureaucrats tend to be more concerned about the public interest than individuals in the private sector.
  **c** argues that the public choices of government maximize net benefits.
  **d** applies economic tools used to analyse markets to the analysis of government behaviour.
  **e** applies the tools of political analysis to the analysis of economic markets.

**14** Competitors who make themselves identical to appeal to the maximum number of voters illustrate
  **a** the principle of maximum differentiation.
  **b** the principle of minimum differentiation.
  **c** the principle of rational ignorance.
  **d** non-rivalry.
  **e** the Niskanen theory of bureaucratic behaviour.

**15** Public choice theory assumes that those involved in the political process are generally motivated by
  **a** self-interest.
  **b** the desire to achieve allocative efficiency.
  **c** dishonesty.
  **d** public spirit.
  **e** the desire for maximum profit.

**16** Competition between two political parties will cause those parties to propose policies
  **a** that are quite different.
  **b** that are quite similar.
  **c** of rational ignorance.
  **d** that reduce the well-being of middle-income families and benefit the rich and the poor.
  **e** that equate total benefits and total costs.

## SHORT ANSWER

**1** Explain the *non-rivalry* and *non-excludability* features of a pure public good.

**2** What is the free-rider problem?

**3** Explain how a tax can be used to achieve efficiency in the face of external costs.

**4** Briefly compare an equilibrium in a political market with an equilibrium in the market for goods and services.

**5** The health service reforms discussed in the *Reading Between the Lines* article were meant to increase efficiency by simulating a market. Why do you think that one result has been an increase in bureaucracy?

## PROBLEMS

**1** The first two columns of Table 18.1 give the demand schedule for education while the third column gives the marginal private cost. Since education generates external benefits, marginal social benefit, given in the last column, is greater than marginal private benefit.

**Table 18.1**

| Quantity (number of students) | Marginal private benefit (pounds) | Marginal private cost (pounds) | Marginal social benefit (pounds) |
|---|---|---|---|
| 100 | 500 | 200 | 800 |
| 200 | 400 | 250 | 700 |
| 300 | 300 | 300 | 600 |
| 400 | 200 | 350 | 500 |
| 500 | 100 | 400 | 400 |
| 600 | 0 | 450 | 350 |

  **a** Represent the data in Table 18.1 graphically.
  **b** What equilibrium price and quantity would result if the market for education is unregulated?
  **c** What is the allocatively efficient number of students?

**2** In an attempt to address the inefficient level of education the government has decided to subsidize schooling.
  **a** The government offers £200 to each student who buys a year of education.
    **i** Draw the new marginal private benefit curve, which includes the subsidy, on your graph and label it $MPB_2$.
    **ii** What are the approximate new equilibrium price and number of students?

**b** The government increases the subsidy to £400.
  **i** Draw another marginal private benefit curve, which includes the subsidy, on your graph and label it $MPB_2$.
  **ii** What are the approximate corresponding equilibrium price and number of students?
**c** What level of subsidy will achieve the efficient number of students in education?

**3** Two candidates are competing in an election for president of the Economics Club. The only issue dividing them is how much will be spent on the annual club party. The seven members of the club (*A* to *G*) have preferences as shown in Table 18.2 regarding how much should be spent on the party.

**Table 18.2**

| Voting member | Proposed amount (pounds) |
| --- | --- |
| A | 10 |
| B | 20 |
| C | 30 |
| D | 40 |
| E | 50 |
| F | 60 |
| G | 70 |

**a** How much will each candidate propose to spend?
**b** To demonstrate that your answer to **a** is correct, consider the outcome of the following two contests.

  **i** Candidate 1 proposes the amount you gave in **a** and candidate 2 proposes £1 less. Which candidate will win? Why?
  **ii** Candidate 1 proposes the amount you gave in **a** and candidate 2 proposes £1 more. Which candidate will win? Why?

## DISCUSSION QUESTION

**1** How might governments take action that would create inefficiency?

## DATA QUESTIONS

In recent years there has been growing opposition to the building of new motorways and other roads. For example, the decision to build a bypass round Newbury provoked widespread opposition from conservationists.

Rather than leaving it to the market, the government decides the quantity of motorways to be built, largely because motorways can be regarded as a semi-public good.

**1** Explain what is meant by a 'public good' and show why motorways might be regarded as a semi-public good.

**2** Why do conservationists oppose the building of motorways?

# ANSWERS

## CONCEPT REVIEW

**1** market failure
**2** interest; choice
**3** private; rivalry; excludability

**4** pure public
**5** free rider; less
**6** marginal benefit
**7** externality; cost; benefit
**8** private property right

**9** private; social

**10** greater

**11** median; benefit; marginal

**12** excise

## TRUE OR FALSE

**1 T** Allocatively inefficient output.

**2 T** Believe government agents act in their own interest, not necessarily public interest.

**3 T** Non-excludability means no incentive to pay.

**4 F** 'Public good' has precise meaning.

**5 T** Definition.

**6 T** Because it ignores external benefits.

**7 T** $MSC = MPC$ + externality.

**8 F** Output should be cut.

**9 T** This will equalize $MSC$ and $MSB$.

**10 F** The theory assumes that they are concerned for their own self-interest.

**11 T** Because this will maximize votes.

**12 F** There are costs involved in acquiring information, so it may be rational to stay ignorant.

## MULTIPLE CHOICE

**1 d** Any income distribution can be associated with allocative efficiency.

**2 a** Definition.

**3 b** Providing public goods would not be profitable for private firms.

**4 c** Cannot exclude ships from seeing the light.

**5 d** See Figure 18.5, text page 449.

**6 a** b–d involve irrelevant costs.

**7 b** Vertical distance between $MSC$ and $MPC$ at $Q = 6$.

**8 d** Where $MPC$ intersects demand.

**9 b** Where $MSC$ intersects demand.

**10 b** Where $MC$ intersects demand.

**11 c** Where $MC$ intersects $MSB$.

**12 d** Shift $MC$ down by vertical distance between $MSB$ and demand.

**13 d** Political marketplace.

**14 b** Definition.

**15 a** It assumes that people are motivated by self-interest.

**16 b** They will maximize their vote according to the principle of minimum differentiation.

## SHORT ANSWER

**1** A good has the non-rivalry feature if its consumption by one person does not reduce the amount available for others. The non-excludability feature means that if the good is produced and consumed by one person, others cannot be excluded from consuming it as well.

**2** The free-rider problem is the problem of unregulated markets producing too little of a pure public good because there is little incentive for individuals to pay for the good. The reason is that the person's payment is likely to have no perceptible effect on the amount the person will be able to consume.

**3** The existence of external costs means that producers do not take into account all costs when deciding how much to produce. If a tax is levied that is exactly the amount of the external cost, the cost will no longer be external. As a result, the producer will take it into account and thus be induced to produce the efficient quantity.

**4** In both cases the equilibrium is a state of rest in the sense that no group has an incentive to change its choices. When a political market is in equilibrium neither demanders (voters) nor suppliers (politicians and bureaucrats) are able to make an alternative choice that will make them better off.

**5** The reason more managers are needed now is that before the reforms only a few people were needed to work on the financial side of the health service. The reforms introduced changes so that GPs bought services from providers such as hospitals. This required more accounts and thus more accountants.

However, supporters of the changes would argue that the reforms made managers more aware of costs and that competition among providers led to increased efficiency in other areas.

## PROBLEMS

**1 a** Figure 18.3 is a graphical representation of the data in Table 18.1. The demand for education is given by the marginal private benefit curve (labelled *MPB*); the marginal private cost curve is labelled *MPC* and the marginal social benefit curve is labelled *MSB*.

**Figure 18.3**

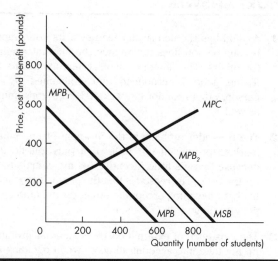

**b** In an unregulated market, equilibrium price and quantity are determined by the intersection of the *MPB* and *MPC* curves. Thus the equilibrium price would be £300 and the equilibrium quantity is 300 students.

**c** Since there are no external costs, the efficient quantity is determined by the intersection of the *MPC* and *MSB* curves. This implies that allocative efficiency is attained at a quantity of 500 students.

**2 a i** The subsidy increases the marginal private benefit to each student by the amount of the subsidy, £200. The new *MPB* curve, labelled *MPB*₁, is included in Fig. 18.3.

    **ii** The new equilibrium after the £200 subsidy is at the intersection of the *MPC* and *MPB*₁ curves. The price of a unit of education will be approximately £370 (£366.67) and there will be approximately 430 (433.33) students.

**b i** With a subsidy of £400 per student, the *MPB* curve will shift to *MPB*₂ in Fig. 18.3.

    **ii** With this subsidy the equilibrium will be at the intersection of the *MPC* and *MPB*₂ curves. The corresponding price of a unit of education will be approximately £430 (£433.33) and the number of students will be approximately 570 (566.67).

**c** In order to achieve an efficient outcome, the subsidy must make the *MPB* curve coincide with the *MSB* curve. This requires a subsidy of £300 per student.

**3 a** Each candidate will propose spending £40 since that is the preference of the median voter (voter *D*)

**b i** Candidate 1 will win because *D*, *E*, *F* and *G* will vote for that candidate since £40 comes closer to matching their preferences than the £39 proposed by candidate 2. Only *A*, *B* and *C* will vote for candidate 2.

    **ii** Candidate 1 will win with the votes of *A*, *B*, *C* and *D*; only *E*, *F* and *G* will vote for candidate 2.

## DISCUSSION QUESTION

**1** The idea that governments won't create inefficiency is called the 'public interest' theory of government. It is based on the assumption that government actions lead to allocative efficiency.

On the other hand, public choice theories assert that well-informed interest groups are able to persuade government to undertake programmes that do not maximize net benefits because most voters are rationally ignorant. For most voters, the costs of gaining information may exceed the benefits obtained. Hence interest groups will have an influence on government that exceeds their size.

# DATA QUESTIONS

**1** A public good is one that can be consumed simultaneously by everyone and from which no one can be excluded. A lighthouse is a good example; one ship looking at the light does not stop others from seeing it, and the owner of the lighthouse cannot stop ships from seeing the light.

Roads can be used simultaneously by many people, and while it is possible to exclude cars it is often impractical to do so. Hence they exhibit some of the characteristics of public goods, but are clearly not 'pure' public goods.

**2** New roads are opposed by conservationists largely because of their undesirable side effects on the environment. Economists call these 'externalities' and they are discussed in detail in Chapter 20.

# Chapter 19 — **Regulation and Privatization**

---

## Chapter in Perspective, Text Pages 465–492

This chapter examines government industrial policy. It focuses in particular on the economic aspects of public corporations and natural monopolies and examines how governments attempt to control such firms. This chapter also describes the competition policies adopted by the United Kingdom and the European Union and the reasons for regional policy.

---

## Helpful Hints

**1** Consider Fig. 19.1, which depicts revenue and marginal cost curves for an industry. Using this figure, it is helpful to think of regulation as determining how the potential total surplus (the area of triangle *abc*) is divided among consumer surplus, producer surplus and deadweight loss.

If the industry is perfectly competitive, then the quantity traded will be $Q_c$ and the market price will be $P_c$. Total surplus is maximized and is given by the area of the triangle *abc*. Total surplus is equal to the sum of consumer surplus given by the area of triangle *dbc* and producer surplus given by the area of the triangle *adc*. There is no deadweight loss.

If the industry is a profit-maximizing monopoly, output will be $Q_m$ and the price will be $P_m$. In this case, total surplus is represented by the area of trapezoid *abfg*. Because of monopoly restriction of output, total surplus under monopoly is less than under competition. The difference is the deadweight loss from monopoly, the amount of total surplus that is lost when we go from competition to monopoly. The deadweight loss is given by the area of the triangle *gfc*. Total surplus can be divided into consumer surplus given by the area of triangle *ebf* and producer surplus given by the area of trapezoid *aefg*. Consumer surplus is quite small but producer surplus is at a maximum.

Of course, actual output may be between these bounds. As output moves from $Q_c$ to $Q_m$, consumer surplus decreases while producer surplus and the deadweight loss both increase. If this industry is regulated, the public interest theory of intervention predicts that the result will be a level of output close to $Q_c$, while the capture theory of intervention predicts a level of output closer to $Q_m$.

**Figure 19.1**

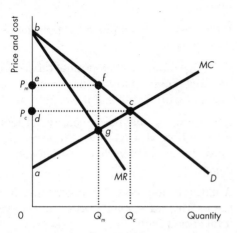

# Key Figures and Table

### Figure 19.2 Natural Monopoly: Marginal Cost Pricing, text page 473

Natural monopolies are heavily regulated. A natural monopoly has decreasing average total cost (*ATC*) over the entire range of market demand. Thus marginal cost (*MC*) is less than *ATC*. This figure illustrates a marginal cost pricing rule as applied to a natural monopoly. Setting the price at marginal cost maximizes total surplus.

### Figure 19.3 Natural Monopoly: Average Cost Pricing, text page 474

This figure uses the same example as Fig. 19.2 to illustrate an average cost pricing rule as applied to a natural monopoly. The price is set equal to average

total cost – at the intersection of the *ATC* curve and the demand curve.

Average cost pricing gives a price of £15 a month and 6 million households are served. The company now breaks even, but consumer surplus is less than under marginal cost pricing and there is a deadweight loss generated equal to the area of the grey triangle. This is the outcome predicted by the public interest theory of intervention.

### Figure 19.4 Natural Monopoly: Profit Maximization, text page 475

If a company is able to maximize profit, it will equate marginal cost (*MC*) and marginal revenue (*MR*). The resulting price will be above average total cost, and the company will now make a profit. Consumer surplus (the area of the green triangle) has declined even further, and the deadweight loss has increased to the area of the grey triangle. This is the outcome predicted by the capture theory of intervention.

### Figure 19.6 Collusive Oligopoly, text page 478

From Chapter 13, we know that an oligopoly industry can make monopoly profits if the firms in the industry form a cartel and enter into a collusive agreement. Because each firm has an incentive to cheat, however, it is difficult to enforce the cartel agreement. As a result, an oligopoly may 'demand' regulation, which has the effect of making the government regulatory agency enforce the collusive agreement that generates monopoly profits for the industry. This is illustrated in the figure.

### Table 19.3 The Main UK Monopoly and Competition Laws, text page 480

This table is a useful summary of the legal position in the United Kingdom.

# SELF-TEST

## CONCEPT REVIEW

**1** There are two principal ways in which the government intervenes in monopolistic and oligopolistic markets. The first of these is _____ , which consists of rules administered by a government agency and

intended to restrict the behaviour of firms. The second is _____ _____ _____ , which legally prohibits certain kinds of monopoly practice.

**2** The difference between the most that consumers are willing to pay and the amount they actually pay is called _____ _____ .

The difference between the revenue received by a producer and the opportunity cost of production is called _____ _____ . The sum of these is _____ _____ .

**3** Allocative efficiency is achieved when total surplus is _____ .

**4** The larger the consumer surplus per buyer resulting from intervention, the _____ is the demand for intervention by buyers. The larger the producer surplus per seller resulting from intervention, the _____ is the demand for intervention by sellers.

**5** The _____ _____ theory of intervention claims that intervention is supplied in order to attain allocative efficiency. The _____ theory of intervention states that intervention is intended to maximize producer surplus.

**6** The process of selling a publicly owned corporation to private shareholders is called _____ .

**7** The pricing rule that maximizes total surplus and achieves allocative efficiency is the _____ _____ pricing rule.

**8** When a regulatory agency sets the price of a regulated natural monopolist so that the regulated firm is able to earn a specified target percentage return on its capital, it is using _____ _____ _____ regulation. If the target rate of return is a normal rate of return, this form of regulation gives the same result as the _____ _____ pricing rule.

**9** British regulatory bodies such as OFTEL have adopted _____ cap regulation using the RPI _____ formula.

## TRUE OR FALSE

**1** Regulation and privatization are the two main ways that the government intervenes in the operation of monopolistic and oligopolistic markets.

**2** In a monopoly industry, producer surplus is maximized at the profit-maximizing level of output.

**3** In a monopoly industry, total surplus is maximized at the profit-maximizing level of output.

**4** Intervention is supplied by politicians and bureaucrats.

**5** Evidence of higher-than-normal rates of return for regulated natural monopolies would match the predictions of the capture theory.

**6** According to the public interest theory of intervention, all government intervention will move the economy closer to allocative efficiency.

**7** A natural monopoly will always produce on the downward sloping portion of its average total cost curve.

**8** For a natural monopoly, marginal cost will always be less than average total cost.

**9** An average cost pricing rule will achieve allocative efficiency.

**10** Under rate of return regulation, firms can get closer to maximizing producer surplus if they inflate their costs.

**11** According to the public interest theory, regulators will regulate a cartel to make sure that firms do not cheat on the collusive cartel agreement to restrict output.

## MULTIPLE CHOICE

**1** The difference between the maximum amount consumers are willing to pay and the amount they actually do pay for a given quantity of a good is called
**a** government surplus.
**b** consumer surplus.
**c** producer surplus.
**d** total surplus.
**e** deadweight surplus.

**2** Total surplus is given by the sum of
**a** the gain from trade accruing to consumers and the gain from trade accruing to producers.
**b** the gain from regulation and the gain from anti-combination laws.
**c** revenues received by firms and government subsidies.
**d** consumer payments and producer profit.
**e** none of the above.

**3** Total surplus is maximized when
   **a** marginal cost equals marginal revenue.
   **b** marginal cost equals average total cost.
   **c** price equals marginal cost.
   **d** price equals average total cost.
   **e** price equals average variable cost.

**4** A large demand for intervention by *producers* will result when there is a
   **a** small consumer surplus per buyer.
   **b** large consumer surplus per buyer.
   **c** large number of buyers.
   **d** small producer surplus per firm.
   **e** large producer surplus per firm.

**5** Which of the following is consistent with the public interest theory of intervention?
   **a** regulation of a natural monopolist by setting price equal to marginal cost
   **b** regulation of a competitive industry in order to increase output
   **c** regulation of the airline industry by establishing minimum airfares
   **d** regulation of agriculture by establishing barriers to exit from the industry
   **e** none of the above

**6** Which of the following is consistent with the capture theory of intervention?
   **a** regulation of a natural monopolist by setting price equal to marginal cost
   **b** regulation of a competitive industry in order to increase output
   **c** regulation of the airline industry by establishing minimum airfares
   **d** regulation of agriculture by establishing barriers to exit from the industry
   **e** none of the above

**7** Figure 19.2 gives the revenue and cost curves for an industry. This industry will become a natural monopoly because
   **a** one firm can supply the entire market at a lower price than can two or more firms.
   **b** there are decreasing returns to scale over the entire range of demand.
   **c** there are diseconomies of scale over the entire range of demand.
   **d** even a single firm will be unable to earn a positive profit in this industry.
   **e** all of the above are true.

**Figure 19.2**

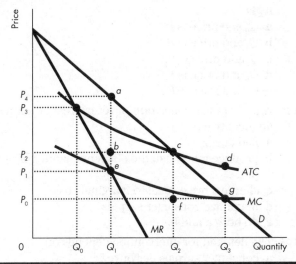

**8** Consider the natural monopoly depicted in Fig. 19.2. If the firm is unregulated and operates as a private profit-maximizer, what output will it produce?
   **a** 0, because the firm suffers economic losses when $P = MC$.
   **b** $Q_0$
   **c** $Q_1$
   **d** $Q_2$
   **e** $Q_3$

**9** Consider the natural monopoly depicted in Fig. 19.2. If a regulatory agency sets a price just sufficient for the firm to earn normal profits, what output will it produce?
   **a** 0, because the firm suffers economic losses when $P = MC$.
   **b** $Q_0$
   **c** $Q_1$
   **d** $Q_2$
   **e** $Q_3$

**10** Consider the natural monopoly depicted in Fig. 19.2. Total surplus is a maximum when quantity is
   **a** $Q_0$ and price is $P_3$.
   **b** $Q_1$ and price is $P_1$.
   **c** $Q_1$ and price is $P_4$.
   **d** $Q_2$ and price is $P_2$.
   **e** $Q_3$ and price is $P_0$.

**11** Consider the natural monopoly depicted in Fig. 19.2. Producer surplus is a maximum when quantity is
  **a** $Q_0$ and price is $P_3$.
  **b** $Q_1$ and price is $P_1$.
  **c** $Q_1$ and price is $P_4$.
  **d** $Q_2$ and price is $P_2$.
  **e** $Q_3$ and price is $P_0$.

**12** A monopolist under rate of return regulation has an incentive to
  **a** pad costs.
  **b** produce more than the efficient quantity of output.
  **c** charge a price equal to marginal cost.
  **d** maximize consumer surplus.
  **e** do both **a** and **b**.

**13** The demand for intervention depends on
  **a** consumer surplus per buyer.
  **b** number of buyers.
  **c** producer surplus per firm.
  **d** number of firms.
  **e** all of the above.

## SHORT ANSWER

**1** Regulation of monopoly is necessary because of the tension between the public interest and the producer's interest. Explain.

**2** In the regulation of a natural monopoly, when would an average cost pricing rule be better than a marginal cost pricing rule?

**3** Why is rate of return regulation equivalent to average cost pricing?

**4** Explain the problem that the recent deregulation process poses for the capture theory of intervention.

**5** With reference to the *Reading Between the Lines* article in this chapter, why do you think that gas prices have fallen in the United Kingdom?

## PROBLEMS

**1 a** It has been suggested that government should eliminate monopoly profit by taxing each unit of monopoly output. What effect would such a policy have on the quantity a monopolist produces and the price it charges?
  **b** What is the effect on economic efficiency?

**2** The demand for Aerodiscs, a disc made from a unique material that flies a considerable distance when thrown, is given by this equation:

$$P = 10 - 0.01 \, Q_D.$$

The corresponding marginal revenue (*MR*) equation is:

$$MR = 10 - 0.02 \, Q.$$

The Aerodisc Company is a natural monopoly. The firm's total fixed cost is £700 and the marginal cost is constant at £2 per disc. (*Note*: This implies that average variable cost is also constant at £2 per disc.) Suppose that the Aerodisc Company is not regulated.
  **a** What will be the quantity sold and the price of an Aerodisc?
  **b** How much is total profit or loss?
  **c** How much is producer surplus?
  **d** How much is consumer surplus?
  **e** How much is total surplus?

**3** Now suppose that the Aerodisc Company becomes regulated and that the regulator uses a marginal cost pricing rule.
  **a** What will be the quantity sold and the price of an Aerodisc?
  **b** How much is total profit or loss?
  **c** How much is producer surplus?
  **d** How much is consumer surplus?
  **e** How much is total surplus?

**4** Suppose that the regulator of the Aerodisc Company uses an average cost pricing rule.
  **a** What will be the price of an Aerodisc and how many will be sold?
  **b** How much is total profit or loss?
  **c** How much is producer surplus?
  **d** How much is consumer surplus?
  **e** How much is total surplus?

**5** Figure 19.3 illustrates the industry demand, marginal revenue (*MR*) and marginal cost (*MC*) curves in an oligopoly industry. The industry is regulated.
  **a** What price and quantity will be predicted by the public interest theory of regulation? Why?
  **b** What price and quantity will be predicted by the capture theory of regulation? Why?
  **c** Can you explain why the firms in this industry might be demanders of regulation?

**Figure 19.3**

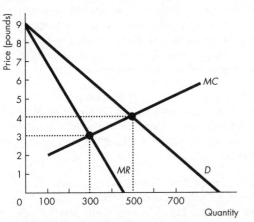

## DISCUSSION QUESTION

**1** How do natural monopolies originate?

## DATA QUESTIONS

**Regulating the United Kingdom's Privatized Monopolies**
A small number of important industries in market economies need to be regulated to prevent monopoly abuse. These industries are natural monopolies where competition cannot exist or must remain limited. A regulatory structure is intended to provide a fair balance between the interests of consumers and the interests of shareholders. A further purpose is to replicate the static and dynamic efficiency incentives that exist in competitive markets.

The United Kingdom adopted a price cap rather than a rate of return regulation precisely to allow the regulated firms to make higher profits (until the next review) if they become more efficient. However, public concern about high profits and management salaries has led the regulatory offices to respond with price cap revisions outside the normal price review periods. But if the regulated firms believe that higher profits will trigger a mid-term price review, they are unlikely to seek the cost savings that lead to the higher profits.

*Source:* Adapted from David Parker, 'Regulating the UK's privatised monopolies', in *Developments in Economics*, GBJ Atkinson (ed.), **12**, 1996, Causeway Press.

**1** Explain what is meant by a natural monopoly and say why its existence requires regulation.

**2** Explain the difference between price cap and rate of return regulation.

**3** What do you think are the desirable and the undesirable consequences of mid-term price reviews?

# ANSWERS

## CONCEPT REVIEW

**1** regulation; general competition policy

**2** consumer surplus; producer surplus; total surplus

**3** maximized

**4** larger; larger

**5** public interest; capture

**6** privatization

**7** marginal cost

**8** rate of return; average cost

**9** price; –X

## TRUE OR FALSE

**1 F** Regulation but not privatization.

**2 T** Definition.

**3 F** True for competition.

**4 T** Definition.

**5 T** Regulators are captured and act in the interests of the monopoly.

**6 T** In this theory governments act in the public interest.

**7 T** To maximize profits.

**8 T** This is why *ATC* is always downward sloping.

**9 F** Marginal cost pricing will do this.

**10 T** Increased costs will allow them to increase profits.

**11 F** Regulators will prohibit collusive cartels.

## MULTIPLE CHOICE

**1 b** Definition.

**2 a** Consumer surplus plus producer surplus.

**3 c** Pricing rule for allocative efficiency.

**4 e** **b, c** lead to increased demand by buyers.

**5 a** This is the only option which will lead to increased efficiency.

**6 c** Helps airline firms, not consumers.

**7 a** Definition of natural monopoly.

**8 c** Where $MC = MR$.

**9 d** Where $P = ATC$.

**10 e** Where $P = MC$.

**11 c** Private monopoly outcome.

**12 a** Higher costs will allow higher profits.

**13 e** Definition.

## SHORT ANSWER

**1** It is in the public interest to achieve allocative efficiency; to expand output to the level that maximizes total surplus. On the other hand, it is in the interest of the monopoly producer to restrict output in order to maximize producer surplus and thus monopoly profit.

Since these interests are not the same, monopoly must be regulated in order to achieve allocative efficiency. The public interest theory of regulation suggests that this is the principle that guides regulation of monopoly industries.

**2** An average cost pricing rule will create a deadweight loss, but so will a marginal cost pricing rule, through the need to impose a tax.

Since for a natural monopoly marginal cost is less than average total cost, regulation by use of a marginal cost pricing rule requires the government to pay a subsidy in order for the firm to be willing to produce at all.

To pay that subsidy the government must levy a tax, which will impose a deadweight loss on the economy. If the deadweight loss associated with the tax (for example, the deadweight loss of the marginal cost pricing rule with its attendant subsidy) is greater than the deadweight loss of an average cost pricing rule, the average cost pricing rule is superior.

**3** The key here is to recall that economic cost includes a normal rate of return. Thus because rate of return regulation sets a price that allows the firm to achieve a normal rate of return, it is setting the price equal to average total cost.

**4** The capture theory predicts that producers will capture the regulatory process and use it to maximize producer surplus. But if the producer lobby was strong enough to achieve regulation, why have producers been unable to stop deregulation? A further question is why do many producers *favour* deregulation? The capture theory has no good answers to these questions.

**5** There are several reasons why gas prices have fallen in the United Kingdom. One is that new gasfields have come onstream. This increase in supply would have led to a fall in price whatever the ownership of the industry. Second, the gas regulator has imposed price controls on British Gas. Lastly, competition has been introduced in the industry, and as would be predicted from economic theory, increased competition tends to mean lower prices.

## PROBLEMS

**1 a** Imposing a tax on each unit sold by a monopolist will increase marginal cost. As a consequence the profit-maximizing monopolist will raise the price and reduce the quantity produced.

**b** The tax will certainly reduce the profit of the monopolist and may even eliminate it, but the consequence will be to make the inefficiency owing to monopoly even worse. This is illustrated in Fig. 19.4. The curve *MC* is the marginal cost curve before the tax. An unregulated monopolist will produce amount $Q_2$, while the economically efficient output is $Q_3$. The tax, however, causes the monopolist to reduce output from $Q_1$ to $Q_2$, which moves the market outcome further away from efficiency.

**2** Figure 19.5 will be helpful in answering questions about the Aerodisc market. It gives the relevant revenue and cost curves for the Aerodisc Company.

**Figure 19.4**

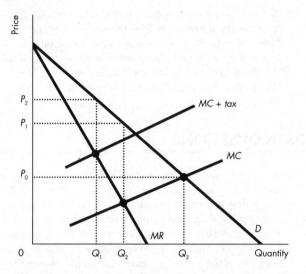

**Figure 19.5**

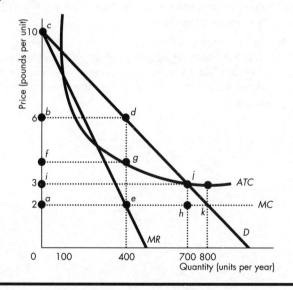

**a** In an unregulated market, the Aerodisc Company will choose output so as to maximize profit, where $MR = MC$. To calculate this output, set $MR = MC = 2$ and solve for $Q$:

$$10 - 0.02Q = 2$$
$$8 = 0.02Q$$
$$400 = Q$$

To calculate price, substitute $Q = 400$ into the demand equation:

$$P = 10 - 0.01Q_D$$
$$= 10 - 0.01\,(400)$$
$$= 10 - 4$$
$$= 6$$

So 400 Aerodiscs will be produced and sold at a price of £6 each.

**b** To determine total profit we first determine average total cost ($ATC$) when output ($Q$) is 400 units.

$$ATC = AFC + AVC$$
$$= (TFC/Q) + AVC$$
$$= (700/400) + 2$$
$$= 3.75.$$

Therefore, total profit is the difference between price (average revenue) and $ATC$ times the quantity sold. This is equal to £90 and is represented in Fig. 19.5 by the region *fbdg*.

**c** Producer surplus is the difference between the producer's revenue and the opportunity cost of production. Total revenue is £2,400 (£6 × 400 units) and total opportunity cost is £800 (£2 × 400 units). Thus producer surplus is £1,600. Graphically, producer surplus is the area of the rectangle *abde* in Fig. 19.5.

**d** Consumer surplus is readily obtained graphically as the area in the triangle denoted *bcd* in Fig. 19.5. The area of that triangle is £800.

**e** Total surplus is £2,400, the sum of producer and consumer surplus.

**3 a** Under a marginal cost pricing rule, the price of an Aerodisc will be equal to marginal cost or £2. To calculate the quantity sold, substitute the price into the demand equation:

$$P = 10 - 0.01Q_D$$
$$2 = 10 - 0.01Q_D$$
$$0.01Q_D = 8$$
$$Q_D = 800.$$

**b** To determine the amount of profit or loss, we must first determine $ATC$ when output is 800. Using the procedure in the previous problem we find that at $Q = 800$, $ATC$ is £2.875 which is greater than price by £0.875 (87.5 pence). Therefore, the Aerodisc Company will make a loss of £700 (£0.875 × 800). Alternatively, since $MC$, is constant, if the price is set equal to $MC$, which is equal to $AVC$, the total loss will be just $TFC$ or £700.

**c** Producer surplus is zero.

**d** Consumer surplus is given by the area of the triangle *ach* in Fig. 19.5, which is £3,200.

**e** Total surplus is £3,200 (a maximum).

**4 a** Computation of $ATC$ at various levels of output allows us to determine that the $ATC$ curve crosses the demand curve when $Q = 700$ and $ATC = £3$. Thus under an average cost pricing rule, the price of an Aerodisc will be £3 and 700 units will be sold.

**b** Since price is equal to average total cost, profit is zero.

**c** Producer surplus is £700, the area of the rectangle *aijh* in Fig. 19.5.

**d** Consumer surplus is £2,450, the area of the triangle *ijc* in Fig. 19.5.

**e** Total surplus is £3,150.

**5 a** The public interest theory predicts that regulators will set price and quantity so as to maximize total surplus. This means that they will choose quantity (and price) where *MC* is equal to demand. This corresponds to a quantity of 500 units and a price of £4 per unit.

**b** The capture theory predicts that the regulator will choose quantity and price so as to maximize the profit of the industry. This is the quantity that would be chosen by a profit-maximizing monopolist, 300 units, where *MC = MR*. The highest price that could be charged and still sell that quantity can be read from the demand curve: £6 per unit.

**c** Firms in the industry would be demanders of regulation if the regulation had the effect of increasing profit to the industry. As we discovered in Chapter 13, cartels are unstable because there is always an incentive to cheat on output restriction agreements and it is very difficult to enforce the agreements. If, however, the firms in an industry can get the government, through regulation, to enforce a cartel agreement, they will want to do it.

## DISCUSSION QUESTION

**1** Natural monopolies occur when the technology within an industry allows one firm to serve the market at a lower cost than more than one firm. For example, the technology of supplying water to a street is such that the fixed costs of laying pipes are extremely high, so that it would be inefficient for a second firm to lay pipes in the same street.

## DATA QUESTIONS

**1** A natural monopoly is a monopoly that occurs when there is a unique source of supply of a raw material or when one large firm can supply the entire market at a lower price than two or more firms. Such monopolies require regulation because competition is not normally possible, so firms may make monopoly profits at the expense of the consumer, as explained in Chapter 12.

**2** Price cap regulation is the phrase used to describe the process whereby a regulator fixes the price that a firm can charge. Its advantage is that it creates an incentive for firms to cut costs. Rate of return regulation occurs when the regulator fixes the rate of return a firm can make on its investment.

**3** The benefit of a mid-term price review is that it may prevent firms making excess profits, reassure the public and enable the regulator to correct any mistakes. Its disadvantage is that it removes the incentive for firms to cut costs.

# Chapter 20 Externalities, the Environment and Knowledge

Text Pages 493–516

## Chapter in Perspective, Text Pages 493–516

This chapter focuses on the economist's approach to the environment and knowledge. It discusses important concepts such as externalities and property rights and shows how they can be used to analyse the environment and can lead to better policies.

The chapter also discusses intellectual property rights.

## Helpful Hints

1  The equilibrium quantity in a competitive market is the amount at which the marginal private cost equals the marginal private benefit. The efficient quantity is the amount at which the marginal social cost and the marginal social benefit are equal.

If the marginal private cost equals the marginal social cost and the marginal private benefit equals the marginal social benefit, the equilibrium amount that is produced equals the efficient amount. This outcome reflects Adam Smith's idea of the invisible hand – that people, seeking to do only what is best for themselves, will be led to do what is best for society 'as if by an invisible hand'.

In most transactions, there are no affected third parties and so there are no external costs or benefits. In other words, private and social costs along with private and social benefits coincide and competitive markets are efficient.

But when third parties are affected, external costs or benefits arise and competitive markets will not be efficient. With external benefits, the marginal private benefit curve lies to the left of the marginal social benefit curve. With external costs, the marginal private cost curve lies to the right of the marginal social cost curve. In both instances, the amount produced in an unregulated market – the level at which the marginal private benefit and private cost curves intersect – is not the efficient amount.

2  If the production of a good or service produces external costs, a competitive market results in a quantity that exceeds the allocatively efficient level. This conclusion makes sense in terms of marginal analysis. People continue an action as

long as the marginal benefit from it exceeds the marginal cost. If they ignore some of the marginal costs of the action, they will do 'too much' of it; that is, more than the efficient amount of the product is produced. Similarly, with external benefits, some of the marginal benefits from the action are ignored. As a result, too little of the action is undertaken, and less than the efficient amount is produced. If you keep this explanation in mind, you will not go wrong when thinking about the impact of externalities on a private market.

**3** Competitive markets with externalities are not efficient because some of the costs or benefits are external. If those costs or benefits could be internalized somehow, the market would be efficient. The chapter discusses two general approaches to internalizing externalities.

The first is to define property rights clearly and enforce them strictly. Then costs (or benefits) imposed on (enjoyed by) non-participants in a transaction will no longer be external. The affected individual will have a voice in the transaction because some of his or her property is affected and the costs (or benefits) become internal through this voice.

The second is to tax or otherwise charge activities that generate external costs and subsidize or otherwise reward activities that generate external benefits. Charging a tax equal to the external cost makes the entire cost internal. Similarly, paying a subsidy in the amount of the external benefit makes the entire benefit internal.

Both of these general methods strive to ensure that the private marginal cost and private marginal benefit accurately reflect the social marginal cost and social marginal benefit. If the private marginal cost and benefit curves correctly mirror the social marginal cost and benefit curves, the level of the good that will be produced is the efficient amount.

## Key Figures

**Figure 20.3 Externalities and The Coase Theorem, text page 499**
This figure shows how it is possible to calculate the efficient quantity of pollution. This will occur when the marginal social cost equals the marginal social benefit.

**Figure 20.5 Marketable Pollution Permits, text page 502**
This three part figure shows how marketable permits can achieve efficiency. Firms with low marginal benefits from pollution will sell their permits to firms with high marginal benefits. If the market works well, the result will be an efficient equilibrium where $MSB = MC$.

# SELF-TEST

## CONCEPT REVIEW

**1** An _____ is a cost or benefit arising from a transaction that affects someone who is not part of the original transaction. Externalities create market _____ .

**2** The _____ theorem holds that if property rights exist and _____ costs are low, there are no externalities.

**3** To maximize society's well-being, the government should aim at producing the level of output at which _____ social cost equals marginal _____ benefit.

**4** One way to tackle externalities is to issue _____ permits which give polluters tradable permits. Alternatively, the government can levy a tax equal to the marginal _____ cost.

**5** Three policies the government can use to achieve an efficient allocation of resources in the presence of external benefits from education and development are subsidies, _____ - _____ _____ and patents.

**6** A subsidy is a payment to producers that depends on the level of _____ .

**7** Patents increase the incentive to _____ .

# TRUE OR FALSE

___ **1** If negative externalities exist, marginal social cost and marginal external cost are equivalent.

___ **2** Externalities arise from the absence of private property rights.

___ **3** Knowledge is an example of a product with external benefits.

___ **4** Assigning a property right will cure the problem of an externality.

___ **5** The efficient amount of pollution is always no pollution.

___ **6** The private market produces more than the efficient amount of a good having a positive externality.

___ **7** One reason that there is not a high tax on carbon fuels is that the cost of the tax is incurred now but any benefits from the tax would be obtained in the future.

___ **8** If the production of a good involves no external costs, the marginal social cost equals the marginal private cost.

___ **9** The inefficiency created by an external cost in the production of a good can be overcome if the government subsidizes production of the good.

___ **10** The Coase theorem states that externalities do not exist if property rights are defined and transactions costs are low.

___ **11** Externalities can create market failure.

# MULTIPLE CHOICE

**1** An externality is a cost or benefit arising from an economic transaction that falls on
  **a** consumers but not producers.
  **b** producers but not consumers.
  **c** someone not party to the transaction.
  **d** rivals.

**2** The production of too many goods with negative externalities is an example of
  **a** consumer sovereignty.
  **b** producer sovereignty.
  **c** public failure.
  **d** market failure.

**3** A copper ore refiner pollutes the water upstream from a brewery. The transactions costs of reaching an agreement between the two are low. When will the amount of water pollution be at its efficient level?
  **a** only if the property right to the stream is assigned to the ore refiner
  **b** only if the property right to the stream is assigned to the brewery
  **c** whenever the property right to the stream is assigned to either the refiner or the brewer
  **d** none of the above because the premise of the question is wrong: there is no such thing as the efficient level of pollution

**4** Suppose that production of rubber for trainers creates an external cost of $2 per tonne of rubber but no external benefits. Then the efficient amount of rubber will be produced when the government imposes a
  **a** subsidy of more than $2 per tonne of rubber.
  **b** subsidy of $2 per tonne of rubber.
  **c** tax of more than $2 per tonne of rubber.
  **d** tax of $2 per tonne of rubber.

**5** Which of the following illustrates the concept of external cost?
  **a** Bad weather decreases the size of the wheat crop.
  **b** A reduction in the size of the wheat crop causes the income of wheat farmers to fall.
  **c** Smoking harms the health of the smoker.
  **d** Smoking harms the health of nearby non-smokers.

**6** A reason for not enacting a high carbon-fuel tax in the United Kingdom is that
  **a** both the costs of and benefits from the tax will occur sometime in the future.
  **b** less developed nations may not decrease their consumption of fuels.
  **c** the costs of global warming have been accurately estimated to be small.
  **d** scientific evidence no longer supports the hypothesis that carbon dioxide adds to global warming.

Use Fig. 20.1 for questions 7–11.

**Figure 20.1**

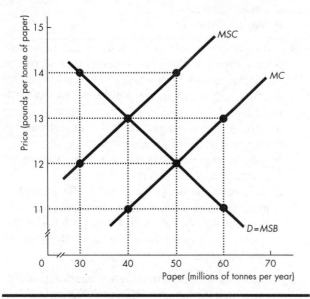

7 As illustrated in Fig. 20.1, the production of paper creates
   a only a positive externality.
   b only a negative externality.
   c both positive and negative externalities.
   d no externalities.

8 The amount of the externality illustrated in Fig. 20.1 is
   a £14 per tonne.
   b £12 per tonne.
   c £2 per tonne.
   d £0 per tonne because no externality is produced.

9 In the absence of any government intervention, how many tonnes of paper are produced in a year?
   a 60 million tonnes
   b 50 million tonnes
   c 40 million tonnes
   d 30 million tonnes

10 The allocatively efficient amount of paper produced in a year is
   a 60 million tonnes.
   b 50 million tonnes.
   c 40 million tonnes.
   d 30 million tonnes.

11 What amount of tax is necessary to cause the efficient amount of paper to be produced?
   a £14 per tonne
   b £12 per tonne

c £2 per tonne
d £0 per tonne because the efficient amount is produced without any government intervention

12 An externality is
   a the amount by which price exceeds marginal private cost.
   b the amount by which price exceeds marginal social cost.
   c the effect of government regulation on market price and output.
   d a cost or benefit that arises from a decision but is not borne by the decision maker.

13 Patents are a solution to the
   a positive externality from attending college.
   b positive externality from discovering new knowledge.
   c negative externality from attending college.
   d negative externality from discovering new knowledge.

Use Table 20.1 for the next four questions.

**Table 20.1**

| Quantity | Marginal private cost (pounds) | Marginal private benefit (pounds) | Marginal social benefit (pounds) |
|---|---|---|---|
| 500 | 5 | 9 | 11 |
| 550 | 6 | 8 | 10 |
| 600 | 7 | 7 | 9 |
| 650 | 8 | 6 | 8 |
| 700 | 9 | 5 | 7 |

14 Table 20.1 represents the market for a good with
   a only a negative externality.
   b only a positive externality
   c both positive and negative externalities.
   d no externalities.

15 Left alone, the equilibrium amount produced is
   a 550.
   b 600.
   c 650.
   d 700.

16 The allocatively efficient level of output is
   a 550.
   b 600.

c 650.

d 700.

**17** What can the government do to cause the efficient amount to be produced?

  a subsidize suppliers £8 per unit

  b subsidize suppliers £2 per unit

  c tax suppliers £2 per unit

  d tax suppliers £8 per unit

**18** Which of the following statements about property rights is correct?

  a Property rights have nothing to do with externalities.

  b The absence of property rights creates negative externalities but has nothing to do with the creation of positive externalities.

  c Property rights pertain only to the rights of owners of real estate.

  d Copyrights are a method of assigning intellectual property rights.

## SHORT ANSWER

**1** Governments provide education at a price (tuition fee) less than cost. What economic argument supports this policy?

**2** Explain how a tax can be used to achieve efficiency in the face of external costs.

**3** What is the marginal social benefit of pollution?

**4** Can you relate the idea of externalities to the *Reading Between the Lines* article in this chapter?

## PROBLEMS

**1** In a small town two factories – factory $A$ and factory $B$ – each produce 10 units of pollution so that the total pollution is 20 units. Factory $A$ can decrease its pollution at a constant marginal cost of £50 per unit; factory $B$ can reduce its pollution at a constant marginal cost of £100 per unit.

  a If both factory $A$ and factory $B$ decrease their pollution by 5 units, what is the total amount of pollution in the town and what is the total cost of attaining this level of pollution?

  b If factory $A$ decreases its level of pollution by 10 units and factory $B$ does not decrease its pollution, what is the total amount of pollution in the town and what is the total cost of achieving this level of pollution?

  b From a social standpoint, to obtain a total of 10 units of pollution, which is more desirable: both factories cutting back by 5 units each or $A$ cutting back by 10 units and $B$ not cutting back? Why?

**2** Vaccination creates a positive externality. Use Fig. 20.2 to illustrate the market for chicken pox vaccination. Label as $Q_0$ the doses that will be taken in the absence of any government intervention and as $Q_1$ the efficient number of doses. How might the government move this market towards allocative efficiency?

**Figure 20.2**

**3** The first two columns of Table 20.2 give the demand schedule for education in Transylvania, and the third column gives the marginal private cost. Because education generates external benefits, the marginal social benefit shown in the last column is greater than marginal private benefit.

  a What equilibrium price and quantity would result if the market for education is unregulated?

  b What is the allocatively efficient quantity of students in Transylvania?

**4** In an attempt to address the inefficient level of education in his country, Igor – the newly appointed minister of education – has decided to provide a low-cost public university, Igor Omphesus (Igor's middle name is Omphesus) University.

**a** To attain the efficient level of schooling, what must tuition fees be at the new university, IOU?

**b** What is the marginal cost of schooling the last student at this university?

**Table 20.2   Education in Transylvania**

| Quantity (number of students) | Marginal private benefit (Euros) | Marginal private cost (Euros) | Marginal social benefit (Euros) |
|---|---|---|---|
| 1 | 500 | 200 | 800 |
| 2 | 400 | 250 | 700 |
| 3 | 300 | 300 | 600 |
| 4 | 200 | 350 | 500 |
| 5 | 100 | 400 | 400 |
| 6 | 0 | 450 | 300 |

## DISCUSSION QUESTIONS

**1** Explain how it can be efficient to allow some pollution.

**2** How can we decide what is an efficient level of pollution?

## DATA QUESTION

### Urban Congestion

There are several reasons why the market is unable to supply transport services which would be regarded as 'efficient' in terms of relative quantities and qualities. For instance, road space is not sold in the usual manner, nor is it supplied whenever and wherever it makes a profit. Public transport systems follow price and supply policies which are very different from what would result in the absence of severe regulation of any alternative suppliers. Intervention by several institutions takes place to control, regulate, encourage, and often to discourage, various transport activities.

Because road space is not sold in the usual way, high-demand road space has a 'price' that is similar to low-demand road space. Therefore high-demand road space is rationed not by price, but by congestion and overcrowding. The failure to ration by price has caused the use of private motor vehicles to increase and that of public transport to decrease during off-peak periods.

*Source:* Adapted from B. Atkinson, P. Baker and B. Milward, *Economic Policy*, Macmillan, 1996.

**1** Why are markets not used to determine the quantity of transport services?

**2** How would an increase in fuel tax affect this market?

**3** Explain what is meant by 'the failure to ration by price'.

# ANSWERS

## CONCEPT REVIEW

**1** externality; failure

**2** Coase; transactions

**3** marginal; social benefit

**4** marketable; external

**5** below-cost provision

**6** output

**7** innovate

## TRUE OR FALSE

**1 F** Marginal social cost equals the marginal private cost plus the marginal externality cost.

**2 T** The fundamental reason for the existence of externalities is that property rights are not well defined.

**3 T** Because knowledge has external benefits, the unregulated private market produces less than the efficient amount.

**4 F** As the Coase theorem points out, assigning property rights will cure the problem of an externality only when transactions costs are low.

**5 F** The efficient amount of pollution is the amount that equalizes the marginal social benefit and cost from pollution.

**6 F** The private market produces *less* than the efficient amount of a good that has a positive externality.

**7 T** Because the benefits are obtained in the future, to take any actions at present to reap these benefits may not be worthwhile.

**8 T** The marginal social cost equals the marginal private cost plus the marginal externality cost. If there is no marginal externality cost, the marginal social cost equals the marginal private cost.

**9 F** If a good creates a negative externality, to attain allocative efficiency its production needs to be taxed, not subsidized.

**10 T** This essentially is the definition of the Coase theorem.

**11 T** Externalities are a reason for market failure; that is, the private, unregulated market does not produce the allocatively efficient level of a good.

## MULTIPLE CHOICE

**1 c** Definition.

**2 d** By producing more than the allocatively efficient amount, the private market has failed.

**3 c** The Coase theorem shows that, when transactions costs are low, to whom a property right is assigned makes no difference. The externality will be internalized, and the efficient level of production will result.

**4 d** Imposing a tax equal to the marginal external cost will set equal the marginal private cost – which includes the tax – and the marginal social cost, thereby ensuring that the efficient amount of rubber will be produced.

**5 d** Bystanders are not part of the initial transaction (the smoking), so the harm that befalls them is an external cost.

**6 b** The equilibrium in this prisoners' dilemma game may be that neither developed nor less-developed nations impose a carbon-fuel tax.

**7 b** Because the *MSC* curve is leftward of the *MC* curve, the figure indicates that the good is creating a negative externality.

**8 c** The vertical difference between the *MSC* curve and the *MC* curve is the marginal external cost, which in this case is £2 per tonne.

**9 b** In the absence of any intervention, the private market produces where the private demand curve (which is the same as the private marginal benefit curve) crosses the private supply curve (which is the same as the private marginal cost curve).

**10 c** Allocative efficiency requires that production be at the level where marginal social cost, *MSC*, equals marginal social benefit, *MSB*.

**11 c** The tax must shift the private *MC* curve until it is the same as the *MSC* curve. Imposing a £2 tax will shift the *MC* curve higher by the amount of the tax, £2, which is the amount desired. More generally, by imposing a tax equal to the marginal externality cost, the new marginal private cost, which includes the tax, is the same as the marginal social cost.

**12 d** Because the cost or benefit is not borne by the decision maker, the cost or benefit is *external* to the decision maker's choice. Being external, the cost or benefit is ignored by the decision maker.

**13 b** New discoveries often may be used by many people, which is an externality from the point of view of the discoverer.

**14 b** At any level of output, the marginal social benefit exceeds the marginal private benefit, which indicates that there must be a positive external benefit.

**15 b** The private market produces the level of output that equalizes the marginal private cost (the private supply curve) and the marginal private benefit (the private demand curve).

**16 e** Efficiency requires that the amount of the good produced equalize the marginal social cost and the marginal social benefit. In this case, efficiency requires that output be 650.

**17 b** If suppliers are granted a £2 per unit subsidy, the marginal private cost schedule drops by £2 at every unit of output. Hence to produce 650 units of output the new marginal private cost becomes £6. This equals the marginal private benefit of 650 units, so the (new) equilibrium price is £6 and the quantity produced is the efficient amount, or 650 units.

**18 d** Definition.

## SHORT ANSWER

**1** The economic argument is that education generates external benefits. In particular, when individuals are educated, society at large receives benefits beyond the private benefits that accrue to those choosing how much education to obtain. The presence of this positive externality means that in the absence of government intervention, the private sector would provide too little education for allocative efficiency. Hence to attain efficiency in the market for education, the government provides below-cost education at public colleges and universities.

**2** The existence of external costs means that producers do not take into account all costs when deciding how much to produce. If a tax is levied that is exactly the amount of the external cost, the cost is no longer external. As a result, the producer takes it into account and thus is induced to produce the efficient quantity.

**3** The marginal social benefit of pollution is the benefit firms receive from being able to pollute. For instance, by polluting the air, an electric utility reduces its costs because it does not have to install expensive pollution reduction devices, such as scrubbers, to decrease air pollution. Hence society benefits from pollution because firms are part of society. (More basically, the fact that the firm does not need to install pollution reduction devices means that the resources that might have been used to produce these devices can be used to produce other goods and services.) The fact that society benefits from pollution must be balanced against the fact that pollution imposes a cost on society, expressed as the marginal social cost of pollution.

**4** An externality is an effect of production or consumption which is not taken into account by the consumer or producer and which affects the utility or costs of other producers or consumers. In this case the externalities are pollution and congestion. Unfortunately, the problem is easier to analyse than to solve, since the solutions involve a loss of utility for a large group – in this case, motorists.

## PROBLEMS

**1 a** The total amount of pollution is 10 units, 5 (remaining) units from factory $A$ and 5 (remaining) units from factory $B$. The total cost of achieving this level of pollution is £750, the cost of £250 incurred by factory $A$ plus the cost of £500 incurred by factory $B$.

 **b** The total amount of pollution (again) is 10 units, comprising no pollution from factory $A$ and 10 units from factory $B$. The total cost of attaining this level of pollution is £500, all incurred by factory $A$.

 **c** From a social standpoint, having factory $A$ decrease its pollution by 10 units and factory $B$ do nothing is the most desirable. This solution has the lowest total social cost – £500 compared with £750 for an equal

reduction at each factory – which means that eliminating the 10 units of pollution has inflicted the lowest possible total cost on society, which certainly is a desirable outcome.

**Figure 20.3**

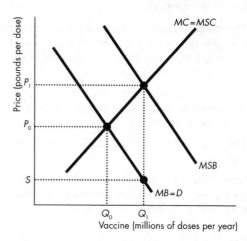

Vaccine (millions of doses per year)

**2** Figure 20.3 shows the market for chicken pox vaccine. Because there are no negative externalities, the marginal social cost curve equals the marginal private cost. This curve is labelled $MC = MSC$ in the figure. It is also the private supply curve. However, the presence of the positive externality means that the marginal social benefit *(MSB)* curve lies rightward of the marginal private benefit curve, which is the same as the private demand curve (labelled $MB = D$). The vertical distance between the curves equals the marginal externality; that is, it is the additional (external) benefit to society over and above the benefit to the private individual. In the absence of government intervention, $Q_0$ is produced, and the efficient amount is $Q_1$.

To move this market closer to the efficient level of output, the government might subsidize production or use of the vaccine. This policy could take the form of paying producers to produce more vaccine. The aim is to shift the private supply curve rightward so that it intersects the private demand curve at output $Q_1$, the efficient amount, and price $S$.

Alternatively, the government might buy $Q_1$ worth of doses and then resell them to consumers below cost at price $S$, the price necessary to induce consumers to buy $Q_1$ doses.

**3 a** In an unregulated market, the equilibrium price and quantity are determined by the intersection of the marginal private benefit and cost curves because these are the demand and supply curves, respectively. Thus the equilibrium price is E300, and the equilibrium quantity is 3 students.

b Because there are no external costs, the efficient quantity is determined by the intersection of the marginal private cost and marginal *social* benefit curves. This result implies that allocative efficiency is attained at a quantity of 5 students attending college.

**4 a** Igor wants 5 students to attend his new university, I.O.U. Five students will attend only when the tuition fee is E100.

b When 5 students attend the university, the marginal cost of the fifth student is E400. By charging the student only E100 in tuition, Igor appears to be losing money on this student. However, the loss is only apparent. Five students are the efficient level of education because the *total* marginal social benefit from the fifth student is E400, which equals the marginal cost of educating this student.

# DISCUSSION QUESTIONS

**1** Pollution is undesirable, but clearly to eliminate it totally isn't optimal. Society could get rid of all air pollution by outlawing all cars, all trains, all planes, shutting down all factories and eliminating all cows. (Cows produce methane.) But we won't do this. The reason is obvious: it's just too expensive. The cost to achieve zero pollution is prohibitive – a whole lot more than the benefit! Moreover, some pollution may be desirable – we get to drive rather than walk, have pizza delivered rather than doing without, and heat our homes rather than freeze.

**2** The 'efficient' level of pollution is the level at which the marginal social cost of pollution reduction equals the marginal social benefit. Suppose that we're at the benefit from the reduction point where the marginal social cost of reducing pollution equals the marginal social benefit. If we decreased pollution any more, the marginal social cost would *exceed* the marginal social benefit. In other words, the cost of any further reduction would exceed the benefit from the reduction

# DATA QUESTIONS

**1** Markets are not used to determine the quantity of road transport services because this industry has several characteristics which would lead to market failure. In particular, roads are semi-public goods – it would be almost impossible to prevent people having access without paying. Moreover, transport has major externalities such as pollution, congestion and the likelihood of road accidents.

**2** An increase in fuel tax would reduce the distance travelled by private cars. Some people would walk; others would use public transport. The effect would depend on the price elasticity of demand.

**3** By 'the failure to ration by price' the author means that market forces are not used to determine the quantity. Since no system of allocating resources can produce all the goods that people might like, in a market system prices act as a rationing device to limit the quantity of goods.

# Chapter 21 Inequality, Redistribution and Welfare

---

## Chapter in Perspective, Text Pages 517–542

Income is the payment to owners of factors of production for the use of those resources. Individuals with more resources to sell or whose resources sell for a higher price will receive larger incomes. Thus the distribution of income depends on the distribution of ownership of resources used in production and the market prices of those resources.

This chapter discusses the distribution of income and wealth in the United Kingdom, and addresses the following questions. How unequally are income and wealth actually distributed? What accounts for this inequality? What are the consequences of government policies intended to redistribute income or wealth? What are the major ideas that constitute a 'fair' distribution of income?

The chapter also analyses one of the largest and most important industries – health. This industry has significant implications for equality.

---

## Helpful Hints

**1** The major tool used by economists to depict the degree of inequality of income or wealth in an economy is the Lorenz curve.

**2** A major message of this chapter is that statistics used to construct Lorenz curves do not always give an accurate picture of inequality.

For example, distribution of wealth that excludes the value of human capital will give a distorted picture relative to the distribution of income.

You should also understand why the distribution of annual (static) income will give a distorted picture relative to the distribution of lifetime (dynamic) income.

Finally, you should understand why the distribution of before-tax, before-transfer income will give a distorted picture relative to the distribution of after-tax, after-transfer income.

**3** The issue of fairness discussed in this chapter is a normative issue. Note, however, that the trade-off between equity and economic efficiency (the so-called big trade-off) is a positive issue.

## Key Figures

**Figure 21.1 Lorenz Curves for Income and Wealth, text page 519**

A Lorenz curve is a useful way to represent the distribution of income or wealth. It plots the cumulative percentage of income or wealth received by a given cumulative percentage of families. This figure gives Lorenz curves for the UK and shows that the distribution of wealth is less equal than the distribution of income.

**Figure 21.2 UK Income Inequality: 1961–1991, text page 520**

An alternative measure of inequality is the Gini coefficient. This is used here to show that inequality has been increasing steadily over the last 20 years.

# SELF-TEST

## CONCEPT REVIEW

**1** Of the three basic factors of production, _____ earns the largest share of total income.

**2** The diagram used by economists to illustrate the cumulative percentage of households ranked from the poorest to the richest is called a(n) _____ _____ . The straight line running through the middle of the diagram is called the line of _____.

**3** The most important factor in determining whether a person receives a high income or a low income is _____.

**4** An income tax system in which the marginal tax rate rises as income rises is called a(n) _____ income tax. A(n) _____ income tax is one in which the marginal tax rate falls with the level of income while for a(n) _____ income tax, the marginal tax rate is constant for all levels of income.

**5** The distribution of income that would prevail in the absence of government policies is called the _____ distribution. The distribution that takes account of government policies is called the distribution after _____ and _____ .

**6** A gift from one generation to the next is called a(n) _____ .

**7** The three types of health-care systems are _____ supply and finance, private supply and _____ finance and government finance and supply.

**8** Private insurance faces _____ hazard and _____ selection problems. National health services face _____ problems but are the most equitable.

**9** Theories of distributive justice that emphasize the equality of the outcomes of economic activity are called _____ - _____ theories while those emphasizing the equality of opportunity are called _____ theories.

**10** The _____ theory states that the fairest outcome is the one that maximizes the sum of the utilities of all individuals in society.

**11** According to the _____ theory, the fairest distribution of income gives the poorest member of society the largest income possible.

## TRUE OR FALSE

—— **1** In the United Kingdom income is more unequally distributed than wealth.

**2** The further the Lorenz curve is from the line of equality, the more equal is the distribution of income.

**3** Under a proportional income tax, the marginal tax rate does not change as income rises.

**4** A regressive income tax redistributes income from rich people to poor people.

**5** Compared with the market distribution of income, government benefits and taxes reduce the inequality of income distribution.

**6** A national health service avoids the problems of third-party payments, economies of scale and insurance markets.

**7** A normal distribution is bell-shaped and is symmetric around the average.

**8** The utilitarian theory is an example of an end-state theory of distributive justice.

## MULTIPLE CHOICE

**1** Differences in the wage rates received by different individuals reflect differences in
**a** marginal product of labour.
**b** natural ability.
**c** human capital.
**d** all of the above.
**e** none of the above.

**2** The inequality in the distribution of wealth is
**a** less than the inequality in the distribution of income.
**b** decreased by the existence of assortative mating.
**c** a better measure of the inequality in the distribution of economic resources than is the inequality in the distribution of income.
**d** even greater if we look at the distribution of wealth among the richest 1 per cent of all families.
**e** all of the above.

**3** A reason for rising health-care prices is
**a** decreased demand owing to higher health-care insurance premiums.
**b** increased supply owing to lower labour costs.

**c** increased demand owing to growth of ailments that can be treated.
**d** increased supply owing to improved technology.

**4** Consider the Lorenz curves in Fig. 21.1. Which Lorenz curve corresponds to the greatest income *inequality*?
**a** A
**b** B
**c** C
**d** D
**e** impossible to tell without additional information

**Figure 21.1**

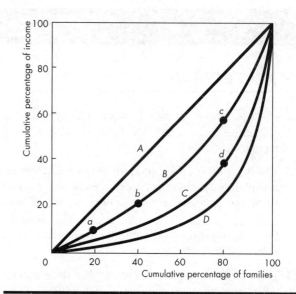

**5** In Fig. 21.1, what is curve A (a straight line) called?
**a** market distribution line
**b** line of equality
**c** fairness line
**d** Okun trade-off curve
**e** none of the above

**6** Which point in Fig. 21.1 indicates that the richest 20 per cent of families earn 40 per cent of the income?
**a** a
**b** b
**c** c
**d** d
**e** none of the above

**7** If the marginal tax rate increases as income increases, the income tax is defined as
  **a** progressive.
  **b** proportional.
  **c** negative.
  **d** regressive.
  **e** excessive.

**8** The distribution of *annual income*
  **a** understates the degree of inequality because it does not take into account the family's stage in its life cycle.
  **b** understates the degree of inequality because it does not take into account the distribution of human capital.
  **c** overstates the degree of inequality because it does not take into account the family's stage in its life cycle.
  **d** overstates the degree of inequality because it does not take into account the distribution of human capital.
  **e** is an accurate measure of the degree of inequality.

**9** Which of the following *reduces* the inequality of income or wealth relative to the market distribution?
  **a** government payments to poor people
  **b** a regressive income tax
  **c** large bequests
  **d** assortative mating
  **e** all of the above

**10** According to the Rawlsian theory, income should be redistributed if the
  **a** average person can be made better off.
  **b** poorest person can be made better off.
  **c** richest person can be made worse off.
  **d** wage rate is greater than the marginal product of labour.
  **e** wage rate is less than the marginal product of labour.

**11** Which of the following is an example of an end-state theory of distributive justice?
  **a** marginal product theory
  **b** the theory of Robert Nozick
  **c** the utilitarian theory
  **d** the process theory
  **e** none of the above

## SHORT ANSWER

**1 a** What is a Lorenz curve?
  **b** What does it illustrate?

**2** Explain the differences and connections between the concepts of wealth and income.

**3 a** What are the two factors that determine a person's income?
  **b** To what extent are these factors the result of forces beyond the control of the individual and to what extent are they the result of individual choice?

**4** The two classes of theories of distributive justice are process theories and end-state theories.
  **a** What is the principal characteristic of a process theory of distributive justice?
  **b** Why is the utilitarian theory an end-state theory of distributive justice?

**5** With reference to the *Reading Between the Lines* article, why do you think that some countries spend much more on health care than others?

## PROBLEMS

**1** Table 21.1 gives information regarding the distribution of income in an economy which generates £100 billion in total annual income.

**Table 21.1   Total Family Income**

| Percentage of families | Total income (billions of pounds) | Income share (per cent) | Cumulative percentage of families | Cumulative percentage of income |
|---|---|---|---|---|
| Poorest 20% | 5 | | | |
| Second 20% | 10 | | | |
| Third 20% | 15 | | | |
| Fourth 20% | 20 | | | |
| Richest 20% | 50 | | | |

  **a** Complete Table 21.1 by computing the entries in the last three columns.
  **b** Draw the Lorenz curve for income in this economy and label it *A*.

**2** Now suppose that a progressive income tax is levied on the economy. The distribution of after-tax income is given in Table 21.2. We have assumed that none of the revenue is redistributed to families in the economy. Note that total after-tax income is £71 billion.

Table 21.2    After-tax Family Income

| Percentage of families | After-tax income (billions of pounds) | After-tax income share (per cent) | Cumulative percentage of families | Cumulative percentage of after-tax income |
|---|---|---|---|---|
| Poorest 20% | 5 | | | |
| Second 20% | 9 | | | |
| Third 20% | 12 | | | |
| Fourth 20% | 15 | | | |
| Richest 20% | 30 | | | |

**a** Complete Table 21.2.

**b** Draw the Lorenz curve for after-tax income on the same graph you used for **1b** and label it *B*.

**c** What effect has the progressive income tax had on inequality?

**3** Lastly, suppose that, in addition, the government redistributes all of the tax revenue so that the after-transfer (after-tax) income distribution is that given in Table 21.3. For example, those in the poorest group receive transfer income of £10 billion so that their after-transfer income becomes £15 billion.

Table 21.3    After-transfer Family Income

| Percentage of families | After-transfer income (billions of pounds) | After-transfer income share (per cent) | Cumulative percentage of families | Cumulative percentage of after-transfer income |
|---|---|---|---|---|
| Poorest 20% | 15 | | | |
| Second 20% | 16 | | | |
| Third 20% | 18 | | | |
| Fourth 20% | 20 | | | |
| Richest 20% | 31 | | | |

**a** Complete Table 21.3.

**b** Draw the Lorenz curve for after-transfer income on the same graph you used for **1b** and **2b** and label it *C*.

**c** What effect has income redistribution through transfer payments had on inequality?

## DISCUSSION QUESTION

**1** Discuss the proposition that no one ought to be denied the best health care possible.

## DATA QUESTIONS

**The Redistribution of Income Through Taxes and Benefits in 1994–95**

Table 21.4 shows how the wide range of household incomes is modified by the tax and benefit system in the United Kingdom. There are various measures of income used in the table; for example, original income, which shows income before benefits are received and taxes deducted. Cash benefits can be either contributory (such as old age pensions) or non-contributory (such as child benefit). Non-cash benefits such as free or subsidized education also affect the distribution of income.

**1 a** Use the data in the table to compare the distribution of original income with the distribution of final income.

**b** Account for the inequalities in original income which are shown in the table.

**2** Compare the relative importance of the different categories of government expenditure and revenue as methods of reducing inequalities in the distribution of income.

**3** Discuss the economic consequences of policies which result in a less equal distribution of income and wealth.

*Source:* Updated and adapted from an Associated Examining Board question for GCE A-Level, June 1989.

**Table 21.4**

| Average per household (£ per year) | Bottom fifth | Next fifth | Middle fifth | Next fifth | Top fifth | All households |
|---|---|---|---|---|---|---|
| Wages and salaries | 1,180 | 3,830 | 10,230 | 17,820 | 28,250 | 12,260 |
| Imputed income from benefits in kind | 10 | 20 | 100 | 310 | 950 | 280 |
| Self-employment income | 260 | 510 | 1,050 | 1,550 | 6,160 | 1,910 |
| Occupational pensions, annuities | 280 | 780 | 1,300 | 1,520 | 2,220 | 1,220 |
| Investment income | 170 | 260 | 500 | 800 | 2,420 | 830 |
| Other income | 140 | 200 | 190 | 250 | 340 | 230 |
| **Total original income** | 2,040 | 5,600 | 13,380 | 22,250 | 40,330 | 16,720 |
| + Benefits in cash | | | | | | |
| Contributory | 1,930 | 2,290 | 1,620 | 1,050 | 680 | 1,510 |
| Non-contributory | 2,730 | 2,180 | 1,540 | 900 | 490 | 1,570 |
| **Gross income** | 6,700 | 10,080 | 16,540 | 24,200 | 41,510 | 19,800 |
| − Income tax and NIC | 270 | 760 | 2,300 | 4,360 | 9,350 | 3,410 |
| − Domestic rates (gross) | 570 | 550 | 630 | 680 | 790 | 640 |
| **Disposable income** | 5,860 | 8,760 | 13,610 | 19,150 | 31,370 | 15,750 |
| − Indirect taxes | 1,740 | 2,070 | 3,090 | 3,960 | 4,810 | 3,130 |
| **Post-tax income** | 4,120 | 6,700 | 10,520 | 15,190 | 26,570 | 12,620 |
| + Benefits in kind | | | | | | |
| Education | 1,600 | 1,250 | 1,390 | 1,200 | 670 | 1,220 |
| National Health Service | 1,790 | 1,720 | 1,660 | 1,460 | 1,270 | 1,580 |
| Housing subsidy | 80 | 80 | 40 | 20 | 10 | 50 |
| Travel subsidies | 50 | 60 | 60 | 90 | 130 | 80 |
| School meals and welfare milk | 80 | 20 | 10 | 10 | – | 30 |
| **Final income** | 7,720 | 9,840 | 13,690 | 17,970 | 28,640 | 15,570 |

*Source: Social Trends*, Central Statistical Office, 1996.

# ANSWERS

## CONCEPT REVIEW

1 labour
2 Lorenz curve; equality
3 education
4 progressive; regressive; proportional
5 market; taxes; transfers
6 bequest
7 private; government
8 moral; adverse; monopoly
9 end-state; process
10 utilitarian
11 Rawlsian

## TRUE OR FALSE

1 F Wealth distribution is more unequal.
2 F Further away = more unequal.
3 T Definition.
4 F Regressive = from poor to rich.
5 T See Table 21.4 in Data Question.
6 T But it has other forms of inefficiency.
7 T Definition.
8 T Sum of all individual utility outcomes maximized.

## MULTIPLE CHOICE

**1 d** All affect marginal revenue product of labour.

**2 d** The very rich are very rich!

**3 c** The health industry is characterized by rising demand.

**4 d** Curve furthest from 45° line.

**5 b** Definition.

**6 c** Moving from 80 per cent to 100 per cent of families (richest 20 per cent) moves income from 60 per cent of total to 100 per cent (40 per cent).

**7 a** Definition.

**8 c** People who are poor at some stage may be rich at other times.

**9 a** Others increase inequality.

**10 b** Definition.

**11 c** Maximizes sum of utilities (end-states) of individuals.

## SHORT ANSWER

**1 a** The Lorenz curve gives a graphical representation of the distribution of income or wealth across some population.

**b** The horizontal axis measures the cumulative percentage of families ranked from the poorest to the richest. The vertical axis measures the cumulative percentages of income or wealth. The further the Lorenz curve is from the line of equality, the more unequal is the distribution of income or wealth.

**2** Wealth is the *stock* of assets owned by an individual while income is the *flow* of earnings received by an individual. The concepts are connected in that an individual's income is the earnings that flow from the person's stock of wealth.

**3 a** A person's income is determined by the market prices for productive resource services and the quantity of resource services the person is able and willing to sell at those prices.

**b** These two factors depend on a number of things, some of which are (at least partially) under the control of the individual and some of which are not.

The price of labour services, the wage rate, is determined in the market for labour. But the wage rate will depend on the marginal product of labour, which is affected by individual choices about training and education as well as inherent personal ability.

The quantity of labour services supplied will also depend on personal choices about how to spend one's time. The quantity of other resource services supplied will depend on personal choices as well as the individual's endowment of the factor.

**4 a** A process theory of distributive justice focuses on the fairness of the process or mechanisms by which results are achieved instead of focusing on the results themselves.

**b** The utilitarian theory suggests that the fairest system is one in which the sum of the utilities in the society is a maximum. Since the theory focuses on the outcome or the ends, it is an end-state theory of distributive justice.

**5** Health care has a high income elasticity of demand. This means that rich countries spend proportionately more on health than poor countries. But there are other factors. For example, the United States spends fairly large amounts on health because of the structure of its health-care system – many people have private health insurance so there is no financial cost to the user for consuming more health care. Moreover, the propensity of Americans to litigate means that medical staff protect themselves by undertaking more tests than would be done in other countries.

## PROBLEMS

**1 a** Table 21.1 is completed as Table 21.5. The income share for each group of families is the total income of that group as a percentage of total income in the economy (£100 billion). The cumulative percentage of income (last column) is obtained by adding the percentage income share of the group (from the third column) to the total percentage income share of all poorer groups of families.

**Table 21.5 Total Family Income**

| Percentage of families | Total income (billions of pounds) | Income share (per cent) | Cumulative percentage of families | Cumulative percentage of income |
|---|---|---|---|---|
| Poorest 20% | 5 | 5 | 20 | 5 |
| Second 20% | 10 | 10 | 40 | 15 |
| Third 20% | 15 | 15 | 60 | 30 |
| Fourth 20% | 20 | 20 | 80 | 50 |
| Richest 20% | 50 | 50 | 100 | 100 |

**b** The curve labelled *A* in Fig. 21.2 is the Lorenz curve for total family income. This simply plots the values in the last two columns of Table 21.5.

**Figure 21.2**

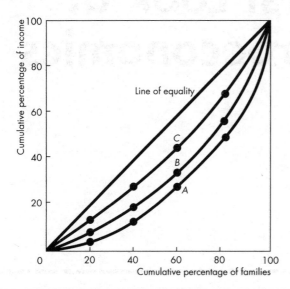

**2 a** Table 21.2 is completed as Table 21.6.

**b** The curve labelled *B* in Fig. 21.2 is the Lorenz curve for after-tax family income.

**c** The progressive income tax has reduced inequality by taking a larger percentage of income from higher income groups.

**Table 21.6   Solution After-tax Family Income**

| Percentage of families | After-tax income (billions of pounds) | After-tax income share (per cent) | Cumulative percentage of families | Cumulative percentage of after-tax income |
|---|---|---|---|---|
| Poorest 20% | 5 | 7 | 20 | 7 |
| Second 20% | 9 | 13 | 40 | 20 |
| Third 20% | 12 | 17 | 60 | 37 |
| Fourth 20% | 15 | 21 | 80 | 58 |
| Richest 20% | 30 | 42 | 100 | 100 |

**3 a** Table 21.3 is completed as Table 21.7.

**b** The curve labelled *C* in Fig. 21.2 is the Lorenz curve for (after-tax) after-transfer family income.

**c** Income redistribution through transfer payments has reduced inequality.

**Table 21.7   After-transfer Family Income**

| Percentage of families | After-transfer income (billions of pounds) | After-transfer income share (per cent) | Cumulative percentage of families | Cumulative percentage of after-transfer income |
|---|---|---|---|---|
| Poorest 20% | 15 | 15 | 20 | 15 |
| Second 20% | 16 | 16 | 40 | 31 |
| Third 20% | 18 | 18 | 60 | 49 |
| Fourth 20% | 20 | 20 | 80 | 69 |
| Richest 20% | 31 | 31 | 100 | 100 |

## DISCUSSION QUESTION

The opportunity cost of providing everyone with the best health care possible would be the goods and services that could no longer be consumed. The best health care possible would mean many more doctors, nurses and other health-care workers, as well as many more buildings and more equipment. This would mean that other sectors of the economy would become poorer.

## DATA QUESTIONS

**1 a** Final income is much more equally distributed than original income. For example, the bottom fifth saw their gross total income rise from £6,700 to £7,720 as a result of taxes and benefits. The income of the richest fifth fell from £41,510 to £28,640.

**b** The main reason is the difference in earned income. This is caused by factors such as differences in human capital, which were discussed in Chapter 15. These differences are exacerbated by differences in investment income.

**2** Benefits in cash and kind play a substantial part in increasing the incomes of the poorest sections of the community. However, these are outweighed by the income removed from the richest fifth by income tax (£3,410 per household) and indirect taxes (£3,130 per household).

**3** Policies that result in a less equal distribution of income and wealth will increase economic growth if they create incentives to work hard and to invest and if people respond to these incentives. However, less equal distributions of income and wealth may mean that poor people suffer from ill health and become less productive, while better-off people may find that their income rises so much that they do not need to work so hard. Hence the result may be a slower rate of economic growth.

# Chapter 22 A First Look at Macroeconomics

---

## Chapter in Perspective, Text Pages 547–573

This chapter sets the scene for the rest of the course. It begins by discussing the origins of macroeconomics and then focuses on economic growth. It analyses recent economic growth in the United Kingdom and other countries and the benefits and costs of growth.

The chapter discusses major macroeconomic issues such as unemployment, inflation and international payments.

---

## Helpful Hints

**1** The inflation rate is calculated as the percentage change in prices using the formula:

$$\frac{\text{current price level} - \text{previous price level}}{\text{previous price level}} \times 100$$

Thus if the current price level is, say, 110 and the previous price level was 100, the inflation rate between these two price levels equals

$$\frac{110 - 100}{100} \times 100, \text{ or } 10 \text{ per cent}$$

Similarly, if the current price level is 121 and the previous price level is 110, then using the formula shows that the inflation rate again equals 10 per cent. Keep in mind that the inflation rate is calculated by using the formula presented above and is *not* just the difference in the two price levels!

**2** The relationship between the current account and the capital account for a country can be understood by making an analogy with your budget. Suppose that you spend more than you earn. In this event you must borrow from other people to make up the shortfall of income.

Return now to the relationship between the current account and the capital account. A country's current account is its (foreign) spending and earnings on goods and services. Exports are the earnings abroad and imports the spending abroad. If the spending on imports exceeds the earnings from exports, the country must borrow from other countries to make up the difference. The capital account shows precisely this information: it shows how much the country is borrowing from (or lending to) other countries. Thus if a country is spending £100 billion more on imports than it earns on exports – so that the current

200

account has a £100 billion deficit – it must be borrowing the £100 billion from other countries – so that the capital account has a £100 billion surplus.

**3** As Helpful Hint 2 demonstrated, whenever the value of a country's imports exceeds the value of its exports, it must borrow from other countries to make up the difference. In this case, the original country is going into debt. Whether this is 'good' or 'bad' perhaps depends on what the borrowing financed.

A current account deficit, with its associated borrowing from abroad, may be 'good' or 'bad'. For instance, if the country is borrowing to make a lot of investments so that its income will be higher in the future, most observers might suggest that the current account deficit is 'good'. But if it is borrowing to buy a lot of goods and services that it uses immediately, many observers

might think that the deficit is 'bad'. Thus the question of whether a current account deficit helps or harms a country is not a question that always has the same answer.

## Key Figures

**Figure 22.3 Long-term Economic Growth in the United Kingdom, text page 553**
This provides a useful picture of long-term economic growth in the United Kingdom, showing periods when real GDP was above and below potential GDP.

**Figure 22.6 Unemployment in the United Kingdom: 1855–1994, text page 557**
This provides a useful picture of long-term unemployment trends.

# SELF-TEST

## CONCEPT REVIEW

**1** The origin of macroeconomics was the publication of _____'s The General Theory of Employment, Interest and _____.

**2** The long-term trend in economic growth is measured by the growth rate of _____ GDP.

**3** The main benefit of economic growth is expanded _____ possibilities. The main costs are less current _____, resource _____ and environmental pollution.

**4** The total number of jobs in the United Kingdom today is about the same as in _____ .

**5** Inflation is a process of rising _____ and _____ of money.

**6** Fluctuations in the inflation rate bring fluctuations in _____ rates.

**7** To meet macroeconomic policy challenges the government uses _____ policy tools and the Bank of England uses the monetary policy tools of _____ rates and _____ supply.

## TRUE OR FALSE

**___ 1** Ignoring interest income and gifts, if UK exports exceed UK imports, the United Kingdom has a current account deficit.

**___ 2** Discouraged workers are not counted as unemployed.

**___ 3** If the average level of prices doubles, the value of money is half of what it was.

**___ 4** In the recession phase of a business cycle, the unemployment rate rises.

**___ 5** The inflation rate can never be negative.

**___ 6** Fiscal policy refers to changes in the interest rate that are designed to influence the economy.

**___ 7** The trough is the lower turning point of the business cycle.

**___ 8** If the real interest rate does not change, an increase in the inflation rate lowers the nominal interest rate.

**9** Real GDP is the amount of goods and services that are produced when resources are fully employed.

# MULTIPLE CHOICE

**1** If last year the price level was 150 and the current price level is 165, over the year the inflation rate has been
   **a** 10 per cent.
   **b** 15 per cent.
   **c** 150 per cent.
   **d** 165 per cent.

**2** Counting discouraged workers as unemployed would
   **a** not change the unemployment rate.
   **b** lower the unemployment rate.
   **c** raise the unemployment rate.
   **d** probably change the unemployment rate, but in an unpredictable direction.

**3** During the Great Depression,
   **a** the unemployment rate was nearly 25 per cent and the major focus of macroeconomics switched to economic growth.
   **b** a productivity growth slowdown occurred and macroeconomics changed its focus to business cycles.
   **c** economists switched their focus so that macroeconomics began to emphasize business cycles.
   **d** John Maynard Keynes suggested that long-term economic growth was the major problem facing capitalist nations.

**4** Real GDP
   **a** measures only the output of real goods, such as machines, not 'unreal' things such as services.
   **b** includes all the goods and services produced in the economy, including those produced in the home.
   **c** is measured by using prices from a single year in order to eliminate the effects of inflation.
   **d** is the amount of goods and services that the country is able to produce when its resources are fully employed.

**5** Real GDP rose in all four quarters of 1995; thus 1995 was definitely a year
   **a** of expansion.
   **b** with a business cycle peak.

   **c** of recession.
   **d** with a business cycle trough.

**6** Which of the following is *not* a cost of more rapid economic growth?
   **a** current consumption that is lost
   **b** environmental damage may increase
   **c** consumption possibilities expand in the future
   **d** jobs and consumption patterns change more rapidly

**7** The unemployment rate generally rises during _____ in the business cycle.
   **a** a peak
   **b** a recession
   **c** a trough
   **d** an expansion

**8** The real interest rate equals the
   **a** interest rate in terms of money.
   **b** interest rate in terms of the goods and services that it will buy.
   **c** nominal interest rate minus the inflation rate.
   **d** both **b** and **c** are correct.

**9** Which of the following is *not* a cost of unemployment?
   **a** increased incidence of theft
   **b** increased numbers of unemployed workers entering college
   **c** increased amounts of domestic violence
   **d** decreased future job prospects

**10** If the United Kingdom has a current account deficit, the
   **a** value of UK exports must exceed the value of UK imports.
   **b** United Kingdom is lending to other countries.
   **c** United Kingdom has a capital account surplus.
   **d** None of the above.

**11** Which of the following is an example of monetary policy?
   **a** changing the interest rate
   **b** changing government spending
   **c** changing tax rates
   **d** changing the government's deficit

**12** During a period of high inflation people increasingly devote resources to predict the inflation rate, which represents
   **a** the 'high nominal interest rate' effect.
   **b** why unemployment rises substantially during these episodes.

c why the foreign exchange rate falls in value during these times.

d a cost of inflation.

**13** Potential real GDP

a falls during a recession.

b grows less rapidly because of the slowdown in productivity growth.

c can never be attained.

d equals actual real GDP.

## SHORT ANSWER

**1** What are the costs of unemployment?

**2** What is meant by the value of money? Why does the value of money fall when there is inflation?

**3** What happens to real GDP and the unemployment rate during each of the four phases of the business cycle?

**4** With regard to the *Reading Between the Lines* article, what do you think is meant by 'The forces bearing on the price level … are now being more balanced than they have been in some decades'?

## PROBLEMS

**1** a At the end of 1995 the price level is 120. At the end of 1996 the price level is 135. What is the inflation rate in 1996?

b At the end of 1997 the price level is 150. What is the inflation rate in 1997?

c At the end of 1998 the price level is 160. What is the inflation rate in 1998?

**2** Complete Table 22.1.

**Table 22.1  Interest Rates and the Inflation Rate**

| Real interest rate (per cent) | Inflation rate (per cent) | Nominal interest rate (per cent) |
|---|---|---|
| 3 | 4 | |
| 3 | 8 | |
| | 1 | 4 |

## DISCUSSION QUESTION

**1** Which is more important, stabilizing the business cycle or boosting long-term economic growth?

## DATA QUESTIONS

Economic growth is wonderful – or is it? Growth brings undeniable advantages. If an economy produces more goods and services, then it can afford to spend more on desirable services such as education and health. It can also spend more on relieving poverty. Moreover, ordinary citizens will have higher standards of living.

However, it also brings costs. Suppose the government decides to build a new road. This will raise GDP but it will also impose environmental damage. In addition, local people may have to install double glazing to cut out noise. This will also increase GDP. Local children may be hurt in traffic accidents on the road. Their medical costs will also increase GDP.

**1** How do we measure economic growth?

**2** Summarize the advantages of economic growth.

**3** Summarize the disadvantages of economic growth.

**4** Do you think economic growth is a desirable objective for government?

# ANSWERS

## CONCEPT REVIEW

**1** Keynes; Money

**2** potential

**3** consumption; consumption; depletion

**4** 1979

**5** prices; value

**6** interest

**7** fiscal; interest; money

# TRUE OR FALSE

**1 F** If exports exceed imports, the United Kingdom has a current account *surplus*.

**2 T** Discouraged workers are not looking for a job and so are not counted as unemployed.

**3 T** When the price level doubles, each pound buys half as many goods as before.

**4 T** As real GDP falls during a recession, the unemployment rate rises.

**5 F** The inflation rate can be negative (called deflation), although in recent years inflation has rarely been negative.

**6 F** Interest rate changes are part of monetary policy.

**7 T** After the trough, the economy enters the expansion phase of the business cycle.

**8 F** The nominal interest rate equals the real interest rate plus the inflation rate, so an increase in the inflation rate raises the nominal interest rate.

**9 F** Potential real GDP is the amount of goods and services produced when all resources are fully employed.

# MULTIPLE CHOICE

**1 a** The inflation rate between these years equals $\frac{165 - 150}{150} \times 100$, or 10 per cent.

**2 c** Counting discouraged workers among unemployed people would boost the unemployment rate.

**3 c** During the Great Depression, the extraordinarily high unemployment rates caused economists to stress short-term, business cycle factors, such as reducing the severity of recessions or depressions.

**4 c** By using prices from a single year, real GDP eliminates the effects of changes in prices, such as inflation.

**5 a** By definition, an expansion is a period of time during which real GDP increases.

**6 c** The expansion in future consumption possibilities is a benefit of economic growth.

**7 b** As real GDP falls in a recession, unemployment rates rise.

**8 d** The real interest rate indicates the amount of goods and services that can be purchased with the money (or nominal) interest rate.

**9 b** Some unemployed workers start college, but this is not a cost of unemployment.

**10 c** A current account deficit must be matched by an equal capital account surplus.

**11 a** Monetary policy includes changing the interest rate and/or the country's money supply. The other answers are examples of fiscal policy.

**12 d** By becoming 'amateur inflation predictors', people take time and effort away from their occupations and so the country produces fewer goods and services.

**13 b** By slowing the growth rate of potential real GDP, the productivity growth slowdown harmed people because it significantly lowered their consumption possibilities in future years.

# SHORT ANSWER

**1** One important personal cost is that when workers are unemployed for long periods of time, their skills and abilities deteriorate, hurting their future job prospects. In addition, substantial social costs are incurred, such as higher theft rates, greater alcohol and drug abuse, more domestic violence and, in general, a loss of human dignity.

**2** The value of money is the quantity of goods and services that can be purchased with one pound of money. Because inflation means that prices are rising on average, one pound of money will buy less. Thus the value of money falls when there is inflation.

**3** During the recession phase of the business cycle, real GDP falls. During this phase the unemployment rate rises, although the rise in unemployment lags behind the fall in real GDP somewhat. At the trough, real GDP reaches its lowest point below trend, and soon thereafter the unemployment rate is at its highest point over the business cycle. The trough is the turning point between the recession phase and the expansion phase. During expansion, real GDP grows and the unemployment rate generally falls. At the end of an expansion, the economy reaches the peak of the business cycle. The peak is characterized by real GDP at its highest point above its trend and the rate of unemployment is either then or soon thereafter at its lowest point over the business cycle.

**4** In this case, the forces bearing on the price level can be analysed in similar terms to those which affect the price level of individual goods, that is demand and supply. However, one of the differences is that at the macro level government policy, in this case monetary policy, can affect demand and supply.

# PROBLEMS

**1 a** The inflation rate in 1996 is 12.5 per cent.
   **b** In 1997 the inflation rate is 11.1 per cent, from

$$\frac{150 - 135}{135} \times 100.$$

Note that, even though the price level changed by the same amount in 1997 as in 1996 (15, or 135 − 120 in 1996 and 150 − 135 in 1997), the inflation rate in the two years is different.

   **c** In 1998 the inflation rate is 6.7 per cent.

**Table 22.2   Interest Rates and the Inflation Rate**

| Real interest rate (per cent) | Inflation rate (per cent) | Nominal interest rate (per cent) |
|---|---|---|
| 3 | 4 | 7 |
| 3 | 8 | 11 |
| 3 | 1 | 4 |

**2** The answers are in Table 22.2. The real interest rate equals the nominal interest rate minus the inflation rate. Alternatively, the nominal interest rate equals the real interest rate plus the inflation rate. Thus for the first row, the nominal interest rate equals the real interest rate, 3 per cent, plus the inflation rate, 4 per cent, or 7 per cent. The first two rows demonstrate the point that when the inflation rate increases, so too does the (nominal) interest rate. Hence the correlation between the inflation rate and the nominal interest rate should be positive.

# DISCUSSION QUESTION

**1** Economists don't agree about which of these macroeconomic challenges is more important.

Some economists think that boosting long-term growth is more important. They point out that if we are able to increase the growth rate of potential real GDP by 1 percentage point, after one generation, or two decades, real GDP per person will be over 22 per cent higher than otherwise. This means that our consumption possibilities will expand by 22 per cent so that, on average, we could buy 22 per cent more goods and services than otherwise. These economists also point out that this 22 per cent increase in consumption possibilities dwarfs the fall of real GDP per person in a recession. Thus they argue that increasing the growth rate of potential GDP is significantly more important than eliminating business cycles.

Other economists disagree. Although they agree that boosting the growth rate of potential real GDP is important, they point out that sustaining even a 1 per cent increase in real GDP over 20 years is extremely difficult. Instead, they argue that taming the business cycle should be considered the major goal of macroeconomic policy. They contend that this task is easier than increasing the growth rate of potential real GDP. Indeed, some of these economists suggest that we have tamed the business cycle a bit because there hasn't been a recession nearly as severe as the Great Depression.

# DATA QUESTIONS

**1** Economists usually measure economic growth by using GDP.

**2** The advantages are usually given as higher living standards, so more goods and services are produced, making it possible to devote more resources to such problems as pollution and poverty.

**3** The disadvantages are that the environment may be harmed; for example, by the depletion of resources such as oil. Growth may also cause pollution and it is often associated with social and economic change, ,which may cause problems.

**4** There is no correct answer to the question of whether or not growth is desirable. The answer largely depends on the values of the person answering the question.

# Chapter 23 · Measuring GDP, Inflation and Economic Growth

**Chapter in Perspective,** Text Pages 574–599

How do we measure aggregate economic activity or the price level? In this chapter we address these questions in some detail.

The most widely used measure of economic activity is gross domestic product, or GDP. Here we discuss what it is and how it is measured. We will also examine the Retail Price Index and the GDP deflator, two measures of the price level. As indicated in Chapter 1, one of the components of any science is careful and systematic measurement. In this chapter, we will see how measurements of the behaviour of the aggregate economy are made and also discuss their limitations. The concepts measured here will lay a foundation for our analysis of macroeconomic theory.

## Helpful Hints

**1** Be sure to distinguish carefully between intermediate goods and investment goods. Both are typically goods sold by one firm to another, but they differ in terms of their use. Intermediate goods are goods that are processed and then resold, while investment goods are final goods themselves. Also note that the national income accounts include purchases of residential housing as investment because housing, like business capital stock, provides a continuous stream of value over time.

**2** Note the difference between government spending on goods and services ($G$) and government transfer payments. Both involve payments by the government, but transfer payments are not payments for currently produced goods and services. Instead, they are simply a flow of money, just like taxes. Indeed it is often useful to think of transfer payments as negative taxes. Therefore, we define net taxes ($NT$) as taxes minus transfer payments.

**3** Figure 23.2 on text page 578 is particularly important and leads to a fundamental equation:

$$Y = C + I + G + EX - IM$$

This equation reflects the expenditure approach to measuring GDP. It tells us that GDP is equal to the total amount of spending on domestic output in the economy by households, firms, government and foreigners. Spending on imports is subtracted to account for the fact that imports are not domestically produced. You need to ensure that you understand this equation.

**4** A price index for the current year is computed as the ratio of the value of a basket of goods in the current year to the value of the *same* basket of goods in a base year, multiplied by 100. It therefore attempts to calculate the cost of purchasing the same choice of goods in two different years. Note that the basket of goods used to calculate the Retail Price Index (RPI) contains goods that are purchased by a typical household. The basket of goods used to calculate the GDP deflator, on the other hand, contains all goods and services included in GDP. It would, therefore, include capital goods.

## Key Figure and Tables

### Figure 23.2 The Circular Flow of Income and Expenditure, text page 578

Households pay taxes to government and receive transfer payments from government, with the resulting net flow of net taxes (*NT*). The government also purchases goods and services from firms (*G*). Firms sell goods and services to the rest of the world (exports = *EX*) and also buy goods and services from the rest of the world (imports = *IM*), with a resulting net flow of net exports (*NX*).

This diagram illustrates the basic relationships in national income accounting. The flows from firms to factor markets illustrate the factor incomes approach, while the flows from goods markets to firms illustrate the expenditure approach.

### Table 23.1 GDP: The Expenditure Approach, text page 581

The expenditure approach to measuring GDP divides the economy into four expenditure sectors and then adds together the spending of these sectors. GDP is obtained as the sum of consumption expenditures (*C*), gross private domestic investment (*I*), government purchases of goods and services (*G*) and net exports (*NX*).

This table illustrates the expenditure approach by reporting GDP for the different sectors in the United Kingdom.

### Table 23.2 GDP: The Factor Incomes Approach, text page 584

GDP can also be measured using an income approach. All of the payments to households for the services of factors of production they hire are added together to obtain net national income at factor cost and then some adjustments are made. This approach to measuring GDP is illustrated using UK data. The percentage contribution to GDP for each of the entries is indicated in the final column of the table.

# SELF-TEST

## CONCEPT REVIEW

**1** Gross _____ _____ is the value of total production of goods and services in an economy during a given period.

**2** Capital and wealth are macroeconomic _____ .

**3** The aggregate expenditure by households on consumption goods and services is called _____ _____ . Total spending by firms on new plant, equipment and buildings, and additions to stocks is called _____ .

**4** Payments from the government to households which are not payments for currently produced goods and services are called _____ _____ .

**5** _____ is equal to disposable income minus consumers' expenditure. Disposable income equals aggregate income minus net _____ .

**6** Investment, government spending on goods and services, and exports are examples of _____ into the circular flow of income. Taxes, saving and imports are examples of _____ from the circular flow of income.

**7** The method of measuring GDP which adds consumption expenditure, investment, government purchases of goods and services and net exports is called the _____ approach. The _____ _____ approach measures GDP by adding together all incomes paid to households by firms. The _____ approach measures GDP by adding together the value added by each firm in the economy.

**8** The amount by which the value of the capital stock is reduced from wear and tear and passage of time is called _____ . When we subtract this amount from gross investment we have _____ investment. Gross domestic product is equal to net domestic product plus _____ .

**9** The value of the output of a firm minus the value of its inputs is called _____ _____ . We are double counting if we include expenditures on _____ goods as well as final goods in our calculation of GDP.

**10** We refer to economic activity that is legal but not reported to the government as the _____ _____ .

**11** The _____ _____ _____ is a measure of the average level of prices of consumption goods and services purchased by a 'typical' urban household. The _____ _____ measures the average level of prices of all final goods and services produced in the economy.

## TRUE OR FALSE

**1** In the aggregate economy, income is equal to expenditure and to GDP.

**2** The government pays High Flyer Aircraft Company for a military jet. This is an example of a transfer payment.

**3** Disposable income is equal to consumption expenditure plus saving.

**4** Imports is an example of an injection into the circular flow of income.

**5** Net domestic product equals gross domestic product minus depreciation.

**6** If two economies have the same GDP, then the standard of living is the same in each economy.

**7** The GDP deflator is calculated as real GDP divided by nominal GDP, multiplied by 100.

**8** If you are interested in knowing whether the economy is producing a greater physical volume of output, you would want to look at real GDP rather than nominal GDP.

**9** If the price of good *A* rises much more rapidly than the prices of other goods, then good *A* is responsible for high inflation.

**10** Consumers shift their purchases away from goods whose relative prices increase and therefore cause the RPI to overstate the actual inflation rate.

## MULTIPLE CHOICE

**1** Which of the following is *not* an example of investment in the expenditure approach to measuring GDP? Peugeot
 **a** buys a new auto stamping machine.
 **b** adds 500 new cars to stocks.
 **c** buys French government bonds.
 **d** builds another assembly plant.
 **e** replaces some worn-out stamping machines.

**2** Which of the following is true for the aggregate economy? Income equals
 **a** expenditure, but these are not generally equal to GDP.
 **b** GDP, but expenditure is generally less than these.
 **c** expenditure equals GDP.
 **d** expenditure equals GDP only if there are no government or foreign sectors.
 **e** expenditure equals GDP only if there is no depreciation.

**3** Saving can be measured as income minus
 **a** taxes.
 **b** transfer payments.
 **c** taxes minus consumers' expenditure.
 **d** net taxes minus consumers' expenditure.
 **e** net taxes plus subsidies.

**4** Interest plus miscellaneous investment income is a component of which approach to measuring GDP?
 **a** factor incomes approach
 **b** expenditure approach
 **c** injections approach
 **d** output approach
 **e** opportunity cost approach

**5** To obtain the factor cost of a good from its market price, one must
 **a** add indirect taxes and subtract subsidies.
 **b** subtract indirect taxes and add subsidies.
 **c** subtract both indirect taxes and subsidies.
 **d** add both indirect taxes and subsidies.
 **e** subtract depreciation.

**6** Which of the following is an example of a leakage from the circular flow of income?
 **a** exports
 **b** investment
 **c** saving
 **d** subsidies
 **e** government purchases

**7** The value of a firm's output minus the value of inputs purchased is
 **a** net exports.
 **b** value added.
 **c** net profit.
 **d** indirect production.
 **e** capital consumption allowance.

**8** The existence of which of the following is *not* a reason for the fact that GDP gives an underestimate of the value of total output in the economy?
 **a** crime
 **b** non-market activities
 **c** the underground economy
 **d** capital consumption allowance
 **e** externalities such as pollution

**Table 23.1**

| Item | Price (pounds) Base | Current | Quantity Base | Current |
|---|---|---|---|---|
| Deck chairs | 1.00 | 1.25 | 100 | 100 |
| Beach towels | 9.00 | 6.00 | 12 | 14 |

**9** Table 23.1 gives price and quantity data for an economy with only two consumers' goods: deck chairs and beach towels. What is the RPI for the current year?
 **a** 100
 **b** 112
 **c** 105.6
 **d** 100.5
 **e** 94.7

**10** Refer to the data in Table 23.1. Between the base year and the current year, what happened to the relative price of deck chairs?

**a** remained unchanged
**b** fell
**c** rose
**d** cannot be determined with the amount of information given
**e** depends on what happens to the RPI

**11** If 1997 is the base year for the GDP deflator, we know that nominal GDP
 **a** equals real GDP in 1996.
 **b** is greater than real GDP in 1996.
 **c** is less than real GDP in 1996.
 **d** in 1997 will be greater than real GDP in 1996.
 **e** in 1997 will be greater than nominal GDP in 1996.

**12** Consider the data in Table 23.2. What is the GDP deflator in 1996?
 **a** 160
 **b** 250
 **c** 200
 **d** 88.89
 **e** 125

**Table 23.2**

| Year | Nominal GDP (billions of pounds) | Real GDP (billions of 1990 pounds) | GDP deflator (1990=100) |
|---|---|---|---|
| 1990 | 125 | 125 | 100 |
| 1996 | 250 | 200 | |
| 1997 | 279 | | 122.22 |

**13** Use the data in Table 23.2. What is real GDP in 1996?
 **a** 225
 **b** 275
 **c** 220
 **d** 336.22
 **e** 110

## SHORT ANSWER

**1** In the aggregate economy, why does income equal expenditure?

**2** In obtaining GDP we count expenditure only on final goods. Why do we *not* count expenditure on intermediate goods?

**3 a** What productive activities are not measured and thus are not included in GDP?
 **b** Is this a serious problem?

**4** Does a 5 per cent increase in the RPI mean that the cost of living has increased by 5 per cent? Why or why not?

**5** Why do you think that the *Reading Between the Lines* article refers to GDP and unemployment figures as 'seasonally' adjusted?

# PROBLEMS

**1** Use the data for an imaginary economy given in Table 23.3 to compute the following.
 **a** GDP
 **b** net investment
 **c** net exports
 **d** disposable income
 **e** saving
 **f** total leakages from and total injections into the circular flow of income. (Are they equal?)

**Table 23.3**

| Item | Amount (billions of pounds) |
|---|---|
| Consumers' expenditure *(C)* | 600 |
| Taxes *(TX)* | 400 |
| Transfer payments *(TR)* | 250 |
| Exports *(EX)* | 240 |
| Imports *(IM)* | 220 |
| Government spending on goods and services *(G)* | 200 |
| Gross investment *(I)* | 150 |
| Depreciation *(Depr)* | 60 |

**2** Table 23.4 gives data for an economy in which there are three consumers' goods: bananas, coconuts and grapes.

**Table 23.4**

| Good | Base period Quantity in basket (boxes) | Base period Price (pounds per box) | Base period Expenditure (pounds) | Current period Price (pounds per box) | Current period Value of quantities (pounds) |
|---|---|---|---|---|---|
| Bananas | 120 | 6 | | 8 | |
| Coconuts | 60 | 8 | | 10 | |
| Grapes | 40 | 10 | | 9 | |

**a** Complete the table by computing expenditures for the base period and the appropriate value of quantities in the current year for computing the RPI.
 **b** What is the value of the basket of consumers' goods in the base period? In the current period?
 **c** What is the RPI for the current period?

**3** Table 23.5 gives data for an economy in which there are three final goods included in GDP: pizzas, staplers and shoes.

**Table 23.5**

| Good | Base period Quantity in basket | Base period Price (pounds) | Base period Expenditure (pounds) | Current period Price (pounds) | Current period Expenditure (pounds) |
|---|---|---|---|---|---|
| Pizzas | 110 | 6 | | 8 | 880 |
| Staplers | 50 | 8 | | 10 | 500 |
| Shoes | 50 | 10 | | 9 | 450 |

**a** Complete the table by computing expenditure on each good evaluated at base period prices.
 **b** What is the value of nominal GDP in the current period?
 **c** What is the value of real GDP in the current period?
 **d** What is the GDP deflator in the current period?

**4** Complete Table 23.6.

**Table 23.6**

| Year | Nominal GDP (pounds) | Real GDP (pounds) | GDP deflator |
|---|---|---|---|
| 1994 | 3,055 | | 94 |
| 1995 | | 3,170 | 100 |
| 1996 | 3,410 | 3,280 | |
| 1997 | | 3,500 | 108 |

# DISCUSSION QUESTION

**1** Why is it important to be able to measure variables such as GDP and inflation?

# DATA QUESTIONS

**Table 23.7   Prices and GDP in Europe**

| Country | GDP by volume 1995 (1990 = 100) | Consumer prices (1990 = 100) |
|---|---|---|
| Denmark | 110.4 | 110.2 |
| Finland | 96.2 | 112.0 |
| France | 105.7 | 111.6 |
| Germany | 118.9 | 119.0 |
| Netherlands | 109.9 | 114.4 |
| Norway | 119.0 | 112.5 |
| Spain | 107.0 | 128.6 |
| Sweden | 100.8 | 124.2 |
| United Kingdom | 106.6 | 118.2 |

Source: *Main Economic Indicators*, OECD, 1996.

**1** Explain what is meant by 'GDP by volume, 1990=100'.

**2** Which country had (a) the highest, and (b) the lowest rate of economic growth in the period 1990–95?

**3** Which country had (a) the largest, and (b) the smallest rise in consumer prices?

**4** To what extent are GDP statistics a good measure of living standards?

# ANSWERS

## CONCEPT REVIEW

**1** domestic product

**2** stocks

**3** consumers' expenditure; investment

**4** transfer payments

**5** Saving; taxes

**6** injections; leakages

**7** expenditure; factor incomes; output

**8** depreciation; net; depreciation

**9** value added; intermediate

**10** hidden economy

**11** Retail Prices Index; GDP deflator

## TRUE OR FALSE

**1 T** From circular flow diagram, production is sold (expenditure) and earnings used to pay out income.

**2 F** It is payment for a good.

**3 T** $Y = C + S + T$ so $Y - T$ (that is, disposable income) = $C + S$.

**4 F** Imports are a withdrawal.

**5 T** Definition.

**6 F** Standard of living depends on level of GDP divided by population.

**7 F** GDP deflator = [(Nominal GDP)/(Real GDP)] × 100.

**8 T** Real GDP measures amount of goods and services while nominal GDP measures current money value and includes impact of inflation.

**9 F** Changes in relative prices do not cause inflation.

**10 T** The RPI is based on a fixed basket of goods and assumes that people continue to buy the same goods (although the RPI basket is periodically changed).

## MULTIPLE CHOICE

**1 c** This is purchase of a capital asset, not capital stock.

**2 c** Definition; the three ways of measuring the nation's accounts should be equal.

**3 d** Income after tax must be either spent or saved.

**4 a** Definition.

**5 b** Market price = Factor cost + Indirect taxes – Subsidies.

**6 c** Savings take money out of the circular flow; others are injections.

**7 b** Definition.

**8 d** This is depreciation and is part of GDP.

**9  e**  RPI = [(Sum of current prices × Base quantities)/ (Sum of base prices × Base quantities)] × 100.

**10  c**  Relative price = Change in price (deck chairs) – Inflation rate = 25% – (–5.3%) = 30.3%, where inflation rate = 94.7 – 100.

**11  a**  Definition of a base year.

**12  e**  GDP deflator = [(Nominal GDP/(Real GDP)] × 100.

**13  a**  Real GDP = [(Nominal GDP)/(GDP deflator)] × 100.

# SHORT ANSWER

**1**  When an expenditure is made, firms receive money payments. The amount received by firms in the aggregate is aggregate expenditure. All that firms receive is distributed as income to households who own the factors of production. Remember that profit is income. Since the aggregate amount firms receive is expenditure and firms pay out all they receive as income, in the aggregate economy, income equals expenditure.

**2**  Counting both final goods and the intermediate goods that were combined to produce them will result in 'double counting'. For example, counting the value of the steel that is sold to a car manufacturer to build a car and then counting it again when the car is sold as a final good will overstate the value of final goods and services since the steel is counted twice.

**3  a**  Activities that produce goods and services that are not included in GDP are criminal activities, production in the underground economy and non-market activities. The first are not reported because the activities themselves are illegal. The second refer to goods and services that are legal but are not reported to circumvent taxes or government regulations. The third include those productive activities which households perform for themselves. Because they do not hire someone else to mow the lawn or wash the car, these are not included in GDP.

**b**  The seriousness of the problem depends on the actual size of activity and this is difficult to measure precisely.

**4**  A 5 per cent increase in the RPI does not mean that the cost of living has increased by 5 per cent if relative prices also change (and they generally will). Changes in relative prices will cause consumers to make substitutions from goods whose relative price has risen to goods whose relative price has fallen. This reduces the effect on the cost of living. The fact that some goods disappear from use and new goods appear also means that changes in the RPI do not precisely reflect changes in the cost of living.

**5**  Economic activity does not take place at an even pace throughout the year. For example, production falls during the Christmas period. Unemployment always rises during the winter months when there are fewer jobs in such industries as tourism, construction and farming. Hence statisticians adjust the actual figures to allow for this.

# PROBLEMS

**1  a**  GDP = $C + I + G + (EX - IM)$ = £970 billion
**b**  Net $I = I - Depr$ = £90 billion
**c**  $NX = EX - IM$ = £20 billion
**d**  Disposable income = GDP + TR – TX = £820 billion
**e**  Saving = Disposable income – C = £220 billion
**f**  Total leakages = $(TX - TR) + IM + S$ = £590 billion
Total injections = $I + G + X$ = £590 billion
So total leakages = total injections.

**2  a**  Table 23.4 is completed here as Table 23.8. Note that the base period quantities are evaluated at current prices to find the value of quantities in the current year.

**Table 23.8**

| Good | Base period Quantity in basket (boxes) | Price (pounds per box) | Expenditure (pounds) | Current period Price (pounds per box) | Value of quantities (pounds) |
|---|---|---|---|---|---|
| Bananas | 120 | 6 | 720 | 8 | 960 |
| Coconuts | 60 | 8 | 480 | 10 | 600 |
| Grapes | 40 | 10 | 400 | 9 | 360 |

**b**  The value of the basket of consumers' goods in the base period is the sum of the expenditures in that period: £1,600. The value of the basket of consumers' goods is obtained as the sum of the values of quantities in that period: £1,920.

**c**  The consumer price index is the ratio of the value of quantities in the current period to the base period expenditure, times 100:

RPI = (1,920/1,600) × 100 = 120.

**3  a**  Table 23.5 is completed as Table 23.9. Base period expenditure for each item is obtained by evaluating the current period quantity at the base year price.

**Table 23.9**

| Good | Base period Quantity in basket | Base period Price (pounds) | Base period Expenditure (pounds) | Current period Price (pounds) | Current period Expenditure (pounds) |
|------|------|------|------|------|------|
| Pizzas | 110 | 660 | 6 | 8 | 880 |
| Staplers | 50 | 400 | 8 | 10 | 500 |
| Shoes | 50 | 500 | 10 | 9 | 450 |

**b** The value of nominal GDP in the current period is the sum of expenditures in the current period: £1,830.

**c** The value of real GDP in the current period is the sum of the current period quantities evaluated at base period prices; in other words, what the expenditures would have been at base year prices: £1,560.

**d** The GDP deflator for the current period is the ratio of nominal GDP to real GDP, times 100:

GDP deflator = $(1,830/1,560) \times 100 = 117.3$.

**4** Table 23.6 is completed as Table 23.10. The following equation is used:

GDP deflator = (Nominal GDP/Real GDP) $\times$ 100.

**Table 23.10**

| Year | Nominal GDP (pounds) | Real GDP (pounds) | GDP deflator |
|------|------|------|------|
| 1994 | 3,055 | 3,250 | 94 |
| 1995 | 3,170 | 3,170 | 100 |
| 1996 | 3,410 | 3,280 | 104 |
| 1997 | 3,780 | 3,500 | 108 |

## DISCUSSION QUESTION

**1** We have to know what GDP is in order to understand growth and business cycles, since we're going to study what makes GDP grow faster and what makes it fluctu-ate. Similarly, other material in this chapter will lay the foundation for much of what follows. More generally, good economics often depends on knowing the uses and the limitations of statistics.

## DATA QUESTIONS

**1** 'GDP' is an abbreviation for 'Gross Domestic Product', which is a measure of the output produced by a country, usually over one year. 'Volume' implies that the figures are in real terms, that is, excluding the effects of inflation. '1990=100' means that 1990 is the base year so that, for example, in the United Kingdom GDP rose by 6 per cent in the period 1990–95.

**2 a** The highest rate of growth of GDP was in Norway.
**b** The lowest rate of economic growth was in Finland.

**3 a** Inflation was highest in Spain.
**b** Inflation was lowest in Denmark.

**4** GDP is probably the best measure of living standards, but it has serious inadequacies. First, a number of economic activities are not included in the figures for GDP; for example, non-market activities such as DIY and housework. Second, the underground economy is excluded, and this may amount to 5 per cent of GDP, although there are no precise estimates. Third, the figures contain errors, and it is not possible to estimate these accurately.

Even if all these limitations were overcome, the figures would not be a precise measure of living standards. GDP often rises in times of war because the economy is producing at full capacity, but living standards may be low because the goods produced are weapons of war. Other factors affecting living standards include the amount of leisure time, the quality of the environment, and the amount of crime. These are not included in the statistics of GDP. Lastly, an average figure for GDP per head says nothing about the distribution of that income. In some countries a small minority may take a large share of the national income.

# Chapter 24 | Employment, Unemployment and Wages

---

## Chapter in Perspective, Text Pages 600–624

In this chapter we focus on one of the principal topics of macroeconomics – employment and unemployment. We define some of the main concepts and the labour market is analysed using demand and supply to explain what determines the level of employment and wages.

The chapter also discusses some of the main ideas used to explain unemployment.

---

## Helpful Hints

**1** Note that there is no perfect way to measure unemployment. One way is to use a survey of the labour force; alternatively the number of people seeking work and claiming benefit can be used.

**2** In a dynamic economy, not all unemployment is inefficient. In fact, frictional unemployment benefits both the individual and society.

Younger workers typically experience periods of unemployment as they try to find jobs that match their skills and interests. The benefit to them of the resulting frictional unemployment is a much more satisfying and productive work life. Society benefits because the frictional unemployment that accompanies such a job-search process allows workers to find jobs in which they are most productive. As a result, the total production of goods and services in the economy rises. (Compare this case with that for most graduates in China. They are assigned jobs upon graduation, with little personal input about type of job or location.)

Structural unemployment is different from frictional unemployment because structurally unemployed workers will not get a new job without retraining or relocation. Thus the cost to the worker is much greater – for example, structurally unemployed workers typically are unemployed for long time periods. These workers bear the brunt of the cost of restructuring industries in our economy. So although society may ultimately benefit in that goods and services in higher demand are produced, structural unemployment can impose a significant cost on the worker.

**3** When economists use the term 'full employment', they do not mean that everyone has a job. Rather, they mean that the only unemployment is frictional and structural in nature. When there is no cyclical unemployment, the rate of unemployment is called the natural rate of unemployment.

The actual rate of unemployment may be less than the natural rate of unemployment. This statement is the same as saying that the level of employment can exceed full employment. In these situations, people are spending too little time searching for jobs, and therefore less productive job matches are being made.

## Key Figures

**Figure 24.6  Labour Market Flows, text page 607**
Unemployment is often presented as a stock (so many people unemployed), but in reality it is made up of flows of people into and out of the labour market. This figure illustrates these flows.

**Figure 24.11  The Labour Market, text page 613**
This figure uses curves for the demand and supply of labour to examine the idea of equilibrium in the labour market.

# SELF-TEST

## CONCEPT REVIEW

**1** Two measures of unemployment are published in the United Kingdom. One is based on the _____ _____ _____ , the other makes use of a _____ count.

**2** The unemployment rate is the percentage of people in the _____ - _____ who are _____ .

**3** Unemployment can be classified into three types, _____ , _____ and _____ .

**4** _____ unemployment is the fluctuating unemployment that coincides with the _____ cycle.

**5** Economists disagree about the magnitude of the _____ rate of unemployment.

**6** Labour _____ and labour _____ interact to determine the level of employment and the _____ real wage rate.

**7** Unemployment is always present because of job _____ .

**8** The natural rate of unemployment depends on the _____ distribution of the population, _____ benefit and technological _____ .

**9** Unemployment arises from job _____ , job _____ and _____ wages.

## TRUE OR FALSE

___ **1** The unemployment rate equals the total number of unemployed people divided by the total working-age population.

___ **2** Full-time students not looking for work are unemployed.

___ **3** Mary lost her job and looked for a new job for eight months. Mary stopped looking for work because she believes she cannot find a job. Mary is frictionally unemployed.

___ **4** A rise in the real wage increases the quantity of labour supplied.

___ **5** Sticky wages are a cause of cyclical unemployment.

___ **6** At full employment, there is no unemployment.

___ **7** An increase in the demand for labour raises the real wage rate.

___ **8** The natural rate of unemployment equals the sum of frictional and cyclical unemployment.

___ **9** Bill has just graduated and is looking for his first job. Bill is frictionally unemployed.

# MULTIPLE CHOICE

**1** Who of the following is cyclically unemployed?

  **a** Cara, a farmer who lost her farm because of foreign competition and is unemployed until retrained

  **b** Omar, a fishery worker who is searching for a better job closer to home

  **c** Eugene, a steelworker who was laid off but has stopped looking for a new job because the economy is in a recession and he thinks he won't be able to find a job

  **d** Amanda, an office worker who lost her job because of a general slowdown in economic activity

**2** Who of the following is frictionally unemployed?

  **a** Cara, a farmer who lost her farm because of foreign competition and is unemployed until retrained

  **b** Omar, a fishery worker who is searching for a better job closer to home

  **c** Eugene, a steelworker who was laid off but has stopped looking for a new job because the economy is in a recession and he thinks he won't be able to find a job

  **d** Amanda, an office worker who lost her job because of a general slowdown in economic activity

**3** If the economy is at full employment, the

  **a** entire population is employed.

  **b** entire work-force is employed.

  **c** only unemployment is frictional unemployment plus discouraged workers.

  **d** only unemployment is frictional and structural unemployment.

**4** One possible cause of unemployment is that

  **a** flexible wages lead to too many fluctuations in real wages.

  **b** sticky wages lead to too many fluctuations in real wages.

  **c** unemployment compensation payments are too low.

  **d** insiders will not allow firms to hire outsiders if that means lower wages.

**5** The demand for labour and the supply of labour are both increasing over time, but the demand for labour is increasing at a faster rate. Over time therefore you would expect to see the

  **a** real wage rate rising and employment falling.

  **b** real wage rate rising and employment rising.

  **c** real wage rate falling and employment rising.

  **d** real wage rate falling and employment falling.

**6** In a country with a working-age population of 200 million, 130 million workers are employed and 10 million workers are unemployed. What is the size of the work-force?

  **a** 200 million

  **b** 140 million

  **c** 130 million

  **d** 10 million

**7** In a country with a working-age population of 200 million, 130 million workers are employed and 10 million workers are unemployed. What is the work-force participation rate?

  **a** 100 per cent

  **b** 70 per cent

  **c** 65 per cent

  **d** 5 per cent

**8** In a country with a working-age population of 200 million, 130 million workers are employed and 10 million workers are unemployed. What is the unemployment rate?

  **a** 5 per cent

  **b** 7.1 per cent

  **c** 7.7 per cent

  **d** 65 per cent

**9** The insider–outsider theory

  **a** explains why wages are sticky.

  **b** refers to the idea that unemployed workers (workers 'outside employment') must search for jobs.

  **c** is not related to the presence of unemployment.

  **d** suggests that unions bargain so that their employed members are paid high wages even though other workers remain unemployed.

**10** An increase in the demand for labour causes the real wage to _____ and the quantity of employment to _____ .

  **a** rise; increase

  **b** rise; decrease

  **c** fall; increase

  **d** fall; decrease

**11** Suppose that the money wage rate is E5 per hour and that the price level is 100. If the money wage

rate rises to E10 per hour and the price level rises to 200, what happens to the real wage rate?
a the real wage rate doubles
b the real wage rate rises but does not double
c the real wage rate does not change
d the real wage rate falls

12 In a recession, what is the largest source of unemployment?
a job leavers
b job losers
c new entrants to the work-force
d re-entrants to the work-force

13 At the natural rate of unemployment, there is no
a frictional unemployment.
b structural unemployment.
c cyclical unemployment.
d unemployment.

14 Which of the following best characterizes a recession?
a Real GDP falls, aggregate hours rise and the unemployment rate falls.
b Real GDP rises, aggregate hours fall and the unemployment rate rises.
c Real GDP, aggregate hours and the unemployment rate all fall.
d Real GDP and aggregate hours fall and the unemployment rate rises.

15 The work-force equals the number of
a employed plus unemployed workers.
b employed people.
c people 16 years old and older who are not in jail.
d employed minus unemployed workers.

16 An efficiency wage refers to
a workers being paid wages below the equilibrium wage rate in order to increase the economy's efficiency.
b wages being set to generate the efficient level of unemployment.
c workers being paid wages above the equilibrium wage rate in order to increase their productivity.
d None of the above.

## SHORT ANSWER

1 For the following time periods, describe Igor's labour market status. When Igor is unemployed, say whether it is frictional, structural, or cyclical unemployment.
a From January 1 to June 30, 1996, Igor was a full-time student pursuing his bachelor's degree.
b On July 1, Igor graduated with his degree in body building. He spent three months looking for work before Dr Frankenstein hired him on October 1.
c From October 1 to January 1, 1997, Igor worked full-time on the night shift.
d On January 1, because of generally worsening economic conditions, Igor was put on part-time work on the night shift even though he wanted to work full time.
e On February 28, as economic conditions worsened, Dr Frankenstein fired Igor. Igor looked for work until May 1.
f On May 1, Igor became convinced that he couldn't find a job, so until October 31 he looked after the house but did not look for work.
g On October 31, Count Dracula dropped by for a bite and offered Igor a job, which he accepted.

2 Can the unemployment rate increase while the total amount of employment also increases?

3 In the *Reading Between the Lines* article, explain what is meant by 'the European social chapter and a national minimum wage'.

## PROBLEMS

Table 24.1

| Employed workers | Unemployed workers | Work-force | Unemployment rate (%) |
|---|---|---|---|
| 100 | 10 | | |
| 80 | | 100 | |
| | | 200 | 5.0 |
| 130 | 8 | | |

1 Complete Table 24.1.

2 Suppose that the initial money wage rate is E5 an hour and that the initial price level is 100. Now assume that both the money wage rate and the price level double.

a What happens to the real wage rate?

b What happens to the quantity of labour supplied; does it increase, decrease, or not change? Why?

c What happens to the quantity of labour demanded; does it increase, decrease, or not change? Why?

**3 a** In Fig. 24.1 illustrate a real wage rate at which jobs are rationed. Indicate the amount of unemployment.

b What can account for job rationing?

**Figure 24.1**

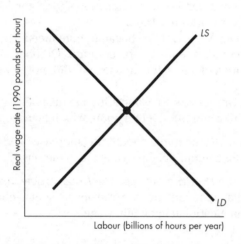

# DISCUSSION QUESTIONS

**1** Explain why understanding the different types of unemployment is useful.

**2** Why is a goal of zero unemployment neither realistic nor desirable?

# DATA QUESTIONS

**Structural Unemployment**

We can differentiate different types of structural unemployment:

◆ Regional – some regions have been over-reliant on particular industries such as coal.

◆ Occupational – some industries suffer disproportionately so far as unemployment is concerned. The construction industry is an example.

◆ Technological – this allows more to be produced with fewer workers and it makes some skills obsolete.

◆ Seasonal – in some cases workers are required for only part of the year. The tourism industry is an example.

*Source:* B. Atkinson, P. Baker and B. Milward, *Economic Policy*, Macmillan, 1996, pp. 239–40.

**1** Explain what is meant by structural unemployment.

**2** What policy measures can be taken to reduce structural unemployment?

# ANSWERS

## CONCEPT REVIEW

**1** Labour Force Survey; claimant

**2** work-force; unemployed

**3** structural; cyclical; frictional

**4** Cyclical; business

**5** natural

**6** demand; supply; equilibrium

**7** search

**8** age; unemployment; change

**9** search; rationing; sticky

## TRUE OR FALSE

**1 F** The unemployment rate equals the total number of unemployed workers divided by the work-force, not the total working-age population.

**2 F** These students are not in the work-force.

**3 F** Mary is a discouraged worker because she stopped looking for a job.

**4 T** A rise in the real wage rate boosts the amount of goods and services that can be purchased by working, so the quantity of labour supplied increases.

**5 T** If wages are sticky, changes in economic activity that affect the price level will cause changes in real wage rates and can create unemployment.

**6 F** At full employment, the unemployment rate equals the natural rate, comprising frictional and structural unemployment.

**7 T** An increase in the demand for labour means that the demand curve of labour shifts rightward, thereby raising the real wage rate.

**8 T** The natural rate of unemployment is *defined* as the sum of frictional and structural unemployment.

**9 T** Bill is part of the normal turnover in the labour market and thus is frictionally unemployed.

# MULTIPLE CHOICE

**1 d** Amanda's job was lost because of a recession, so Amanda is cyclically unemployed.

**2 b** Omar is part of the normal turnover in the work-force, so he is frictionally unemployed.

**3 d** At full employment, the unemployment rate is the natural rate, which equals the sum of frictional and structural unemployment.

**4 d** Insider–outsider theory states a potential cause of unemployment.

**5 b** When demand rises faster than supply, then price will rise.

**6 b** The work-force equals the sum of employed workers (130 million) and unemployed workers (10 million), or 140 million.

**7 b** The work-force participation rate equals the percentage of the working-age population in the work-force, that is, the total work-force (140 million) divided by the total working-age population (200 million), multiplied by 100.

**8 b** The unemployment rate equals the number of unemployed workers divided by the work-force, multiplied by 100.

**9 d** Because unions negotiate on behalf of their employed members, unions do not bargain for lower wage rates even though lower wage rates would reduce the unemployment rate.

**10 a** As Fig. 24.2 illustrates, the rightward shift in the demand curve from $LD_0$ to $LD_1$ raises the wage rate to $W_1$ and increases the level of employment to $L_1$.

**11 c** The real wage rate equals the money wage rate divided by the price level. Thus when both the money wage rate and price level double, the real wage rate does not change.

**Figure 24.2**

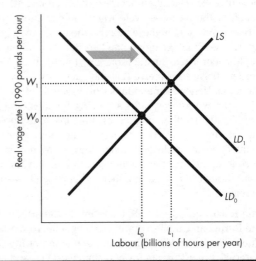

**12 b** Job losers include workers who have been fired or laid off, and these workers account for the majority of unemployment during a recession.

**13 c** The natural rate comprises only frictional and structural unemployment.

**14 d** In a recession, economic activity slows so that real GDP and aggregate hours of work fall and the unemployment rate rises.

**15 a** The definition of the work-force is the sum of employed and unemployed workers.

**16 c** Definition.

# SHORT ANSWER

**1 a** As a full-time student, Igor was not in the work-force.
**b** While Igor searched for his first job, he was frictionally unemployed.
**c** When working full-time for Dr Frankenstein, Igor was an employed worker.
**d** Even though Igor wanted full-time work, he none the less was still counted as (fully) employed when he was on the part-time night shift.
**e** From February 28 to May 1, Igor was cyclically unemployed because his unemployment was the result of a downturn in the economy.
**f** From May 1 to October 31, Igor was not in the work-force because he was not looking for work. Igor was a discouraged worker.
**g** Igor is employed after October 31.

**2** Although it is not common, both the number of employed workers and the unemployment rate can increase at the same time. This situation occurs most often just after the trough of the business cycle when the economy moves into an expansion. In these months, the economy is growing, real GDP is expanding, and so the total amount of employment rises. In addition, previously discouraged workers begin to perceive that they may now be able to find a job. Hence a large number of discouraged workers rejoin the work-force, start searching for jobs, and add significantly to the number of unemployed workers. (Recall that as discouraged workers they were not counted as unemployed; rather they were not in the work-force.) Hence the unemployment rate may increase even though the total number of employed workers increases.

**3** The European Social Chapter refers to the attempts of the European Union to grant social benefits to workers. These can be wide ranging and include maternity (and paternity) rights, rights for part-time workers, and companies operating in several countries have to call annual meetings of workers' representatives.

A national minimum wage is found in almost every advanced country except the United Kingdom. It attempts to help relieve the poverty of low-paid workers by preventing employers paying low wages.

# PROBLEMS

**Table 24.2**

| Employed workers | Unemployed workers | Work-force | Unemployment rate (per cent) |
|---|---|---|---|
| 100 | 10 | 110 | 9.1 |
| 80 | 20 | 100 | 20.0 |
| 190 | 10 | 200 | 5.0 |
| 130 | 8 | 138 | 5.8 |

**1** The answers are in Table 24.2. To calculate them, recall that the work-force equals the sum of employed and unemployed workers. Hence in the first line the total work-force equals 100 + 10 or 110. In the second line, the number of unemployed workers equals the work-force, 100, minus the total number of employed workers, 80. Thus unemployed workers number 20. The unemployment rate equals the total number of unemployed workers divided by the work-force, multiplied by 100. Thus in the first row the unemployment rate equals

$$\frac{10}{100} \times 100 = 9.1 \text{ per cent.}$$

In the third row, rearranging the definition of the unemployment rate shows that the total number of unemployed workers equals the unemployment rate multiplied by the work-force. Hence in the third row the total number of unemployed workers is 5 per cent × 200 so that unemployment is 10. The number of employed workers in that row is therefore 190.

**2 a** The real wage rate does not change. The real wage rate is defined as the money wage rate divided by the price level. Because both the money wage rate and price level double, the doubling 'cancels' so that the real wage rate is unaffected. Alternatively, if the money wage rate doubles and the price level doubles, people receive twice as much money for each hour's work, but the money buys only half what it did before. Hence the real wage rate – the number of goods and services that can be purchased with an hour's work – does not change.

**b** Because the real wage rate does not change, neither does the quantity of labour supplied. The quantity of labour supplied depends on the real wage rate, *not* the money wage rate, because the real wage rate indicates how many goods and services can be purchased with an hour's work.

**c** The quantity of labour demanded does not change. Similar to the supply of labour, the demand for labour depends on the real wage rate, not the money wage rate. Essentially, the real wage rate shows the cost of hiring labour (the money wage) relative to the price of the firm's output (the price level). When both the cost of hiring labour and the price of the firm's output double, the firm has no incentive to hire either more or less labour because the profit from hiring workers has not changed.

**Figure 24.3**

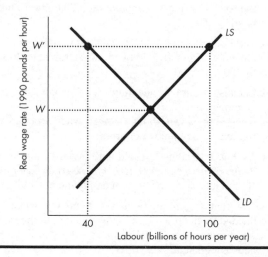

**3 a** In Fig. 24.3, any wage rate higher than the equilibrium wage rate, $W$, creates some job rationing. For instance, at the wage rate $W'$, the demand for labour is only 40 billion hours of labour, yet at this wage rate 100 billion hours of labour are supplied. At this wage rate unemployment is 60 billion hours of labour. More generally, the extent of unemployment equals the difference between the quantity of labour supplied and the quantity demanded.

**b** Three factors can account for job rationing: efficiency wages, insider interest and the minimum wage.

Efficiency wages occur when firms pay above-equilibrium wage rates to increase their workers' productivity. Hence firms might pay a wage rate of $W'$ knowing that, although the higher wage rate increases their costs, this effect is more than offset by the higher productivity of the workers receiving the higher wage rate.

The idea of insider interest indicates that unions may bargain to further *only* the interests of their employed members. Hence unions bargain for a high wage rate because the union does not represent the workers remaining unemployed by an above-equilibrium wage rate.

Lastly, the minimum wage may be at a level that is above the equilibrium wage rate. In this case the quantity of labour demanded is less than that supplied, and jobs are rationed because not everyone who wants to work at the going (minimum) wage rate can find employment.

# DISCUSSION QUESTIONS

**1** The classification of unemployment can be extremely useful for us, as students, because it makes clear some of the causes of unemployment. Once we know the causes, we can also get a lot of insight into what we should do about them.

For example, take the idea of structural unemployment. Structurally unemployed workers will need a different type of help than those who are cyclically unemployed. A worker who is cyclically unemployed doesn't necessarily need a lot of retraining. But a worker who is structurally unemployed may benefit from this type of training. So by recognizing that structural reasons are one cause of unemployment, we can see that offering retraining may be a good idea if we want to reduce the unemployment rate.

**2** Reducing frictional unemployment to zero would be costly, since some people are always looking for work and the economy needs some flexibility. It would probably be equally impossible to reduce structural unemployment to zero. But cyclical unemployment is a different issue. The more we can tame the business cycle, the more we can reduce cyclical unemployment.

# DATA QUESTIONS

**1** Structural unemployment is caused by changes in the structure of the economy which lead to changes in the demand for and supply of labour in particular industries and occupations.

**2** No policies can completely eliminate structural unemployment since the structure of the economy will continue to change. However, retraining workers so that they can change jobs is a useful policy. Some economists would argue that this should be augmented by regional policy to help depressed areas; for example, giving grants to firms moving into the area and using other measures to help particular industries.

# Chapter 25 Investment, Capital and Interest

---

## Chapter in Perspective, Text Pages 625–652

Our future living standards depend, at least in part, on the level of investment. This chapter analyses the factors that influence investment. It also looks at the factors that influence households' saving and consumption decisions – which also have a large impact on future living standards, as does the effect of net imports.

The chapter integrates these factors to discuss equilibrium in the national economy.

---

## Helpful Hints

**1** This chapter is important for at least two reasons.

First, it is a key building block to an understanding of economic growth. Economic growth results from growth in productive inputs and from growth in technology. The two most important inputs are labour, which was discussed in Chapter 24, and capital, which is examined in this chapter. Chapter 26 integrates the topics in this chapter and those in Chapter 24 with some new material (the role of technology and incentives that help foster economic growth) to permit a thorough analysis of economic growth.

Second, it is helpful in understanding business cycles, that is, the recurring fluctuations in economic activity. Investment, and particularly fluctuations in investment, play a crucial role in business cycles. Thus the discussion of the demand for investment is significant in terms of several key issues concerning the causes of business cycles and potential cures for business cycles.

**2** The saving supply and investment demand model is another supply and demand model. The saving supply curve is just another supply curve, and the investment demand curve is simply another demand curve. Thus all the lessons and rules that you have learned about 'ordinary' supply and demand curves directly apply to the saving supply curve and the investment demand curve. For instance, the difference between a movement along a curve and a shift in a curve is exactly the same as before. A change in the variable on the vertical axis (the real interest rate in this case) causes a movement along the (saving) supply curve and (investment) demand curve. A change in any other relevant variable (such as disposable income) shifts the curve(s).

3 Always remember that the marginal propensity to consume and marginal propensity to save refer to *changes* in consumption expenditure and saving that are caused by *changes* in disposable income. One way to remember these relationships is to think of the question that, say, the marginal propensity to consume answers: if a person's disposable income increases by £100, how much more will the person spend on consumption?

The marginal propensity to consume and marginal propensity to save are important in later chapters because we are often interested in how consumption (and saving) respond to changes in income. For instance, during a recession, income falls and hence we may want to know how that causes consumption to change. For this purpose, the marginal propensity to consume is crucial.

# Key Figures

## Figure 25.4 Investment Demand, text page 631

Part (a) shows that the demand for investment curve is shaped like an ordinary demand curve – at lower interest rates more will be demanded.

Part (b) shows the effect of a shift in the curve, in this case caused by a change in expectations. When firms expect higher profits they will invest more at all levels of interest.

## Figure 25.6 Consumption Demand Curve and Saving Supply Curve, text page 635

Part (a) shows a movement along a curve caused by a change in the real interest rate. Part (b) also shows a movement along a curve, in this case indicating that a rise in real interest rates causes a rise in saving.

Note that subsequent figures show other influences which shift these curves.

# SELF-TEST

## CONCEPT REVIEW

1 Net investment (gross investment minus _____ ) increases the capital stock.

2 The return on capital is the _____ interest rate.

3 Interest depends on the expected _____ rate and the real _____ rate.

4 When the expected profit rate increases, the investment demand curve shifts _____ .

5 Consumption expenditure and saving decisions are influenced by the real interest rate, _____ income, the purchasing power of net _____ and _____ future income.

6 The consumption demand curve is the relationship between consumption expenditure and the _____ _____ rate.

7 Other things remaining the same, net exports adjust to fill the gap between _____ GDP and $C + I + G$.

## TRUE OR FALSE

__ 1 The real interest rate equals the interest rate on a loan plus the inflation rate.

__ 2 An increase in the expected profit rate shifts the saving supply curve rightward.

__ 3 An increase in the real interest rate increases the quantity of people's saving.

__ 4 On average, the investment rate in developing countries has been higher than that in developed countries.

__ 5 If a £100 increase in disposable income causes an increase in saving of £40, the *MPS* is 0.40.

__ 6 The amount of net investment is smaller during recessions and larger during expansio ns.

__ 7 An increase in the real exchange rate increases net exports.

__ 8 When an individual's consumption demand curve shifts rightward, the person's saving supply curve shifts leftward.

**9** If the world saving supply curve shifts rightward more rapidly than the investment demand curve, the real interest rate falls.

## MULTIPLE CHOICE

**1** An increase in the expected profit rate shifts the _____ _____ curve rightward and _____ the real interest rate.
  **a** saving supply; lowers
  **b** investment demand; raises
  **c** saving supply; raises
  **d** investment demand; lowers

**2** If the interest rate on a loan is 8 per cent and the inflation rate is 2 per cent, the real interest rate is
  **a** 16 per cent.
  **b** 10 per cent.
  **c** 6 per cent.
  **d** 4 per cent.

**3** In the long run, the sum of a country's consumption expenditure, investment and government purchases is less than the country's potential GDP. Then in that country
  **a** the real interest rate rises.
  **b** net exports are positive.
  **c** the government raises its spending.
  **d** the investment demand curve will shift rightward.

**4** Which of the following does *not* increase consumption expenditure?
  **a** an increase in disposable income
  **b** an increase in the purchasing power of net assets
  **c** an increase in expected future income
  **d** an increase in the expected profit rate

**5** Which of the following has the smallest fluctuations?
  **a** gross investment
  **b** net investment
  **c** capital stock
  **d** fluctuations in gross investment and capital are the same and are the smallest

**6** An increase in a country's consumption expenditure _____ its real exchange rate and _____ its net exports.
  **a** lowers; decreases
  **b** lowers; increases

**c** raises; increases
**d** raises; decreases

**7** A household's *MPC* is 0.90. Hence an increase of £100 of disposable income causes
  **a** consumption expenditure to increase by £100.
  **b** consumption expenditure to increase by £90.
  **c** saving to decrease by £90.
  **d** Both **b** and **c** occur.

---

**Figure 25.1**

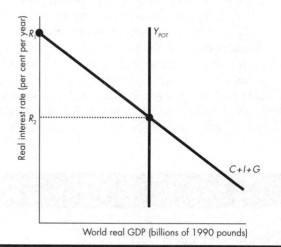

**8** In Fig. 25.1, the equilibrium real interest rate is
  **a** $R_1$.
  **b** between $R_1$ and $R_2$.
  **c** $R_2$.
  **d** less than $R_2$.

**9** Which of the following increases both consumption demand and saving supply?
  **a** an increase in the real interest rate
  **b** a decrease in future expected income
  **c** an increase in net assets
  **d** an increase in disposable income

**10** If the real interest rate is less than the equilibrium real interest rate, the quantity of
  **a** saving exceeds the quantity of investment and the real interest rate rises.
  **b** saving exceeds the quantity of investment and the real interest rate falls.
  **c** investment exceeds the quantity of saving and the real interest rate falls.
  **d** investment exceeds the quantity of saving and the real interest rate rises.

**11** What could raise the equilibrium real interest rate and increase the equilibrium quantity of investment?

    **a** a rightward shift of the saving supply curve

    **b** a leftward shift of the saving supply curve

    **c** a leftward shift of the investment demand curve

    **d** a rightward shift of the investment demand curve

**12** The marginal propensity to save is

    **a** the total amount of saving by a household.

    **b** the fraction of a household's disposable income that is saved.

    **c** the fraction of a change in disposable income that is saved.

    **d** slightly greater than 1.0 for the UK economy.

**13** In the long run, net exports equal

    **a** potential real GDP minus $C + I + G$.

    **b** the exchange rate minus the inflation rate.

    **c** investment.

    **d** potential real GDP.

**14** The opportunity cost of consumption expenditure this year versus next year is

    **a** the real interest rate.

    **b** the real exchange rate.

    **c** the expected profit rate.

    **d** None of the above.

## SHORT ANSWER

**1** The interest rate on a loan in 1977 was 12 per cent; in 1997 the interest rate on a comparable loan was 8 per cent. Based on this information alone, in which year was the real interest rate the highest?

**2** Table 25.1 shows how Igor's consumption depends on the real interest rate when his disposable income is £20,000.

    **a** Complete the table.

    **b** In Fig. 25.2 illustrate Igor's consumption demand curve; in Fig. 25.3 show his saving supply curve.

    **c** Suppose that Igor expects his income to increase in the future, which causes his consumption expenditure to increase by £50 at every real interest rate. What happens to his saving at each real interest rate?

    **d** If Igor's current disposable income increases by £100, his consumption expenditure increases by £80 at every interest rate. What is

Igor's marginal propensity to consume? His marginal propensity to save?

**Table 25.1   Igor's Consumption and Saving**

| Real interest rate (per cent) | Consumption expenditure (pounds) | Saving (pounds) |
|---|---|---|
| 3 | 19,500 | |
| 4 | 19,200 | |
| 5 | 18,900 | |
| 6 | 18,600 | |
| 7 | 18,300 | |

**Figure 25.2**

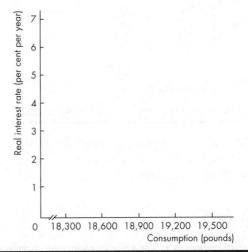

**Figure 25.3**

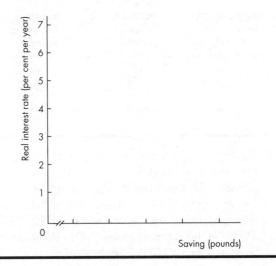

**3** In Fig. 25.4, draw a world investment demand and saving supply curve. Show the equilibrium real interest rate and the amount of saving and investment. Use the figure to illustrate what happens when the expected profit rate increases.

**Figure 25.4**

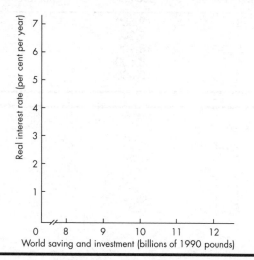

**4** Re-read the *Reading Between the Lines* article, and explain the relationship between consumer credit and consumer spending.

## PROBLEMS

**Table 25.2   Expenditures in Nirvana**

| Real interest rate (per cent) | Consumption expenditure (C) (billions of pounds) | Investment (I) (billions of pounds) |
|---|---|---|
| 3 | 26 | 24 |
| 4 | 24 | 21 |
| 5 | 22 | 18 |
| 6 | 20 | 15 |
| 7 | 18 | 12 |

**1** Table 25.2 gives the consumption demand and the investment demand for the country of Nirvana. At any interest rate, the government of Nirvana buys goods and services worth £10 billion and levies net taxes equal to £10 billion. There is no international trade. Potential real GDP in Nirvana is £45 billion.

**a** Complete the investment demand and saving supply schedules in Table 25.3. What is the equilibrium real interest rate?

**b** Complete Table 25.4, showing the sum of consumption expenditure plus investment plus government purchases of goods and services, $C + I + G$, and potential real GDP. What is the equilibrium real interest rate?

**c** How do your answers for **a** and **b** compare? Why?

**Table 25.3   Investment and Saving in Nirvana**

| Real interest rate (per cent) | Investment demand (I) (billions of pounds) | Saving supply (billions of pounds) |
|---|---|---|
| 3 | | |
| 4 | | |
| 5 | | |
| 6 | | |
| 7 | | |

**Table 25.4   $C + I + G$ and Potential Real GDP in Nirvana**

| Real interest rate (per cent) | $C + I + G$ (billions of pounds) | Potential real GDP (billions of pounds) |
|---|---|---|
| 3 | | |
| 4 | | |
| 5 | | |
| 6 | | |
| 7 | | |

**2** Initially, the small country of Primus is in long-run equilibrium and net exports equal zero. Then the expected profit rate in Primus increases. Because Primus is a small part of the world economy, the world real interest rate does not change. How does this change affect Primus's

**a** investment demand curve?

**b** $C + I + G$ curve?

**c** equilibrium quantity of investment?

**d** equilibrium quantity of net exports?

Illustrate your answer to this part with a sketch.

**3** In 2, how does Primus finance the change in its investment?

**Table 25.5   Expenditures in Weezer**

| Real interest rate (per cent) | Consumption expenditure (billions of pounds) | Investment (billions of pounds) |
|---|---|---|
| 3 | 40 | 22 |
| 4 | 38 | 21 |
| 5 | 36 | 20 |
| 6 | 34 | 19 |
| 7 | 32 | 18 |
| 8 | 30 | 17 |

**Table 25.6   C + I + G and Net Exports in Weezer**

| Real interest rate (per cent) | C + I + G (billions of pounds) | Potential real GDP (billions of pounds) | Net exports (billions of pounds) |
|---|---|---|---|
| 3 | | | |
| 4 | | | |
| 5 | | | |
| 6 | | | |
| 7 | | | |
| 8 | | | |

**4** Table 25.5 shows the schedules of consumption expenditure and investment in the country of Weezer. Government purchases of goods and services are £24 billion, and potential GDP is £80 billion.

**a** Complete Table 25.6.

**b** What do positive net exports mean? And negative net exports?

**c** If the world real interest rate is 5 per cent, what are the levels of consumption, investment and net exports in this economy?

**d** If the world real interest rate rises to 7 per cent, what happens in this economy?

**e** If the government in Weezer increases its purchases, what happens to the country's net exports?

## DISCUSSION QUESTION

**1** Why does investment decrease when the real interest rate rises?

## DATA QUESTIONS

**Consumption and Income**
The data in Table 25.7 refer to the UK economy.

**Table 25.7**

| | Real personal disposable income (billions 1990 pounds) | Real consumers' expenditure (1990=100) |
|---|---|---|
| 1990 | 381 | 100 |
| 1991 | 378 | 107 |
| 1992 | 388 | 112 |
| 1993 | 384 | 116 |
| 1994 | 396 | 119 |
| 1995 | 405 | 122 |

*Source: Economic Trends*, HMSO, 1996.

**1** What is meant by 'real personal disposable income'?

**2** What factors might have caused real personal disposable income to change over this period?

**3** What is meant by 'real consumers' expenditure 1990=100'?

**4** What factors other than current disposable income might affect consumption?

# ANSWERS

## CONCEPT REVIEW

**1** depreciation

**2** real

**3** profit; interest

**4** rightward

**5** disposable; assets; expected

**6** real interest

**7** potential

# TRUE OR FALSE

**1 F** The real interest rate equals the interest rate on a loan *minus* the inflation rate.

**2 F** An increase in the expected profit rate shifts the investment demand curve rightward; it does not shift the saving supply curve.

**3 T** As the real interest rate rises, the 'reward' from saving increases, so people increase the quantity they save.

**4 T** Although not true for all developing countries, on average in developing countries the investment rate exceeds that in developed countries.

**5 T** The *MPS* is defined as the ratio of the change in saving caused by a change in disposable income or, in this question, $40/$100 = 0.40.

**6 T** Net investment fluctuates with the business cycle; it is higher during expansions and lower during recessions.

**7 F** A rise in the real exchange rate reduces net exports because it makes UK exports more expensive and UK imports less expensive.

**8 F** This may be true. The shift in the saving supply depends on the reason for the shift in the consumption demand curve. For instance, if the consumption demand curve shifted rightward because disposable income increased, the increase in disposable income also shifts the saving supply curve rightward. If the shift in the consumption demand curve was caused by an increase in net assets, the increase in net assets shifts the saving supply curve leftward.

**9 T** The rightward shift in the saving supply curve lowers the equilibrium real interest rate.

# MULTIPLE CHOICE

**1 b** As Fig. 25.5 shows, the shift in the investment demand curve to the right raises the equilibrium real interest rate from $R_0$ to $R_1$.

**2 c** The real interest rate equals the interest rate on the loan, 8 per cent, minus the inflation rate, 2 per cent.

**3 b** Net exports are positive as the country exports the excess of its potential GDP over the domestic demand $(C + I + G)$ for it.

**4 d** An increase in the expected profit rate increases investment, not consumption expenditure.

## Figure 25.5

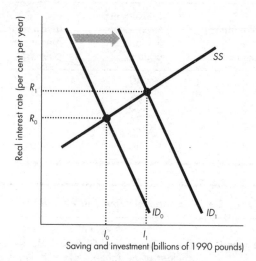

**5 c** The capital stock's fluctuations are a much smaller fraction of the total capital stock than fluctuations in either measure of investment.

**6 d** The increase in consumption expenditure lowers net exports (fewer goods are left to export), and the increase in net exports is associated with a drop in the real exchange rate.

**7 b** The change in consumption expenditure equals the *MPC* multiplied by the change in disposable income, or $0.90 \times $100$.

**8 c** The equilibrium real interest rate is the real interest rate that sets the quantity of world real GDP demanded equal to world potential real GDP.

**9 d** An increase in disposable income shifts both the consumption demand and saving supply curves rightward.

**10 d** The excess of the quantity demanded of investment over the quantity supplied of saving creates upward pressure on the real interest rate that moves the real interest rate towards its equilibrium.

**11 d** The rightward shift in the investment demand curve raises both the equilibrium real interest rate and equilibrium quantity of investment.

**12 c** Definition.

**13 a** Net exports adjust so that the *total* demand for real GDP, $C + I + G + NX$, equals potential real GDP.

**14 a** By consuming this year, the household loses the opportunity to save the funds and consume more next year. The amount of increased consumption forgone equals the real interest rate, which essentially is the gain in the purchasing power of savings.

# SHORT ANSWER

**1** Determining when the real interest rate was the highest is impossible. The real interest rate equals the interest rate on the loan minus the inflation rate. If the inflation rates in the two years were the same, the real interest rate in 1977 was higher. But if the inflation rate was sufficiently higher in 1977 than in 1997, the real interest rate in 1977 would be lower than in 1997. For instance, suppose that the inflation rate in 1977 was 11 per cent and in 1997 was 3 per cent. Then the real interest rate in 1977 was 1 per cent and in 1997 was 5 per cent.

**Table 25.8   Igor's Consumption and Saving**

| Real interest rate (per cent) | Consumption expenditure (pounds) | Saving (pounds) |
|:---:|:---:|:---:|
| 3 | 19,500 | 500 |
| 4 | 19,200 | 800 |
| 5 | 18,900 | 1,180 |
| 6 | 18,600 | 1,400 |
| 7 | 18,300 | 1,700 |

**2 a** Table 25.8 shows Igor's saving. At any real interest rate, Igor's saving equals his disposable income, £20,000, minus his consumption expenditure. Thus at the real interest rate of 3 per cent, Igor's saving equals £20,000 – £19,500, or £500.

**b** Figure 25.6 illustrates Igor's consumption demand curve, and Fig. 25.7 shows his saving supply curve.

**Figure 25.7**

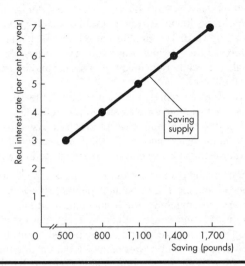

**c** Igor's saving falls by £50 at every real interest rate. Thus at a real interest rate of 3 per cent, Igor now saves £450 and at a real interest rate of 4 per cent, Igor saves £750.

**d** The marginal propensity to consume, or *MPC*, is $\Delta C/\Delta YD$ where $\Delta$ means 'change in', $C$ is consumption expenditure, and $YD$ is disposable income. Thus Igor's *MPC* equals £80/£100, or 0.80.

Igor's marginal propensity to save, *MPS*, is defined as $\Delta S/\Delta YD$ , where $S$ is saving. Because Igor's consumption expenditure increases by £80 when his disposable income increases by £100, Igor's saving must increase by £20. Thus Igor's *MPS* is £20/£100, or 0.20.

**Figure 25.6**

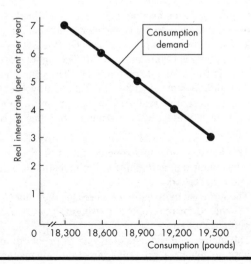

**Figure 25.8**

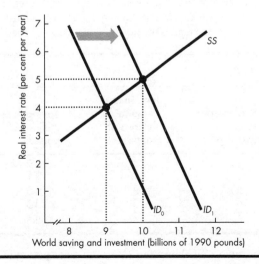

**3** Figure 25.8 shows an investment demand $ID_0$ and saving supply curve $SS$. The curves do not need to be identical to those shown; however, the investment demand curve must slope downward and the saving supply curve must slope upward. The equilibrium real interest rate is the interest rate at which the two curves cross, or 4 per cent. The equilibrium quantity of saving and investment is £9 billion.

An increase in the expected profit rate shifts the investment demand curve rightward, to $ID_1$ in the figure. As a result, the equilibrium real interest rate rises, to 5 per cent in the figure, and the equilibrium quantity of saving and investment also increases, to £10 billion in the figure.

**4** The availability and cost of credit is an important influence on the level of consumer spending, but it does not determine spending. Much spending is done without any credit, and is determined by other factors such as the level of disposable income, expected future income and the purchasing power of net assets. Despite this, figures for credit are a useful guide to what is happening to consumer spending.

## PROBLEMS

**1 a** Table 25.8 shows the investment demand and saving supply schedules for Nirvana. The investment demand schedule was given in the problem question. To get the saving supply schedule, first note that disposable income equals aggregate income of £45 billion (potential real GDP) minus net taxes of £10 billion, or £35 billion. From this amount, at each real interest rate, subtract the consumption expenditure to get saving. Thus at the real interest rate of 3 per cent, households spend £26 billion on consumption, leaving £9 billion for saving. The equilibrium real interest rate is 6 per cent because it is the real interest rate at which the quantity of investment demanded equals the quantity of saving supplied.

**Table 25.8**

| Real interest rate (per cent) | Investment demand (billions of pounds) | Saving supply (billions of pounds) |
|---|---|---|
| 3 | 24 | 9 |
| 4 | 21 | 11 |
| 5 | 18 | 13 |
| 6 | 15 | 15 |
| 7 | 12 | 17 |

**b** Table 25.9 shows the $C + I + G$ and potential real GDP schedules. Potential real GDP was given in the

problem question as £45 billion. The $C + I + G$ schedule is obtained at each real interest rate by adding consumption expenditure, investment and government purchases of goods and services. For instance, when the interest rate is 3 per cent, consumption expenditure is £26 billion, investment is £24 billion and government purchases are £10 billion for a total real demand of £60 billion. From Table 25.9, the equilibrium real interest rate is 6 per cent because this real interest rate sets the quantity of consumption expenditure plus investment plus government purchases equal to the potential real GDP.

**Table 25.9**

| Real interest rate (per cent) | $C + I + G$ (billions of pounds) | Potential real GDP (billions of pounds) |
|---|---|---|
| 3 | 60 | 45 |
| 4 | 55 | 45 |
| 5 | 50 | 45 |
| 6 | 45 | 45 |
| 7 | 40 | 45 |

**c** The equilibrium real interest rate in **a** is identical to that in **b**. They are identical because the two approaches (the saving supply/investment demand and the $C + I + G$/potential real GDP) are equivalent. To see the equivalency, take the equality between saving and investment, that is, $S = I$. To both sides, add consumption expenditure, $C$, which gives $C + S = C + I$. Next, recall that net taxes equal government purchases of goods and services, $NT = G$. Then, to the left side of the formula, $C + S$, add $NT$ and to the right side, $C + I$, add $G$, giving $C + S + NT = C + I + G$. Now, $C + S$ equals disposable income, and adding taxes to disposable income gives aggregate income. As aggregate income equals potential real GDP, the left side of the equality is potential real GDP. The right side, $C + I + G$, is the demand for real GDP. Thus the equality that initially started as $S = I$, the **a** equality, is equivalent to potential real GDP = consumption demand plus investment plus government purchases, the **b** equality.

**2 a** The increase in the expected profit rate increases investment demand, shifting the investment demand curve rightward.

**b** The increase in investment increases the total $C + I + G$ demand for real GDP, and Primus's $C + I + G$ curve shifts rightward.

**c** The increase in the expected rate of profit combined with no change in the real interest rate means that the quantity of investment increases.

**d** Because $C + I + G$ in Primus increases, net exports decrease and become negative. This situation is illustrated in Fig. 25.9, where the $C + I + G$ line shifts to $C + I' + G$. At the initial real interest rate of $R$, net exports were zero. After the increase in $C + I + G$, net exports are negative (so that imports exceed exports) and are equal to the distance between points $a$ and $b$ shown by the dashed line. In other words, at the real interest rate of $R$, an amount of 'net imports' equal to the distance between $a$ and $b$ must be subtracted from the $C + I + G$ demand for real GDP in order to set the total demand for GDP equal to potential real GDP.

**Figure 25.9**

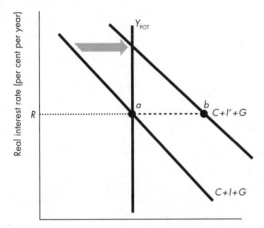

Real GDP in Primus (billions of 1990 pounds)

**3** Investment can be financed by national saving and borrowing from the rest of the world. In Primus's case, national saving does not change because the real interest rate is constant. Thus the increase in investment is financed by borrowing from the rest of the world, as Primus runs a current account deficit and capital account surplus.

**Table 25.10   $C + I + G$ and Net Exports**

| Real interest rate (per cent) | $C + I + G$ (billions of pounds) | Potential real GDP (billions of pounds) | Net exports (billions of pounds) |
|---|---|---|---|
| 3 | 86 | 80 | –6 |
| 4 | 83 | 80 | –3 |
| 5 | 80 | 80 | 0 |
| 6 | 77 | 80 | 3 |
| 7 | 74 | 80 | 6 |
| 8 | 71 | 80 | 9 |

**4 a** Table 25.10 shows the schedules of $C + I + G$, potential real GDP and net exports for the country of Weezer. For the $C + I + G$ column, take the row with the real interest rate of 5 per cent as an example. At this interest rate, $C + I + G$ equals the sum of £36 billion (consumption expenditures) plus £20 billion (investment) plus £24 billion (government purchases of goods and services), or £80 billion. For the potential real GDP column, potential real GDP is given as £80 billion, and this amount does not depend on the real interest rate. Hence at all interest rates potential GDP is £80 billion. Lastly, net exports equal potential real GDP minus $C + I + G$. For instance, when the real interest rate is 6 per cent, net exports equal £80 billion (potential real GDP) minus £77 billion ($C + I + G$), or £3 billion.

**b** When net exports are positive, Weezer exports more goods and services than it imports. For instance, at the real interest rate of 6 per cent, residents of Weezer buy only £77 billion of Weezer's £80 billion of goods and services. The remaining £3 billion of goods and services are exported to other countries. When net exports are negative, Weezer imports more goods and services than it exports. Take the situation at the real interest rate of 3 per cent. Weezer's residents, firms and government demand £86 billion of goods and services. However, Weezer produces only £80 billion of goods and services. Thus the extra £6 billion of goods and services demanded are imported so that net exports are –£6 billion.

**c** If the real interest rate is 5 per cent, then Table 25.10 shows that net exports are 0.

**d** If the world real interest rate rises to 7 per cent, consumption and investment in Weezer decrease so that $C + I + G$ decreases by £6 billion. In other words, domestic spending within Weezer decreases by £6 billion. Potential GDP does not change, so net exports from Weezer rise by £6 billion.

**e** If the government in Weezer increases its purchases, the demand for GDP from domestic residents, $C + I + G$, increases. Hence Weezer's net exports decrease.

## DISCUSSION QUESTION

**1** Investment means the purchase of new capital goods; that is, investment refers to buying the actual capital good.

If the real interest rate goes up, people are less likely to borrow to buy a car or anything else. Companies behave in the same way. If the real interest rate goes up, companies will borrow less, cutting back on their investments. So when the real interest rate rises, the quantity of investment that firms demand decreases.

# DATA QUESTIONS

1 In 'real personal disposable income', the 'real' refers to data that have been adjusted to remove the effects of inflation. 'Disposable income' is income after income tax has been removed.

2 Any of the factors which cause shifts in aggregate demand or aggregate supply might cause shifts in real income. The fall in real income in 1991 was caused by the recession. The subsequent rise to recovery was caused by a variety of factors such as the fall in the value of the pound.

3 'Real consumers' expenditure' means that the effects of inflation have been removed. '1990' prices means that 1990 has been used as a base year. Rather surprisingly, consumers continued to spend more even though real incomes fell in 1991.

4 Apart from current disposable income, the factors that might affect consumption are such things as expected future income. They are discussed in detail in the main text on pages 633–639.

# Chapter 26 Long-term Economic Growth

---

## Chapter in Perspective, Text Pages 653–680

Why do economies grow? This question is at the heart of this chapter. The sources are varied – markets, property rights and monetary exchange provide a foundation, but technology is also crucial. Various theories of economic growth are discussed here as are the policies needed to achieve growth.

---

## Helpful Hints

**1** Economics is sometimes called the 'dismal science'. This nickname came about because of the classical growth theory. The main conclusion from the classical approach is that, in the long run, workers are bound to earn only a subsistence wage. This result is, indeed, dismal! And, from our perspective near the start of a new millennium, it also must seem odd. The fact that the classical model of growth was developed at the beginning of the industrial revolution is somewhat ironic. The classical model of growth focuses on population growth and does not allow for continuing technological change and capital growth, two features of the industrial revolution that were to become an increasingly important aspect of the world in which we live. It is these omissions that account for the dismal, subsistence-wage conclusion of the classical model.

One of the advancements made by the neoclassical growth theory was its emphasis on technological growth as an engine of economic development. The new growth theory goes even further by examining the factors that lead to technological change in the form of increasing society's stock of knowledge. In the new growth theory, economic growth can persist indefinitely because the incentive to accumulate more knowledge persists indefinitely. In a real sense, then, the nickname for economics might be changed, perhaps to the 'happy science'!

**2** In the neoclassical model, an increase in technology sets off a spurt of economic growth. However, this growth does not continue forever; eventually, unless another technological change occurs, economic growth dies out. The reason that growth eventually stops is important to understand and can be summed up in one phrase: 'the law of diminishing returns'. The law of diminishing returns is a key assumption of the neoclassical theory; it accounts for the downward slope of the capital demand curve.

To understand this law, we need to examine how the 'return' (the additional output that additional capital creates) of 'ordinary' capital changes as more capital is accumulated. A concrete example is industrial robots. When an industrial robot is installed in a factory, only that particular factory can use the robot. The first such robot may be quite valuable as it fits well into the factory's operations, a fairly large number of workers are available to service it, and it can produce a lot of output. Thus its return is quite high and, because it's producing a lot of additional output, economic growth is robust. The second robot in the factory may be almost as valuable, but now consider, say, the twentieth robot installed in the plant. With 20 robots, the factory is starting to get crowded. Workers servicing the robots are starting to be spread thin, with the result that the robots may spend a substantial period waiting to be repaired or reprogrammed. Thus the twentieth robot is likely to produce significantly less additional output than the first robot. Essentially, the amount of economic growth created by the twentieth robot is substantially less than that created by the first robot. As more and more robots are installed, the return continues to fall until eventually it reaches zero and economic growth ceases.

In addition, because the return from additional robots diminishes, the return from installing additional robots falls as more robots are obtained. As a result, more robots are installed only if the opportunity cost of buying them (the real interest rate) falls, which means that the demand curve for industrial robots – or, more generally, ordinary capital – slopes downward.

**3** In contrast to the neoclassical theory of growth, discussed in Helpful Hint 2, in the new growth theory, economic growth can persist forever. The crucial ingredient in the new growth theory is the assumption that the demand for knowledge capital curve is horizontal. What accounts for the assumption? That is, why doesn't this demand curve slope downward like other demand curves, such as the demand curve for (ordinary) capital?

The answers to these questions lie in the behaviour of the return from knowledge capital compared with the return from ordinary capital.

Think of knowledge capital as 'a better way to produce output', that is, a new technology. When the first 'better way' is developed, it can be applied to all similar factories in the economy, not just the one that developed it. The new technology will increase output so that economic growth occurs. The second 'better way' also will increase output. Now consider the twentieth new technology. This new technology will continue to increase output. But (unlike the twentieth industrial robot discussed in Helpful Hint 2), nothing diminishes the amount of additional output created. Factories are not getting more crowded, and workers are not being spread more thinly. In other words, *all* similar factories anywhere can use the new technology as can workers in *all* these factories. The twentieth 'new way' may well replace, say, the nineteenth 'new way' so that the gain in output from the twentieth unit of knowledge capital may be as large as the gain in output from the first. Hence, unlike ordinary capital, the return from additional new knowledge capital does not diminish. New knowledge capital will continue to be developed even if the opportunity cost of developing it (the real interest rate) does not fall. Hence the knowledge capital demand curve does not slope downward; it is horizontal, which indicates that, even if the real interest rate does not fall, more knowledge capital will be developed and economic growth will continue.

# Key Figures

**Figure 26.9 Neoclassical Growth Theory, text page 668**
This figure shows the effect of technological change. In part (a) higher productivity increases the demand for capital but puts up interest rates. In part (b) higher savings lower interest rates and increase the quantity of capital per person.

**Figure 29.10 New Growth Theory, text page 670**
In new growth theory, growth continues because the returns to capital in the form of knowledge do not decrease.

# SELF-TEST

## CONCEPT REVIEW

1 Over the 150 years from 1855 to 1995 real GDP per person in the United Kingdom increased at an average of _____ per cent a year.

2 Three institutions are crucial to the creation of incentives. They are markets, _____ _____ and _____ exchange.

3 Growth accounting separates the contribution to economic growth of the growth of aggregate _____ , of _____ per hour and of _____ change.

4 Economic growth arises from improvements in _____ capital, increases in the _____ stock and improvements in _____ .

5 New growth theory is that the growth rate depends on the costs and benefits of developing new _____ .

6 To achieve faster growth we must increase the growth of _____ per hour or increase the pace of _____ advance.

## TRUE OR FALSE

___ 1 In the new theory of economic growth, economic growth can continue indefinitely.

___ 2 The neoclassical growth theory stressed the role played by people's incentives for discovering new technology.

___ 3 Limiting the extent of international trade increases the rate of economic growth.

___ 4 The lower the real interest rate, the larger is the quantity supplied of capital.

___ 5 Energy price hikes are one of the causes of the productivity growth slowdown.

___ 6 The law of diminishing returns states that, as more capital is used, the total output produced diminishes.

___ 7 An increase in the amount of capital per hour of work shifts the productivity function upward.

___ 8 An assumption of the classical growth theory is that an increase in real wages and incomes increases the population growth rate.

___ 9 In the neoclassical theory of growth, a technological advance that increases the productivity of capital shifts the capital demand curve rightward.

## MULTIPLE CHOICE

1 Which of the following is *not* a source of economic growth?
 a saving and investment in new capital
 b the productivity function
 c investment in human capital
 d discovery of new technologies

2 The demand curve for knowledge capital
 a is vertical.
 b slopes downward.
 c slopes upward.
 d is horizontal.

3 Growth accounting divides changes in productivity into changes resulting from
 a markets and property rights.
 b saving and investment.
 c capital per hour of labour and technology.
 d human capital and other capital.

4 With no technological change, a 10 per cent increase in capital per hour of work causes approximately a _____ per cent increase in output per hour of labour.
 a 30
 b 10
 c 3.3
 d 1

5 Which theory of economic growth concludes that growth can be a 'perpetual motion machine'?
 a the classical theory
 b the neoclassical theory
 c the new theory
 d all of the theories

236 *CHAPTER TWENTY SIX*

**6** Which theory of economic growth concludes that in the long run people will be paid only a subsistence real wage?
  **a** the classical theory
  **b** the neoclassical theory
  **c** the new theory
  **d** all of the theories

**7** An increase in the amount of capital per hour of work causes
  **a** the productivity function to shift upward.
  **b** the productivity function to shift downward.
  **c** a movement along the productivity function to a higher level of output per hour of work.
  **d** a movement along the productivity function to a lower level of output per hour of work.

**8** Technological advancement causes
  **a** the productivity function to shift upward.
  **b** the productivity function to shift downward.
  **c** a movement along the productivity function to a higher level of output per hour of work.
  **d** a movement along the productivity function to a lower level of output per hour of work.

**9** A key assumption of new growth theory is that
  **a** all technological change is exogenous.
  **b** higher incomes lead to a higher birth rate.
  **c** a successful innovator has the opportunity to earn a temporary, above-average profit.
  **d** the rate of time preference is less than the real interest rate.

**10** If the real interest rate exceeds the rate of time preference, the capital _____ _____ shifts _____ .
  **a** demand curve; rightward
  **b** demand curve; leftward
  **c** supply curve; rightward
  **d** supply curve; leftward

**11** Suppose that capital per hour of work increases by 30 per cent and that real GDP per hour of work increases by 18 per cent. What is the contribution to the increase in real GDP per hour of work from the change in capital per hour of work?
  **a** the increase in capital per hour of work increased real GDP per hour of work by 30 per cent
  **b** the increase in capital per hour of work increased real GDP per hour of work by 18 per cent
  **c** the increase in capital per hour of work increased real GDP per hour of work by 10 per cent
  **d** the increase in capital per hour of work increased real GDP per hour of work by 8 per cent

**12** Suppose that capital per hour of work increases by 30 per cent while real GDP per hour of work increases by 18 per cent. What is the contribution to the increase in real GDP per hour of work from changing technology?
  **a** the change in technology increased real GDP per hour of work by 30 per cent
  **b** the change in technology increased real GDP per hour of work by 18 per cent
  **c** the change in technology increased real GDP per hour of work by 10 per cent
  **d** the change in technology increased real GDP per hour of work by 8 per cent

**13** Of the following types of capital, which does *not* have diminishing returns?
  **a** personal computers
  **b** knowledge
  **c** new oil discoveries
  **d** industrial robots

**14** A classical growth theory assumption was that
  **a** the population growth rate increases when real GDP per person increases.
  **b** saving is more important than investment in determining economic growth.
  **c** capital plays a major role in determining how rapidly the economy grows.
  **d** human capital is the ultimate cause of economic growth.

**15** In the new theory of economic growth, as long as the real interest rate is greater than the rate of time preference
  **a** the population growth rate increases.
  **b** saving is less than investment.
  **c** international trade is necessary.
  **d** more knowledge capital is acquired.

**16** Dynamic comparative advantage
  **a** can boost a country's economic growth rate permanently.
  **b** is temporary and often goes to the supplier that is first in the market.
  **c** had no role in contributing to the growth of the 'miracle economies'.
  **d** is a source of permanently higher profits for a firm.

# SHORT ANSWER

**1** What are the three basic preconditions for economic growth? Explain the role that each plays in promoting economic growth. Are these preconditions sufficient for economic growth to continue for ever? Why or why not?

**2** Would the slowdown in productivity growth have been as large if real GDP had included the value of improving the environment?

**3** Igor was recently named minister for the economy. His first task is to predict his country's long-term growth prospects. Igor expects that capital per hour of labour will grow at 1 per cent per year. Moreover, he expects technological change of 1 per cent per year. What productivity growth rate will Igor predict?

**4** Re-read the *Reading Between the Lines* article. Do you think that high rates of saving cause faster economic growth, or does fast growth lead to higher savings rates?

# PROBLEMS

**1** **a** In Fig. 26.1, illustrate a productivity function that shows when capital per hour of work is £30 then £20 of real GDP per hour of work is produced. Label this point *a*.

**Figure 26.1**

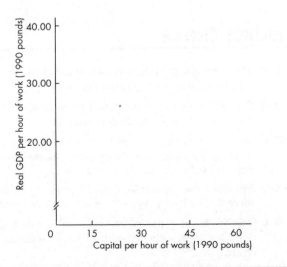

**b** In Fig. 26.1, show what happens to the amount of real GDP per hour of work when the amount of capital per hour of work increases from £30 to £60. After the increase in capital per hour of work, what is the new amount of real GDP per hour of work? (Use the one-third rule.)

**c** In Fig. 26.1, show what happens to the productivity function when new technology is developed?

**2** **a** In 1996, real GDP per person in the country of Slow is £2,000 and is growing at the rate of 1 per cent per year. After 1 year, what is real GDP per person? After 2 years? After 10 years? After 25 years?

**b** Real GDP per person in Fast is £2,000 and is growing at the rate of 3 per cent per year. After 1 year, what is real GDP per person? After 2 years? After 10 years? After 25 years?

**c** Initially the ratio of GDP per person in Fast to GDP per person in Slow is 1.00. What is the ratio after 1 year? After 25 years?

**Figure 26.2**

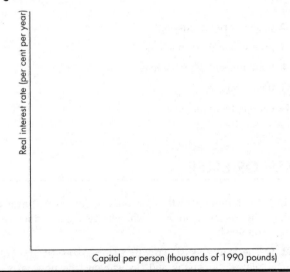

**3** In Fig. 26.2, draw a demand curve for physical capital, such as machine tools. Label this curve $KD_0$. Also in Fig. 26.2, draw a demand for knowledge capital curve and label it $KD_1$. If these curves are similar, explain why; if they are dissimilar, explain why.

# DISCUSSION QUESTIONS

**1** Explain the relationship between the saving supply curve and capital supply curve.

**2** Can you relate shifts in the capital supply curve to the saving supply curve?

# DATA QUESTIONS

## Economic growth

Over the long term, output is determined by the characteristics of the supply side of the economy. Thus in seeking an explanation for international differences in economic growth over long periods, it is natural to look at supply side conditions such as the level of investment in both physical capital and the skills of the workforce. This is the approach of those who espouse the

new models of endogenous growth. These growth models argue that growth leads to an increased demand for education, which, through its impact on worker productivity, stimulates future growth. This implies that economic growth stimulates further growth.

*Source:* G. Johnes and J. Taylor, 'The Structure of the UK Economy', in M. J. Artis, *The UK Economy*, 14th ed, 1996, Oxford, p. 35, by permission of Oxford University Press.

**1** What is meant by 'endogenous growth'?

**2** Why should economic growth lead to an increased demand for education?

**3** What are the four facts which are the starting point of new growth theory?

# ANSWERS

## CONCEPT REVIEW

**1** 1.3

**2** property rights; market

**3** hours; capital; technological

**4** human; capital; technology

**5** technologies

**6** capital; technological

## TRUE OR FALSE

**1 T** Economic growth can persist for ever because the return from new knowledge capital does not diminish.

**2 F** The neoclassical growth theory stressed the role played by saving and investment; the new growth theory emphasizes people's incentives.

**3 F** The rapidly growing miracle economies demonstrate that allowing international trade is good economic growth policy.

**4 F** The lower the real interest rate, the smaller is the quantity of capital supplied.

**5 T** As a result of massive hikes in the price of energy, technological development was devoted to reducing the amount of energy used in production rather than increasing overall productivity.

**6 F** The law of diminishing returns states that as more capital is used the *additional* output produced diminishes.

**7 F** An increase in the quantity of capital per hour of work causes a movement along a productivity function, not a shift in the function.

**8 T** The data, however, show just the opposite: an increase in real wages and incomes is associated with a decrease in the population growth rate.

**9 T** By increasing the demand for capital, the equilibrium quantity of capital increases and so, too, does the country's real GDP

## MULTIPLE CHOICE

**1 b** The productivity function can illustrate economic growth, but it is not a source of growth.

**2 d** The demand curve is horizontal because knowledge capital is not subject to diminishing returns.

**3 c** Growth accounting is used to divide changes in productivity into different factors so that the factors responsible for growth can be identified.

**4 c** From the one-third rule, output per hour of labour increases by 10 per cent $\times \frac{1}{3}$, or 3.3 per cent.

**5 c** Only in the new theory can economic growth continue for ever without some exogenous source of change.

**6 a** This conclusion of the classical theory for the long run was based on the assumption that population growth rises when income increases.

**7 c** An increase in capital per hour of work causes a movement along the productivity function.

**8 a** Technological advances shift the productivity function upward.

**9 c** The opportunity to earn an above-average profit gives innovators the incentive to develop new technologies.

**10 c** When the real interest rate exceeds the rate of time preference, people save and the supply of capital increases.

**11 c** The one-third rule states that the increase in real GDP per hour of work from the increase in capital per hour of work is $^{1}/_{3} \times 30$ per cent, or 10 per cent.

**12 d** Based on the answer to **11**, the increase in capital per hour of work raised productivity by 10 per cent, leaving technology to account for the remaining 8 per cent.

**13 b** Knowledge capital does not have diminishing returns, so its demand curve is horizontal.

**14 a** The data, however, show that this assumption is false. Population growth *decreases* when income increases.

**15 d** When the real interest rate exceeds the rate of time preference, saving occurs; this saving allows more knowledge capital to be accumulated.

**16 b** Dynamic comparative advantage refers to the point that the costs of the first supplier in a market often are temporarily lower than those of the latecomers.

## SHORT ANSWER

**1** The three necessary preconditions for economic growth are markets, property rights and monetary exchange. Markets enable people to buy and sell at low cost. In addition, markets create and convey important information in the form of prices. Monetary exchange also facilities buying and selling. Thus markets and monetary exchange help promote specialization, which can vastly increase the amount of goods and services produced. Property rights are a key to specialization. Without secure property rights, people would be less willing to specialize because the good they produce might be taken from them without their deriving any personal benefit from it.

These preconditions are not sufficient for growth to continue for ever. To have persistent growth, saving, investing in new capital (both physical and human) and

developing new technologies must occur. Without the necessary three preconditions, saving, investing and developing new technologies will not occur. But simply having the three preconditions in place is no guarantee that saving, investing and developing new technologies will occur.

**2** No, the slowdown in productivity growth would not have been as large. One of the reasons for the slowdown was that the value of an improved environment is not included in real GDP. During the 1970s, investment often was aimed at reducing pollution. If the benefit of the resulting cleaner environment had been included, real GDP would have been larger and, as a result, productivity – which equals real GDP divided by aggregate hours of work – also would have been larger.

**3** Use the one-third rule to predict the productivity growth rate. Capital per hour of labour is growing at 1 per cent and will contribute productivity growth of $^{1}/_{3}$ per cent. Technological change contributes another 1 per cent, so Igor will predict that total productivity growth will be $1^{1}/_{3}$ per cent.

**4** The relationship between savings and growth is complex. In many cases high savings rates and high growth rates are found together, and it is difficult to say which causes which. There are also exceptions where high growth is not accompanied by high savings rates (partly because capital often flows to such countries); and there are countries where high savings rates have not led to rapid growth.

## PROBLEMS

**Figure 26.3**

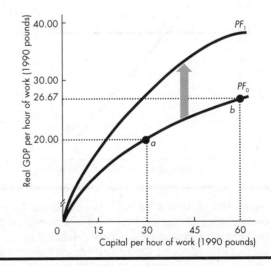

**1 a** Figure 26.3 shows the initial productivity function $PF_0$, going through point $a$.

**b** An increase in the amount of capital per hour – say, from £30 to £60 – causes a movement along productivity function $PF_0$ from point $a$ (real GDP of £20 per hour) to point $b$. The increase in capital per hour is 100 per cent. Thus the one-third rule states that real GDP per hour of work will increase by one-third of 100 per cent, or 33 per cent. The new level of real GDP per hour of work is £26.67.

**c** An increase in technology shifts the productivity function upward. This shift is from productivity function $PF_0$ to the new productivity function $PF_1$.

**2 a** After 1 year, real GDP per person in Slow is £2,000 × 1.01 = £2,020.00. After 2 years, real GDP per person in Slow is £2,000 × (1.01)² = £2,040.20. Similarly, after 10 years real GDP per person is £2,209.24 and after 25 years is £2,564.86.

**b** Real GDP per person in Fast after 1 year is £2,060.00; after 2 years is £2,121.80; after 10 years is £2,687.83; and after 25 years is £4,187.56.

**c** After 1 year, the ratio of real GDP per person in Fast to real GDP per person in Slow is £2,060.00/£2,020.00 = 1.02. After 25 years the ratio is £4,187.56/£2,564.86 = 1.63. In other words, after 25 years, real GDP per person in Fast is 63 per cent higher than in Slow. This result demonstrates how a slightly more rapid growth rate compounds over time to create a large difference in real GDP per person.

**Figure 26.4**

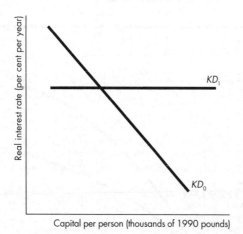

Capital per person (thousands of 1990 pounds)

**3** Figure 26.4 illustrates the two types of capital. There is an important difference between the two curves: the demand for physical capital curve slopes downward, whereas the demand for knowledge capital curve is horizontal. The difference in the slopes of the curves reflects the difference in how their returns change when more capital is acquired. As more physical capital is acquired, the return from the capital falls. Thus the quantity demanded of physical capital increases only if the opportunity cost of the new capital decreases, that is, only if the real interest rate falls. However, the return from knowledge capital does not diminish. So if the real interest rate is below the return from knowledge capital, people will demand additional knowledge capital even if the real interest rate does not fall further.

## DISCUSSION QUESTION

**1** Stocks and flows are the key to the relationship between the saving supply and the capital supply curves.

The capital supply curve shows us the stock of capital, that is, the total amount of capital in the economy. The saving supply curve shows us the flow of saving, that is, the flow of new capital. So the amount of saving – which we get from the saving supply curve – shows us the addition to the capital stock – which we measure from the capital supply curve.

**Figure 26.5**

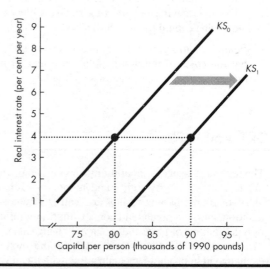

Capital per person (thousands of 1990 pounds)

**2** If we assume no depreciation the relationship can be illustrated by Fig. 26.5. Suppose that at the beginning of this year the capital supply curve is $KS_0$. Also, let's say that the real interest rate is 4 per cent so that the quantity of capital supplied is £80,000 per person. During the year, suppose that the real interest rate remains at 4 per cent and that people save an additional £10,000 of capital per person. Thus at the end of the year, the supply curve of capital will shift rightward to $KS_1$, which shows that, at a real interest rate of 4 per cent, £90,000 of capital per worker now is supplied. In other words, the deal is that when people save, more total capital is available, so the supply curve of capital shifts rightward and it shifts rightward by the amount of the saving.

# DATA QUESTIONS

1 In economics an 'exogenous' variable is one which is determined by other variables in the model. In this case the phrase 'growth stimulates further growth' implies that growth is endogenous.

2 Economic growth leads to an increased demand for education by individuals because they hope that it will lead to better jobs which become available as growth progresses. For firms, growth requires a more skilled labour force.

3 The four facts are:
   ◆ Discoveries result from choices and actions
   ◆ Discoveries bring profits
   ◆ Discoveries can be used by many people at the same time
   ◆ Physical activities can be replicated

These are discussed in more detail in the main text, page 669.

# Chapter 27 Aggregate Supply and Aggregate Demand

---

## Chapter in Perspective, Text Pages 684–709

What determines the amount of goods and services that an economy produces? What causes inflation and how can it be controlled? What are the causes of unemployment, and why does the unemployment rate fluctuate over time? The fundamental purpose of macroeconomic analysis is to address these kinds of issues; issues regarding the behaviour of the national economy as a whole.

In this chapter we begin to build the basic tool of macroeconomic analysis: the aggregate demand and aggregate supply model. This model will prove to be extremely helpful as we attempt to explain the growth of real GDP and inflation as well as business cycle fluctuations in real GDP and unemployment. In subsequent chapters we develop in more detail the underlying principles of aggregate demand and aggregate supply.

---

## Helpful Hints

**1** This chapter discusses the fundamental concepts of aggregate demand, aggregate supply and macroeconomic equilibrium. The model developed is the principal means by which we interpret macroeconomic activity. While later chapters will refine our understanding of these concepts, the basic model is introduced here. As a result, this chapter should be reviewed until it is mastered.

**2** Three separate reasons for the negative slope of the aggregate demand curve are discussed: the real money balances effect, the intertemporal substitution effect and the international substitution effect.

The first two of these are consequences of the fact that a change in the price level will change the level of real money. A change in real money has a direct effect on aggregate expenditure (the real money balances effect) as well as an indirect effect: a change in real money will lead to a change in interest rates which then affects aggregate expenditure (the intertemporal substitution effect).

The third effect is a consequence of the fact that a change in the UK price level changes the relative prices of UK goods and services in terms of the prices of goods and services in the rest of the world. In each of these cases, an increase in the price level will cause a decrease in the aggregate quantity of goods and services demanded, thus explaining a negatively sloped *AD* curve.

**3** There is one important reason for the positive slope of the short-run aggregate supply curve: input prices are held constant. Given constant input prices, a change in the price level, that is the price of output, will affect the amount of goods and services that producers are willing to supply. For example, if the price of output rises but the price of input remains constant, profit-maximizing firms will increase output.

**4** As in our study of microeconomics, in macroeconomics we do not define the short run and long run in terms of a length of calendar time but rather in terms of whether or not key variables can change. Here, in the short run the prices of factors of production do not change, whereas in the long run they do change. The principal implication is that, in the short run, a change in the price level causes the price of output relative to the price of input to change and thus firms will change their rate of output. On the other hand, in the long run, input prices adjust and there is no long-run change in output because the initial price of output relative to input prices is restored.

**5** The distinction between the short run and the long run gives rise to the differences among the various factors that affect the short-run and long-run aggregate supply curves. Since input prices are held constant for the short-run aggregate supply curve but not for the long-run aggregate supply curve, a change in input prices will shift the short-run curve but not the long-run curve.

## Key Figures

**Figure 27.2 Short-run Aggregate Supply, text page 687**
This figure shows the relationship between the short-run aggregate supply curve, which slopes upward to the right, and the long-run aggregate supply curve, which is vertical at the full-employment level.

**Figure 27.6 Changes in the Quantity of Real GDP Demanded, text page 693**
The table in this figure simply lists the factors that will cause the aggregate demand curve to shift. Changes in these factors will cause the aggregate quantity of goods and services demanded either to increase or to decrease *at a given price level.*

**Figure 27.8 Short-run Macroeconomic Equilibrium, text page 697**
Short-run macroeconomic equilibrium occurs when the level of aggregate GDP demanded is equal to aggregate real GDP supplied. Graphically, this occurs at the intersection of the aggregate demand and short-run aggregate supply curves. This intersection gives the equilibrium value of real GDP and the price level.

# SELF-TEST

## CONCEPT REVIEW

**1** A firm's _____ output is the output at which its cost per unit produced is minimized. The level of real GDP that results when all firms are producing at this level of output and when there is full employment is _____ - _____ aggregate supply.

**2** With input prices held constant and the economy producing below its physical limit, an increase in the price level will cause the quantity of real GDP supplied to _____ . Thus the _____ - _____ aggregate supply curve is _____ sloped. When the economy reaches its physical limit to produce, this curve becomes _____ .

**3** If the quantity of real GDP demanded equals the quantity of real GDP supplied, the economy is in _____ _____ . If this occurs when the economy is on its long-run aggregate supply curve, then the economy is said to be in _____ - _____ equilibrium. If this occurs at a level of real GDP below long-run aggregate supply, a(n) _____ equilibrium has occurred.

**4** The graphical representation of the relationship between the quantity of real GDP demanded and the price level is called the _____ _____ curve. As the price level increases, the quantity of real GDP demanded _____ .

**5** There are three separate effects of the price level on the quantity of real GDP demanded. The first of these is the real money balances effect. As the price level rises, the quantity of real money _____ , which causes the quantity of real GDP demanded to _____ .

**6** The second effect involves the substitution of goods now for goods later or vice versa; this is the _____ _____ effect. A lower price level will tend to lead to _____ interest rates, which causes the quantity of real GDP demanded to _____ .

**7** The third effect is the _____ substitution effect. If the UK price level rises (holding everything else constant), the quantity of UK-produced goods demanded will _____ and the quantity of foreign-produced goods demanded will _____ .

**8** If the quantity of money increases (holding everything else constant), the aggregate demand curve will shift to the _____ . The aggregate demand curve will shift to the right if the government _____ taxes.

**9** If the economy is producing below its physical limit, an increase in aggregate demand (other things remaining the same, including input prices) will result in a(n) _____ in the price level and a(n) _____ in the level of real GDP.

**10** An increase in the price of raw materials (other things remaining constant) will result in a(n) _____ in the price level and a(n) _____ in the level of real GDP.

# TRUE OR FALSE

___ **1** According to the real money balances effect, the lower the quantity of real money, the larger is the quantity of real GDP demanded.

___ **2** As interest rates decline, the aggregate quantity of goods and services demanded rises.

___ **3** An increase in the expected rate of inflation will decrease aggregate demand.

___ **4** If the government decides to increase its expenditures on goods and services, the aggregate demand curve will shift to the right.

___ **5** An increase in income taxes will cause the aggregate demand curve to shift to the right.

___ **6** If the economy is on its long-run aggregate supply curve, there is full employment.

___ **7** If the stock of capital increases, both the long-run and short-run aggregate supply curves will shift to the right.

___ **8** It is possible to have a macroeconomic equilibrium at a level of real GDP above full employment.

___ **9** If there is a significant technological advance (other things remaining the same), the long-run aggregate supply curve will shift to the right but the short-run aggregate supply curve will not shift.

___ **10** If there is significant technological advance (other things remaining the same), the price level will rise.

___ **11** The main force generating the underlying tendency of real GDP to expand over time is increases in long-run aggregate supply.

___ **12** The main force generating a long period of inflation is persistent increases in aggregate demand.

___ **13** A large increase in the price of oil, such as in 1973, will generally result in an inflationary recession.

---

## MULTIPLE CHOICE

**1** The aggregate demand curve (*AD*) illustrates that, as the price level falls, the quantity of
  **a** real GDP demanded increases.
  **b** real GDP demanded decreases.
  **c** nominal GDP demanded increases.
  **d** nominal GDP demanded decreases.
  **e** real money balances falls.

**2** Which of the following is a reason for the downward slope of the aggregate demand curve?
  **a** the intertemporal substitution effect
  **b** the international substitution effect
  **c** the expected inflation effect
  **d** the nominal balance effect
  **e** both **a** and **b**.

**3** As the price level rises, the quantity of real money balances
  **a** increases, and thus the aggregate quantity of goods and services demanded increases.
  **b** increases, and thus the aggregate quantity of goods and services demanded decreases.
  **c** decreases, and thus the aggregate quantity of goods and services demanded increases.
  **d** decreases, and thus the aggregate quantity of goods and services demanded decreases.
  **e** decreases, and this has no effect on the aggregate quantity of goods and services demanded.

**4** Which of the following will cause the aggregate demand curve to shift to the right?
  **a** an increase in interest rates (at a given price level)
  **b** an increase in expected inflation
  **c** an increase in taxes
  **d** a decrease in the price level
  **e** an increase in the price level

**5** Long-run aggregate supply is the level of real GDP at which
  **a** each firm is producing its capacity output.
  **b** there is full employment.
  **c** the economy is producing its physical limit.
  **d** each firm is producing its capacity output and there is full employment.
  **e** prices are sure to rise.

**6** Short-run aggregate supply is the relationship between the price level and the quantity of real GDP supplied, holding constant the

**a** wage rate.
**b** quantities of factors of production.
**c** level of government spending.
**d** price level.
**e** prices of factors of production.

**7** The short-run aggregate supply curve (*SAS*) is positively sloped but becomes vertical at the level of real GDP at which
  **a** each firm is producing its capacity output.
  **b** each firm is producing output at its physical limit.
  **c** there is full employment.
  **d** it intersects the aggregate demand curve.
  **e** hyperinflation starts.

**8** A technological improvement will shift
  **a** both the short-run aggregate supply and the aggregate demand curves to the right.
  **b** both the short-run aggregate supply and long-run aggregate supply curves to the left.
  **c** the short-run aggregate supply curve to the right but leave the long-run aggregate supply curve unchanged.
  **d** the long-run aggregate supply curve to the right but leave the short-run aggregate supply curve unchanged.
  **e** both the short-run aggregate supply and long-run aggregate supply curves to the right.

**9** Macroeconomic equilibrium occurs when the
  **a** economy is at full employment.
  **b** economy is producing at its physical limit.
  **c** aggregate demand curve intersects the short-run aggregate supply curve along its vertical portion.
  **d** quantity of real GDP demanded equals the quantity of real GDP supplied.
  **e** aggregate demand curve intersects the long-run aggregate supply curve.

**10** Which of the graphs in Fig. 27.1 illustrates an unemployment equilibrium?
  **a** (a)
  **b** (b)
  **c** (c)
  **d** (d)
  **e** both (c) and (d)

**11** Which of the graphs in Fig. 27.1 illustrates an above full-employment equilibrium?

**Figure 27.1**

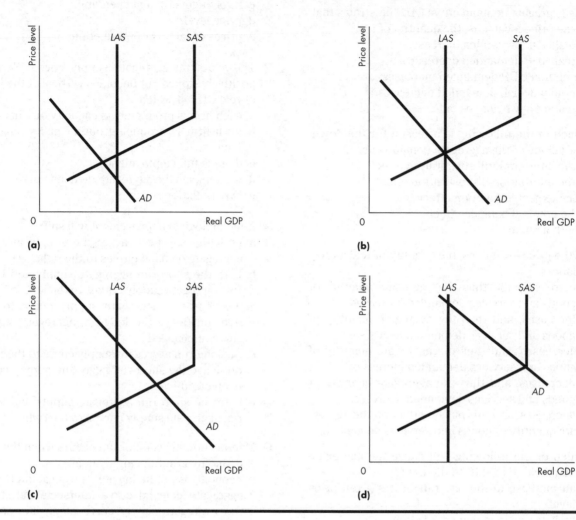

(a)

(b)

(c)

(d)

**a** (a)
**b** (b)
**c** (c)
**d** (d)
**e** both (c) and (d)

**12** If real GDP is greater than long-run aggregate supply, then the economy is
  **a** not in macroeconomic equilibrium.
  **b** in a full-employment equilibrium.
  **c** in an above full-employment equilibrium.
  **d** in an unemployment equilibrium.
  **e** in long-run equilibrium.

**13** If input prices remain constant and firms are producing at levels less than their physical limits, an increase in aggregate demand will cause
  **a** an increase in the price level and an increase in real GDP.
  **b** an increase in the price level and a decrease in real GDP.
  **c** a decrease in the price level and an increase in real GDP.
  **d** a decrease in the price level and a decrease in real GDP.
  **e** an increase in the price level but no change in real GDP.

## SHORT ANSWER

**1** The intertemporal substitution effect implies that an increase in the price level will lead to a decrease in the aggregate quantity of goods and services demanded. Explain.

**2** The international substitution effect implies that an increase in the price level will lead to a decrease in the aggregate quantity of goods and services demanded. Explain.

**3** Why is the long-run aggregate supply curve vertical?

**4** Why is the short-run aggregate supply curve positively sloped over most of its range?

**5** Re-read the *Reading Between the Lines* article. Why should people 'become twitchy' when consumer spending rises and the housing market lifts itself off the floor?

## PROBLEMS

**1** Suppose the economy is initially in full-employment equilibrium. Assuming that input prices remain constant, graphically illustrate the effect of an increase in foreign income. What happens to the price level and the level of real GDP?

**2** Suppose the economy is initially in full-employment equilibrium. Assuming that input prices remain constant, graphically illustrate the effect of an increase in the stock of human capital. What happens to the price level and the level of real GDP?

**3** Suppose the economy is initially in full-employment equilibrium. Graphically illustrate the effect of an increase in wages. What happens to the price level and the level of real GDP?

**4** Consider an economy that is initially at a full-employment equilibrium. In each of four successive years, an economic event occurs:

Year 1: The government increases its expenditures on goods and services.
Year 2: OPEC increases the price of oil.
Year 3: The government increases the money supply.
Year 4: The government decreases the money supply.

**a** Graphically illustrate the successive consequences of these four events on a diagram similar to that shown in Fig. 27.2(a). Label the initial equilibrium point *a* and label the new equilibrium points after years 1, 2, 3 and 4, *b*, *c*, *d* and *e*, respectively.

**b** Suppose that each new equilibrium is achieved gradually over one year. In Fig. 27.2(b), point *a* refers to the initial level of real GDP; time is measured on the horizontal axis. Plot the behaviour of real GDP during the succeeding four years. Comment on the pattern of that behaviour.

**Figure 27.2**

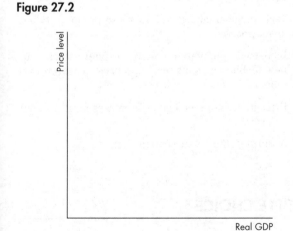

**(a)**

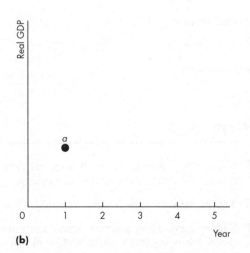

**(b)**

## DISCUSSION QUESTIONS

**1** Why does a drop in the price level not shift the *SAS* curve?

**2** Draw a diagram to show what happens in the long run after an initial decrease in aggregate demand has occurred.

## DATA QUESTION

Draw diagrams to illustrate the effect on UK price levels and real GDP of the following changes (assume that the economy is originally below full-employment equilibrium).

**a** Quantity of money (£M4)

| 1992 | 1995 |
|------|------|
| £507 billion | £597 billion |

**b** In the 1991 budget the VAT rate was increased from 15 per cent to 17.5 per cent.

**c** Population of OECD countries (the OECD is the organization of the richest countries)

| 1980 | 1992 |
|------|------|
| 780 million | 867 million |

**d** UK average weekly earnings (male)

| 1992 | 1995 |
|------|------|
| £333 | £375 |

# ANSWERS

## CONCEPT REVIEW

**1** capacity; long-run

**2** increase; short-run; positively; vertical

**3** macroeconomic equilibrium; full-employment; unemployment

**4** aggregate demand; decreases

**5** falls; decrease

**6** intertemporal substitution; lower; increase

**7** international; fall; rise

**8** right; decreases

**9** increase; increase

**10** increase; decrease

## TRUE OR FALSE

**1 F** With a lower quantity of real money, individuals cut spending to increase the level of real money.

**2 T** People will have more money to spend.

**3 F** If individuals expect a higher inflation rate they will spend more today to avoid higher prices in the future.

**4 T** Government spending is an injection into the circular flow.

**5 F** Curve will shift to left because people will have less money to spend.

**6 T** Definition.

**7 T** Increase in capital will lead to rise in productivity so that more output is produced at every price.

**8 T** Equilibrium may be at, above or below full-employment level.

**9 F** Anything that shifts the *LAS* curve also shifts the *SAS* curve.

**10 F** Technological change will increase productivity and lower prices.

**11 T** Increased population, more capital stock and new technology shift the *LAS* curve rightward over time.

**12 T** Rises in *AD* not matched by increases in *AS* will pull up prices.

**13 T** It will shift the *AS* curve to the left.

## MULTIPLE CHOICE

**1 a** *AD* curve is downward sloping owing to three substitution effects. It is real GDP by definition, not nominal. Also real money balances increase here.

**2 c** **c** shifts *AD* curve, and **d** doesn't exist.

**3 d** Price rises so money buys fewer goods (real money balances fall), so *AD* falls.

**4 b** People will buy now before prices rise.

**5 b** Definition.

**6 e** Definition.

**7 b** At vertical portion of *SAS* curve firms cannot produce more output because they are at their physical limits.

**8 e** Technological improvements mean that labour is more productive leading to increase in supply in both short and long run.

**9 d** Macroeconomic equilibrium always occurs where *AD* = *SAS*; equilibrium *may* occur at answers **a–c**, but it doesn't always occur there.

**10 a** Unemployment equilibrium occurs when *AD* = *SAS* to left of *LAS*.

**11 e** Above full-employment equilibrium occurs when *AD* = *SAS* to right of *LAS*.

**12 c** Equilibrium is where *AD* = *SAS*; if this is greater than *LAS* then there is above full-employment equilibrium.

**13 a** Firms will increase output and prices will also rise (*AD* curve shifts to right).

## SHORT ANSWER

**1** Intertemporal substitution means the substitution of goods now for goods later or vice versa. There are two keys to understanding the intertemporal substitution effect.

The first of these is that changes in interest rates influence households to engage in intertemporal substitution. For example, if interest rates rise, households will tend to borrow and spend less now, thus decreasing the aggregate quantity of goods and services demanded.

The second key is that interest rates are determined by the demand for loans and the supply of loans and that these are affected by changes in the quantity of real money. In particular, a decrease in real money will make households less willing to lend. This means that the supply of loans will decrease, which will cause the interest rate to rise.

Combining these keys, the intertemporal substitution effect is described as follows: an increase in the price level decreases the quantity of real money, which reduces the supply of loans and thus raises interest rates. The rise in interest rates will lead to a decrease in the aggregate quantity of goods and services demanded.

**2** International substitution means substituting domestically produced goods for foreign-produced goods or vice versa. If the price of domestic goods rises and foreign prices remain constant, domestic goods become relatively more expensive, and so households will buy fewer domestic goods and more foreign goods.

This means that there will be a decrease in the quantity of real GDP demanded. Thus an increase in the price level (the prices of domestic goods) will lead to a decrease in the aggregate quantity of (domestic) goods and services demanded through the international substitution effect.

**3** Long-run aggregate supply is the level of real GDP supplied when each firm in the economy is producing at its capacity output and there is full employment. Since this level of real GDP is independent of the price level, the long-run aggregate supply curve is vertical. It should also be noted that this is the level of real GDP attained when input prices are free to adjust so as to clear factor markets.

**4** The short-run aggregate supply curve is positively sloped because it holds input prices constant. Thus when the price level rises, firms see the prices of their output rising, but the prices of their inputs remain unchanged. Each firm is then induced to increase output and so aggregate output increases.

**5** Improvements in the housing market and rising consumer spending are positive signs for an economy in many ways – they suggest rising GNP and falling unemployment. However, they can also be indicators that the rate of inflation may start to rise. For those people who worry about inflation and believe that it has many undesirable effects, this may cause concern – 'twitching' for the author.

## PROBLEMS

**1** In Fig. 27.3, the economy is initially at point *a* on the original *AD* curve, $AD_0$. An increase in foreign income will shift the *AD* curve to the right, from $AD_0$ to $AD_1$. At the new equilibrium, point *b*, the price level has risen and the level of real GDP has increased.

**2** The economy in Fig. 27.4 is initially at point *a* on the $LAS_0$ and $SAS_0$ curves. An increase in the stock of human capital will shift both the *LAS* and *SAS* curves to the right, to $LAS_1$ and $SAS_1$, respectively. At the new equilibrium, point *b*, the price level has fallen and the level of real GDP has increased.

**Figure 27.3**

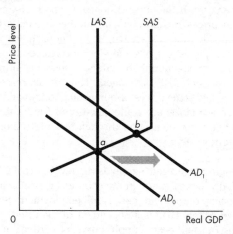

**Figure 27.4**

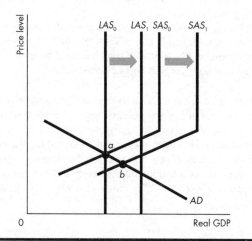

**Figure 27.5**

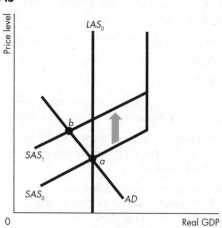

At the beginning of year 2, OPEC increases the price of oil, which shifts the SAS curve from $SAS_0$ to $SAS_2$. Real GDP falls, producing a new equilibrium at point c.

At the beginning of year 3, the government increases the money supply (perhaps to combat the fall in output), which causes the AD curve to shift from $AD_1$ to $AD_3$. The new equilibrium is at point d and real GDP has risen.

Lastly, in year 4, the government decreases the money supply (perhaps to combat the continuing increase in the price level) and the AD curve shifts to the left, from $AD_3$ to $AD_4$, say. The consequence is a decline in real GDP and a new equilibrium at point e.

**b** The behaviour of real GDP over time is illustrated in Fig. 27.6(b). At the beginning of year 1, the output level is given by point a but the shift in AD causes output to rise by the beginning of year 2 (point b). Similarly, as indicated in **a**, in years 2, 3 and 4, real GDP falls, rises and falls again (points c, d and e). These real GDP movements are characteristic of the business cycle movements in real GDP.

## DISCUSSION QUESTIONS

**1** A change in the price level does not shift the AD or AS curves; instead the price level itself changes in response to a shift in the AD or AS curves. For example, if firms lose confidence in future profits they will cut investment. This will shift the AD curve leftward along the SAS curve. The result will be a fall in prices.

**3** In Fig. 27.5, the economy is initially at point a on the $SAS_0$ curve. An increase in wages will shift the SAS curve upward, to $SAS_1$. At the new equilibrium, point b, the price level has risen and the level of real GDP has decreased.

**4 a** The required diagram is shown in Fig. 27.6(a). The initial equilibrium is at point a with $AD_0$, $SAS_0$, and LAS.

At the beginning of year 1, the increase in government spending shifts the AD curve from $AD_0$ to $AD_1$ producing a new equilibrium (by the end of the year) at point b. We note that real GDP has increased.

**Figure 27.6**

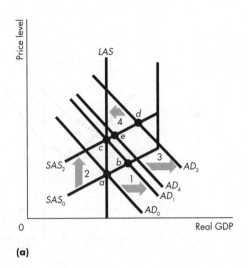

**(a)**

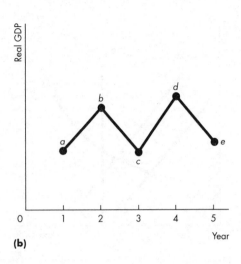

**(b)**

**2** The fall in price reached in **1** is a short-term effect because unemployment is below the natural rate. The result will be a series of adjustments such as a fall in wages and other input costs. Thus firms are willing to increase their supply of goods even if the price level does not change. This causes the *SAS* curve to shift rightward as shown in Fig. 27.7. The new equilibrium will be where $SAS_1$ intersects $AD_1$. The new long-run equilibrium is at point $c$ where the new equilibrium level

of GDP equals potential real GDP. Compared with the original equilibrium, the long-term result of the fall in investment is that the price level is lower, but real GDP is the same.

## DATA QUESTION

**a** Other factors remaining the same, an increase in the quantity of money will increase aggregate demand as shown in Fig. 27.8(a). The result will be a move from $a$ to $b$, giving a rise in prices and in GDP. Note that if the economy had been at full employment there would have been no rise in GDP.

**b** An increase in VAT will shift the aggregate supply curve upward as shown in Fig. 27.8(b). The result will be a move from equilibrium $a$ to $b$, a rise in prices and a fall in GDP.

**c** An increase in population in OECD countries will increase demand for UK goods and services and the result will be identical to that described in part **a**.

**d** A rise in weekly earnings that is not accompanied by any change in productivity will increase firms' costs and shift the short-run *AS* curve upward, and the result will be that described in **b**. There may also be an increase in aggregate demand if people expect the inflation rate to increase. This would further push up prices but would also increase GDP.

**Figure 27.7**

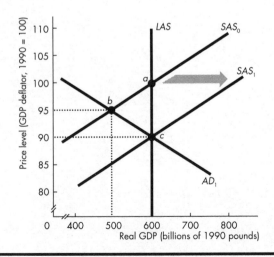

**Figure 27.8**

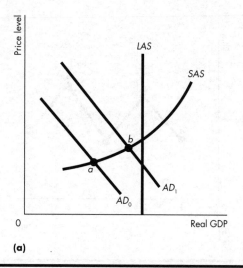

(a)

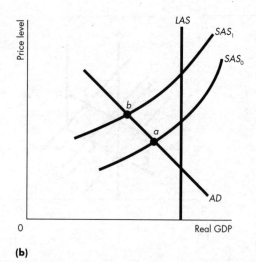

(b)

# Chapter 28    Expenditure Multipliers

---

## Chapter in Perspective, Text Pages 710–740

This chapter introduces several important concepts. The marginal propensity to consume and marginal propensity to save are linked to changes in disposable income and their relationship needs to be understood. Another important concept is the aggregate expenditure schedule which shows how aggregate expenditure depends on real GDP.

However, the focus of the chapter is on the multiplier which shows that a change in autonomous expenditure creates an additional change in induced expenditure.

---

## Helpful Hints

**1** This chapter distinguishes between autonomous expenditure and induced expenditure. Autonomous expenditure is independent of changes in real GDP, whereas induced expenditure will vary as real GDP varies. In general, a change in autonomous expenditure creates a change in real GDP, which in turn creates a change in induced expenditure. The induced changes are at the heart of the multiplier effect.

However, even though autonomous expenditure may be independent of changes in real GDP, it will not be independent of changes in other variables (for example, the price level).

**2** Note that the *AD* curve is derived from the *AE* curve. In other words, the *AE* curve shows the equilibrium level of expenditure for a particular price level. This price level together with the equilibrium level of expenditure (which equals real GDP) is a point on the *AD* curve. Hence not only are the *AE* and *AD* curves quite different, but we actually use one to derive the other!

**3** The concept of the multiplier is extremely important. It is a result of the interaction of the various components of aggregate expenditure. In particular, an initial increase in autonomous expenditure, such as investment, increases real GDP directly, but that is not the end of the story. The initial increase in real GDP generates an increase in induced expenditure, which further increases real GDP and thus induces further increases in (induced) expenditure.

The total effect on real GDP is larger than the initial increase in autonomous expenditure because of the induced expenditure.

Induced expenditure occurs because the initial increase in real GDP (created by the increase in autonomous expenditure) raises people's disposable incomes. For instance, an increase in investment purchases of personal computers raises the incomes of workers who are hired to manufacture the additional personal computers. Then, because the marginal propensity to consume is greater than zero, the increase in disposable income increases these workers' (induced!) consumption expenditures. You should become thoroughly familiar with both the concept of and the mathematics behind the multiplier.

Income taxes have a stabilizing effect. The higher the income tax rate, the less any change in GDP translates into a change in disposable income. In turn, the smaller change in disposable income creates a smaller change in (induced) consumption expenditure and therefore makes the multiplier smaller. This automatic stabilizer effect works by reducing the induced effects in the multiplier process.

**4** The multiplier shows the change in equilibrium expenditure. Thus if the multiplier is, say, 5.0 and investment (a component of autonomous expenditure) increases by £10 billion, equilibrium expenditure increases by £50 billion.

However, an increase in equilibrium expenditure of £50 billion does not necessarily mean that equilibrium real GDP also increases by £50 billion. The change in equilibrium real GDP depends on the interaction of aggregate demand and aggregate supply. The £50 billion increase in equilibrium expenditure implies that the *AD* curve shifts rightward by £50 billion, but this shift is only one part of the picture. Depending on the aggregate supply curve, real GDP could increase by an amount close to £50 billion (if the *SAS* curve is relatively flat) or by an amount less than £50 billion (how much less depends on the steepness of the *SAS* curve) or £0 (which is the case in the long run, when the *LAS* curve is vertical).

The multiplier generally overstates the change in GDP because the multiplier ignores the effect of changing prices. But when the *AD* curve shifts rightward, the price level rises. The rise in the price level decreases equilibrium expenditure, an effect ignored by the multiplier. Thus always keep in mind that the multiplier gives the shift in the *AD* curve, that is, the change in equilibrium aggregate expenditure. However, the multiplier does *not* necessarily give the change in equilibrium GDP.

**5** Distinguishing between two types of changes in autonomous spending is crucial. One type adds to the instability of the economy; it includes changes in autonomous consumption, investment and exports. The other type of change usually is a planned shock that will (its proponents hope) reduce the instability of the economy; it includes changes in government spending and taxes. As both types of changes work through the same multiplier process, the same process that creates instability also is available to reduce instability.

## Key Figures

### Figure 28.1 Consumption Function and Saving Function, text page 713
The relationship between disposable income on the one hand and consumption and saving on the other is crucial in macroeconomics. This figure shows how consumption and saving are affected by increases in disposable income.

### Figure 28.2 Marginal Propensities to Consume and Save, text page 715
The idea of the margin lies at the heart of economics and this figure shows how *increases* in disposable income lead to changes in saving and consumption.

### Figure 28.8 The Multiplier, text page 724
This shows how an increase in some component of autonomous expenditure (such as government spending or investment) leads to a multiplied increase in GDP.

# SELF-TEST

## CONCEPT REVIEW

**1** The components of aggregate expenditure are ————————— expenditure, investment, government purchases and net ——————— .

**2** Consumption and saving are influenced by several factors including ——————— interest rates, disposal ——————— , assets minus ————————————————— , and expected ——————— ——————— .

**3** The marginal propensity to consume is a fraction of the _____ in disposable income that is _____ .

**4** Imports are determined by _____ GDP, comparative prices and foreign _____ rates.

**5** With a steady price level, aggregate _____ determines real GDP.

**6** Equilibrium expenditure occurs when aggregate _____ expenditure equals real _____ .

**7** A change in autonomous expenditure changes real GDP by an amount determined by the _____ .

**8** The greater the marginal propensity to _____ the greater is the multiplier.

**9** A change in the price level shifts the *AE* curve and brings a movement along the _____ curve.

## TRUE OR FALSE

**___  1** In the short run, an increase in investment expenditure of £1 billion will generate an increase in equilibrium expenditure of more than £1 billion.

**___  2** In the long run, an increase in investment expenditure of £1 billion will generate an increase in equilibrium expenditure of more than £1 billion.

**___  3** When real GDP increases, induced expenditure also increases along the *AE* curve.

**___  4** When aggregate planned expenditure exceeds real GDP, stocks rise more than planned.

**___  5** The multiplier is greater than one because an increase in autonomous expenditure leads to an induced increase in consumption expenditure.

**___  6** An increase in investment shifts the *AE* curve upward and the *AD* curve rightward.

**___  7** The multiplier equals $\dfrac{1}{(1 - MPS)}$.

**___  8** Equilibrium expenditure occurs when aggregate planned expenditure equals real GDP.

**___  9** Planned aggregate expenditure can be different from actual aggregate expenditure.

**___ 10** The sum of the marginal propensity to consume and the marginal propensity to save equals 1.

**___ 11** If the marginal propensity to consume is 0.8 and there are no income taxes or imports, the multiplier equals 5.0.

## MULTIPLE CHOICE

**1** An increase in the price level shifts the *AE* curve _____ and _____ equilibrium expenditure.
   **a** upward; increases
   **b** upward; decreases
   **c** downward; increases
   **d** downward; decreases

**2** Autonomous expenditure is *not* influenced by
   **a** the interest rate.
   **b** the foreign exchange rate.
   **c** real GDP.
   **d** any variable.

**3** The aggregate expenditure curve shows the relationship between aggregate planned expenditure and
   **a** government purchases.
   **b** real GDP.
   **c** the interest rate.
   **d** the price level.

**4** If unplanned stocks rise, aggregate planned expenditure is
   **a** greater than real GDP and firms will increase output.
   **b** greater than real GDP and firms will decrease output.
   **c** less than real GDP and firms will increase output.
   **d** less than real GDP and firms will decrease output.

**5** Which of the following conditions shifts the consumption function downward?
a an increase in current disposable income
b an increase in future expected income
c an increase in the purchasing power of net assets
d a decrease in the purchasing power of net assets

**6** When the marginal propensity to consume is 0.50 and there are no income taxes or imports, the multiplier equals
a 10.0.
b 5.0.
c 2.0.
d 0.5.

**7** If the marginal propensity to consume is 0.75 and there are no income taxes nor imports, what is the multiplier?
a 1.33
b 1.50
c 2.00
d 4.00

**8** The fraction of the last pound of disposable income saved is called the
a marginal propensity to consume.
b marginal propensity to save.
c marginal tax rate.
d None of the above.

**9** The multiplier is 2.0 and, owing to an increase in expected future profit, investment increases by £10 billion. The *AD* curve
a shifts rightward by £20 billion.
b shifts rightward by more than £20 billion.
c shifts rightward by less than £20 billion.
d shifts upward by £20 billion.

**10** The multiplier is 2.0 and, owing to an increase in expected future profit, investment increases by £10 billion. In the short run, equilibrium real GDP will
a increase by £20 billion.
b increase by more than £20 billion.
c increase by less than £20 billion.
d be unaffected.

**11** The multiplier is 2.0 and, owing to an increase in expected future profit, investment increases by £10 billion. If potential real GDP is unaffected, in the long run, equilibrium real GDP will
a increase by £20 billion.
b increase by more than £20 billion.

c increase by less than £20 billion.
d be unaffected.

**12** An increase in autonomous expenditure shifts the *AE* curve
a upward and leaves its slope unchanged.
b upward and makes it steeper.
c upward and makes it flatter.
d downward and makes it steeper.

**Figure 28.1**

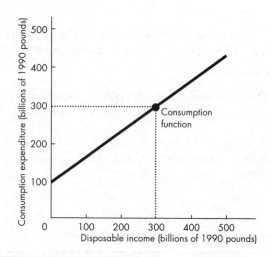

**13** What is the marginal propensity to consume, *MPC*, in Fig. 28.1?
a 1.00
b 0.90
c 0.67
d £3 billion

**14** The multiplier equals
a $1/(MPC)$.
b $MPC/(1 - MPC)$.
c $MPS/MPC$.
d $1/(1 - MPC)$.

## SHORT ANSWER

**1** What is the difference between autonomous expenditure and induced expenditure?

**2** Explain why the *MPC* plus the *MPS* must total 1.

**3** Explain why the multiplier is larger if the marginal propensity to consume is larger.

**4** Suppose that aggregate planned expenditure is greater than real GDP so that stocks are decreasing. If prices are sticky, explain the process by which equilibrium expenditure is achieved.

**5** Briefly explain what the *AE* curve illustrates and how it is related to the *AD* curve.

**6** The *Reading Between the Lines* article suggests that the fall in demand will reduce tax revenues. Why?

## PROBLEMS

**1** The island country of Wet has no international trade and no income taxes. The marginal propensity to consume in Wet is 0.75.
  **a** Investment increases by £20 billion. Before prices change, what is the change in equilibrium expenditure?
  **b** By how much and in what direction does the aggregate demand curve shift?
  **c** Suppose that, instead of being 0.75, the marginal propensity to consume was 0.90. With this marginal propensity to consume, what is the change in equilibrium expenditure? The shift in the aggregate demand curve?
  **d** In the short run, prices rise. Without giving a precise numeric answer, what is the effect of the higher price level on the change in equilibrium expenditure? The shift in the aggregate demand curve?

**2 a** Complete Table 28.1.
  **b** Based on Table 28.1 how does a decrease in the size of the *MPC* affect the multiplier?

**Table 28.1 The *MPC*, *MPS* and Multiplier**

| MPC | MPS | Multiplier |
|-----|-----|------------|
| 0.9 | | |
| 0.8 | | |
| 0.7 | | |
| 0.6 | | |
| 0.5 | | |

**Table 28.2  Aggregate Expenditure Components**

| Real GDP | Consumption expenditure (billions of 1990 pounds) | Investment | Government purchases |
|----------|-----|-----|-----|
| 0.5 | 0.2 | 0.3 | 0.2 |
| 1.0 | 0.6 | 0.3 | 0.2 |
| 1.5 | 1.0 | 0.3 | 0.2 |
| 2.0 | 1.4 | 0.3 | 0.2 |
| 2.5 | 1.8 | 0.3 | 0.2 |

**Figure 28.2**

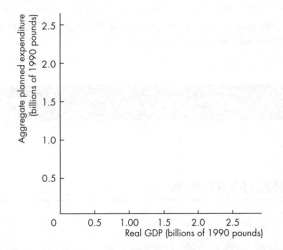

**3** Table 28.2 shows the components of aggregate expenditure in the country of Woodstock. Woodstock has no foreign trade and no taxes.
  **a** Plot these components of aggregate expenditure in Fig. 28.2. Label the consumption line *C*, the investment line *I*, and the government purchases line *G*.
  **b** Complete Table 28.3 to show aggregate expenditure in Woodstock.
  **c** Use Table 28.3 and plot the aggregate expenditure line in Fig. 28.2. Label it *AE*.
  **d** Draw a 45° line in Fig. 28.2. What is equilibrium expenditure in Woodstock?
  **e** Use either Fig. 28.2 or Table 28.3 to determine the equilibrium amount of consumption expenditure, investment and government purchases.

**Table 28.3 Aggregate Expenditure**

| Real GDP (billions of 1990 pounds) | Aggregate expenditure (billions of 1990 pounds) |
| --- | --- |
| 0.5 | |
| 1.0 | |
| 1.5 | |
| 2.0 | |
| 2.5 | |

## DISCUSSION QUESTION

1 Explain how the shift in the *AD* curve is determined, what the short-run effects are on the price level and real GDP, and what the long-run effects are on the price level and GDP.

## DATA QUESTIONS

### Investment and GDP

The amount of bread we eat next year will be fairly similar to the amount we ate last year. This is because consumption patterns of staple foods such as bread are fairly stable. The pattern of investment is different. When incomes and expenditures are rising, firms buy more machines and put in orders for new offices and factories. When national income is constant or falling, firms do not need extra machines and so investment falls. Thus gross fixed capital formation at constant prices was £107,577 million in 1990 but fell to £97,403 million in 1991. By 1995 it had risen to £100,081. These changes in investment have a multiplied effect on national income.

1 How do changes in investment affect GDP?

2 What factors affect the size of the effect on GDP?

# ANSWERS

## CONCEPT REVIEW

1 consumption; exports

2 real; income; debts; future income

3 change; consumed

4 real; exchange

5 demand

6 planned; GDP

7 multiplier

8 consume

9 *AD*

## TRUE OR FALSE

1 **T** An increase in investment creates a larger increase in equilibrium expenditure because of the action of the multiplier.

2 **F** In the long run, the economy returns to potential GDP, so the long-run multiplier is zero.

3 **T** The increase in GDP *induces* increases in aggregate expenditure. Indeed, that is why the *AE* curve has a positive slope.

4 **F** When aggregate planned expenditure exceeds real GDP, stocks fall because more goods and services are being purchased than are being produced.

5 **T** This is why a multiplier exists.

6 **T** Any increase in autonomous expenditure *not* caused by a change in the price level shifts the *AE* curve upward and the *AD* curve rightward.

7 **F** With the *MPC*, the multiplier is $\dfrac{1}{(1-MPC)}$, with the *MPS*, the multiplier is $\dfrac{1}{MPS}$.

8 **T** Definition.

9 **T** If the economy is not in equilibrium, actual aggregate expenditure is different from planned aggregate expenditure.

10 **T** Because $MPC + MPS = 1$, the two formulas for the multiplier, $\dfrac{1}{(1-MPC)}$ and $\dfrac{1}{MPS}$, are equivalent.

11 **T** The multiplier is $\dfrac{1}{(1-MPC)}$, so when the *MPC* is 0.8, the multiplier is 5.0.

# MULTIPLE CHOICE

**1 d** An increase in the price level decreases consumption expenditure, thereby shifting the *AE* line downward and hence decreasing the equilibrium level of expenditure.

**2 c** The definition of autonomous expenditure is expenditure that is not affected by changes in real GDP.

**3 b** The aggregate expenditure curve shows that, as real GDP increases, so too does the quantity of planned expenditure.

**4 d** If unplanned stocks rise, aggregate planned expenditure is less than production, that is, less than GDP. In response to the unplanned rise in stocks, firms reduce their level of production and real GDP decreases.

**5 d** A decline in the purchasing power of net assets makes people poorer, so they decrease their consumption expenditure.

**6 c** The multiplier is $\dfrac{1}{(1 - MPC)}$ , which means that, here, the multiplier equals 2.0.

**7 d** Comparing the answer to this question with the answer to **6** shows that as the *MPC* increases in magnitude, so does the multiplier.

**8 b** Definition.

**9 a** The rightward shift in the *AD* curve equals the multiplied impact on equilibrium expenditure, which in this case is 2.0 × £10 billion = £20 billion.

**10 c** Even though the *AD* curve shifts rightward by £20 billion, the *SAS* curve slopes upward. Hence in the short run, the increase in the equilibrium level of real GDP is less than £20 billion. Figure 28.3 illustrates this situation, where the £20 billion rightward shift in the *AD* curve creates only a £10 billion increase in equilibrium GDP.

**11 d** In the long run, GDP returns to potential GDP without any long-run effect on real GDP. In Fig. 28.3, in the long run GDP returns to the potential GDP of £50 billion.

**12 a** An increase in autonomous expenditure shifts the *AE* curve upward; a decrease shifts it downward.

**13 c** The *MPC* is $\Delta C/\Delta YD$, which here is £2 billion/£3 billion = 0.67.

**14 d** Definition.

## Figure 28.3

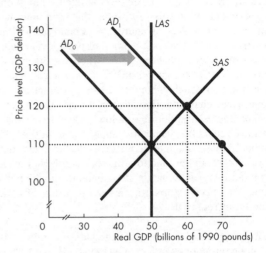

# SHORT ANSWER

**1** Autonomous expenditure does not change when real GDP changes, whereas induced expenditure does change.

**2** Only two things can be done with an additional pound of disposable income: spend all or part of it or save all or part of it. The *MPC*, or marginal propensity to consume, indicates the fraction of the additional pound of disposable income that is spent on consumption, whereas the *MPS*, or marginal propensity to save, indicates the fraction of the additional pound that is saved. Because consumption and saving are the only two uses to which the pound can be put, the two fractions must sum to 1.

**3** Any initial increase in autonomous expenditure generates a direct increase in equilibrium expenditure. The basic idea of the multiplier is that this initial increase in aggregate expenditure generates *further* increases in aggregate expenditure as increases in consumption expenditure are induced. In each round of the multiplier process, the increase in spending, and thus the further increase in aggregate expenditure, are determined by the marginal propensity to consume. Because a larger marginal propensity to consume means a larger increase in aggregate expenditure at each round, the total increase in equilibrium expenditure is greater. Thus the multiplier is larger if the marginal propensity to consume is larger.

**4** In the discussion of aggregate expenditure and equilibrium expenditure in this chapter, we assume that prices are sticky so that the price level is fixed. This 'thought experiment' allows us to develop the economic model of the components of aggregate expenditure without worrying about the complication of price level changes. As a result of this assumption, when we discuss how firms adjust to unwanted decreases in their stocks, we assume that firms respond by raising production, without prices changing. However, in the *AS/AD* model, we relax this assumption and 'allow' prices to change by reintroducing the aggregate supply curve. In the *AS/AD* model, we get the more realistic result that firms change both prices and production. In other words, in the short run, an increase in aggregate expenditure, which shifts the *AD* curve rightward, raises the price level *and* increases real GDP.

**5** The purpose of investigating aggregate expenditure is to deepen our understanding of aggregate demand. The *AE* curve answers the question: for a given price level, how is equilibrium expenditure determined? For instance, when the price level rises, aggregate expenditure decreases (so that the *AE* curve shifts downward) and equilibrium expenditure decreases. Aggregate demand is different. It relates the quantity of real GDP demanded to differing values of the price level. In other words, the *AD* curve uses the results derived using the *AE* curve to show how equilibrium expenditure changes when the price level changes.

**6** Essentially, a fall in demand will reduce tax revenues because it means that people will spend less; hence the government will receive less in VAT and excise duties. Moreover, the fall in demand will reduce incomes, so the government will receive less in income tax.

## PROBLEMS

**1 a** The multiplier in Wet is

$$\frac{1}{(1 - \text{MPC})} \text{ , or}$$

$$\frac{1}{(1 - 0.75)} = 40.$$

Thus the change in equilibrium expenditure is $4.0 \times$ £20 billion, or £80 billion.

**b** The aggregate demand curve shifts by an amount equal to the change in equilibrium expenditure. Hence because equilibrium expenditure increases by £80 billion, the aggregate demand curve shifts rightward by £80 billion.

**c** If the marginal propensity to consume is 0.90, the multiplier is 10.0. Hence in this case, equilibrium expenditure increases by $10.0 \times$ £20 billion = £200 billion, and the aggregate demand curve shifts rightward by £200 billion.

**d** When prices start to rise, the aggregate expenditure curve shifts downward. (The higher prices decrease people's consumption expenditure.) The downward shift in the aggregate expenditure curve reduces equilibrium expenditure. However, the aggregate demand curve does *not* shift. Instead, a movement occurs along the aggregate demand curve to a lower level of equilibrium real GDP.

**2 a** Table 28.1 is completed here as Table 28.4. Because $MPC + MPS = 1.0$, $MPS = 1.0 - MPC$. Thus for the first row, $MPS = 1.0 - 0.9 = 0.1$. The multipliers can be calculated using either of two equivalent formulas, namely,

$$\text{multiplier} = \frac{1}{(1 - MPC)} = \frac{1}{MPS}.$$

**b** As Table 28.4 shows, when the *MPC* falls in size, so too does the multiplier.

**Table 28.4 The *MPC*, *MPS* and Multiplier**

| MPC | MPS | Multiplier |
|-----|-----|------------|
| 0.9 | 0.1 | 10.0 |
| 0.8 | 0.2 | 5.0 |
| 0.7 | 0.3 | 3.3 |
| 0.6 | 0.4 | 2.5 |
| 0.5 | 0.5 | 2.0 |

**Figure 28.4**

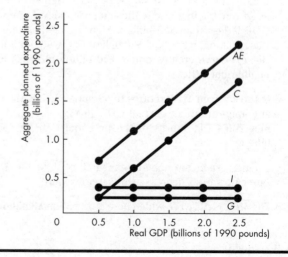

**3 a** Figure 28.4 shows the consumption line, *C*, the investment line, *I*, and the government purchases line, *G*.

**b** Table 28.5 shows the schedule of aggregate expenditure. Aggregate expenditure equals the sum of consumption expenditure, investment, and government purchases. Thus when GDP is, say, £1.0 billion, aggregate expenditure equals £0.6 billion + £0.3 billion + £0.2 billion, or £1.1 billion.

## Table 28.5  Aggregate Expenditure

| Real GDP (billions of 1990 pounds) | Aggregate expenditure (billions of 1990 pounds) |
|---|---|
| 0.5 | 0.7 |
| 1.0 | 1.1 |
| 1.5 | 1.5 |
| 2.0 | 1.9 |
| 2.5 | 2.3 |

## Figure 28.5

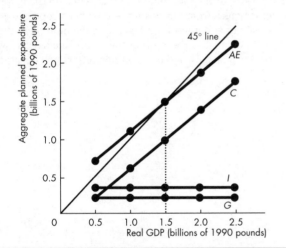

**c** The aggregate expenditure curve, *AE*, is plotted in Fig. 28.4. It is the vertical sum of the *C* + *I* + *G* curves in the figure.

**d** Figure 28.5 shows the 45° line. The equilibrium level of expenditure equals £1.5 billion because the *AE* line crosses the 45° line at that point.

**e** In Fig. 28.5 the dotted line indicating the equilibrium level of expenditure shows that the equilibrium level of consumption is £1.0 billion, the equilibrium level of investment is £0.3 billion, and the equilibrium level of government purchases is £0.2 billion. Alternatively, in Table 28.2, the data in row 3 – the row for which GDP is £1.5 billion – give the same answers for consumption, investment and government purchases.

## DISCUSSION QUESTION

### Figure 28.6

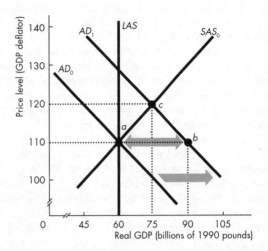

**1** Assume that investment increases by £10 billion. Let's also assume that the *MPC* equals 0.67.

First, we calculate the multiplier. We know that the multiplier equals

$$\frac{1}{(1-MPC)}$$

so in this case we get

$$\frac{1}{(1-0.67)} = 3.0.$$

In other words, we know that the multiplier is 3.0 and that the £10 billion increase in investment leads to a 3.0 × £10.0 billion = £30.0 billion increase in equilibrium expenditure.

In Figure 28.6, before investment increased, the economy was in equilibrium at point *a*. The initial aggregate demand curve, $AD_0$, crossed the short-run aggregate supply curve, $SAS_0$, and the long-run aggregate supply curve, *LAS*. The equilibrium price level was 110 and real GDP was £60 billion.

The increase in investment shifts the *AD* curve rightward, and the size of the shift equals the change in equilibrium expenditure. In other words, the *AD* curve shifts rightward to $AD_1$, and the size of the shift equals £30 billion. The shift is the difference between point *b* and point *a* along the double headed arrow; this difference is £30 billion. So the *AD* curve shifts rightward by the multiplied impact on equilibrium expenditure.

A key point is that, in the short run, real GDP doesn't increase by the whole £30 billion. It would increase by the whole £30 billion only if prices didn't change. But, in the short run, prices will start to change. As they rise, people reduce their consumption expenditure, and the equilibrium amount of expenditure doesn't change by the whole £30 billion; it changes by something less. Figure 28.6 shows that the short-run equilibrium – where $AD_1$ crosses $SAS_0$ – is at point $c$. At point $c$, real GDP increases by (only) £15 billion, to £75 billion. Why don't we go to point $b$? Because, in the short run, the price level has increased, from 110 to 120.

But, point $c$ is not the end of the story. At point $c$, the price level has increased but money wages haven't changed. As more time passes, workers negotiate higher wages, which take into account the higher prices. And, as money wage rates rise, the short-run aggregate supply curve shifts leftward.

The last part of the story is illustrated in Fig. 28.7. Here the $SAS$ curve has shifted leftward and the new, long-run equilibrium point is $d$, where the $AD$ curve crosses the $LAS$ curve and the $SAS$ curve, $SAS_1$. Thus at point $d$, we've returned to the long-run equilibrium because prices *and* money wages have both adjusted: real GDP has returned to its potential level (£60 billion) and the price level has increased to 130.

Table 28.6 shows some results that can help you tie all these changes together. It lists the four points shown in Figs 28.6 and 28.7. We begin at point $a$. Then the increase in investment starts to move us to point $b$. If prices are sticky long enough, the multiplier process will have time to complete itself and we'll get to point $b$. But in the short run prices rise, so if we do reach $b$ we move pretty quickly to point $c$, where prices – but not money wages – have changed. Then, from point $c$, money wages start to adjust and we eventually move from point $c$ to point $d$, where both prices and money wages have risen. Point $d$ is the final, long-run equilibrium.

**Table 28.6  Different Points**

| Point | Situation |
|---|---|
| $a$ | Initial equilibrium |
| $b$ | Price level constant, money wage constant |
| $c$ | Price level increased, money wage constant |
| $d$ | Price level increased, money wage increased |

## DATA QUESTIONS

**1** Changes in the level of investment affect GDP through the multiplier process. This process occurs because when investment rises the people who benefit from the investment will in turn increase their spending, and the process will be repeated. The process also occurs when there is a fall in investment.

**2** The size of the multiplier effect depends on the amount of leakages from the system. If marginal propensities to save, tax and import are high, then the multiplier effect will be small. If these propensities are small, there will be few leakages, and the multiplier effect will be large.

**Figure 28.7**

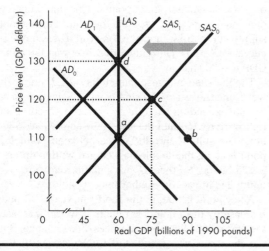

# Chapter 29

# The Government Budget and Fiscal Policy

Chapter 29

---

## Chapter in Perspective, Text Pages 741–766

Fiscal policy – government policy concerning taxes and public spending – is the subject of this chapter. The background to fiscal policy is described and the effects in both the short run and the long run are discussed.

---

## Helpful Hints

**1** In Chapter 28 the idea behind the multiplier was discussed. This chapter continues the discussion by introducing additional multipliers, including the government purchases multiplier and the lump-sum tax multiplier. These multipliers exist for the same reason that the multiplier existed in the preceding chapter. An initial autonomous change that affects people's disposable income leads them to change their consumption expenditure, which further affects disposable income and thereby induces further changes.

**2** That the multipliers in this chapter exist for the same reasons as those in Chapter 28 is reinforced by the fact that the investment multiplier (derived in Chapter 28) is identical to the government spending multiplier. In the simplest case without income taxes or imports, both multipliers are

$$\frac{1}{(1 - MPC)}.$$

The reason is that, for example, a £1 billion increase in either investment or government purchases initially adds £1 billion to the stream of aggregate expenditure. In other words, the effect on aggregate expenditure from a change in investment spending is identical to the effect of a similar change in government purchases.

**3** The fact that the investment multiplier equals the government purchases multiplier occasionally leads to confusion among students, who realize that an increase in investment spending will increase the country's capital stock but that an increase in government purchases may not affect the country's capital stock. These students argue that the capital stock changes must therefore cause the effect of an increase in investment to differ from the effect of an increase in government spending.

Although this analysis has some long-run merit, it is incorrect in its application to aggregate demand and is incorrect in the short run.

First, remember that multipliers calculate the amount by which the *aggregate demand* curve shifts when autonomous spending changes. The total demand for goods and services changes by the same amount regardless of whether the initial change in expenditure was by firms (for their investment) or by the government (for its purchases of goods and services). Hence the multiplier – which measures the size of this shift – is identical for investment and government spending.

Second, remember that the aggregate demand curve does not depend on the amount of the country's capital. The aggregate supply curve(s) shifts when the country's capital stock changes. An increase in investment spending will change the capital stock, whereas an increase in government purchases does not necessarily change the capital stock. Thus the response of the aggregate supply curve(s) may be different for the two increases in spending.

Even though the aggregate supply curve(s) might respond differently, ignoring any differences is convenient for two reasons. First, for the short run, time is needed for the capital to be installed and come online. Thus in the short run, the country's capital stock does not change when investment increases and so, in the short run, the aggregate supply curve(s) does not shift. Second, even in the long run the change in investment spending creates only a minuscule fraction of a change in the country's total capital stock. In the analysis of business cycle fluctuations in economic activity, that amount of change generally is ignored as too small to matter. Thus although it is important for the topic of long-term economic growth, for multiplier analysis a change in investment spending is treated the same as a change in government purchases.

## Key Figures

### Figure 29.5 The Government Purchases Multiplier, text page 750

This shows the effect of an increase in government spending. The *AE* curve shifts up by the amount of the increase, the economy moves to a new equilibrium where *AE* = real GDP and the effect is a multiplied rise in GDP.

### Figure 29.12 Supply Side Effects of Fiscal Policy, text page 759

This figure compares two views. Traditionally, a tax cut had been seen to increase *AD* and have only a small effect on supply. However, supply siders argue that a tax cut increases incentives and so has a considerable supply side effect.

# SELF-TEST

## CONCEPT REVIEW

1 For many years the United Kingdom, like almost all other countries, has run a budget _____ .

2 Like changes in investment, changes in government spending have a(n) _____ effect.

3 Automatic _____ are mechanisms that operate without the need for action by government. For example, if real GDP begins to fall, government _____ increases and _____ revenues fall.

4 In the short run, when prices are sticky, a change in government spending will have a(n) _____ effect on GDP.

5 Crowding out is the tendency for an increase in government spending to bring a(n) _____ in investment. It does not occur if real GDP is _____ than potential GDP.

## TRUE OR FALSE

___ 1 Raising government spending and lump-sum taxes at the same time and by the same amount will increase aggregate demand.

___ 2 Changes in lump-sum taxes are an example of an automatic stabilizer.

__ **3** The government purchases multiplier is greater than 1 because an increase in government purchases leads to an induced increase in consumption expenditure.

__ **4** If the marginal propensity to consume is 0.8 and there are no income taxes or imports, the government purchases multiplier is 5.0.

__ **5** If the marginal propensity to consume is 0.8 and there are no income taxes or imports, the lump-sum tax multiplier is –4.0.

__ **6** If the marginal propensity to consume is 0.8 and there are no income taxes or imports, the balanced budget multiplier is 1.0.

__ **7** In the short run, an increase in government purchases increases real GDP.

__ **8** In the long run, expansionary fiscal policy increases real GDP.

__ **9** Taxes and transfer payments that vary as income varies act as automatic stabilizers in the economy.

__ **10** An increase in lump-sum taxes shifts the *AE* curve upward and the *AD* curve leftward.

__ **11** The larger the marginal propensity to consume, the larger the government purchases multiplier becomes.

## MULTIPLE CHOICE

**1** Which of the following happens automatically if the economy goes into a recession?
  **a** government purchases of goods and services increase
  **b** net taxes rise
  **c** the deficit rises
  **d** lump-sum taxes fall

**2** Suppose that the government purchases multiplier is 2. If government purchases increase by £10 billion but prices do not change, equilibrium expenditure
  **a** increases by £20 billion.
  **b** increases by more than £20 billion.
  **c** increases by less than £20 billion.
  **d** is unaffected.

**3** Suppose that the government purchases multiplier is 2. If government purchases increase by £10 billion, in the short run, equilibrium GDP
  **a** increases by £20 billion.
  **b** increases by more than £20 billion.
  **c** increases by less than £20 billion.
  **d** is unaffected.

**4** Suppose that the government purchases multiplier is 2. If government purchases increase by £10 billion and potential real GDP does not change, in the long run, equilibrium GDP
  **a** increases by £20 billion.
  **b** increases by more than £20 billion.
  **c** increases by less than £20 billion.
  **d** is unaffected.

**5** Which of the following increases the multiplier?
  **a** an increase in the marginal propensity to import
  **b** an increase in the marginal tax rate
  **c** a decrease in the marginal propensity to consume
  **d** an increase in the marginal propensity to consume

Table 29.1 shows consumption, investment and government purchases in a country that has no taxes and no foreign trade (both imports and exports equal zero). Use Table 29.1 for the next five questions.

**Table 29.1 Aggregate Expenditure**

| Real GDP | Consumption expenditure (billions of 1990 pounds) | Investment | Government purchases |
|---|---|---|---|
| 4 | 2.0 | 1 | 1 |
| 5 | 2.5 | 1 | 1 |
| 6 | 3.0 | 1 | 1 |
| 7 | 3.5 | 1 | 1 |
| 8 | 4.0 | 1 | 1 |

**6** What is the aggregate expenditure when GDP equals £7 billion?
  **a** £7 billion
  **b** £5.5 billion
  **c** £3.5 billion
  **d** £1 billion

**7** What is the equilibrium level of expenditure?
  **a** $7 billion
  **b** $6 billion
  **c** $5 billion
  **d** $4 billion

**8** What is the *MPC*?
  **a** 1.00
  **b** 0.90
  **c** 0.50
  **d** $4 billion

**9** What is the government purchases multiplier?
  **a** 0.5
  **b** 2.0
  **c** 5.0
  **d** 10.0

**10** If government purchases increase by $1 billion, before the price level changes, what is the new equilibrium level of expenditure?
  **a** $7 billion
  **b** $6 billion
  **c** $5 billion
  **d** $4 billion

For the next three questions, there are no income taxes and no foreign trade.

**11** If the *MPC* is 0.9, what is the lump-sum multiplier?
  **a** 10.0
  **b** 9.0
  **c** –9.0
  **d** –10.0

**12** If the *MPC* is 0.9, what is the government purchases multiplier?
  **a** 10.0
  **b** 9.0
  **c** –9.0
  **d** –10.0

**13** If the *MPC* is 0.8, what is the government purchases multiplier?
  **a** 10.0
  **b** 8.0
  **c** 5.0
  **d** –9.0

## SHORT ANSWER

**1** Explain why the multiplier effect on real GDP from an expansionary fiscal policy is smaller when the aggregate supply curve is considered. If the expansionary policy has no incentive effects on aggregate supply, what is the long-run multiplier for real GDP?

**2** Suppose that an expansionary fiscal policy has incentive effects that increase aggregate supply. How does the effect on the price level and real GDP of this policy compare with that of a policy that has no supply side effects? What is the long-run multiplier when the policy has incentive effects?

**3** Briefly explain whether the following events will shift the *AE* curve and/or the *AD* curve. (For each case, assume that other variables remain constant.)
  **a** a rise in the price level
  **b** a rise in expected future profits for businesses
  **c** a tax cut
  **d** an increase in government purchases
  **e** an increase in government purchases combined with an equal increase in lump-sum taxes

**4** With reference to the *Reading Between the Lines* article, why do governments find it difficult to cut government spending?

## PROBLEMS

**1** Igor has been elected finance minister of Transylvania. Igor's first action is to hire a crack team of economists and to tell them that he wants a prediction of Transylvania's equilibrium expenditure for next year.
  **a** The economists compile their estimates of next year's real GDP, consumption expenditure, investment and government purchases. These data are shown in Table 29.2. (The stake is the unit of currency in Transylvania.) Transylvania has no foreign trade. Unfortunately, the economists lost their calculator and need your help to complete Table 29.3, which lists real GDP and aggregate expenditure.
  **b** Based on Table 29.3, what is equilibrium expenditure in Transylvania predicted to be?

**2** The economy is in long-run equilibrium. The aggregate supply curve is $AE_0$, as shown in Fig. 29.1, and the aggregate demand curve is $AD_0$, as shown in Fig. 29.2. The *MPC* is 0.75, and the government then lowers its lump-sum taxes by $2 billion. There are no income taxes and no imports.

**Table 29.2  Expenditure in Transylvania**

| Real GDP | Consumption expenditure (billions of 1990 pounds) | Investment | Government purchases |
|---|---|---|---|
| 1.0 | 0.8 | 0.3 | 0.1 |
| 1.5 | 1.2 | 0.3 | 0.1 |
| 2.0 | 1.6 | 0.3 | 0.1 |
| 2.5 | 2.0 | 0.3 | 0.1 |
| 3.0 | 2.4 | 0.3 | 0.1 |
| 3.5 | 2.8 | 0.3 | 0.1 |

**Table 29.3  Aggregate Expenditure in Transylvania**

| Real GDP (billions of 1990 stakes) | Aggregate expenditure (billions of 1990 stakes) |
|---|---|
| 1.0 | |
| 1.5 | |
| 2.0 | |
| 2.5 | |
| 3.0 | |
| 3.5 | |

**Figure 29.1**

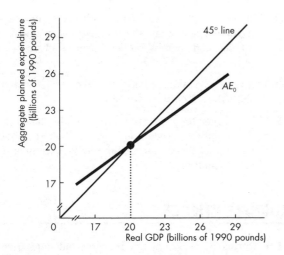

**Figure 29.2**

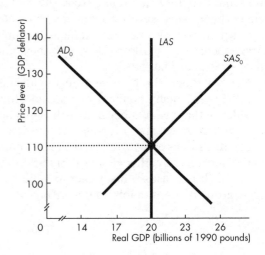

**a** In Figs 29.1 and 29.2, show the initial effect of the decrease in lump-sum taxes on the aggregate expenditure curve and aggregate demand curve. Draw your answers for the period of time over which the price level does not change.

**b** From Fig. 29.2, what is the short-run effect on the price level and real GDP? Label the short-run equilibrium *a*. Without drawing it, explain the effect of the change in the price level on the *AE* curve in Fig. 29.1.

**c** In the long run, ignoring any incentive effects on the supply side, what is the effect on the price level? On real GDP? Without drawing it, what happens to the *AE* curve in Fig. 29.1? Does the *AD* curve in Fig. 29.2 shift as a result of the change in the price level?

## DISCUSSION QUESTION

**1** Explain why the interest payments on the government debt are not necessarily harmful to the economy as a whole.

## DATA QUESTIONS

**Do Tax Cuts Promote Economic Growth?**
Economic theory suggests that lower tax rates could boost growth in several ways. For example, they might encourage people to work harder, and they might stimulate savings and investment.

So much for theory. Is there empirical evidence to support it? Cross-country comparisons do not provide much evidence that tax cuts boost growth. Comparing average growth rates and average tax burdens of OECD countries does appear to give some support to the idea. Unfortunately, this simple correlation does not mean much because so many factors influence a country's growth rate, notably initial income levels.

Poorer countries are more likely to grow faster than rich ones.

Such intercountry studies also have a big drawback: they typically measure a country's average tax burden when it is the marginal ones which matter. So even if spending is cut, the economic evidence still suggests that, on their own, tax cuts will make little difference to long-term growth.

*Source:* Adapted from *The Economist*, 24 August 1996, p. 74. Copyright © *The Economist*, London, 24 August 1996.

1 Summarize the theory which suggests that lower taxes might encourage growth.

2 Why do marginal tax rates matter more than average rates?

# ANSWERS

## CONCEPT REVIEW

1 deficit

2 multiplier

3 stabilizers; spending; tax

4 multiplier

5 decrease; less

## TRUE OR FALSE

**1 T** Simultaneously increasing government spending and lump-sum taxes is an example of a balanced budget change; equilibrium aggregate expenditure – and hence aggregate demand – increases by an amount equal to the change in spending (and taxes).

**2 F** *Income* taxes are automatic stabilizers, falling when income decreases and rising when income increases.

**3 T** Definition.

**4 T** The government purchases multiplier is $\frac{1}{(1-MPC)}$ or, in this case, $\frac{1}{(1-0.8)} = 5.0$.

**5 T** The lump-sum tax multiplier is $-\frac{MPC}{(1-MPC)}$, or $-\frac{0.8}{(1-0.8)} = -4.0$.

**6 T** The balanced budget multiplier always equals 1.0.

**7 T** An increase in government purchases shifts the *AD* curve rightward and, in the short run, increases real GDP.

**8 T** If incentive effects increase potential GDP and thereby shift the *LAS* curve rightward, real GDP increases in the long run. But with no incentive effects, potential GDP does not change and real GDP does not increase in the long run.

**9 T** By changing with real GDP, both taxes and transfer payments help limit the fluctuations in disposable income and thereby reduce business cycle fluctuations.

**10 F** An increase in taxes shifts the *AD* curve leftward but shifts the *AE* curve downward.

**11 T** The larger the *MPC*, the more people change their consumption expenditure when their disposable income changes, increasing the government purchases multiplier.

## MULTIPLE CHOICE

**1 c** During a recession, tax revenues fall and transfer expenditures rise, thereby increasing the budget deficit.

**2 a** When the price level is constant, equilibrium expenditure (or, equivalently, the shift in the *AD* curve) equals the government purchases multiplier times the change in government purchases, or $2 \times £10$ billion = £20 billion.

**3 c** The *AD* curve shifts rightward by £20 billion and, in the short run, the equilibrium point moves along the upward-sloping *SAS* curve so that the equilibrium level of real GDP increases by less than £20 billion.

**4 d** In the long run, the equilibrium returns to potential GDP, so if potential GDP does not change, neither does real GDP.

**5 d** When the marginal propensity to consume increases, each change in disposable income induces a larger change in consumption expenditure, so the multiplier is larger.

**6 b** Aggregate expenditure equals the sum of consumption expenditure, investment and government purchases, so when real GDP equals £7 billion, aggregate expenditure equals £3.5 billion + £1 billion + £1 billion, or £5.5 billion.

**7 d** Equilibrium expenditure is the level of aggregate expenditure that equals real GDP. In Table 29.1, when real GDP is £4 billion, aggregate expenditure also equals £4 billion, the level of equilibrium expenditure.

**8 c** The *MPC* equals $(\Delta C)/(\Delta YD)$. With no taxes, real GDP equals disposable income. Hence when real GDP changes by £1 billion, consumption expenditure changes by £0.5 billion, so the *MPC* equals £0.5 billion/£1 billion, or 0.50.

**9 b** The government purchases multiplier is
$$\frac{1}{(1 - MPC)}.$$
Hence, with an *MPC* of 0.50, the government purchases multiplier is 2.0.

**10 b** The equilibrium level of expenditure has increased by an amount equal to the government purchases multiplier times the change in government purchases, or $2 \times £1$ billion, so the new equilibrium is £6 billion. Alternatively, £1 billion can be added to the schedule of government purchases in Table 29.1. Then the equilibrium expenditure becomes £6 billion, the level of real GDP that creates a (new) level of aggregate expenditure equal to real GDP.

**11 c** The lump-sum tax multiplier is
$$-\frac{MPC}{(1 - MPC)}, \text{ which equals } -\frac{9.0}{(1 - 0.9)} = -9.0.$$

**12 a** The government purchases multiplier is
$$\frac{1}{(1 - MPC)}.$$
When $MPC = 0.9$, this multiplier is
$$\frac{1}{(1 - 0.9)} = 10.0.$$

**13 c** The answer to **12** shows how to calculate the government spending multiplier. Comparing the answers to **12** and **13** shows that the smaller the *MPC* is, the smaller the government purchases multiplier becomes.

## SHORT ANSWER

**1** The multiplier indicates the size of the change in real GDP relative to the size of an initial change in autonomous expenditure, as long as the price level does not change. More generally, the multiplier indicates the size of the shift in the *AD* curve. The *AS* curve shows that the price level rises as aggregate demand increases. The rise in the price level lowers aggregate expenditure, leading to a smaller increase in real GDP than if the price level had remained constant. Indeed, in the long run, the economy returns to potential GDP. In the absence of effects on aggregate supply, the long-run multiplier is zero.

**2** If the expansionary fiscal policy has incentive effects that increase aggregate supply, not only does the *AD* curve shift rightward, but so too do the aggregate supply curves. As a result, the rise in the price level is less and the increase in real GDP is greater when the aggregate supply curves shift. Indeed, if potential real GDP increases as a result of the incentive effects, the long-run multiplier exceeds zero because real GDP increases in the long run.

**3** In general, any change that changes autonomous spending shifts the *AE* curve. Therefore all the changes shift the *AE* curve. Any change in autonomous expenditure not caused by a change in the price level shifts the *AD* curve. Therefore **a** involves a movement along the *AD* curve, and **b–e** create shifts in the *AD* curve.
  **a** The rise in the price level shifts the *AE* curve downward and creates a movement upward along the *AD* curve.
  **b** The rise in future expected profits increases investment, thereby shifting the *AE* curve upward and the *AD* curve rightward.
  **c** The decrease in taxes increases consumption expenditure, and shifts the *AE* curve upward and the *AD* curve rightward.

**d** An increase in government purchases shifts the *AE* curve upward and the *AD* curve rightward.

**e** A simultaneous increase in government purchases and lump-sum taxes shifts the *AE* curve upward and the *AD* curve rightward.

**4** Some of the reasons governments find it difficult to cut spending were discussed in Chapter 18, which described public choice theory. This suggests that the interaction of voters, politicians and bureaucrats will lead to over-provision of goods by the public sector and that there will be considerable resistance to cuts. Even if this theory is not accepted, cutting spending is difficult since it often means people losing their jobs.

## PROBLEMS

**Table 29.4  Aggregate Expenditure in Transylvania**

| Real GDP (billions of 1990 stakes) | Aggregate expenditure (billions of 1990 stakes) |
|---|---|
| 1.0 | 1.2 |
| 1.5 | 1.6 |
| 2.0 | 2.0 |
| 2.5 | 2.4 |
| 3.0 | 2.8 |
| 3.5 | 3.2 |

**1 a** Table 29.4 shows the aggregate expenditure schedule in Transylvania. The schedule is computed by adding consumption expenditure, investment and government purchases. For example, when real GDP is 3.5 billion stakes, aggregate expenditure equals the sum of consumption expenditure, 2.8 billion stakes, investment, 0.3 billion stakes, and government purchases, 0.1 billion stakes, or 3.2 billion stakes.

**b** Equilibrium expenditure is 2 billion stakes, because that level of real GDP equals aggregate expenditure.

**2 a** Figures 29.3 and 29.4 show the effect of the tax reduction on the *AE* and *AD* curves.

In Fig. 29.3, the £2 billion reduction in taxes raises disposable income by £2 billion. From the £2 billion increase, with the *MPC* equal to 0.75, 0.75 × £2 billion, or £1.5 billion goes to increased consumption expenditure. Hence, as shown in Fig. 29.3, the *AE* curve shifts upward (by £1.5 billion, the length of the small arrow) to $AE_1$. Figure 29.3 also shows that the increase in equilibrium expenditure is £6 billion, from £20 billion to £26 billion. Alternatively, the £6 billion increase in equilibrium expenditure equals the reduction in taxes, –£2 billion, multiplied by the lump-sum tax multiplier,

$$-\frac{MPC}{(1 - MPC)}$$ , which is –3.0.

In Fig. 29.4, the aggregate demand curve shifts rightward, from $AD_0$ to $AD_1$. As shown by the length of the double-headed arrow, the extent of the rightward shift is £6 billion, the increase in equilibrium expenditure.

**Figure 29.3**

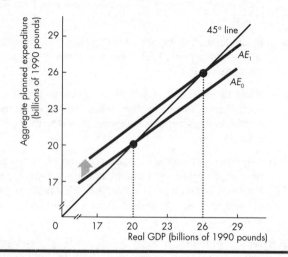

**Figure 29.4**

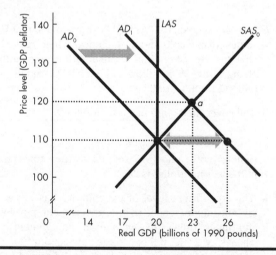

**b** In Fig. 29.4, the short-run equilibrium point is at *a*. The price level rises to 120, and real GDP increases to £23 billion. The increase in the price level from 110 to 120 decreases aggregate expenditure; that is, in Fig. 29.3, the *AE* curve shifts downward from $AE_1$. Indeed, the *AE* curve shifts downward enough so that the equilibrium level of expenditure is £23 billion, the same level as real GDP in Fig. 29.4.

**Figure 29.5**

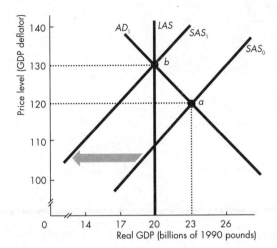

c In the long run, the economy returns to potential GDP. Hence in the absence of any supply side effects, as money wages rise and the *SAS* curve shifts leftward, the equilibrium eventually returns to the point where the *AD* curve crosses the *LAS* curve (point *b* in Fig. 29.5). In the long run, the price level equals 130 and real GDP equals £20 billion. The rise in the price level decreases aggregate expenditure, so the *AE* curve in Fig. 29.3 continues to shift downward. Eventually, when the long-run equilibrium is reached, the *AE* curve has shifted all the way back to $AE_0$. At this point, equilibrium expenditure is the same as

initially, £20 billion, which also equals the level of potential GDP. The *AD* curve does *not* shift as a result of the higher price level.

## DISCUSSION QUESTION

**1** Who exactly receives the interest that is paid on government debt? It's the people who own the debt, who are mainly nationals of the country concerned. Look at the issue like this. UK citizens pay taxes that go towards paying the interest on the government's debt. However, UK citizens also receive most of these interest payments. So some people pay the interest (through taxes) and other people receive the interest payments.

## DATA QUESTIONS

**1** The theory that tax cuts lead to economic growth depends in large part on how the labour market reacts. A tax cut will cause some people, particularly women, to join the labour market, and also cause others to work more since they will receive more money. On the other hand, this higher income will cause some people to choose more leisure. There will also be effects on savings and investment. The main text, page 630–632 deals with the determinants of investment in some detail.

**2** Marginal matters more than average because decisions are taken at the margin. Whatever the average rate of tax, a person will ask the question: 'If I work extra hours, how will this affect my income?' In other words, the crucial factor will be the marginal effect.

# Chapter 30   Money

---

## Chapter in Perspective, Text Pages 767–798

What exactly is money and what are its functions? How does a particular monetary system arise? What role do banks play in the creation of money? These are a few of the important issues addressed in this chapter.

Our major reason for pursuing a deeper understanding of money and banks, however, is to help us understand the connection between money and macroeconomic activity, especially the behaviour of the price level. This is done using one of the most famous and influential theories in economics: the quantity theory of money.

---

## Helpful Hints

**1** What is money? You should be able to answer this question on several levels. First, at the level of general definition: money is a medium of exchange, and so on. Second, at the level of classification: currency notes are money but cheques are not. Third, at the level of specific definitions such as M4.

**2** One of the most important concepts presented in this chapter is the money multiplier process by which banks create money. There are two fundamental facts that allow banks to create money.

First, one of the liabilities of banks is money: chequeable deposits. Banks create money by creating new chequeable deposits. Second, banks hold fractional reserves. This means that when a bank receives a deposit, it will hold only part of it as reserves and can loan out the rest. Note that the bank is not indulging in a scam – it is still maintaining assets (reserves plus loans) to match its liabilities (the deposits). When that loan is spent, at least part of the proceeds are likely to be deposited in another bank, creating a new deposit (money).

The money multiplier process follows from this last fact: banks make loans when they receive new deposits and these loans are spent and will return to another bank, creating another new deposit. The process then repeats itself, adding more money (but in progressively smaller amounts) in each round. Practise going through examples until the process becomes second nature.

**3** Why does the aggregate demand curve shift to the right when there is an increase in the quantity of money?

For the answer, we return to the discussion of aggregate demand in Chapter 27. There we discovered that an increase in the quantity of *real* money caused aggregate demand to increase for two reasons. The first was the real money balances effect and the second was the intertemporal substitution effect, which is a result of the fact that interest rates will fall when real money increases.

272

*At a given price level*, an increase in the quantity of money is an increase in the quantity of real money. Thus aggregate demand increases through these two effects and, since the price level is given, the aggregate demand curve shifts to the right.

4 Analysts often use the quantity theory to help shape their thinking about future inflation. In particular, they look at the rate of growth of money supply to help predict whether the inflation rate is likely to rise or fall, although you should note that the relationship is not always precise or constant.

## Key Figures and Table

### Figure 30.3 Creating Money at the One-and-Only Bank, text page 782

Since most of us think of money as notes and coins, it is often hard to understand how banks can create money. This figure gives a simplified account assuming that the bank always keeps 25 per cent of any deposit and so lends out 75 per cent. Note that bank assets always equal liabilities.

### Figure 30.6 Long-run Effects of a Change the Quantity of Money, text page 786

Figure 30.5 showed that in the short run an increase in the money supply will raise prices and GDP. However, Figure 30.6 shows that in the long run this will cause money wages to rise, so causing the *SAS* curve to move to the left so that in the long run raising money supply has no effect on real GDP; it only raises prices.

### Table 30.2 Two Measures of Money, text page 772

This gives a useful summary of the components of M0 and M4.

# SELF-TEST

## CONCEPT REVIEW

1 Money is defined by its main function: money is a(n) _____ _____ _____ . This means that money is anything that is generally acceptable in exchange for goods and services.

2 Money has four functions, the first of which gives the definition of money. It also serves as a medium of _____ , a(n) _____ of account and a(n)_____ _____ _____ .

3 Money takes four different forms. A physical commodity that is valued in its own right and also serves as a medium of exchange is called _____ money. A paper claim to a commodity that circulates as money is called _____ _____ money. An intrinsically worthless (or almost worthless) commodity that serves the functions of money is called _____ money. Lastly, a loan that the borrower promises to pay on demand which is used by the lender in exchange for goods and services is called _____ _____ money.

4 A firm that takes deposits from households and firms and makes loans to other households and firms is called a(n)_____ _____ .

5 Assets that can be quickly converted into a medium of exchange at a reasonably certain price are known as _____ assets. The degree to which an asset has this property is known as _____ .

6 The fraction of a bank's total deposits that are actually held in reserves is called the _____ _____ . The ratio of reserves to deposits that a bank regards as necessary to conduct business is called the _____ _____ _____ . Actual reserves minus desired reserves equal _____ _____ .

7 The proposition that an increase in money leads to an equal percentage increase in the price level is the _____ theory of _____ . Its original basis follows from certain propositions about the equation of _____ . This equation is true by definition since one of its components is defined by it. This component, the _____ of circulation, is the average number of times a pound is used annually to buy the goods and services that make up GDP.

# TRUE OR FALSE

__ **1** Barter can take place only if there is a double coincidence of wants.

__ **2** Money is anything that is generally acceptable as a medium of exchange.

__ **3** Unpredictable changes in the rate of inflation enhance the function of money as a standard of deferred payment.

__ **4** Only money serves as a store of value.

__ **5** Gresham's law implies that money that has *not* been debased (good money) will tend to drive debased money (bad money) out of circulation.

__ **6** If a depositor withdraws currency from a bank, that bank's reserve ratio declines.

__ **7** The simple money multiplier is equal to 1 divided by the desired reserve ratio.

__ **8** Other things remaining the same, the currency drain makes the real-world money multiplier larger than the simple money multiplier.

__ **9** An increase in the quantity of money shifts the aggregate demand curve rightward.

__ **10** According to the quantity theory of money, in the long run, an increase in the quantity of money will cause the price level to rise but will leave real GDP unchanged.

__ **11** The quantity theory of money implies that a 10 per cent increase in the quantity of money will cause a 10 per cent increase in the price level.

__ **12** If the quantity of money is £50 billion and nominal GDP is £200 billion, the velocity of circulation is $\frac{1}{4}$.

__ **13** On average, the money supply growth rate is exceeded by the inflation rate.

# MULTIPLE CHOICE

**1** Which of the following is *not* one of the four functions of money?
 **a** medium of exchange
 **b** measure of liquidity

 **c** standard of deferred payment
 **d** store of value
 **e** unit of account

**2** When a contract specifies that a certain number of pounds are to be paid in the future for services rendered, money is functioning as a
 **a** medium of exchange.
 **b** measure of liquidity.
 **c** unit of account.
 **d** store of value.
 **e** standard of deferred payment.

**3** If the prices of goods and services were stated in terms of pounds of salt, then salt is a
 **a** unit of account.
 **b** standard of deferred payment.
 **c** store of value.
 **d** quasi-money.
 **e** medium of exchange.

**4** UK currency today is an example of
 **a** fiat money.
 **b** commodity money.
 **c** convertible paper money.
 **d** private debt money.
 **e** fractionally backed gold-convertible money.

**5** A chequeable deposit in a financial institution is an example of
 **a** commodity money.
 **b** fiat money.
 **c** convertible paper money.
 **d** private debt money.
 **e** public debt money.

**6** Which of the following is an example of quasi-money or 'almost' money?
 **a** credit cards
 **b** demand deposits
 **c** term deposits
 **d** other chequeable deposits
 **e** savings deposits

**7** A bank can create money by
 **a** selling some of its investment securities.
 **b** increasing its reserves.
 **c** lending its excess reserves.
 **d** printing more cheques.
 **e** converting reserves into securities.

**8** If all banks hold 100 per cent reserves, what is the simple money multiplier?

**a** 0
**b** 1
**c** 10
**d** 100
**e** infinite

# SHORT ANSWER

**1** What is meant by a double coincidence of wants?

**2** What are the four principal functions of money?

**3** Explain why credit cards are not money.

**4** How do banks create money?

**5** According to the quantity theory of money, what is the effect of an increase in the quantity of money?

**6** Which of the functions of money does the inflation discussed in the *Reading Between the Lines* article prevent from functioning?

# PROBLEMS

**1** Suppose an individual sells £1,000 worth of government securities to the Bank of England and deposits the proceeds (£1,000) in Bank 1. Note that this new deposit initially increases the quantity of money by £1,000. Assume that the desired reserve ratio for all banks is 20 per cent (0.2). Also assume that there is no currency drain. As it stands, Table 30.1 gives information for the first round of the money expansion process that will be generated by this new deposit.

**a** Follow the first six rounds of the money creation process by completing the six rows of Table 30.1.

**Table 30.1 Money Creation Process – No Currency Drain**

| Bank number | New deposits (pounds) | New loans (pounds) | New reserves (pounds) | Cumulative Increase in money (pounds) | Increase (pounds) |
|---|---|---|---|---|---|
| 1 | 1,000 | 800 | 200 | 1,000 | 1,000 |
| 2 | | | | | |
| 3 | | | | | |
| 4 | | | | | |
| 5 | | | | | |
| 6 | | | | | |

**b** What is the total increase in the quantity of money after six rounds?

**c** What is the money multiplier?

**d** After all rounds have been completed, what will the total increase in money be?

**2** Suppose there is a decrease in the quantity of money. Using an aggregate demand–aggregate supply model, show what happens to the price level and the level of real GDP in the short run and in the long run.

**3** We observe an economy in which the price level is 1.5, real GDP is £240 billion and the money supply is £60 billion.

**a** What is the velocity of circulation?

**b** According to the quantity theory of money, what will be the result of an increase in the quantity of money to £80 billion?

# DISCUSSION QUESTION

**1** Explain how fractional reserve banking works, and how a deposit of (say) £100 will be there awaiting withdrawal.

# DATA QUESTIONS

**Money & Prices**

**Table 30.2**

| Year | Quantity of money (M4 £000 million) | Index of Retail Prices (1985 = 100) |
|---|---|---|
| 1981 | 129 | 79.1 |
| 1982 | 155 | 85.8 |
| 1983 | 175 | 89.8 |
| 1984 | 199 | 94.3 |
| 1985 | 226 | 100 |
| 1986 | 262 | 103.4 |
| 1987 | 304 | 107.7 |
| 1988 | 358 | 113.0 |
| 1989 | 422 | 121.8 |
| 1990 | 473 | 133.3 |
| 1991 | 501 | 141.1 |
| 1992 | 519 | 146.4 |
| 1993 | 545 | 149.2 |
| 1994 | 568 | 152.8 |

Source: *Economic Trends*, HMSO, 1996.

1 Explain what is meant by
   a M4
   b Index of Retail Prices (1985=100)

2 Outline the quantity theory of money. Comment on this theory in the light of the figures in Table 30.2.

# ANSWERS

## CONCEPT REVIEW

1 means of payment

2 exchange; unit; store of value

3 commodity; convertible paper; fiat; private debt

4 financial intermediary

5 liquid; liquidity

6 reserve ratio; desired reserve ratio; excess reserves

7 quantity; money; exchange; velocity

## TRUE OR FALSE

1 **T** Buyer must be selling what seller wants to buy and vice versa.

2 **T** Basic function of money.

3 **F** Unpredictable inflation makes it difficult to to sign long-term contracts eroding value of money as a standard of deferred payments.

4 **F** Other assets (such as land) can act as store of value.

5 **F** Agents keep more valuable good money and circulate less valuable bad money.

6 **T** Currency is part of reserve ratio.

7 **T** Definition – see text for explanation.

8 **F** Currency drain makes money multiplier smaller.

9 **T** Increase in money supply causes $MD$ to shift to rightward for real money balances effect and intertemporal substitution effect.

10 **T** True in the very long run.

11 **T** Theory assumes that $V$ and $Y$ are independent of money supply so that change in money leads to proportionate change in prices.

12 **F** $V = PT/M = 200/50 = 4$.

13 **F** See Data Questions for evidence.

## MULTIPLE CHOICE

1 **b** Definition of a function.

2 **e** Payment is deferred.

3 **a** Definition.

4 **a** Definition.

5 **d** Definition.

6 **a** Most readily changed into currency.

7 **c** Lending its reserves is done by crediting borrower's deposits, creating more deposits = more money.

8 **b** Multiplier = 1/(desired reserve ratio) = 1/1 = 1.

## SHORT ANSWER

1 A double coincidence of wants occurs in barter when an individual who has good $A$ and wants to trade for good $B$ finds an individual who has good $B$ and wants to trade for good $A$.

2 The four principal functions of money are: medium of exchange; unit of account; standard of deferred payment; store of value.

3 A credit card is not money, but rather a mechanism for borrowing money, which must later be repaid. The repayment of money takes place when the credit card bill is paid by cheque.

4 Banks create money by making new loans. When the proceeds of these loans are spent, the person receiving the money will deposit much of it in a bank deposit which is new money.

5 According to the quantity theory of money, an increase in the quantity of money will cause the price level to increase by an equal percentage amount.

6 Rampant inflation such as that which occurred in Brazil is harmful largely because it prevents money fulfilling its functions. In this case, money cannot be used as a store of value or as a standard for deferred payment

because it loses its value. It can be used as a unit of account, but with difficulty; for example, account holders have to be compensated for inflation. Money can still be used as a medium of exchange, but again with difficulty since no one wants to hold money.

# PROBLEMS

**1 a** Table 30.1 is completed as Table 30.3. Note that 80 per cent of each new deposit will be loaned out and 20 per cent will be held as reserves. When a new loan is deposited in a bank, it becomes a new deposit and thus money.

## Table 30.3 Money Creation Process – No Currency Drain

| Bank number | New deposits (pounds) | New loans (pounds) | New reserves (pounds) | Cumulative Increase in money (pounds) | Increase (pounds) |
|---|---|---|---|---|---|
| 1 | 1,000.00 | 800.00 | 200.00 | 1,000.00 | 1,000.00 |
| 2 | 800.00 | 640.00 | 160.00 | 800.00 | 1,800.00 |
| 3 | 640.00 | 512.00 | 128.00 | 640.00 | 2,440.00 |
| 4 | 512.00 | 409.60 | 102.40 | 512.00 | 2,952.00 |
| 5 | 409.60 | 327.68 | 81.92 | 409.60 | 3,361.60 |
| 6 | 327.68 | 262.14 | 65.54 | 327.68 | 3,689.28 |

**b** After six rounds the total (cumulative) increase in the quantity of money is £3,689.28. This is obtained from the last column of Table 30.3.

**c** The money multiplier in this case is the simple money multiplier given by:

$$\text{Simple money multiplier} = \frac{1}{\text{Desired reserve ratio}}$$

Since the desired reserve ratio is 0.2, the simple money multiplier is 5.

**d** The total increase in money will be £5,000 after all rounds are completed. This is obtained by multiplying the initial increase in deposits (£1,000) by the simple money multiplier (5).

**2** The consequences of a decrease in the quantity of money are illustrated in Fig. 30.1. The economy is initially in long-run equilibrium at point $a$, the intersection of $AD_0$ and $SAS_0$ (and $LAS$). The price level is $P_0$ and GDP is at its full-employment level, $Y$.

A decrease in the quantity of money will shift the $AD$ curve to the left, from $AD_0$ to $AD_1$. The new short-run equilibrium is at point $b$. The price level falls to $P_1$ and

real GDP falls to $Y_1$. In the long run, however, input prices will also fall, which will shift the $SAS$ curve down, from $SAS_0$ to $SAS_1$. A new long-run equilibrium is achieved at point $c$. Thus in the long run, the price level falls further to $P_2$, while real GDP returns to its initial level, $Y$.

**Figure 30.1**

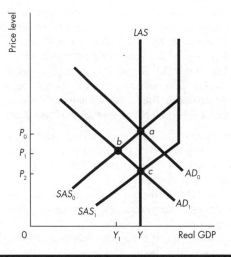

**3 a** From the equation of exchange, we know that the velocity of circulation is defined by:

$$\text{Velocity of circulation} = \frac{\text{Price level} \times \text{Real GDP}}{\text{Quantity of money}}$$

With the values for the price level, real GDP and the quantity of money given in this problem, we have:

$$\text{Velocity of circulation} = \frac{1.5 \times 240}{60} = \frac{360}{60} = 6$$

**b** The quantity theory of money predicts that an increase in the quantity of money will cause an equal percentage increase in the price level. An increase in money from £60 billion to £80 billion is a one-third (33 per cent) increase. Thus the quantity theory of money predicts that the price level will rise by one-third (33 per cent). Since the initial price level is 1.5, the predicted price level will be 2.0.

# DISCUSSION QUESTION

**1** In the past, many banks have gone bust because they have not kept sufficient reserves and there has been a crisis of confidence so that savers have wanted their money back. Since this had been lent out, the banks were unable to repay depositors and so became bankrupt.

This does not happen now; bank supervision is better and the government guarantees deposits.

# DATA QUESTIONS

**1 a** 'M4' is a measure of the money supply in the United Kingdom, which includes cash held outside the Bank of England by the public as well as all sterling deposits at banks and building societies.

  **b** The Index of Retail Prices is a measure of the change in consumer prices bought by a typical household in the United Kingdom. '1985=100' means that 1985 has been chosen as the base year.

**2** The quantity theory of money suggests that an increase in the quantity of money leads to an equal increase in the price level. The theory is discussed in detail in the main text, pages 788–791.

Figure 30.2 takes the data in Table 30.2 and converts the figures into percentage changes in order to make comparisons.

At first sight, the diagram does not give any support to the quantity theory. The increases in the quantity of money are always larger than the changes in the retail price index. However, supporters of the quantity theory

**Figure 30.2**

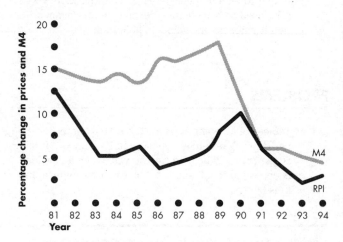

would point out that the pattern of the curves is similar; for example, M4 began rising in 1985 and the rate of inflation rose in the years after 1986. Moreover, the theory suggests that price rises will be equal to changes in the money supply *in the long run*, and this may not be apparent in a fairly short set of figures. Also, M4 may not be the most appropriate measure of money, and the Retail Price Index may not be an accurate measure of price changes.

# Chapter 31

# The Central Bank and Monetary Policy

---

## Chapter in Perspective, Text Pages 799–830

In Chapter 30 we discovered that a new bank deposit will, as it works its way through the banking system, cause a total increase in the quantity of money that is a multiple of the initial new deposit. But how might that new money-creating deposit arise? In this chapter, we find that a central bank, through its use of monetary policy tools, can create such new deposits and thus influence the quantity of money.

The reason we are so interested in the quantity of money, of course, is that changes in the quantity of money can have important effects on real GDP and the price level. For example, an increase in the quantity of money will increase aggregate demand, thus causing the price level to increase and the level of real GDP to increase, at least in the short run.

How does an increase in the quantity of money affect aggregate demand? We will learn that an increase in the quantity of money will cause an increase in aggregate expenditure primarily through its ability to lower interest rates. Then the question becomes: how does a change in the quantity of money cause interest rates to change? A major purpose of this chapter is to present a model that will allow us to explain the determination of interest rates and how these affect the economy.

---

## Helpful Hints

**1** One restriction on UK monetary policy is created by the international nature of the UK economy – this will be discussed in later chapters. The fact that UK citizens and foreigners can easily switch between UK and foreign assets is a crucial constraint on policy choices, as we shall see.

**2** One of a central bank's most important tasks is to control the money supply. It uses four methods: credit ceilings, changing asset requirements, changing interest rates and open market operations. Since no method is perfect, the actual methods adopted vary over the years, and you should understand all four.

To remember whether an open market purchase will lead to a decrease or an increase in money, it may be helpful to think of open market operations as an exchange of government securities for cash. For example, think of an open market purchase as the Bank of England acquiring government securities by giving cash to the public. Thus the money supply will increase.

**3** Ordinary use of the term *money* does not make some of the important distinctions that are made in economics. To avoid confusion regarding the concept of the demand for money, it is important that these distinctions are clear.

For example, we often talk about our income as the amount of *money* we make over a certain period of time. When we use the term in this context, we are speaking of money as a flow – a quantity received over some period of time.

On the other hand, we may talk about how much money we have in our bank account or in our wallet at a certain point in time. In this context we are speaking of money as a stock – a quantity at a point in time. The distinction between these two concepts can be important.

To avoid potential confusion, economists rarely use the term money when referring to a flow. Instead, they will use less ambiguous alternative terms like income or wage. In this chapter, money always refers to a stock. When we talk about the demand for money we are talking about the desire to hold a stock of money and not spend it. (However, it *is* being held for future spending purposes.)

## Key Figures

**Figure 31.4  A Round in the Multiplier Process Following an Open Market Operation, text page 810**

This shows what happens when the government buys assets from commercial banks. The ultimate result is an increase in bankers' reserves and therefore in their ability to create money.

Note that selling securities by the government would have the opposite effect.

**Figure 31.10 Money Market Equilibrium, text page 819**

This illustrates an equilibrium in the money market. The supply of real money does not vary as the interest rate varies. The real money supply curve is thus a vertical line. However, the demand for real money is inversely related to the interest rate, and therefore the real money demand curve is negatively sloped. The equilibrium interest rate is determined by the intersection of the demand curve for real money and the supply curve of real money.

At interest rates higher than the equilibrium, the fixed supply of real money is greater than the quantity of real money demanded; households and firms are holding more money than they desire at these higher interest rates. They will therefore try to reduce the excess supply by buying financial assets. As a result of this increase in the demand for financial assets, the price of financial assets will rise and the interest rates earned on these assets will fall. As interest rates fall, the quantity of money demanded increases, reducing the excess supply of money. This process will continue until interest rates have fallen sufficiently so that the quantity of real money demanded is equal to the quantity of real money supplied. Similarly, at interest rates below equilibrium, the same process will occur, but in the opposite direction, pushing the interest rate back to equilibrium. Note that the demand for money must do the adjusting, as the supply of money is fixed.

# SELF-TEST

## CONCEPT REVIEW

**1** The attempt by the Bank of England to control inflation and reduce business cycle fluctuations by changing the quantity of money and adjusting interest rates is called _____ .

**2** The Bank of England is an example of a(n) _____ central bank.

**3** The Bank of England uses three main policy tools. It can change _____ requirements and also the _____ _____ on lending of last resort. The third tool involves the purchase and sale of government securities by the Bank of England. It is called _____ _____ _____ .

**4** There are three main motives for holding money. The first motive, to undertake transactions and minimize the cost of transacting, is called the _____ motive. Money held as a precaution against unforeseen events and required unplanned purchases corresponds to the _____ motive. The last motive, to avoid predicted losses from holding stocks and bonds that are expected to fall in value, is called the _____ motive.

**5** The relationship between the quantity of real money demanded and the interest rate, holding other things constant, is called the _____ for _____ _____ .

**6** An increase in real income will shift the demand curve for real money to the _____ , and, if the supply of real money is constant, will cause the equilibrium interest rate to _____ .

**7** The amount by which an initial increase in bank reserves is multiplied to calculate the effect on total bank deposits is called the _____ _____ multiplier. This multiplier will be larger, the _____ is the desired reserve ratio.

**8** If the Bank of England buys government securities in the open market, the interest rate is likely to _____ .

**6** If the price level increases, there will be an increase in the nominal quantity of money people will want to hold.

**7** If the price level increases, there will be an increase in the real quantity of money people will want to hold.

**8** The velocity of circulation is given by the ratio of real GDP to real money supply.

**9** If interest rates rise, the velocity of circulation is likely to increase.

**10** If interest rates rise, the quantity of money demanded is likely to decrease.

**11** The development of near-money deposits and growth in the use of credit cards in recent years have caused the demand curve for real money to shift to the right.

**12** If the price of a bond rises, the interest rate earned on the bond falls.

**13** An increase in the demand for real money will cause the interest rate to fall.

**14** If households or firms find that they have more money than they want to hold, they will buy financial assets. This will cause the prices of financial assets to rise and the interest rates earned on those assets to fall.

**15** If the Bank of England wants to lower interest rates, it should sell government securities in the open market.

## TRUE OR FALSE

**1** An increase in reserve requirements is intended to increase lending by banks.

**2** Bank of England notes are non-convertible.

**3** The money multiplier is given as the ratio of the quantity of money to the monetary base.

**4** If there is an increase in the fraction of deposits that households and firms hold as currency, the money multiplier will decrease.

**5** The higher the banks' desired reserve ratio, the larger is the money multiplier.

## MULTIPLE CHOICE

**1** The international nature of the UK economy
  **a** means the Bank of England has an expanded range of actions to choose from.
  **b** means the Bank of England must ignore exchange rate determination.
  **c** is due to the many restrictions on capital mobility set by the government.
  **d** means the Bank of England has no independence.
  **e** means the Bank of England cannot ignore interest rate pressures from EU countries.

**2** A flexible exchange rate regime is one in which the
  **a** supply of pounds remains flexible.
  **b** demand for pounds remains flexible.
  **c** value of the exchange rate is determined by market forces.
  **d** value of the exchange rate is influenced by the central bank.
  **e** central bank defines and maintains a flexible exchange rate value.

**3** A managed exchange rate regime is one in which the
  **a** supply of the pound is managed.
  **b** demand for the pound is managed.
  **c** value of the exchange rate is determined by market forces.
  **d** value of the exchange rate is influenced by the central bank.
  **e** central bank defines and maintains a fixed exchange rate value.

**4** Which of the following would *not* affect the size of the monetary base?
  **a** A bank exchanges government securities for a deposit at the Bank of England.
  **b** A bank exchanges vault cash for a deposit at the Bank of England.
  **c** The Bank of England buys government securities from a bank.
  **d** The Bank of England buys government securities from someone other than a bank.
  **e** The Bank of England sells government securities to a bank.

**5** An open market purchase of government securities by the Bank of England will
  **a** increase bank reserves and thus increase the monetary base.
  **b** decrease bank reserves and thus decrease the monetary base.
  **c** increase bank reserves and thus decrease the monetary base.
  **d** decrease bank reserves and thus increase the monetary base.
  **e** decrease bank reserves but increase the money supply if banks have excess reserves.

**6** If banks want to hold 3 per cent of deposits as reserves and households and firms want to hold 10 per cent of deposits as currency, what is the money multiplier?
  **a** 8.5
  **b** 11.0

  **c** 36.7
  **d** 10.0
  **e** 33.3

**7** The money multiplier will increase if either the fraction of deposits that households and firms want to hold as currency
  **a** increases or the desired reserve ratio increases.
  **b** decreases or the desired reserve ratio decreases.
  **c** decreases or the desired reserve ratio increases.
  **d** increases or the desired reserve ratio decreases.
  **e** None of the above.

**8** The quantity of real money demanded will increase if either real income increases or the
  **a** price level increases.
  **b** price level decreases.
  **c** interest rate increases.
  **d** interest rate decreases.
  **e** price of bonds falls.

**9** Real money is equal to nominal money
  **a** divided by real GDP.
  **b** minus real GDP.
  **c** divided by the price level.
  **d** minus the price level.
  **e** divided by velocity.

**10** The higher the interest rate, the
  **a** lower the quantity of money demanded, and the higher is the velocity of circulation.
  **b** lower the quantity of money demanded, and the lower is the velocity of circulation.
  **c** higher the quantity of money demanded, and the higher is the velocity of circulation.
  **d** higher the quantity of money demanded, and the lower is the velocity of circulation.
  **e** higher the quantity of money demanded, but the money supply remains unaffected.

**11** Which of the following will cause the demand curve for real money to shift leftward?
  **a** an increase in real GDP
  **b** a decrease in interest rates
  **c** the expanded use of credit cards
  **d** an increase in the quantity of money supplied
  **e** an increase in the price level

**12** If households and firms find that their holdings of real money are less than desired, they will
  **a** sell financial assets, which will cause interest rates to rise.
  **b** sell financial assets, which will cause interest rates to fall.

**c** buy financial assets, which will cause interest rates to rise.

**d** buy financial assets, which will cause interest rates to fall.

**e** buy goods, which will cause the price level to rise.

**13** If the Bank of England buys government securities in the open market, the supply curve of real money will shift

**a** leftward, and the interest rate will rise.

**b** leftward, and the interest rate will fall.

**c** rightward, and the interest rate will rise.

**d** rightward, and the interest rate will remain constant as money demand will shift to the right as well.

**e** None of the above.

**14** If real GDP increases, the demand curve for real money will shift

**a** leftward, and the interest rate will rise.

**b** leftward, and the interest rate will fall.

**c** rightward, and the interest rate will rise.

**d** rightward, and the interest rate will fall.

**e** rightward, and the interest rate will remain constant.

**15** Money market equilibrium occurs

**a** when interest rates are constant.

**b** when the level of real GDP is constant.

**c** when money supply equals money demand.

**d** only under a fixed exchange rate.

**e** when both **a** and **b** are true.

## SHORT ANSWER

**1** Why do international considerations constrain the Bank of England's actions?

**2** How does an open market purchase of government securities lead to an increase in the monetary base?

**3** What are the three main motives for holding money?

**4** Why do people care about the quantity of real money they hold rather than the quantity of nominal money they hold?

**5** Why will the quantity of real money demanded fall when the interest rate rises?

**6** The market for money is initially in equilibrium when the Bank of England increases the supply of money. Explain the adjustment to a new equilibrium interest rate.

**7** With regard to the *Reading Between the Lines* article, why do you think that a small cut in interest rates of $\frac{1}{4}$ per cent matters?

## PROBLEMS

**1** Let $D$ = deposits, $C$ = currency, and $R$ = reserves. Then let $a = C/D$, the ratio of currency to deposits, and $b = R/D$, the ratio of reserves to deposits. Table 31.1 gives alternative values for $a$ across its top margin and alternative values for $b$ down its left margin.

Complete the nine cells of Table 31.1 by computing the money multiplier for each of the nine combinations of $a$ and $b$ and note what happens to the money multiplier as the currency to deposits ratio increases. Note what happens to the money multiplier as the reserves to deposits ratio increases.

**Table 31.1   Money Multipliers**

|  | | $a$ | |
|---|---|---|---|
| $b$ | 0.1 | 0.2 | 0.3 |
| 0.05 | | | |
| 0.10 | | | |
| 0.15 | | | |

**2** Calculate the money multipliers in each of the following cases.

**a** The money supply is £50 billion and the monetary base is £20 billion.

**b** Deposits = £50 billion, currency = £10 billion and reserves = £5 billion.

**c** Reserves = £5 billion, currency = £15 billion and the reserve to deposits ratio = 0.1.

**3** Figure 31.1 illustrates the current equilibrium in the money market where *MD* is the demand curve for real money and *MS* is the supply curve for real money. Suppose that the Bank of England wants to stimulate aggregate expenditure by lowering the interest rate to 6 per cent. By how much must the Bank of England increase the nominal money supply if the price level is 2?

**Figure 31.1**

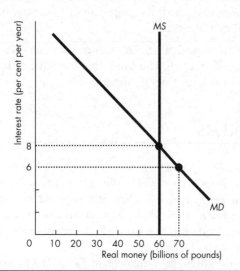

rounds of the process, then specify the effects in all other rounds, and finally give the total effects.

**b** What is the total change in money after six rounds?

**c** What is the total change in the money supply? Does this number agree with the desired change from Problem **3**?

**4** Having determined the amount by which the Bank of England must increase the nominal supply of money, we now want to determine the open market operation that will be necessary if the currency to deposits ratio is 0.2 and the desired reserve ratio is 0.1. Will the Bank of England need to buy or sell government securities in the open market and in what amount?

**5** Given the values for the currency to deposits and desired reserve ratios assumed in Problem **4**, the round-by-round money multiplier process is examined here.

**a** For the open market operation in Problem **4**, complete Table 31.2 by following the first six

## DISCUSSION QUESTION

**1** 'Whenever the government runs a deficit and has to sell government securities it automatically increases the money supply.' Is this true?

## DATA QUESTIONS

### The Central Bank of the United Kingdom

What does a central bank do? Essentially it has three functions. The first is to advise on and execute monetary policy – that is, policies aimed at safeguarding the value of money in the economy. The second is to ensure the soundness of the country's financial system, including direct supervision of banks and other participants in City financial markets. The third is to promote the efficiency and competitiveness of the financial system….

**Table 31.2  Money Multiplier Effects (billions of pounds)**

| Round | Excess reserves at start of round | New loans | Change in deposits | Change in currency | Excess reserves at end of round | Change in quantity of money |
|---|---|---|---|---|---|---|
| 1 | | | | | | |
| 2 | | | | | | |
| 3 | | | | | | |
| 4 | | | | | | |
| 5 | | | | | | |
| 6 | | | | | | |
| All others | – | | | | – | |
| Totals | – | | | | – | |

The bank is a significant participant in both the domestic money markets and the foreign exchange markets. This means it is able to influence interest rates domestically and, in certain circumstances, to carry out operations in the foreign exchange markets to smooth fluctuations in the level of sterling. This in turn enables it to use its market operations to put into effect the government's policies for interest rates and the exchange rate, which are the major elements of monetary policy.

*Source:* Adapted from *Economic Briefing*, May 1991, HM Treasury.

**1** Explain what is meant by
  **a** 'monetary policy', and
  **b** 'City'.

**2** What participants other than banks are there in the City?

**3** How does the government put into effect its 'policies for interest rates'?

# ANSWERS

## CONCEPT REVIEW

**1** monetary policy
**2** subservient
**3** asset; interest rate; open market operations
**4** transactions; precautionary; speculative
**5** demand; real money
**6** right; rise
**7** simple money; smaller
**8** fall

## TRUE OR FALSE

**1 F** It will decrease lending.
**2 T** They are not backed by gold.
**3 T** Definition.
**4 T** $mm = (1 + \Delta C/\Delta D)/(\Delta C/\Delta D + \Delta R/\Delta D)$ causes increase in $CD$ and fall in $mm$.
**5 F** High reserve ratio means banks can lend less and so create less money.
**6 T** People will want to hold more money to pay higher prices.
**7 F** They will want to hold more money in nominal terms.
**8 F** $V$ = Nominal GDP/$M$.
**9 T** People will spend money more quickly.
**10 T** Because the opportunity cost of holding money will rise.
**11 F** Demand for money is determined by factors such as level of incomes.

**12 T** Inverse ratio between bond price and interest rate.
**13 F** Increases in demand push up prices.
**14 T** If demand for money exceeds supply, people will use excess to buy assets, so pushing up their price.
**15 F** Selling government bonds leads to fall in banks' reserves and so to fall in banks' ability to create money.

## MULTIPLE CHOICE

**1 e** Financial markets are interdependent; hence so are interest rates.
**2 c** Definition.
**3 d** Definition.
**4 b** Others are all examples of open market operations.
**5 a** Bank of England pays for securities by crediting banks' reserves, which are part of monetary base.
**6 a** $mm = (1 + 0.1)/(0.1 + 0.03) = 8.5$.
**7 b** Both decreases mean there are more reserves to create new loans at each stage of the multiplier process.
**8 d** Opportunity cost of holding money will fall, so people will hold more.
**9 c** Definition.
**10 a** Rise in interest rate means rise in opportunity cost of holding money, leading to fall in demand for money and increase in velocity since velocity = $Y/MD$.
**11 c** Credit cards will facilitate transactions.
**12 a** People will sell assets to obtain money; fall in asset prices will lead to higher interest rates.

**13 e** Buying bonds leads to rise in deposits, reserves and money supply; excess supply of money leads to fall in interest rates.

**14 c** Rise in GDP means people want more money to finance transactions. Increase in demand for money pushes up its price.

**15 c** Definition.

## SHORT ANSWER

**1** The Bank of England is constrained by international considerations because UK citizens and foreigners can each hold deposits in the other's country. As a result, interest rates are related across borders, a factor that constrains the Bank of England's ability to manipulate domestic interest rates through monetary policy. It is also constrained by membership of the European Union.

**2** An open market purchase of government securities by the Bank of England increases the monetary base by increasing one of its components: banks' deposits at the Bank of England. The process by which this takes place depends on whether the securities are purchased from banks or from the non-bank public.

If the purchase is from banks, the process is direct: the Bank of England pays for the securities by crediting the bank's deposit at the Bank of England, which directly increases the monetary base.

If the purchase is from the non-bank public, the Bank of England pays by writing cheques on itself which the sellers of the securities deposit in their banks. The banks in turn present the cheques to the Bank of England, which credits the banks' deposits at the Bank of England. Thus in either case, the monetary base increases by the amount of the open market purchase.

**3** The three main motives for holding money are the transactions motive, the precautionary motive and the speculative motive.

**4** Nominal money is simply the number of pounds. Real money is a measure of what money will buy because it will fall as the price level rises and the number of pounds is constant.

What matters to people is the quantity of goods and services that money will buy, not the number of pounds. If the price level rises by 10 per cent, people will want to hold 10 per cent more pounds (given real income and interest rates) in order to retain the same purchasing power.

**5** Much of what constitutes money pays no interest; for example, currency and demand deposits. The interest rate is the opportunity cost of holding money, which pays no interest since interest income on alternative financial assets that could have been held is forgone. When interest rates rise, it becomes more costly to hold money, and so people will reduce their money holdings in order to buy other financial assets and take advantage of the higher interest rates.

**6** An increase in the supply of real money means that, at the current interest rate, the quantity of money supplied will be greater than the quantity of money demanded. Money holders will want to reduce their money holdings and will attempt to do so by buying bonds. The increase in the demand for bonds will cause the price of bonds to rise and thus interest rates on bonds to fall. As interest rates fall, the quantity of money demanded increases, which reduces the excess supply of money. This process continues until the interest rate has fallen sufficiently that the quantity of money demanded is the same as the quantity of money supplied.

**7** Changes in interest rates can have a significant effect on the economy, but a cut of only $\frac{1}{4}$ per cent will have little direct effect. Its importance therefore lies in its effect on expectations; for example, it gives an indication of what changes might be expected in the future.

## PROBLEMS

**1** The completed table is shown as Table 31.3. The entries are values of the money multiplier obtained from the following formula:

$$mm = \frac{1 + a}{a + b}$$

where $mm$ is the money multiplier. For example, for the cell of the table corresponding to $a = 0.2$ and $b = 0.05$, we have:

$$mm = \frac{1 + 0.2}{0.2 + 0.05} = \frac{1.2}{0.25} = 4.8$$

We note that for a given currency to deposits ratio, as the desired reserve ratio increases, the money multiplier decreases. For a given desired reserve ratio, as the currency to deposits ratio increases, the money multiplier also decreases.

**Table 31.3  Money Multipliers**

| | a | | |
| --- | --- | --- | --- |
| b | 0.1 | 0.2 | 0.3 |
| 0.05 | 7.33 | 4.80 | 3.71 |
| 0.10 | 5.50 | 4.00 | 3.25 |
| 0.15 | 4.40 | 3.43 | 2.89 |

**2 a** The money multiplier is the ratio of the money supply *(M)* to the monetary base *(MB)*:

$$mm = M/MB = 50/20 = 2.5$$

**b** Here we calculate $a = \Delta C/\Delta D$ and $b = \Delta R/\Delta D$ and use the formula:

$$a = \Delta C/\Delta D = 10/50 = 0.2$$
$$b = \Delta R/\Delta D = 5/50 = 0.1$$
$$mm = \frac{1 + a}{a + b} = \frac{1 + 0.2}{0.2 + 0.1} = 4$$

**c** Here we are given that $b = 0.1$ but we must find $a = \Delta C/\Delta D$. We know the value of $\Delta C$ but not the value of $\Delta D$. We can find the value of $\Delta D$, however, from our knowledge of $b$ and $\Delta R$: $\Delta D = \Delta R/b$. Therefore,

$$\Delta D = \Delta R/b = \pounds 5 \text{ billion}/0.1 = \pounds 50 \text{ billion}$$
$$a = \Delta C/\Delta D = 15/50 = 0.3$$
$$mm = \frac{1 + a}{a + b} = \frac{1 + 0.3}{0.3 + 0.1} = 3.25$$

**3** The current equilibrium interest rate is 8 per cent and the Bank of England would like to increase the money supply sufficiently to lower the interest rate to 6 per cent. Since the quantity of real money demanded at an interest rate of 6 per cent is £70 billion, the Bank of England will want to increase the supply of real money by £10 billion: from £60 billion to £70 billion.

Real money is nominal money divided by the price level and the Bank of England controls only the supply of nominal money. Since the price level is 2, the supply of nominal money must rise by £20 billion in order to increase the supply of real money by £10 billion. Therefore, the Bank of England will need to increase the nominal money supply by £20 billion.

**4** In order to increase the supply of money, the Bank of England will need to buy government securities in the open market because buying government securities will increase bank reserves and the monetary base. The amount of the open market purchase will depend on the money multiplier. Since $a = 0.2$ and $b = 0.1$, we can calculate the money multiplier as follows:

$$mm = \frac{1 + a}{a + b} = \frac{1 + 0.2}{0.2 + 0.1} = 4$$

This means that any initial increase in the monetary base will generate a total increase in money equal to 4 times its size. Thus if we want a total increase in money of £20 billion, we need a £5 billion increase in the monetary base. This requires an open market purchase of £5 billion in government securities.

**5 a** The completed table is shown as Table 31.4. The £5 billion open market purchase will create excess reserves of £5 billion which will be loaned out; 20 per cent of the loan or £1 billion will be held as currency, the remainder will be added to deposits (£4 billion). Of this increase in deposits, 10 per cent or £0.4 billion will be held as desired reserves, and the rest (£3.6 billion) will be excess reserves at the end of round 1. This then becomes the excess reserves at the beginning of round 2 and the process continues.

In subsequent rounds we compute the various entries in the table as follows:

– Excess reserves at start of round = excess reserves at end of previous round
– New loans = excess reserves at start of round
– Change in deposits = 0.8 times new loans
– Change in currency = 0.2 times new loans
– Excess reserves at end of round = 0.9 times change in deposits
– Change in quantity of money = change in deposits + change in currency

The total effects for each relevant column are obtained by using the fact that the money multiplier is 4 (from Problem 4) and the effect of all other rounds is the difference between the final total and the total after six rounds.

## Table 31.4 Money Multiplier Effects (billions of pounds)

| Round | Excess reserves at start of round | New loans | Change in deposits | Change in currency | Excess reserves at end of round | Change in quantity of money |
|---|---|---|---|---|---|---|
| 1 | 5.00 | 5.00 | 4.00 | 1.00 | 3.60 | 5.00 |
| 2 | 3.60 | 3.60 | 2.88 | 0.72 | 2.59 | 3.60 |
| 3 | 2.59 | 2.59 | 2.07 | 0.52 | 1.86 | 2.59 |
| 4 | 1.86 | 1.86 | 1.49 | 0.37 | 1.34 | 1.86 |
| 5 | 1.34 | 1.34 | 1.07 | 0.27 | 0.96 | 1.34 |
| 6 | 0.96 | 0.96 | 0.77 | 0.19 | 0.69 | 0.96 |
| All others | – | 4.65 | 3.72 | 0.93 | – | 4.65 |
| Totals | – | 20 | 16 | 4 | – | 20 |

**b** The total change in money after six rounds is £15.25 billion, the sum of the changes in the quantity of money for rounds 1 to 6.

**c** The total change in the money supply is £20 billion, which can be obtained by using a money multiplier of 4. This is exactly the desired increase in the money supply from Problem **3**.

# DISCUSSION QUESTION

**1** The effect depends on how the deficit is funded. If the government funds a deficit by selling securities such as bonds to the commercial banks, then this will also decrease the banks' ability to create money (unless they have excess reserves). This is because they will be able to buy government bonds only at the expense of other securities or making fewer loans and in this case the money supply is not increased. However, if the banks have excess reserves, they will be able to buy bonds without reducing their holdings of other assets, so the money supply would increase. If the government sells bonds to the general public then the public gives money to the government which then spends it, that is, gives it back to the public, so there is no effect on the money supply.

However, if the government funds the deficit by selling bonds to the Bank of England, the result will be a rise in the money supply since the bank uses newly created money to buy the bonds.

# DATA QUESTIONS

**1 a** As the article suggests, 'monetary policy' is aimed at safeguarding the value of money in the economy, but it is also used as a means of achieving other economic goals such as a stable exchange rate. It involves controlling the quantity of money, and influencing interest and exchange rates.

**b** The 'City' sometimes refers to that part of London where banks and insurance companies are concentrated, but usually it refers to the financial institutions themselves.

**2** Apart from banks (there are over 500 authorized banks in the United Kingdom), the other participants in the financial market include discount houses, building societies, the stock exchange and insurance firms.

**3** The interest rate is determined by the demand for money and its supply. The government influences the interest rate by using methods such as open market operations and by altering the rate on last resort lending. These methods are discussed in detail in the main text, pages 818–824.

# Chapter 32  Inflation

---

## Chapter in Perspective, Text Pages 831–859

In previous chapters we have discussed equilibrium real GDP, equilibrium aggregate expenditure, the equilibrium interest rate and the equilibrium real wage rate. In this chapter we bring all of these things together to examine macroeconomic equilibrium.

We find that the nature of macroeconomic equilibrium depends critically on expectations, especially price level (or inflation) expectations. It thus becomes important to consider how expectations are formed and how expectations affect macroeconomic behaviour. The model developed in this chapter is a powerful tool in explaining the wide variety of macroeconomic events.

---

## Helpful Hints

**1** This chapter will be difficult for some students, but it is important because it finalizes the development of the complete modern macroeconomic model. The model developed here is the basic model generally used by macroeconomists as they analyse the economy. It has proved to be a powerful tool for such analysis.

**2** The fourth condition for a macroeconomic equilibrium deserves some additional comment. This condition is that the quantity of labour demanded equals the quantity of labour supplied. It is important to note, however, that this does not mean that employment is determined by the intersection of the demand for labour curve and the supply of labour curve. If this had to be the case, contrary to statements in the text, macroeconomic equilibrium would require full employment. The quantity of labour supplied should be understood to mean the quantity of labour that households want to supply, given the wages that prevail, information that they have about available jobs, and the wage and employment contracts that they have accepted. This last condition indicates that employment can be above or below full employment if wages are sticky and the price level is not correctly anticipated.

**3** Recall also that if the expected price level turns out to be correct, employment will turn out to be at the full-employment level and thus real GDP supplied will be equal to full-employment (capacity) real GDP. This is why a short-run aggregate supply curve intersects the long-run aggregate supply curve at the expected price level. If the price level is actually equal to the expected price level, the economy must be at full employment; that is, the economy must be on its long-run aggregate supply curve.

**4** Note that the rational expectation of the price level will be at the intersection of the expected aggregate demand curve and the expected long-run aggregate supply curve. (This will yield the best possible forecast, the one most likely to be correct on average.) The rational expectations equilibrium, which determines the actual price level, is at the intersection of the actual aggregate demand curve and the actual short-run aggregate supply curve.

**5** Be sure you know why each of the following is true.

– If the actual price level is greater than the expected price level, real GDP is above capacity.
– If the actual price level is less than the expected price level, real GDP is below capacity.
– If the actual price level is equal to the expected price level, real GDP is at capacity.

The wise student will understand all nine possible cases that lead to these three outcomes.

**6** An important implication of the rational expectations hypothesis is that the consequences of any macroeconomic event (such as a monetary or fiscal policy) depends on expectations. The effect on the price level and real GDP of a given increase in the money supply will be different for different price level expectations. Its effect on the position of the aggregate demand curve does not depend on the expected price level, but the position of the short-run aggregate supply curve does depend on the expected price level and thus so does the macroeconomic equilibrium. The crucial point is whether the actual level of aggregate demand is anticipated or unanticipated.

## Key Figures

**Figure 32.2 A Demand-pull Rise in the Price Level, text page 834**

In part (a), an increase in aggregate demand (caused by such factors as increased consumer or government spending) shifts the *AD* curve leading to a rise in prices. Part (b) shows that in turn this forces up wages, causing firms to supply less at each price level and shifting the *SAS* curve leftward. The result is a further increase in prices.

**Figure 32.4 A Cost-push Rise in the Price Level, text page 837**

Costs rise – perhaps from an increase in wages, or in the price of raw materials such as oil. The consequence is that the short-run aggregate supply curve moves leftward and the result is higher prices.

**Figure 32.7 Rational Expectation of the Price Level, text page 841**

The construction of a rational expectation of the price level is illustrated here. The rational expectation of the price level is the forecast obtained by the intersection of the expected aggregate demand curve and the expected long-run aggregate supply curve. The first step is to obtain forecasts of the aggregate demand and long-run aggregate supply curves. These are indicated in the figure by *EAD* and *ELAS* respectively. The rational expectation of the price level occurs at the intersection of these two curves. Since the expected price level is at this intersection, the expected short-run aggregate supply curve also intersects these curves at the same point. (This is because its position is determined by the rational expectation of the price level.)

**Figure 32.9 A Short-run Phillips Curve, text page 845**

This is a well-known diagram in economics, and worth remembering. It shows that in the short run there is a trade-off between inflation and unemployment. Figure 32.11 (text page 847) develops this by adding a long-run curve.

# SELF-TEST

## CONCEPT REVIEW

**1** Four conditions must be satisfied when the economy is in macroeconomic equilibrium.

– Real GDP demanded equals _____ _____.

– Aggregate planned expenditure equals _____ _____.

- Real money demanded equals _____ _____ _____ .

- Quantity of labour demanded equals _____ _____ _____ _____ .

**2** The short-run aggregate supply curve intersects the long-run aggregate supply curve at a price level equal to the _____ _____ _____ . If the price level is higher than expected, then real GDP is _____ than capacity output.

**3** If inflation turns out to be higher than expected, borrowers _____ and lenders _____ .

**4** A forecast that is based on all the available information, is correct on average and minimizes the range of the forecast error is called a(n) _____ expectation. The proposition that the forecasts people make are the same as the forecasts made by an economist using the relevant economic theory as well as all information available is called the _____ _____ hypothesis.

**5** The rational expectation of the price level is given by the intersection of the expected aggregate demand curve and the expected _____ - _____ _____ _____ curve.

**6** A macroeconomic equilibrium based on expectations that are the best available forecasts is called a(n) _____ _____ equilibrium.

**7** The definition of inflation is: the percentage rise in the _____ _____ from one year to another. When aggregate demand is expected to increase and it doesn't, actual inflation is _____ its expected level and actual GDP is _____ capacity output.

**8** An unanticipated increase in the money supply will cause the price level to _____ and real GDP to _____ .

**9** During periods when the rate of inflation is high, nominal interest rates tend to be _____ . If the Bank of England unexpectedly increases the money supply, the immediate effect is to _____ interest rates. If the Bank of England conducts an anticipated and continuous increase in the money supply, interest rates will _____ .

## TRUE AND FALSE

___ **1** In a macroeconomic equilibrium the economy will exhibit full employment.

___ **2** The short-run aggregate supply curve intersects the long-run aggregate supply curve at the expected price level.

___ **3** If the expected price level falls, the short-run aggregate supply curve will shift downward by the amount of the fall.

___ **4** Expectations of inflation are partially self-fulfilling.

___ **5** If people expect aggregate demand to increase but it doesn't, the price level will fall and real GDP will increase.

___ **6** A rational expectation is a forecast that is always correct.

___ **7** The rational expectations hypothesis states that people make forecasts in the same way economists do.

___ **8** In a rational expectations equilibrium the economy will exhibit full employment.

___ **9** If the price level at the beginning of 1996 is 120 and the price level at the beginning of 1997 is 130, the rate of inflation is 8.3 per cent.

___ **10** If the inflation rate rises but nominal interest rates remain unchanged, then real interest rates have fallen.

___ **11** If the inflation rate rises but real interest rates remain unchanged, then nominal interest rates have fallen.

___ **12** If an increase in the money supply is unanticipated, its immediate effect will be to raise interest rates.

## MULTIPLE CHOICE

**1** Figure 32.1 illustrates an economy initially in equilibrium at point *a*. What would cause the short-run aggregate supply curve to shift from $SAS_0$ to $SAS_1$?
   **a** an expected increase in the money supply
   **b** an increase in the price level
   **c** an increase in the marginal product of labour
   **d** an increase in the demand for money
   **e** a decrease in wages

**Figure 32.1**

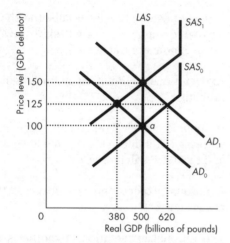

**2** Figure 32.1 illustrates an economy initially in equilibrium at point *a*. If the *AD* curve is correctly expected to shift from $AD_0$ to $AD_1$, the new macroeconomic equilibrium will be real GDP =
   **a** £380 billion and price level = 125.
   **b** £500 billion and price level = 150.
   **c** £500 billion and price level = 100.
   **d** £620 billion and price level = 125.
   **e** £500 billion and price level = 125.

**3** Figure 32.1 illustrates an economy initially in equilibrium at point *a*. If the *AD* curve is expected to shift from $AD_0$ to $AD_1$ but it actually remains at $AD_0$, the new macroeconomic equilibrium will be real GDP =
   **a** £380 billion and price level = 100.
   **b** £500 billion and price level = 150.
   **c** £500 billion and price level = 100.
   **d** £620 billion and price level = 125.
   **e** £380 billion and price level = 125.

**4** Figure 32.1 illustrates an economy initially in equilibrium at point *a*. If the *AD* curve is expected to remain at $AD_0$, but in fact, shifts to $AD_1$, the new macroeconomic equilibrium will be real GDP =
   **a** £380 billion and price level = 125.
   **b** £500 billion and price level = 150.
   **c** £500 billion and price level = 100.
   **d** £620 billion and price level = 125.
   **e** £500 billion and price level = 125.

**5** If the rate of inflation turns out to be lower than expected, borrowers
   **a** and lenders both lose.
   **b** and lenders both gain.
   **c** gain but lenders lose.
   **d** lose but lenders gain.
   **e** lose but lenders are just as well off.

**6** If the rate of inflation turns out to be lower than expected, then
   **a** expectations could not be rational expectations.
   **b** real GDP will be less than full-employment (capacity) real GDP.
   **c** the real interest rate will be lower than expected.
   **d** the real wage rate will be lower than expected.
   **e** the money wage rate will be higher than expected.

**7** A rational expectations equilibrium is the price level and real GDP given by the intersection of the
   **a** actual aggregate demand curve and the actual long-run aggregate supply curve.
   **b** actual aggregate demand curve and the expected short-run aggregate supply curve.
   **c** expected aggregate demand curve and the expected short-run aggregate supply curve.
   **d** expected aggregate demand curve and the expected long-run aggregate supply curve.
   **e** aggregate demand curve and the actual short-run aggregate supply curve.

**8** According to the rational expectations hypothesis, a correctly anticipated increase in the money supply in an economy with a given long-run aggregate supply will result in
   **a** an increase in the price level and an increase in real GDP.

**b** an increase in the price level and a decrease in real GDP.

**c** a proportional increase in the price level and no change in real GDP.

**d** no change in the price level and an increase in real GDP.

**e** no change in the price level and no change in real GDP.

**9** Suppose OPEC unexpectedly increases the price of oil. This is a negative aggregate supply shock. As a result, the price level will

**a** rise and real GDP will increase.

**b** rise and real GDP will decrease.

**c** fall and real GDP will increase.

**d** fall and real GDP will decrease.

**e** rise and real GDP will stay the same.

**10** The current year's price level is 180 and the rate of inflation over the past year has been 20 per cent. What was last year's price level?

**a** 144

**b** 150

**c** 160

**d** 216

**e** 100

**11** Which of the following would cause the aggregate demand curve to keep shifting upward year after year?

**a** a tax cut

**b** an increase in government purchases of goods and services

**c** inflation

**d** excess wage demands

**e** a positive rate of growth in the quantity of money

**12** Suppose aggregate demand increases by less than anticipated. This will result in an unanticipated

**a** rise in inflation and real GDP falls below capacity.

**b** rise in inflation and real GDP rises above capacity.

**c** fall in inflation and real GDP falls below capacity.

**d** fall in inflation and real GDP rises above capacity.

**e** fall in inflation and real GDP stays at capacity.

**13** If the actual price level is higher than the expected price level, then real GDP

**a** must be above capacity.

**b** must be below capacity.

**c** must be equal to capacity.

**d** can be above, below, or equal to capacity depending on the position of the aggregate demand curve.

**e** can be above or equal to capacity depending on the position of the aggregate demand curve.

## SHORT ANSWER

**1** What will happen to the price level and real GDP if the government increases its purchases of goods and services and that increase is not anticipated (that is, the price level is not expected to change)?

**2** What will happen to the price level and real GDP if the government increases its purchases of goods and services and that increase is anticipated?

**3** How is a rational expectation of the price level calculated?

**4** What is the relationship between the expected rate of inflation and interest rates?

**5** It is frequently argued that high wage demands by workers (based on high price expectations) cause inflation. According to the rational expectations model developed in this chapter, is this true or not? Explain briefly.

**6** Why do you think the author of the *Reading Between the Lines* article says that while inflation 'looks set to fall further for several months at least, the longer-term prospect is less rosy'?

## PROBLEMS

**1** Table 32.1 gives the initial aggregate demand and short-run aggregate supply schedules for an economy in which the expected price level is 80.

**a** What is capacity real GDP?

**b** What is actual real GDP and the actual price level?

**Table 32.1 Aggregate Demand and Supply**

| Price level (GDP deflator) | Real GDP demanded | Real GDP supplied |
|---|---|---|
| 60 | 600 | 400 |
| 80 | 500 | 500 |
| 100 | 400 | 600 |
| 120 | 300 | 700 |
| 140 | 200 | 700 |

**2** In year 1 the economy is in the macroeconomic equilibrium characterized in Problem **1**. It is expected that in year 2, aggregate demand will be as given in Table 32.2.

   **a** What is the vertical amount of the expected shift in the aggregate demand curve when real GDP is £500 billion?

**Table 32.2 Aggregate Demand and Supply**

| Price level (GDP deflator) | Real GDP demanded | Real GDP supplied |
|---|---|---|
| 60 | 800 | |
| 80 | 700 | |
| 100 | 600 | |
| 120 | 500 | |
| 140 | 400 | |

   **b** What is the rational expectation of the price level for year 2?

   **c** The expected shift in aggregate demand will cause the short-run aggregate supply *(SAS)* curve to shift. What will the new *SAS* curve be? For each price level, give the new values of real GDP supplied in the last column of Table 32.2.

   **d** Suppose that, in fact, aggregate demand does not change but remains as given in Table 32.1. What will real GDP and the price level be in year 2?

   **e** Compare the actual change in the price level with the expected change.

**3** In year 1 the economy is in the macroeconomic equilibrium characterized by Problem **1**. It is expected that in year 2, aggregate demand will be as given in Table 32.2. It turns out that expectations are correct: the actual aggregate demand in year 2 is as given in Table 32.2.

   **a** What is the rational expectation of the price level for year 2?

   **b** What will real GDP and the price level turn out to be in year 2?

   **c** Compare the actual change in the price level with the expected change.

**4** Graphically illustrate the rational expectations equilibrium in an economy for which aggregate demand is higher than expected. Compare the actual equilibrium with the expected equilibrium.

**5** Graphically illustrate the rational expectations equilibrium in an economy for which aggregate demand is higher than expected and long-run aggregate supply is lower than expected. Compare the actual equilibrium .with the expected equilibrium.

## DISCUSSION QUESTION

**1** Why does an increase in the monetary growth rate sometimes lower the rate of interest and sometimes raise it?

## DATA QUESTIONS

**Shooting at Inflation**

Economic pundits talk about 'slaying' inflation as if inflation fighting were like elephant hunting: first find your elephant, then fire. This is how policy makers tend to behave; they shoot only when they see inflation rising. But by then it is almost always too late, because monetary policy takes up to two years to take effect. Indeed, central bankers need to squeeze the interest rate trigger well before inflation rises. That requires skill, luck and a tough political hide; for if they succeed in killing inflation before everyone can see that it is an obvious threat, they will get little credit for it. Indeed, they will often be accused of holding back a growing economy.

*Source:* Copyright © *The Economist*, London, 15 June 1996, p. 18.

**1** Why does monetary policy take up to two years to have its effect?

**2** How does 'squeezing the interest rate trigger' bring down inflation?

# ANSWERS

## CONCEPT REVIEW

**1** real GDP supplied; real GDP; real money supplied; quantity of labour supplied

**2** expected price level; greater

**3** gain; lose

**4** rational; rational expectations

**5** long-run aggregate supply

**6** rational expectations

**7** price level; below; below

**8** increase; increase

**9** high; lower; rise

## TRUE OR FALSE

**1** F Equilibrium can be at, below or above the full-employment level.

**2** T When expectations are correct, actual real GDP = natural rate.

**3** T Changes in expected prices cause changes in supply.

**4** T If people expect higher inflation, firms will put up prices and workers will seek higher wages.

**5** F See Helpful Hint 5.

**6** F Rational expectations are correct *on average*.

**7** F Make forecasts in a different way.

**8** F Equilibrium may not be at full-employment level – depends on expectations.

**9** T Inflation rate = $[(P_1 - P_0)/P_0] \times 100 = [(130 - 120)/120] \times 100 = 8.3$.

**10** T Actual real interest rate = Nominal interest rate – Inflation rate.

**11** F Nominal rates would have to rise to keep real rate the same.

**12** F Immediate effect is rise in real money supply leading to fall in nominal interest rates.

## MULTIPLE CHOICE

**1** a A rise in the price of a crucial input would lead to leftward shift in *SAS* curve.

**2** b Expected $P$ found from intersection of $EAD = AD_1$, and actual *SAS* is set here leading to new equilibrium where actual *AD* and *SAS* curves cross.

**3** e Expected $P$ found from intersection of $EAD = AD_1$ and actual *SAS* is set here leading to equilibrium where actual *AD* and *SAS* curves cross.

**4** d Expected $P$ found from intersection of $EAD = AD_1$ and actual *SAS* is set here, so new equilibrium where actual *AS* and *SAS* curves cross.

**5** d Borrowers will lose because they will have expected to pay back less.

**6** b Economy will be in equilibrium at less than full-employment level.

**7** e Definition.

**8** c Increase in money supply leads to rise in aggregate demand. Since this is anticipated it causes leftward shift in *SAS* curve of equivalent amount so rise in price level and no change in real GDP.

**9** b *SAS* curve will shift leftward.

**10** b Invert formula. Inflation rate = $[(P_1 - P_0)/P_0] \times 100$.

**11** e Others would have only a one-off effect.

**12** c Because actual price level = expected when *SAS* curve crosses *LAS* curve, and equilibrium occurs when $AS = SAS$ – try drawing a graph.

**13** a Because actual price level = expected when *SAS* curve crosses *LAS* curve, and equilibrium occurs when $LAS = AD$.

## SHORT ANSWER

**1** An increase in government purchases of goods and services will shift the aggregate demand curve to the right. If the price level is not expected to change, the short-run aggregate supply curve remains unchanged and the increase in aggregate demand will cause the price level to rise and real GDP to increase.

**2** If the shift in the aggregate demand curve is anticipated, the expected price level will rise by the amount of the vertical shift in the aggregate demand curve and thus the short-run aggregate supply curve will shift up by that amount. So when an increase in aggregate demand is fully anticipated, the aggregate demand curve and the short-run aggregate supply curve will shift upward by the same amount. As a result, the price level will rise and real GDP will remain unchanged.

**3** A rational expectation of the price level is obtained by using the aggregate demand–aggregate supply model to predict the price level. The actual price level will be given by the intersection of the aggregate demand curve and the short-run aggregate supply curve. Therefore we want to determine where we expect these curves to be and then see where they intersect. The problem is that the short-run aggregate supply curve depends on the expected price level and that is what we are trying to find. We resolve this problem by recognizing that if the price level turns out to be equal to the expected price level, the short-run aggregate supply curve intersects the aggregate demand curve at the point where the latter curve intersects the long-run aggregate supply curve. Since the long-run aggregate supply curve does not depend on the expected price level, the rational expectation of the price level is obtained at the intersection of the aggregate demand curve and the long-run aggregate supply curve.

**4** When the rate of inflation is expected to rise, the interest rate will also rise to compensate for the increased rate at which the purchasing power of money is eroding. The essential point is that lenders and borrowers are interested in the quantity of goods and services that a unit of money will buy. Lenders will insist on the higher interest rate (to compensate for the loss of purchasing power of money) and borrowers will be willing to pay it because they realize that the pounds they pay back will buy fewer goods and services.

**5** In the short run, a rise in wages will shift the short-run aggregate supply curve to the left, raising the price level. However, a continuing rise in the price level (that is, an inflation), requires a continuing rise in both the *AD* and the *SAS* curves. This therefore requires a positive growth rate of the money supply to sustain or validate the inflation.

**6** The author thinks that short-run inflation will continue to fall because labour costs 'are subdued'. Also commodity prices have fallen. However, in the longer run the economy is picking up speed, largely because of a rise in consumer spending and because inflation in services has accelerated.

# PROBLEMS

**1 a** Capacity real GDP is the quantity of real GDP supplied when the expected price level is equal to the actual price level. The last column of Table 32.1 gives the quantity of real GDP supplied at various price levels assuming that the expected price level is constant at 80. When the actual price level is also 80 the quantity of real GDP supplied is £500 billion, so that is the value of capacity real GDP.

**b** Actual real GDP and the actual price level are determined by the intersection of the aggregate demand curve and the short-run aggregate supply curve. Real GDP is £500 billion and the price level is 80, since at a price level of 80, the quantity of real GDP demanded equals the quantity of real GDP supplied (£500 billion).

**2 a** The price level associated with £500 billion of real GDP demanded for the original aggregate curve (Table 32.1) is 80. The price level associated with £500 billion of real GDP demanded for the new expected aggregate demand curve (Table 32.2) is 120. Therefore the aggregate demand curve is expected to shift upward by 40.

**b** The rational expectation of the price level is given by the intersection of the expected aggregate demand curve (Table 32.2) and the expected long-run aggregate supply curve. Long-run aggregate supply is equal to £500 billion and is not expected to change. Since the price level associated with £500 billion of real GDP demanded is 120, the rational expectation of the price level is 120.

**c** The quantities of real GDP supplied for the new *SAS* curve are given in Table 32.3. The original expected price level is 80. From **b** we know that the new expected price level is 120, which implies that the *SAS* curve shifts upward by 40. Thus at each quantity of real GDP supplied, the price level on the new *SAS* curve is 40 points higher than on the original *SAS* curve (Table 32.1). For example, real GDP supplied of £500 billion now requires a price level of 120 rather than 80. Similarly, real GDP supplied of £400 billion now requires a price level of 100 rather than 60. (Note that the values in parentheses in the table are inferred by extrapolation rather than calculated from Table 32.1.)

**Table 32.3 Aggregate Demand and Supply**

| Price level (GDP deflator) | Real GDP demanded | Real GDP supplied |
|---|---|---|
| 60 | 800 | (200) |
| 80 | 700 | (300) |
| 100 | 600 | 400 |
| 120 | 500 | 500 |
| 140 | 400 | 600 |

**d** The new macroeconomic equilibrium in year 2 will occur at the intersection of the actual *AD* curve and the relevant *SAS* curve. Since the *AD* curve was expected to shift, the relevant *SAS* curve is the one associated with the expected price level of 120 (the *SAS* curve is completed Table 30.3). But the *AD* curve did not actually shift, so the *AD* curve is given in Table 32.1. The intersection of these curves is at real GDP equals $400 billion and price level equals 100 (that is, when the price level is 100, the quantity of real GDP demanded is equal to the quantity of real GDP supplied at $400 billion).

  **e** The price level was expected to rise from 80 to 120, but in fact it only rises from 80 to 100.

**3 a** Since aggregate demand is expected to increase, the rational expectation of the price level for year 2 is the same as in Problem **2** above: 120.

  **b** The rational expectations equilibrium will occur at the intersection of the actual *AD* curve and the relevant *SAS* curve. Since the expected price level is 120, the relevant *SAS* curve is the one given in completed Table 30.3. The actual *AD* curve is also given in Table 32.2. Thus real GDP will be $500 billion and the price level will be 120.

  **c** The price level was expected to rise from 80 to 120, which is exactly what happens.

**4** Figure 32.2 illustrates the rational expectations equilibrium. The expected aggregate demand curve is given by *EAD* which intersects the expected long-run aggregate supply curve, *ELAS*, at point *a*. Thus the rational expectation of the price level is $P_0$, which implies that the relevant short-run aggregate supply curve is *ESAS*. The actual aggregate demand curve, *AD*, is higher than expected and the actual short-run aggregate supply curve is the same as *ESAS*. The rational expectations equilibrium occurs at point *b*, the intersection of *AD* and *ESAS*. The equilibrium price level, $P_1$, is higher than expected and thus real GDP is above capacity (that is, above $Y_0$).

**5** Figure 32.3 illustrates the rational expectations equilibrium in this case. The expected aggregate demand curve, *EAD*, intersects the expected long-run aggregate supply curve, *ELAS*, at point *a*. Thus the rational expectation of the price level is $P_0$, which implies that the expected short-run aggregate supply curve is *ESAS*. The actual aggregate demand curve, *AD*, is higher than expected. Also, the actual long-run aggregate supply curve, *LAS*, is lower than expected, which means that the actual short-run aggregate supply curve corresponding to an expected price level of $P_0$ is given by *SAS*. The rational expectations equilibrium occurs at point *b*, the intersection of the *AD* and *SAS* curves. The equilibrium price level is $P_1$, which is much higher than expected. Real GDP can be above, below, or at the expected

capacity real GDP, $Y_0$, depending on the relative magnitudes of the unanticipated shifts (Fig. 32.3 shows real GDP above expected capacity GDP), but real GDP will be above the new actual capacity real GDP, $Y_1$.

**Figure 32.2**

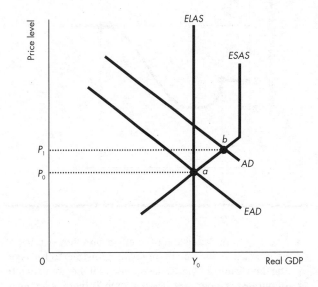

**Figure 32.3**

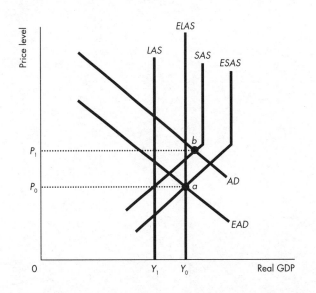

# DISCUSSION QUESTION

**Figure 32.4**

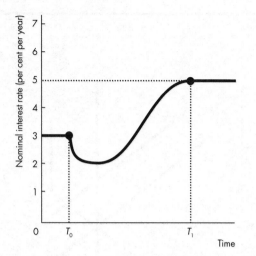

1 The key to understanding the effect on interest rates of an increase in the rate of monetary growth is to focus on the time frame. In Fig. 32.4, suppose that the nominal rate of interest is 3 per cent. Then at time $T_0$ there is an unanticipated increase in the money supply which leads to an unexpectedly high level of the real money supply. As we saw in Chapter 31, this will lead to a fall in the interest rate. In Fig. 32.4 this is shown as a fall to 2 per cent.

However, in the long run this will lead to a rise in investment demand and inflation so that at time $T_1$ people raise their forecasts of inflation and this raises the nominal interest rate to 5 per cent.

Hence assuming that the economy is running at the full employment level, an increase in the money supply will lower and then increase the rate of interest.

# DATA QUESTIONS

1 Monetary policy takes a long time to have an effect because there are so many agents involved and the interactions among them are often slow. For example, if the government decided to fight inflation by putting up interest rates, it would be some time before people's expectations about inflation changed. Also, the labour market is often slow to react to changes in policy since it is not particularly flexible.

2 Figure 32.14, main text (p. 850), shows the relationship between money growth, inflation and the interest rate. Essentially, monetary policy works in the short term through its effects on demand and supply, causing an economic slowdown. For example, a rise in interest rates would reduce aggregate demand and so lead to a fall in prices. In the long run, monetarists would argue that there would be little or no effect on the real economy, since this is determined by real factors such as the size of the work-force and its productivity.

# Chapter 33  The Business Cycle

---

## Chapter in Perspective, Text Pages 860–889

If economic growth was constant, with, for example, GDP rising by 3 per cent every year, then economic life would be much simpler. Unfortunately, it is characterized by boom and recession. This chapter explores several theories of the business cycle and then uses these theories to analyse recent economic history.

---

## Helpful Hints

1  This chapter should be rewarding for those who have expended the effort required to understand the preceding six chapters because it introduces no new analytic methods. Instead, the fully developed aggregate demand and aggregate supply model is applied to the analysis of some interesting macroeconomic episodes, including the Great Depression.

2  As you examine various macroeconomic episodes, focus on a key question: are the primary changes in aggregate demand, in aggregate supply, or possibly in both? Also, as you follow the various changes, be sure that you understand what is going on in the labour market that underlies the goods and services market. The labour market will tell you what is happening to two key variables: employment and unemployment.

3  Two competing theories (flexible wages and sticky wages) are used to explain real-world labour market events. Facts, such as the level of wages or employment, are not in dispute. The dispute centres on the changes in the economy that caused the facts. It also touches on the government policies that might affect the economy.

Remember, these are theories, not statements of fact, and their explanations could be incorrect. Only proper empirical investigation over time will determine their validity.

4  The real business cycle theory is closely linked to the flexible wage theory of the labour market. In particular, the real business cycle theory is based on the assumption that the economy is always producing on its long-run aggregate supply curve; that is, the economy is always at potential GDP. Because potential GDP is also the full-employment level of GDP, the real business cycle theory asserts that, in the labour market, wages (or other mechanisms) are sufficiently flexible so that the economy is always at full employment. Thus the real business cycle/flexible wage theory view is that fluctuations in employment represent fluctuations in the level of full employment. The level of full employment changes when labour demand and/or labour supply changes. For instance, a decrease in labour demand decreases the level of full-employment equilibrium and actual employment in the economy decreases.

As the text indicates, the real business cycle theory of the economy is highly controversial. The assumptions underlying this approach seem extreme to many economists. In particular, the views that money wages are so flexible that the economy is always at full employment, that the impulse creating business cycles is fluctuations in technology, and that changes in the money supply do not affect real GDP are rejected by the majority of economists. Nonetheless, real business cycle theory has had a surprising amount of success in explaining various facts about business cycles, and a sizeable minority of economists believe that the real business cycle theory is a good way to analyse the business cycle. Which group of economists is correct? At this time, it is impossible to tell because the evidence on the real business cycle theory is still accumulating.

But if this approach ultimately is accepted, it will represent a major change from the more conventional aggregate demand theories.

## Key Figures

**Figure 33.2 A Keynesian Recession, text page 865**
In this view of the economy, recession is caused by a fall in some component of aggregate demand. The result is a fall in GDP. Figure 33.3 shows Keynesian expansion caused by a rise in aggregate demand.

**Figure 33.4 A Monetarist Business Cycle, text page 867**
In this two-part diagram the key feature is a change in the rate of monetary growth which shifts the *SAS* curve.

# SELF-TEST

## CONCEPT REVIEW

**1** Three types of aggregate demand theories are discussed. They are _____ theory, _____ theory and _____ expectations theory.

**2** _____ theory says the business cycle is caused by volatile _____ , a multiplier effect and _____ wages.

**3** Monetarist theory explains the theory in terms of changes in the growth rate of _____ .

**4** Rational expectations theories say the cycle is caused by _____ fluctuations in aggregate _____ .

**5** The _____ business cycle theory says economic fluctuations are caused by _____ change that makes productivity growth fluctuate.

**6** A 1930s style of depression is unlikely today because of factors such as _____ deposit protection, the Bank of England's role as _____ of last resort and the greater importance of _____ and spending in the economy.

## TRUE AND FALSE

__ **1** One reason that a recession is likely to be much less severe than during the 1930s is because the government sector is much larger now than it was then.

__ **2** The stock market crash of 1929 was the most important cause of the Great Depression.

__ **3** The real business cycle theory is based on the assumption that money wages are flexible and adjust quickly.

__ **4** The data show that recessions start when investment slows or decreases.

__ **5** The new Keynesian theory of the business cycle stresses intertemporal substitution.

__ **6** The impulse in the Keynesian theory of business cycles is a change in firms' expectations of future sales and profits.

__ **7** Keynesian, monetarist and rational expectations theories of business cycles focus on fluctuations in aggregate demand as the cause of business cycles.

___ **8** According to the real business cycle theory, a drop in productivity increases the demand for labour.

___ **9** The primary cause of the recession in 1973–75 was the large increase in oil prices.

___ **10** In the Keynesian theory, money wages do not fall in response to a decrease in aggregate demand.

## MULTIPLE CHOICE

**1** Monetarists and Keynesians assert that the Great Depression reflected a _____ shift of the aggregate _____ curve.
**a** leftward; supply
**b** rightward; supply
**c** rightward; demand
**d** leftward; demand

**2** According to monetarists such as Milton Friedman, the Great Depression was caused by
**a** the stock market crash of 1929.
**b** a massive contraction of the money supply, leading to large decreases in aggregate demand.
**c** an expansion of the money supply, leading to higher inflation.
**d** loss of business and consumer confidence.

**3** Which of the following is the impulse in the Keynesian business cycle theory?
**a** an unexpected change in aggregate demand
**b** a change in the growth rate of the money supply
**c** a change in expectations about future sales and profits
**d** a change in the growth rate of productivity

**4** Which of the following is the impulse in the monetarist business cycle theory?
**a** an unexpected change in aggregate demand
**b** a change in the growth rate of the money supply
**c** a change in expectations about future sales and profits
**d** a change in the growth rate of productivity

**5** Which of the following is the impulse in the rational expectations business cycle theories?
**a** an unexpected change in aggregate demand
**b** a change in the growth rate of the money supply
**c** a change in expectations about future sales and profits
**d** a change in the growth rate of productivity

**6** Which of the following is the impulse in the real business cycle theory?
**a** an unexpected change in aggregate demand
**b** a change in the growth rate of the money supply
**c** a change in expectations about future sales and profits
**d** a change in the growth rate of productivity

**7** An increase in aggregate demand increases GDP by the least amount in the _____ .
**a** Keynesian theory
**b** monetarist theory
**c** new Keynesian theory
**d** real business cycle theory

**8** Multi-income families reduce the probability of another Great Depression by
**a** reducing the probability of everyone in the family being simultaneously unemployed.
**b** investing more in the economy.
**c** paying more taxes.
**d** increasing fluctuations in consumption.

**9** The intertemporal substitution effect refers to the idea that
**a** a higher real wage rate increases the quantity of labour supplied.
**b** a higher real wage rate decreases the quantity of labour supplied.
**c** a higher real interest rate increases the supply of labour.
**d** the demand for labour depends on the money wage rate, not the real wage rate.

**10** According to the _____ theory of business cycles, a change in the monetary growth rate has no effect on real GDP.
**a** Keynesian
**b** monetarist
**c** new Keynesian
**d** real business cycle

**11** An average recession lasts for about _____ ; an average expansion lasts for about _____ .
  **a** 1 year; 1 year
  **b** 4 years; 1 year
  **c** 1 year; 4 years
  **d** 4 years; 4 years

**12** In an average recession, real GDP falls by about _____ ; in an average expansion real GDP climbs by about _____ .
  **a** 6 per cent; 6 per cent
  **b** 22 per cent; 6 per cent
  **c** 6 per cent; 22 per cent
  **d** 22 per cent; 22 per cent

**13** Which theory of the business cycle has a mechanism that allows the economy to remain in a recession indefinitely?
  **a** Keynesian
  **b** monetarist
  **c** new classical
  **d** new Keynesian

**14** The sticky wage explanation of the labour market in the 1973–75 recession explains the drop in employment as the result of a decrease in
  **a** labour supply only.
  **b** labour demand only.
  **c** both labour demand and labour supply.
  **d** neither labour demand nor labour supply.

**15** The flexible wage theory of the labour market explains the decrease in employment during the 1973–75 recession as the result of a decrease in
  **a** labour supply only.
  **b** labour demand only.
  **c** both labour demand and labour supply.
  **d** neither labour demand nor labour supply.

**16** Which of the following is *not* a criticism of the real business cycle theory?
  **a** The impulse assumed for the real business cycle theory is implausible.
  **b** The long-run aggregate supply curve is vertical.
  **c** Money wages are sticky.
  **d** The changes in productivity ascribed to technological advances actually are caused by changes in aggregate demand.

## SHORT ANSWER

**1** What caused the recession that became the Great Depression? What changed the recession into the Great Depression?

**2** What is the basic controversy among economists about the behaviour of the labour market during a recession? What is each theory's position in this controversy? Why is the controversy important in terms of designing an appropriate anti-recessionary economic policy?

**3** How do government transfer payments help reduce the severity of a recession caused by an unexpected decrease in aggregate demand?

**4** List four important features of the economy that make severe depression less likely today. Explain how each factor helps stabilize the economy.

**5** The *Reading Between the Lines* article suggests that German forecasters have been unable to forecast a downturn. Why do you think that forecasters cannot always forecast the future successfully?

## PROBLEMS

**Figure 33.1**

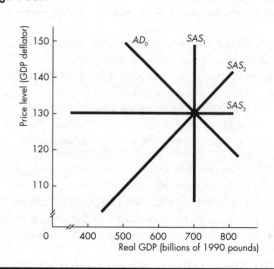

**1** Figure 33.1 shows the initial aggregate demand curve, $AD_0$, and three aggregate supply curves.

   **a** Which aggregate supply curve is consistent with Keynesian theory?

   **b** Which aggregate supply curve is consistent with monetarist theory?

   **c** Which aggregate supply curve is consistent with real business cycle theory?

**2** Suppose that the aggregate demand curve in Fig. 33.1 shifts leftward by £200 billion at every price level.

   **a** Draw this shift in Fig. 33.1.

   **b** Along which aggregate supply curve is the decrease in GDP the largest? The least?

   **c** Relate your answers to **b** to your answers to Problem 1. In particular, for a shift in aggregate demand, which theory predicts the largest decrease in GDP? The smallest decrease in GDP? The largest change in the price level? The smallest?

**3** Complete Table 33.1 by listing the impulse that each theory stresses as the primary cause of business cycles.

### Table 33.1 Theories and Impulses

| Theory | Impulse |
| --- | --- |
| Keynesian | |
| Monetarist | |
| New classical | |
| New Keynesian | |
| Real business cycle | |

## DISCUSSION QUESTION

**1** Why are the cause(s) of business cycles not fully understood?

## DATA QUESTIONS

### The Trade Cycle

The United Kingdom, along with other industrialized countries, has suffered from regular fluctuations in the level of economic activity at least since the nineteenth century.

The most recent recession, that of 1990–92, was longer than the 1980–82 recession. The economy suffered eight quarters of negative year-on-year growth (10 if the two quarters of zero change in GDP are included). In the 1980–82 recession, the level of real GDP reached in the second quarter of 1979 was not reached again till the second quarter of 1983, four years later. In the 1990–92 recession, real GDP peaked in the second quarter of 1990.

The length of the recession has in part contributed to the lower level of inflation at the start of the recovery phase compared with the 1980–82 recession. However, unemployment began to fall in 1993. This makes unemployment almost a coincident indicator in the trade cycle rather than a lagged indicator.

*Source*: Adapted from A. Anderton, *The Student's Economy in Focus 1993/4*, Causeway Press, 1993, p. 54.

**1** Why do some recessions last longer than others?

**2** Explain why unemployment is normally a lagged indicator of the trade cycle.

# ANSWERS

## CONCEPT REVIEW

**1** Keynesian; monetarist; rational

**2** Keynesian; expectations; sticky

**3** money

**4** unanticipated; demand

**5** real; technological

**6** bank; lender; taxes

## TRUE OR FALSE

**1 T** The government sector tends to stabilize the economy because government purchases do not decline in a recession.

**2 F** The stock market crash may have increased uncertainty and helped spur the initial recession in 1929, but it was not the cause of the Great Depression.

**3 T** With rapidly and efficiently adjusting money wages, the real business cycle theory asserts that the economy is always at full employment.

**4 T** Recessions start when investment slows and expansions begin when investment accelerates.

**5 F** The real business cycle theory stresses intertemporal substitution.

**6 T** Because these expectations can change so rapidly, Keynes called them 'animal spirits'.

**7 T** The sole exception to the focus on aggregate demand is the real business cycle theory, which focuses on fluctuations in aggregate supply.

**8 F** A decline in productivity *decreases* the demand for labour.

**9 T** The huge increase in oil prices delivered a severe shock to the country's aggregate supply and helped create a recession.

**10 T** Because money wages do not fall, the economy remains stuck in a recession until aggregate demand increases.

## MULTIPLE CHOICE

**1 d** Although monetarists and Keynesians disagree about what shifted the aggregate demand curve, both agree that the Great Depression reflected massive leftward shifts in the aggregate demand curve.

**2 b** Monetarists point to the Great Depression as evidence that changes in monetary growth are a major impulse in creating business cycles.

**3 c** The Keynesian theory emphasizes the 'animal spirits' of future sales and profit expectations.

**4 b** Monetarists assert that the major impulse in creating business cycles is changes in the growth rate of the money supply.

**5 a** Rational expectations theories point to unexpected changes in aggregate demand as the impulse that causes business cycles.

**6 d** The real business cycle theory suggests that the impulse that creates business cycles is changes in the growth rate of productivity.

**7 d** In the real business cycle theory, changes in aggregate demand have *no* effect on real GDP; instead, they affect only the price level.

**8 a** Because everyone in the family is not likely to be unemployed simultaneously, the family's income is much less likely to fall to zero. As a result, the family's consumption expenditures are more stable.

**9 c** Basically, the higher real interest rate boosts the return from saving, so in order to earn more and thus save more, people increase their supply of labour when the real interest rate rises.

**10 d** Real business cycle theory asserts that only real factors – not monetary factors – can affect real GDP.

**11 c** Recessions are shorter than expansions.

**12 c** Generally, after each recession GDP climbs during the next expansion to new heights.

**13 a** Because money wages are assumed not to respond to decreases in aggregate demand, after a decrease in aggregate demand the economy remains mired in a recession until some other factor causes an increase in aggregate demand.

**14 b** Because the oil price hike lowered labour productivity, the demand for labour decreased, which decreased employment.

**15 c** The demand for labour decreased for the same reason as in 14. In addition, the lower real interest decreased the supply of labour as people substituted away from working in 1973–75 and towards working in other periods when the real interest rate would be higher.

**16 b** The long-run aggregate supply *is* vertical because it reflects potential real GDP.

## SHORT ANSWER

**1** The major cause of the Great Depression was an unanticipated decrease in aggregate demand, which was the consequence of reduced investment and consumer expenditure (especially on durable goods), owing to uncertainty and pessimism. However, these changes created only a 'typical' recession, not the Great Depression. The reason(s) given for the recession's worsening are controversial. Some economists contend that further decreases in aggregate demand caused by uncertainty led to the Great Depression. Other economists assert that governments failed to act in a timely and proper manner. In particular, these economists point to the massive contraction in the money supply and the waves of bank failures in many countries as the factors that converted a recession into the Great Depression.

**2** Economists disagree about the speed with which the money (and hence also the real) wage rate adjusts in the labour market.

Some economists (Keynesians and new Keynesians) believe that money wages are sticky and adjust only slowly to price level changes; indeed, Keynesian economists think that money wages do not adjust to decreases in aggregate demand. Monetarists also think that money wages are sticky but not as sticky as Keynesian and new Keynesian economists think. In particular, money wages will adjust to changes in the price level, but not immediately, in the monetarist view. New classical economists also may acknowledge some stickiness in money wages but less so than monetarists do. However, real business cycle economists think that the money wage is flexible and quickly adjusts to changes in the price level. As a result, the labour market always is in equilibrium and any changes in employment reflect changes in full employment.

This issue has a significant implication for the design of an appropriate policy to respond to recession. If the Keynesians and new Keynesians are correct, expansionary monetary or fiscal policies may be useful in counteracting recession because the recessionary decrease in employment is a sign that money wages are failing to adjust rapidly. However, if the real business cycle position is correct (the economy is always at full employment, so the decline in employment during the recession is a sign that the level of full employment has fallen), expansionary monetary or fiscal policy will simply increase the rate of inflation and have no effect on real GDP or unemployment.

**3** When a recession arises, unemployment increases and disposable income declines. Less disposable income leads to a reduction in consumption expenditure, which has a further multiplier effect (negatively) on aggregate demand. Transfer payments reduce the secondary effects of a recession by reducing the amount by which disposable income falls. As incomes fall and unemployment increases, government transfer payments increase in the form of higher unemployment benefits or other welfare payments. As a result, the decline in both disposable income and consumption is reduced.

**4** The four important features of the economy that make severe depression less likely today are that:

1 bank deposits are insured;
2 national banks are better prepared to be the 'lender of last resort';
3 taxes and government spending are a larger fraction of GDP; and
4 multi-income families are more economically secure.

Reasons (1) and (2) make a collapse of the money supply and the banking system much less likely today. With deposit insurance, bank failures do not feed on each other; that is, if a bank fails today, its depositors are not afraid that they will lose all the deposits that have been entrusted to the bank. Hence bank failures do not feed on each other. The fact that national central banks are more determined to play an active 'lender of last resort' role means that, when banks need emergency funds, the central bank will loan them the funds rather than allow the banks to fail. Hence, for both reasons, a massive wave of bank failures and contraction of the money supply, as occurred during the Great Depression, is unlikely.

The larger size of the government sector helps stabilize aggregate demand. Government purchases do not (automatically) decline during recessions, so aggregate demand may decrease less. In addition, as incomes fall during a recession, so too do income taxes, which helps moderate the drop in disposable incomes and thus stabilizes consumption expenditures.

Finally, the increased number of multi-income families also helps stabilize the economy. In a multi-income family, when one worker becomes unemployed during a recession, the family still has income from its other wage earner(s). Thus this family's consumption expenditures do not decrease as much during a recession and overall consumption expenditure – and hence aggregate demand – becomes more stable.

**5** Economic forecasting is difficult for several reasons. First, the real world is extremely complex, and the future depends on the actions of millions of agents, some of whom will act differently tomorrow than they did today. Another reason is that forecasts depend on theories, and as we have seen, there is often disagreement among theories.

## PROBLEMS

**1** **a** Aggregate supply curve $SAS_3$ is consistent with the Keynesian view of a horizontal aggregate supply curve.

   **b** Aggregate supply curve $SAS_2$ is a monetarist, upward-sloping aggregate supply curve.

   **c** Real business cycle theory asserts that the economy is always on its vertical long-run aggregate supply, so the real business cycle aggregate supply curve is $SAS_1$.

**2** **a** Figure 33.2 shows the £2 billion decrease in aggregate demand.

   **b** Along aggregate supply $SAS_3$ the new equilibrium is at point $a$. The price level has stayed constant (at 130), but GDP has declined by £200 billion. The smallest change in GDP occurs with aggregate supply curve $SAS_1$. Along this aggregate supply curve, the new equilibrium is at point $c$, so the price level falls the most (from 130 to 110) but GDP does not change; it remains at £700 billion.

**Figure 33.2**

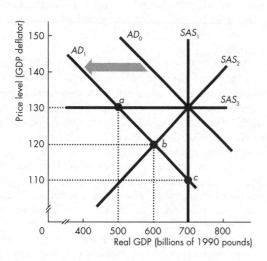

c Figure 33.2 shows that for a change in aggregate demand, the Keynesian theory (with its new equilibrium at point *a*) predicts the largest change in GDP and the smallest change in the price level. The real business cycle theory (with its new equilibrium at point *c*) predicts the largest change in the price level and the smallest change in GDP. Lastly, the monetarist theory (with its new equilibrium at point *b*) is midway between the two extremes.

**Table 33.2 Theories and Impulses**

| Theory | Impulse |
|---|---|
| Keynesian | Changes in expectations about future sales and profits |
| Monetarist | Changes in the monetary growth rate |
| New classical | Unexpected changes in aggregate demand |
| New Keynesian | Changes in aggregate demand that were unexpected when labour contracts were signed |
| Real business cycle | Changes in productivity growth |

3 Table 33.2 shows the impulse that each theory stresses as the primary cause of business cycles. You may find this table a helpful summary of the different theories.

## DISCUSSION QUESTION

1 The real world is incredibly complex. For example, economists would like to know how much a change in the money supply affects real GDP. Think of all the different possibilities. Keynesians and monetarists say that changes in the money supply can have large effects. Rational expectations economists think that only unexpected changes can affect real GDP. The real business cycle theory says that changes in the money supply have no effect.

But think about what we'd have to do to determine which answer is correct. Basically, we'd have to change the money supply and nothing else. That is, government spending couldn't change, the price of oil couldn't change, technology couldn't change – nothing could change. If any of these other things changed, real GDP might change because of that factor, not because of the change in the money supply. If we could conduct this type of 'controlled' experiment, we could figure out exactly how the change in the money supply affected real GDP.

However, this kind of experiment is not possible. So economists have to try to disentangle all the different factors that affect real GDP and unemployment. All these things – taxes, government spending, technology, oil prices, interest rates and the money supply – change every day, and each may have an impact on GDP. Isolating the effect of any one of them is nearly impossible.

## DATA QUESTIONS

1 Some recessions last longer than others because the factors that influence the business cycle are stronger than in other recessions. For example, for Keynesian economists, a recession would last longer if the fall in aggregate demand was severe or was prolonged, perhaps because business pessimism was prolonged. Table 33.2 lists the impulses that have been identified by various theorists; an increase in the severity of any of these impulses would be listed as a cause of prolonging a recession by supporters of a particular theory.

2 Unemployment is normally a lagged indicator because it follows a change in GDP, but in the opposite direction. Thus it usually rises following a fall in GDP. As recovery occurs and GDP rises, then unemployment falls after the rise in GDP.

# Chapter 34 | Macroeconomic Policy Challenges

---

## Chapter in Perspective, Text Pages 890–915

This chapter begins by discussing the *objectives* of economic policy – what the government should try to achieve. It then looks at the policies that can be adopted to achieve these goals, and in particular it distinguishes between fixed and feedback rules.

---

## Helpful Hints

**1** As in Chapter 33, only a few new concepts are introduced, and the aggregate demand–aggregate supply model developed in many of the preceding chapters is used to analyse the effects of policy. This use represents a payoff for all the effort required to master that model!

This chapter asks the most important macroeconomic policy question: can the government and the Bank of England carry out successful policies to make individuals' lives better?

The answer to this question makes a great deal of difference to the quality of everyone's life. For instance, if activist policies can be used to avoid business cycles, no college student needs to fear graduating just when a recession hits. However, if activist policies actually worsen the severity of recessions, their use may condemn many students to search for work in the face of a severe recession. So the answer to the question of whether the government can carry out policies to improve our lives is tremendously important – and is currently unknown!

**2** Numerous complications arise in real-world use of the aggregate demand–aggregate supply model to make policy decisions. In previous chapters the problems were simplified to maximize learning. Now a more realistic perspective of problems that confront a policy maker is given.

The macroeconomic model that we are using is a good indicator of the *qualitative* effects of changes in factors that affect aggregate demand and aggregate supply. For example, we know that an increase in the money supply shifts the aggregate demand curve rightward. However, in the development and implementation of policy, qualitative knowledge is not sufficient. Policy makers must also have quantitative knowledge. They must know how much an increase in the money supply will increase aggregate demand.

Although economists understand the direction of the effect, knowledge of the magnitude of the effect is much more limited and difficult to obtain. This lack of knowledge reduces the potential for policy to be used to 'fine tune' the economy.

In addition to direction and magnitude, policy makers must also know when to implement a policy. The full effect on aggregate demand of policy changes made today is not immediate. Much, if not most, of that effect occurs only with considerable time lags. Thus policy makers must be able to predict these time lags to ensure that the future effect of a policy change will be appropriate when the effect actually occurs.

Unfortunately, this is extremely difficult. These lags often are long and variable, making them difficult to predict. As a result, policy makers may initiate a policy today that sometime in the future actually shifts aggregate demand in the 'wrong' direction because circumstances have changed. In that case, the policy will be destabilizing and therefore worse than doing nothing.

**3** This chapter presents two opposing views of the usefulness of countercyclical policy. Apart from the 'practical' problems discussed so clearly in the text, these differing views come partially from differing assumptions about one crucial factor: the speed with which the private sector reacts to macroeconomic shocks relative to the speed with which government reacts.

The advocates of fixed rules (real business cycle theorists, monetarists and flexible wage theorists) believe that the private sector generally reacts quickly – people have rational expectations and process new information quickly because there are economic incentives to do so, such as signing flexible wage contracts that allow wages to react quickly to changes in the price level. These advocates also believe that government reacts slowly because of lags in recognizing problems, developing policy and implementing policy. Fixed-rule advocates therefore logically arrive at the conclusion that feedback rules at best make no difference and at worst can actually harm the economy.

The advocates of flexible rules (Keynesians and sticky wage theorists) believe that the private sector reacts slowly – people sign long-term contracts that prevent wages from reacting quickly to changes in the price level. They also believe that the government can react more quickly than the private sector and therefore arrive logically at the conclusion that feedback rules can make the economy better off by speeding recovery from a recession.

## Key Figure

**Figure 34.6  Two Stabilization Policies: Aggregate Demand Shock, text page 902**
This compares the results of fixed and feedback rules when faced by a fall in aggregate demand. Parts (a) and (b) show the results of a fixed rule policy, and part (b) shows the result of a feedback rule.

# SELF-TEST

## CONCEPT REVIEW

**1** The goals of macroeconomic policy are: the highest sustainable rate of _____ _____, small business _____, low _____ and _____.

**2** A(n) _____ - _____ policy specifies an action to be pursued independently of the state of the economy.

**3** A(n) _____ - _____ policy specifies how policy action responds to changes in the state of the economy.

**4** _____ policies involve government action to stimulate the economy when it is in recession.

**5** When inflation is tamed, a _____ usually results because people form policy _____ based on past policy actions.

# TRUE AND FALSE

__ **1** Cost-push inflation is particularly a problem for an economy if it follows monetarist fixed rules.

__ **2** Nominal GDP targeting is an example of a fixed-rule policy.

__ **3** One of the goals (targets) of economic policy is to reduce the unemployment rate below its natural rate.

__ **4** Reducing the inflation rate usually leads to a recession.

__ **5** Increasing national saving is likely to increase the economic growth rate.

__ **6** Discretionary policy can be characterized as a type of sophisticated feedback policy.

__ **7** The use of feedback rules cannot make business cycle fluctuations in economic activity more severe.

__ **8** The statement 'allow the money supply to grow at the constant rate of 3 per cent per year', is an example of a feedback-rule policy.

# MULTIPLE CHOICE

**1** Which of the following is an example of a fixed-rule policy?
  **a** Wear your boots if it snows.
  **b** Leave your boots at home if it does not snow.
  **c** Wear your boots every day.
  **d** Listen to the weather forecast and then decide whether to wear your boots.

**2** Monetary policy affects the economy _____ , and fiscal policy affects the economy_____ .
  **a** immediately; immediately
  **b** immediately; after a lag
  **c** after a lag; immediately
  **d** after a lag; after a lag

**3** According to the real business cycle theory, if the government increases the money supply when real GDP declines, real GDP will
  **a** increase, but only temporarily.
  **b** increase permanently.
  **c** not change and neither will the price level.
  **d** not change but the price level will rise.

**4** OPEC once again succeeds in drastically raising the price of oil. This is an aggregate _____ shock, and a _____ policy runs the risk of creating a cost-push inflation.
  **a** demand; fixed-rule
  **b** demand; feedback-rule
  **c** supply; feedback-rule
  **d** supply; fixed-rule

**5** Businesses become convinced that future profits from investment will be less than initially believed. This conviction is an aggregate _____ shock and a _____ policy may be able to keep real GDP from falling below potential GDP.
  **a** demand; fixed-rule
  **b** demand; feedback-rule
  **c** supply; feedback-rule
  **d** supply; fixed-rule

**6** Tax changes that raise the return from private saving can be used to help
  **a** reduce inflation.
  **b** eliminate the business cycle.
  **c** increase the rate of economic growth.
  **d** increase the natural rate of unemployment.

**7** The data show that, in the year before an election, monetary policy generally is _____ , and in the year after an election, monetary policy generally is _____ .
  **a** expansionary; expansionary
  **b** expansionary; contractionary
  **c** contractionary; expansionary
  **d** contractionary; contractionary

**8** A fixed-rule policy that sets the growth rate of the money supply at 4 per cent per year
  **a** ensures that persisting inflation does not occur.
  **b** counteracts temporary increases in aggregate demand.
  **c** counteracts temporary decreases in real output.
  **d** offsets supply shocks.

**9** A fixed-rule monetary policy
  **a** requires considerable knowledge of how changes in the money supply affect the economy.
  **b** would be impossible for the government to achieve.
  **c** would result in constant real GDP.
  **d** minimizes the threat of cost-push inflation.

**10** Expanding the money supply when the economy is in a recession is a policy that may
  **a** reduce inflation.
  **b** help smooth the business cycle.
  **c** increase the rate of economic growth.
  **d** increase the natural rate of unemployment.

**11** Which of the following is one of the two core macroeconomic policy targets?
  **a** unemployment constant at 6 per cent
  **b** steady growth in real GDP
  **c** steady growth in nominal GDP
  **d** inflation at the natural rate

**12** According to real business cycle theory,
  **a** any decrease in real GDP is the result of a decrease in long-run aggregate supply.
  **b** fluctuations in aggregate demand change potential real GDP.
  **c** fluctuations in aggregate demand cannot affect the price level.
  **d** feedback-rule policies are best.

**13** The rule, 'Reduce taxes in a recession', is an example of a
  **a** Keynesian fixed-rule policy.
  **b** Keynesian feedback-rule policy.
  **c** monetarist fixed-rule policy.
  **d** monetarist feedback-rule policy.

**14** Which type of economist believes that fluctuations in aggregate demand combined with sticky money wages are the main source of business cycles and that activist feedback-rule policies should be followed?
  **a** a Keynesian economist
  **b** a monetarist economist
  **c** a real business cycle economist
  **d** all economists

**15** Economists who favour fixed-rule policies over feedback-rule policies over feedback-rule policies argue that policy lags are

  **a** shorter than the forecast horizon and that potential GDP is known reasonably well.
  **b** shorter than the forecast horizon and that potential GDP is not known.
  **c** longer than the forecast horizon and that potential GDP is known reasonably well.
  **d** longer than the forecast horizon and that potential GDP is not known.

**16** The usual result when inflation is reduced is
  **a** an immediate strong expansion.
  **b** a recession.
  **c** more rapid growth in aggregate demand.
  **d** The premise of the question is wrong because there is no *usual* result when inflation is reduced.

## SHORT ANSWER

**1** What are the two core macroeconomic policy targets? How are they achieved theoretically with nominal GDP targeting?

**2** Distinguish between fixed-rule policy and feedback-rule policy.

**3** The purpose of policy is to stabilize. How, then, can feedback rules result in even greater variability in aggregate demand?

**4** What is the relationship between policies designed to foster more rapid growth in potential GDP and policies designed to limit business cycle fluctuations in economic activity? Do any of these policies overlap? Explain. Is there a source of potential conflict between the policy goal of more rapid growth and the policy goal of limiting business cycles? If so, what is it?

**5** The *Reading Between the Lines* article gives different estimates for the natural rate of unemployment. If economists cannot agree what the natural rate is, does this diminish its usefulness?

## PROBLEMS

**1** Assume that the government knows exactly how much and when the aggregate demand curve will shift, both in the absence of monetary policy and when the government changes the money supply. Moreover, assume that, in 1996, a one-year decrease in aggregate demand occurs because of a drop in government purchases of goods and services but that, in 1997, government purchases return to normal. Between 1996 and 1997, potential GDP does not grow.

**a** If the government follows the fixed rule, 'Hold the money supply constant', in Fig. 34.1 show how the temporary decrease in aggregate demand affects real GDP and the price level in 1996.

**b** The government continues to follow the fixed rule in **a**. In Fig. 34.2, show the effect on real GDP and the price level in 1997.

**c** Assume that the government follows the feedback rule, 'Raise the money supply whenever aggregate demand decreases and lower it whenever aggregate demand increases'. The government's target is to hold real GDP equal to potential GDP. If there are no lags in the effect of monetary policy, in Fig. 34.3 show the effect in 1996 of the temporary decrease in government spending on real GDP and the price level.

**d** The government continues to follow the feedback rule in **c**. In Fig. 34.4, show the effect in 1997 on real GDP and the price level.

**e** Assume that holding GDP as close as possible to potential GDP is a target for policy makers. Which policy – the fixed-rule policy or the feedback-rule policy – is best?

**Figure 34.1**

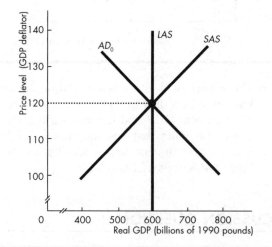

**Figure 34.2**

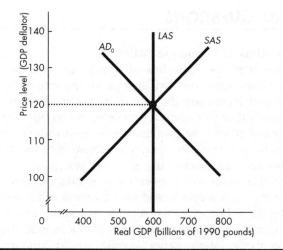

**Figure 34.3**

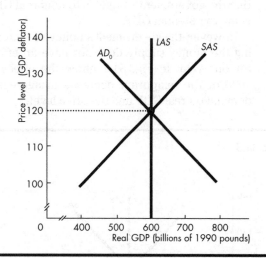

**2** As in Problem **1**, the government knows exactly how much the aggregate demand curve will shift. In 1996, a one-year drop in government purchases of goods and services occurs, but in 1997, government purchases return to normal. Between 1996 and 1997, potential GDP does not grow. But now assume that the government does not know when a change in the money supply will shift the aggregate demand curve.

**Figure 34.4**

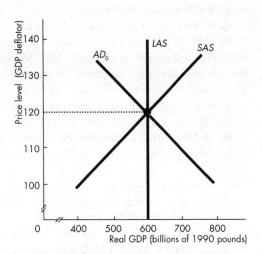

**a** Assume that the government follows the feedback rule, 'Increase the money supply whenever aggregate demand decreases and decrease it whenever aggregate demand increases', and that the government's target is to hold real GDP equal to potential GDP.

However, the government's policy of increasing the money supply does not have an effect for one year. In Fig. 34.5, show the effect in 1996 of the temporary decrease in aggregate demand on real GDP and the price level.

**Figure 34.5**

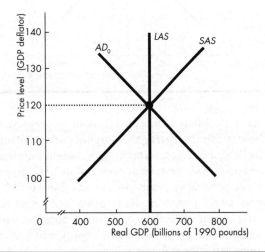

**b** The government continues to follow the feedback rule in **a**. In Fig. 34.6, show the effect in 1997 on real GDP and the price level. (Remember the policy that was undertaken in 1996.)

**c** Has the government helped stabilize or destabilize the economy? Explain.

## DISCUSSION QUESTION

**1** Should the government conduct activist, feedback-rule policies or should it stick to non-activist, fixed-rule policies?

## DATA QUESTIONS

### The Aims of Economic Policy

If we read the speeches of politicians, two policy objectives stand out: bringing down the rate of inflation and increasing the rate of economic growth. Of course, other objectives are sometimes mentioned, but they are given little prominence or seen to be dependent on these two. For example, ministers claim credit when unemployment falls, but even this is often presented as a result of a strong counter-inflation policy.

Many economists would also mention other policy objectives. For example, some would claim that governments should aim to reduce fluctuations in the business cycle. Many other people would emphasize

**Figure 34.6**

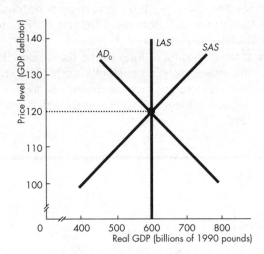

environmental objectives, even though this might mean slower economic growth, or even no economic growth at all.

1 Can governments succeed in achieving all their economic objectives at the same time?
2 Can you think of other economic objectives?

# ANSWERS

## CONCEPT REVIEW

1 economic growth; fluctuations; unemployment; inflation
2 fixed-rule;
3 feedback-rule
4 Feedback
5 recession; expectations

## TRUE OR FALSE

1 **F** Fixed rules do not allow the money supply to react to cost changes, so fixed rules basically eliminate the possibility of cost-push inflation.

2 **F** Nominal GDP targeting is a feedback rule because policy responds to current changes in nominal GDP.

3 **F** One of the goals is to hold the unemployment rate equal to the natural rate.

4 **T** In practice, inflation reduction most often leads to a recession.

5 **T** By increasing the national saving rate, the country can accumulate more capital, which would increase its rate of economic growth.

6 **T** Discretionary policy means that policy makers respond to the current state of the economy, which is a form of feedback policy.

7 **F** Feedback rules can worsen the severity of business cycles if substantial and unpredictable lags occur before the policies can have an effect on the economy.

8 **F** The statement in the question is a fixed rule because the monetary growth rate is fixed regardless of the current state of the economy.

## MULTIPLE CHOICE

1 **c** This is a fixed rule because it does not depend on the day's weather.

2 **d** Both monetary and fiscal policies have lags before they affect the economy. These lags offer the possibility that the effect of the policy will be perverse; that is, a policy could have a contractionary effect when the economy is already in a recession.

3 **d** In the real business cycle view, real GDP is determined solely by long-run aggregate supply, so monetary policy, which affects only aggregate demand, cannot change real GDP. Instead, monetary policy affects only the price level.

4 **c** By decreasing aggregate supply, the increase in oil prices raises the price level and decreases real GDP. If the government's feedback rule conducts an expansionary monetary policy, the price level will rise still more, leading OPEC, in turn, to again raise the price of oil, which can create a cost-push inflation.

5 **b** A feedback-rule policy in this case increases aggregate demand. Such a policy offsets the initial decrease in aggregate demand and can keep production at potential real GDP.

6 **c** By increasing the return from private saving, private saving will increase and the country will accumulate more capital.

7 **b** The tendency for monetary policy to be expansionary before an election raises the possibility of a 'political business cycle' whereby monetary policy is conducted on the basis of politics rather than economics.

8 **a** A major benefit of fixed rules that specify low rates of monetary growth is that they eliminate the possibility of high and persisting inflation.

9 **d** 8 deals with the general result that fixed monetary policy rules limit inflation; **9** covers the specific result that fixed monetary policy rules eliminate the possibility of cost-push inflation.

10 **b** By increasing aggregate demand, an expansionary monetary policy may reduce the high unemployment rate that results in a recession.

11 **b** The other core macroeconomic policy target is keeping the inflation rate low.

12 **a** Real business cycle theory asserts that the economy always produces on its long-run aggregate supply curve.

13 **b** The rule has taxes that depend on the state of the economy and thus is a feedback rule, the type of rule advocated by Keynesian economists.

**14 a** The main impulse that causes business cycles in the Keynesian theory is fluctuations in aggregate demand caused by fluctuations in investment. Keynesians also recommend that these fluctuations be countered by activist feedback rules.

**15 d** Both long lags and uncertainty about potential GDP increase the possibility that fixed rules would be superior to feedback rules.

**16 b** In theory, a credible, announced policy of reducing inflation might not affect real GDP, but in practice reductions in inflation generally are accompanied by a recession.

## SHORT ANSWER

**1** The two core macroeconomic policy targets are steady growth in real GDP at the maximum sustainable rate and keeping inflation low and predictable.

Nominal GDP targeting uses feedback rules to try to keep nominal GDP at the target level. Supporters of nominal GDP targeting argue that, if nominal GDP falls below the target, it is the result of falling real GDP, and if nominal GDP rises above the target, it is the result of inflation. Hence conducting expansionary policy when nominal GDP growth is low will increase the growth rate of real GDP so that it moves closer to its maximum sustainable rate. Conducting contractionary policy when nominal GDP growth is high will reduce the inflation rate and keep it low. Hence meeting the target growth rate for nominal GDP will meet both core targets.

**2** The difference between a fixed-rule policy and a feedback-rule policy is whether the specified action depends on the state of the economy. A fixed-rule policy specifies an action that will be pursued regardless of the state of the economy. For instance, a fixed-rule policy of increasing the money supply by 3 per cent per year implies that the money supply will be increased by 3 per cent regardless of whether the economy is in an expansion or a recession. In contrast, a feedback-rule policy specifies actions that may change, depending on the state of the economy. For instance, a feedback-rule policy of increasing the growth rate of the money supply if the economy is in a recession and decreasing the growth rate if the economy is in an expansion means that the growth rate of the money supply will change according to the state of the economy.

**3** Policy actions affect aggregate demand only after a time lag. This means that a policy action taken today will have its intended effect sometime in the future. Therefore policy makers must forecast the state of the economy a year or two ahead to be confident that the effect of the policy action taken today will be appropriate when the effect occurs. Such forecasting is extremely difficult, both because the lags are long and because they are unpredictable. As a result, policy makers face the likelihood that the policy action taken today will have an inappropriate future effect. For instance, an expansionary monetary policy designed to counter a current recession may actually affect the economy in two years when it is already enjoying a robust expansion. Thus the expansionary policy may lead to accelerating inflation, which could destabilize rather than stabilize aggregate demand.

**4** Policies designed to increase the long-term growth of potential GDP generally are quite different from policies designed to combat business cycle fluctuations in economic activity. To increase the growth rate of potential GDP, policies must be designed to increase national saving, to spur investment in human capital, and to increase research and investment in new technologies. Conversely, to reduce business cycle fluctuations, policies must be designed to offset fluctuations in aggregate demand (if, indeed, fluctuations in aggregate demand are the source of the business cycle and if policies can successfully limit the fluctuations). Thus tax policies that increase the return from private saving, policies that increase the quality and access to schooling, and tax policies that increase the return from investment in new technologies may increase the rate of growth in potential GDP. They are quite different from the fiscal and monetary policies that might be used to limit business cycles.

However, one source of overlap and possible conflict may exist between the two sets of policies. To increase national saving and hence the growth rate of potential GDP, reducing the government's budget deficit is a potential policy. But to combat a recession, a tax cut and an increase in government spending are potential policies, and these policies increase the government's budget deficit. Thus fiscal policy designed to stabilize the business cycle also may have an impact on the growth rate of potential GDP.

**5** The natural rate of unemployment was discussed in Chapter 24 where it was suggested that it was composed of frictional and structural unemployment. If these could be estimated precisely, then governments could expand the economy until unemployment fell to its natural rate without causing inflation. However, the inability to agree on a method of measurement means that the government cannot know exactly the point at which inflation will rise, and this diminishes the usefulness of the concept of a natural rate of unemployment.

# PROBLEMS

### Figure 34.7

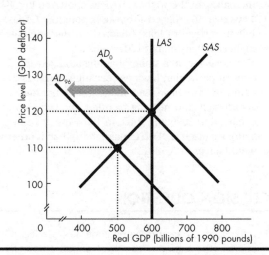

**1 a** Figure 34.7 shows the effect. With a fixed rule, nothing offsets the decline in government purchases. Hence the decrease in aggregate demand decreases real GDP (from £600 billion to £500 billion) and the price level falls (from 120 to 110).

### Figure 34.8

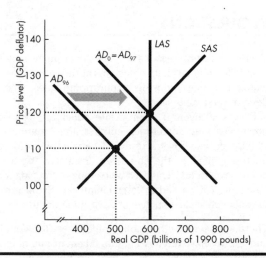

**b** As Fig. 34.8 shows, in 1997 the aggregate demand curve returns to its initial level of $AD_0$. Hence real GDP returns to its initial, full-employment level of £600 billion, and the price level returns to the initial level of 120.

### Figure 34.9

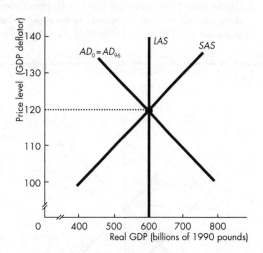

**c** A feedback rule enables the government to offset the initial decrease in aggregate demand. Hence the government's expansionary policy keeps aggregate demand stationary at $AD_0$. As a result, Fig. 34.9 shows how real GDP remains at its full-employment level (£600 billion), with the price level remaining unchanged.

**d** In 1997, as aggregate demand returns to normal, the feedback rule will lead the government to terminate its expansionary policy. Hence aggregate demand in 1997 remains at $AD_0$. Thus as Fig. 34.10 shows, real GDP (again) equals potential GDP, £600 billion, and the price level (again) equals 120.

### Figure 34.10

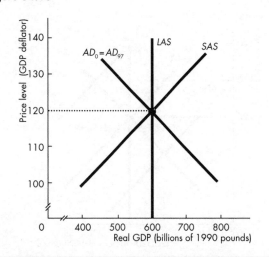

**e** The feedback-rule policy was best for the economy. With the feedback-rule policy, in neither year did real GDP deviate from potential GDP. With the fixed-rule policy, **a** shows that when aggregate demand decreased in 1996, real GDP fell below potential GDP.

**Figure 34.11**

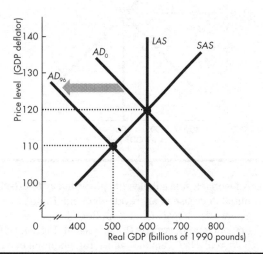

**2 a** In 1996, the government conducts an expansionary policy, but because the policy does not take effect until after a one-year lag, the policy has no effect in 1996. Hence as Fig. 34.11 demonstrates, in 1996, aggregate demand falls to $AD_{96}$, real GDP decreases to £500 billion, and the price level falls to 110.

**Figure 34.12**

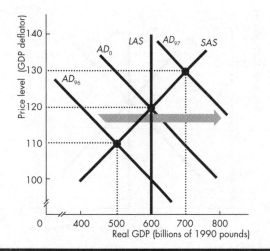

**b** In 1997, with the increase in aggregate demand back to normal, the government's feedback rule causes it to end the expansionary policy. But in 1997, the expansionary policy that was conducted in 1996 affects the economy. Hence aggregate demand increases all the way to $AD_{97}$, as shown in Fig. 34.12. Thus in 1997, real GDP exceeds potential GDP (£700 billion instead of £600 billion) and the price level is higher (130 instead of 120).

**c** The government's policy has destabilized the economy. In particular, business cycle fluctuations in economic activity have been made worse, not better. The government did nothing to offset the recession that occurred in 1996 and then, in 1997, the government's actions caused GDP to expand more than it otherwise would have.

## DISCUSSION QUESTION

**1** Feedback rules require very good knowledge of the economy (for example, the level of full employment), introduce unpredictability into the economy, can generate bigger fluctuations in aggregate demand because of lags and do not work for aggregate supply. Consequently, they can lead to worse results than fixed rules.

However, fixed rules also have disadvantages. What if bad fixed rules are applied over long periods? Moreover, active government intervention can sometimes lead to better results than fixed rules. So the debate continues.

## DATA QUESTIONS

**1** There are several reasons why the government might be unable to achieve all its objectives at the same time. For example, it may be using inappropriate rules, whether fixed or feedback.

However, even if appropriate rules are followed, objectives may sometimes conflict. For example, the Phillips curve shows a trade-off between inflation and unemployment in the short run. Similarly, rapid economic growth may lead to a worsening of the balance of payments (discussed in later chapters). Rapid growth may also be at the expense of environmental progress.

**2** There are several other policy objectives that could be chosen. We have already mentioned environmental considerations. Others might stress the need for a more equal society. This would require higher taxation of rich people and more spending on welfare. In the United States in particular, there is considerable pressure for the government to aim to balance the budget. All these questions are matters of value.

# Chapter 35 Trading with the World

---

## Chapter in Perspective, Text Pages 919–949

Why do nations trade? What is the nature of the gains that make trade worthwhile? What determines which goods a country will import and which it will export? In this chapter we also turn to more difficult issues such as: if there are significant gains to free trade, why do countries frequently restrict imports? What are the effects of a tariff or a quota or some other trade restriction?

---

## Helpful Hints

**1** It may be useful to recall the discussion in Chapter 3 of opportunity cost, comparative advantage and gains from trade. The current chapter applies the fundamental concepts of opportunity cost and comparative advantage to the problem of trade between countries. The basic principles are the same whether we are talking about trade between individuals in the same country or between individuals in different countries.

Many students seem confused by the concept of comparative advantage, partly because they implicitly consider absolute advantage as the sole reason for trade. A country has an absolute advantage if it can produce all goods using less inputs than another country. However, such a country can still gain from trade if it concentrates its resources where it is *relatively* more efficient.

**2** In addition to the gains from trade, this chapter also discusses the economic effects of trade restrictions. One of the important things we learn is that the economic effects of a tariff and a quota are similar. A voluntary export restraint (VER) is also a quota, but one imposed by the exporting country rather than the importing country. All these trade restrictions raise the domestic price of the imported good, and reduce the volume of and value of imports. They will also reduce the value of exports by the same amount as the reduction in the value of imports. The increase in price that results from each of these trade restrictions produces a gap between the domestic price of the imported good and the foreign supply price of the good. The difference between the alternative trade restrictions lies in which party captures this excess. In the case of a tariff, the government receives the tariff revenue. In the case of a quota imposed by the importing country, domestic importers who have been awarded a licence to import capture this excess through increased profit. When a VER is imposed, the excess is captured by foreign exporters who have been awarded licences to export by their governments.

**3** The major point of this chapter is that the gains from free trade can be considerable. Why then do countries have such a strong tendency to impose trade restrictions? The key is that while free trade creates overall benefits to the economy as a whole, there are both winners and losers. The winners gain more in total than the losers lose, but the latter tend to be concentrated in a few industries. We are therefore not surprised that free trade will be resisted by some acting on the basis of rational self-interest. Even though only a small minority benefit from any given trade restriction while the overwhelming majority will be hurt, we are not surprised to see trade restrictions implemented. The reason is that the cost of a given trade restriction to each of the many is indvidually quite small while the benefit to each of the few will be individually large. Thus the few will have a significant incentive to see that restriction takes place while the many will have little incentive to expend time and energy in resisting trade restriction.

# Key Figures

## Figure 35.6 International Trade in Cars, text page 926

The price at which a good trades internationally and the quantity traded are determined by the international market for the good. This figure illustrates a hypothetical international market for cars using the example of Farmland and Mobilia. Mobilia has a comparative advantage in the production of cars and so supplies cars to the world market. At higher prices, Mobilia is willing to supply more cars although it must receive at least 1,000 kilograms of grain (its opportunity cost of a car) to be willing to produce. The supply curve in the figure gives Mobilia's export supply of cars. Similarly, the demand curve in the figure gives Farmland's import demand for cars. It shows that as the price of a car falls, the quantity of cars that Farmland wants to import increases, although it will not buy any cars at a

price above 9,000 kilograms of grain (its opportunity cost of a car). The equilibrium price when trade takes place is at the intersection of these two curves. The price of a car (under free trade) is 3,000 kilograms of grain, and 4 million cars per year are imported by Farmland from Mobilia.

## Figure 35.7 Expanding Consumption Possibilities, text page 927

This clearly illustrates the gains from trade experienced by Farmland and Mobilia. Without trade, each country consumes what it produces. Its consumption is constrained by the production possibility frontier. The gain from trade for each country is that, with trade, while production is constrained by the production possibility frontier, consumption can exceed that frontier. Consumption is constrained only by the consumption possibility curve which (except for a single point) lies beyond the production possibility curve. Part (a) shows the situation for Farmland. Without trade, Farmland produces and consumes at point $a$: 8 million cars and 15 billion kilograms of grain. With trade (at 1 car trading for 3,000 kilograms of grain), Farmland produces at point $b$: 5 million cars and 30 billion kilograms of grain. But because of trade, consumption can be different. Indeed, with trade Farmland consumes at point $c$: 9 million cars and 18 billion kilograms of grain. This is 1 million more cars and 3 billion more kilograms of grain than were consumed without trade (at point $a$). This additional consumption is the gain from trade for Farmland. A similar analysis in part (b) illustrates that Mobilia also gains from trade.

## Figure 35.9 The Effects of a Tariff, text page 933

The effects of a tariff on the price of a good and the quantity traded are shown in this figure by using the Farmland and Mobilia example of trade in cars. Farmland imposes a tariff of $4,000 per car on cars imported from Mobilia. This shifts the export supply curve upward by $4,000 since the price must include the supply price received by Mobilia and the tariff. Thus the price of a car in Farmland increases from $3,000 to $6,000 and the quantity of cars traded falls to 2 million per year. The total revenue from the tariff (which is received by the government of Farmland) is $8 billion: $4,000 per car times 2 million cars. Although this figure does not show it directly, Farmland's grain exports will also decrease because Mobilia's income from export of cars has fallen.

# SELF-TEST

## CONCEPT REVIEW

**1** The goods and services purchased from people in foreign countries are called _____. The goods and services sold to people in foreign countries are called_____. The value of exports minus the value of imports is called the _____ of _____ .

**2** A country is said to have a(n) _____ _____ in the production of a good if it can produce that good at a lower opportunity cost than any other country. A country is said to have a(n) _____ _____ if for all goods its output per unit of inputs is higher than any other country.

**3** The restriction of international trade is called _____ . A tax imposed by the importing country on an imported good is called a(n) _____ . The result of imposing such a tax is to _____ the price that consumers in the importing country pay and _____ the quantity traded. When such a tax is imposed the tax revenue is received by the _____ .

**4** A restriction that specifies a limit on the quantity of a particular good that can be imported is called a(n) _____ . The result of such a limit is to _____ the price that consumers in the importing country pay. The extra revenue from such a limit is received by the _____ .

**5** An agreement between two governments in which the government of the exporting country agrees to restrict the quantity of its exports to the importing country is called a(n) _____ _____ . Such an agreement will _____ the price that consumers in the importing country pay for the good.

**6** When a good is sold in a foreign market at a lower price than in a domestic market or for a price that is lower than the cost of production it is called _____ .

## TRUE OR FALSE

**1** When a UK citizen stays in a hotel in France, the United Kingdom is exporting a service.

**2** If there are two countries, $A$ and $B$, and two goods, $x$ and $y$, and country $A$ has a comparative advantage in the production of $x$, then country $B$ must have a comparative advantage in the production of $y$.

**3** If country $A$ must give up 3 units of $y$ to produce 1 unit of $x$ and $B$ must give up 4 units of $y$ to produce 1 unit of $x$, then $A$ has a comparative advantage in the production of $x$.

**4** If countries specialize in goods for which they have a comparative advantage, then some countries will gain and others will lose but the gains will be larger than the losses.

**5** Trading according to comparative advantage allows all trading countries to consume outside their production possibility frontier.

**6** If a country has an absolute advantage, it will not benefit from trade.

**7** Countries may exchange similar goods for each other because of economies of scale in the face of diversified tastes.

**8** When governments impose tariffs, they are increasing their country's gain from trade.

**9** A tariff on a good will raise its price and reduce the quantity traded.

**10** A tariff not only reduces the total value of imports but it reduces the total value of exports as well.

**11** A quota will cause the price of the imported good to fall.

# MULTIPLE CHOICE

**1** Suppose there are two countries, $A$ and $B$, producing two goods, $x$ and $y$. Country $A$ has a comparative advantage in the production of good $x$ if less

  **a** of good $y$ must be given up to produce one unit of $x$ than in country $B$.

  **b** labour is required to produce one unit of $x$ than in country $B$.

  **c** capital is required to produce one unit of $x$ than in country $B$.

  **d** labour and capital are required to produce one unit of $x$ than in country $B$.

  **e** of good $x$ must be given up to produce one unit of $y$ than in country $B$.

**2** Suppose there are two countries, $A$ and $B$, producing two goods, $x$ and $y$, and that country $A$ has a comparative advantage in the production of $x$. If the countries trade, the price of $x$ in terms of $y$ will be

  **a** greater than the opportunity cost of $x$ in country $A$ and less than the opportunity cost of $x$ in country $B$.

  **b** less than the opportunity cost of $x$ in country $A$ and greater than the opportunity cost of $x$ in country $B$.

  **c** greater than the opportunity cost of $x$ in both countries.

  **d** less than the opportunity cost of $x$ in both countries.

  **e** dependent on the relative size of each economy.

**3** International trade according to comparative advantage allows each country to consume

  **a** more of the goods it exports but less of the goods it imports than without trade.

  **b** more of the goods it imports but less of the goods it exports than without trade.

  **c** more of both goods it exports and goods it imports than without trade.

  **d** less of both goods it exports and goods it imports than without trade.

  **e** either **a** or **b**; it depends on the price of the goods.

**4** In country $A$, it requires one unit of capital and one unit of labour to produce a unit of $x$ and it requires two units of capital and two units of labour to produce a unit of $y$. What is the opportunity cost of good $x$?

  **a** the price of a unit of capital plus the price of a unit of labour

  **b** one unit of capital and one unit of labour

  **c** two units of capital and two units of labour

  **d** one half unit of $y$

  **e** two units of $y$

**5** If country $A$ has an absolute advantage in the production of everything,

  **a** no trade will take place because country $A$ will have a comparative advantage in everything.

  **b** no trade will take place because no country will have a comparative advantage in anything.

  **c** trade will probably take place and all countries will gain.

  **d** trade will probably take place but country $A$ will not gain.

  **e** trade will probably take place but country $A$ will be the only one to gain.

**6** The imposition of a tariff on imported goods will increase the price consumers pay for imported goods and

  **a** reduce the volume of imports and the volume of exports.

  **b** reduce the volume of imports and increase the volume of exports.

  **c** reduce the volume of imports and leave the volume of exports unchanged.

  **d** will not affect either the volume of imports or the volume of exports.

  **e** increase the volume of imports but decrease the volume of exports.

**7** Who benefits from a tariff on good $x$?

  **a** domestic consumers of good $x$

  **b** domestic producers of good $x$

  **c** foreign consumers of good $x$

  **d** foreign producers of good $x$

  **e** no one

**8** A tariff on good $x$ which is imported by country $A$ will cause the

  **a** demand curve for $x$ in country $A$ to shift upward.

  **b** demand curve for $x$ in country $A$ to shift downward.

  **c** supply curve of $x$ in country $A$ to shift upward.

  **d** supply curve of $x$ in country $A$ to shift downward.

  **e** demand and the supply curve of $x$ in country $A$ to shift upward.

**9** Country $A$ and country $B$ are currently engaging in free trade. Country $A$ imports good $x$ from country $B$ and exports $y$ to $B$. If country $A$ imposes a tariff on $x$, country $A$'s $x$-producing industry will

   **a** expand and its $y$-producing industry will contract.

   **b** expand and its $y$-producing industry will expand.

   **c** contract and its $y$-producing industry will contract.

   **d** contract and its $y$-producing industry will expand.

   **e** expand and its $y$-producing industry will be unchanged.

**10** Country $A$ and country $B$ are currently engaging in free trade. Country $A$ imports good $x$ from country $B$ and exports $y$ to $B$. If country $A$ imposes a quota on $x$, country $A$'s $x$-producing industry will

   **a** expand and its $y$-producing industry will contract.

   **b** expand and its $y$-producing industry will expand.

   **c** contract and its $y$-producing industry will contract.

   **d** contract and its $y$-producing industry will expand.

   **e** expand and its $y$-producing industry will be unchanged.

**11** When a tariff is imposed, the gap between the domestic price and the export price is captured by

   **a** consumers in the importing country.

   **b** the person with the right to import the good.

   **c** the domestic producers of the good.

   **d** foreign exporters.

   **e** the government of the importing country.

**12** When a quota is imposed, the gap between the domestic price and the export price is captured by

   **a** consumers in the importing country.

   **b** the domestic producers of the good.

   **c** the government of the importing country.

   **d** foreign exporters.

   **e** the person with the right to import the good.

**13** When a voluntary export restraint agreement is reached, the gap between the domestic price and the export price is captured by

   **a** consumers in the importing country.

   **b** the person with the right to import the good.

   **c** the government of the importing country.

   **d** foreign exporters.

   **e** the domestic producers of the good.

**14** If we import more than we export, then

   **a** we are going to be unable to buy as many foreign goods as we desire.

   **b** we will make loans to foreigners fo enable them to buy our goods.

   **c** we will have to finance the difference by borrowing from foreigners.

   **d** our patterns of trade, including the direction of exports and imports, will be different than if exports equal imports.

   **e** both **c** and **d**.

## SHORT ANSWER

**1** What is meant by comparative advantage?

**2** How is it that both parties involved in trade can gain?

**3** How does a tariff on a particular imported good affect the domestic price of the good, the export price, the quantity imported and the quantity of the good produced domestically?

**4** How does a tariff on imports affect the exports of the country?

**5** How does a quota on a particular imported good affect the domestic price of the good, the export price, the quantity imported and the quantity of the good produced domestically?

**6** Why might a government prefer a quota to a tariff?

**7** Re-read the *Reading Between the Lines* article. Why do you think that African governments have adopted protectionist policies despite these economic arguments?

## PROBLEMS

**1** Consider a simple world in which there are two countries, Atlantis and Beltran, each producing two goods, food and cloth. The production possibility frontier for each country is given in Table 35.1.

a Assuming a constant opportunity cost in each country, fill in the rest of the table.

b What is the opportunity cost of food in Atlantis? of cloth?

c What is the opportunity cost of food in Beltran? of cloth?

d Draw the production possibility frontiers on separate graphs.

Table 35.1

| Atlantis | | Beltran | |
|---|---|---|---|
| Food (units) | Cloth (units) | Food (units) | Cloth (units) |
| 0 | 500 | 0 | 800 |
| 200 | 400 | 100 | 600 |
| 400 | | 200 | |
| 600 | | 300 | |
| 800 | | 400 | |
| 1,000 | | | |

**2** Suppose that Atlantis and Beltran engage in trade.

a In which good will each country specialize?

b If 1 unit of food trades for 1 unit of cloth, what will happen to the production of each good in each country?

c If 1 unit of food trades for 1 unit of cloth, draw the consumption possibility frontiers for each country on the corresponding graph from Problem **1d**.

d Before trade, if Atlantis consumed 600 units of good, the most cloth it could consume was 200 units. After trade, how many units of cloth can be consumed if 600 units of food are consumed?

**3** Figure 35.1 gives the import demand curve for shirts for country $A$, labelled $D$, and the export supply curve of shirts for country $B$, labelled $S$.

a What is the price of a shirt under free trade?

b How many shirts will be imported by country $A$?

**4** Suppose the shirtmakers in country $A$ (of Problem 3) are concerned about foreign competition and so the government of country $A$ imposes a tariff of £9 per shirt.

Figure 35.1

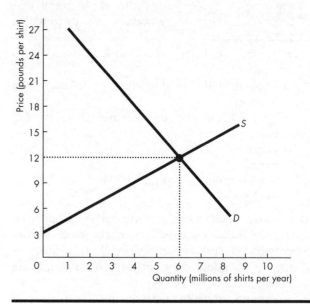

a What will happen to the price of a shirt in country $A$?

b What is the price the exporter will actually receive?

c How many shirts will be imported by country $A$?

d What is the revenue from the tariff? Who captures it?

**5** Suppose that instead of a tariff, country $A$ imposes a quota of 4 million shirts per year.

a What will be the price of a shirt in country $A$?

b What price will the exporter actually receive?

c How many shirts will be imported by country $A$?

d What is the difference between the total amount paid by consumers and the total amount received by exporters – the 'excess profit'? Who captures it?

## DISCUSSION QUESTION

**1** How can firms in rich countries compete with firms in poorer countries that pay much lower wages?

## DATA QUESTIONS

### South Korean Cars

It is a modest aim. Emboldened by last month's truce between American and South Korean trade negotiators, Detroit's Big Three car makers are pushing ahead with plans to grab a less-than-towering 5 per cent of the South Korean market, up from today's puny 0.27 per cent. Despite the recent deal, pushing up their share will be hard.

True, barriers are coming down. South Korea's tariff on cars has been cut from 10 per cent to 8 per cent. Also from next year, South Korea will abolish five of its 38 car safety tests; of the remainder, American cars will be exempted from 28 and European cars from 23.

However, customs' procedures remain notoriously lengthy and the EU Chamber of Commerce in Seoul argues that Korea should recognise tests carried out in exporting countries. And all Japanese cars are banned.

Three obstacles face foreign car makers. One is loyalty to domestic products. Another is the growing power of the home team. The third is taste. Koreans like their cars small; Americans tend to make them big.

*Source:* Copyright © *The Economist*, London, 21 October 1996, p. 108.

**1** Describe the economic consequences of tariff barriers.

**2** Give examples of non-tariff barriers.

# ANSWERS

## CONCEPT REVIEW

**1** imports; exports; balance; trade

**2** comparative advantage; absolute advantage

**3** protectionism; tariff; increase; decrease; government

**4** quota; raise; importer

**5** voluntary export restraint; raise

**6** dumping

## TRUE OR FALSE

**1 F** The United Kingdom is importing (using) a service.

**2 T** $A$'s comparative advantage means lower units of $y$ lost per unit of $x$ than $B$, higher units of $x$ lost per unit of $y$ produced than $B$, hence $B$ has comparative advantage of $y$.

**3 T** $A$ has lower opportunity cost $(3y < 4y)$ = lost $y$ per unit of gained $y$.

**4 F** All countries gain from specialization and trade, although some groups within countries lose.

**5 T** Countries will specialize and trade to consume outside $PPF$.

**6 F** If comparative advantage exists, so do gains from trade.

**7 T** Diversified tastes mean that many products are demanded. These can be provided efficiently only if there is specialization and trade.

**8 F** Trade restrictions reduce gains from trade.

**9 T** A tariff leads to shift in export supply curve leading to increase in price and fall in quantity.

**10 T** Since a tariff reduces imports it will reduce incomes in other countries and so foreigners' ability to import will fall.

**11 F** Quota means fall in supply and so rise in price.

## MULTIPLE CHOICE

**1 a** Opportunity cost will be less.

**2 a** Ignoring taxes and so on, prices will be in between differing opportunity costs.

**3 c** Consumption possibilities frontier is outside *PPF*.

**4 d** Inputs to make one $X$ could make $^1/_2$ $Y$.

**5 c** All countries will gain if they specialize where they have *comparative* advantage.

**6 a** It will reduce volume of imports because their price has increased; it will reduce exports since foreigners' incomes will fall and so they will import less.

**7 b** Domestic producers will benefit from higher price.

**8 c** Tariff leads to rise in domestic price = export price + tariff, leading to upward shift of supply curve.

**9 a** Tariff will reduce imports of $x$ so its $x$-producing industry will expand; but $y$ industry will contract since foreigners will have less money to buy $y$.

**10 a** Quota will reduce imports of $x$ so domestic industry will benefit from higher price, but $y$ industry will suffer because foreigners will have less money to buy $y$.

**11 e** Government collects tariff revenue = import price – export price.

**12 e** Under a quota system, domestic government allocates the licence to import.

**13 d** Because they have the right to export.

**14 c** Since imports have to be paid for, in long run country has to borrow from foreigners to get foreign exchange to pay for imports.

# SHORT ANSWER

**1** A country is said to have a comparative advantage in the production of some good if it can produce that good at a lower opportunity cost than any other country.

**2** For two potential trading partners to be willing to trade, they must have different comparative advantages; that is, different opportunity costs. If they do, then they will trade and both parties will gain. If the parties do not trade, they will each face their own opportunity costs. A price at which trade takes place must be somewhere between the opportunity costs of the two traders. This means that the party with the lower opportunity cost of the good in question will gain because it will receive a price above its opportunity cost. Similarly, the party with the higher opportunity cost will gain because it will pay a price below its opportunity cost.

**3** A tariff on an imported good will raise its price to domestic consumers as the export supply curve shifts upward. The export price is determined by the original export supply curve. As the domestic price of the good rises, the quantity of the good demanded falls and thus the relevant point on the original export supply curve is at a lower quantity and a lower export price. This lower quantity means that the quantity imported falls. The rise in the domestic price will also lead to an increase in the quantity of the good supplied domestically.

**4** When country $A$ imposes a tariff on its imports of good $x$, not only does the volume of imports shrink but the volume of exports of $y$ to country $B$ will shrink by the same amount. Thus a balance of trade is maintained. As indicated in the answer to **3**, the export price of good $x$ falls when a tariff is imposed. This fall in the price received by the exporter means that the price of imports in the foreign country has risen; that is, if the amount of $y$ that country $B$ gets for an $x$ has fallen, the quantity of $x$ that must be given up to obtain a $y$ has increased. This implies that the quantity of $y$ ($A$'s export) demanded by country $B$ will fall and thus $A$'s exports will decline.

**5** The effect of a quota on the domestic price of the good, the export price, the quantity imported and the quantity of the good produced domestically are exactly the same as the effects of a tariff discussed in the answer to **3**. The only difference is that the increase in the domestic price is here not the result of a vertical shift in the export supply curve but the result of the fact that the quota forces a vertical effective export supply curve at the quota amount.

**6** The effects of tariffs and quotas on prices and quantities have been discussed in the answers to **3** and **5**. The difference is that the excess revenue raised by a tariff is captured by the government whereas the excess revenue raised by a quota is captured by the people who have been given the right to import by the government. In either case the government is in a position to benefit. It may prefer to use quotas to reward political supporters by giving them rights to import and thus allowing them to capture large profits. Quotas give the government more precise control over the quantity of imports. Also, it is politically easier to impose a quota than a tariff.

**7** African governments, like many others, adopt protectionist policies partly because they are not economists and do not understand theories such as comparative advantage. In addition, they are faced with political pressures to support particular industries or sections of the economy. These pressures can be strong, and their great importance to a few people can outweigh the benefits which would accrue to the many if protectionist policies were abandoned.

# PROBLEMS

**1 a** Completed Table 35.1 is shown here as Table 35.2. The values in the table are calculated using the opportunity cost of each good in each country (see **b** and **c**).

**Table 35.2**

| Atlantis | | Beltran | |
|---|---|---|---|
| Food (units) | Cloth (units) | Food (units) | Cloth (units) |
| 0 | 500 | 0 | 800 |
| 200 | 400 | 100 | 600 |
| 400 | 300 | 200 | 400 |
| 600 | 200 | 300 | 200 |
| 800 | 100 | 400 | 0 |
| 1,000 | 0 | – | – |

**b** In order to increase the output (consumption) of food by 200 units, cloth production (consumption) falls by 100 units in Atlantis. Thus the opportunity cost of a unit of food is $^1/_2$ unit of cloth. This opportunity cost is constant (as are all others in this problem, for simplicity). Similarly, the opportunity cost of cloth in Atlantis is 2 units of food.

**c** In Beltran a 100 unit increase in the production (consumption) of food requires a reduction in the output (consumption) of cloth of 200 units. Thus the opportunity cost of food is 2 units of cloth. Similarly the opportunity cost of cloth in Beltran is $^1/_2$ unit of food.

**d** Figure 35.2 parts (a) and (b) illustrate the production possibility frontiers for Atlantis and Beltran, respectively (labelled $PPF_A$ and $PPF_B$). The rest of the diagram is discussed in Problem 2.

**2 a** Since (from Problem **1b** and **c**) we see that Atlantis has lower opportunity cost ($^1/_2$ unit of cloth) in the production of food, Atlantis will specialize in the production of food. Beltran, with the lower opportunity cost for cloth ($^1/_2$ unit of food) will specialize in cloth.

**b** Each country will want to produce every unit of the good in which it specializes as long as the amount it receives in trade exceeds its opportunity cost. For Atlantis, the opportunity cost of a unit of food is $^1/_2$ unit of cloth but it can obtain 1 unit of cloth in trade. Since the opportunity cost is constant (in this simple example), Atlantis will totally specialize by producing all of the food it can: 1,000 units per year (point *b* in

Fig. 35.2a). Similarly, in Beltran, the opportunity cost of 1 unit of cloth is $^1/_2$ unit of food but 1 unit of cloth will trade for 1 unit of food. Since the opportunity cost is constant, Beltran will totally specialize in the production of cloth and will produce 800 units per year (point *b'* in Fig. 35.2b).

**c** The consumption possibility frontiers for Atlantis and Beltran (labelled $CPF_A$ and $CPF_B$) are illustrated in Fig. 35.2, parts (a) and (b), respectively. These frontiers are straight lines that indicate all the combinations of food and cloth that can be consumed with trade. The position and slope of the consumption possibility frontier for an economy depends on the terms of trade between the goods and the production point of the economy. The consumption possibility frontier for Atlantis ($CPF_A$), for example, is obtained by starting at point *b* on $PPF_A$, the production point, and examining possible trades. For example, if Atlantis traded 400 units of the food it produces for 400 units of cloth, it would be able to consume 600 units of food (1,000 units produced minus 400 units traded) and 400 units of cloth, which is represented by point *c*.

**d** If Atlantis consumes 600 units of food, trade allows consumption of cloth to be 400 units, 200 units more than possible without trade. The maximum amount of cloth that can be consumed without trade is given by the production possibility frontier. If food consumption is 600 units, this is indicated by point *a*

**Figure 35.2**

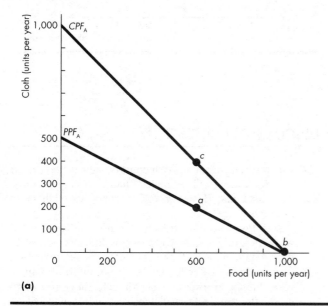

(a)

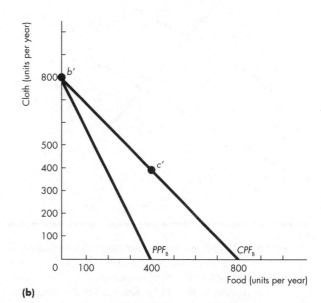

(b)

on $PPF_A$. The maximum amount of cloth consumption for any level of food consumption with trade is given by the consumption possibility frontier. If food consumption is 600 units, this is indicated by point $c$ on $CPF_A$.

**3 a** The price of a shirt under free trade will occur at the intersection of country $A$'s import demand curve for shirts and country $B$'s export supply curve of shirts. This occurs at a price of £12 per shirt.
**b** Country $A$ will import 6 million shirts per year.

**4 a** The effect of the £9 per shirt tariff is to shift the export supply curve ($S$) upward by £9. This is shown as a shift from $S$ to $S'$ in Fig. 35.3. The price is now determined by the intersection of the $D$ curve (which is unaffected by the tariff) and the $S'$ curve. The new price of a shirt is £18.
**b** Of this £18, £9 is the tariff, so the exporter receives only the remaining £9.
**c** Country $A$ will now import only 4 million shirts per year.
**d** The tariff revenue is £9 (the tariff per shirt) times 4 million (the number of shirts imported), which is £36 million. This money is received by the government of country $A$.

**Figure 35.3**

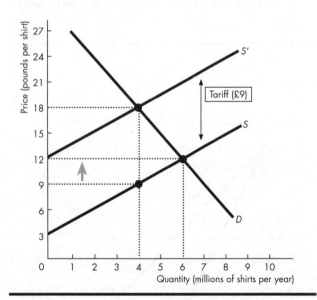

**5 a** The quota restricts the quantity that can be imported to 4 million shirts per year regardless of the price and is represented by a vertical line in Fig. 35.4 (which corresponds to Fig. 35.1). The market for shirts will thus clear at a price of £18 per shirt.

**b** This £18 price is received by the people who are given the right to import shirts under the quota. The amount received by the exporter is £9, given by the height of the $S$ curve at a quantity of 4 million shirts per year.
**c** Country $A$ will import 4 million shirts per year, the quota limit.
**d** The 'excess profit' is £9 per shirt (the £18 received by the importer minus the £9 received by the exporter) times 4 million shirts, which is £36 million. This is captured by the importers who have been rewarded by the government of country $A$ since they have been given the right to import under the quota. This is essentially a right to make an 'excess profit'.

**Figure 35.4**

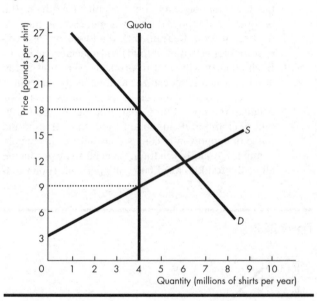

## DISCUSSION QUESTION

**1** Assume that wages in a rich country, such as the United Kingdom, are 10 times higher than in a poor country, such as India. However, UK workers are also more productive.

Let's take two industries. In the first, industry $A$, UK workers are twice as productive as Indian workers. In the second, industry $B$, they are 20 times as productive. In industry $A$, UK workers won't be able to compete with Indian workers, even though they are more productive. So UK firms will lose out in this industry.

However, in industry *B* UK firms will drive Indian firms out of business even though they are paid 10 times as much. This is because they are so much more productive that unit costs are lower.

This simplified example illustrates comparative advantage.

## DATA QUESTIONS

**1** Tariff barriers always result in higher prices and a fall in the quantity of goods bought in the country imposing the tariff. Figure 35.9 in the main text illustrates this. Hence we would expect the cut in tariff barriers by South Korea to result in a rise in the number of imported cars. However, this is likely to be small since the cut in the tariff is small, and other barriers remain.

**2** The non-tariff barrier in this example is one ostensibly designed to maintain safety standards. However, such administrative regulations are frequently used to restrict imports.

Quotas and VERs are other examples of non-tariff barriers. They also result in lower sales and higher prices, but non-tariff barriers are often worse than tariffs because they are less easy to negotiate away.

# Chapter 36 The Balance of Payments and the Exchange Rate

---

## Chapter in Perspective, Text Pages 950–979

The world is becoming increasingly more interrelated, through both international trade and international finance. In Chapter 35 we examined international trade. In this chapter we continue to explore the international economy by further exploring international finance and its relation to international trade.

What determines the value of the balance of trade and the balance of payments? What is the relation between the balance of trade and international lending or borrowing? Does a government budget deficit have any effect on the balance of trade? What role does the value of the pound have in determining the balance of trade? Or is the relationship in the opposite direction – does the balance of trade determine the value of the pound? What are the implications of the move towards a single currency in the European Union? These are some of the basic questions addressed in this chapter.

---

## Helpful Hints

1 The previous chapter demonstrated the gains from trade between countries. Indeed, as noted in Chapter 3, these are the same gains that result from trade within countries as well. However, there is an important difference between trade within a single country and trade between countries. When individuals in the same country engage in trade, they use the same currency and so trade is straightforward. On the other hand, international trade is complicated by the fact that individuals in different countries use different currencies. The person selling the good from Japan will want payment to be in Japanese yen, but the person buying the good in the United Kingdom will probably be holding only UK pounds. This problem complicates trade between individuals in different countries. This chapter addresses this complication by looking at the balance of payments of a country as well as the relation of the balance of payments to the foreign exchange rate.

2 Note that the balance of payments must balance. Individual accounts in the balance of payments can be in deficit or surplus but this will be offset by a surplus or deficit in another account.

**3** It is important to understand foreign exchange rates as prices determined by supply and demand. They are prices of currency determined in markets for currency. The demand for UK pounds in the foreign exchange market, for example, is the demand for pound sterling (denominated) assets, including UK money. That demand will arise from the desire on the part of foreigners to purchase UK goods and services (which requires pounds) and the desire on the part of foreigners to purchase UK financial or real assets. The supply of sterling assets is determined by the government and depends on the exchange rate regime.

**4** The law of one price is not relevant only in the context of international trade. Any time there is a discrepancy in the price of the same good in two markets, natural economic forces (unless restricted) will eliminate that discrepancy and thus establish a single price.

**5** Purchasing power parity is the manifestation of the law of one price in international trade. Purchasing power parity implies that, as long as exchange rates can adjust, they will adjust so that money (of whatever country) will have the same purchasing power in all countries. This means that if one country experiences inflation while others do not, exchange rates will adjust so that the purchasing power of money will be the same in all countries.

**6** Note that it is not the edict of a government which fixes the exchange rate of its currency but rather the willingness of its central bank to supply all of the domestic currency denominated assets that are demanded at the fixed exchange rate.

**7** With a fixed exchange rate, a country cannot use monetary policy to control inflation. With a flexible exchange rate a country can insulate itself from external shocks by varying the exchange rate. Within the European Union, the exchange rates of the various countries are largely fixed against each other. One reason is that this gives stability and encourages intra-country trade. The introduction of a single currency would strengthen this process.

# Key Figures and Tables

## Figure 36.1 The Balance of Payments, 1975–1994, text page 953
The historical record of the balance of payments account is given here.

## Figure 36.6 Three Exchange Rate Systems, text page 967
This illustrates the effects of an increase in the demand for sterling assets under the three exchange rate systems. Part (a) shows the effects under a fixed exchange rate system, part (b) shows the effects under a flexible exchange rate system, and part (c) examines the consequences under a managed exchange rate system. The difference in the effects arises from the difference in the supply curve of sterling assets under each of the three regimes.

## Table 36.4 The Demand for Sterling Assets, text page 966
The demand for sterling assets is characterized in this table. The first part indicates that, just like any other case, the demand for sterling assets obeys the law of demand: the quantity of sterling assets demanded is negatively related to the price of a pound in terms of foreign currency. For example, if the yen price of the pound rises, the quantity of sterling assets demanded declines. The second part of the figure lists several factors that will cause the demand curve for sterling assets to shift.

## Table 36.5 The Supply of Sterling Assets, text page 966
This is a counterpart to Table 36.4. It characterizes the other half of the foreign exchange market, the supply of sterling assets. As discussed in the text, the slope of the supply curve for sterling assets depends on the type of exchange rate regime. Under a fixed exchange rate system, the supply curve of sterling assets is horizontal at the fixed exchange rate. Under a flexible exchange rate system, the supply curve of sterling assets is vertical, and under a managed exchange rate system, it is positively sloped. The bottom section of the table indicates that the supply curve of sterling assets will shift if the Bank of England changes the money supply or if there is a government budget surplus/deficit.

# SELF-TEST

## CONCEPT REVIEW

**1** The international trading, borrowing and lending activities of a country are recorded in its _____ of _____. The expenditures on imported goods and services and the receipts from the sale of exported goods and services are recorded in the _____ account. The _____ account records lending to and borrowing from the rest of the world. The change in a country's holdings of foreign currency is shown in the _____ _____ account.

**2** A country that is borrowing more from the rest of the world than it is lending is called a(n) _____ _____ . A country that is lending more to the rest of the world than it is borrowing is called a(n) _____ _____ .

**3** A country that during its entire history has borrowed more from the rest of the world than it has loaned is called a(n) _____ country.

**4** The balance of trade deficit is _____ _____ the sum of the government budget deficit and the private sector deficit.

**5** Relative prices are determined by _____ and _____ in the _____ market. Money prices are determined by the value of the _____ _____ given the relative prices.

**6** The higher the value of the exchange rate, the _____ is the balance of _____ . The equilibrium value of the exchange rate is determined by the demand and supply of _____ _____ .

**7** If the private sector surplus is constant, a higher government sector deficit means a higher _____ _____ _____ _____ .

**8** The market in which the currencies of different countries are exchanged for each other is called the _____ _____ market. The price at which one currency exchanges for another is called the _____ _____ _____ .

**9** There are three foreign exchange systems. In the first of these the value of the exchange rate is pegged by a central bank. This is a(n) _____ exchange rate. A(n) _____ exchange rate is a system in which the exchange rate is determined by market forces without government intervention. A(n) _____ exchange rate is a system in which the government does not peg the exchange rate but does intervene in the foreign exchange market in order to influence the price of its currency.

**10** The conversion criteria for entry to a single currency in the European Union include low inflation, that the government deficit should be no more than _____ per cent of GDP and that government debt should be no more than _____ per cent of GDP.

## TRUE OR FALSE

**___  1** The sale of Scotch whisky to the United States will be recorded in the current account of the balance of payments accounts.

**___  2** If there is a current account deficit then there must also be a deficit in either the capital account or the official settlements account.

**___  3** The official settlements account balance must always be equal to zero.

**___  4** If a country is a net borrower from the rest of the world, it must be a debtor country.

**___  5** If a country is a net borrower for consumption purposes, this is nothing to worry about.

**___  6** If a country has a large government budget deficit and the private sector deficit is small, the balance of trade deficit will be large.

**___  7** If investment is greater than saving, the private sector has a deficit.

**___  8** Net exports is the same as the current account balance.

**___  9** A larger government sector deficit always leads to a higher current account deficit.

___ **10** Money prices are set by the exchange rate, while relative prices are set on the world market.

___ **11** If the Bank of England wishes to prevent the exchange rate from depreciating in value, the best way is to lower the growth rate of the money supply.

___ **12** If the exchange rate between the UK pound and the Japanese yen changes from 130 yen per pound to 140 yen per pound, the UK pound has appreciated.

___ **13** If the foreign exchange value of the pound is expected to rise, the demand for sterling denominated assets increases.

___ **14** Under a fixed exchange rate system, the supply curve of assets valued in the currency is horizontal at the pegged exchange rate.

## MULTIPLE CHOICE

**1** Which of the following is one of the balance of payments accounts?
**a** current account
**b** non-traded goods account
**c** official reserves account
**d** net interest account
**e** public account

**2** Suppose the United Kingdom initially has all balance of payments accounts in balance (no surplus or deficit). Then UK firms increase the amount they import from Japan, financing that increase in imports by borrowing from Japan. There will now be a current account
**a** surplus and a capital account surplus.
**b** surplus and a capital account deficit.
**c** deficit and a capital account surplus.
**d** deficit and a capital account deficit.
**e** deficit and a capital account balance.

**3** The country Plato came into existence at the beginning of year 1. Given the information in Table 36.1, in year 4 Plato is a
**a** net lender and a creditor country.
**b** net lender and a debtor country.
**c** net borrower and a creditor country.

**d** net borrower and a debtor country.
**e** net lender and neither a creditor nor a debtor country.

**Table 36.1**

| Year | Borrowed from rest of world (billions of pounds) | Loaned to rest of world (billions of pounds) |
|------|--------------------------------------------------|----------------------------------------------|
| 1 | 60 | 20 |
| 2 | 60 | 40 |
| 3 | 60 | 60 |
| 4 | 60 | 80 |

**4** Assuming that Plato is on a floating exchange rate, in which year or years in Table 36.1 did Plato have a current account surplus?
**a** year 1
**b** year 2
**c** years 1, 2 and 3
**d** years 1 and 2
**e** year 4 only

**5** A country is currently a net lender and a debtor country. Which of the following statements applies to that country?
**a** It has loaned more capital than it borrowed from abroad this year, but borrowed more than it loaned during its history.
**b** It has borrowed more capital from abroad than it loaned this year and also borrowed more than it loaned during its history.
**c** It has loaned more capital than it borrowed from abroad this year and has loaned more than it borrowed during its history.
**d** Its accounting system must be in error if it shows this country to be a net lender and a debtor country at the same time.
**e** Its debts must be currently growing.

**6** The distinction between a debtor or creditor country and a net borrower or net lender country depends on
**a** the distinction between the level of saving in the economy and the saving rate.
**b** the distinction between the level of saving in the economy and the rate of borrowing.

**c** the distinction between the stock of investments and the flow of interest payments on those investments.

**d** the distinction between exports and imports.

**e** really nothing; they are the same.

**7** Suppose that in a country, government purchases of goods and services are £400 billion, taxes (net of transfer payments) is £300 billion, saving is £300 billion and investment is £250 billion. Net exports are in a

**a** surplus of £150 billion.

**b** surplus of £50 billion.

**c** deficit of £150 billion.

**d** deficit of £50 billion.

**e** deficit of £250 billion.

**8** The country in **7** has a government budget

**a** surplus and a private sector surplus.

**b** surplus and a private sector deficit.

**c** deficit and a private sector surplus.

**d** deficit and a private sector deficit.

**e** surplus and a private sector balance.

**9** The link between the public sector deficit and the private sector surplus can be weak because

**a** the interest rate will tend to do the adjusting to a change in public deficits rather than the private sector.

**b** real GDP will tend to do the adjusting to a change in public deficits rather than the private sector.

**c** the economy may not be operating at close to capacity, and changes in public deficits will not affect the private sector.

**d** international capital mobility may cut any strong link between changes in the public sector deficit and changes in interest rates.

**e** the government's deficit is partly caused by borrowing abroad.

**10** Under a flexible exchange rate regime, if the foreign exchange value of a country's currency starts to rise, that country's central bank will

**a** increase the supply of assets denominated in its own currency.

**b** decrease the supply of assets denominated in its own currency.

**c** decrease the demand for assets denominated in its own currency.

**d** do nothing.

**e** do nothing unless there is a government budget deficit, in which case it will increase the supply of assets denominated in its own currency.

**11** Which of the following will shift the supply curve of sterling assets rightward under flexible exchange rates?

**a** an increase in the demand for foreign goods by UK citizens

**b** a decrease in the demand for UK goods by foreigners

**c** the pound is expected to appreciate

**d** the government has a budget deficit

**e** none of the above

**12** Under a managed exchange rate system, a UK government budget deficit will cause the foreign exchange price of the pound to

**a** fall and the quantity of sterling assets held to fall.

**b** fall and the quantity of sterling assets held to rise.

**c** rise and the quantity of sterling assets held to fall.

**d** rise and the quantity of sterling assets held to rise.

**e** stay constant, but the quantity of sterling assets held will rise.

**13** Which of the following would cause the pound to depreciate against the yen?

**a** an increase in UK money supply

**b** an increase in interest rates in the United Kingdom

**c** a decrease in interest rates in Japan

**d** an increase in imports from the United Kingdom purchased by Japan

**e** a government budget surplus

## SHORT ANSWER

**1** What is the relationship between a country's trade deficit, its government budget deficit and its private sector deficit?

**2** What is purchasing power parity?

**3** The *Reading Between the Lines* article discusses a rise in the value of the pound. Why do currencies fluctuate in price?

# PROBLEMS

**1** The international transactions of a country for a given year are reported in Table 36.2.

### Table 36.2

| Transaction | Amount (billions of pounds) |
|---|---|
| Exports of goods and services | 100 |
| Imports of goods and services | 130 |
| Transfers to the rest of the world | 20 |
| Loans to the rest of the world | 60 |
| Loans from the rest of the world | |
| Increase in official reserves | 10 |

**a** What is the amount of loans from the rest of the world?

**b** What is the current account balance?

**c** What is the capital account balance?

**d** Does this country have a flexible exchange rate?

**2** The information in Table 36.3 is for a country during a given year.

### Table 36.3

| Variable | Amount (billions of pounds) |
|---|---|
| GDP | 800 |
| Taxes (net of transfer payments) | 200 |
| Government budget deficit | 50 |
| Consumption | 500 |
| Investment | 150 |
| Imports | 150 |

**a** What is the level of government expenditure on goods and services?

**b** What is the private sector surplus or deficit?

**c** What is the value of exports?

**d** What is the balance of trade surplus or deficit?

**3** Tables 36.4 and 36.5 give the domestic demand and supply for imaginary products called widgets and toffs.

### Table 36.4

| Price of toffs (£ each) | Supply of toffs | Demand for toffs |
|---|---|---|
| 2 | 1,000 | 7,000 |
| 4 | 3,000 | 5,000 |
| 6 | 5,000 | 3,000 |
| 8 | 7,000 | 1,000 |
| 10 | 9,000 | 0 |

### Table 36.5

| Price of widgets (£ each) | Supply of widgets | Demand for widgets |
|---|---|---|
| 6 | 2,000 | 64,000 |
| 8 | 4,000 | 12,000 |
| 12 | 6,000 | 10,000 |
| 16 | 8,000 | 8,000 |
| 20 | 10,000 | 6,000 |
| 24 | 12,000 | 4,000 |

**a** Draw a graph of the two markets, clearly identifying the domestic equilibrium if there is no international trade.

**b** Suppose that the world price for toffs is £4 each and for widgets is £6 each. Calculate what exchange rate would lead to a balance of trade that is neither a deficit nor a surplus. Show this equilibrium on your graph.

**4** Suppose that the exchange rate between the UK pound and the Deutschemark is DM3 per pound.

**a** What is the exchange rate in terms of pounds per Deutschemark?

**b** What is the price in pounds of a camera selling for DM250?

**c** What is the price in Deutschemarks of a computer selling for £1,000.

## DISCUSSION QUESTION

**1** Why is a deficit on the current account often called 'unfavourable'?

## DATA QUESTIONS

### Influences on the Balance of Payments

**1** Summarize the trends in the three variables.

**2** What relationship would you expect to find between the unemployment rate and the exchange rate on the one hand and the balance of payments on the other? Do these statistics confirm your expectations?

**Table 36.6**

| Year | Unemployment (millions) | Sterling exchange rate (1985 = 100) | Current balance (millions of pounds) |
|---|---|---|---|
| 1979 | 1,312 | 107 | −453 |
| 1980 | 1,611 | 116 | 2,843 |
| 1981 | 2,482 | 123 | 6,748 |
| 1982 | 2,901 | 113 | 4,649 |
| 1983 | 3,127 | 106 | 3,787 |
| 1984 | 3,158 | 102 | 1,832 |
| 1985 | 3,281 | 100 | 2,750 |
| 1986 | 3,312 | 96 | −24 |
| 1987 | 2,993 | 90 | −4,182 |
| 1988 | 2,426 | 97 | −15,151 |
| 1989 | 1,784 | 93 | −22,515 |
| 1990 | 1,664 | 91 | −18,268 |
| 1991 | 2,292 | 92 | −8,533 |
| 1992 | 2,279 | 88 | −9,468 |
| 1993 | 2,919 | 81 | −11,042 |
| 1994 | 2,637 | 84 | −1,684 |

*Source:* Central Statistical Office, *Economic Trends, 1996.* HMSO.

# ANSWERS

## CONCEPT REVIEW

**1** balance; payments; current; capital; official settlements

**2** net borrower; net lender

**3** debtor

**4** equal to

**5** demand; supply; world; exchange rate

**6** higher; trade; sterling assets

**7** balance of trade deficit

**8** foreign exchange; foreign exchange rate

**9** fixed; flexible; managed

**10** 3; 60

## TRUE OR FALSE

**1 T** Whisky is a visible export.

**2 F** There must be a surplus to offset the current deficit.

**3 F** Settlements vary according to what happens elsewhere in the accounts.

**4 F** May be true or untrue. Net borrower means that current account net borrowing > 0. Debtor country means that sum of all net borrowing > 0.

**5 F** Borrowing will have to be repaid.

**6 T** Balance of trade (negative) = Government balance (large negative) + Private balance (small negative).

**7 T** Definition.

**8 F** See definition.

**9 F** Perhaps 'uncertain' – it depends on reaction of private sector surplus/deficit.

**10 T** Exchange rate affects price of goods in international trade.

**11 T** Lower rate of money supply will increase interest rate and so persuade people to invest in currency to receive higher interest.

**12 T** Pound is more valuable, so rise in demand for sterling assets.

**13 T** Rise in foreign exchange value of pound leads to rise in foreign exchange value of sterling assets and so a rise in demand for sterling assets.

**14 T** Because Bank of England is willing to buy or sell pounds in order to keep exchange rate fixed.

# MULTIPLE CHOICE

**1 a** Definition.

**2 c** Imports > exports, therefore current account deficit. Borrowing > lending, so capital account surplus (think about which way money is flowing).

**3 b** Current lending > borrowing, so net lender. Sum of past borrowing > sum of lending, so debtor country.

**4 e** Flexible exchange rate leads to official settlements balance = 0; hence current account surplus = capital account deficit – occurs only when lending > borrowing.

**5 a** Definitions of net lender and debtor country. Debts are shrinking.

**6 c** Net lender – stock of investments rising. Debtor country – negative flow of interest payments on investments.

**7 d** Net exports = $(T - G) + (S - I) = 300 - 400 + 300 - 250 = -50$.

**8 c** Government sector deficit = $G - T = 400 - 300 = 100$. Private sector surplus = $S - I = 300 - 250 = +50$.

**9 d** Link between government sector deficit and private sector surplus is via higher interest rates – international capital mobility restricts changes in interest rates.

**10 d** Definition of flexible exchange rate regime.

**11 d** Others all affect demand for pounds.

**12 b** Rightward shift positively sloped supply curve. Draw a graph to check.

**13 a** This increases the supply of pounds. **b**, **c** and **d** increase demand, **e** leads to fall in supply.

# SHORT ANSWER

**1** The national income accounting identities allow us to show that a country's balance of trade deficit is equal to the sum of its government budget deficit and its private sector deficit.

**2** Purchasing power parity follows from arbitrage and the law of one price. It means that the value of money is the same in all countries once the differences in risk are taken into account. For example, if the exchange rate between the pound and the yen is 120 yen per pound, purchasing power parity says that a good that sells for 120 yen in Japan will sell for £1 in the United Kingdom. Thus the exchange rate is such that money (pounds or yen) has the same purchasing power in both countries.

**3** In a market economy, currencies fluctuate in value for similar reasons as the prices of other goods fluctuate; in other words, because of fluctuations in demand and supply. But there are differences. For most currencies, demand fluctuations can be quite large as speculators

buy and sell particular currencies. In these decisions, expectations about the future play a large part. For example, in the article, the Chancellor's pledge about future policy has affected expectations.

# PROBLEMS

**1 a** The amount of loans from the rest of the world is £100 billion. This is obtained by recognizing that the overall balance of payments must balance; the sum of the positive entries (exports, loans from the rest of the world and increase in official reserves) must equal the sum of the negative entries (imports, transfers to the rest of the world and loans to the rest of the world).

**b** The current account balance is a £50 billion deficit: exports minus imports minus transfers to the rest of the world.

**c** The capital account balance is a surplus of £40 billion: loans from the rest of the world minus loans to the rest of the world.

**d** This country does not have a flexible exchange rate because official reserves increased. Official reserves would have remained unchanged under flexible exchange rates.

**2 a** Since we know that the government budget deficit is £50 billion and the taxes (net of transfer payments) are £200 billion, we can infer that government expenditure on goods and services is £250 billion.

**b** The private sector surplus or deficit is given by saving minus investment. Investment is given as £150 billion but we must compute saving. Saving is equal to GDP minus taxes minus consumption: £100 billion. Thus there is a private sector deficit of £50 billion.

**c** We know that GDP is consumption plus investment plus government expenditure on goods and services plus net exports (exports minus imports). Since we know all these values except exports, we can obtain that value by solving for exports. The value of exports equals GDP plus imports minus consumption minus investment minus government expenditure on goods and services; the value of exports equals £50 billion.

**d** There is a balance of trade deficit of £100 billion. This can be obtained in two ways. First, we can recognize that the balance of trade surplus or deficit is given by the value of exports (£50 billion) minus the value of imports (£150 billion). The other method is to recognize that the balance of trade deficit is equal to the sum of the government budget deficit (£50 billion) and the private sector deficit (£50 billion).

**3 a** Equilibrium in the market for toffs occurs at a price of £5 each, shown in Fig. 36.1(a), with 4,000 units traded (point *a*), while equilibrium in the market for widgets occurs at a price of £16 each, with 8,000 units traded (point *a'*), shown in Fig. 36.1(b).

**Figure 36.1**

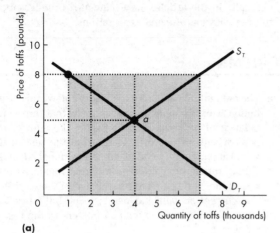

**(a)**

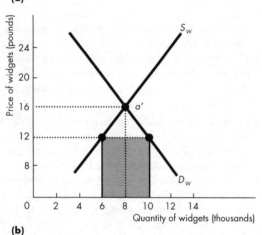

**(b)**

b A balance of trade will have the amount earned by exports equal to the amount paid out for imports. To start, pick an exchange rate and see what happens to exports and imports. For example, pick £1 equals $1. In this case, the world price of a toff is equivalent to £4, so UK demand is 5,000 units and UK supply is only 3,000 units, leading to imports of 2,000 units at £4 per unit, for a net payment of £8,000. The world price of a widget is £6, so demand is 14,000 units and supply is only 2,000 units, leading to imports of 10,000 units at £6 per unit, for a total payment of £60,000.

Clearly, at this exchange rate we do not have a balance of trade, since the United Kingdom is trying to import both goods. To get rid of a deficit, recall that the exchange rate must fall in value. We would therefore try lower and lower values (for example, £1.50 per $1), until by trial and error we arrive at the correct value of £2 per $1. In this case, the price of a toff is £8, so that demand is 1,000 units and supply is 7,000 units, leading to exports of 6,000 units, earning £48,000. The price of a widget is £12, leading to a

demand of 10,000 units and a supply of 6,000 units, and we import 4,000 units, at a total payment of £48,000, for a balance of trade.

We can see this balance demonstrated on the graphs, with the shaded areas showing the export earnings equal to the import payments.

4 a If £1 can be purchased for DM3, then the price of a Deutschemark is £$\frac{1}{3}$ per Deutschemark.

b At an exchange rate of DM3 per pound, it takes £83.30 to obtain the DM250 needed to buy the camera.

c At an exchange rate of DM3 per pound, it takes DM3,000 to obtain the £1,000 needed to buy the computer.

## DISCUSSION QUESTION

1 A deficit on the current account is called unfavourable because it almost always means that the value of imports exceeds the value of exports and this can create the impression that a country is living beyond its means. However, note that a deficit on the current account must be balanced by a surplus on the capital account. In turn, this is seen as unfavourable by some people since it means that foreigners are buying UK assets.

## DATA QUESTIONS

1 Unemployment rose until 1986, then declined, subsequently rose and fell again after 1993. The exchange rate rose rapidly in the first part of the period, then declined substantially, with a small rise in 1988. It fell rapidly in 1993. The balance of payments on current account improved until the mid-1980s, then moved into a substantial deficit.

2 As unemployment rises consumer spending falls. We should therefore expect to find that as unemployment rises, imports will fall and the balance of payments moves towards a surplus. Figure 36.2(a) shows a clear relationship between unemployment and the balance of payments. In the period 1979–81 unemployment rose sharply and this was reflected in a rise in the current balance. In the middle part of the graph the relationship is less clear. After 1986, unemployment fell and the current deficit rose as we would expect.

As the exchange rate of the pound rises, each pound can buy more foreign goods while UK goods rise in price in foreign markets. We would therefore expect to find that a rise in the exchange rate leads to an increase in imports and a fall in exports, that is, the current account moves towards a deficit. However, there may be time lags while consumers adjust to new prices and producers develop new markets. Thus we can argue that the sharp rise in the exchange rate after 1979 was one reason why the balance of payments moved towards a deficit after 1981. The subsequent fall in the value of the pound could be expected to lead to an improvement in the balance of payments. This does not seem to have happened; the exchange rate effect may have been outweighed by the fall in unemployment, although in the last few years the relationship is as we would expect.

**Figure 36.2**

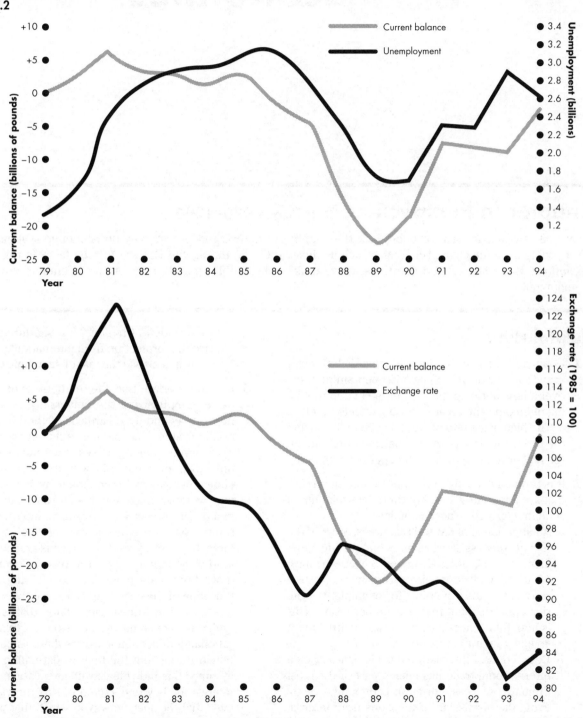

# Chapter 37  Emerging Economies

---

## Chapter in Perspective, Text Pages 980–1006

What makes countries rich or poor? Is it the quantity of natural resources? Why do economic systems differ? What problems do changing economies such as those in China, Russia and Eastern Europe face? In this chapter we address these and related questions as we look at the problems and prospects for economic growth and development.

---

## Helpful Hints

1 Countries become rich by achieving high rates of growth in per head income and maintaining them over a long period of time. The role of compounding of income can create startling effects here!

   The higher the rate of capital accumulation and the faster the pace of technological improvement, the higher the rate of growth in per head income.

2 It is probably equally important to note the things that are apparently not important determinants of economic growth. These include:

   a An abundance of natural resources. Most of the recent success stories of economic development (that is, Hong Kong and Singapore) have occurred with few natural resources. Natural resources can be helpful (for example, the oil-rich countries) but they are not necessary. This is hopeful because a country can do little about its lack of natural resources.

   b Restriction of international trade. Unrestricted international trade has been a part of the most dramatic success stories of economic growth. From the discussion of the gains from interna-

tional trade in Chapter 35, it should be no surprise that protection from international competition will decrease the rate of economic growth.

3 It is appropriate that the textbook ends where it began, emphasizing the universal problems that face any economy regardless of the kind of economic system that organizes its economic activity. Foremost among these is the fundamental and universal problem of scarcity, which makes choice necessary. No economic system can eliminate scarcity. Each simply confronts the problem in a different way. Once again we find that opportunity cost is a consequence of choice necessitated by scarcity and not a consequence of the kind of economic system in place. Regardless of how choices are made, the cost of any action is the value of the best forgone alternative.

   An additional underlying notion that is relevant under any economic system is the postulate of the rationality of economic agents that has been maintained throughout the text. In particular, we have assumed that individuals will pursue their own best interest as they understand it. It is the case, however, that the specific way in which that pursuit of

EMERGING ECONOMIES 339

self-interest will be manifest will be different under different economic systems since alternative systems provide different incentives and constraints.

## Key Figures

**Figure 37.6 Capitalism's Solution to the Economic Problem, text page 988**

This illustrates the interaction between households and firms and shows that markets are at the heart of the system.

**Figure 37.7 Socialism's Solution to the Economic Problem, text page 989**

This is the counterpart to Figure 37.6 and shows that in socialism planning takes the place of markets.

# SELF-TEST

## CONCEPT REVIEW

1  A country in which there is little industrialization, little capital equipment and low per head incomes is called a(n) _____ country. A country that is poor but is accumulating capital and developing an industrial base is called a(n) _____ country.

2  Countries in which there is a rapidly developing broad industrial base and per head income is growing quickly are called _____ _____ countries. A country with a large amount of capital equipment and in which people are highly specialized, enabling them to earn high per head incomes, is called a(n) _____ country.

3  The distribution of income among countries is _____ unequal than the distribution of income among families in the United Kingdom.

4  If poor countries have a slow growth rate of real per head GDP and rich countries have a faster growth rate, the gap between the rich and poor countries_____ .

5  The relationship between inputs and outputs is called the _____ function. There are three classes of inputs. The first, _____, includes non-produced natural resources. The second, _____, increases as the number of workers increases. The third, _____, includes machines and factories as well as human skills and knowledge.

6  The relationship between per head output and the per head stock of capital in a given state of technology is called the _____ _____ _____ function. It will

shift _____ if there is a technological advance.

7  Other things remaining the same, the larger saving is, the _____ will be the rate of capital accumulation. Other things remaining the same, the larger the government budget deficit, the _____ will be the rate of capital accumulation.

8  The situation in which a country is locked into a low income condition that reinforces itself is called a(n) _____ _____ .

9  The universal fundamental economic problem of _____ cannot be abolished by any economic system.

10  Private ownership of capital and reliance on market allocation of resources are the principal characteristics of the economic system known as _____ . The economic system based on public ownership of capital and centrally planned allocation of resources is called _____ .

11  An in-between economic system that combines public ownership of capital with market allocation of resources is called _____ _____ . Another in-between economic system with private ownership of capital but a high degree of state intervention in the allocation of resources is called _____ _____ _____ .

## TRUE OR FALSE

___  1  The poorest countries in the world are underdeveloped countries.

___ **2** For a poor country to close the real per head income gap between itself and rich countries, it must attain and maintain a high rate of economic growth.

___ **3** Higher levels of average human capital, but with the same level of per head physical capital, will not raise per head income.

___ **4** Faster growing countries typically have lower rates of capital accumulation.

___ **5** Countries with higher population growth rates generally have a smaller percentage of the population under age 15.

___ **6** Scarcity is not a problem for capitalist economies.

___ **7** The United Kingdom is an example of a pure capitalist economy.

## MULTIPLE CHOICE

**1** Which of the following is not an attribute of a developing country?
**a** poverty
**b** a low stock of capital
**c** a developing industrial base
**d** a developing commercial base
**e** a stable and high stock of capital

**2** The poorest countries are typically characterized by all of the following except
**a** high literacy rates.
**b** high birth rates.
**c** limited availability of capital.
**d** low per head incomes.
**e** poor capital accumulation.

**3** The Lorenz curve depicting the distribution of average per head income across countries lies
**a** on the 45° line.
**b** to the left of the 45° line.
**c** to the right of the 45° line but not as far out as the Lorenz curve depicting the distribution of income of families within the United Kingdom.
**d** to the right of the 45° line and further out than the Lorenz curve depicting the distribution of income of families within the United Kingdom.

**e** to the right of the 45° line, roughly as far out as the Lorenz curve depicting the distribution of income of families within the United Kingdom.

**4** Suppose rich country *A* enjoys a per head income of £100,000 per year and poorer country *B* has a per head income of only £1,000. With constant populations, what happens to the income gap between the two countries (initially £99,000) if per head income in the poor country grows at a rate of 100 per cent, while growth in the rich country is only 2 per cent?
**a** The income gap between gap between the two must narrow since the poor country grows faster.
**b** The income gap stays the same.
**c** The income gap widens despite the faster growth in the poor country.
**d** The income gap initially narrows, then widens.
**e** The income gap initially widens, then narrows.

**5** Which of the following is not a characteristic of a per head production function?
**a** Per head output increases as the per head stock of capital increases.
**b** The state of technology is held constant for a given per head production function.
**c** The law of diminishing returns applies to the per head production function.
**d** As the stock of capital increases, the per head production function shifts upward.
**e** As technological knowledge advances, the per head production function shifts upward.

**6** As capital is accumulated and capital per unit of labour increases,
**a** this leads to less output since workers tend to become less hard working when working with big machines.
**b** this increases the productivity of labour and economic growth.
**c** the marginal productivity of capital increases.
**d** this leads to a reduced rate of economic growth as workers lose their jobs to the machines.
**e** population growth typically increases as a result.

**7** As the work-force grows with a constant capital stock, a there is less output in total since the capital–labour ratio declines.

b the marginal productivity of labour is increased as the marginal productivity of capital is decreased.

c the marginal productivity of labour and capital both increase.

d the marginal productivity of labour and capital both decrease.

e the marginal productivity of labour is reduced.

**8** There is a limit to growth induced by capital accumulation in the short run since

a labour growth rates may become negative.

b even as capital per head increases, the rate of increase in total output will eventually begin to diminish.

c even as capital per head increases, the rate of increase in total output will eventually begin to increase causing excessive inflation.

d there is a strong limit to the amount of capital that can be accumulated.

e low population growth means too few workers for the amount of new capital.

**9** Which of the following is not a principal obstacle to economic growth for poor countries?

a population growth

b high number of dependants as a percentage of population

c low saving rates

d international debt

e multinational corporations

**10** Population growth can reduce economic growth if

a per head productivity increases as well.

b the population increase consists of able-bodied workers.

c the population increase consists of children or other dependants not yet in the work-force.

d too many workers push up wages.

e the population increase consists of immigrants.

**11** For a given level of saving, investment will be higher the

a higher is the government budget deficit and the higher is the current account deficit.

b higher is the government budget deficit and the lower is the current account deficit.

c lower is the government budget deficit and the higher is the current account deficit.

d lower is the government budget deficit and the lower is the current account deficit.

e higher is the income level.

**12** The best any economic system can do is to

a produce on its production possibility frontier.

b produce above its production possibility frontier.

c produce below its production possibility frontier.

d eliminate scarcity.

e produce a fair distribution of individual incentives.

**13** Which economic system is characterized by private ownership of capital and considerable state intervention in the allocation of resources?

a capitalism

b socialism

c market socialism

d communism

e welfare state capitalism

**14** Which economic system is characterized by private ownership of capital and reliance on market allocation of resources?

a capitalism

b socialism

c market socialism

d welfare state capitalism

e communism

**15** During the Great Leap Forward in China under Mao Zedong,

a there was a dramatic increase in agricultural production but not industrial production.

b the application of new technologies resulted in a significant general increase in production.

c China experienced extremely slow economic growth.

d China became a major exporter of grains and cotton.

e China's educational sector boomed.

**16** The economic reforms of 1978 under Deng Xiaoping

a moved China off the 'capitalist road' it had been on under Mao Zedong.

b abolished collectivized agriculture.

c have resulted in slower economic growth in China.

d have made China more dependent on food imports.

e led to the closing of universities and schools.

# SHORT ANSWER

**1** Use the concept of a per head production function to explain why an increase in the rate of capital accumulation will lead to faster economic growth.

**2** Why is international debt generally an obstacle to the economic growth of a poor country?

**3** How can an underdevelopment status be self-reinforcing?

**4** Briefly describe the economic reforms proclaimed by Deng Xiaoping in China in 1978. What has been their effect?

**5** What do you think was the cause of the 'three years of economic decline' mentioned in the *Reading Between the Lines* article?

# PROBLEMS

**1** Consider two countries, High and Low. High currently has a real per head income of £10,000 while Low currently has real per head income of only £5,000. The rate of growth of real per head income in High is 1 per cent per year.

   **a** Suppose the rate of growth of real per head income in Low is 10 per cent per year. What will the gap in real per head income between High and Low be after 1 year? After 4 years?

   **b** Suppose the rate of growth of real per head income in Low is 20 per cent per year. What will the gap in real per head income between High and Low be after 4 years? How many years will it take for Low to surpass High?

**2** This problem illustrates the effect of capital accumulation and technological growth on economic growth. Figure 37.1 shows two per head production functions for an economy. Suppose we begin on the curve labelled $PF_1$.

   **a** What is the effect on output per head of an increase in capital per head from 1 machine per worker to 3 machines per worker? From 3 machines per worker to 5 machines per worker? From 1 machine per worker to 5 machines per worker directly?

   **b** Now suppose that there is a technological improvement that shifts the per head production function from $PF_1$ to $PF_2$. What is the effect on output per head of this technological

improvement if there is 1 machine per worker? If there are 5 machines per worker?

   **c** Now suppose that the technological improvement that shifts the *PF* curve occurs at the same time as the capital per head increases from 1 machine per worker to 5 machines per worker. What is the effect on output per head?

**Figure 37.1**

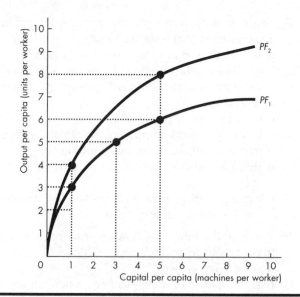

**3** Graveland is a poor country with no natural resources except gravel. Initially, income is £500 per year, taxes (and government spending) are £100 per year, all of disposable income is consumed, there are no exports or imports and there is no technological change (all figures are per head).

   **a** In this economy, what is the level of saving and of investment? Is there economic growth?

   **b** Suddenly, there is a worldwide gravel shortage, and Graveland is able to export gravel at a huge profit. Exports soar from zero to £700, income rises to £1,900 and consumption rises to £1,100 per year. There are still no imports, and initially government spending and taxes are constant. What happens to the current account? What is investment now? Is the growth rate now positive?

   **c** Suppose that Graveland starts to import capital goods at a rate of £500 per year. What happens to the current account? Savings? Investment? Future growth?

# DISCUSSION QUESTION

**1** Is the world economic system fair?

# DATA QUESTIONS

### Inflation in Poland

Poland introduced a market economy at the beginning of 1990. During the first week of the year, the Polish people saw the price of bread rise by 40 per cent, ham by 50 per cent, petrol by 100 per cent, electricity by 400 per cent and coal by a staggering 600 per cent. Although all prices increased, some increased by more than others, changing relative prices as shown in Fig. 37.2. The average price increase in January 1990 was 77 per cent. Goods and services with prices that increased by more than this amount experienced an increase in their relative price; goods and services with prices that increased by less than this amount experienced a decrease in their relative price. Thus the relative prices of bread and of ham each decreased and the relative price of fuel increased. This led to a substitution effect; many Polish people decided to stop driving their cars altogether.

Inflation on the scale experienced in Poland resulted from one main factor – too much money chasing too few goods. When money supply increases quickly, so does aggregate demand. When aggregate demand grows faster than aggregate supply, the result is inflation.

**Figure 37.2**

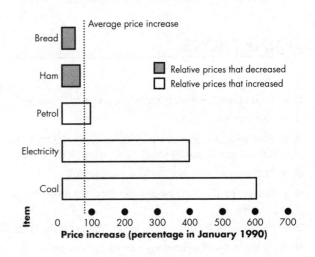

*Source:* Adapted from M. Parkin, 'Inflation in Eastern Europe', *Economic Times*, Fall 1991.

**1** Explain what is meant by
  **a** market economy
  **b** substitution effect

**2** Why should aggregate demand increase when money supply increases?

# ANSWERS

## CONCEPT REVIEW

**1** underdeveloped; developing

**2** newly industrialized; industrial

**3** more

**4** widens

**5** production; land; labour; capital

**6** per head production; upward

**7** larger; smaller

**8** underdevelopment trap

**9** scarcity

**10** capitalism; socialism

**11** market socialism; welfare state capitalism

## TRUE OR FALSE

**1 T** Definition.

**2 T** To close the gap, poor countries must grow at a faster rate than rich countries.

**3 F** Increase in human capital leads to increased productivity and higher per head incomes.

**4 F** High rates of capital accumulation are associated with rapid growth.

**5 T** High population growth means many children.

**6 F** Scarcity is a problem for all economies.

**7 F** The United Kingdom is a mixed economy.

## MULTIPLE CHOICE

**1 e** Definition.

**2 a** Poor countries usually have low levels of literacy.

**3 d** See text discussion.

**4 e** First year: $A$'s growth = $2,000, while $B$'s = $1,000. By third year $A$'s growth = $2,080.80, while $B$'s = $4,000.

**5 d** This creates a movement along a function.

**6 b** More capital means labour can produce more output per unit.

**7 e** Fall in capital–labour ratio means fall in productivity.

**8 b** Owing to fixed technology and labour resources.

**9 e** Multinational corporations can foster growth.

**10 c** Because resources must be spent on child care.

**11 c** From formula for investment.

**12 a** Cannot be above the frontier because of resource constraints (scarcity); can do better than just a fair distribution.

**13 e** Definition.

**14 a** Pure capitalism relies on market allocation.

**15 c** See text discussion – slow growth owing to resource misallocation.

**16 b** See text discussion.

## SHORT ANSWER

**1** The per head production function illustrates how per head output increases as the per head stock of capital increases, given the state of technology. If the rate of capital accumulation increases, then the per head stock of capital is increasing more rapidly, which means that per head output is increasing more rapidly; that is, there is faster economic growth. This is illustrated graphically by more rapid movements up along the graph of the per head production function.

**2** If a poor country has a large international debt, it needs a current account surplus in order to make interest payments and pay back the debt.

**3** The problem with many poor countries is that they have a low per head stock of capital. In order to increase it, they must increase the saving rate, but the saving rate

will not increase because a low per head stock of capital results in low per head output which implies low saving. Thus the existence of a low per head capital stock leads to conditions that generate a low per head capital stock.

**4** In 1978 Deng Xiaoping abolished collective agriculture (state-owned and state-operated farms) and raised prices paid to farmers for many crops. Agricultural land was leased to farmers for the payment of a fixed tax and a commitment to sell part of its output to the state. The main thing is that individual farmers were free to decide what to plant and how to produce. Since farmers now were able to profit from their productivity, there were new incentives for efficiency. The effects have been striking. The production of agricultural products increased dramatically with the output of some products (those for which the set price was increased the most) increasing by many times their previous level. China went from being the world's largest importer of agricultural products to being an exporter of these products. The overall growth rate in the economy increased to 7 per cent per year.

**5** Changing from one economic system to another is difficult. In the former Soviet Union prices were fixed and everyone had a job. This meant that as market prices were introduced some firms could not compete and so had to close. To prevent this the government often bailed them out by increasing the money supply, so increasing inflation. In addition, there were other difficulties; for example, a huge cut in the imports of particular goods since foreigners were not willing to accept payment in roubles which were losing their value. This meant that essential raw materials were difficult to obtain.

## PROBLEMS

**1 a** Since the rate of growth is 1 per cent per year in High, real per head income will increase from $10,000 to $10,100 after 1 year. Since the rate of growth is 10 per cent per year in Low, real per head income will increase from $5,000 to $5,500. Thus the real per head income gap between High and Low has fallen from $5,000 to $4,600. In High, real per head income next year will be 1.01 times real per head income this year. In Low, real per head income next year will be 1.10 times real per head income this year. If we carry this out for 4 years, we find that after 4 years, real per head income will be $10,406 in High and $7,320 in Low. Thus after 4 years, the real per head income gap will have fallen to $3,086.

**b** If the growth rate in Low is 20 per cent, after 4 years real per head income will be $10,368, while real per head income in High will be £10,406 (since the growth rate in High is still 1 per cent per year). Thus after 4 years, the real per head income gap between High and Low will have fallen from £5,000 to £38. Real per head income in Low will surpass real per head income in High early in year 5.

**2 a** From $PF_1$ in Fig. 37.1 we see that as the capital per head increases from 1 machine per worker to 3 machines per worker, output per worker increases from 3 units to 5 units. As the machines per worker increase from 3 to 5, output per worker increases from 5 to 6 units. Thus the law of diminishing returns holds. We note that if we increase the machines per worker from 1 directly to 5, output per worker increases from 3 directly to 6 units.

**b** If there is 1 machine per worker, the upward shift from $PF_1$ to $PF_2$ implies that output per worker increases from 3 units to 4 units. If, however, there are 5 machines per worker, the upward shift from $PF_1$ to $PF_2$ implies that output per worker increases from 6 units to 8 units.

**c** If we increase the machines per worker from 1 to 5 at the same time as the shift from $PF_1$ to $PF_2$ occurs, output per worker will increase from 3 units to 8 units.

**3 a** Given the equation Investment = Saving plus Current account deficit minus Government deficit, since there are initially no deficits, clearly investment equals saving. However, consumption equals disposable income, so saving is zero, as is investment.

**b** If exports are £700 and imports are still zero, then net exports (the current account in this case) are £700. From our equation, we can see that investment equals saving of £700 plus a current account deficit of –£700 minus government deficit of zero, or investment equals zero. Since investment equals zero and there is no technological change, growth stays constant at zero after Graveland reaches the new level of income.

**c** Net exports now equal £700 – £500 or £200. Saving and income are initially unchanged, as is the government deficit, so that investment equals £700 + (–£200) – 0 = £500. Clearly this investment will raise the capital stock and create future growth.

## DISCUSSION QUESTION

**1** It all depends on what is meant by 'fair'. Certainly, the world economic system is not fair if by fair we mean that incomes are equally distributed. However, you will also note that incomes are not equally distributed within countries. Issues of fairness are normative; that is, they involve value judgements and are not easily resolved by the positivist methods adopted by many economists. If you are interested in questions of fairness you should read the works of writers such as Rawls and Sen which are probably in your library.

## DATA QUESTIONS

**1 a** A market economy is one where resources are allocated as a result of the forces of demand and supply. The price system conveys information which allows decentralized decision making. Market economies usually also involve private ownership of most of the means of production.

**b** A substitution effect is the effect on the demand for a good or service of a change in the price of a good or service assuming that real income remains unchanged. Thus individuals will move along an indifference curve – in the example above they will consume less of goods such as fuel where the price has increased and more of goods whose relative price has fallen.

**2** At least two of the components of aggregate demand will be affected by a rise in the supply of money. Other things remaining the same, the rise in money supply will bring down the rate of interest and so stimulate investment.

The rise in money supply will mean that the demand for money is less than the supply of money; consumers will use the excess supply to buy more consumer goods, hence aggregate demand will rise.